AUTOMOBILE ELECTRONICS

AND BASIC ELECTRICAL SYSTEMS

VOLUME 1: TEXT

KEN LAYNE CMAT, SAE

AUTOMOBILE ELECTRONICS
AND BASIC ELECTRICAL SYSTEMS
VOLUME 1: TEXT

REGENTS/PRENTICE HALL
Englewood Cliffs, New Jersey 07632

Library of Congress Cataloging-in-Publication Data:

Layne, Ken.
    Automobile electronics and basic electrical systems / Ken Layne.
      p.   cm.
    Includes bibliographical references.

     1. Automobiles—Electric equipment—Maintenance and repair.
2. Automobiles—Electronic equipment—Maintenance and repair.
I. Title.
TL272.L38 1990
629.25'48—dc20
                                                     89–36409
                                                      CIP

Cover design: Karin Gerdes Kincheloe
Cover illustration photo: Alex Pietersen

All illustrations credited to automobile and
component manufacturers and to suppliers and
manufacturers of parts, tools, and equipment are
held in copyright by the individual contributors. No
illustration may be reproduced in any way without
the explicit, written permission of the copyright
owner.

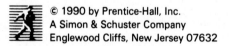 © 1990 by Prentice-Hall, Inc.
A Simon & Schuster Company
Englewood Cliffs, New Jersey 07632

Printed in the United States of America

10 9 8 7 6 5 4 3 2 1

ISBN   0-13-053281-9

Prentice-Hall International (UK) Limited, *London*
Prentice-Hall of Australia Pty. Limited, *Sydney*
Prentice-Hall Canada Inc., *Toronto*
Prentice-Hall Hispanoamericana, S.A., *Mexico*
Prentice-Hall of India Private Limited, *New Delhi*
Prentice-Hall of Japan, Inc., *Tokyo*
Simon & Schuster Asia Pte. Ltd., *Singapore*
Editora Prentice-Hall do Brasil, Ltda., *Rio de Janeiro*

DEDICATION

Paul Norman Hebert

(1939–1988)

The best damn mechanic,
The best damn engineer
I ever knew.

PREFACE

No technical service profession demands more knowledge and higher skills from its members than the automobile service profession. In the early days of the automobile, a person could do a lot of service jobs with a good measure of horse sense and a box full of blacksmith's tools. Basic mechanical skills are still essential for professional automobile service, but a new element has been added: you have to be able to work on the electronic controls!

The age of electronics in the auto industry began in the 1970's when electronic controls were applied to engine systems to reduce emissions and improve fuel economy. The 1980's saw these engine control systems grow and become more complex. The 1980's also saw electronic instrumentation and accessory systems become common throughout the new-car market. In the late 1980's, electronic controls began to appear for a wide range of vehicle accessories and other systems.

You can approach the growing field of electrical and electronic service from several backgrounds. If you have studied or specialized in other vehicle systems, you know the mechanical principles and service needs of these systems. If you have studied electronic systems, you have been introduced to electronic principles and troubleshooting requirements. In either case, this book will help you learn how electronic controls are being applied throughout all systems of modern automobiles.

We cannot underestimate the knowledge and skills of an oldtime mechanic. Professional mechanics of past generations laid the foundation for modern automobile service. A professional service technician today, though, must have equal measures of:

1. Knowledge of automobile system operation.
2. The service skills necessary to keep those systems operating correctly.

TWO VOLUMES— SYSTEM DESCRIPTION AND SERVICE

Because a professional technician must know how systems operate and how to service them, this text is divided into two volumes. The first volume will help you learn how automobile electrical and electronic systems operate. The second volume will help you learn the service skills that are the true measure of a master mechanic.

The first volume of *Automobile Electronics* explains the principles of electricity and electronics that operate in all modern electrical systems. The first volume also surveys the common electrical and electronic systems on late-model vehicles. It progresses from the fundamental sources of electricity through specific examples of systems from major carmakers. These descriptions emphasize the similarities among various systems and the basic principles used by all manufacturers.

The second volume of *Automobile Electronics*, the *Practice Manual*, provides the testing and repair instructions that will be the foundation of your professional service skills. This volume contains step-by-step procedures similar to those you will find in service manuals from carmakers and service guide publishers. These instructions will help you to understand professional reference manuals and use them as basic tools in your service work. Moreover, the second volume of this text explains the *reasons* for different service procedures and the common features of all carmakers' service methods.

SERVICE INSTRUCTIONS COMPLEMENT INDUSTRY REFERENCE MANUALS

We do not have the room in this book to include every manufacturer's specific test and service procedures. No textbook can do that. The service procedures in the *Practice Manual* are basic guidelines for electrical and electronic system testing and service. They will familiarize you with the principles and common points of these skills. These service instructions also will acquaint you with the ways in which carmakers and independent manual publishers produce service procedures and specifications.

Reference manuals are essential tools for service of late-model cars. The second chapter of the *Practice Manual* explains how to use various service publications. For every job that you do, you will need the following information from factory shop manuals or independent service guides:

• Specifications for parts, adjustments, and electrical operating conditions

• Step-by-step test and service procedures

• Carmakers' maintenance schedules

• Test and service equipment operating instructions

• Flat-rate labor time standards

The basic service skills that you learn as you study electrical and electronic service will lay the foundation for your career as a professional automobile service technician.

SYSTEM ENGINEERING AND SYSTEM SERVICE

This text applies a system-engineering and system-service viewpoint to electrical and electronic service. On today's cars, fuel delivery, ignition, and emission control are fully integrated combustion control systems, regulated by onboard computers. The same is true of driver convenience and accessory systems such as air conditioning, cruise control, and vehicle instrumentation. For example, you can't think of emission controls as items that are separate from fuel and ignition components. Also, when you work on fuel and ignition components, you must know how a change in one part or system will affect other systems. And, you must know how the operation on any one part will affect overall system operation.

Don't get the idea that a good mechanic ever ignored any one component when servicing a vehicle system. The point is that on today's cars, you can't think about individual parts separately for a moment. You have to understand complete system operation. Electrical service has always been an interesting and profitable automotive service field. Whether you specialize in this area or in general automobile service, this book will help you understand modern automotive electronic principles.

Each volume is divided into five major parts that contain chapters on related subjects and systems:

• An introduction to the principles of electricity and electronic systems, including computer applications to automotive control and instrumentation systems. Additionally, the first part of the *Practice Manual* surveys common shop practices, tools, materials, and test methods used throughout electrical and electronic system service.

• Engine electrical system operation and maintenence: the principles of batteries, starting systems, and charging systems; as well as the basic service skills needed to troubleshoot and repair these systems.

• Ignition system and electronic engine control systems operation and service.

• Lighting systems, instrumentation, and safety systems.

• Electrical and electronic accessories: power windows, seats, door locks, navigation systems, and air-conditioning controls.

These divisions follow the traditional viewpoint toward comprehensive electrical system service. Throughout the major parts of this two-volume set, the distinction is maintained between traditional electrical system and late-model electronic counterparts. The arrangement of the subjects in this two-volume text also highlights the fact that many electrical systems on today's cars are fully integrated through electronic controls.

INDUSTRY TESTING AND TRAINING STANDARDS

The arrangement of the subjects in these volumes covers the skill requirements outlined in the specifications for the Automotive Service Excellence (ASE) electrical systems certification test and most of the engine performance test. Review questions at the end of the chapters are written in the style of ASE test questions. These will not only help you review the chapter contents, they will help you to prepare for the actual certification tests.

Additionally, the organization and contents of these volumes are based on automotive industry training standards contained in American National Standards Institute (ANSI) publication D18.1–1980. This is your assurance that this text covers the knowledge and skills that the service industry requires of its members.

FULLY ILLUSTRATED TEXT

The two volumes of this book contain almost 2,000 illustrations. Many are original drawings and photographs, prepared expressly for these volumes. Others have been selected from carmakers' late-model service manuals and adapted to illustrate the contents of these books. The result is a fully integrated combination of text and illustrations that *shows and tells* you how vehicle systems operate and how to service them.

The second volume contains several step-by-step photographic overhaul procedures for alternators, starter motors, and ignition distributors. These procedures provide detailed illustrations and instructions for typical methods required to service these vital electrical components.

Major sections of the chapters in the second volume, the *Practice Manual*, also explain the use of electrical diagrams, troubleshooting charts, and carmaker's illustrated service procedures.

OTHER FEATURES OF THESE VOLUMES

In addition to the fully illustrated text, these volumes contain the following features that will help you learn and practice professional electrical and electronic system service:

• *Safety*—Safety is good business, and following all necessary precautions will ensure the safety of yourself, your shop, and your customers. The first chapter of the second volume summarizes the general safety practices for electrical system service. Specific CAUTIONS and WARNINGS appear in the procedures of other chapters to help you do various repair jobs safely.

• *Learning Objectives*—Each chapter begins with a list of basic knowledge or skills that you should acquire from studying the chapter. Again, these objectives follow the general requirements of ASE certification testing and industry training standards.

• *Technical Terms*—Key words and phrases important to a service technician are printed in boldface type. These terms are explained in the text and collected in the glossary at the end of each volume. Studying and understanding these will help you build the vocabulary of a professional mechanic.

• *Essays on Related Topics*—Short essays on topics related to electrical service are included throughout the first volume. These short subjects deal with specific service tips, system designs, and the historical development of automobile electrical systems. They will add depth to your understanding of the automobile industry and help you in the service profession.

FOR FURTHER STUDY

The manufacturers of automobiles have made rapid progress in the application of electronic controls to suspensions, brakes, steering systems, transmissions, and cruise controls. For those interested in the operation and service of these systems, the textbook *Automotive Chassis Electronic Systems*, also by Ken Layne, is available from John Wiley & Sons.

ACKNOWLEDGMENTS

The author and the publisher wish to thank the vehicle manufacturers and other companies in the automotive service industry that contributed information and illustrations for this book. Automobile service is a highly technical, rapidly advancing profession. This book would not have been possible without the assistance of the following companies.

American Honda Motor Company

American Isuzu Motors, Inc.

Atlas Supply Company

Automotive Technician Associates, Inc. (An Organization Dedicated to Better Mechanics)

Balco, Inc. (the entire engineering staff)

Champion Spark Plug Company

Chilton Book Company

Chrysler Corporation

Clayton Industries

Clymer Publications

Ford Motor Company (Ford Parts and Service Division)

Garrett Air Research Industrial Division

The Gates Rubber Company

General Motors Corporation:
    AC-Delco Division
    Buick Motor Division
    Cadillac Motor Car Division
    Chevrolet Motor Divison
    Delco-Remy Division
    Oldsmobile Division
    Pontiac Motor Division
    Rochester Products Division
    Saginaw Steering Gear Division

Hennessy Industries, Inc.:
    Coats Diagnostic Division

K-D Manufacturing Company

Kent-Moore Tool Division

Mazda Motor Corporation

Mitchell Manuals, Inc.

Mitsubishi Motor Sales of America, Inc.

Motor Publications (The Hearst Corporation)

National Institute for Occupational Safety and Health

Nissan Motor Corporation in U.S.A.

Porsche + Audi

Prestolite Division of Bunker Ramo-Eltra Corporation (A Subsidiary of Allied Corporation)

Robert Bosch Sales Corporation (Robert Bosch GmbH)

Snap-on Tools Corporation

Stanley Proto Industrial Tools

Society of Automotive Engineers (SAE)

The L. S. Starrett Company

Sun Electric Corporation

Toyota Motor Sales, U.S.A., Incorporated

Volkswagen of America, Inc.

Volvo of America Corporation

Additionally, the following individuals contributed information and research materials or reviewed selected parts of the manuscript. The author wishes to thank:

James Geddes

Carlton Hardy—Ford Motor Company Training Center, Milpitas, CA

Bob Kruse—Larry Hopkins Pontiac, Sunnyvale, CA

Kalton C. Lahue—photographs for the component overhaul sequences

Robert J. Mahaffay

Don Nilson

Armando Nogueiras, Jr.

Thomas M. Terrell—Garrett AirResearch Industrial Division, Torrance, CA

Russ Ostler—Chrysler Corporation, Livermore, CA

Chris Wood—Grant & El Camino Chevron, Mountain View, CA

Most importantly:

Mary Douglas did a masterful job of managing the overall production of both volumes of this text.

Ruth Cottrell kept track of thousands of illustrations and other bits.

Joan Pendleton did a thoroughly professional job of copyediting all the manuscript.

The manuscript for this book was reviewed by the following automotive educators. Their advice and counsel were invaluable.

Al Engeldahl
Automotive Technology Department
College of DuPage
Glen Ellyn, IL

Mike Hartley
Automotive Technology Department
Automotive High School
Brooklyn, NY

Gerald Helsley
Automotive Technology Department
Kalamazoo Valley College
Kalamzoo, MI

Gilbert James
Automotive Technology Department
Long Beach City College
Long Beach, CA

Robert Lehmann
Automotive Technology Department
San Bernardino Valley College
San Bernardino, CA

Skip Merrick
Automotive Technology Department
Alfred State College
Wellsville, NY

Russ Molaski
Automotive Technology Department
Northeast Wisconsin Technical Institute
Green Bay, WI

Donald Nilson
Automotive Technology Department
Las Positas College
Livermore, CA

CONTENTS

EXPANDED CONTENTS

INTRODUCTION

PART ONE
ELECTRICAL AND ELECTRONIC PRINCIPLES

INTRODUCTION

INTRODUCTION

This textbook is about automobile electrical and electronic systems, and it has two main themes:

1. Understand the system.
   a. The best way to understand how any single part of an automobile works is to know how it operates as part of a complete system.
   b. The best way to test and service a part is to treat it as part of a larger system.
   c. The best way to understand any system is to understand its overall purpose and how each part works to help the system do its job.
2. Understand the common principles.
   a. All systems of an automobile operate on common scientific principles.
   b. If you understand some of the basic facts of science, you can recognize them in different systems.
   c. This, in turn, will help you understand how the systems and their parts work.

The electrical and electronic systems on late-model cars are some of the best examples of the system concept in modern technology. If you remember the ideas summarized above as you study these systems, you will be on your way to becoming a professional service technician.

In Part One of this text, you will learn about basic electricity and electronics. The earliest automobiles at the turn of the century had no electrical systems. Electrical systems became essential parts of the automobile, however, by the second decade of the industry's growth. The basic reasons are obvious. Electric power provides the best way to light a lamp, crank an engine, and operate dozens of accessories. Since Charles "Pop" Kettering invented the electric self-starter and the battery-powered, inductive-discharge ignition, electrical systems have been integral parts of our automobiles.

Today, solid-state electronic systems are equally important parts of our cars. A skilled service technician must understand the basics of electricity and the principles of solid-state electronics to do his or her job professionally on late-model vehicles.

Chapters 1 and 2 in Part One review the principles of automobile electrical and electronic systems. As you study the starting, charging, ignition, and electronic systems in later chapters, you will see these fundamental principles repeated in various applications.

Chapter 3 introduces most of the common electrical parts used throughout the automobile. No electrical circuit can exist without conductors (wiring) and switches, relays, solenoids, motors, or other devices for system control and operation.

Chapters 4, 5, and 6 introduce the principles of solid-state electronics and computer systems found on all modern vehicles. The automobile industry entered the electronic age in the 1970's. For two decades, new electronic control and display systems have appeared each model year at a bewildering rate.

The principles that you will learn in chapters 4, 5, and 6 are *critical* to your understanding of the various electronic systems that you will study in later chapters. All of the electronic systems on late-model cars are variations on the application of basic solid-state electronic and computer system principles.

1 ELECTRICAL AND ELECTRONIC PRINCIPLES

WHAT

Even the most complex electronic system operates on the basic ideas that you studied in a high school science class. Nineteenth-century scientists discovered the principles of electricity, and twentieth-century engineers put them to work in our homes, our shops, and our automobiles. You don't have to be a scientist or an engineer to understand these ideas and put them to work in the automotive service profession. You do have to understand the fundamentals of electricity, however, to understand how electrical systems operate and to service them accurately. This chapter summarizes the basic facts of electron movement in atoms, electric current, voltage, resistance, and other principles with which you will work daily.

WHY

People used to consider that the electrical system of a car consisted of the battery, the alternator, the starter motor, the ignition, and the vehicle lighting. Electrical systems on modern cars are far more complex, and electronic systems provide sophisticated control for many vehicle functions. On late-model cars, electrical and electronic controls integrate the operation of all combustion control systems. Other electronic systems monitor and control antilock braking systems, automatic transmission or transaxle shifting, suspension operation, air conditioning, and vehicle instruments. Although these systems may seem complicated at first, they operate on the basic electrical principles explained in this chapter. If you understand the fundamentals of current, voltage, and resistance, you can recognize their operation in several vehicle systems and make your service work easy and accurate.

GOALS

After studying this chapter, you should be able to:

1. Define current, voltage, and resistance and the units for measuring each.

2. Explain the conventional current and electron flow theories.

3. Explain and give examples of materials that are conductors, insulators, and semiconductors.

4. Explain Ohm's and Kirchhoff's laws.

5. Explain and illustrate series, parallel, and series-parallel circuits.

6. Explain electric power.

7. Explain capacitance and capacitor uses.

MATTER AND ATOMS— CHEMICAL BUILDING BLOCKS

One of the simplest scientific principles is that everything in the universe consists of **matter** and that matter exists in three physical forms: solid, liquid, and gas. Metals in an engine are solid. Gasoline and engine coolant are liquids. The air that an engine takes in and the exhaust it gives off are gaseous matter. Matter can change its form, of course. Water is normally liquid, but it can freeze to solid ice or **vaporize** to gaseous steam.

Atoms and Elements

Whether it exists as a solid, a liquid, or a gas, all matter begins with simple building blocks called **atoms**. There are only a few more than 100 different kinds of atoms. Of these, 92 exist in nature, and another dozen or so have been created in laboratories.

Each different atom is called an **element**. Although the atoms of one element are different from the atoms of all other elements, all have the same basic parts. The atomic parts are the things that let atoms of one element join with each other or combine with atoms of other elements. The actions of atomic parts also are the basis for electricity. The abilities of some materials to conduct electricity and of other materials to insulate against conduction are based on atomic structure. Electrical properties include the structure of a single atom and the interaction among atoms.

Electrons, Protons, and Neutrons

As simple as an atom is, its parts are even simpler. They are the **electron**; the **proton**; and, in most atoms, the **neutron**. Protons and neutrons are at

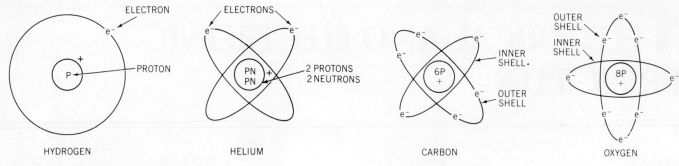

Figure 1-1. Hydrogen is the simplest element. It has one electron and one proton. Helium has two electrons, two protons, and two neutrons.

Figure 1-2. A carbon atom has six protons and electrons. An oxygen atom has eight of each. Carbon and oxygen both have two electron shells.

the center, or **nucleus**, of every atom. The electrons of an atom circle, or orbit, the nucleus, figure 1-1. The differences between atoms of different elements are the numbers of electrons and protons in each element. The simplest element is hydrogen, represented by the letter "H." It has one electron and one proton. Its atomic number is 1. Helium (He) is the second simplest element. It has a nucleus of two protons and two neutrons, with two electrons in its orbit, figure 1-1. The atomic number for helium is 2.

Electrons and protons have opposing electrical charges. This basic atomic theory is the foundation for electrical theory. An electron has a negative charge, shown by a minus sign (−). A proton has a positive charge, shown by a plus (+) sign. A neutron has no charge; it is neutral.

In a balanced atom, the number of electrons equals the number of protons. The balance of the opposing negative and positive charges holds the atom together. The principle of charges is:

• Like charges (+ and +, or − and −) repel each other.

• Opposite charges (+ and −) attract each other.

The positive proton in the nucleus attracts the negative electron and keeps it from flying out of the atom. Because the electron is moving in orbit, **centrifugal force** keeps it from being drawn into the nucleus by the proton. The positive charges on pro-

tons in the nucleus do not force the protons apart, because the neutrons neutralize the effects of the positive charges on each other. That's why all atoms—except hydrogen, with only one proton—have neutrons.

Simple and Complex Atoms

More complex atoms have more electrons, protons, and neutrons. Carbon (C) and oxygen (O) are common elements, figure 1-2, but are more complex than hydrogen and helium. Carbon has six protons in its nucleus and six electrons in orbit. Oxygen has eight of each. These atoms are still balanced because they have equal numbers of electrons and protons. Atoms can become unbalanced by giving up or taking on electrons. An atom cannot give up or take on protons, however. Only electrons can be lost or gained.

An unbalanced atom with more or fewer electrons than protons is an **ion**. An atom with more electrons than protons is a negative ion. One with fewer electrons is a positive ion. Electron movement is the basis for electricity and for chemical combinations.

Electron Movement. Atoms of different elements can link together chemically by sharing electrons with each other. Look again at the carbon and oxygen atoms in figure 1-2. The electrons are not all in the same orbit. The orbits are arranged in shells, and

each shell is progressively farther from the nucleus. Carbon and oxygen have two electron shells. More complex atoms have more shells. Each shell of any atom can hold certain maximum numbers of electrons. From the inner shell outward, there are seven possible shells. The maximum numbers of electrons in each shell are: 2, 8, 18, 32, 32, 9, and 2.

The outer shell, whether it is the second or the seventh, never has more than eight electrons. The next higher element forms another shell or adds an electron to an inner shell that is yet unfilled. The outer electron shell, or **valence shell**, is the most important for understanding both chemistry and electricity.

Scientists say that the electron shells of an atom are energy levels. Atoms use this energy to try to complete their outer electron shells. An atom with few electrons in its outer, or valence, shell combines easily with other atoms. This allows each atom in the combination to complete its outer shell by sharing electrons. Atoms with full outer shells do not combine with other atoms.

Atoms with only one or two valence electrons in their outer shells require little energy to cause these electrons to move to the shells of other atoms. Most such elements are metals like gold, silver, copper, aluminum, iron, and so on. Because it takes little energy to move the valence electrons of these atoms into other orbits, these elements combine easily with other

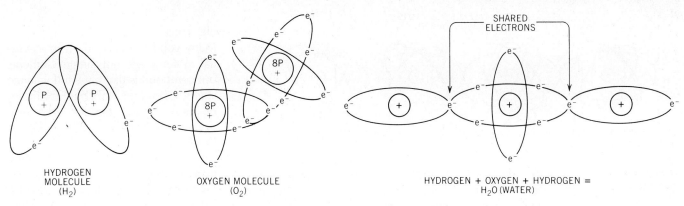

Figure 1-3. Hydrogen and oxygen in their natural states both exist as molecules of two atoms: H_2 and O_2.

Figure 1-4. Water is a compound of two hydrogen atoms and one oxygen atom: H_2O.

elements, and they are good conductors of electric current.

Elements with six or seven valence electrons combine selectively with elements that have one or two valence electrons. But atoms with many outer electrons need more energy to move the electrons into other orbits. Many of these elements are gases, and they are poor conductors of electricity because they need so much energy to move their electrons. These examples show that electron energy is the basis for chemical reactions and for electric current.

CHEMICAL REACTIONS

Atoms share valence electrons in two ways. They combine with another atom of the same element, or they combine with an atom of another element. When two or more atoms join together, they form a **molecule**. Some elements in their natural state exist as molecules of two identical atoms. Hydrogen and oxygen exist naturally as molecules of two identical atoms, H_2 and O_2, figure 1-3.

Compounds and Mixtures

Atoms of one element can combine with those of another in a **compound**. Two hydrogen atoms, each with one electron, can combine with one oxygen atom, which lacks two electrons

in its outer shell. In this way the atoms are chemically bound together in a molecule of the compound H_2O, figure 1-4. Another form of matter, in addition to elements and compounds, is a **mixture**. Mixtures are formed when molecules of elements or compounds mix together but do not share electrons.

Water (H_2O) is a simple compound. Sulfuric acid (H_2SO_4) is another compound. When we put water and sulfuric acid together in a battery, we do not form another compound. Instead, we have a mixture that we call an electrolyte. Similarly, silicon (Si) is another common element. When you study solid-state electronics, you will learn that silicon can become a controlled conductor of electric current by mixing it with very small amounts of other elements. Also, when electronic devices are built, silicon can be made to combine with oxygen or nitrogen into the compounds silicon dioxide (SiO_2) or silicon nitride (Si_3N_4).

The important things to remember about elements, compounds, and mixtures are:

• Elements are matter in its purest form. You can't break an atom of an element into smaller pieces and still have recognizable matter.

• Molecules are two or more atoms joined together by sharing their electrons in their outer shells. They can be atoms of the same or different elements.

• Compounds are molecules of atoms of two or more different elements joined by sharing the electrons in their outer shells.

• Mixtures are two or more elements or compounds that join together physically but do not share electrons in a chemical bond.

Elements, compounds, and mixtures are equally important forms of matter in electrical system design. And this brings us to our next subject.

CONDUCTORS, INSULATORS, AND SEMICONDUCTORS

Remember that the outer, valence, electron shell of an atom never has more than eight electrons. If an atom has three or fewer valence electrons, they are loosely held **free electrons**. These electrons will move easily into the electron shells of other atoms.

If an atom has five or more valence electrons, they are held tightly in the valence shell. It takes more electron energy to dislodge them or to let another electron enter the shell. These are called **bound electrons**.

Remember also that electrons are constantly in motion, either around the nucleus of their own atom or among the valence shells of other atoms. This electron movement can be a random drift, or it can be a controlled movement from one point

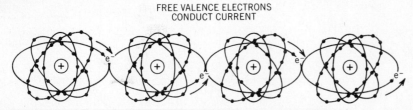

FREE VALENCE ELECTRONS
CONDUCT CURRENT

Figure 1-5. Copper is a good conductor because its free valence electrons move easily from atom to atom.

to another. If it is controlled, this electron movement becomes **electric current**. Electric current produces electric power. Also, for any energy to produce useful work and power, some force must be applied to it. The **electromotive force** that produces current flow is **voltage**. Before we look at current and voltage more closely, however, we should examine a few facts about the materials that conduct and insulate current flow.

Materials with three or fewer valence electrons are good **conductors** of electric current because little force is needed to move the free electrons from one atom to another. Most metals, such as gold, copper, aluminum, and iron, are good conductors because of their valence electron structure, figure 1-5.

Materials with five or more valence electrons are poor conductors because it takes more force to move the bound outer electrons from one atom to another. These materials are **insulators**. Most gases, such as oxygen and nitrogen, have five or more valence electrons and are good insulators. Many good insulators used in electrical systems are not single elements but compounds that have full valence shells. Glass and rubber are examples of these. Many plastics are compounds created especially for use as insulators.

Five elements have just four electrons in their outer shells. These are neither good conductors nor good insulators. These elements are called **semiconductors**, and electric current can flow in them under controlled conditions. Silicon is the most important semiconductor from an electrical viewpoint. Silicon-based semiconductors are the foundation of solid-state electronic devices, which you will study later.

DO YOU KNOW YOUR WEIGHTS AND NUMBERS?

The three principal parts of an atom—electrons, protons, and neutrons—are the things that distinguish one element from another and allow elements to react chemically and conduct electricity. This atomic structure has other features that allow scientists to identify other features of elements.

Because atoms never give up protons and the number of protons in an atom's nucleus remains constant, the number of protons is a good way to identify atoms of different elements. The number of protons is called the atomic number. Hydrogen has one proton; its atomic number is 1. Oxygen has eight protons; its atomic number is 8. Uranium has 92 protons; its atomic number is 92.

Remember that a balanced atom has equal amounts of protons and electrons, but an atom can become electrically unbalanced. An unbalanced atom with more or fewer electrons than protons is an ion. An atom with more electrons than protons is a negative ion. One with fewer electrons than protons is a positive ion.

Atoms of the same element differ in another way. They can have different numbers of neutrons, and this is the basis for two other important terms: atomic weight and isotope. Protons and neutrons are the heaviest parts of an atom by far. Therefore, scientists have said that the total number of protons and neutrons equals the atomic weight of an element. Helium has two of each; its atomic weight is 4. Oxygen has eight protons and eight neutrons; its atomic weight is 16.

Isotopes are atoms that have the same number of protons but different amounts of neutrons. Carbon, for example, in its most common form has six protons and six neutrons. Its atomic number is 6, and its weight is 12. Carbon can also exist with eight neutrons. Its number is still 6, but its weight is 14. The two atoms are chemically identical (same number of positive and negative charges), but they are physically different. Carbon with six neutrons is the isotope carbon-12. With eight neutrons, it is the isotope carbon-14.

SOME BASIC PHYSICS

Up to this point, we have looked at atoms and their parts in terms of chemical properties. Chemistry is the science of the structure of matter. Chemistry is half of electricity; physics is the other half. When you understand how an electrical system works, you will see that you cannot separate chemistry and physics.

In a basic science class, you will learn that physics is the study of matter and energy and their interaction. Energy, however, is not matter. It is a feature, or ability, of matter. The relationships between energy and matter allow us to use electric power to do useful work.

If you ever have trouble understanding what happens when an alternator charges a battery, remember that an alternator only changes mechanical energy into electrical energy, figure 1-6. You change electrical energy back to mechanical energy when you use the battery to power the starter motor and crank the engine. Before examining electricity further, we should review a few other principles that operate in electrical systems.

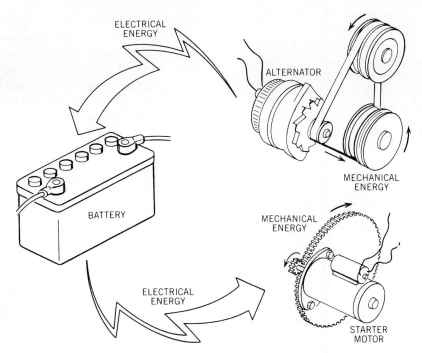

Figure 1-6. An alternator changes mechanical energy of rotation into electrical energy when it charges a battery. A starter motor changes electrical energy to mechanical energy when it cranks the engine.

Energy

Energy is the ability to do work, and we can view it in several ways. All atoms have electrical energy in the form of attraction and repulsion among their positive and negative charges. Additionally, electrons are in constant motion. The normal electron movement in most molecules is a random drift. It has no direction. When an outside force is imposed on this random electron drift, the electron movement takes on a definite direction. Then we have electric current. The same electron energy that binds atoms together becomes useful electricity only when a direction of current flow is established.

Potential and Specific Energy.
The difference between electron energy and useful electricity illustrates one way that energy is classified: by whether it is released for work or whether it is stored. Unreleased, stored energy is **potential energy**. When it is released to do work, it becomes **specific energy** and takes

other forms. When we apply one kind of force to potential electron energy, we create specific electrical energy that can perform work.

Energy can change its form as different forces are applied to it. Chemical energy can become electrical energy or thermal energy. Either of these can become mechanical energy used to move an object. Whenever energy changes its form, some kind of force is involved. Force and energy combine to produce **work**.

Work

If energy is the ability to do work, work itself is the result of using that ability. When energy is released to move a car, work is produced as motion. When energy is released to light an electric lamp, that's another form of work. Here are some other definitions that relate to energy, work, and—ultimately—power:

Mechanical force acts on an object to start, stop, or change the direction of motion.

Inertia is the tendency of an object in motion to keep moving and the tendency of an object at rest to remain at rest.

Momentum is the force of continuing motion.

Friction is the force that resists motion between the surfaces of two objects or forms of matter.

Torque is twisting or turning force that produces rotating mechanical work around an axis. Like work, torque can be measured in a combination of distance and force measurement.

You have probably read these terms when studying automobile engines and drivetrains. Many people, however, do not think of inertia, momentum, and friction in the context of electrical systems. Remember, though, that electrons are matter; and all the principles of physical energy, motion, and work apply to electrical systems. Electrons must overcome inertia when current starts to flow, and current itself has momentum and dynamic inertia that work to keep it flowing. Friction between moving electrons and parts of a circuit is part of electrical resistance.

You have probably read torque ratings for various automobile engines or for electric motors. An engine or a motor can be rated at 200 foot-pounds of torque at 3,000 revolutions per minute, or 10 foot-pounds of torque at 1,750 revolutions per minute, or some other measurement depending on its size and design. You may have asked yourself, "Is torque a measure of power?" The answer, of course, is no, it isn't; but torque and power are both related to doing work.

Power

Torque measures how much work an engine or a motor can do. **Power** measures the rate, or speed, of doing that work. The power of an engine or an electric motor is commonly measured in horsepower or in watts or kilowatts. The customary English sys-

The Scotsman James Watt (1736–1819) was one of history's most prolific inventors and engineers. Although he didn't invent the steam engine, his improved engine with a separate condenser (which he patented in 1769) improved the engine's efficiency by more than 70 percent. Watt also developed a furnace that consumed its own smoke (a leader in air pollution control) and an early copying machine. (He didn't invent Xerox, however.) A little-known fact is that he was the first scientist to prove that water is a compound of oxygen and hydrogen, not an element.

Remember that Watt worked out the calculations that gave us the horsepower as a standard unit of power measurement. His formula for computing horsepower was based on the fact that a horse could move 200 pounds 165 feet in one minute. Now, 165 feet may seem like an odd unit of distance measurement, but was it? Watt started with a traditional English unit, the rod, which was used in surveying and mining engineering during his time. One rod equals 16.5 feet, and a convenient distance measurement for his calculations was 10 rods, or 165 feet. Do you suppose he was thinking metric and actually invented a standard unit we could call "one dekarod"?

horsepower can do it in one-quarter minute (four times as fast). The power unit of a watt also measures the rate of work, and you will learn more about electric power measurements later in this chapter. First, however, we must continue with basic electric current, voltage, and resistance.

CURRENT

To understand the electron flow that is electric current, you should remember the rules of positive and negative charges. Unlike charges (+ and −) attract each other. Like charges (+ and +, or − and −) repel each other. The electrons of an atom have negative charges and are attracted to positive charges. The free electrons in a good conductor, like a piece of copper wire, are attracted by positive charges and will move easily from atom to atom. To create electric current in a copper wire, we need a positive charge at one end and a negative charge at the other.

Later in this chapter, we will explain how these charges develop at opposite ends of a wire. For now, just assume that they exist, figure 1-8. The free electron of an atom near the positive end of the wire is attracted by the positive charge. As the electron leaves its valence shell and moves toward the positive charge, the atom becomes unbalanced; it becomes positively charged. This atom then attracts the electron from another nearby atom. The electrons of neighboring atoms move toward the positive end of the wire. They are helped along by the negative charges at the other end of the wire. The result is controlled, directed current flow. Current will continue to flow as long as the positive and negative charges exist at opposite ends of the wire.

Current Theories

Historically, electrical current has been described by two theories. These are the **conventional theory** and the

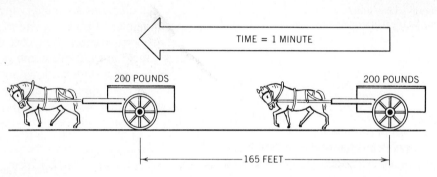

Figure 1-7. One horsepower equals 33,000 foot-pounds of work (165 feet × 200 pounds) done in 1 minute.

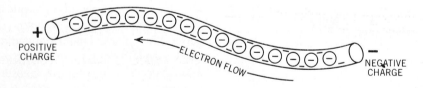

Figure 1-8. Electrons can be forced through a wire by placing a positive charge at one end and a negative charge at the other.

tem measures power in **horsepower** because a Scotsman, James Watt, was the first person to scientifically calculate power. He based his calculations on the amount of work that a horse could do in a specific amount of time. Watt determined that in one minute, one horse could move 200 pounds 165 feet, figure 1-7.

When you multiply 165 feet times 200 pounds, you have 33,000 foot-pounds of work. If one horse can do that amount of work in one minute, then one horsepower equals 33,000 foot-pounds of work per minute, or 550 foot-pounds per second. Two horsepower can do the same work in one-half minute (twice as fast). Four

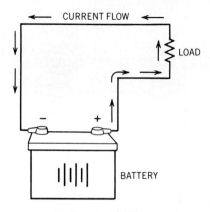

Figure 1-9. The conventional theory says that current flows from positive to negative.

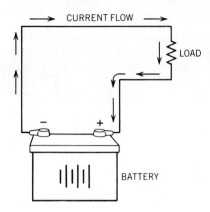

Figure 1-10. The electron theory says that current flows from negative to positive.

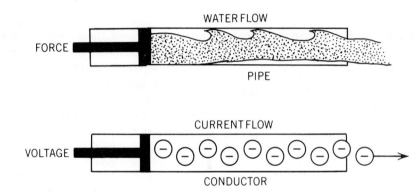

Figure 1-11. Voltage causes current to flow in a conductor just as force causes water to flow in a pipe.

electron theory. The conventional theory is the older of the two. It says that current flows from a positive charge to a negative charge, figure 1-9. The electron theory says that current flows from a negative charge to a positive charge, figure 1-10.

Traditionally, the conventional theory has been used to describe current flow in automotive systems, and it is still the more commonly used theory. Since the development of automotive electronic systems, such as on-board computers, the electron theory has also been used in automotive service. You can use either theory accurately as long as you use it consistently and do not mix the two. For some examples in this chapter, we will use both; but we will identify each theory as we use it.

The Ampere

Current flow in a conductor is similar to water flow in a pipe, figure 1-11. When we measure water flow, we count ounces or gallons of water moving past one point in a given time: gallons per minute, for example. When we measure current flow, we count electrons moving past one point in a given time. Since electrons are so small and move so fast, we don't count individual electrons to measure current. We use the **ampere** as the unit to measure current. An ampere is to one electron what a gallon is to a single molecule of water. One ampere equals 6.28 billion billion electrons. When that many electrons pass one point in a conductor in one second, one ampere of current flows.

Direct and Alternating Current

There are two kinds of current flow that we use for practical electric power: **direct current (dc)** and **alternating current (ac)**. Direct current is current that always flows in the same direction. It is the kind of current obtained from batteries. Alternating current changes directions between two points from positive to negative and back to positive. Each cycle of alternating current occurs in an equal amount of time. The electric power in our homes and shops is ac power and alternates at 60 cycles per second, or 60 **hertz (Hz)**.

Both ac and dc systems have advantages and disadvantages for different uses, and both exist in an automobile. Most of the electrical devices in a car are 12-volt dc devices. They receive voltage and current from a 12-volt battery, which is a source of dc power. The battery, however, is charged by an alternating current generator, or alternator. The alternating current from the alternator is changed to direct current before it leaves the alternator and gets to the battery.

The Circuit—A Current Path

The single wire in figure 1-8 is not a complete electrical circuit. For current to flow, it must have a complete **circuit**, or circular path, from negative charge to positive and back to negative again. Figure 1-12 shows a simple circuit that consists of an energy source (a battery), conductors (wires), and a unit to do work (a lamp).

Following the electron flow theory, the energy of the battery causes current to flow from the negative terminal, through the wires, to the lamp. The lamp changes electrical energy into light and heat energy. Current then flows back to the positive terminal of the battery. The battery itself completes the circuit as current flows from the positive terminal to the negative terminal. For current to flow, a circuit must have **continuity**; that is, it must be continuous. If the circuit is

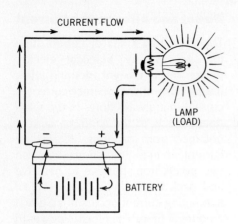

Figure 1-12. Current flow requires a complete circuit.

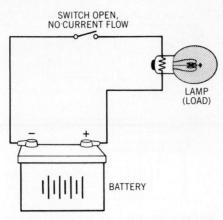

Figure 1-13. If a circuit is broken, no current will flow.

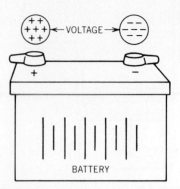

Figure 1-14. Voltage is a potential difference in force between two points.

broken at any point, current will not flow, figure 1-13. To open and close a circuit, we use a switch, as shown in figure 1-13.

VOLTAGE

Voltage is the electromotive force, or pressure, that causes current to flow. Voltage is a form of energy. When a circuit is complete and current is flowing, voltage is released electrical energy. Voltage also is potential energy. When a battery is not connected to a circuit, it still contains potential voltage in the form of a negatively charged terminal at one end and a positively charged terminal at the other, figure 1-14. The strength of this energy, or the amount of force, depends on the strength of the positive and negative charges and the difference between them. Voltage is high if the charges are strong with a large difference between them. Voltage is low if the charges are weak and have little difference. A potential of 120 volts is 10 times as strong as a potential of 12 volts.

Voltage also exists between any two points in a circuit when current is flowing. The only time voltage does not exist is when the potential difference in force falls to zero. You will often hear voltage referred to simply as "potential" because of this.

The Volt and Voltage Sources

Just as the ampere is the unit used to measure current, the **volt** is the unit used to measure voltage. One volt is the amount of energy, or force, needed to move one ampere through one ohm of resistance. You will learn about resistance and ohms in the next section.

In an automobile, the principal voltage sources are the battery and the alternator. In a battery, chemical energy creates the potential electrical energy between the two battery terminals. Mechanical energy creates the voltage potential between two terminals of the alternator.

RESISTANCE

An electric circuit must contain resistance to current flow to change electrical energy to heat, light, or movement. If a circuit contained no resistance, the flow of electrons would be like a flood of water from a broken dam. It would do more damage than good.

All conductors have some resistance to current, just as all pipes have some resistance to fluid flow. This resistance is the friction of the moving electrons. In electrical wire, it is almost negligible. The important resistance in an electric circuit is in the

form of the working devices such as lamps and motors. These are often called the **electrical load** of the circuit. The lamp in figures 1-12 and 1-13 is the load on the circuit. It has more resistance than the conductors or switches. Current flows through the lamp, however; and the same amount that enters one side leaves the other. Voltage, though, decreases from one side of the lamp to the other because the lamp is the point where electrical energy is changed to heat and light energy.

Resistance also exists at a point where a circuit is broken, or opened by a switch, figure 1-13. This is infinite resistance. It prevents current flow but does no useful work because electrical energy is not changed to any other form of energy. The important differences between the resistance of a load and the resistance of a broken, or open, circuit are:

• Current flows through a load, and voltage decreases from one side of the load to the other.

• Current does not flow through a break, and the same potential voltage exists on both sides of the break as exists at the voltage source.

The Ohm and Factors of Resistance

The unit used to measure the amount of resistance in a circuit is the **ohm**.

One ohm is the resistance present when one volt is required to move one ampere of current through a circuit. Five factors determine the amount of resistance in any part of a circuit. The following examples refer to conductors, but remember that loads are also conductors even though they have resistance.

1. *Conductor condition*—A completely broken conductor has infinite resistance. Anything that similarly reduces the area for current flow through a conductor also increases resistance—including corrosion, looseness, or a partially broken conductor.

2. *Conductor cross-sectional area*—A thin conductor has a narrow current flow path and more resistance than a thick conductor.

3. *Conductor length*—Moving electrons constantly collide with the atoms of a conductor. The longer the conductor, the farther current must flow and the more collisions occur.

4. *Conductor temperature*—High temperature causes high resistance in most conductors.

5. *Atomic structure*—Conductors with many free electrons allow easy current flow. Insulators with few free electrons have high resistance to current.

ELECTRICAL MEASUREMENTS AND METRIC PREFIXES

The two measurement systems widely used in the automotive industry are the U.S. customary system and the international metric system. While the United States still uses U.S. customary units for many measurements, the metric system is the most widely used system in the world.

Electrical units such as the ampere, volt, ohm, farad, and others are used interchangeably in the metric and customary systems. Therefore, you do not have to worry about converting metric volts to customary volts. A volt is a volt. You will, however, use metric prefixes with electrical units for

Prefix	Symbol	Relation to Basic Unit	Examples
mega	M	1,000,000	8MΩ (megohms) = 8,000,000 ohms
kilo	k	1,000	20 kV (kilovolts) = 20,000 volts
milli	m	0.001 OR $\frac{1}{1,000}$	50 mV (millivolts) = 0.050 volts
micro	μ	0.000 001 OR $\frac{1}{1,000,000}$	18 μA (microamps) = 0.000018 A
nano	η	0.000000001	20 nV (nanovolts) = 0.000000020 volts
pico (micro-micro)	ρ	0.000000000001	20 pF (picofarads) = 0.000000000020 farads

Figure 1-15. These are the metric prefixes and the symbols used with electrical units of measurement in automotive service.

easier measurements. Therefore, 8,000,000 ohms is expressed as 8 megohms (8 MΩ), which is 8 × 1,000,000 ohms. You will also work with measurements such as 15 milliamperes (15 mA), which is 0.015 ampere, and 25 kilovolts (25 kV), which is 25,000 volts. Most electrical test equipment is built with switches that do the multiplying and dividing for you. Figure 1-15 summarizes common electrical units of measurement.

OHM'S AND KIRCHHOFF'S LAWS

The work of two 19th-century German scientists gave us some principles, or laws, that explain the relationships of current, voltage, and resistance in circuits. These laws have practical value in your automotive electrical service work.

Ohm's Law

The measurement of electrical resistance was named after George Simon Ohm, and we touched on his law when we said that one ohm is the amount of resistance present when one volt moves one ampere of current through a circuit. Ohm stated the relationship of voltage, current, and resistance as a simple equation that can be written three ways:

1. Voltage = current × resistance.
2. Current = voltage ÷ resistance.
3. Resistance = voltage ÷ current.

These equations usually are written with voltage abbreviated as *E* for "electromotive force," current (amperes) abbreviated as *I* for "intensity," and resistance abbreviated as *R*. The equations above can be written:

1. $E = IR$.
2. $I = E \div R$.
3. $R = E \div I$.

Figure 1-16 shows that if you know any two values for a circuit, you can find the third through simple multiplication or division.

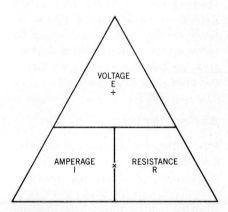

Figure 1-16. Use Ohm's law to calculate voltage, current, or resistance in a circuit if you know two of the values. Cover the unknown value and multiply or divide the other two.

Kirchhoff's Laws

Another 19th-century German scientist, Gustave Robert Kirchhoff, discovered two more facts about voltage and current. His laws are really examples of the principles of conservation of matter and energy. Neither matter nor energy can be created or destroyed, only changed. Kirchhoff's voltage law says:

> The sum of the voltage drops across all of the loads (items of resistance) in a circuit must equal the source voltage.

Kirchhoff's current law is:

> The sum of the currents flowing into any point in a circuit equals the sum of the currents flowing out of the same point.

> Electrons do not collect at any load or other point in a circuit and stop flowing. This is one reason that a circuit must be unbroken for any current to flow at all.

SIMPLE CIRCUITS

Ohm's and Kirchhoff's laws may seem a little abstract; but by looking at some simple circuits, you can see how they work. When you study and troubleshoot specific electrical systems, you will put these laws to work. To understand these laws better, we will look at three basic kinds of circuits: series, parallel, and series-parallel. To follow the diagrams for each circuit, you must recognize some symbols for electrical devices, such as batteries, loads, resistance, switches, and so on, figure 1-17.

Series Circuit

In a **series circuit,** current flow has only one path, figure 1-18. Following conventional current flow theory (+ to −), you can see that current flows from the battery, through the load (the resistance), and back to the battery. Figure 1-19 shows a circuit of a battery, two motors, and a switch in series. When the switch is closed and

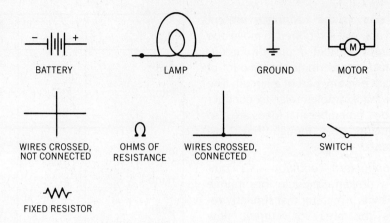

Figure 1-17. These are just a few of the electrical symbols you will learn as you study automotive electrical systems.

the circuit complete, current flows through both motors. Here are some applications of Ohm's and Kirchhoff's laws to a series circuit:

1. Because there is only one path for current flow, amperage is the same at every point in the circuit.

2. The total resistance of the circuit is the sum of the individual loads (resistors) in series. This can be one or any number of separate loads.

3. The total source voltage must be dropped across the total resistance load of the circuit. If the load is just one resistor, all voltage must be dropped across that one load. If there are several loads in the circuit, voltage drop across each is proportional to its resistance. Total voltage drop equals total source voltage.

Using Ohm's law, you can calculate the voltage, current, and resistance of the circuits shown in figures 1-18 and 1-19. Assume that the switches have no resistance when closed. In figure 1-18, you have a 4-ohm resistor connected to a 12-volt battery. You can calculate the amperage using Ohm's law thus:

$$E \div R = I$$
$$12 \div 4 = 3 \text{ amperes}$$

In figure 1-19, you have two 3-ohm resistors in the form of motors. Total series resistance equals 6 ohms. Voltage is again 12 volts, and again you calculate the circuit amperage:

$$E \div R = I$$
$$12 \div 6 = 2 \text{ amperes}$$

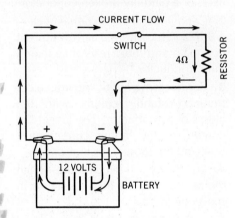

Figure 1-18. In a series circuit, all current flows equally through every part of the circuit. There is only one current path.

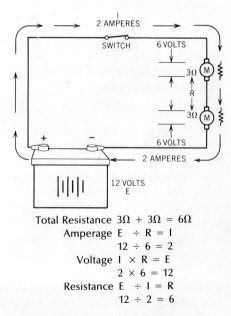

Total Resistance $3\Omega + 3\Omega = 6\Omega$
Amperage $E \div R = I$
$12 \div 6 = 2$
Voltage $I \times R = E$
$2 \times 6 = 12$
Resistance $E \div I = R$
$12 \div 2 = 6$

Figure 1-19. When the switch is closed and the circuit complete, current flows equally through both motors in series.

If you know the amount of current and the individual resistance of each load, you can calculate the source voltage or the voltage drop across each load.

For figure 1-18:

$$I = 3 \text{ amperes}, \quad R = 4 \text{ ohms}$$
$$I \times R = E$$
$$3 \times 4 = 12 \text{ volts}$$

For figure 1-19:

$$I = 2 \text{ amperes}, \quad R_1 = 3 \text{ ohms}, \quad R_2 = 3 \text{ ohms}$$
$$R_t \text{ (total)} = 3 + 3 = 6 \text{ ohms}$$
$$I \times R = E$$
$$2 \times 6 = 12 \text{ volts}$$

For figure 1-19, the voltage drop across each motor equals 2 amperes × 3 ohms, or 6 volts. The drop of 6 volts across each of two motors equals the source voltage of 12 volts, which proves Kirchhoff's voltage law.

If you know the current flow in a series circuit and the source voltage, you can calculate the total resistance as follows:

For figure 1-18:

$$E \div I = R$$
$$12 \div 3 = 4 \text{ ohms}$$

For figure 1-19:

$$12 \div 2 = 6 \text{ ohms total for both motors}$$

You can use the same formula to calculate the resistance of each motor in series; but to do so, you must know the voltage drop across each motor. The 6 ohms of total resistance in figure 1-19 could be 4 ohms and 2 ohms. To prove this calculation, you would have to know that one motor dropped 8 volts and the other dropped 4 volts.

Parallel Circuit

In a **parallel circuit**, current has two or more paths that it can follow. Current splits into parallel branches at junction points. The parallel branches are **shunt** circuits. Here are some applications of Ohm's and Kirchhoff's laws in parallel circuits:

1. The voltage across each branch, or applied to each parallel branch, is the same.

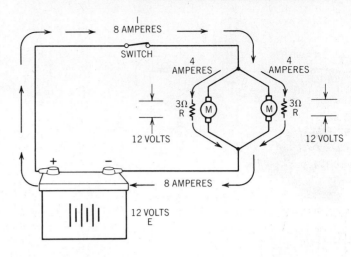

Total (Equivalent) Resistance
$$\frac{3\Omega \times 3\Omega}{3\Omega + 3\Omega}$$
$$\frac{9\Omega}{6\Omega}$$
$$1.5\Omega$$

Total Amperage $E \div R = I$
$$12 \div 1.5 = 8$$
Total Voltage $I \times R = E$
$$8 \times 1.5 = 12$$
Total Resistance $E \div I = R$
$$12 \div 8 = 1.5$$

Branch Amperage $E \div R = I$
$$12 \div 3 = 4$$
Branch Voltage $I \times R = E$
$$4 \times 3 = 12$$
Branch Resistance $E \div I = R$
$$12 \div 4 = 3$$

Figure 1-20. In a parallel circuit, current flow has two or more alternate paths.

2. Total resistance of a parallel circuit is less than the lowest individual resistance, because as you add resistors (or loads), in parallel, you are adding more conductors.

3. Total amperage in a parallel circuit equals the sum of the branch amperages.

Let's take the two motors from figure 1-19 and put them in parallel to see how it affects current flow and total circuit resistance, figure 1-20. Current now flows independently through each motor. If you remove one, you still have a complete circuit through the other.

Total resistance of a parallel circuit is called **equivalent resistance** because it is equivalent to the resistance of a single load in series with the voltage source. You can calculate this equivalent resistance in two ways. If the circuit has only two loads, as in figure 1-20, you can use the product-over-the-sum method:

$$\frac{3 \text{ ohms} \times 3 \text{ ohms}}{3 \text{ ohms} + 3 \text{ ohms}} = \frac{9}{6} = 1.5 \text{ ohms}$$

To use this method to calculate the equivalent resistance for a parallel circuit with more than two loads, repeat the formula for two resistances at a time until you determine one final resistance for the complete circuit. You also can use a formula that allows you to calculate the equivalent resistance for any number of parallel loads:

$$R_t = \frac{1}{R_1} + \frac{1}{R_2} + \frac{1}{R_3} + \cdots + \frac{1}{R_n}$$

To calculate amperage in a parallel circuit, you must treat each branch as a separate circuit because current in each branch is different. Voltage is equal across each branch, so divide the source voltage by the branch resistance to determine the branch amperage. For either motor in figure 1-20: do it like this:

$$E \div R = I$$
$$12 \div 3 = 4 \text{ amperes in each branch}$$

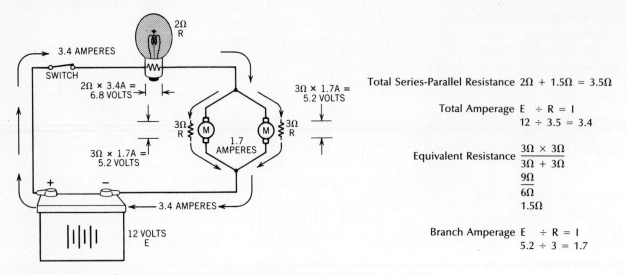

Figure 1-21. In a series-parallel circuit, some loads are in series; others are in parallel.

Total current flow for the complete circuit is 8 amperes because there are two identical branches. If you didn't know the resistance of each branch but did know the source voltage and the branch amperages, you could calculate each resistance as follows:

$$E \div I = R$$
$$12 \div 4 = 3 \text{ ohms}$$

You also can calculate the equivalent resistance for both motors in parallel as follows, using the source voltage and the total circuit amperage:

$$E \div I = R$$
$$12 \div 8 = 1.5 \text{ ohms}$$

That is the same value you obtained earlier, using the product-over-the-sum method with the two branch resistances.

If you know the resistance and current flow of any part of the circuit, or of the entire circuit, you can determine source voltage two ways. Using the resistance and amperage for one branch:

$$I \times R = E$$
$$4 \times 3 = 12 \text{ volts}$$

Using the total circuit amperage and equivalent resistance:

$$I \times R = E$$
$$8 \times 1.5 = 12 \text{ volts}$$

Series-Parallel Circuits

To troubleshoot automotive circuits, you sometimes test one part of a large system as a simple series circuit. Other times, you will have to test loads in parallel as in the preceding examples. Most complete automotive circuits, however, are **series-parallel circuits**. Some loads are in series with others, and some are in parallel. Let's take the same two motors in parallel from figure 1-20 and add an indicator lamp in series with them, figure 1-21. The two 3-ohm motors remain in parallel with each other, but the 2-ohm indictor is in series with both.

All of the rules you have learned for series circuits and for parallel circuits apply in series-parallel circuits. To calculate the voltage, amperage, or resistance for any part, or all, of the circuit, begin by reducing the parallel branches to equivalent series loads. Then combine the equivalent values with any actual series loads.

The 3-ohm motors in parallel, figure 1-21, have an equivalent resistance of 1.5 ohms. Now, add this value to the 2-ohm resistance of the lamp to determine total circuit resistance:

$$1.5 + 2 = 3.5 \text{ ohms}$$

You know that the source voltage is 12 volts, so divide 12 volts by 3.5 ohms total resistance to determine total current:

$$12 \div 3.5 = 3.4 \text{ amperes}$$

Total current in figure 1-21 is less than in figure 1-20 because total resistance is greater. Also, voltage across the parallel branches is less than 12 volts because part of the source voltage is dropped across the 2-ohm lamp. To calculate the voltage drop across the lamp, multiply the total current by the resistance of the lamp:

$$I \times R = E$$
$$3.4 \times 2 = 6.8 \text{ volts dropped across the indicator lamp}$$

This leaves 5.2 volts across both parallel branches. Current in each branch is:

$$E \div R = I$$
$$5.2 \div 3 = 1.7 \text{ amperes}$$

All values balance as they are supposed to. The sum of the voltage drops equals the source voltage (6.8 + 5.2 = 12). The amperage in each parallel branch adds up to the total circuit amperage (1.7 + 1.7 = 3.4).

This has been a brief introduction to basic electrical circuits. Testing and repairing electrical systems are not difficult if you understand the principles of circuits and take one troubleshooting step at a time.

CAPACITANCE

Capacitance is the ability, or capacity, of two conducting surfaces to store an electric charge, or voltage, when they are separated by an insulator. A device that has this ability is a capacitor. A capacitor also is called a **condenser** because electric charges collect, or condense, on the plates as water vapor condenses on a cold glass.

Capacitance is an electrical feature that operates in many areas of an automobile. The principle that opposite + and − charges attract each other leads to the idea that there is a field of electrical energy, or potential voltage, between any two oppositely charged points. This is called an **electrostatic field** because the charges do not move. They are stored on the two points as a form of static electricity. If you can cause opposite charges to collect on two surfaces, you can build a simple capacitor to store voltage.

A simple capacitor consists of two conductive plates, usually metal such as aluminum, zinc, steel, or copper. A conductor is attached to each plate, and an insulator is placed between them, figure 1-22. The insulator might be nothing more than the air in the space between the plates, or it might be some nonconductive material such as ceramic, glass, paper, or plastic. This insulator is called a **dielectric**.

If you install this capacitor in a circuit and start current flow by closing the switch, figure 1-23, electrons begin to flow from the battery around the circuit toward one plate of the capacitor. Because electrons cannot flow through the dielectric, they collect on one plate, which becomes negatively charged. Simultaneously, electrons also flow from the opposite plate of the capacitor toward the positive terminal of the battery. This plate then becomes positively charged.

Current flows only as long as it takes for the positive and negative voltage difference across the capacitor plates to equal the positive and negative difference of the source volt-

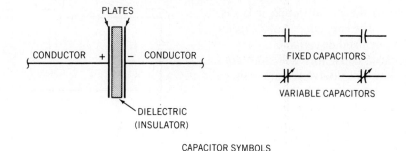

CAPACITOR SYMBOLS

Figure 1-22. A capacitor is two conductive surfaces, or plates, separated by an insulator.

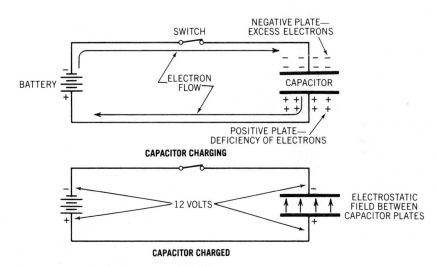

Figure 1-23. Current flow charges the capacitor to the same voltage as the battery; then current flow stops.

age. At that point, the negative terminal of the battery and the negative plate of the capacitor are at the same negative potential. The positive plate and the positive battery terminal are at equal positive potential. The voltage charges across the capacitor and across the battery are equal, and no more current will flow because the dielectric of the capacitor creates an open circuit. The charges on the capacitor will not change as long as the plates are not connected to each other or to some other point with a different potential.

Capacitors are rated in **farads** (F). One farad is an enormous voltage charge, so the capacitors in automobiles and other electronic systems have capacitance of microfarads (μF),

which is one-millionth (0.000001) of a farad. Three factors affect capacitance:

1. The larger the plate areas, the larger the charge the capacitor can hold, because there is a larger area on which the charge can collect.

2. The closer the plates, the larger the charge, because a strong electrostatic field exists between opposite charges that are close together.

3. The better the insulating qualities of the dielectric, the higher the capacitance.

Unlike a resistor, a capacitor does not consume any power or change any energy in a circuit. All of the voltage stored on a capacitor is returned to the circuit when it is discharged. The capacitance of a capacitor can be fixed or variable.

Because capacitors will store voltage, they will slow down any voltage change in a circuit. They often are used to absorb voltage changes in a circuit and are thus "shock absorbers." A capacitor has low resistance to current flow until it is charged, and then its resistance is infinite.

If you connect a capacitor in parallel across a 12-volt circuit, initial current flow charges the capacitor, then flows through other devices in the circuit, figure 1-24. If a high-voltage pulse hits the circuit (as can happen in an automobile), the capacitor absorbs the extra voltage as an additional charge before the current can damage any other part of the circuit. Capacitors are also used as short-circuit shunts to cause current to stop quickly when a circuit is opened. This is one of the jobs of an ignition condenser. A capacitor can also store a high-voltage charge and then discharge it quickly when connected across a circuit that needs the voltage. These are a few of the general uses for capacitors in automotive systems that you will discover in this text.

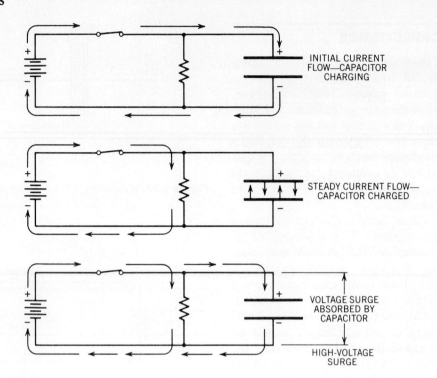

Figure 1-24. The capacitor absorbs voltage changes in this circuit and acts as a voltage shock absorber.

ELECTRIC POWER—WATTS

You have just reviewed the principles of electric current, voltage, and resistance and have seen how they operate together in basic circuits. You have also seen how electric current is the controlled flow of electrons among atoms. Atoms and their electrons are basic forms of matter. You have learned that current flow is electricity at work and that voltage is the force, or energy, that causes the work to be done. You also learned earlier in this chapter that power is the rate at which work is done. The unit of electric power is the **watt**. You calculate watts by multiplying current times voltage. Using the symbol P for power, the formula is:

$$P = E \times I$$

Thus, a circuit with 3 amperes of

current flowing and a source voltage of 12 volts produces 36 watts of power. This power can be an electric motor, or a lamp, or some other device that does work, figure 1-25. If you are wondering where the time factor (rate of doing work) enters the power equation, remember that it is part of the definition of current. One ampere of current equals 6.28 billion billion (6.28×10^{18}) electrons moving past a single point per second. For simplicity, engineers call this quantity of electrons one coulomb. An ampere, therefore, equals electron movement of one coulomb per second.

To prove the relationship between mechanical and electric power, you can substitute coulombs per second for amperes in the power equation. In this example, t equals the rate of time (one second):

$$P = E \times \frac{Q}{t}$$

Whether power is developed as mechanical motion or as heat or light, energy does work over a specific period of time.

Wattage ratings are often given for bulbs, motors, and other devices. Using this rating and the formulas of Ohm's law, you can calculate other circuit values. For example, a 36-watt lamp in a 12-volt circuit draws 3 amperes of current because:

If $P = E \times I$, then $I = P \div E$
36 watts $\div$ 12 volts = 3 amperes

Therefore, the resistance of that 36-watt bulb must be 4 ohms because, using Ohm's law:

$$E \div I = R$$
$$12 \div 3 = 4 \text{ ohms}$$

The electric power formula ($P = E \times I$) relates directly to Ohm's law:

If $E = IR$, then $P = (IR)I$ or
$$P = I^2R$$
If $I = E \div R$, then $P = E(E \div R)$ or
$$P = E^2 \div R$$

These formulas can help your electrical troubleshooting. If you know the wattage rating of a bulb, you can calculate what the circuit resistance ought to be and compare that to the measured resistance of the circuit.

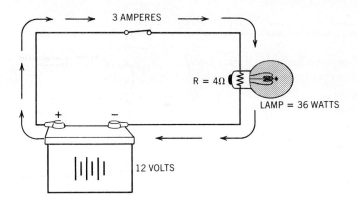

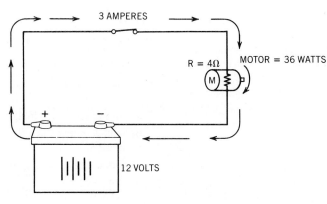

Figure 1-25. Watts, or wattage, is the measurement of electrical power. Watts = amperes × volts.

Watts and Horsepower

Since the watt and the horsepower are both units for measuring the rate at which work is done, there is a relationship between them. Horsepower equals force times distance times time. One horsepower equals 200 pounds moved 165 feet in one minute, or 33,000 foot-pounds per minute. This equals 550 foot-pounds per second. Voltage is a measure of force, similar to pounds. Amperage is a measurement of rate of movement, similar to feet per minute. (One ampere = 6.28 x 10^{18} electrons per second). When one volt of force moves that many electrons per second (one ampere), we have one watt of power. To think of the difference between one watt and one horsepower very simply, one electron is much smaller than a foot. Therefore, one watt is smaller than one horsepower. In fact, 1 horsepower = 746 watts.

SUMMARY

This chapter has summarized a basic course in dc electrical systems in a few pages. Its purpose is to help you understand the basics of all automotive electrical devices. Whether the next subject you study is batteries, alternators, starter motors, or ignition systems, remember these basic facts:

1. Current is the flow of electrons measured in amperes. It flows through a complete path called a circuit.

2. Current is either direct or alternating. The conventional current flow theory says that current flows from + to −; the electron flow theory says it flows from − to +.

3. Voltage is force applied to or across a circuit that causes current to flow.

4. Resistance opposes current and is measured in ohms. It is contained within a circuit.

5. Circuits are either series, parallel, or series-parallel. A series circuit has only one current path. A parallel circuit has several current paths. A series-parallel circuit has some loads in series and others in parallel.

6. Ohm's law says: "One ohm of resistance is present when one volt forces one ampere to flow in a circuit." Mathematically, Ohm's law is written:

- Voltage (E) = Current (I) × Resistance (R)
- Current (I) = Voltage (E) ÷ Resistance (R)
- Resistance (R) = Voltage (E) ÷ Current (I)

7. Capacitance is the ability of two surfaces to store voltage as an electrostatic charge.

8. The unit of electric power is the watt. Wattage equals current (I) times voltage (E).

REVIEW QUESTIONS

Multiple Choice

1. Student A says that good electrical conductors are materials with few electrons in the outer shell. Student B says that good conductors have full valence shells. Who is right?

a. A only
b. B only
c. both A and B
d. neither A nor B

2. Student A says that two hydrogen atoms joined with one oxygen atom form a molecule. Student B says that two hydrogen atoms joined with one oxygen atom form a compound. Who is right?

a. A only
b. B only
c. both A and B
d. neither A nor B

3. Electron energy becomes useful electricity when:

a. the negative charge is high enough
b. the positive charge is high enough
c. atoms share many valence electrons
d. all free electrons are forced to move in the same direction from point to point.

4. Student A says that power is a measurement of the distance that force moves an object. Student B says that power is a measurement of the rate, or speed, at which work is done. Who is right?

a. A only
b. B only
c. both A and B
d. neither A nor B

5. Good electrical conductors have how many free electrons in the outer shells of their atoms or molecules?

a. 3 or fewer
b. 4 or fewer
c. 6 or more
d. 8 or more

6. Controlled movement of electrons from one point to another is:

a. voltage
b. current
c. resistance
d. capacitance

7. Electromotive force that moves electrons from point to point is:

a. voltage
b. current
c. resistance
d. capacitance

8. Student A says that conventional current moves from positive (+) to negative (−). Student B says the electron theory states that electrons flow from negative (−) to positive (+). Who is right?

a. A only
b. B only
c. both A and B
d. neither A nor B

9. Student A says that an alternator generates direct current. Student B says that automotive electrical systems operate on alternating current. Who is right?

a. A only
b. B only
c. both A and B
d. neither A nor B

10. For current to flow and produce useful work, every circuit must have:

a. capacitance
b. inductance
c. resistance
d. reluctance

11. An open circuit has no:

a. resistance
b. reluctance
c. voltage
d. continuity

12. Student A says that voltage across a circuit equals current times resistance of the circuit. Student B says that power consumed by a circuit equals voltage times current. Who is right?

a. A only
b. B only
c. both A and B
d. neither A nor B

13. If voltage across a series circuit is 12 volts and current is 3 amperes, resistance must be:

a. 36 ohms
b. 4 ohms

c. 0.25 ohm
d. 6 ohms

14. If current in a circuit is 10 amperes and resistance is 1.4 ohms, voltage must be:

a. 7 volts
b. 12 volts
c. 14 volts
d. 10 volts

15. Student A says that a parallel circuit has several current paths. Student B says that a series-parallel circuit has several current paths. Who is right?

a. A only
b. B only
c. both A and B
d. neither A nor B

16. Total current in a parallel circuit equals the:

a. sum of resistance in each branch
b. voltage minus the resistance of each branch
c. sum of the amperage in each branch
d. sum of the voltage across each branch

17. If total circuit resistance is 5 ohms, 9 volts will deliver how much current?

a. 1.8 amperes
b. 2.4 amperes
c. 0.55 ampere
d. 0.41 ampere

18. A 12-volt circuit with 6 amperes of current consumes how much power?

a. 2 watts
b. 20 watts
c. 48 watts
d. 72 watts

19. The field of electrical energy between two oppositely charged points (+ and −) is:

a. magnetic flux
b. a dielectric
c. an electrostatic field
d. permeability

Fill in the Blank

20. When a liquid becomes a gas, it is _Vaporized_

21. A balanced atom has equal numbers of _Electrons_ and _Protons_ .

22. An unbalanced atom is an _____ .

23. The outer electron orbit, or shell, of an atom is the _Valence_ shell.

24. Electrons that move easily from their _shell_ to the _shell_ of other atoms are free electrons.

25. Atoms or molecules with many bound electrons are good electrical _insulators_

26. Force multiplied by distance equals _watts_ .

27. A rate of 550 foot-pounds of work per second equals one _Amp_ .

28. Loosely held valence electrons that move easily into the electron shells of other atoms are called _free_ electrons.

29. Tightly held valence electrons that take quite a bit of energy to dislodge them are called _____ electrons.

30. The electromotive force that produces current flow is called _Voltage_ .

31. Elements with four valence electrons that are neither good conductors nor good insulators are called _Semi Conductors_

32. To conduct electricity, a copper wire must have a positive charge at one end and a _Negative_ charge at the other end.

33. The unit of current measurement is the _Amps_ .

34. Current that flows, at equal intervals, from positive to negative and back to positive is called _Direct_ current.

35. The principal voltage sources in an automobile are the battery and the _Alternator_

36. The unit used to measure the amount of resistance in a circuit is the _Ohm's_ .

37. To calculate the voltage across a circuit, you must know the current and the _resistance_

38. Total resistance of a parallel circuit is called _total_ resistance.

39. To calculate electric power (watts), you need to know current and _Voltage_ .

40. The unit used to rate capacitors is the _____ .

2 SOURCES OF ELECTRICITY AND ELECTROMAGNETIC INDUCTION

WHAT

Chapter 1 introduced the principles that are the foundation for our knowledge and use of electricity. The first chapter also explained basic circuits and the fundamentals of electric current, voltage, and resistance. This chapter continues with the principles of electricity by examining the sources used to generate electric current and voltage.

Among these sources, electrochemistry and electromagnetism are the most important for automotive use. This chapter explains the relationships between electricity and magnetism and how electromagnetism is used on an automobile.

WHY

An automobile uses electric power to crank the engine, ignite the air-fuel mixture, light lamps, provide heat, and perform several kinds of mechanical work. To do these jobs, the automobile must generate its own electricity. A modern automobile is a complex, self-contained electric power system.

To understand automotive electrical systems completely, you must understand the sources of electric power. Several methods can be used to generate electric current and voltage. Chief among these for automotive uses are electrochemistry and electromagnetism. Moreover, electromagnetism allows electric power to do mechanical work in various systems. Knowing the principles of electromagnetism will help you to understand the similarities among different electrical systems.

GOALS

After studying this chapter, you should be able to:

1. Explain how electricity is generated by friction, heat, light, pressure, chemistry, and magnetism.

2. Explain the basic operation of a voltage cell and the difference between primary and secondary batteries.

3. Explain magnetic lines of force, polarity, permeability, and reluctance.

4. Explain electromagnetic principles and electromagnetic induction.

SOURCES OF ELECTRICITY

Up to this point, we have talked about voltage and current simply as existing without giving much thought to how electricity is generated. Remember that electrical energy, like any energy, is generated by changing the form of some other energy. There are six common ways to do this. Examples of all six exist in your car, but chemistry and magnetism are the most important.

1. *Friction*—If you rub some materials together, friction transfers electrons from one surface to another. One surface becomes positively charged; the other becomes negatively charged. These charges are stationary, or static, so this kind of voltage is called **static electricity**. The surfaces remain positively and negatively charged until they are connected or brought close enough together so that the potential difference can discharge through brief current flow. Tires rolling on pavement can build up a static charge on a vehicle frame that might be discharged if the frame is connected back to the ground. That's why gasoline trucks have straps connected to the frame that drag on the ground to eliminate the static charge as fast as it collects.

2. *Heat*—If you join two pieces of two different metals and heat the junction, you can create a voltage difference between the other ends of the wires. If you connect the unheated ends of the wires to a circuit, a small amount of current will flow. The voltage may be only a few thousandths of a volt (millivolt), and the current might be only a few millionths of an ampere (microampere). This voltage and current, however, can be used in a temperature-sensing device called a **thermocouple**. This kind of electricity is **thermoelectricity**, and it is used in some engine temperature sensors in engineering laboratories. Thermocouples also can be used in electronic control systems, but extra amplifying circuits are needed to increase the signal voltage. Therefore, simpler kinds of sensors are generally used for automotive on-board applications.

3. *Pressure*—When you apply pressure to some crystals, such as quartz or a diamond, voltage develops between the surfaces of the crystal. This is **piezoelectricity** and is how a phonograph needle and some microphones work. Piezoelectricity also is used to create voltage or to vary resistance in many electronic engine control systems. Piezoresistance is used in engine detonation sensors. Voltage is applied to a sensor that changes its resistance as pressure is applied to it. This changing resistance causes a variable voltage drop across the resistor and, thus, a variable-voltage sensor signal.

4. *Light*—If you expose certain metals to light, some of the light energy releases free electrons in the metal. If you connect one end of a conductor to the metal and the other end to a point with a different potential charge, the free electrons will flow as current. This is called **photoelectricity**, and it is used in automatic headlamp dimmers, speed sensors, and other devices.

Some photoelectric cells are made of iron and selenium with a translucent insulator between the two metals. When light strikes the cell, the iron releases electrons, and the selenium collects them. This creates a voltage between the two metals. If you connect the iron and selenium sides of the photoelectric sandwich to opposite sides of a circuit, current will flow as long as the light source is present. If you remove the light, current stops, and voltage returns to zero.

Photoelectricity also is used in many electronic sensors. In such a sensor, a light-emitting diode (LED) directs a light beam toward a phototransistor. When the light beam is interrupted by a rotating shutter or a reflector, the phototransistor turns off and on to generate a timing or speed signal. You will see this application of photoelectricity in some electronic ignitions and many vehicle speed sensors.

5. *Chemistry*—If you put two different conductive materials (usually metals or metal compounds) in a conductive and reactive solution (such as an acid), you can create a voltage between the two materials. One becomes positively charged; the other becomes negatively charged. This happens because of the action of the valence electrons of the two conductive materials and the conductive solution. The action is based on the principles you learned in chapter 1 and is called **electrochemistry**. This is the way an automotive battery develops voltage. This also is the way an engine exhaust gas oxygen sensor develops a signal voltage for an electronic feedback control system.

6. *Magnetism*—If you pass an electrical conductor through the lines of force that surround a magnet, you can cause current to flow in the conductor. Similarly, current flowing in a conductor creates a magnetic field around the conductor. **Electromagnetic** action is an important source of electricity in an automobile. It is also the basis for changing electrical energy to mechanical energy. Magnetic principles generate electricity in an alternator and allow the electrical energy to do work in various electric motors. Electromagnetic action also provides the high voltage necessary to ignite the air-fuel mixture in an engine. Solenoids, relays, and other electromagnetic devices change electrical energy to mechanical force. A later section of this chapter outlines the electromagnetic principles that operate in different automotive systems.

ELECTROCHEMISTRY

Because an automobile uses electric power to start the internal-combustion engine, it must have one electric power source that does not depend upon mechanical energy to generate current and voltage. That electric power source is the battery.

This may seem obvious today, but it was not obvious in the early days of the automobile. The first self-propelled vehicles with internal-combustion engines were built in the 1890's. It wasn't until 1908 that Charles Kettering patented the electrical inductive-discharge ignition with a battery as the power source. It was another four years (1912) before Kettering perfected the electric starter motor. For almost two decades, automotive engineers concentrated on developing the engine and chassis. They didn't worry too much about luxuries such as self-starters and electric lights. When Kettering and other pioneer engineers proved the practicality of putting a battery on board an automobile, mobile electric power became common.

Today, the engineering logic is simple. Use a battery and a small, but powerful, electric motor to start the engine. Use the same battery for initial power for the ignition system. Use a battery that can be recharged after it provides the initial starting and ignition power. Once the engine is running, use some of its power to generate electric power.

Electrochemical Action

Historically, automotive batteries have been called "storage batteries," but a battery does more than store electricity. A battery changes chemical energy to electrical energy and is thus a source of electric power. A battery produces electricity through the chemical reaction that occurs in a **voltage cell**. The name "battery" really means a collection of voltage cells, but we use the name to identify anything from a single-cell flashlight battery to a multicell automobile battery.

The Voltage Cell. A voltage cell consists of two dissimilar materials placed in a third material (usually a liquid or a paste) that is both conductive and reactive. The conductive and reactive liquid or paste is the **electrolyte**. The two dissimilar materials are the cell **electrodes**. The electrolyte is the medium through which the electrodes react. One of the electrodes releases electrons and becomes positively charged. This is called the **anode**. The other electrode collects electrons and becomes negatively charged. This is called the **cathode**.

This electrochemical reaction creates a difference in potential electrical energy—a voltage—between the two electrodes. The electrodes of a voltage cell have terminals for connection to an external circuit. When the terminals are connected to a circuit, the voltage causes electrons to flow through the circuit. This current flow makes the voltage cell a source of electric power. The cell stores energy in chemical form and releases the electricity in electrical form when it is connected to a circuit.

The first practical voltage cell was developed about 1800 by Alessandro Volta, from whose name we get the words, "volt" and "voltage." He used zinc and copper as the dissimilar electrodes and deposited the electrolyte on moist paper between the two metals. Today, we use several kinds and sizes of voltage cells, or batteries of cells, as common sources of electric power. The electrodes may be two different metals, or they may be metal and carbon. The electrolyte may be in liquid form, or it may be in semisolid paste form.

Cells and Batteries. A dry-cell battery has a carbon positive electrode (anode) and a zinc negative electrode (cathode). The cathode is usually the cell case, and the anode is a carbon rod in the center. The electrolyte is not truly "dry" but is contained in a damp paste inside the cell. The electrolyte reacts with the carbon anode and drives electrons to the zinc cathode.

An automotive battery is a wet-cell battery. The electrolyte is a liquid mixture of water (H_2O) and sulfuric acid (H_2SO_4). The electrodes are dissimilar metals: soft, or spongy, lead (Pb) and lead dioxide (PbO_2). In a fully charged automotive battery, the lead (Pb) electrodes are the cathode, with surplus electrons and a negative ($-$) charge. The lead dioxide (PbO_2) electrodes are the anode with a deficiency of electrons and a positive ($+$) charge.

Whether a battery is based on a carbon-zinc dry cell or a lead-acid wet cell, the electrochemical reaction is basically the same. When any voltage cell is fully charged, the positive

anode reacts with the negative cathode through the electrolyte. The anode gives up electrons to the cathode to develop the voltage between the two terminals of the cell. When the cell terminals are connected to each other through an outside circuit, electrons flow from the cathode, through the circuit, and back to the anode. The cathode becomes less negative, and the anode becomes less positive. When the positive and negative charges of the anode ($+$) and cathode ($-$) become equal, no voltage difference exists between them. Electrons then cease to flow through the outside circuit, and the cell is discharged.

While electrons were flowing in the circuit, the electrochemical energy of the cell was changed to heat, light, or mechanical energy in the circuit. Because electrochemistry produces electron flow in only one direction, a battery can produce only direct-current (dc) power.

Voltage and Current in Battery Cells. The chemical structure of the materials used as electrodes and electrolyte in any cell determines the maximum voltage available from the cell. Typical dry-cell batteries with zinc and carbon electrodes develop about 1.5 volts per cell. Automotive batteries with dissimilar lead materials as electrodes and sulfuric acid as the electrolyte develop about 2.1 volts per cell. A single cell may be large or small, but it always develops about the same maximum voltage, depending on the materials used in its construction. To obtain higher voltage, we must connect several cells together in a battery.

If we connect several cells in series, the cell voltages add together to produce total battery voltage. A 12-volt automotive battery has six 2.1-volt, lead-acid cells in series: + terminal of one cell connected to − terminal of the next cell. (Total maximum voltage of a 12-volt battery is actually about 12.6 volts.) A 9-volt dry-cell battery for a transistor radio actually has six small cells of 1.5 volts each, connected in series.

While cell materials determine the maximum voltage, cell size determines the maximum current. There is a very simple physical explanation for this. Current is the flow of electrons (a form of matter) between the electrodes. The larger the electrodes, the more electrons are available to flow as current. Therefore, a large battery can deliver more total current than a small battery. For example, a D-size dry-cell battery and a AA-size dry-cell battery both produce 1.5 volts. The larger D-size, however, produces more current to operate a flashlight longer or brighter than the smaller AA-size.

By connecting several voltage cells in parallel, you can increase current capacity as if you built a larger cell. Connecting all + electrodes to each other and all − electrodes to each other has the same effect as building larger electrodes. Parallel cell connections provide more electrons for electric current, but the total voltage between the final + and − terminals is the same as that of a single cell.

We have an example of series and parallel connections of battery cells in the battery installations on some diesel automobiles. Six battery cells in series form a 12-volt battery. Two 12-volt batteries in parallel provide 12 volts to crank the engine, but the parallel connection doubles the current available from a single battery.

Primary and Secondary Batteries

Every battery—dry cell or wet cell, large or small—is either a **primary battery** or a **secondary battery**. In a primary battery, the electrochemical action is not reversible. Eventually, one or both of the electrodes is destroyed. The electrochemical action ceases, and the battery can no longer produce voltage and current. The most common dry-cell batteries are primary batteries. When they no longer provide enough power for our flashlights or radios, we throw them away. Some dry-cell batteries, such as nickel-cadmium batteries, can be recharged. These are secondary batteries.

In a secondary battery, the electrochemical action is reversible. The chemical structure of the electrodes in a secondary battery changes as the battery discharges and delivers current. We can reverse the discharging action, however, by applying charging current to the battery in the opposite direction. The charging current reverses the electrochemical action and restores the battery electrodes and electrolyte to their original conditions. The battery again stores chemical energy that can be converted to electrical energy.

Chapter 7 explains the operation and construction of automotive batteries in more detail. Chapters 6 and 13 explain electrochemistry in exhaust gas oxygen sensors. At this point in your study of electricity, it is important to recognize electrochemistry as one basic source of electric power on an automobile. Because a battery must be recharged and because the automobile requires continuous electric power for long periods, the vehicle must have another source of electricity. This brings us to the subjects of magnetism and electromagnetism.

MAGNETISM

Magnetism is caused by the movement of electrons in some materials and is recognized by the force it exerts on other materials. The properties of **magnetism** are similar to, but not the same as, the properties of electricity. All materials have electrical conductivity and resistance. All materials have the magnetic properties of permeability and reluctance. Although these properties are not the same, their relationships are similar. Also, electric current flow depends upon the force of potential energy between opposite positive and negative terminals. Magnetic lines of force depend on the attraction and repulsion of opposite magnetic poles. Every electric principle has a magnetic **analogy**.

Magnetic Field (Flux)

Iron is the most common magnetic material. Some other metals have magnetic properties but not nearly as strong as those of iron. Still other materials—elements or compounds—such as aluminum, glass, wood, and all gases, cannot be magnetized at all. We recognize magnetism by the presence of magnetic lines of force around an object. These lines of force are a **magnetic field** caused by the alignment of atoms within the material. One theory says that the electrons of an atom have circles of force around them. When the electrons of an iron bar are aligned so that the circles of force add together, the iron is magnetized.

In a bar of iron that is magnetized, the lines of force in the magnetic field concentrate at the ends of the bar and form closed parallel loops around the bar, figure 2-1. The lines have direction and exist between the opposite ends, or poles, of the magnet. The

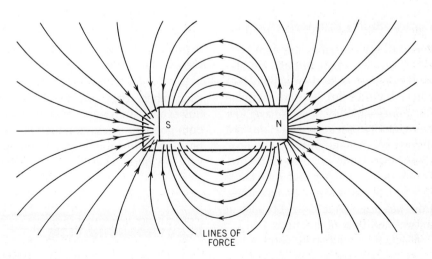

LINES OF FORCE

Figure 2-1. Magnetic lines of force form a magnetic field that surrounds a magnet.

lines are called **flux lines**, and a magnetic field is often called **magnetic flux**. The **flux density** of a magnetic field indicates the number of flux lines per square centimeter of any area. If 100 flux lines pass through 10 square centimeters, the flux density of that area is 100 divided by 10, or simply 10, figure 2-2. Flux density is strongest near the poles of a magnet.

Magnetic Polarity

Every magnet has a north (N) and a south (S) **pole**. The poles of a magnet relate to each other as positive and negative charges relate to each other. Unlike poles (N and S) attract each other; like poles (N and N, or S and S) repel each other, figure 2-3. We call this magnetic **polarity**. We also use the term polarity to describe the opposite + and − terminals of an electric circuit.

Flux lines exit from the north pole of a magnet and enter the south pole. Flux density is equal at each pole because an equal number of lines enter and exit. The flow of flux lines is what causes the poles to attract and repel each other. If you bring two south poles close together, flux lines try to enter both, and the flux density forces the poles apart. If you bring a north and a south pole close together, flux lines exit from one and enter the other, so their natural flow draws the poles together.

Permeability and Reluctance

Permeability describes the ease with which flux lines pass through a material. Iron has high permeability because it allows flux lines to pass easily. Gases—including air—have low permeability because they do not allow easy passage of magnetic flux. **Reluctance** is the opposite of permeability. A material has high reluctance if it resists the passage of flux lines. Iron has low reluctance because it allows easy flow of flux lines.

Magnetic permeability and reluctance relate to each other as electrical conductivity and resistance relate to

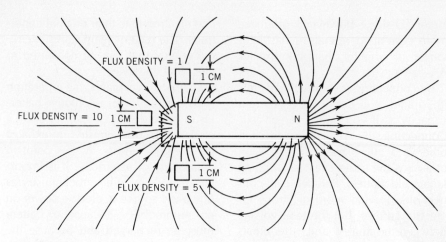

Figure 2-2. Flux density is the number of flux lines per square centimeter. It is strongest near the poles of a magnet.

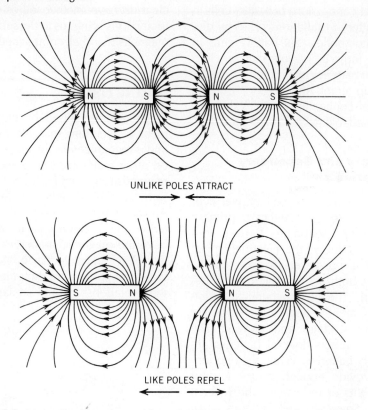

UNLIKE POLES ATTRACT

LIKE POLES REPEL

Figure 2-3. Magnetic poles attract and repel each other just as + and − electrical charges do.

each other. They are not the same, however. Aluminum and iron are both good electrical conductors. Iron has high permeability; aluminum has very low permeability.

ELECTROMAGNETISM

An important relationship between electricity and magnetism provides the major source of electric power in an automobile. As current flows through a conductor, a magnetic field forms around the conductor. There is a direct relationship between the amount of current in amperes and the strength (flux density) of the field. Moreover, there is a relationship between the direction of current flow and the polarity of the field. Magnetism that develops because of current flow is called **electromagnetism**.

Drill

#1 Explain in your own words.

Basically if you grabbed a bar with both hands with negative being on the ~~l~~ palm side of the ~~left~~ left hand and stretching your thumb out on the left hand you have demonstrated the conventional ~~flow~~ theory of current ~~flow~~. But if you look at your right hand and think of your palm being the ~~+~~ positive and with the thumb stretched out and being negative you have demonstrated the electron theory of current flow.

#2 Polarity

3 Reluctance

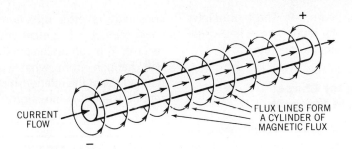

Figure 2-4. Current flow in a conductor forms cylinders of magnetic flux.

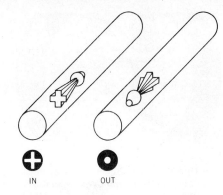

Figure 2-5. We use these current flow direction symbols in electrical and electromagnetic diagrams.

Electromagnetic Field

The magnetic field around a current-carrying wire is a series of concentric cylinders of flux lines, figure 2-4. The greater the current flow, the greater the flux density. The flux lines of the cylinders have direction like the flux lines of a bar magnet. The direction of current flow in the wire determines the direction of the flux lines.

We use arrows to show the direction of current flow, which you can see easily in the side view. If you look at the end of a wire in which current is flowing toward you, you see the head of an arrow, shown by a dot, figure 2-5. If you look at the end of a wire with current flowing away from you, you see the tail of an arrow, shown by a cross or a +.

If you know the direction of current, you can figure out the direction of the flux lines by using the right-hand rule or the left-hand rule. Using the conventional current theory from + to −, if you grasp a wire with your right hand so that your thumb points in the direction of current flow, your fingers wrap around the wire in the direction of the flux lines. This is the **right-hand rule**, figure 2-6.

Using the electron theory of current flow from − to +, if you grasp a wire with your left hand so that your thumb points toward current flow, your fingers again wrap around the wire in the direction of the flux lines. This is the **left-hand rule**, figure 2-7. You can use either the right-hand or the left-hand rule for current flow and magnetic field relationships as long as you

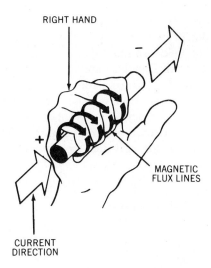

Figure 2-6. The right-hand rule of current flow and field direction is based on the conventional theory of current flow. (Delco-Remy)

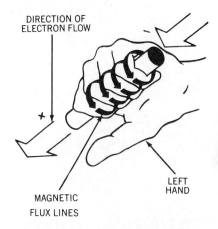

Figure 2-7. The left-hand rule of current flow and field direction is based on the electron current flow theory. (Delco-Remy)

use the correct rule for each current flow theory and don't mix them.

Field Interaction

The flux cylinders around conductors react with each other just as the fields around bar magnets do because all flux lines have direction and set up magnetic poles. If you bring two wires with current flowing in opposite directions close together, their fields oppose each other and force the wires apart, figure 2-8. If you bring two wires with current flowing in the same direction close together, their fields attract each other and draw the wires closer. You can do the same things with the electromagnetic fields of conductors and the fields of permanent

STRONG FIELD BETWEEN CONDUCTORS

CONDUCTORS TEND TO MOVE APART

Figure 2-8. When current flows in opposite directions, the resulting magnetic fields oppose each other and force the conductors apart. (Delco-Remy)

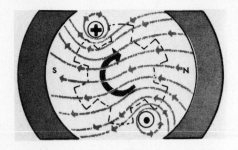

Figure 2-9. The interaction of magnetic fields causes electric motors to operate. (Delco-Remy)

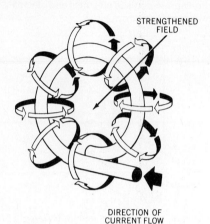

STRENGTHENED FIELD

DIRECTION OF CURRENT FLOW

Figure 2-10. The magnetic field in the center of a loop is strengthened because the flux lines combine their strength. (Delco-Remy)

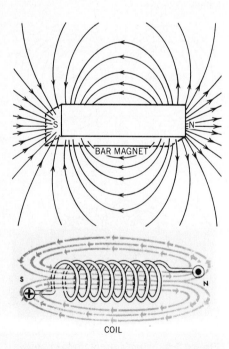

BAR MAGNET

COIL

Figure 2-11. The magnetic field around a coil has north and south poles similar to those of a bar magnet. (Delco-Remy)

magnets, figure 2-9. These principles of field interaction are what cause electric motors to operate.

Conductor Shape and Field Strength

You can strengthen the field around a conductor by bending it into a loop, figure 2-10. This causes the fields that meet in the center of the loop to attract each other or combine their strengths. You can strengthen the field even more by continuing to wind the conductor into a coil. When you do this, the field around the coil takes the shape of a field around a bar magnet, figure 2-11. The coil forms a north and a south pole from which the flux lines exit and enter. The strength of this field is determined by the number of turns in the coil and the amount of current flowing into it.

Electromagnets

You can further strengthen the field of a coil by placing an iron bar inside it. Because the iron is more permeable than air, flux lines concentrate in the iron. When you do this, you create an **electromagnet**, figure 2-12. Electromagnets are used in **relays** and **solenoids** in many automotive systems. Relays are used as remote switches that allow a small amount of current in one circuit to open or close a switch in a circuit with more current. Solenoids are used to create mechanical motion. Chapter 3 explains relay and solenoid operation in detail.

Simple electromagnets operate on direct current. Alternating current that

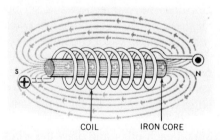

COIL   IRON CORE

Figure 2-12. An iron bar placed in a current-carrying coil becomes an electromagnet. (Delco-Remy)

constantly reverses directions would cause the field of an electromagnet to reverse. You can understand why this will happen from what you have learned about the relationships of current flow and flux direction.

ELECTROMAGNETIC INDUCTION

Magnetic flux lines generate current and voltage in a conductor if either the field or the conductor is moving. The resulting current and voltage are called **induced current** and **induced voltage**. The process is called **electromagnetic induction** and is the principle of all commercial electric power generation.

Voltage is induced by **relative motion** between the conductor and the field. This can occur in three ways:

1. The conductor can move through a stationary field, figure 2-13.
2. The field can move past or around a stationary conductor, figure 2-14.
3. The flux lines of a magnetic field expand or collapse as current flow increases or decreases through a conductor, figure 2-15.

All three methods are used to induce voltage in automotive electrical systems. The first two ways depend on mechanical movement of a conductor or a magnet and are easy to visualize. The third way depends on the motion of increasing or decreasing magnetic energy and is not as easy to visualize.

Rotating Conductor—The Generator

If you put a loop conductor in the field between two stationary magnets and rotate the conductor, you will induce a voltage in the conductor, figure 2-13. The polarity of the voltage changes every half revolution because the rotating conductor cuts the flux lines in opposite directions.

1. At point A, the conductors move parallel with the field. No voltage is induced.

2. At point B, the conductors have rotated 90 degrees and cut the maximum number of flux lines. This induces maximum positive voltage.

3. At point C, the conductors are again parallel with the field. Again, no voltage is induced.

4. At point D, the conductors have rotated another 90 degrees and cut the maximum number of flux lines, but in the opposite direction. This induces maximum negative voltage.

5. At point E, the conductors have returned to the same position as in point A, and no voltage is induced. One induction cycle is finished, and another is about to start.

Generator Rectification. Current that results from the induced voltage is alternating current (ac). The induced alternating current and voltage must be changed, or **rectified**, to direct current (dc) and a regulated dc voltage. Remember that the battery is the

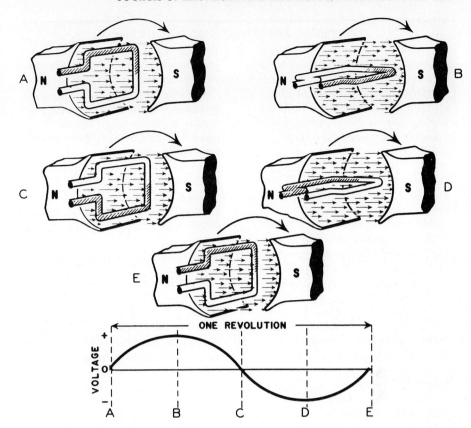

Figure 2-13. An ac voltage is induced as a rotating conductor cuts through the flux lines of a stationary magnetic field. (Prestolite)

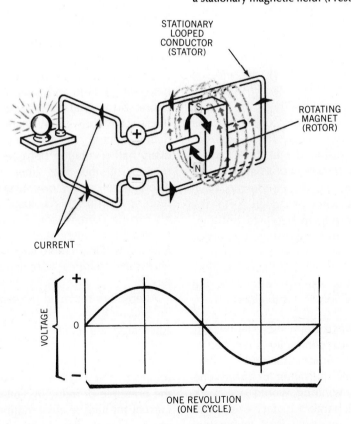

Figure 2-14. An ac voltage is induced as the flux lines of a rotating magnet cut through a stationary conductor. (Delco-Remy)

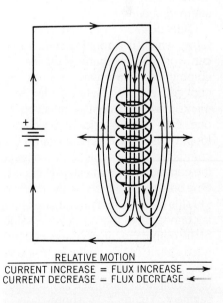

Figure 2-15. As a magnetic field expands and contracts, the relative motion of the changing flux density induces voltage in a conductor.

NATURAL AND ARTIFICIAL MAGNETS

There are two different types of magnets: natural and artificial. Natural magnets are formed by nature and are found in the form of a black iron ore called magnetite. Since the demand for inexpensive magnetic material far exceeds the limited availability of natural magnets, scientists discovered that by placing certain types of metals or alloys in an intense magnetic field, they could produce artificial magnets.

When subjected to such a magnetic field, substances such as iron, steel, or alloys of aluminum and nickel (known as "Alnico") will acquire the same magnetic properties as magnetite, but with considerably more magnetic strength.

Artificial magnets made from softer metals such as iron will gradually lose their magnetic properties. These are known as "temporary" magnets. When harder substances such as steel or Alnico are used to create magnets, they tend to retain the magnetic properties over a very long period of time. They are known as "permanent" magnets.

The latest development in magnet technology is the use of an artificial magnet material called Magnequench®. This material possesses magnetic properties that are far superior to other forms of permanent magnet material. This means that a smaller, stronger magnet can be used to do the same work as the larger, heavier magnets formerly used.

Developed by General Motors, Magnequench® magnets have replaced the current-carrying field coils mounted on the iron pole pieces in Delco-Remy starter motors. Use of Magnequench® magnets allows downsizing of the starter motor to about 50 percent of the size of a field coil motor without sacrificing any of the cranking performance.

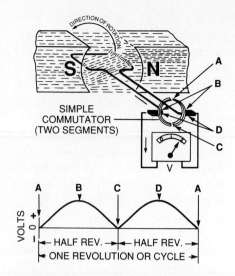

Figure 2-16. A simple commutator rectifies alternating current to pulsating direct current.

winding is connected to a pair of commutator segments. The pulsating dc voltages overlap to produce an almost continuous dc voltage at the output terminal, figure 2-17.

source of initial electric power for an automobile, and a battery can produce only direct current. Therefore, all electrical and electronic devices on almost all vehicles are dc devices. Furthermore, a battery can be recharged only with direct current, not alternating current.

Older dc generators used a **commutator**, which is a rotating switch that can work as a mechanical rectifier. A commutator is a metal ring (usually copper), cut into semicircular segments. Each segment is attached to one end of a generator conductor loop. Carbon brushes bear against the commutator segments and connect the commutator to an external circuit. One brush is connected to the positive (+) side of the output circuit; the other is connected to the negative (−) side of the output circuit. As the conductor turns, each brush contacts first one end and then the other end of the revolving loop through a commutator segment. Figure 2-16 shows how a commutator rectifies ac to dc.

1. At point A, the conductor loops are at the zero-voltage position. The brushes are at the gaps between the commutator segments.

2. At point B, the conductors have rotated 90 degrees to maximum positive voltage. Current flows from the commutator segments, through the brushes, to the circuit.

3. At point C, the conductors are again at the zero-voltage position, and the brushes are at the gaps between the commutator segments.

4. At point D, the conductors have rotated another 90 degrees to the maximum negative-voltage position. However, the opposite commutator segments are against the + and − brushes. Current continues to flow through the external circuit in the same direction as it did at point B.

The voltage graph shows how ac in the generator conductor is rectified to dc by the commutator and brushes. This simple pulsating dc from one generator winding would not work well to recharge a battery or operate electrical devices. Real generators have many conductor windings mounted on a rotating armature. Each

Rotating Field— The Alternator

If you put a magnet inside a stationary conductor loop and rotate the magnet, you also create relative motion between the field and the conductor, figure 2-14. The voltage graph in figure 2-14 shows that again the induced voltage changes polarity with every half revolution because the direction of the flux lines passing through the conductor changes. Current flow from this voltage is also alternating current (ac). This method is used in the alternator of your car, and you will learn more about it when you study charging systems in chapter 9.

Alternators replaced dc generators on automobiles in the early 1960's. Alternators are lighter, more efficient, and can operate at higher speeds than dc generators. Whether the conductor rotates or the field rotates, however, the principle of inducing voltage and current through relative motion is the same. A generator or an alternator always produces alternating current in its conductor windings.

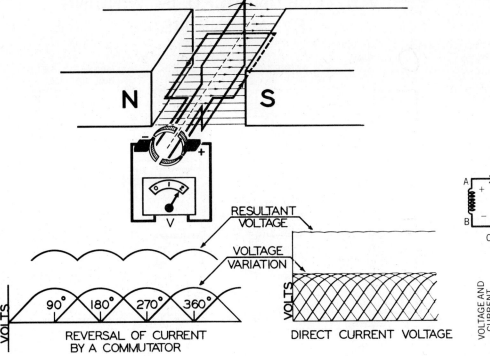

Figure 2-17. A generator commutator delivers steady direct current with a slight ac "ripple."

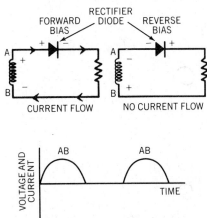

Figure 2-18. One diode provides half-wave rectification from one output winding. (Delco-Remy)

Alternator Rectification. An alternator also must have a way to rectify alternating current and voltage to dc output. Because the conductors do not rotate, you can't use a commutator to rectify alternator output. Fortunately, you don't need one. There is a better way to do the job. Automotive alternators use solid-state electronic diodes to rectify ac to dc.

Chapter 4 explains the construction and operation of semiconductor diodes, and chapter 9 explains the construction and operation of alternators. You can understand diode rectification, however, if you simply think of the diode as an electrical 1-way check valve. It allows current to flow in one direction and blocks it in the opposite direction. If we connect a diode to one end of the stationary conductor in figure 2-14 and then connect an external circuit, the diode allows current in one direction and blocks it in the other, figure 2-18. The result is pulsating dc similar to the output from a simple 2-segment commutator.

The single diode in figure 2-18 rectifies only the positive (+) half of the voltage cycle. Adding more diodes and making the final output connection in parallel allows us to rectify the negative (−) half of the cycle as well, figure 2-19. Like a generator, an alternator has more than one conductor to generate current and voltage. A series of stationary conductor windings and an arrangement of six diodes produces a rectified dc output with only a trace of ac fluctuation, figure 2-20. Semiconductor diodes produce this dc output with no moving rectifier parts and no mechanical wear between brushes and a rotating commutator.

We will leave further study of alternators until chapter 9, but there is one final point to understand about electromagnetic induction in a generator or an alternator. The magnetic field for a generator or an alternator could be formed with permanent magnets. If it were, the magnets would have to be very large and heavy to produce enough magnetic flux to generate the necessary current. This is not practical, so generators and alternators have electromagnetic fields. Direct current flows from the battery through

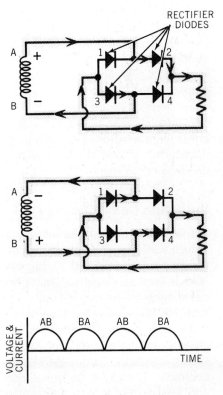

Figure 2-19. Four diodes provide full-wave rectification from one output winding. (Delco-Remy)

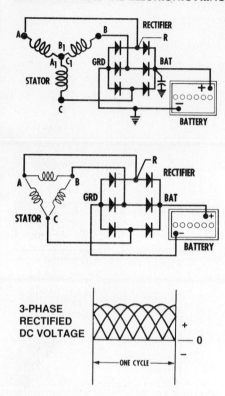

Figure 2-20. Six diodes produce rectified dc from three alternator windings.

VOLTAGE INDUCED IN WINDING BY MAGNETISM

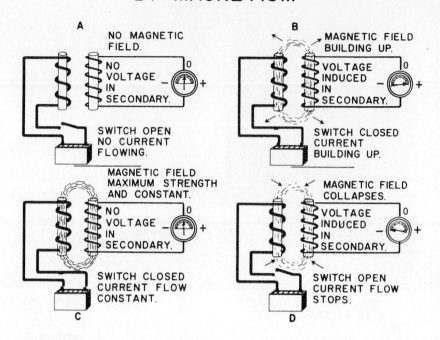

Figure 2-21. Mutual induction results as a changing field, caused by current flow in one coil, induces voltage in a second coil. (Prestolite)

the windings around the field poles to establish the magnetic field. When the generator or alternator starts to produce current and voltage, field current comes from its own dc output terminal. Controlling the amount of current in the field controls the magnetic strength of the field. This, in turn, regulates the output of the generator or alternator. Controlling the field current is the basis for regulating the induced voltage.

Induction Coil Principles

We said earlier that the third way to induce voltage by relative motion between a conductor and a magnetic field is hard to visualize. That's because there are no moving parts. The magnetic field, however, does move.

As current flow increases and decreases through a conductor, the resulting magnetic field expands and contracts. That is, it becomes more and less dense. If you put another conductor within the field created by current flow in the first and then vary

the current flow in the first conductor, you create relative motion between the magnetic field and the second conductor, figure 2-15. This is the kind of relative motion that exists in ignition coils and transformers.

If you wind the two conductors into coils and place one inside the other, you have built an **induction coil**. Ignition coils and transformers are induction coils because one coil winding induces voltage and current in the other. This induction process includes the actions of self-induction and mutual induction.

Self-induction. As current flows through a coil, the magnetic field expands and induces a voltage in the coil that opposes the direction of current that created the field in the first place. This countervoltage is called **counterelectromotive force (CEMF)**. As original current increases, CEMF opposes its increase. As original current decreases, CEMF opposes the decrease. If current is steady, there is no relative motion between the coil and

the field, and there is no induced voltage. Induction occurs only when the field expands or collapses.

Mutual Induction. If you place two coils close together, you can transfer energy from one to the other through **mutual induction**. As current flows through the first coil, its increase or decrease causes the field around the first coil to increase or decrease. This changing field will induce a voltage in a second coil, figure 2-21. In practice, the two coils are wound around each other and around an iron core to increase the field strength, figure 2-22. One coil is connected to a current and voltage source and is called the **primary winding**. This is the coil winding that induces the voltage. The second coil is connected to another circuit. This is the coil winding in which the voltage is induced and is called the **secondary winding**.

Changing current in the primary winding induces a countervoltage in both the primary and secondary windings. Figure 2-21 shows how this

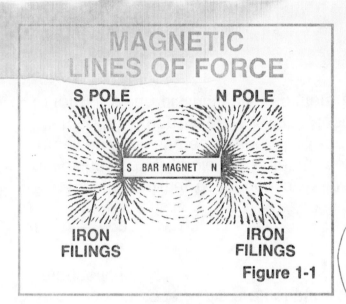

MAGNETIC LINES OF FORCE

S POLE   N POLE

S BAR MAGNET N

IRON FILINGS   IRON FILINGS

Figure 1-1

The lines of force are heavily concentrated at the north (N) and south (S) poles of the magnet, and then spread out into the surrounding air between the poles. There are relatively few lines of force when a magnet is weak, and many lines of force when a magnet is strong. Lines of force are referred to collectively as magnetic flux. When a magnet is strong, the field is said to have a high flux density. When the magnet is weak, the flux density is low.

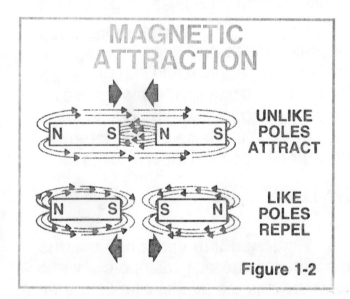

MAGNETIC ATTRACTION

N S   N S   UNLIKE POLES ATTRACT

N S   S N   LIKE POLES REPEL

Figure 1-2

A force of attraction exists between any two magnets lying end to end with a north and south pole facing each other. When unlike poles are brought close to each other, the magnetic lines of force pass from the north to the south poles. They try to shorten (like releasing a stretched rubber band) and therefore try to pull the two poles together.

As long as the two bar magnets are lying end to end with a north and south pole facing each other, an attractive force will exist. If, however, one of the magnetic poles were reversed, so that either both north poles or both south poles were facing each other, the result would be a repelling force. The repelling force would increase as the two like poles were moved closer to each other and the lines of force going in the same direction would be drawn closer to each other. Since these lines of force attempt to push apart, a repelling effect results between the like poles. One of the fundamental laws of magnetism can be stated: "Unlike" poles attract each other, and "like" poles repel each other. See Figure 1-2.

Fundamentals of Magnetism

INTRODUCTION

Magnetism is a connecting link between electricity and mechanical energy. Through the use of magnetism in an automobile alternator, some of the power developed by the engine is changed into an electron flow. This electron flow (current) keeps the battery charged, illuminates the headlamps and operates the ignition.

Electrons flowing from the battery are also changed by magnetism into mechanical power. This can be seen in the operation of the starter motor. Electrical energy sets up a magnetic field in the starter, which is then converted to mechanical power to crank the engine. Therefore, magnetism produces current (electron flow) and current produces magnetism.

MAGNETISM – THE BEGINNING

Magnetism was first discovered when pieces of iron ore called lodestone were seen to attract other pieces of iron. Later it was learned that a bar of this iron ore, if suspended in air, would rotate itself so that one end always pointed to the north pole of the earth. This end of the bar became known as north (N), the other end south (S). From this piece of iron ore the compass was developed. The earth, a huge magnet with north and south poles, causes the compass needle to swing into the north-south position.

Continued research into the bar magnet disclosed that an attractive force existed around the magnet. This area of attraction became known as the "field of force" or "magnetic field."

MAGNETIC FIELD AND FLUX

A magnetic field may be thought of as lines of force which we arbitrarily assume come out of the north (N) pole and enter the south (S) pole. The theory of magnetic lines of force can be illustrated by sprinkling iron filings on a piece of glass resting on top of a bar magnet. When the glass is lightly tapped by hand, the iron filings align themselves to form a clear, distinctive line pattern around the bar magnet (Figure 1-1).

GM Product Service Training

18001.02-1A

11-1-86

1-1

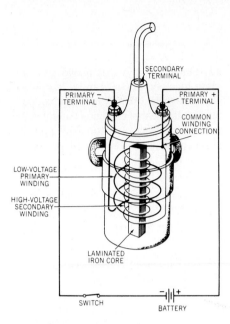

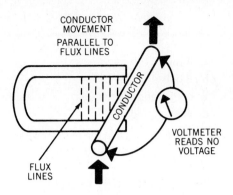

Figure 2-23. No voltage is induced if the conductor and the flux lines are parallel and no flux lines are cut. (Delco-Remy)

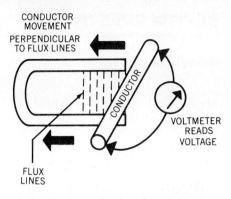

Figure 2-24. Maximum voltage is induced when the conductor and the flux lines intersect at 90 degrees. (Delco-Remy)

Figure 2-22. Induction coils have two concentric windings around an iron core. (Robert Bosch).

works as current starts and stops in the primary winding. There is a direct relationship between the number of turns in a coil and the voltage that can be induced. Therefore, induction coils are made with secondary windings that have many more turns than the primary windings. In this way, low voltage in the primary can induce much higher voltage in the secondary. An ignition coil is an excellent example of this. When you study ignition systems and electronic engine controls later in this volume, you will learn more about how induction coils can increase voltage.

Induced Voltage Strength

Four factors affect the strength of the voltage induced in any of the three ways explained here:

1. The amount of current in a coil and thus the strength of the magnetic field. High current and a strong field induce a high voltage.

2. The number of conductors cutting the flux lines. Many turns in a coil secondary winding or many conductors in an alternator will cause a higher induced voltage.

3. The speed of relative motion between the conductor and the flux

lines. A rapidly expanding or collapsing field or a fast-moving conductor will cause a higher induced voltage.

4. The angle at which the conductor and flux lines intersect. If the conductor and the flux lines are parallel, the conductor does not cut any of the lines, and no voltage is induced, figure 2-23. If the conductor and the flux lines move at 90 degrees to each other, the conductor cuts the most possible lines, and the greatest voltage is induced, figure 2-24.

SUMMARY

Electrochemistry and electromagnetism are the most important sources of electricity in an automobile. Electrochemistry is the basis for voltage cells and batteries. Electrochemistry generates current and develops voltage through the reaction of two dissimilar materials in an electrolyte. The chemical structures of the anode (+ electrode), the cathode (− electrode), and the electrolyte determine the voltage produced by a cell. The size of the electrodes determines the current capacity.

The battery is the primary electric power source on an automobile. Automotive batteries are lead-acid, wet-cell batteries. They are also secondary batteries, which means that they can be recharged. To recharge a battery and provide additional elec-

tricity, an automobile needs other electric power sources.

Electromagnetism is the second major source of electricity on an automobile. Magnetism is the energy caused by the alignment of atoms in some materials. Magnetic flux lines form a magnetic field with lines of force concentrated at the magnet's north and south poles. Unlike magnetic poles (N and S) attract each other; like poles (S and S, or N and N) repel each other. These are the principles of magnetic polarity.

An electromagnetic field forms around a current-carrying conductor. The field can generate voltage through electromagnetic induction. Relative motion must exist between the field and the conductor. Motion can occur in three ways:

1. The conductor can move through a stationary field as in a dc generator.

2. The field can move past or around a stationary conductor as in an alternator.

3. The flux lines of a magnetic field can expand and collapse as current flow increases and decreases through a conductor as in an induction coil.

Electromagnetism is an important source of electric current and voltage in an automobile. Through relays, solenoids, and motors, electromagnetism can also change electrical energy into mechanical energy. You will learn how this is done in the next chapter.

REVIEW QUESTIONS

Multiple Choice

1. Student A says that the left-hand rule is used with the conventional current flow theory to determine direction of current flow. Student B says that the right-hand rule is used with the electron theory of current flow. Who is right?

  a. A only
  b. B only
  c. both A and B
  d. neither A nor B

2. Student A says that an induction coil has a primary and a secondary winding. Student B says that a coil produces voltage by rotating a conductor within a magnetic field. Who is right?

  a. A only
  b. B only
  c. both A and B
  d. neither A nor B

3. Which of the following actions will cause a magnetic field to induce voltage in a conductor?

  a. The conductor moves through the stationary magnetic field.
  b. The magnetic field moves past the stationary conductor.
  c. The magnetic field expands and collapses around the conductor.
  d. all of the above

4. An automotive battery cell in a normal state of charge produces:

  a. about 3 volts
  b. about 2.5 volts
  c. about 2.1 volts
  d. about 2.9 volts

5. Student A says that the positive electrode in a voltage cell is called a cathode. Student B says the conductive and reactive liquid or paste in a voltage cell is called the electrolyte. Who is right?

  a. A only
  b. B only
  c. both A and B
  d. neither A nor B

6. Student A says that a wet-cell battery contains a lead (Pb) cathode and a lead dioxide (PbO_2) anode. Student B says that this describes a dry-cell battery. Who is right?

  a. A only
  b. B only
  c. both A and B
  d. neither A nor B

7. Student A says that the electrochemical action is not reversible in a primary battery. Student B says that the electrochemical action is reversible in a secondary battery. Who is right?

  a. A only
  b. B only
  c. both A and B
  d. neither A nor B

8. Student A says that magnetism is caused by the movement of electrons in certain materials. Student B says that magnetism can be recognized by the force it exerts on other materials. Who is right?

  a. A only
  b. B only
  c. both A and B
  d. neither A nor B

9. Student A says that iron has high reluctance because it resists easy flow of flux lines. Student B says that iron has high permeability because it allows flux lines to pass easily. Who is right?

  a. A only
  b. B only
  c. both A and B
  d. neither A nor B

10. Student A says that you can create an electromagnet by placing an iron bar inside the field of a coil. Student B says that simple electromagnets operate on alternating current. Who is right?

  a. A only
  b. B only
  c. both A and B
  d. neither A nor B

11. Student A says that a magnetic field is strongest nearest the poles and becomes progressively weaker as you move away from the poles. Student B says that the strength of a magnetic field can be increased by increasing the current flow. Who is right?

  a. A only
  b. B only
  c. both A and B
  d. neither A nor B

12. Student A says that if two coils are close together, energy can be transferred from one to the other by mutual induction. Student B says that changing current in the primary winding of a coil will induce a countervoltage in both coil windings. Who is right?

  a. A only
  b. B only
  c. both A and B
  d. neither A nor B

Fill in the Blank

13. Current that flows, at equal intervals, from positive to negative and back to positive is called _____ current.

14. The principal voltage sources in an automobile are the battery and the _____ .

15. The lines of force in a magnetic field are called _____ lines.

16. Magnetism that develops because of current flow is called _____ .

17. A battery is really a collection of _____ .

18. Since electrochemistry produces electron flow in only one direction, a battery can produce only _____ power.

19. Cell materials determine maximum voltage; cell size determines maximum _____ .

20. Like magnetic poles _____ , unlike magnetic poles _____ .

21. Flux lines pass easily through a material with high _____ .

22. Magnetic flux lines generate current and voltage in a conductor if either the field or conductor is moving. This process is called _____ .

23. The _____ in a dc generator is a rotating switch that can work as a mechanical rectifier.

24. Alternators rectify ac current to dc current through the use of solid-state _____ .

3 BASIC ELECTRICAL SYSTEM PARTS

WHAT

Chapter 1 introduced the principles of electric current, voltage, and resistance, as well as basic circuits. Chapter 2 outlined the sources of electric power in an automobile and some ways in which it is used. Now we can introduce some of the common parts used in automotive electrical systems. We can also start to examine some typical automobile circuits.

This chapter explains how current, voltage, resistance, and electromagnetism operate in typical automotive electrical and electronic systems.

WHY

All electrical and electronic circuits have many features in common. Whether it is a high-current circuit for a starter motor or a low-current circuit for a computer, every circuit has electrical conductors, connectors, switching devices, circuit protection devices, and various parts that do some kind of work.

Automobile electrical systems have used electric motors and electromechanical switches, relays, and solenoids for 75 years or more. Fuses and other circuit protection devices are common to all systems.

If you understand the common parts of all systems and how they work, you can test and repair electrical circuits faster and more accurately. More importantly, understanding basic circuits, switches, relays, and solenoids will help you understand automotive computer systems later in this book. You will find that computer-controlled systems are simply refinements of electromechanical systems that have existed for years.

As a service technician, you will never have to design or test the systems used to suppress electronic interference on a car. You must, however, be able to recognize them and ensure that they are installed correctly. This chapter ends with a summary of the interference suppression methods used on late-model vehicles.

GOALS

After studying this chapter, you should be able to:

1. Understand metric and American Wire Gauge (AWG) sizes for wiring.

2. Recognize different kinds of connectors and wiring harnesses.

3. Explain the differences between primary wiring and other kinds of conductors in automotive electrical systems.

4. Explain the principles of circuit resistance and loads.

5. Identify common automotive circuit protection devices.

6. Explain the operation of switches, relays, solenoids, motors, and other common electrical system parts.

7. Understand the difference between a traditional electrical wiring system and a multiplex wiring system.

8. Understand the principles of electromagnetic interference (EMI) suppression.

ELECTRICAL SYSTEM POLARITY

In chapter 1, you learned the two theories of current flow:

• The conventional theory says that current flows from positive (+) to negative (−).

• The electron theory says that current flows as electrons from negative (−) to positive (+).

We almost always use the conventional current flow theory for automotive electrical systems. This will help you understand system polarity.

Electrical polarity indicates the + and − connections of the voltage source to the system. The primary voltage source on a vehicle is the battery, and the battery connections establish system polarity. Since 1956, all domestic passenger cars and light trucks have used positive-polarity sys-

tems. The battery + terminal is connected to the insulated, or "hot," side of the system. This is the point of highest voltage in the system. The battery − terminal is connected to the ground side of the system, which is the lowest voltage point. Current flows from the + terminal of the battery, through the system, to the − terminal. Voltage is highest at the + terminal, drops through the circuit, and is lowest at the − terminal. A positive-polarity system is also called a negative-ground system.

Before 1956, 6-volt Ford and Chrysler vehicles had negative-polarity, positive-ground systems. As late as 1969, some imported cars also had positive-ground systems.

System polarity affects the operation of electrical components. An alternator must be installed so that its output terminal connects to the battery + terminal, or the insulated side of the system. If alternator and battery connections are reversed, the alternator can be damaged. Ignition coils and other electromagnetic parts are also sensitive to system polarity. Some motors may run backwards, and some relays and solenoids may not work properly if their connections are reversed in relation to system polarity. Expensive electronic modules can be destroyed if their polarity is reversed. Electrical test equipment must be connected to the vehicle system in relation to system polarity. The positive lead from a test instrument must be connected to the + side of the system and the negative lead to the − side of the system.

You will learn more about specific effects of electrical polarity in later chapters of this book. Although all late-model vehicles have positive-polarity, negative-ground electrical systems, you should always double-check all connections to be sure that they are correct in relation to system polarity. Understanding the principle of electrical polarity also will help you follow the explanations of circuit conductors and electrical parts in the rest of this chapter.

CIRCUIT CONDUCTORS

Every circuit must have:

1. A power source
2. Circuit conductors
3. Circuit loads
4. A circuit protection device

The power source is the battery or the alternator. Circuit conductors are the wires, cables, printed circuit

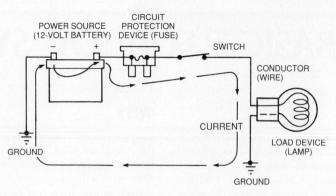

Figure 3-1. A simple circuit showing the complete path through which current flows. (Chrysler)

boards, and other low-resistance parts that carry the current from the power source to the loads. The circuit loads are the devices that change electrical energy into heat, light, sound, and mechanical energy. Circuit loads provide the necessary resistance for the circuit. Circuit protection devices prevent excessive current from overheating or damaging the conductors or circuit loads. Figure 3-1 shows a typical circuit.

When we think of conductors in automotive systems, we usually think of the thousands of feet of wire that run throughout the vehicle. However, circuit load devices and the vehicle chassis also conduct current. Important differences between conductors and loads are:

• Conductors should have low resistance; loads have higher resistance.

• Conductors should cause a very slight voltage drop; all measurable circuit voltage should drop across circuit loads.

Except for the ignition secondary circuit from the coil to the spark plugs, all automotive circuits are low-voltage circuits. The battery and the alternator supply 12 to 15 volts. Even the 24-volt systems on some trucks are considered low-voltage systems. We don't consider a circuit to be a high-voltage system until it operates with hundreds or thousands of volts.

Automotive Wiring

Most of the wiring in automotive circuits consists of copper wire covered

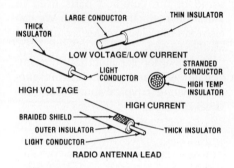

Figure 3-2. Construction of typical body wiring. (Chrysler)

with plastic insulation. Copper is used as the conductor because of its good conductivity, flexibility, and low cost. The conductor may be a single strand of copper, but most often it is formed of several strands wound together to improve flexibility. Single strands or solid wires are found in low-voltage, low-current circuits and in circuits where flexibility is not required. Multistrand wires are used in high-voltage, high-current circuits or in circuits where vibration or component movement makes flexibility a requirement. Figure 3-2 shows the construction of both types of wiring, as well as the special wiring used for radio antenna leads.

Some General Motors vehicles have aluminum wiring in some circuits. Aluminum is less expensive than copper, but it is also less flexible. Aluminum also is less conductive than copper, so aluminum wiring must be larger than copper wiring to carry equivalent current. Circuits with aluminum wiring in GM vehicles are in the lower part of the forward body where they are not subject to much flexing and carry current for only a short distance.

Insulation. Modern insulation materials are high-resistance plastic compounds. Older wiring had cloth and paper insulation. Insulation not only protects the conductivity of individual wires, but it also resists heat, moisture, corrosion, and vibration that could damage the circuit. The insulation is colored to aid circuit assembly and circuit testing.

A thin plastic insulation is used on low-voltage, low-amperage conductors, except when they are placed in areas of high temperatures or other poor environmental conditions. High-voltage wires require a tougher, temperature-resistant insulation that will not fail when the circuit heats up.

Wire routing and retention are also important factors in circuit protection. Conductors often require additional protection that cannot be provided by insulation alone. Special clips, straps, tubing, sleeves, or boots may be used to position and protect conductors, figure 3-3. Whenever you remove these to service a conductor or component, you must replace them or you might create new problems in the circuit.

All of the low-voltage wiring in an automobile is often called **primary**

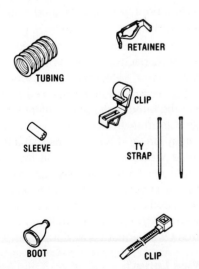

Figure 3-3. A variety of wiring protective devices are used in automotive circuits. (Chrysler)

wiring because it is the kind used for low-voltage, low-current ignition primary circuits. Battery cables, ignition spark plug cables, and printed circuit boards are also circuit conductors. Because of their purposes and special construction, however, they are not called primary wiring.

To accurately test and repair circuit wiring, you must know about wire sizes and how wire size and length affect circuit operation.

Wire Size

Wire size indicates the cross-sectional area of the conductor. The cross-sectional area directly affects the amount of current a wire can carry. As the cross-sectional area of a conductor increases, its resistance decreases. A conductor with a large cross section has less resistance and can carry more current than one with a small cross section. High-current circuits need larger wiring than low-current circuits need.

American Wire Gauge (AWG) Sizes.
Two standard systems for wire sizes are the **American Wire Gauge (AWG)** and the metric systems. In the AWG system, wire diameter is measured in mils, and cross-sectional area is measured in circular mils. A mil is 0.001 inch. A circular mil is the area of a circle that is 0.001 inch in diameter. The cross section of a round conductor in circular mils equals the square of the diameter. That is, if the diameter is 200 mils (0.200 inch), the area in square mils is 200 × 200, or 40,000 circular mils. The total cross section of stranded wire equals the cross sections of all individual strands. It does not include any space between strands. The cross section and current-carrying capacity of a single strand wire and a multistrand wire of the same size number are the same.

Fortunately, we don't have to worry about wire diameter in mils or area in circular mils to identify or select wire sizes. AWG wire sizes are indicated by number. The numbers are based

AWG Gauge Size	Conductor Diameter (Inch)	Cross-Sectional Area (Circular Mils)
20	0.032	1,020
18	0.040	1,620
16	0.051	2,580
14	0.064	4,110
12	0.081	6,530
10	0.102	10,400
8	0.128	16,500
6	0.162	26,300
4	0.204	41,700
2	0.258	66,400
1	0.289	83,700
0	0.325	106,000
2/0	0.365	133,000
4/0	0.460	211,600

Figure 3-4. The smallest wiring used in an automobile is number 18 or 20 for low-current applications. Number 2/0 or 4/0 wire is battery cable size.

on the cross section, and they also relate to the diameter of the wire. In the AWG system, the higher the number, the smaller the wire cross-sectional area and diameter. Number 18 wire is smaller than number 14 wire, for example. Engineers determine wire size by the current loads of each circuit.

AWG wire sizes based on circular mils range from number 40 (the smallest) through number 0000, or 4/0 (the largest). Number 20 is the smallest that you usually find in an automobile, figure 3-4. Wires larger than 4/0 are identified by their cross section in thousands of circular mils, but you will never deal with such heavy wire on an automobile. Automobile electrical system wiring typically uses number 14, 16, and 18 wire. High-current power distribution circuits may use number 10 or 12 wire. Low-current electronic circuits may use number 20 wire. For comparison, battery cables are typically number 2, 4, or 6 wire. You also will see AWG wire sizes identified as 20-gauge, 16-gauge, 12-gauge, or 6-gauge wire.

You need not memorize all AWG wire sizes and corresponding diameters or cross sections, but you must be able to recognize gauge sizes listed on diagrams. The following facts will

PROBLEMS, PROBLEMS, PROBLEMS

Just when you thought you had mastered all of the intricate ins and outs of electrical troubleshooting, along come electronics, computers, and a whole host of new little problems that service technicians have never had to deal with before. Many such problems involve the circuit ground, electromagnetic interference (EMI), and voltage surges.

It used to be pretty simple to determine if you had a good ground, but grounds have changed, like everything else. Proper grounds are important to an onboard computer, since the computer operates many functions by removing or restoring ground to a circuit.

This means that connector pin contacts can be extremely important, especially since connectors that handle 40 or more terminals have become commonplace in automotive wiring systems. Pin contacts are crucial in modern circuits. Connectors must be checked for bent pins, pins that have backed out of the connector, and corrosion caused by the introduction of water or other fluids, among other defects.

The type of ground used also has become very important on vehicles with many electronic systems. Automakers have found it necessary to provide two different types of

grounds to avoid EMI that can damage the sensitive electronic circuits. One type of ground is called the "clean" ground and is used for the electronic circuits. The other or "dirty" ground handles those circuits containing components that cause interference as they operate, such as relays, switches, and solenoids.

The problems of voltage surge and EMI even affect optional equipment accessories installed on a vehicle. Some automakers are now recommending that such accessories be installed with separate grounds and power supplied by direct connection to the battery via special cable adapters, instead of cutting into another circuit or connecting the accessory to the ignition switch. The idea is to keep the accessory circuit power connection and ground as far away from the computer as possible. If not, the EMI created by such accessories can induce voltage surges into the computer circuit wiring.

As you learn more about electronic circuits and onboard computers, you'll discover other problems due to the use of automotive electronic circuits and learn the simple precautions required to prevent system damage.

Metric Size	AWG Size
.22	24
.35	22
.5	20
.8	18
1.0	16
2.0	14
3.0	12
5.0	10
8.0	8
13.0	6
19.0	4
32.0	2

Figure 3-5. These are approximately equivalent AWG and metric wire sizes.

ifications in AWG or metric sizes, or both, and the two systems have equivalent sizes. Metric 8.0 wire has a current-carrying capacity of AWG 18-gauge wire. Figure 3-5 lists equivalent metric and AWG wire sizes.

Remember these final points about wire sizes:

1. The size number—AWG or metric—refers to the conductor size, not the complete size of the conductor plus the insulation. Two 18-gauge wires, for example, will have different outside diameters if one has thicker insulation.

2. Gauge sizes specified for automotive wiring are usually based on using copper wire. If aluminum wire is used, it must be a larger gauge because aluminum is not as good a conductor as copper.

3. Although wire sizes are based on current capacity, system voltage also affects wire selection. Low source voltage requires less resistance to deliver the same current that higher voltage can deliver. A 24-volt electrical system on a truck can use smaller gauge wiring than a 12-volt system would need for equal current. Similarly, a circuit for a computer sensor that operates on 5 volts may have heavier wiring than a similar 12-volt circuit with equally low current.

Wire Length

Wire length affects the resistance and current-carrying ability of conductors

help you understand the principles of wire sizes and wiring for various circuits.

• A wire with twice the cross section of another has a gauge number that is three numbers different. For example, a number 15 wire has twice the cross section of a number 18 wire.

• A wire with 10 times the cross section of another has a gauge number that is 10 times different. For example, a number 6 wire has 10 times the cross section of a number 16 wire.

Metric Wire Sizes. In the metric system, wire sizes are identified by the cross-sectional area of the wire in square millimeters (mm^2). The smaller the number, the smaller the wire.

Metric wire sizes are determined by calculating the cross section of the conductor by the standard formula for the area of a circle:

$$Area = radius^2 \times 3.14$$

You can determine the metric size of a wire with a diameter of 3.2 mm (radius of 1.6 mm) as follows:

$$Area = (1.6 \text{ mm})^2 \times 3.14$$
$$Area = 2.56 \text{ mm}^2 \times 3.14$$
$$Area = 8.0 \text{ mm}^2$$

The metric size is, therefore, 8.0. You can determine an unknown metric wire size by measuring the conductor with a micrometer and using this formula. Fortunately, you don't have to calculate wire sizes too often. They are listed in carmakers' spec-

just as does wire size, or gauge number. Number 18 wire can conduct 15 amperes for 10 feet with no significant voltage drop. If the circuit must reach 15 feet, it requires number 14 wire for the same 15 amperes. Figure 3-6 lists the wire sizes required to conduct various amounts of current for different lengths in circuits grounded to the vehicle chassis.

Wiring Harness and Connectors

A modern automobile may contain almost half a mile of wiring and 500 or more separate circuit connections. If that amount of wiring were installed as individual wires, each with a separate terminal, manufacturing costs would be excessive. To simplify vehicle assembly, engineers group wires into harness assemblies. Harnesses have a variety of connectors to join wires to other harnesses and to individual circuit parts. Wiring harnesses and connectors are the circuit conductors that you will work with for electrical service.

Wiring Harnesses. A **wiring harness** contains circuit wiring for a general

Total Current at 12 Volts (Amperes)	Wire Gauge for Length in Feet											
	3'	5'	7'	10'	15'	20'	25'	30'	40'	50'	75'	100'
1	18	18	18	18	18	18	18	18	18	18	18	18
2	18	18	18	18	18	18	18	18	18	18	16	16
3	18	18	18	18	18	18	18	18	18	18	14	14
4	18	18	18	18	18	18	18	18	16	16	12	12
5	18	18	18	18	18	18	18	18	16	14	12	12
6	18	18	18	18	18	18	16	16	16	14	12	10
7	18	18	18	18	18	18	16	16	14	14	10	10
8	18	18	18	18	18	16	16	16	14	12	10	10
10	18	18	18	18	16	16	16	14	12	12	10	10
11	18	18	18	18	16	16	14	14	12	12	10	8
12	18	18	18	18	16	16	14	14	12	12	10	8
15	18	18	18	18	14	14	12	12	12	10	8	8
18	18	18	16	16	14	14	12	12	10	10	8	8
20	18	18	16	16	14	12	10	10	10	10	8	6
22	18	18	16	16	12	12	10	10	10	8	6	6
24	18	18	16	16	12	12	10	10	10	8	6	6
30	18	16	16	14	10	10	10	10	10	6	4	4
40	18	16	14	12	10	10	8	8	6	6	4	2
50	16	14	12	12	10	10	8	8	6	6	2	2
100	12	12	10	10	6	6	4	4	4	2	1	1/0
150	10	10	8	8	4	4	2	2	2	1	2/0	2/0
200	10	8	8	6	4	4	2	2	1	1/0	4/0	4/0

Figure 3-6. For a given amount of current, larger wire must be used for longer distances to avoid excessive voltage drop.

LOCATING SHORTS TO GROUND THE EASY WAY

Locating a short to ground in a circuit can be a headache when fuses blow as fast as you install them. Commercial short detectors are available, but a circuit breaker and a compass are sufficient to solve the problem. Used together, these act as a short detector, working on the principle of the magnetic field created around a conductor by current flow.

To keep the circuit operating long enough to find the problem, solder a pair of short leads to the terminals of a 25- to 30-ampere cycling circuit breaker. If the vehicle you are troubleshooting uses glass fuses, attach a pair of alligator clips on the other ends of the leads. Use spade terminals instead of alligator clips if the vehicle uses minifuses. Connect the alligator clips or spade terminals

to the fuse position in the fuse box. When the circuit is operated, the circuit breaker will open and close the circuit as it heats up and cools down.

Once the circuit is functioning on a partial basis, you can trace its path with a compass. As the circuit breaker cycles, the compass needle

will deflect. (This will work even through trim panels.) However, the needle will stop deflecting once you've passed the point of the short, because there is no current flowing in that part of the circuit. Now that you've found the problem area, you can correct it and then install a new fuse of the correct value.

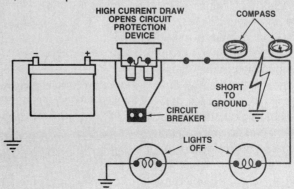

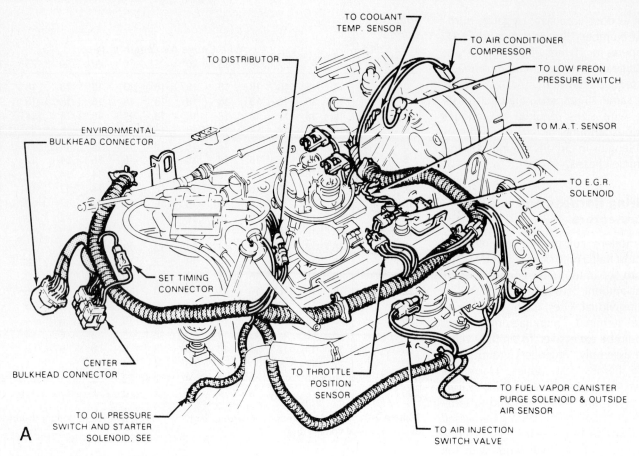

TO COOLANT TEMP. SENSOR

TO DISTRIBUTOR

TO AIR CONDITIONER COMPRESSOR

TO LOW FREON PRESSURE SWITCH

TO M.A.T. SENSOR

TO E.G.R. SOLENOID

ENVIRONMENTAL BULKHEAD CONNECTOR

SET TIMING CONNECTOR

CENTER BULKHEAD CONNECTOR

TO THROTTLE POSITION SENSOR

TO FUEL VAPOR CANISTER PURGE SOLENOID & OUTSIDE AIR SENSOR

TO OIL PRESSURE SWITCH AND STARTER SOLENOID, SEE

TO AIR INJECTION SWITCH VALVE

A

area of the vehicle. You will see typical harnesses identified as:

- Forward body harness
- Engine harness
- Engine compartment harness
- Instrument panel (IP) harness
- Main body harness
- Rear body harness

The wires in each harness are wrapped in tape or enclosed in insulated tubing or conduit. A complex harness serves many circuits and branches out to many electrical components throughout the vehicle, as in the engine compartment, figure 3-7A, or behind the instrument panel. A simple harness services one or a few circuits, as in the taillamp circuit or an individual component circuit, figure 3-7B. Some wires for individual circuits enter and leave a complex harness at specific points along its length. Often, branch harnesses are routed from main harnesses to other parts of the car. Most wires in main harnesses are terminated in large multiple-pin connectors at each end of the harness. A multiple-pin connector may have

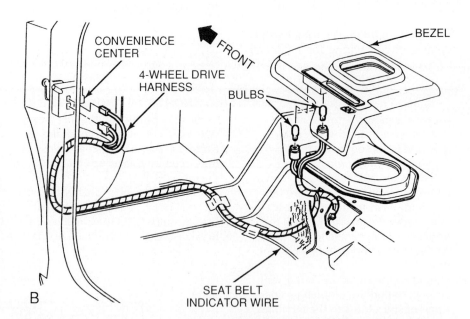

CONVENIENCE CENTER

4-WHEEL DRIVE HARNESS

FRONT

BEZEL

BULBS

B

SEAT BELT INDICATOR WIRE

Figure 3-7. Automotive wiring harnesses vary from the complex engine harness shown in position **A** to the simple 4-wheel-drive indicator harness shown in position **B**. (General Motors)

40, 60, or more individual wire connection terminals. Some harness connectors attach directly to other harnesses. Others attach to bulkhead connectors at the firewall or the rear of the passenger compartment.

Connectors. Automotive electrical systems have connectors that range from simple single-terminal connectors to large multiple-terminal harness connectors. The following are examples of typical connectors that you will work with.

• *Single-wire connectors*—Single-wire connectors connect one wire to another or one wire to an electrical component. Ring, hook, and forked terminals connect a wire to a terminal on a device in the circuit, figure 3-8. Male and female bullet and slide, or spade, terminals connect two wires together, figure 3-9. On original-equipment wiring, a single-wire connector may be molded to the end of a wire. Replacement connectors are usually installed by soldering or crimping the connector terminal to the wire.

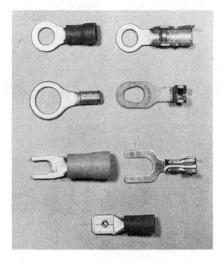

Figure 3-8. Typical ring, fork, and spade connectors.

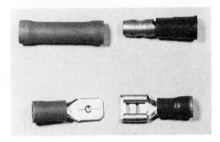

Figure 3-9. Typical male and female bullet and spade connectors.

Figure 3-10. Typical molded connector halves with multiple circuit wires.

• *Molded connectors*—Some connectors (usually with 1 to 4 wires) are 1-piece molded parts, figure 3-10. Individual wires and terminals cannot be separated for repair.

• *Multiple-wire (hard-shell) connectors*—Many multiple-wire connectors

have hard plastic shells that hold the mating pins and sockets (male and female terminals) of individual connectors. Figure 3-11 shows several common types. Individual wires and their terminals can be removed from the connectors for repair. These con-

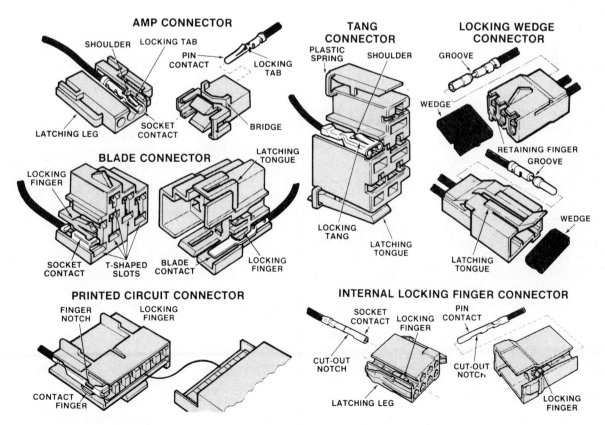

Figure 3-11. Typical hard-shell connectors used in automotive wiring systems. (Ford)

40-WAY BULKHEAD DISCONNECT

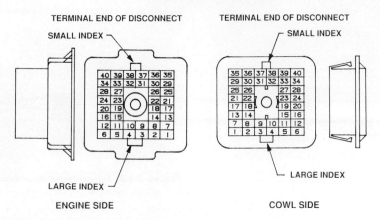

ENGINE SIDE

COWL SIDE

Figure 3-12. Bulkhead connectors join wiring harnesses through firewalls and other bulkhead separations on a vehicle. (Chrysler)

Figure 3-13. Weather-Pack connectors used on GM vehicles have a rubber seal at the rear of the connector, as well as primary and secondary locks that must be loosened to separate the connector halves.

Figure 3-14. Metri-Pack connectors used on GM vehicles use a different sealing arrangement and a single connector lock. These are used where environmental factors are not as critical.

nectors also allow you to probe the rear of the individual connections to test circuit operation without separating the connector.

• *Bulkhead connectors*—Bulkhead connectors are used where many circuits in a wiring harness must pass through a barrier such as the firewall. The bulkhead connector is installed through the firewall and multiple-wire connectors on separate harnesses are attached to each side, figure 3-12.

• *Weather-Pack connectors*—Late-model GM cars have special environmental or weatherproof connectors throughout the engine and body harnesses. These Weather-Pack connectors have rubber seals on the wire ends of the terminals and secondary sealing covers on the rear of each connector half, figure 3-13. One connector half is generally attached to a component; the other half is attached to the wiring harness. Weather-Pack connectors may be single or multiple connectors and are used in electronic systems where any voltage drop due

to connector corrosion can cause problems.

• *Metri-Pack and Micro-Pack connectors*—Also used on GM cars, Metri-Pack and Micro-Pack connectors, figure 3-14, are similar in design to Weather-Pack connectors but lack the secondary sealing cover. They are designed for use with smaller terminals.

All of the requirements for good conductivity and low resistance that apply to circuit conductors also apply to connectors. Connectors are simply extensions of the wiring. Poor connections are common causes of electrical system problems. Corrosion, a loose connection, or broken wire strands at a connector can cause high resistance and resulting voltage drop that will upset circuit operation. For example, a 10-percent voltage drop in a 12-volt lighting circuit (1.2 volts) due to a bad connection can reduce lighting efficiency by 30 percent. A similar 10-percent voltage drop in an air conditioning system can reduce blower motor speed or stop motor

operation completely. Circuit connections are important test-and-repair points for electrical service.

Other Conductors

We have mentioned battery cables, printed circuit boards, and ignition spark plug cables as specialized kinds of circuit conductors. Although they are not considered primary wiring, battery cables and printed circuit boards are low-resistance, low-voltage conductors. Ignition cables are high-resistance, high-voltage conductors.

Battery Cables. The battery cables are the starting and ending points for almost all electrical circuits on a vehicle. The positive (+) cable carries current to distribution points for other electrical systems. The negative (−) cable is the ground return path for current to flow back to the battery.

Because the battery must deliver several hundred amperes of current to the starter motor, battery cables are heavy number 4 or number 6 wire. Some long cables may be even heavier. If the battery did not have to supply high current to the starter motor, its cables could be number 10 or 12 primary wire.

Most battery cables are made with an insulated, braided copper conductor, permanently attached to lead or tinned copper terminals. The cable terminal that attaches to the battery terminal is usually made of lead to reduce corrosion when fastened to the lead battery terminal. The terminal at the other end of the cable is usually tinned copper.

Some vehicles have battery ground cables made of flat, braided, uninsulated copper. Insulation is not required for the low-voltage ground side of the system. These cables, or straps, have the same resistance and current capacity as equivalent round cables.

As with other vehicle wiring, a replacement battery cable must always be the same gauge or larger than the original cable.

Printed Circuit Boards. Printed circuit boards are used as circuit conductors in most instrument panels, figure 3-15, and inside components such as radios, computer assemblies, and some voltage regulators and windshield washer motors. They are used for low-current circuits in locations with limited space.

A printed circuit board is made by printing a thin film of a copper conductor on an insulated plastic board. Further manufacturing steps add connectors to the board for gauges, lamp bulbs, and other loads.

Printed circuit boards do the same jobs as primary wiring. Their compact size and ease of manufacture in large quantities reduce the cost and manufacturing time of the assemblies where they are used. Interestingly, the manufacturing principles used for printed circuit boards are the basis for manufacturing the miniature electronic integrated circuits that you will learn about later.

A unique kind of connector, called a card-edge connector, is used for

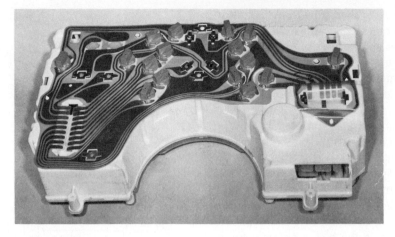

Figure 3-15. Printed circuit boards are universally used in automotive instrument panels.

many printed circuit boards. The circuit connectors, or traces, are printed out to one edge of the board. The trace ends are aligned, and the edges are left exposed with no insulation. The edge of the board is then plugged into a socket to complete the circuits to the power supply and to other loads away from the board. You will see edge connectors on circuit boards in many of your test instruments and in a few components on late-model vehicles.

Ignition (Spark Plug) Cables. The ignition cables, or spark plug cables, are the only high-voltage conductors used on most vehicles. These wires carry current at voltages from 10,000 to 40,000 volts in the ignition secondary circuit. This high voltage is necessary to create the spark that ignites the air-fuel mixture in the engine.

Ignition cables are installed from the distributor cap to the spark plug and, on most engines, between the ignition coil and the distributor cap. The cables are 7 or 8 millimeters in diameter, but the conductor is a small core in the center of the cable. Most of the cable diameter is heavy insulation needed to withstand the high voltage and to protect the conductor from heat, oil, dirt, and moisture. The insulation on many cables is made of silicone rubber, which has:

• Excellent insulating (dielectric) ability

• Good flexibility
• Excellent resistance to heat, water, and oil

Silicone rubber insulation also is fragile and must be handled carefully. Other ignition cables use insulation material known by the trademarked name Hypalon. Many cables have several layers of insulating material for the best combination of strength, flexibility, and good insulation.

Over 30 years ago, most ignition cables had stranded metallic conductors made of copper or steel wire. Low-resistance metallic conductors allow the high-voltage cables to emit electrical impulses that interfere with radio and television reception. This **radiofrequency interference (RFI)** disrupts radio and television reception and other sensitive electronic circuits. RFI is often called "signal noise" because it interferes with voltage signals in other circuits.

Federal regulations in the United States, Canada, and most other countries limit the amount of RFI that a vehicle can emit. Because metallic-core ignition cables are the largest single RFI source, the easiest way to minimize interference is to eliminate the metal conductor. For over 30 years, most vehicles have used ignition cables with high-resistance conductors made of carbon or of linen or fiberglass strands impregnated with graphite. Because they reduce radio and television interference, the cables often are called **television-radio-suppression (TVRS) cables**. Metallic-conductor cables are still made for some industrial engines and some high-performance uses. They are not recommended for highway vehicles, however.

High-resistance, nonmetallic ignition cables also have a secondary benefit. Resistance in the cables affects ignition secondary voltage and current after the spark plug fires. High resistance raises the voltage applied to the plug when it fires. This improves ignition in the high-resistance conditions inside the cylinder. It also helps ignition of lean air-fuel mixtures or the firing of a dirty spark plug. High resistance in the cables also reduces current after ignition, which could otherwise burn spark plug electrodes and distributor cap terminals.

Circuit Grounds

We said earlier that the vehicle chassis and engine are also electrical conductors. Automotive electrical systems are basically single-wire systems. They use the vehicle chassis and engine as the ground side of all circuits, figure 3-16. This completes the low-voltage return side of each circuit to the battery.

In a positive-polarity, negative-ground system, the battery − cable is fastened to the engine or frame. The battery + cable is connected to the system to deliver current to all loads in all circuits. In this kind of system, the battery + cable is the insulated, or "hot," cable. The insulated, or hot, side of every circuit is the wiring from the battery voltage connection to all loads in the circuit.

Many vehicles have additional ground cables, or **bonding straps** between the engine and the chassis to ensure a low-resistance ground path for various circuits. Many vehicles have battery ground connections to both the chassis and the engine for the same reason.

Resistance on the insulated (hot) side of any circuit varies with the various loads in the circuit. The resistance on the ground side of any circuit

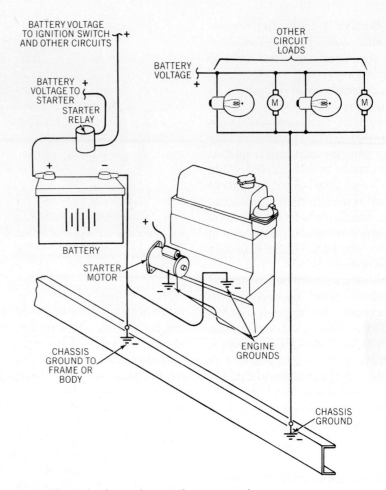

Figure 3-16. All vehicle electrical circuits have a ground connection to the chassis or the engine.

between a load and its ground connection must be virtually zero. All circuit voltage must drop through the loads on the insulated side of a circuit. There should be little or no measurable voltage between any point on the ground side of a circuit and the battery − terminal. The low voltage on the ground side of the electrical system allows the use of the chassis and engine as ground-return paths.

Every ground connection on the vehicle is electrically the same as a connection to the battery − terminal. That is, the ground potential should be zero voltage at every grounding point. Circuit loads can be grounded directly through the case of the device or remotely by system wiring. **Case grounds** are used where a device is installed with electrical continuity to the engine or chassis. The component case should be made of metal if the ground circuit is to be complete, but some components housed in plastic

cases will have a tab or ground strap to serve the same purpose. **Remote grounds** are used where continuity does not exist or where remote ground is used to control the component, as in the case of reversible motors where the current must flow in both directions. Because of the nonmetallic materials used in late-model instrument panels and exterior lamp housings, gauge and lamp circuits usually have remote grounds.

Multiplex Circuits

Conventional electrical circuits have proliferated in late-model automobiles, resulting in wiring harnesses of 50 or more wires, a trend that is likely to continue in the foreseeable future. The more extensive use of electrical systems in the automobile is a direct result of the ever-increasing use of electronic control systems. Some of these control systems are basic to vehicle operation, such as engine management, fuel injection, antilock braking, or suspension control. Others are not directly related to vehicle operation, but are convenience systems for drivers, such as instrument panel displays that calculate trip mileage, fuel economy, and so on, or sound systems incorporating programmable radios.

The great increase in electrical circuits used by solid-state components not only results in a large number of wires and limited space in which to run them, but also contributes to a problem about which you'll learn later in this chapter—electromagnetic interference (EMI). To accommodate the growing need for electrical circuitry in automotive design, engineers are turning to a **multiplex wiring system** that will reduce the number and size of wiring harnesses as well as the problems posed by EMI. We will look at the two major approaches to a multiplex wiring system currently in use.

Bus Data Links. A multiplex wiring system using bus data links consists of a central transmitter and various receivers. The transmitter is a microprocessor that is the control center of the system. Each receiver is located close to the electrical load it controls. The transmitter and receivers are connected to battery power and communicate over a peripheral serial bus, or 2-way data link. You will learn more about a peripheral serial bus and how it functions when you study body control modules in chapter 5.

Control switches for the various circuits (headlamps, windshield wiper, heater, cruise control, etc.) are connected to the transmitter. Each switch has its own individual signal or code. When the transmitter receives a particular code, it knows which switch is calling and immediately communicates a control signal to the proper receiver to carry out the command. For example, if the headlamp switch is activated by the driver, the transmitter will tell the appropriate receiver to turn the lights on or off, as the driver requests. Figure 3-17 shows the basic

arrangement and principles of this system.

The transmitter acts as a traffic control officer. It interprets the request from the switch and decides if the conditions are correct to carry out the request. Suppose that the ignition switch is off but the driver has activated the power window switch. The transmitter will ignore this signal from the switch. If the driver turns the ignition on and reactivates the power window switch, the transmitter will signal the receiver that controls the power windows to carry out the command.

The receivers are slave units that have no decision-making capability of their own. They can only carry out the commands issued by the transmitter. They may, however, send feedback signals to the transmitter concerning a defective bulb or other system failure. Depending upon its design and function, a receiver might operate the

electrical load itself or control a relay that actually operates the load.

While a multiplex wiring system using a peripheral serial bus offers many advantages over conventional wiring systems, it is still prone to interruption by EMI.

Optical Data Links. The second approach to multiplexing uses optical data links or fiberoptic cables instead of the peripheral serial bus. In this type of system, a light-emitting diode (LED) in the transmitter sends signals through the fiberoptic cable to a photodiode in the receiver. (This application of photoelectricity was introduced in chapter 2.) A decoder in the receiver translates the signals and allows the receiver to complete the required output function. Figure 3-18 shows the basic arrangement and principles of an optical data link system.

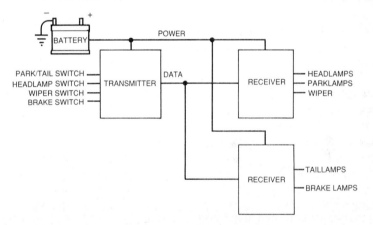

Figure 3-17. In a multiplex wiring system using a peripheral data bus, the transmitter and all receivers are connected to battery power. The transmitter is connected to each receiver by a bidirectional data bus.

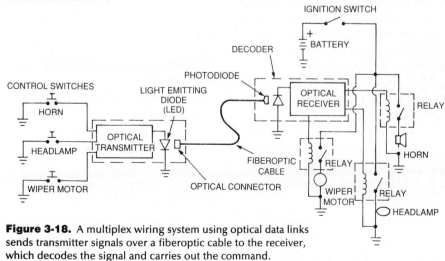

Figure 3-18. A multiplex wiring system using optical data links sends transmitter signals over a fiberoptic cable to the receiver, which decodes the signal and carries out the command.

One form of optical data link system has been used since 1982 on certain Toyota models sold only in Japan. This system connects an optical module in a master body electronic control unit (ECU) with individual ECU's in each door via two fiberoptic cables. The use of two cables makes the Toyota example a bidirectional system, figure 3-19. The master ECU controls the individual ECU's on one cable; the second cable allows the individual ECU to send diagnostic signals back to the master ECU. Special connectors are used to ensure that the optical signals will be properly transmitted.

Activating the switch in any door closes a relay in the master ECU and provides power to the system control circuit. Once the control circuit is powered, the master ECU sends its command to the appropriate door ECU, which executes the command. Figure 3-20 shows the electrical circuit involved in this activity.

Because an optical data link system uses light instead of electricity to transmit signals, EMI will not affect its operation, nor will the system itself create interference that can affect the operation of other electrical systems.

Design Advantages. Whether a multiplex wiring system uses a peripheral serial bus or optical data link design, it offers many advantages over conventional wiring systems. Some of the more common are:

1. The number and size of the wires in a given circuit can be reduced considerably. This, in turn, will reduce the complexity of wiring harnesses.

2. Since the switches in such a system require only a low current capacity, a wide variety of touch-type switches can be integrated into vehicle design.

3. Timing functions can be built into the transmitter or master ECU. This can provide many convenience features, such as:

• Locking all doors above a specified speed

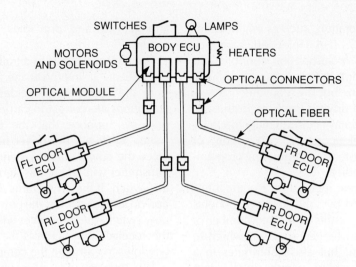

Figure 3-19. A component schematic of the Toyota multiplex system using an optical data link.

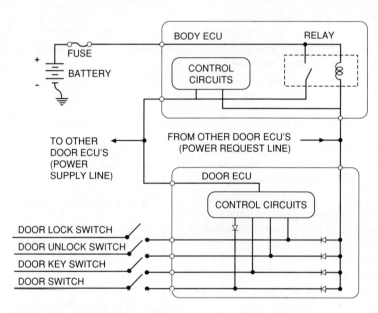

Figure 3-20. This electrical schematic shows how the relay and control circuits work in the Toyota multiplex system.

• Unlocking all doors when the ignition is turned off

• Leaving exterior lighting on briefly after the ignition is turned off

• Leaving interior lighting on briefly after the doors are closed

• Shutting off wiper blade motion in a selected nonpark position for servicing

4. EMI interference can be reduced or eliminated.

CIRCUIT RESISTANCE

Every electrical circuit must have some kind of resistance in order to do any kind of work. That's how electrical energy changes into some other kind of energy. Consider the following example.

A battery produces electric current and develops electrical energy as a voltage difference between its two terminals. It stores the current and volt-

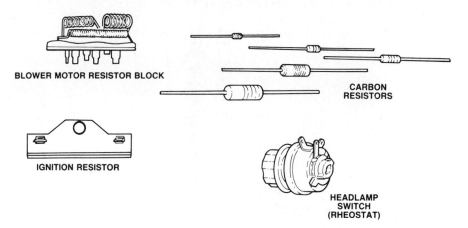

BLOWER MOTOR RESISTOR BLOCK

CARBON RESISTORS

IGNITION RESISTOR

HEADLAMP SWITCH (RHEOSTAT)

Figure 3-21. Some of the wide variety of resistors used in automotive applications.

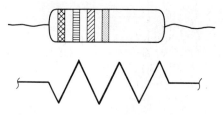

Figure 3-22. The symbol for a resistor (bottom) and a typical axial-lead resistor (top). Color bands on the resistor indicate its resistance in ohms.

age until it is connected to a circuit. This is similar to storing water in a reservoir. We can release the energy of flowing water to do work just as we can release electric current.

If we release the water slowly, with controlled resistance, we can change its energy to some other kind of energy. When we release the water through a water wheel or a rotating turbine, we can use its energy to operate machinery or to turn an electric power generator. If the reservoir bursts, all of the water is released with no resistance, and it does more harm than good.

The same principle applies to electric current. If we connect a battery or other current source to a circuit with resistance (a circuit load), we can control the current and use its energy for some other job. If we build a circuit with no resistance (other than the small resistance of the conductors), current will flood through the circuit like water from a broken dam. The current must release its energy in some way, and the only way available is through heat energy. Uncontrolled current flow can burn up a circuit if the conductors do not provide enough resistance. On an automobile, current from a battery or an alternator will do just that if it is connected to a circuit with no resistance.

Resistors come in many forms. A light bulb is a resistor. It changes electrical energy to light and heat energy. A motor or any electromagnetic coil is

a resistor. It changes electrical energy to magnetic or mechanical energy, or both. A radio amplifier is a resistor; so is a computer. A resistor can be a simple heater, such as an automobile cigarette lighter. Figure 3-21 shows some typical automotive resistors.

Some electrical and electronic circuits use resistors simply to control circuit voltage. Ignition systems have several kinds of resistance to regulate voltage. Many electronic circuits have small resistors to reduce or stabilize voltage applied to other circuit parts. Regardless of a resistor's form or function, the following principles apply to its operation:

1. Voltage always decreases (drops) as current flows from one side of a resistor to the other.

2. Current flow remains constant through a resistor. It does not decrease.

3. All resistors release some energy as heat.

Remembering these facts will help your troubleshooting when you test electrical circuits.

Figure 3-22 shows the standard symbol for a resistor, or resistance, in an electrical circuit diagram. This symbol indicates fixed resistance, and the examples above are types of fixed resistors used in automobiles. Electrical systems also used stepped, or tapped, resistors and variable resistors.

Stepped (Tapped) Resistors

A stepped, or tapped, resistor has two or more fixed resistance values. Circuit resistance can be changed by connecting wires to the different taps on the resistor, usually through a switch, figure 3-23. A heater blower speed control switch is a common example of a stepped resistor. Moving the blower speed control switch adds and subtracts resistors from the blower motor circuit. Low resistance at the switch allows higher voltage at the motor and higher blower speed. High resistance at the switch does just the opposite.

Another kind of stepped resistance is used in computer circuits to convert on-off digital voltage signals to continuously variable analog signals. A digital-to-analog converter circuit can be made from a series of resistors as shown in figure 3-23, but the circuit is microscopic. You will learn more about automotive computer circuits in chapter 5.

Variable Resistance

A stepped resistor allows you to add and subtract circuit resistance in fixed amounts, or steps. A variable resistor provides a range of changeable resistance for a circuit. The switch that controls the brightness of instrument panel lamps contains such a resistor. As you will learn in chapter 6, many sensors in computer-controlled vehicle systems are variable resistors.

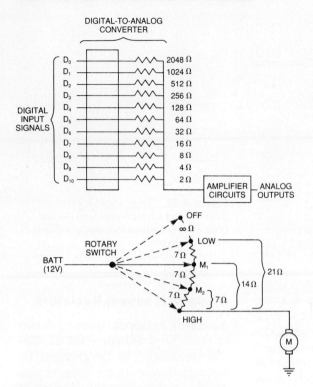

Figure 3-23. The stepped (tapped) series of resistors in the bottom drawing can regulate motor speeds. A similar, but much smaller, series of resistors in the top view is typical of solid-state circuits used for digital-to-analog converter circuits in a computer.

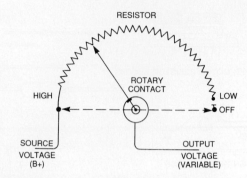

Figure 3-24. A rheostat is a 2-wire variable resistor. Rheostats were often used in older heater motor controls.

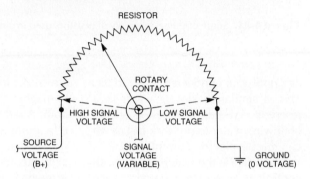

Figure 3-25. A potentiometer is a 3-wire resistor. Source voltage drops across the resistor to ground. Signal voltage is taken from the movable contact. Current stays constant through the entire resistor to minimize the effects of heat on the voltage drop.

Automotive systems commonly use two kinds of variable resistors: **rheostats** and **potentiometers**.

Rheostats. A rheostat has two connecting terminals: one to a fixed end of a resistor coil or other resistive element, the other to a movable contact that slides along the resistor, figure 3-24. Turning the movable contact, or wiper, toward or away from the connection at the fixed end, decreases or increases the resistance at the wiper connection. Rheostats are used on heater-blower motor circuits on some older cars and in instrument panel lighting switches.

Potentiometers. A potentiometer has three connecting terminals, figure 3-25. It gets its name because it varies the potential (voltage) at an output terminal. Each end of the resistor element is connected to a circuit. The third connection is to the movable contact. Again, the movable contact provides a variable voltage drop as it moves across the resistor. Total voltage drop across the resistor is more stable than in a rheostat because current always flows through the same amount of resistance and its temperature remains stable. Therefore, the variable output voltage at the movable contact is more stable and reliable than from a rheostat. Many of the sensors in electronic engine control systems are potentiometers, and you will learn more about them in chapters 5 and 6.

Automotive electrical systems use other kinds of variable resistors, such as thermistors and piezoresistive devices. These are usually used as sensors in computer control systems, and you will learn about them in chapter 6.

CIRCUIT PROTECTION

If we want a reliable circuit, we must provide protection against accidental

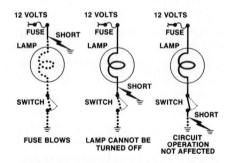

Figure 3-26. Typical short circuits. The results of a short will differ according to where it occurs in the circuit.

high current. If part or all of the circuit resistance fails so that current can still find a complete path, we have a **short circuit**, figure 3-26. Voltage will not drop across resistors in the circuit, and current will increase because of the higher voltage. High current through a short circuit creates heat that can damage circuit devices. To protect a circuit, we can install a device that will melt or burn up or otherwise open the circuit before the excessive heat can damage other components.

All electrical circuits are protected from excessive current by one of three devices: fuses, circuit breakers, and fusible links (fuse links). Any of these devices will open a circuit before high current can cause permanent damage to the circuit or its components. Each circuit protection device is sensitive to current, not voltage, and is thus rated by its current-carrying capacity. A 25-ampere fuse or circuit breaker will conduct up to 25 amperes of current in the electrical system, regardless of whether it is a 6-, 12-, or 24-volt system. Circuit protection devices are installed at, or near, the power source of the circuits they protect. This makes them an important starting point for troubleshooting sequences.

Fuses

A fuse installed in an electrical circuit acts as a safety valve. It performs this function by "blowing" or opening the circuit when excessive current passes through it. Three types of fuses are used in modern automotive electrical circuits:

1. Glass fuses
2. Cartridge fuses
3. Blade-type or minifuses

Glass fuses are small glass cylinders of uniform diameter but varying in length. They contain a thin metal link, figure 3-27. The thickness of the metal link depends upon the current rating. When a heavy electrical load passes through the metal link, the link burns in half. The fuse condition can be determined visually by removing it from its holder and checking the condition of the metal link. If it is broken or if the glass cylinder appears black, the fuse has blown.

Automobile fuse ratings range from 0.5 to 35 amperes, but 4-ampere to 25-ampere fuses are most common. Cylindrical glass fuse sizes and ratings are established by the Society of Fuse Engineers (SFE). All SFE fuses are the

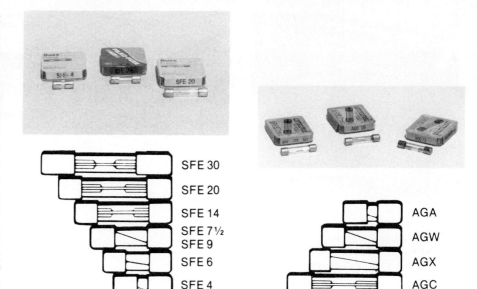

Figure 3-27. Typical SFE fuses (left) and AG-series fuses (right).

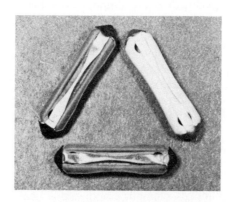

Figure 3-28. Typical cartridge-type fuses.

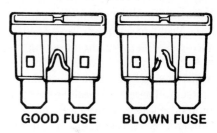

GOOD FUSE   BLOWN FUSE

Figure 3-29. Good and bad blade-type fuses.

same diameter, but the length varies with the current rating, figure 3-27. Some cars have AGA, AGC, and AGW fuses. The lengths of all fuses in one series are the same, even though the current ratings vary.

Cartridge fuses are used in many European vehicles. They have pointed ends that fit into special fuse holders and a thin metal link that extends between the two ends, figure 3-28. They function like glass fuses.

Blade-type fuses, or minifuses, are a flat design encapsulated in plastic. The plastic contains two blades connected by a metal link. The end of each blade is flush with the plastic at the top of the fuse, allowing fuse condition to be checked with test probes without removing it from its slot in the

fuse block. Blade fuses are color coded to indicate current ranges, but some colors make it difficult to visually determine if the fuse is good or bad. Figure 3-29 shows blade fuse design and the difference between a good and a bad fuse.

Fuses are generally installed in a central fuse block or panel located under the instrument panel, figure 3-30, or on the firewall. Some foreign vehicles have the fuse block in the engine compartment. Fuse identification and specifications are often printed on the fuse block itself, figure 3-30, or on the fuse block cover. Power for most circuits except the headlamps, starter motor, and ignition system is supplied through the fuse block. Battery voltage is applied

Figure 3-30. Fuse blocks or panels are generally located under the instrument panel or on the bulkhead or kick panel. Fuse identification is normally provided on the fuse block itself or its cover.

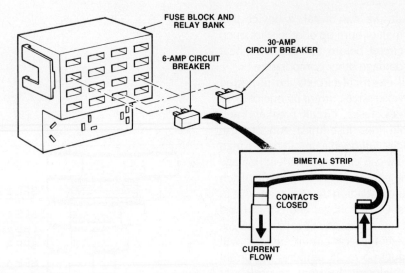

Figure 3-31. Typical self-resetting circuit breaker construction and location. (Chrysler)

to a main **bus bar** in the fuse block, which is connected to one end of the fuse. The other end of the fuse is connected to the circuit, or circuits, it protects. Some circuits may use inline fuses installed in plastic fuse holders and spliced into the circuit wiring.

A blown fuse is a warning that something is wrong in the circuit it protects. There are basic rules that should be followed concerning fuses. Failure to observe them can result in major heat or fire damage and possibly the loss of the entire vehicle.

• Always determine what caused a fuse to blow and correct the problem before installing a replacement.
• Never install a higher capacity fuse in a circuit than specified. A high-amperage fuse may allow excessive current, which will damage circuit parts.
• Never use foil or other metallic materials to bridge the fuse terminals.
• If a fuse of the correct amperage value is not available, remove a fuse of equal amperage value from another circuit that you can do without temporarily, or temporarily install a fuse of slightly lower value.

Circuit Breakers

Circuit breakers are used in circuits where it is important to restore power quickly or where temporary overloads may occur. Circuit breakers may be located in the fuse block or panel, installed in the circuit itself, or within a switch assembly. A circuit breaker contains an arm made of two different types of metal called a **bimetal element**, figure 3-31. Current passing through this bimetal arm causes the two strips of metal to expand at different rates. Low or normal current through the arm will not overheat the bimetal element, and the circuit breaker contacts remain closed. Since one metal expands faster than the other, excessive current will overheat the bimetal element. This causes the arm to move and open the contacts, shutting off the current through the circuit breaker.

There are two types of circuit breakers. Type I is a self-resetting device, also called a cycling circuit breaker. As the arm cools down, the bimetal element contracts and the arm will then close the contacts, allowing current to flow again. This process will repeat the open/close sequence as long as power is applied or until the condition is corrected. Type I circuit breakers are most often used in headlamp circuits.

Type II, or noncycling, circuit breakers remain open when excessive current passes through them. A coil installed around the bimetal arm holds it open until power is shut off or the condition is corrected. A noncycling circuit breaker must be reset before it will function properly.

Fusible Links

Some circuits have fusible links, or fuse links, in addition to fuses and circuit breakers. A fusible link is different from a fuse. It is a short length of wire that is four gauge sizes smaller than the circuit in which it is installed. A fusible link is covered with a special nonflammable insulation. The fusible link will burn out when an overload occurs. The insulation will generally bubble or blister to indicate that the link is burned out and must be replaced, but this may not always happen. When a fusible link appears to be good but the circuit does not work, use an ohmmeter or self-powered test lamp to check the link for continuity.

Some fusible links are spliced into the circuit; others are installed with snap-together connectors. Fusible links are generally located in one or two positions in the engine compartment, figure 3-32. Some foreign cars use a fusible link box containing short links that plug in much like a fuse, figure 3-33.

The first real advance in fusible link design made its appearance on domestic automobiles with the 1988 Lincoln Continental and 1989 Ford

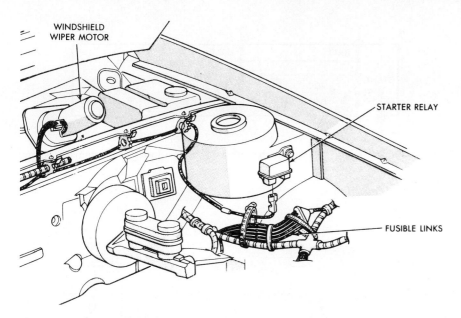

Figure 3-33. Fusible links used with many foreign cars are short lengths of small-gauge wire with terminal ends that plug into a fuse link box located in the engine compartment.

Figure 3-32. Automakers generally locate fusible links in one or two places in the engine compartment. This is a typical Chrysler location. (Chrysler)

Figure 3-34. These color-coded fuse links are used for high-current, 30- to 80-ampere circuits on some 1988 and later vehicles.

Probe. Instead of a length of wire installed in the circuit, this fuse link, as its manufacturer calls it, is a plug-in type that looks much like a long, fat blade-type fuse when installed. The housing contains a short length of wire suitable for the rated current load. As figure 3-34 shows, the top of the fuse link housing is transparent and allows you to visually determine the condition of the link inside. The fuse link has no exposed blades, but plugs into a combination fuse and fuse link box that contains blade terminals. Color coded according to amperage value, fuse links are used in high-amperage circuits (from 30 to 80 amperes).

Factory-installed fusible links are generally color coded to indicate current-carrying capacity, although replacement links may not be color coded. As with fuses, a burned-out fusible link should not be replaced with ordinary wire or a link of greater capacity. The resulting overload could result in a fire or even complete loss of the vehicle.

BASIC ELECTRICAL SYSTEM PARTS

Other basic electrical parts are common to most circuits. These include switches, relays, solenoids, motors, and other electromagnetic devices.

Switches

A switch controls circuit operation by opening and closing the current path. Like a connector, a switch is an extension of the circuit conductors. It should have little or no resistance and little or no measurable voltage drop across it.

The simple switch in figure 3-35A is a single-pole, single-throw (spst) switch. The symbol for a switch can be drawn to show the open (off) or the closed (on) positions. The term "pole" indicates the number of power (input) connections on the switch. The term "throw" indicates the number of output connections on the switch. An spst switch can open and close one circuit. A single-pole, double-throw (spdt) switch, figure 3-35B, can alternately open and close the two output circuits.

A switch can have as many poles and throws as it needs to do its job and as the designer can fit into the switch body. Some switches are "ganged" switches that have multiple poles, throws, and wipers. The wiper is the movable part of the switch that opens and closes circuits. An ignition switch is a ganged switch with several poles,

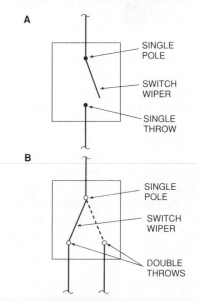

Figure 3-35. The symbol shown in **A** is used for a typical single-pole, single-throw (spst) switch; the symbol shown in **B** is a typical single-pole, double-throw (spdt) switch.

throws, and wipers. Figure 3-36 is a typical ignition switch symbol used by most carmakers. The dashed line between the wipers indicates that they are ganged and move together.

Besides identifying switches by the number of poles and throws, we also identify them by their normal contact positions. "Normal" refers to the switch position when it is not actuated or has no outside force applied to it.

• In a **normally open (NO) switch**, the contacts are open until an outside force closes them to complete the circuit.

• In a **normally closed (NC) switch**, the contacts are closed to complete the circuit until an outside force opens them.

You will find both kinds of switches, NO and NC, in vehicle electrical systems.

Vehicle electrical systems have other switches besides simple and complex manual switches. Many switches are operated by temperature or pressure. A simple temperature switch used to sense coolant temperature has a bimetal element that bends as it heats and cools. The arm opens and closes the switch contacts as the temperature changes. The contacts of oil pressure switches and vacuum switches open and close in response to pressure. Figure 3-37 shows examples of typical temperature and pressure switches.

Mercury switches and inertia switches operate automatically to open and close circuits in response to movement. A mercury switch has a closed capsule partly filled with mercury, which is a good conductor. In a normally open position, the mercury is at the end of the capsule away from the switch contacts. When the capsule rotates or moves in an arc, the mercury flows to the other end of the capsule and closes the switch. Mercury switches are often used as automatic switches to turn on trunk and engine compartment lamps. They also can be used as rollover switches to open electric fuel pump circuits in a vehicle accident.

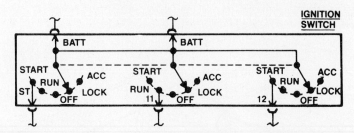

Figure 3-36. This typical ignition switch symbol illustrates a switch with multiple poles and throws and ganged wipers. (Ford)

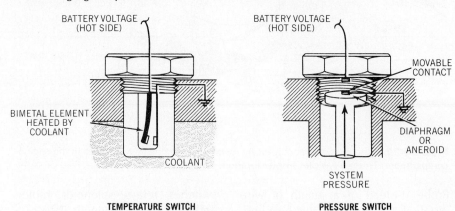

Figure 3-37. Temperature and pressure switches can be normally open or normally closed.

An inertia switch is usually a normally closed switch with its contacts held together by a calculated amount of friction or spring tension. When sudden physical movement overcomes the friction or tension, the contacts open. They respond to a sudden change in inertia. Inertia switches are often used as safety switches to open electric fuel pump circuits upon the impact of a vehicle accident. The switch must be reset to its normally closed position by hand.

Switches can be placed on the hot side or the ground side of circuit devices. The hot side of a circuit has voltage applied to it; the ground side is connected to ground. Switch locations determine the conditions when circuit devices are hot, which is important for accurate testing.

Relays

A relay is an electromagnetic switch that works on the principles you learned in chapter 2. Current through a coil creates an electromagnetic field. Relays have two important features that make them common in automotive systems.

1. A relay provides remote control of one or more other circuits by opening and closing a switch in a control circuit.

2. A relay allows a low-current control circuit to switch high current on and off in a power circuit.

Every relay has two circuits in parallel, figure 3-38. The control circuit of the relay has an electromagnetic coil wound around an iron core. The coil has resistance and is the load on the control circuit. The power circuit, or output circuit, of the relay has two switch contacts, one of which is on a movable armature. In this example, the armature is made of spring steel, and its tension holds the contacts open. The contacts are the switch for the power circuit and contain little or no resistance. Here is how the relay control and power circuits in figure 3-38 work:

1. When the switch in the control circuit closes, current flows through the coil and creates an electromagnetic field in the core.

2. The core attracts the movable armature downward against spring tension to close the contacts.

3. The armature contacts close the circuit for the motor so that current flows through the motor.

4. When the control switch opens, current stops through the relay coil, and the electromagnetic field collapses.

5. Spring tension opens the armature contacts, and current to the motor stops.

Like switches, relays can be normally open or normally closed. Both

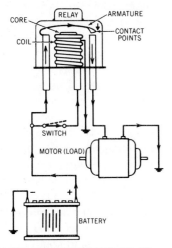

1. SWITCH CLOSES, CURRENT FLOWS THROUGH COIL AND CREATES ELECTROMAGNETIC FIELD IN RELAY CORE.
2. CORE ATTRACTS MOVABLE ARMATURE DOWNWARD AGAINST SPRING TENSION TO CLOSE CONTACT POINTS.
3. ARMATURE CONTACT POINTS CLOSE CIRCUIT TO MOTOR SO THAT CURRENT FLOWS THROUGH MOTOR.
4. WHEN SWITCH OPENS, CURRENT STOPS THROUGH RELAY COIL AND FIELD COLLAPSES.
5. SPRING TENSION OPENS ARMATURE CONTACT POINTS AND CURRENT TO MOTOR STOPS.

Figure 3-38. This relay is a remote control switch that opens and closes a motor circuit.

the control circuit and the power circuit of the relay in figure 3-38 are normally open. This is the kind of relay you will find most often in automotive systems. Normally open relays control horns, starter motors, and electric fuel pumps on many cars.

A relay with a single control winding is generally used only for short-term operation, such as in a horn circuit. Relays for continuous operation usually have two control windings. One winding creates the magnetic field and moves the armature. A second, lighter winding maintains the field and holds the armature. A stronger field is needed to move the armature than to hold it. When the armature moves, it breaks the contacts for the first or pull-in winding. The second or hold-in winding keeps the relay energized with less current.

Using the same electromagnetic principles, engineers can design relays with other operating features.

• The relay in figure 3-39 has two sets of contacts to operate two power circuits with one control circuit.

• The relay in figure 3-40 has normally closed power circuit contacts. The coil field opens the power circuit when the control circuit closes.

• The relay in figure 3-41 has opposing normally open and normally closed contacts. Control circuit operation opens one power circuit and closes the other.

Knowing the operating positions of switches and relays is important for troubleshooting. Switch and relay positions determine which circuit devices are hot (have voltage applied to them) under various conditions. Relay operation is also the basis for computer logic and control operations, as you will learn in chapter 4.

Solenoids

A solenoid is an electromagnetic device that works like a relay. A solenoid, however, uses electromagnetism and a movable plunger or armature to do mechanical work. Like a relay, a solenoid has an electromagnetic coil and a core. The solenoid also has a spring-loaded, movable plunger. Electromagnetism in the coil and core attracts the plunger, which moves mechanical linkage. The solenoid is then energized. When current stops in the coil, the magnetic field collapses, and the spring returns the plunger to the deenergized position. A solenoid is a circuit load device. The resistance of its coil changes electrical energy to magnetic and mechanical energy.

The solenoid plunger can open and close a vacuum valve or a fuel valve. It can also operate linkage for door and trunk locks. The most common solenoids on many cars engage the drive gears for the starter motor. Many

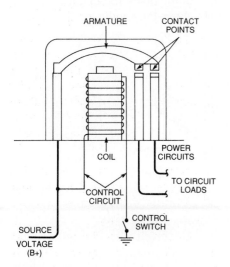

Figure 3-39. A double-contact relay.

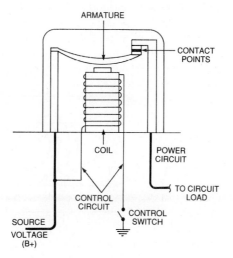

Figure 3-40. A normally closed relay.

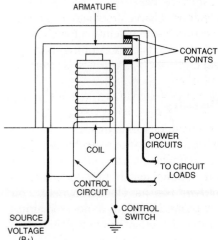

Figure 3-41. A double-acting relay.

starter solenoids also function as relays, or electromagnetic switches. The solenoid plunger moves linkage to engage the starter drive gear with the engine flywheel. The plunger also closes the contacts for the high-current circuit from the battery to the starter motor. Chapter 8 explains starter solenoid design and operation in detail.

High-current starter solenoids and solenoids for continous operation usually have separate pull-in and hold-in windings, similar to those in some relays. Plunger movement opens the contacts on the pull-in winding. The hold-in winding maintains the magnetic field and holds the plunger with less current.

Relays and solenoids are direct current devices. They can operate as described here only if current flows continuously in one direction through their coils. Remember that current direction establishes the direction of a magnetic field. If current reversed continually as it does in ac devices, the field would continually reverse. A relay armature or a solenoid plunger would not stay energized. It would vibrate back and forth. Because automotive electrical systems are dc systems, however, relays and solenoids are ideal devices to use for circuit control and electromechanical operations.

Many solenoids in computer-controlled systems operate with intermittent, on-off direct current. You will learn how these solenoids operate as electromechanical actuators in chapter 6. On-off electromagnetic fields are also used in other common electrical parts, such as warning buzzers.

Buzzers

Many circuits contain buzzers to warn the driver of various conditions, such as seatbelts unfastened, keys left in the ignition switch, and doors ajar. A buzzer has an electromagnetic coil and core, as well as a movable armature and a set of contact points. The coil and the armature contacts are in series, however, figure 3-42. Current flows through the coil and the nor-

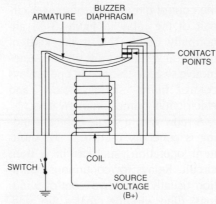

Figure 3-42. In a buzzer, the coil is in series with the armature and contact points. Opening and closing the circuit causes the armature to vibrate against the buzzer diaphragm.

mally closed contacts to ground. Electromagnetism in the core moves the armature to open the contacts and break the circuit. The magnetic field then collapses, and the contacts reclose. The circuit opens and closes many times per second. The resulting vibrations create the buzzing sound.

Motors

In chapter 2, you learned how a magnetic field can induce electric current in a conductor. When current flows through a conductor, a magnetic field forms around the conductor. The strength of the field depends on the amount of current; the magnetic polarity depends on current direction. The preceding explanations of relays and solenoids are examples of how electromagnetic induction is used in

some common electrical parts. This is a good point to introduce the ways in which electromagnetism is used in motors.

If you bring two conductors close to each other, their magnetic fields will interact as any fields will according to the laws of magnetic attraction. The interaction of magnetic fields can change electrical energy to mechanical energy in an electric motor.

If we place a conductor in a strong magnetic field, the field created by conductor current tries to move the conductor out of the surrounding field. The conductor moves from a strong field to a weak field, figure 3-43. The opposing north-north and south-south poles of the two fields repel each other. If we form the conductor into a loop, current flows in opposite directions on each side of the loop, figure 3-44. This forms two opposite magnetic fields. If we then place the loop conductor on a rotating shaft, we have built a simple motor **armature.**

To build a motor, we must place the armature between two stationary magnetic north and south poles. The conductor fields then interact with the surrounding magnetic field, figure 3-45. The clockwise field of the top conductor adds to the field of the poles. This creates a strong field under the conductor, which forces it upward. The counterclockwise field of the lower conductor also adds to the field of the poles and creates a strong field above the conductor. This forces

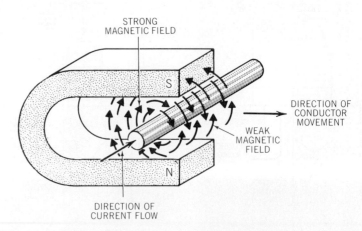

Figure 3-43. A current-carrying conductor in a magnetic field tries to move from the strong field to the weak field.

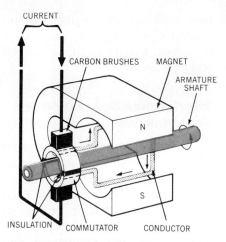

Figure 3-44. A loop conductor on a shaft within a magnetic field is a simple electric motor. (Bosch)

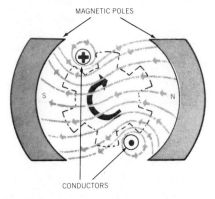

Figure 3-45. The interaction of magnetic fields causes electric motors to operate. (Delco-Remy)

the lower conductor downward. Because the conductor loop is on a rotating armature, field interaction turns the armature.

If the armature had only one conductor loop, it would turn until the magnetic fields balanced each other and then stop. To keep the motor turning, an armature has many conductor loops to react with the stationary magnetic poles. To keep the motor turning steadily in the same direction, current must flow in the same direction through each armature loop, or winding. Moreover, current must flow through each winding in sequence when the winding is at a position where it will react most strongly with the stationary field. That is, we must switch the current on and off rapidly in each winding. To do this, we use a commutator.

Just as a commutator can be a rotating switch to rectify current output

from a generator, it can maintain steady current to the rotating windings of a motor armature. In a simple motor, current flows through a brush to one commutator segment. It then flows through the winding to another commutator segment on the opposite end and out through a second brush. As the armature turns, the first winding and its commutator segment move away from the brushes, and a second pair of segments rotates to contact the brushes. Current then flows through the second winding in the same direction as through the first, and the armature continues to turn. The process continues through each winding in sequence, and the armature rotates steadily as long as current flows through the brushes and commutator.

This example is a very simple 2-brush motor. Motors can be built with several brushes and different combinations of series and parallel connections for armature windings and electromagnetic field windings. Armature and field winding arrangements affect motor speed and torque. Engineers select different combinations for different uses. As you study motors in various electrical systems throughout this book, you will learn how series, parallel, and series-parallel armature and field windings affect motor torque, speed, and power. Understanding the internal connections of a motor is important for testing and repair. No matter how a motor is built, however, all motors work on the principles just outlined.

The stationary magnetic fields of a motor can be a pair of electromagnets

or permanent magnets. Most electric motors have electromagnetic field poles, which can produce a strong field in a compact space. Field strength can be controlled by controlling current through the field windings. Some small motors, however, are built with permanent magnet fields. This allows a simpler motor design by eliminating the electrical connections and windings for the field. Such motors are often used to operate a constant, light load at a constant speed, such as a small electric fan.

Permanent-magnet motors were seldom used for high-torque, high-power automotive applications until Chrysler introduced such a starter motor on its 1986 models, followed by General Motors on 1987 vehicles. These permanent magnet, or PM, starter motors, substitute permanent magnets for the field coils, figure 3-46. A planetary reduction drive, figure 3-47, is used to increase the torque of a high-speed motor with permanent-magnet fields.

Figure 3-46. Permanent magnets replace the field coil in the new lightweight PM starter motors.

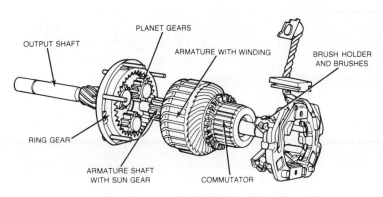

Figure 3-47. A planetary gear system is used to increase the torque of a permanent magnet starter motor. (Chrysler)

INTERFERENCE SUPPRESSION

When we discussed ignition cables earlier in this chapter, we introduced the subject of radiofrequency interference (RFI). RFI is a form of electromagnetic interference (EMI). RFI suppression has been an important part of automotive electrical system design for decades. The purpose is to protect radio and television broadcast signals against interference from vehicle systems, principally the ignition. As the use of electronic systems increases on late-model cars, the area of interference suppression has grown to include the broader field of EMI suppression. Low-power digital integrated circuits are vulnerable to EMI signals that were unimportant a decade ago.

Radio transmission is the generation of high-frequency electromagnetic waves. An electromagnetic field is formed and its strength is varied many thousand or million times per second. As field strength and polarity change, the field passes through a cycle similar to an alternating current cycle. We measure cycles per second with the unit called the hertz (Hz). High-frequency signals of thousands of cycles per second are measured in kilohertz (kHz). Millions of cycles per second are measured in megahertz (MHz). These are the transmission frequencies of AM and FM radio and television broadcasting, figure 3-48. AM transmitters send signals by varying the strength, or amplitude, of the transmission frequencies. FM and TV transmitters send signals by varying the frequency itself. Radio and television receivers change the high-frequency electromagnetic waves back to voltage signals that create sound and pictures.

Interference Generation and Transmission

An electromagnetic field is created whenever current flows in a conductor, and field strength changes whenever current stops and starts. Each change in field strength creates an electromagnetic signal wave. If current changes fast enough, it creates high-frequency electromagnetic waves that interfere with radio transmission or with other electronic systems. EMI is an undesirable form of electromagnetism.

Electromagnetic waves are created whenever current starts and stops in

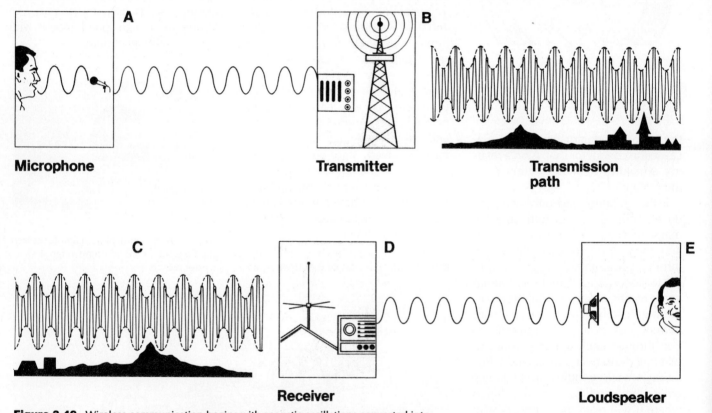

Microphone   **Transmitter**   **Transmission path**

Receiver   **Loudspeaker**

Figure 3-48. Wireless communication begins with acoustic oscillations converted into alternating voltage of the same frequency by a microphone (**A**). The low-frequency signal created in **A** is superimposed on an amplitude-modulated carrier wave (**B**). The high-frequency wave created in **B** is transmitted and received by an antenna (**C**). The receiver separates the low-frequency signal from the high-frequency carrier wave (**D**). The speaker translates the signal back into acoustic oscillations (**E**). These are the principles of radio and tv communication. (Bosch)

a spark plug cable. The length of the cables, the operating frequency of the system, and the high voltage of the spark plug circuits make the ignition system an excellent EMI transmitter.

An electromagnetic wave is also created whenever a switch opens or closes in a circuit. High-frequency waves are created by a revolving commutator in a motor. (A commutator is a rotating switch.) EMI waves are created by the slight ac fluctuations in the alternator output circuit. Relays, solenoids, electromechanical voltage regulators, and vibrating horn contacts all produce electromagnetic waves. Figure 3-49 shows common sources of EMI on a typical automobile.

Additionally, EMI can be generated by static electric charges that develop due to friction at the following locations:

• Tire contact with the road surface
• Engine drive belts
• Drive axles and shafts
• Clutch and brake lining surfaces

EMI is transmitted in four ways:

1. By coupling through circuit conductors, figure 3-50

2. By capacitive coupling in an electrostatic field between two devices or conductors with voltage applied to them, figure 3-51

3. By inductive coupling as magnetic fields form and collapse between two conductors, figure 3-52

4. By electromagnetic radiation, figure 3-53

All of these interference transmission sources exist in an automobile.

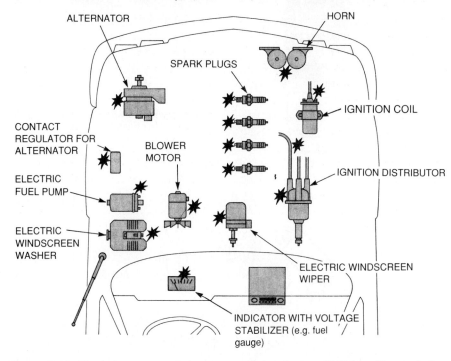

Figure 3-49. The major sources of electromagnetic interference (EMI) found in a typical automobile. (Bosch)

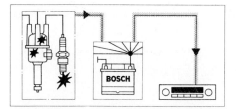

Figure 3-50. In conductive coupling interference, the wiring transmits the interference directly from the source to the receiver. (Bosch)

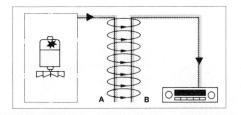

Figure 3-52. An electromagnetic field between adjacent wiring results in inductive coupling interference. (Bosch)

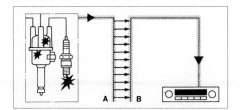

Figure 3-51. A capacitive field between adjacent wiring results in capacitive coupling interference. (Bosch)

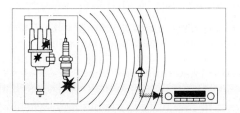

Figure 3-53. In radiation interference, the EMI waves are picked up by wiring that serves as a receiving antenna. (Bosch)

EMI Suppression

There are four general approaches used to reduce EMI:

1. The addition of resistance to conductors to suppress conductive transmission and radiation

2. The installation of capacitors and **choke coil** combinations to reduce an inductive capacitive coupling

3. The installation of ground straps that will bypass signals to ground and thus reduce conductive transmission and radiation

4. The use of various forms of metal shielding to reduce EMI radiation, as well as capacitive and inductive coupling

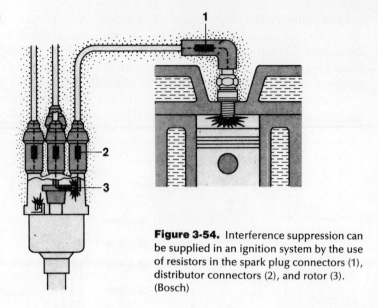

Figure 3-54. Interference suppression can be supplied in an ignition system by the use of resistors in the spark plug connectors (1), distributor connectors (2), and rotor (3). (Bosch)

Suppressing with Resistance. Circuit resistance works only in a high-voltage system to suppress RFI. Interference-suppression resistors are not practical in low-voltage circuits because they create too much voltage drop and power loss.

The ignition secondary circuit is the only high-voltage system on most vehicles and can be the largest source of EMI. The distributor switches thousands of volts across separate spark plug circuits and turns current on and off thousands of times per second. An 8-cylinder engine running at 2,000 rpm produces electromagnetic waves at a frequency of 8 kHz. Current in metallic high-voltage ignition cables can create electromagnetic waves strong enough to interfere with radio and TV signals and other electronic systems. This interference can upset radio reception on a vehicle. It can also disturb public radio and TV transmission, as well as emergency radio service for police and other public service agencies.

Because the ignition system is the largest EMI source on a vehicle, engineers attacked that problem more than 30 years ago. Nonmetallic conductors in ignition cables add resistance and reduce the current in the cables, thus reducing the strength of the magnetic fields. High resistance also reduces voltage fluctuations in

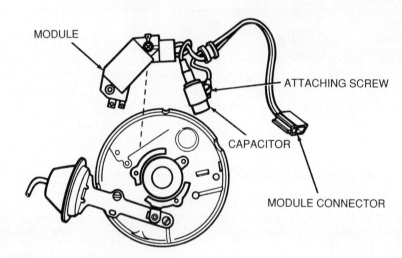

Figure 3-55. The capacitor in this HEI distributor is not an ignition condenser. It suppresses radiofrequency interference.

the circuits. Resistors added to spark plug electrodes and to distributor rotors also help to reduce RFI, figure 3-54. Some electronic ignitions require silicone grease on distributor cap and rotor terminals to suppress RFI radiation.

Suppressing with Coils and Capacitors. Remember from chapter 1 that a capacitor can be used as a voltage "shock absorber." Capacitors are installed in parallel with (across) many circuits and switching points to absorb changing voltage. Electronic ignition systems do not require ignition condensers, or capacitors, as do

breaker-point ignitions. Many, however, have a capacitor across the primary circuit at the ignition module, figure 3-55, to absorb voltage changes as the primary current switches on and off. Breaker-point ignitions often have interference suppression capacitors at the coil + terminal, figure 3-56. Most alternators have a capacitor across the output terminal to smooth out the ac voltage fluctuations, figure 3-57. This not only reduces EMI, but it also smooths the voltage applied to the vehicle electrical system. Electric motors, too, often have capacitors across the armature circuit to reduce voltage pulses at the

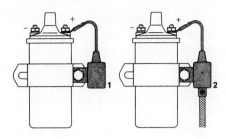

Figure 3-56. Installation of an ignition coil suppression capacitor when the coil is connected directly to the chassis (1). If the coil is not connected directly to the chassis, a separate ground strap is used (2). (Bosch)

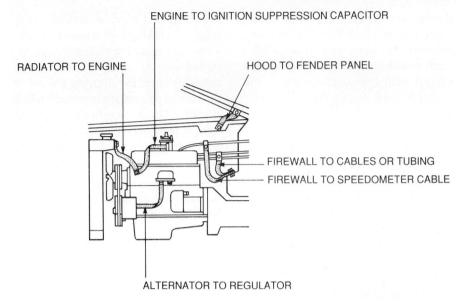

ENGINE TO IGNITION SUPPRESSION CAPACITOR

RADIATOR TO ENGINE

HOOD TO FENDER PANEL

FIREWALL TO CABLES OR TUBING

FIREWALL TO SPEEDOMETER CABLE

ALTERNATOR TO REGULATOR

Figure 3-59. EMI suppression is accomplished in many late-model vehicles by the use of separate ground straps. (Bosch)

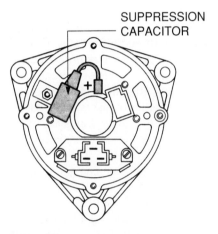

SUPPRESSION CAPACITOR

Figure 3-57. Installation of a suppression capacitor on an alternator. (Bosch)

ATTENTION WARNING VORSICHT

Figure 3-60. This bonding strap reduces the electrostatic field between the hood and the engine compartment.

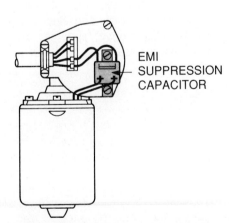

EMI SUPPRESSION CAPACITOR

Figure 3-58. Choke coils and suppression capacitors are often used with automotive electric motors. (Bosch)

commutator. Many horns have capacitors to suppress interference from their vibrating contacts.

Choke coils are installed in some motor circuits and radio power circuits to reduce current fluctuations created by self-induction. On automobiles, choke coils are generally used in combination with capacitors as EMI filter circuits. Wiper motors and electric fuel pump motors often have such filters, figure 3-58.

Suppressing with Ground Straps.
You learned earlier that many automobiles have ground or bonding straps between the chassis and the engine to ensure a low-resistance circuit ground path. These straps also help to suppress EMI conduction and radiation. Resistance in a ground path creates an unwanted voltage drop. It also creates a voltage difference across the resistance, which can be an EMI source. Many vehicles have suppression ground straps between body parts and rubber-mounted components to ensure good conductivity and "short circuit" any interference, figure 3-59.

Some late-model cars have ground straps between body parts where no electrical circuit exists. Figure 3-60 shows such a strap between the hood and a fender panel. This strap is solely an EMI suppression device. Without it, the hood and the car body would form a large capacitor. The opening between the hood and fender would form an electrostatic field that would couple with computer circuits in the wiring harness routed along the fender panel.

Suppressing with Shielding. Metal shields around components that generate RFI signals block the waves. The distributors on a few engines are completely covered by metal shields to reduce RFI radiation from breaker points, condensers, and rotors. The metal housings of most vehicle computers help to shield the circuits from external electromagnetic waves.

The Need for EMI Suppression

Interference suppression has become more important as electronic systems have increased on late-model vehicles. The greater use of citizens-band (CB) and other 2-way radios, as well as mobile telephones, has increased the need for EMI suppression. Electromagnetic interference can also damage the operation of vehicle computer systems. These systems operate on voltage signals of a few millivolts (thousandths of a volt) and milliamperes (thousandths of an ampere) of current. Any of the four kinds of interference transmission listed earlier can generate false voltage signals and excessive current in computer systems. False voltage signals can upset computer operation. Excessive current can destroy microelectronic circuits.

As the use of increasingly sophisticated automotive electronics becomes more widespread with each model year, interference suppression has become a critical engineering

field. Much electrical service work requires working with suppression devices and ensuring that they are installed and operating properly. Engineers are currently studying the use of fiberoptics as a means of reducing EMI signals. Since fiberoptics transmit light instead of electrical signals, they will neither radiate nor be affected by EMI transmissions.

SUMMARY

Electrical polarity can be established with a positive or a negative ground. All late-model automobiles have positive-polarity, negative-ground electrical systems. Many electrical devices are sensitive to system polarity and will not work properly if connected backwards.

Every electrical system must have a power source, conductors, and circuit loads. The battery and the alternator are the electric power sources in automobiles. The circuit wiring and the vehicle chassis and engine are the conductors. Resistive devices are the circuit loads. Loads are also conductors, but they cause voltage to drop through the circuit; conductors do not.

Most wiring on an automobile is low-voltage, primary wiring, identified by AWG or metric wire sizes, which indicate current-carrying capacity. Most primary wiring is grouped into harnesses. Connectors join wires to each other and to circuit loads. Battery cables, printed circuit boards, and ignition cables are specialized conductors. Automotive electrical systems use the vehicle chassis and engine as the ground-return side of all circuits to the battery. All circuit voltage should drop through circuit loads before returning to ground.

Multiplex wiring circuits offer many advantages over conventional wiring circuits. Multiplex circuits may use a peripheral data bus or fiberoptic cables to transmit signals between components. This reduces the number of wires in a circuit.

Any circuit load is a resistor. Resistance allows electric current to do work by changing electrical energy into heat, light, sound, and mechanical energy. Lamp bulbs, inductive coils, motors, and heating elements are all types of fixed resistors used on automobiles. Some fixed resistors are used to control circuit voltage. Stepped (tapped) resistors and variable resistors are also used as voltage-control devices.

Every electrical circuit must have a way to turn current on and off and a device to protect it against excessive current. Many kinds of switches control circuit operation on automobiles. Fuses, circuit breakers, and fusible links are the three kinds of circuit protection devices used in automotive systems.

Electromagnetism can generate voltage and induce current. It can also create a magnetic field to do mechanical work. Relays use electromagnetism to act as remote switches. Solenoids and motors change electrical and magnetic energy to mechanical energy.

Electromagnetism can also generate electromagnetic interference (EMI) and radiofrequency interference (RFI). This interference can disrupt radio and television signals and electronic systems. Automotive systems use many devices to suppress this interference.

REVIEW QUESTIONS

Multiple Choice

1. Mechanic A says that insulation colors indicate wire size, or gauge. Mechanic B says that wire gauge can be listed in either American Wire Gauge (AWG) or metric specifications. Who is right?

a. A only
b. B only
c. both A and B
d. neither A nor B

2. Mechanic A says that a case ground is a ground connection directly to the engine or chassis. Mechanic B says that many lamps and gauges have remote ground. Who is right?

a. A only
b. B only
c. both A and B
d. neither A nor B

3. Mechanic A is installing a 20-gauge fusible link in a 16-gauge circuit wire. Mechanic B is installing a 12-gauge fusible link in a 16-gauge circuit wire. Who is doing the job correctly?

a. A only
b. B only
c. both A and B
d. neither A nor B

4. Many late-model GM cars use special connectors called:

a. molded connectors
b. AMP connectors
c. inverted-tang connectors
d. Metri-Pack connectors

5. Which of the following metals is the most desirable conductor for use in an electric circuit?

a. copper
b. nickel
c. aluminum
d. lead

6. TVRS ignition cables use a conductor made of:

a. carbon
b. linen or fiberglass strands
c. both a and b
d. neither a nor b

7. Mechanic A says that when a fusible link blows, the insulation blisters or bubbles. Mechanic B says that a fusible link suspected of being defective can be checked with an ohmmeter or self-powered test lamp. Who is right?

a. A only
b. B only
c. both A and B
d. neither A nor B

8. Mechanic A says that an inertia switch is normally open and is closed by the force of an impact. Mechanic B says that a mercury switch is normally open and can be used as a rollover switch to close a fuel pump circuit. Who is right?

a. A only
b. B only
c. both A and B
d. neither A nor B

9. Mechanic A says that a solenoid is an electromagnetic device that works like a relay. Mechanic B says that a relay also contains a movable plunger or armature and can do mechanical work. Who is right?

a. A only
b. B only
c. both A and B
d. neither A nor B

10. Mechanic A says that electromagnetic waves are created whenever current starts and stops in a spark plug cable. Mechanic B says that the opening and closing of a switch in a circuit creates EMI. Who is right?

a. A only
b. B only
c. both A and B
d. neither A nor B

11. Mechanic A says that system polarity affects the operation of automotive electrical components. Mechanic B says that polarity is not a concern when using test equipment, except for reversed readings. Who is right?

a. A only
b. B only
c. both A and B
d. neither A nor B

12. Mechanic A says that voltage increases as current flows from one side of a resistor to the other. Mechanic B says that current is rectified as it flows through a resistor. Who is right?

a. A only
b. B only
c. both A and B
d. neither A nor B

13. Which of the following is not used as a circuit conductor in automotive electrical systems?

a. printed circuits
b. integrated circuits
c. single-strand wire
d. multistrand wire

14. Which of the following is not true of a circuit breaker?

a. It is installed in a circuit prone to temporary overloads.
b. It contains a bimetal element to operate the contacts.
c. It may be a cycling or noncycling type.
d. It must be replaced after it has been activated.

15. A TVRS cable is another name for a:

a. spark plug cable
b. battery cable
c. towing cable
d. ground cable

16. Which of the following cannot protect a circuit from excessive current flow?

a. fuse
b. circuit breaker
c. relay
d. fusible link

17. Mechanic A says a multiplex wiring system using a peripheral data bus eliminates EMI interference. Mechanic B says that special connectors are required to prevent signal loss in a multiplex wiring system using optical data links. Who is right?

a. A only
b. B only
c. both A and B
d. neither A nor B

18. Which of the following is not true of a multiplex wiring system?

a. a reduction in the number and size of wires
b. provides two-way communication
c. reduces or eliminates EMI problems
d. is widely used on domestic vehicles

Fill in the Blank

19. Conductors should have _____ resistance; loads should have _____ resistance.

20. Except for the ignition secondary circuit, all automotive electrical circuits are _____ systems.

21. The two standard systems for wire size are the _____ and the _____ systems.

22. While wire sizes are based on current capacity, wire selection is also determined by system _____ .

23. Circuit wiring for a general area of an automobile is contained in a _____ .

24. Printed circuit boards are most commonly used in automotive _____ .

25. A _____ resistor has two or more fixed resistance values.

26. When excessive current passes through a circuit breaker, the internal contacts _____ .

27. A switch should have _____ resistance and _____ measurable voltage drop across it.

28. A _____ provides remote control of a circuit by opening and closing a switch in its control circuit.

29. Relays and solenoids will only operate properly on _____ current.

30. The largest source of EMI on an automobile is the _____ .

31. A fuse is rated by its _____ capacity.

32. The general cause of a blown fuse is excessive _____ .

33. The _____ reverses current flow through the conductor of a motor.

34. Modern automobiles use a _____ -polarity, _____ -ground electrical system.

35. Switches used with a multiplex wiring system require a _____ current capacity.

4 SEMICONDUCTOR ELECTRONIC PRINCIPLES

WHAT

A little more than 100 years ago, the Industrial Revolution of the 19th century brought us the technology that made the automobile possible. For the past 25 years, all industries—and all of us—have been going through an electronic revolution that is equally as important as was the Industrial Revolution. The automobile has been the target of the electronic revolutionaries because it offers the opportunity to put electronics to work in many ways for the comfort, convenience, and safety of motorists.

The preceding three chapters summarized the principles and sources of electricity, as well as basic automotive electrical systems. This chapter introduces the principles of solid-state electronics that operate in modern automobiles. As with other systems, all of our automobile electronic devices operate similarly, regardless of where they are used. The electronic fundamentals are simply an extension of the electrical fundamentals you have learned.

WHY

You can't service any system on a modern car without dealing with some electronic device. That device might be a simple sensor that warns of low oil level, or it might be a sophisticated computer that performs complicated system integration for fuel delivery, ignition, emission control, and transmission shifting. Just as you should understand the fundamentals of electricity before working with switches, circuits, and electric power, you should understand the principles of electronics before dealing with them in different systems.

GOALS

After studying this chapter, you should be able to:

1. Explain solid-state electronics, semiconductor current flow, and the difference between N and P material.

2. Explain the construction, operation, and voltage-current relationships in diodes, bipolar transistors, field-effect transistors, and other electronic devices.

3. Explain the differences between discrete devices, integrated circuits, and hybrid circuits.

SOLID-STATE ELECTRONICS

Both electricity and electronics deal with the controlled movement of electrons to do work. We usually use the word, "electrical" to describe systems in which electric current flows through wires and electromechanical devices such as switches, motors, lamps, and other units to produce light, heat, or motion. Also, an electrical circuit usually does not increase, or amplify, the current or voltage delivered to the circuit by a battery, a generator, or an induction coil.

"Electronic" systems usually involve the transmission of electrons or voltage signals through vacuum or gases or semiconductor materials in at least part of a circuit. Also, many electronic components have no moving electromechanical parts. Electronic devices often amplify voltage or current and can perform logical decision-making functions.

For over 60 years, electronic systems used vacuum tubes, figure 4-1, to transmit electrons between two conductors and to amplify current or voltage. With the invention of the transistor in 1948, scientists had a practical way to do the same thing with solid, crystal materials. These crystal materials are the group of elements called semiconductors. Because they have all of their electrical properties in solid, one-piece forms, the science in which they are used came to be called **solid-state electronics**.

Today, it is difficult to separate electrical from electronic systems. For decades, automotive electrical systems have used induction coils for many purposes. Today, these traditional systems are controlled by solid-state electronic devices. Similarly, electrical generating systems have solid-state rectifiers and electronic voltage regulators. To test electromechanical systems for automatic door locks and other accessories, for example, you will have to recognize the purpose of electronic diodes in the circuits.

Traditionally, the science of electronics began with the study of electron flow in vacuum tubes. Today, it begins with semiconductor materials.

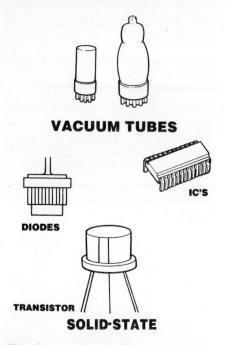

Figure 4-1. Vacuum tubes were the earliest method of transmitting electrons between conductors and amplifying current or voltage. Transistors do the same job much faster, require far less space, and do not overheat. (Chrysler)

SEMICONDUCTORS

Five elements have just four electrons in their valence shells: carbon, silicon, germanium, tin, and lead. They are neither good conductors (three or fewer valence electrons) nor good insulators (five or more valence electrons). They are semiconductors. While all of these elements are chemically semiconductors, the two most important for solid-state electronics are silicon and germanium. Of these two, only silicon is used for modern integrated circuits, and we will concentrate on silicon devices.

As a pure element, silicon is a crystal solid. Each of its atoms shares its four valence electrons with four adjoining atoms, figure 4-2. In this way, every atom has a full valence shell, and elemental silicon is a relatively good insulator. The uniform crystal structure of silicon can be upset, however, by adding impurities to a silicon crystal in the form of atoms of other elements. This process is called **doping**. The amount of other material added to pure silicon is quite small, usually in a ratio of one part **dopant** to 10,000,000 parts silicon.

N-Material

If an element such as phosphorus or arsenic with five free electrons is added to silicon, the resulting mixture has a negative charge because it has

extra free electrons not permanently attached to any valence shell. The extra electrons continuously bump from shell to shell and dislodge other electrons in a random drift, figure 4-3. This kind of doped semiconductor material is called **N-material** because it has a negative charge.

P-Material

If an element such as boron or gallium with three free electrons is added to silicon, the resulting mixture has a shortage of free electrons and, therefore, a positive charge. This is called **P-material**. The places in the incomplete valence shells that would normally be filled by electrons are called **holes**, figure 4-4. Free electrons from adjoining atoms continuously try to fill the holes; and, as they do, they leave other holes behind. Random electron drift also exists in P-material, but as electrons drift, so do holes. Semiconductor electrical theory defines holes as positive charge carriers and electrons as negative charge carriers.

Hole Flow

You can think of electrons in semiconductors as moving in one direction and holes as moving in the other, figure 4-5. Moreover, if an electron has a negative charge (as you have learned), you can think of a hole as having a positive charge. Therefore,

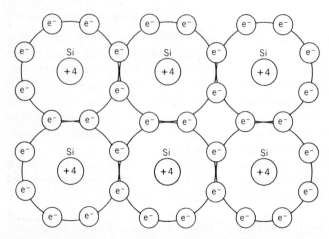

Figure 4-2. Each atom of silicon in its pure form shares its four valence electrons with four adjoining atoms so that each completes its valence shell.

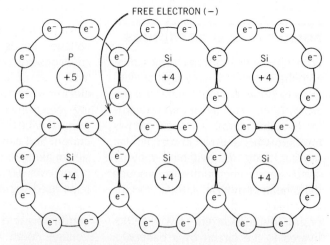

Figure 4-3. N-material has extra free electrons not permanently bound to any valence shells.

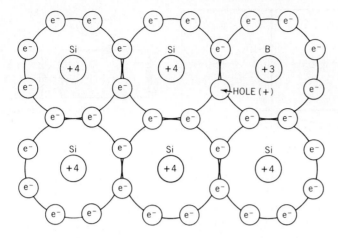

Figure 4-4. P-material has holes in some valence shells that attract electrons from adjoining atoms.

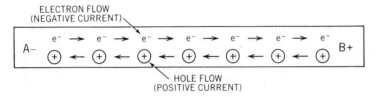

Figure 4-5. Electron flow and hole flow move in opposite directions through a semiconductor.

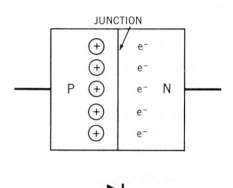

Figure 4-6. A diode is formed by the junction of P-material and N-material.

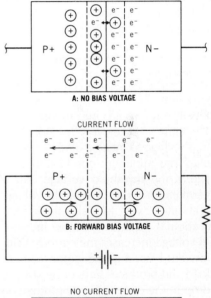

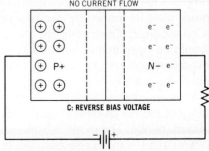

Figure 4-7. Forward bias voltage causes current flow through a diode; reverse bias prevents current flow.

as electron flow carries a negative charge, or negative current, from point A to point B, hole flow carries a positive charge, or positive current, from point B to point A, figure 4-5. Hole flow is simply another way to look at the conventional current flow theory, which says that current flows from positive to negative. To study semiconductors, we use both the electron flow theory (− to +) and the conventional, or hole flow, theory (+ to −).

DIODES

Let's take a piece of semiconductor N-material and a piece of P-material and put them together to see what happens electrically. When we join the two pieces, we form a **PN junction**. Figure 4-6 shows such a junction and the symbol for the device called a **diode**.

The arrowhead in the diode symbol indicates the P-material and the direction of hole flow, or conventional current flow. The same arrowhead indication is used in transistor symbols, as you will see later. In a diode, the

P-material is the anode, with + current carriers (holes); and the N-material is the cathode, with − charge carriers (electrons).

With no voltage applied to the diode, some electrons from the N-material cross the junction to fill holes in the P-material. This forces a few holes in the opposite direction across the junction to be filled by electrons in the N-material. This random hole and electron movement soon reaches a point where the junction stabilizes and no more holes and electrons drift from one side to the other, figure 4-7A.

The stabilized junction is also called the depletion layer because mobile charge carriers (holes and electrons) are not sufficient to overcome the fixed charge density of P- and N- material. In other words, conductivity is depleted, or reduced, at the PN junction. Without voltage applied to the diode, it will not do anything useful electrically. But if we apply voltage across the diode (positive to one side, negative to the other), we change its electrical characteristics. This is called **bias voltage**.

Forward Bias

If we apply positive voltage to the P-material and negative voltage to the N-material, we have **forward bias**, which causes current to flow across the junction and through the diode. This is because the positive voltage repels positively charged holes in the P-material forward and across the junction into the N-material. At the same time, the negative voltage on the N-material attracts the holes and repels electrons toward the junction, where they move into the P-material. Thus, we have current flow: holes in one direction, electrons in the other, figure 4-7B.

Reverse Bias

If we reverse the voltage and apply positive to the N-material and negative to the P-material, we have **reverse bias**, figure 4-7C. The reverse voltage potential, or polarity, attracts holes and free electrons away from the PN junction, and no current flows through the diode.

Junction Diode Operation

The resistance of the PN junction is very low in the forward direction. Ideally, it would be almost zero. Therefore, it takes very low forward-bias voltage to make a diode conductive. The minimum conduction voltage is the **threshold voltage**. For a germanium diode, threshold voltage is about 0.3 volt; for a silicon diode, it is about 0.7 volt. Any further increase in voltage increases the current. With forward bias, a diode is not a circuit load and produces little or no voltage drop in the circuit. Current through a diode must be limited by a resistor or a circuit load. Otherwise, the diode would be operating in a short-circuit condition and would burn up from excessive current.

With reverse bias voltage, the resistance of the PN junction is very high, almost infinite. The diode acts like an open circuit with reverse bias. All of the reverse-bias voltage appears across the PN junction, just as it would across an open switch. Figure

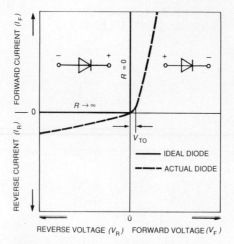

Figure 4-8. The ideal resistance curve of a PN diode.

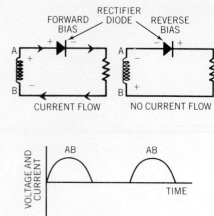

Figure 4-10. One diode allows current to flow in one direction but blocks it in the other. (Delco-Remy)

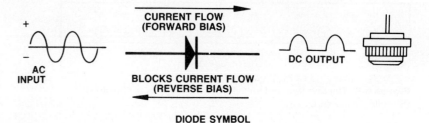

Figure 4-9. Forward bias allows current to flow in one direction in a diode; reverse bias blocks current flow. (Chrysler)

4-8 shows the ideal resistance curve of a PN diode as a 90-degree angle. In the forward direction, resistance drops to zero. The diode conducts full current with any forward bias voltage. Similarly, resistance is infinite with any reverse bias voltage, and no current flows. No diode has the operating characteristics of the ideal curve, but most diodes used in automotive systems operate according to the typical curve shown in figure 4-8.

Junction Diode Uses

Now you see a practical use for diodes. They can be used to control the direction of current flow. In this way, a diode acts in an electrical system as a check valve acts in a hydraulic system. Remember that alternating current changes its direction in regular cycles (+ to − and − to +). The alternator on your car generates alternating current, but the electrical devices need direct current. The first

major use of diodes in automotive electrical systems was to rectify alternating current to direct current.

With forward bias applied to a diode, it allows current to flow in one direction, figure 4-9. With reverse bias, the diode blocks, or checks, current flow, figure 4-9. If we connect a diode to one end of an alternator conductor, figure 4-10, and then connect an external circuit, the diode allows current in one direction and blocks it in the other. The result is pulsating dc current.

The single diode in figure 4-10 rectifies only the positive (+) half of the voltage cycle. Adding more diodes and making the final output connection in parallel allows us to rectify the negative (−) half of the cycle as well, figure 4-11. A series of alternator conductor windings and an arrangement of six diodes produces a rectified dc output with only a trace of ac fluctuation, figure 4-12.

We can also use a diode in a warn-

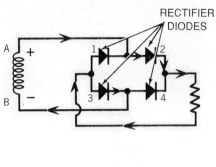

RECTIFIER DIODES

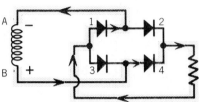

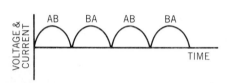

Figure 4-11. Four diodes provide full-wave rectification from one output winding. (Delco-Remy)

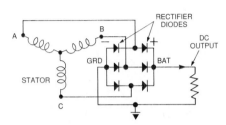

Figure 4-12. Six diodes provide full-wave rectification from three output windings (three-phase rectification).

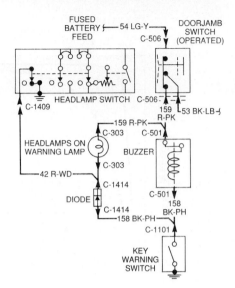

Figure 4-13. This warning circuit uses a diode to light an indicator lamp and sound a buzzer. (Ford)

ing circuit to light an indicator lamp or sound a buzzer, or both. Figure 4-13 shows a circuit that will light a warning lamp if the headlamps are left on or sound a buzzer if the ignition key is left in the lock. Power is supplied through the doorjamb switch. The circuit is grounded through the headlamp switch or through the key-warning switch. Here is how the diode works in the circuit.

• The headlamps are off; the ignition key is left in the lock to close the key switch; the door is opened to close the door switch. Current flows through the door switch, the buzzer, and the key-warning switch to ground. The diode blocks current through the warning lamp so it cannot reach ground at the key switch. The headlamp switch is open, so the warning lamp is not grounded there, either. The buzzer sounds, but the warning lamp does not light.

• The headlamps are on; the door is opened. Current flows through the warning lamp to ground at the head-

lamp switch. The lamp lights. Current also flows through the buzzer, through the diode in the forward direction, to ground at the headlamp switch. The buzzer also sounds.

The diode allows one buzzer to warn of the key left in the ignition and the headlamps left on. The diode allows the warning lamp to light only when the headlamps are left on. In this way, the diode acts as a simple electronic logic device. You will learn more about electronic logic circuits in chapter 5.

The current control of a PN diode is not perfect. Even with reverse bias, there is a small amount of reverse current flow across the junction because holes and electrons attract each other. Normally, this current is so small that it does not matter. There may be occasions, however, when diode leakage current leads to a diode being diagnosed as faulty. The very small test current used by a digital voltmeter may pass through a good diode in each direction. The meter reading then may lead you to reject it as being defective.

If reverse bias is too high, however, the voltage force can overcome the natural resistance of the diode. The covalent bond structure of the diode

then breaks down, allowing full reverse current flow. If the magnitude and duration of the reverse current through the diode is great enough, the excessive heat will damage the diode.

Zener Diodes

The **breakdown voltage** depends on the thickness of the kind of semiconductor material, the amount of doping, and the thickness of the PN junction. The breakdown voltage is called the zener breakdown voltage or the avalanche breakdown voltage, depending on the amount and rate of reverse current. Zener breakdown provides a more gradual reverse current than avalanche breakdown, figure 4-14.

Every diode has three operating regions, figure 4-15:

1. The conducting region with forward bias voltage. Resistance is low, and forward current is high.

2. The blocking region with low reverse bias voltage. The resistance is high, and current is low.

3. The breakdown region with high reverse bias voltage. Resistance breaks down, and reverse current is high.

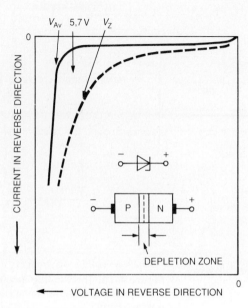

Figure 4-14. Avalanche breakdown (V_{Av}) is more abrupt than zener breakdown (V_Z). (Bosch)

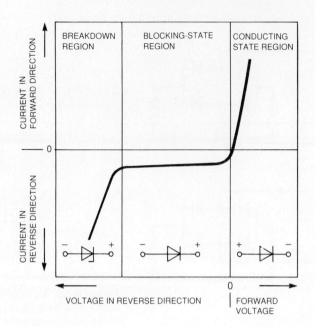

Figure 4-15. The three operating regions of a diode.

ELECTROSTATIC DISCHARGE AND ELECTRONIC CIRCUITS

Walk into the service department of topflight new car dealerships these days and you're likely to see a strange sight—the tuneup technician is wearing a special wrist strap and is plugged into a grounded mat while working on a vehicle. He's probably learned the hard way that you can't be too careful about electrostatic discharge when working around electronic components.

Electrostatic discharge is generated when two dissimilar materials (especially synthetics) rub together or separate. The amount of charge that builds up depends on a variety of factors: the type of materials, their proximity to each other, the speed with which they are separated, and the amount of humidity present.

The static discharge we've all seen and felt has to be greater than about 7,000 volts before we even notice it. Static discharges of less voltage may pass unnoticed by humans, but not by a computer chip. A surge of less than 100 volts can put the computer chip on a junkpile. Under the right conditions, static discharges of

40,000 to 50,000 volts can occur. These give a human a good sting, but are the death knell for electronic circuits and components.

A static-related failure can take one of two forms:

1. It immediately blows a hole in a microcircuit, resulting in a complete failure.

2. It causes only minor damage in the microcircuit at first; but as time passes, the circuit gradually deteriorates and eventually results in a complete failure.

Technicians who slide across the car seat to unplug the computer module first noticed the results of static discharge. Anyone who has blown a computer in that manner has learned his lesson the hard way. But static charges and discharges can also affect solid-state components right from the parts department.

Electronic components are wrapped in static-free packing material and should not be removed from their containers in the usual manner. To prevent any static charge or

discharge problem, ground the wrapping with an alligator clip lead before removing the component. It's also a good idea not to touch the component connections if you're not grounded. Since synthetic materials are especially prone to static charges or discharges, another good idea is to watch the kind of clothing you wear while working on the vehicle.

The technician described at the beginning has learned his lesson. Working on the grounded mat with the special wrist strap provided, he can handle the component in the vehicle, remove the component to be installed from its packing, and install it in the vehicle without fear of electrical reprisal. Of course, once he breaks the continuity that provides a path of equalization for a static charge by removing the wrist strap or stepping off the grounded mat, a static charge can start to build. For this reason, he must remain grounded during the entire repair procedure.

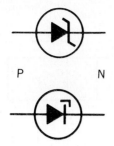

Figure 4-16. These symbols represent zener diodes in circuit diagrams.

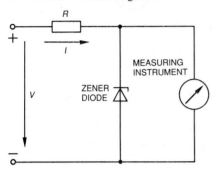

Figure 4-17. Overvoltage protection is provided for the measuring instrument (MI) by inserting a zener diode in parallel. (Bosch)

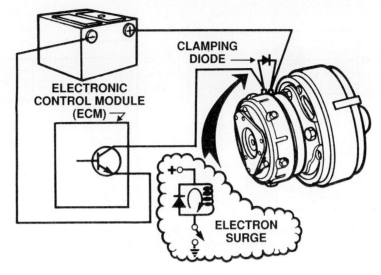

Figure 4-18. A clamping diode acts like a pressure relief valve. It protects a circuit from surge currents caused by abrupt interruption of the current in an electromagnetic device. (Delco-Remy)

Reverse current can destroy a simple PN diode, but special diodes can take advantage of this characteristic.

If we build a diode of heavily doped materials that will withstand reverse current and that will allow reverse current only above a specific voltage, we have a **zener diode**. We might build a zener diode to conduct reverse current only when voltage is above 6 volts, for example. Below that voltage, the diode acts as a simple PN diode. We can use such a zener diode to open and close a circuit at a prescribed voltage. Figure 4-16 shows the symbols for a zener diode.

Figure 4-17 shows a zener diode in parallel with a measuring instrument to protect the instrument from high voltage surges. The diode breakdown voltage equals the maximum safe voltage that can be applied to the instrument. Let's assume that it is 10 volts. When system voltage reaches 10 volts, the zener diode breaks down and conducts reverse current. This causes an additional voltage drop across the resistor and limits voltage at

the instrument to 10 volts. When system voltage drops below 10 volts, the zener diode again blocks reverse current. A silicon zener diode with a steep breakdown curve is ideal for precise voltage control in this kind of circuit. You will find such diodes in electronic voltage regulators, ignition control units, and instrumentation systems. Zener diodes also are used in Chrysler air conditioning systems to prevent compressor clutch circuit surges.

Clamping Diodes

A voltage surge results when current flowing through a solenoid or relay is interrupted. This surge is caused by electrons passing through the solenoid or relay coil that do not want to stop at the open in the circuit. As they run into the open, they attempt to jump it. If successful, a spark results. Installing a diode across the coil provides a bypass for the electrons during the period the circuit is open. In effect, this "clamping diode" acts as an electronic pressure relief valve and prevents the spark, figure 4-18.

One important application is the compressor clutch diode used in late-model air conditioning systems. Release of the electromagnetic compressor clutch coil produces voltage spikes that can damage the onboard

computer. The clutch diode prevents this voltage surge from reaching the computer.

Light-Emitting Diodes

When the two dopant materials, gallium and arsenic, form a gallium-arsenide compound in a diode, an interesting thing happens. When holes and electrons meet, they are neutralized as electrical charge carriers. When this happens, electrical energy is released as light. Such a diode is a **light-emitting diode (LED)**, figure 4-19.

The construction of an LED differs only slightly from that of a standard PN junction diode. A typical silicon diode requires 0.5 to 0.7 volt to turn on; an LED needs about 1.5 to 2.2

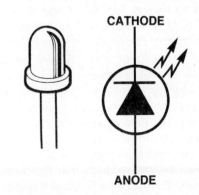

Figure 4-19. A light-emitting diode (LED) is represented by this symbol. (Delco-Remy)

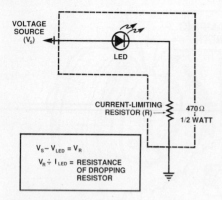

Figure 4-20. A current-limiting resistor is used in series to prevent an LED from failing. (Delco-Remy)

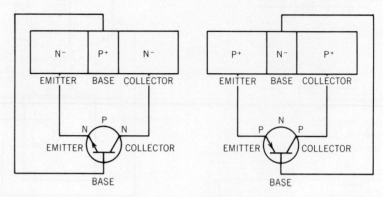

Figure 4-21. A transistor is a 3-element semiconductor made of alternate P and N materials (PNP or NPN).

volts to forward bias it. Although most LED's have no problem handling 20 to 200 mA, a current-limiting resistor is generally connected in series, figure 4-20.

If we arrange such diodes in geometrical shapes and turn current flow on and off through selected diodes in the pattern, we can create the lighted LED displays used in electronic calculators and some automobile instruments.

TRANSISTORS

A diode can control the direction of current and the amount and polarity of voltage applied across all or part of a circuit. It cannot increase, or amplify, current or voltage, however. Electronic systems usually need current or voltage amplification to develop enough power to do useful work. A **transistor** is a semiconductor device that can provide this amplification. A transistor also can work like a relay to switch a high-current circuit on and off in response to a voltage signal across a low-current circuit.

We can build a transistor from a PN diode by adding a third layer of doped semiconductor material. We construct the transistor so that the outer layers are the same kind of material (both P or both N), and the center layer is the opposite. Thus, we can build either an NPN or a PNP transis-

tor, figure 4-21. The name comes from transfer and resistor because a transistor transfers signals across the resistance of two PN junctions. The three parts of a transistor are the **base**, the **emitter**, and the **collector**, figure 4-21. Notice that the arrowhead on a transistor symbol is always on the emitter and, as on a diode symbol, it always points in the direction of hole flow (conventional current flow).

This kind of transistor is a **bipolar** transistor because it uses both electrons and holes as current carriers. Current flows with positive and negative polarity in different circuits. The emitter provides the majority current carriers (either holes or electrons), and the collector receives them when the transistor is switched on, or conducting. Let's look at an NPN transistor to see how it operates.

Because there are two PN junctions (between the emitter and the base, and between the base and the collector), there are two places where we can apply bias voltage. If we apply forward bias to the emitter-base junction (− potential on the N emitter and + potential on the P base), current flows as in a simple PN diode, figure 4-22. If we apply reverse bias to the base-collector junction, current does not flow. This junction again acts like a diode, but with voltage polarity reversed, figure 4-23.

The three parts of a transistor are doped and constructed differently to

affect the amount of current through different parts. The base is thin and doped for just a few carriers—in this case, holes. The emitter is thicker and doped for maximum carriers, free electrons in an NPN transistor. The collector is larger (thicker) than the emitter but doped less. It has fewer majority carriers (electrons in an NPN transistor) and allows reverse current when bias voltage is applied.

To get our NPN transistor to conduct and amplify current, let's assume that the N-type emitter is at a potential of zero volts. If we apply a low forward bias voltage of 2 or 3 volts across the emitter-base junction, electrons flow from the emitter into the base, and holes flow in the opposite direction. Even at a low voltage, there are extra electrons that gather in the base. The base has fewer holes than the emitter has electrons because of the different doping ratios.

Now let's apply a higher positive voltage of 10 or 12 volts to the collector. This creates a reverse bias across the base-collector junction. High positive voltage on the collector attracts electrons away from the base-collector junction, so little or no current flows between the base and collector. However, the extra electrons that have gathered in the base due to forward bias on the emitter-base junction now pass through the base and into the collector toward the high positive voltage, figure 4-24.

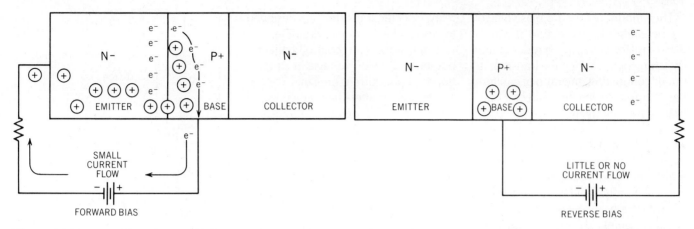

Figure 4-22. Forward bias on the emitter-base junction causes forward current flow, but excess free electrons accumulate in the base.

Figure 4-23. Reverse bias on the base-collector junction prevents current flow unless the emitter-base junction is forward biased.

The 10 or 12 volts across the emitter and collector would not be enough to cause electron flow from emitter to collector. (The voltage examples we are using are purely arbitrary; the actual voltages are a design consideration for each transistor.) However, the forward bias across the emitter-base junction boosts electron flow enough to cause the electrons to flow through the base, through the collector, to the higher voltage. The overall electron flow is forward, from low (or negative) potential to high (or positive) potential.

Transistors as Amplifiers

Figure 4-24 is a simple example of how a transistor can increase current flow through its parts and how a small voltage and current flow across one junction can control a larger current flow through the complete device. For a PNP transistor, the voltages and flows of electrons and holes are reversed, but the principle is the same.

Suppose that the forward bias across the emitter-base is supplied by the low voltage from a radio signal. This low voltage and current represent a fraction of a watt of power. The larger voltage and current flow between the emitter and collector represent several watts of power, enough to drive the electromagnet of a car radio speaker. Moreover, the ratio of emitter-base power and emitter-collector power remains constant. The ratio of amplification is called

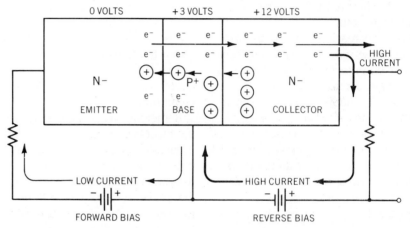

Figure 4-24. A small amount of current flow through the emitter-base junction controls a larger current flow through the emitter and collector.

gain and is a design factor of the transistor.

Consider the forward bias voltage and current between the emitter and base as input power. If it fluctuates between one-tenth and five-tenths of a watt (100 to 500 milliwatts), and the gain of the transistor is 100 (100 to 1), then the output power between the emitter and collector will fluctuate between 1 and 5 watts. Such a transistor can increase power enough to drive a speaker or to switch ignition current on and off in response to low input voltage and current.

Amplifying transistors like this have been used for decades in automobile radios, charging systems, and ignition systems to handle large amounts of current in response to small signal voltages. They are often called power transistors, and figure 4-25 shows several examples.

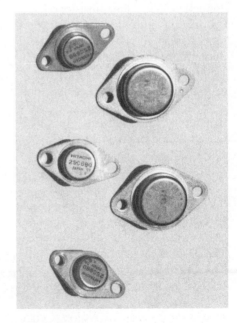

Figure 4-25. Power transistors are used in automotive charging and ignition systems.

The amount of forward bias voltage on the emitter-base junction at which the transistor starts to conduct is the switching point. When the transistor is on, or conducting, the ratio of emitter-base current to emitter-collector current stays relatively constant. This is called the linear conduction region because 0.1 ampere of emitter-base current may equal 1 ampere of emitter-collector current, for example. Eventually, however, the transistor will reach a saturation condition. At this point, large increases in emitter-base current produce only small increases in emitter-collector current. The transistor is simply conducting as much current as it can handle. Increasing the emitter-base bias voltage will not significantly increase output current. Voltage drop across the emitter-collector circuit is very small, and the transistor is operating as a simple relay.

Like a diode, a transistor has three operating conditions; however, they are not the same as those of a diode. In summary, the operating conditions of a transistor are:

1. *Cutoff*—Bias voltage on the base is below the switching point. The transistor is not conducting; it is blocking. It acts as an open switch.

2. *Conduction*—Bias voltage is high enough to switch the transistor on. It is conducting current, but output current changes in proportion to current through the base. This is the amplification stage.

3. *Saturation*—Bias voltage, base current, and output current are at the maximum. The transistor acts as a closed switch or relay.

Transistors as Relays

You might ask what the difference is between a transistor as an amplifier and a transistor as a switch or relay. The answer is, not much electrically. The difference is in how the transistor is used: whether it switches from cutoff to saturation, or whether it operates in the conduction region. Generally, a given transistor is not used as both an amplifier and as a switch or

relay. Specific transistors are designed to work better as one or the other.

A transistor can control collector output current or voltage in proportion to input current or signal voltage across the emitter-base junction. In this conduction region, the transistor amplifies the output in proportion to the input. Amplifying transistors are used in radio systems. The amplified output is an **analog** signal, which means that it changes in direct proportion to the input signal.

When a transistor acts as a switch or relay, it switches directly from cutoff (no conduction) to saturation (full conduction). Such a transistor can be used to switch current on and off in a power circuit. The switching action also is the foundation for digital computers. As you will learn in the next chapter, a **digital** signal is one that is either on or off.

Remember the explanation of simple electromagnetic relays in chapter 3. Electromagnetism in the relay control coil moves the armature to close the contacts of the relay power circuit. The power circuit switches from open (no conduction) to closed (full conduction). A small amount of current in the control circuit can switch a large amount of current in the power circuit.

A transistor can act as a solid-state relay in a circuit, and this is one of the most important uses of transistors in automotive electrical systems. When maximum forward bias voltage and emitter-base current are applied, the collector current goes to complete saturation, and voltage drop across the emitter-collector circuit goes to a minimum. These are the same operating conditions that a relay has.

The emitter-collector circuit is the power circuit. The emitter-base circuit is the control circuit. Base current can be controlled by a simple single-throw switch, figure 4-26, or by a double-throw switch that changes the polarity on the base. When the switch closes, low emitter-base current biases the transistor to allow higher emitter-collector current to flow through a circuit load, figure 4-27. The emitter base circuit has a resistor

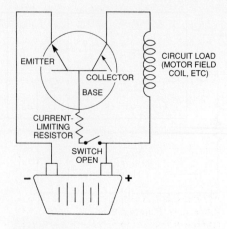

Figure 4-26. A simple diagram of a transistor used as a power relay.

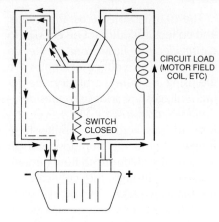

—— EMITTER-COLLECTOR CURRENT

– – – EMITTER-BASE CURRENT

Figure 4-27. Low emitter-base current and bias voltage allow a higher emitter-collector current to flow in the power circuit. This transistor is a solid-state relay.

to limit bias voltage and emitter-base current.

Although figures 4-26 and 4-27 show the symbol for a mechanical switch in the base circuit, combinations of diodes, resistors, and zener diodes can control voltage on the base. This allows a transistor to act as an electronic relay with no moving parts and very fast switching action.

THYRISTORS

A **thyristor** is a semiconductor switching device made up of alternating P and N layers, or regions. Not only can it switch current on and off, but it also can rectify ac to dc. The most com-

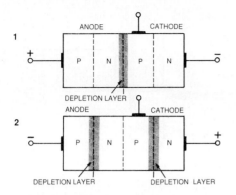

Figure 4-28. The center PN junction blocks current when the P-type anode is connected to the positive voltage side of the circuit and the N-type cathode is connected to the minus side. (Bosch)

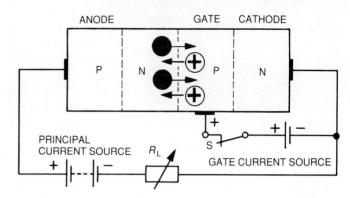

Figure 4-29. Applying a positive voltage to the P-type anode turns the transistor on. (Bosch)

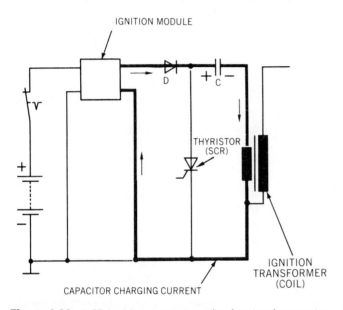

Figure 4-30. A CD ignition stores energy by charging the capacitor. The thyristor, or SCR, blocks the discharge circuit. (Bosch)

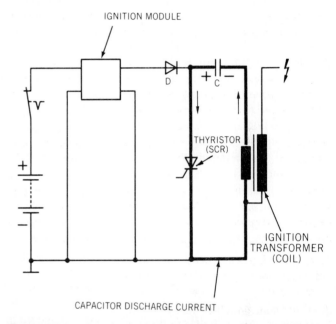

Figure 4-31. When the thyristor, or SCR, receives a trigger voltage from the distributor, it allows the capacitor to discharge energy to the coil primary winding. (Bosch)

mon kind of thyristor used in some automotive systems is the **silicon-controlled rectifier (SCR)**.

An SCR consists of four semiconductor regions, arranged PNPN. Like a transistor, an SCR has two terminals for working current (the power circuit) and one terminal for control current. These are:

- The anode (+), or P-terminal
- The cathode (−), or N-terminal
- The gate, one of the two inner regions

The SCR behaves as a PNP transistor joined to an NPN transistor. Unlike a transistor, however, an SCR does not need continuous control current. It needs only a trigger pulse ap-

plied to the gate to become conductive.

An SCR thyristor can be connected into a circuit in the forward or the reverse direction. The forward direction is the simplest example to show SCR operation, figure 4-28. In this condition, the P-type anode is connected to the + voltage side of the circuit, and the N-type cathode is connected to the − side. The center PN junction then blocks current. When a + voltage pulse is applied to the P-type gate, it acts as base current in an NPN transistor, figure 4-29. The transistor turns on, and its working current acts as base current on the PNP-transistor portion of the SCR. As long as voltage across the anode and

cathode remains high enough, the SCR will continue to conduct. Current continues to flow even with the gate trigger voltage removed. Current stops if gate voltage is reversed or if system voltage falls below the breakdown voltage for the center PN junction.

This kind of thyristor effectively blocks reverse current from cathode (−) to anode (+) under all conditions. Thus it can rectify alternating current and gets the name "silicon-controlled rectifier." SCR's are used as high-power switches. You'll find them in some solid-state voltage regulators and ignition control units. Figures 4-30 and 4-31 show an SCR in a capacitive-discharge ignition circuit. Ignition primary current charges a large capacitor through diode D. The SCR acts as a diode to block current through the capacitor discharge circuit. When a signal voltage is applied to the SCR gate, it closes the capacitor discharge circuit through the ignition coil primary winding. Diode D then blocks reverse current to the ignition control unit and the rest of the system. When capacitor discharge voltage drops below the breakdown voltage of the SCR, the SCR stops conducting and opens the discharge circuit.

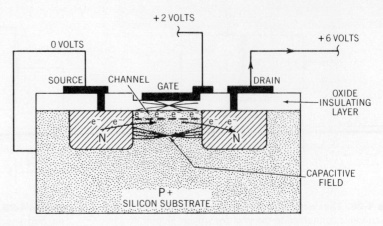

Figure 4-32. A field-effect transistor is controlled by gate voltage that creates a capacitive field and causes current to flow through the channel from source to drain. This is an N-channel enhancement-type FET.

FIELD-EFFECT TRANSISTORS

A **field-effect transistor (FET)** is another 3-element semiconductor device that allows high voltage and large current flow to be controlled by a small signal voltage. The bipolar NPN transistor in the earlier examples is controlled by changing the current through the emitter-base junction. A field-effect transistor is controlled by changing voltage in a capacitive field. Its three parts are:

1. The **source**, which supplies the current-carrying electrons or holes and is similar to the emitter in a bipolar transistor.

2. The **drain**, which collects the current carriers and is similar to the collector.

3. The **gate**, which is similar to the base of a bipolar transistor and which creates the capacitive field that allows current to flow from the source to the drain.

A field-effect transistor is not a bipolar device because current involves only one group of charge carriers, either holes or electrons, and flows between similar materials, N to N or P to P. It does not require bias voltage or forward and reverse current as does a bipolar transistor. Briefly, here is one way in which a field-effect transistor works.

The source and the drain are the same kind of doped material, either N or P. Let's say both are N-material, figure 4-32. The source and drain are separated by a thin channel of either N- or P-material. If we hold the source at zero voltage and apply 6 volts to the drain, no current will flow between the two. Then we install the gate as a metal strip above the channel between the source and drain and apply a lower positive voltage to it. The gate forms a capacitive field between itself and the channel. The voltage of this field attracts electrons from the source just as the base does in a bipolar transistor. The electrons then flow across the channel to the higher positive voltage on the drain.

This kind of FET is called an enhancement-type because the field effect enhances, or improves, current flow from the source to the drain. Another kind of FET is the depletion-type, where the field effect depletes, or cuts off, current flow. In simple terms, you can think of enhancement-type and depletion-type FET's as working like normally open and normally closed switches. Remember that bipolar transistors are controlled by current flow between the emitter and base. FET's are controlled by voltage that forms a capacitive field between the source and the drain.

Like a bipolar transistor, a field-effect transistor can work as an amplifier or as a relay. Many radio and video amplifiers, as well as voltage regulators, use FET's to control output voltage. More importantly, field-effect transistors, built in miniature sizes, act as switching circuits for digital computers. Thousands of FET's can be built on a small silicon chip as an integrated circuit (IC). These IC's form the computing logic circuits of automotive computers, which you will study in the next chapter.

DARLINGTON PAIR

Some control circuits are too small or too sensitive to produce the required output. Increasing the operating current of the control circuit is not effective, because it can cause undesirable effects. To operate the circuit properly and produce the required output, a Darlington pair is used.

A Darlington pair consists of two transistors connected together as shown in figure 4-33. This is often referred to as a "piggyback" transistor. The first transistor acts as a preamplifier. It produces a large operating current for the second transistor, which is isolated from the control circuit. The second transistor functions as a final amplifier, boosting the current to produce the required output. Darlington pairs of transistors are the basis of most electronic ignition control modules, as you will see in chapter 12.

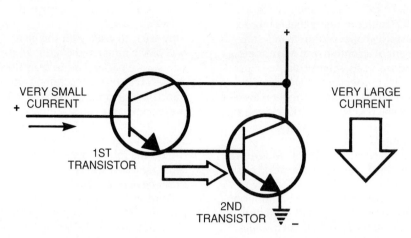

Figure 4-33. A Darlington pair consists of one transistor acting as a preamplifier to create a larger base current for the second transistor, or final amplifier. (Delco-Remy)

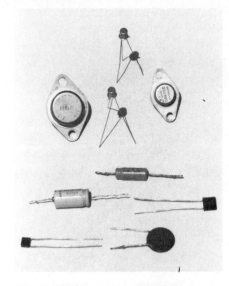

Figure 4-34. These discrete electronic devices are used in various automotive systems.

DISCRETE DEVICES, INTEGRATED AND HYBRID CIRCUITS

All of the electronic devices we have seen so far can be manufactured and assembled into circuits in different ways. Device manufacture and circuit assembly is usually divided into three categories: discrete devices, integrated circuits, and hybrid circuits.

Discrete Devices

Any of the electronic devices we have examined can be made of an individual part. Engineers call these **discrete devices**, which means that each one is made separately and has wire leads for connecting it into a complete circuit. Most early solid-state devices were discrete devices, such as the rectifying diodes on older alternators. You can still find discrete devices in many automotive systems, especially in charging, ignition, and headlamp circuits that handle large amounts of power. Figure 4-34 shows several discrete diodes and transistors from automotive systems.

Integrated Circuits

Although discrete devices are quite small compared to the vacuum tubes of older electronic circuits, they are

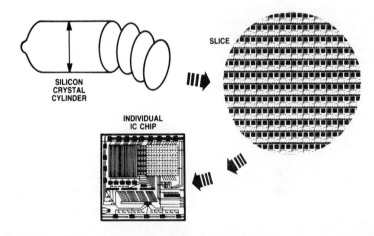

Figure 4-35. Hundreds of IC chips are made on a single slice or wafer of a silicon crystal cylinder. (Chrysler)

enormous compared to a modern **integrated circuit (IC)**. An integrated circuit is a complex electronic circuit of perhaps several thousand transistors and other devices, all formed on a tiny chip of silicon.

Integrated circuits are made by photographically reproducing circuit patterns on a silicon slice or wafer and then depositing various conductive P and N materials and insulating materials. Conductive and insulating materials are formed through chemical reaction of gases and by depositing metals such as aluminum. The doping of alternating silicon layers is carried out during wafer fabrication.

This process often requires more than 100 separate steps to build an IC. Several hundred identical IC's can be built on a single 4-, 5-, or 6-inch silicon slice or wafer, figure 4-35. Each is cut from the wafer as an individual "chip" and installed in a package device that can be plugged into a larger circuit. Figure 4-36 shows the main stages of IC manufacturing from silicon wafer to packaged circuit.

The field-effect transistors that you studied earlier are a major factor in the creation of integrated circuits. FET's can do most of the switching, processing, and amplifying jobs of discrete diodes, resistors, capacitors,

Figure 4-36. (Rear) a silicon ingot from which wafers are sliced for semiconductor manufacture. (Left center) a polished silicon wafer. (Right center) a finished device wafer. Each small square is a complete integrated circuit. (Foreground) each circuit chip is cut from a wafer and packaged as a microprocessor device or as a control chip in an ignition module.

MOORE'S LAW

There's a widely known law in the electronics industry that is more a historical observation than a statement of scientific fact. Nevertheless, Moore's Law seems true.

The modern integrated circuit—several electronic devices on a single silicon chip—was developed at Fairchild Semiconductor in 1959, where Gordon Moore was a research scientist. In 1964, Moore was Fairchild's research director. Looking back over the previous five years, he noted that the number of electronic devices that engineers were able to fabricate on a single chip had been doubling every year.

This observation gave rise to his prediction that integrated circuit complexity would continue to double annually for the foreseeable future—and he was right, for almost 20 years. This came to be known as "Moore's Law."

By 1969, 10 years after the invention of the integrated circuit, engineers were packing more than 1,000 diodes, resistors, capacitors, and transistors on a single chip. By 1974, the number was approaching 20,000 per chip; and by 1977, it had passed 250,000. Today, single IC chips that can do the jobs of one-half million separate transistors, diodes, and other devices are practical.

Gordon Moore, along with his partner, Robert Noyce, and others, is credited with developing the microprocessor—a digital computer on a chip. In 1968, Moore and Noyce founded Intel Corporation, a leading manufacturer of microprocessors and other IC devices.

and other transistors. Thousands of FET's can be built on a tiny chip called a metal-oxide semiconductor (MOS). This kind of IC is called a **MOSFET** and is the heart of modern computer systems—in automobiles and elsewhere.

Diodes, resistors, capacitors, bipolar transistors, and field-effect transistors all can be made as discrete devices, or as parts of integrated circuits, figure 4-37. The only electrical or electronic device that cannot be made as part of an IC is an inductor, or induction coil. To create a usable magnetic field, an induction coil is made by winding a conductor around a permeable core. No way of fabricating a usable induction coil in an integrated circuit has yet been invented.

As sophisticated and versatile as integrated circuits may be, many automotive systems have requirements that IC's cannot meet. These are chiefly systems with either, or both, of the following features:

1. Circuits that carry high current and high power that would overload the small conductors in IC's.

2. Circuits that employ electromagnetic induction.

For these reasons, many automotive systems use solid-state devices in combination with traditional electrical and electromagnetic components. Hybrid circuits also help to solve these problems by combining discrete devices with IC devices.

Hybrid Circuits

A circuit built with several discrete devices and several IC's is called a **hybrid circuit**. Many automotive systems have used, and continue to use, hybrid circuits, figure 4-38. As more and more functions are packed into single IC's, the need for discrete diodes, resistors, capacitors, and transistors is decreasing. Many jobs done by hybrid circuits on cars 10 years ago are now done by one or two IC's. Hybrid circuits continue in use, however, for high-current circuits and for electromagnetic systems.

SUMMARY Electronic System Integration

It's a long way from a PN diode to an engine management system computer; but if it were not for the simple idea of doping silicon atoms, neither one would be possible. You will be dealing with electronic devices regularly when you service late-model vehicles. Don't be surprised if you start out to adjust idle speed and wind up replacing an electronic control unit.

An important point to remember is that you can't repair any electronic control device on a modern car; you can only replace it. You can overhaul a starter motor or repair an alternator,

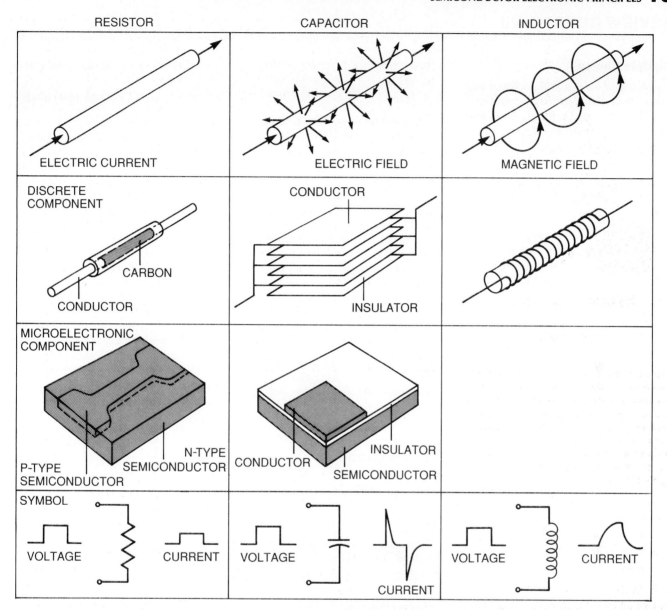

Figure 4-37. With the exception of inductors, discrete devices can be made as parts of an integrated circuit. There is no practical way to fabricate a usable induction coil in an integrated circuit.

but you can't repair or adjust the electronic chips in a computer. You can, however, test system operation, identify good and bad components, and replace only those that you can prove are defective. To do this professionally, you have to understand how they operate.

You have to understand what the input and output signals from sensors to computers to actuators mean. You have to know what they should be, and you have to identify those that are right and wrong. The next two chapters summarize the operation of automotive computers and the sensors and actuators of computer systems. All computer system operations are based on the principles of current flow and voltage levels in electronic semiconductor devices that you have learned here.

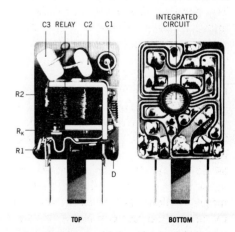

Figure 4-38. Hybrid circuits are made from discrete devices and integrated circuit chips assembled on a printed circuit board. (Bosch)

REVIEW QUESTIONS

Multiple Choice

1. Student A says that phosphorus and arsenic have five valence electrons and are P-dopant materials. Student B says that boron has three valence electrons and is an N-dopant. Who is right?
   a. A only
   b. B only
   c. both A and B
   d. neither A nor B

2. Student A says that hole flow is the opposite of electron flow. Student B says that hole flow is similar to conventional current flow theory. Who is right?
   a. A only
   b. B only
   c. both A and B
   d. neither A nor B

3. A zener diode allows reverse current flow at the point of:
   a. bias voltage
   b. breakdown voltage
   c. system voltage
   d. forward voltage

4. Student A says that a transistor can work like a relay to switch current. Student B says that a transistor can amplify current. Who is right?
   a. A only
   b. B only
   c. both A and B
   d. neither A nor B

5. All of the following are parts of a bipolar transistor, except the:
   a. base
   b. emitter
   c. collector
   d. gate

6. All of the following are parts of a field-effect transistor, except the:
   a. source

   b. collector
   c. drain
   d. gate

7. An individual transistor, diode, capacitor, or other electronic part is:
   a. an integrated circuit
   b. a hybrid circuit
   c. a discrete device
   d. an analog device

8. Student A says that an analog signal is either on or off. Student B says that an analog signal changes proportionally to the quantity measured. Who is right?
   a. A only
   b. B only
   c. both A and B
   d. neither A nor B

9. Student A says that temperature sensors are analog devices. Student B says that temperature sensors are digital devices. Who is right?
   a. A only
   b. B only
   c. both A and B
   d. neither A nor B

10. Student A says that a silicon-controlled rectifier (SCR) is a common type of thyristor that acts like a PNP transistor connected to an NPN transistor. Student B says that a hybrid circuit is built with two or more IC's and discrete devices. Who is right?
   a. A only
   b. B only
   c. both A and B
   d. neither A nor B

11. A major difference between a light-emitting diode (LED) and a standard silicon junction diode is that the LED:
   a. requires about three times as much voltage to turn it on

   b. allows current to pass in either direction
   c. is a specially doped zener diode
   d. none of the above

12. A piggybacked transistor is called a:
   a. bipolar transistor
   b. unipolar transistor
   c. field-effect transistor
   d. Darlington pair

Fill in the Blank

13. The element commonly used as the basis for semiconductor devices is _____ .

14. The device created when N-material and P-material are joined is called a _____ .

15. The method used to induce electrical flow in a diode is called _____ voltage.

16. The process of adding an impurity to a silicon crystal is called _____ .

17. The _____ is used to increase, or amplify, current or voltage.

18. The ratio of current or voltage amplification in a transistor is the _____ .

19. The three parts of a transistor are the base, the _____ , and the collector.

20. In a field-effect transistor, the element that supplies the current-carrying electrons is called the _____ .

21. A circuit built on a single silicon chip without discrete transistors, resistors, diodes, and other devices, is called an _____ .

22. To measure changing temperature continuously across a range, a computer would use an _____ signal.

5 MICROCOMPUTER ELECTRONIC SYSTEMS

WHAT

A modern automobile may have a dozen or more separate "computers" on board to control engine operation, air conditioning, instrument displays, suspension operation, power steering, braking, and other vehicle functions. Engineers use computers to design automobiles and to test their operation. Automobile factories have computers to control automatic manufacturing equipment. Computers do many jobs for different people in different applications. But all computers, whatever their size and purposes, operate on similar principles.

WHY

You probably will never design or build an automotive computer or modify its operation—at least not as a service technician. If you know the basic parts of a computer system and understand its operation, however, you can recognize when it is not operating correctly and what parts are not working properly. This understanding also will help you to recognize how and why a system might malfunction, which lets you apply basic knowledge to specific troubleshooting. If you know the principles of all computers, you will see more similarities than differences among various systems, and you will understand the operation of new systems as carmakers introduce them each year.

GOALS

After studying this chapter, you should be able to:

1. Explain the four basic functions of all computers.

2. Explain the difference between analog and digital computers, as well as analog and digital voltage signals.

3. Understand basic digital logic and how it is similar to operation of simple relays.

4. Explain the principal parts of a computer.

5. Explain the various methods by which computers communicate with each other in a body computer module system.

6. Identify instrumentation and control systems.

7. Explain the difference between open-loop and closed-loop control system operation.

WHAT IS A COMPUTER?

Actually, "computer" is probably not the best name for these devices. The first computers built 50 or more years ago were designed by scientists and mathematicians to do complex mathematical calculations. Their principal job was to compute. The name stuck.

The earliest computers and today's modern versions use the same principles of converting information to combinations of voltage signals that represent combinations of numbers. The number combinations might represent other kinds of information: speed, temperature, or even letters and words, for example. The computer processes the signals by computing

the numbers they represent and then delivering information in computed, or processed, form.

Computer Functions

The operation of any computer is divided into the four basic functions of input, processing, storage, and output. These functions aren't really unique to computers, however. You can identify them in other systems, such as the mechanical drives and hydraulic systems of an automobile. Here is how the four functions operate in a computer.

1. *Input*—The computer receives a voltage signal from an input device. The device might be a pushbutton on

an instrument panel or a **sensor** on an engine component. Keyboard terminals for office computers are also input devices.

Automobiles have many mechanical, electrical, and magnetic sensors that measure things like car speed, engine speed, temperature, air pressure, and airflow. The sensors convert the measurements to voltage input signals for the computer. An input sensor can be something as simple as a switch that opens and closes a circuit to the computer.

2. *Processing*—The computer takes the input signals and switches them through many series of electronic logic circuits in its programmed instructions. These logic circuits pro-

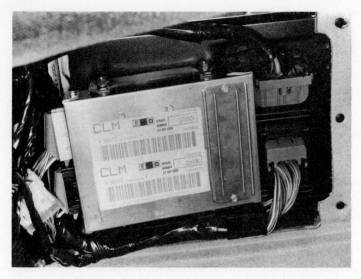

Figure 5-1. Most automobile computers are contained in metal boxes and mounted in the passenger compartment.

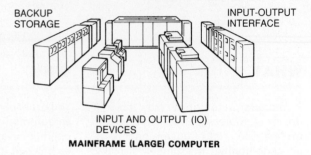

CENTRAL PROCESSING UNIT (CPU)
(TEMPORARY STORAGE UNITS AND CONTROL UNIT).

BACKUP STORAGE

INPUT-OUTPUT INTERFACE

INPUT AND OUTPUT (IO) DEVICES

MAINFRAME (LARGE) COMPUTER

Figure 5-2. Mainframe computers occupy large spaces and are used in commercial, industrial, or scientific applications. (Toyota Motor Company)

cess the input signals into output commands, which are another series of voltage signals that the computer sends to other devices in the system.

3. *Storage*—Every computer has an electronic memory to store its program instructions. Also, many programs require that some input signals be stored and not processed immediately, or be stored for later reference. Some output signals also may be stored momentarily before sending them to other parts of the system. The information storage ability of a computer is its "memory," and we will look at different kinds of memory later.

4. *Output*—All of the information processing and memory ability of a computer would not be worth much if it did not give back some other information or instructions. After processing the input signals, the computer returns output voltage signals to various output devices. On an office computer, the output device might be a printer or a cathode ray tube (CRT) display screen. On an automobile, the output device might be an instrument panel display or a system **actuator**. Actuators are devices that adjust engine idle speed, control air conditioning temperature, regulate fuel meter-

ing, adjust suspension height, and keep brakes from locking.

Another feature of many computer systems is that an output signal from one system can also be an input signal to another. Thus, a temperature-control computer can send an output signal that engages an air conditioning compressor clutch. That same signal can also be an input signal to an engine-control computer. The engine computer then sends an output signal to another actuator to control idle speed with the increased engine load. Not all air conditioning and engine computers work exactly this way, but this example shows how some systems are interconnected through their output and input functions.

Regardless of its purpose, complexity, or size, every computer system operates with the four basic functions of input, processing, storage, and output. Remembering these four functions will help you to organize your troubleshooting. When you test a system, you will be trying to isolate a problem to one of these areas. You can adjust or repair some input and output devices. You can only replace a processing or storage component, as well as some other kinds of input and output devices.

Computer Sizes

Automotive computers are installed in small metal boxes, figure 5-1, and are generally mounted in the passenger compartment under the instrument panel or behind a kick panel. Because of their small size, it's often difficult to visualize the similarities between these small computers and large computer systems. Historically, computer engineers recognize three general sizes, or classes, of computers: mainframe computers, minicomputers, and microcomputers.

Mainframe computers are the large, complex systems built by IBM, Cray Research, and other major manufacturers, figure 5-2. The processing and storage equipment often occupies a large room or an entire building built just to house the computer. A mainframe computer can have thousands of separate input devices, including keyboard terminals, video input devices, system sensors, and connections to output signals from other computers. A large mainframe computer can do several different jobs at once and can send signals to thousands of different output devices, including printers, display screens, system actuators, and other computer systems. Many of the computers used

Figure 5-3. The silicon chip containing the microprocessor can be seen through the window in this GM PROM. The entire circuit package is about 1 1/2 inches long.

to design automobiles and to control automatic factory equipment are mainframe computers. Scientists at research laboratories have used large mainframe supercomputers to do calculations that earlier mathematicians only dreamed about but never lived long enough to do.

Modern minicomputers have the computing power of earlier mainframe computers, but they are much smaller. Many businesses use a single minicomputer system for their accounting records, sales transactions, and word processing. Schools use them to process student and class records. A minicomputer can have many different input and output devices and can do several jobs simultaneously. It does not fill a large room or an entire building, and it usually does not have the processing capacity or speed of a large, modern mainframe computer.

A microcomputer is a computer in a box. Apples, IBM PC's, and other personal computers are all microcomputers. Most are smaller than a large television set but have the computing power of mainframe computers built 30 or 40 years ago. Most personal microcomputers are designed for use by one person at a time, although they can be connected to larger mini or mainframe computers and serve as input terminals or auxiliary computers for a larger system. Most microcomputers can only do one job or "run one program" at a time, but these are often complex processing operations. A microcomputer does not have the computing power, speed, and accuracy of a modern mainframe. It can,

SILICON DIP

If it weren't for silicon DIP's, computers would still be far too expensive to use on automobiles. PROM's could not be replaced to cure driveability problems, and personal computers (IBM PC's and Apples) would cost tens of thousands of dollars and be reserved for very large business offices.

So what is this marvelous DIP? Is it some kind of special chemical? a magic elixir? what?

A DIP is a dual inline package, a standardized way to package IC devices so that they can be plugged into circuit boards on different kinds of computers. When you look at a computer circuit board, you see many small rectangular devices with rows of small metal connector legs projecting downward on each side. These are dual inline packages (DIP's).

Microprocessors, coprocessors, memory chips, input-output circuits, and other integrated circuit chips are installed in the small plastic packages. Their circuit ends are connected to the leg connectors of the dual inline package. In this way, one standard microprocessor or memory chip can be used in a wide variety of computer circuits. Dozens of memory chips can be installed in parallel on a circuit board to give a computer an enormous amount of electronic storage.

Dual inline packages range in size from about 1/4-inch long to 2 or 3 inches long. Widths vary, as does the spacing of the connectors. All sizes, however, conform to a variety of standardized shapes that allow computer engineers to design circuit boards in the most economical way.

When you change a PROM in an engine control or body control computer, you are handling a dual inline package device. Without dual inline package standards—silicon DIP—we wouldn't have the powerful, economical computers that we use in our homes, shops—and cars.

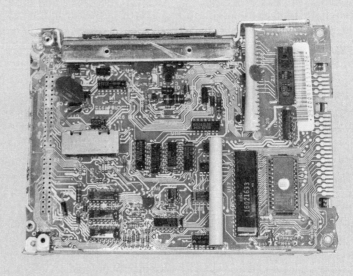

however, do many different jobs very well, including the operation of vehicle systems.

Onboard Computers

This brief summary of computer types and sizes brings us to the microprocessor, or "computer on a chip." Through the electronic technology of very large scale integration (VLSI), engineers can pack tens of thousands of transistor logic circuits on a chip of silicon only one-quarter or three-eights of an inch square. Installed in its circuit package with all connecting leads, a microprocessor is about the size of a small drawing eraser, figure 5-3. The microprocessor receives the computer input signals and sends out the output signals. Its thousands of circuits are the computer for the entire system.

It is interesting to note that the microprocessors used in onboard automobile computers are the same ones used in personal microcomputers. Because of their versatility, microprocessors can be programmed for many different functions. When the microprocessor and other IC memory components are programmed for specific purposes, they can be installed on a circuit board in a computer to control engine operation or to do financial calculations at a businessman's desk.

The early automobile onboard computers handled one function and made 10 engine adjustments per second. A decade later, today's onboard computer can adjust 27 functions while processing up to 2 million instructions per second. When the Cadillac Allanté was introduced, its computer had 90.7 kilobytes of memory, or more than the best personal computer available in 1986.

We have mentioned computer programs, memory, voltage signals, and processing in this introduction. The remaining sections of this chapter explain how these and other computer functions operate in automobile systems.

ANALOG AND DIGITAL PRINCIPLES

Every computer needs instructions to do any job, just as you need written instructions to do a repair job you have never done before. The instructions must be organized into a given sequence to perform a particular task. The instructions for a computer are called its **program**, but a computer cannot read words or even numbers. A computer can only read voltage signals.

Because a computer is based on IC chips with thousands of transistors that can respond to thousands of combinations of voltage signals, all we have to do is "translate" words, numbers, and other information into various combinations or amounts of voltage that the computer can understand. That's what the programming languages do.

Analog and Digital Computers

In chapter 4, we introduced the terms **analog** and **digital** to describe transistor operation as an amplifier or as a relay. Computers and their input and output signals also can be either analog or digital. Understanding these terms will help you understand computer system operation.

Analog means that a voltage signal or a processing function is infinitely variable in relation to something being measured or an adjustment to be made, figure 5-4. Digital means that an input or output signal or a processing decision is either yes-no, high-low, or on-off, figure 5-5. Most automobile system operating conditions are analog variables. Temperature, for example, doesn't change abruptly from zero to 100 or 200 degrees. It varies in infinite steps from high to low. The same is true of engine speeds, vehicle speed, airflow, fuel consumption, and other factors.

A computer may need to measure temperature changes through a range from 0° to 250° F. This can be "translated" for the computer as an analog voltage that varies from 0 volts at 0 degrees to 5 volts at 250°. Any analog signal between 0 and 5 volts represents a proportional temperature between 0 and 250° F.

A digital signal is voltage that is either high or low, or current that is either on or off, with no changing range of voltage or current in between. Suppose that a computer needs to know that engine temperature is either above or below a specific level, say 100° F. It doesn't need to know the exact temperature, only whether it's above or below a certain point. This can be translated to a digital signal of no voltage below 100° F and any arbitrary voltage when temperature exceeds 100° F. In this way, a digital signal is similar to a simple switch that opens and closes a circuit.

This kind of signal is called a digital signal because the on and off signals are processed by the computer as the digits, or numbers, 0 and 1. Digital computers use a mathematical system called the **binary system**, which uses only these two digits. Any number from our conventional decimal number system can be translated into a combination of binary 0's and 1's. So can any word from any language if we use specific combinations of 0's and 1's to represent letters of the alphabet.

A transistor working as an amplifier is the basis for an analog computer. The output current or voltage varies in direct proportion to the input current or voltage. The amplified output is thus analogous to the input. The ratio of input change to output change remains constant.

A transistor working as a relay is the basis for a digital computer. The transistor output switches from cutoff to saturation as the input signal switches from off to on. Output is either high or low, on or off. The on and off output signals represent the binary digits 1 and 0 for a digital computer.

Some early engine computers were analog devices that received and delivered analog input and output signals. Analog computers, however, are susceptible to changing temperature and supply voltage and to signal interference. They also are expensive to build. Digital computers are not as susceptible to changing temperature and supply voltage or signal interference. Digital computers also are less expensive to build and faster than analog computers. Almost all current automobile computers are based on digital microprocessors.

Digital computers change analog input signals to digital **bits** (binary digits) of information through analog-to-digital (AD) converter circuits. The microprocessor processes data as high-low, on-off voltage signals through digital logic networks made of thousands of **MOSFET** transistors. Based on its computations, the computer sends an output voltage to an instrument panel display or to a system actuator to change spark timing,

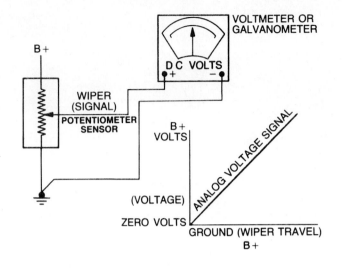

Figure 5-4. An analog sensor circuit. (Ford)

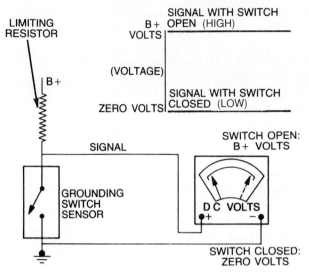

Figure 5-5. A digital sensor circuit. (Ford)

fuel metering, cruise control speed, air conditioning temperature, or another condition.

These onboard computers can process thousands of digital signals per second. They do it faster than humans can respond to corresponding words and numbers because their circuits can switch the voltage signals on and off in billionths of a second.

Binary Numbers

On and off voltage signals can represent the digits 1 and 0 of the binary number system. You may have worked with the binary system in mathematics classes, but let's review how it works in a digital computer.

Our customary decimal system uses the numbers 0 through 9, and we call it a base 10 system. For single numbers from 0 through 9, we write one column of numbers, or numbers in the ones position. When we reach numbers above 9, we add another column or position to the left: the tens position. Thus the number 10 equals one ten and zero ones; 29 equals two tens and nine ones. Each successive position to the left multiplies the number by a power of ten:

$$1 = 10^0$$
$$10 = 10^1$$
$$100 = 10^2$$
$$1000 = 10^3$$

The base 10 decimal system is not the only possible system of numerical notation. Mathematicians do, in fact, use number systems that work on base 8, base 12, base 16, and base 2—the binary system. In the binary system, whole numbers are grouped from right to left as they are in the decimal system. Because the system uses only two digits, the first position must equal 0 or 1. To write the value of 2, we must use the second position. We write it 10, but it equals one two and zero ones. Each successive position to the left multiplies the number by a power of two:

$$1 = 2^0 = \text{decimal number 1}$$
$$10 = 2^1 = \text{decimal number 2}$$
$$100 = 2^2 = \text{decimal number 4}$$
$$1000 = 2^3 = \text{decimal number 8}$$

Similarly, we can change other decimal numbers to binary numbers. For example:

Decimal Number	Binary Equivalent
3	11
5	101
7	111
9	1001

We could go on like this indefinitely, translating any decimal number you can think of into a binary equivalent. It may seem like an academic exercise, but it has a practical use in a digital computer. If we ar-

range several thousand transistor circuits in different series and parallel combinations in a microprocessor, we can make them switch on and off in combinations to equal any binary number faster than you can write the decimal equivalent.

Analog-to-Digital Conversion

Let's go back to our earlier examples of temperature signals for a computer. If a computer only needs to know that temperature is below or above a certain point—100° F, for example—we can connect a digital sensor that acts as a simple switch. Below 100° F, the switch is open and the computer receives no input voltage from that sensor circuit. Above 100° F, the switch closes and the computer receives an input voltage signal. That's a simple digital, on-off circuit: on = 1, off = 0.

Suppose, however, that the computer needs to know the exact temperature (or any temperature in a range) within one degree. Earlier, we used the example of a sensor that measures temperature from 0° F to 250° F. The sensor may send an analog voltage signal that varies from 0 to 5 volts. Each 1-volt change in the signal equals a 50-degree change in temperature. But this computer needs more precise temperature measurements than 50-degree increments. Fortunately, automotive computers and many sensors are precise enough to operate on signals that change by fractions of a volt. The fractions can be as small as 0.001-volt, or 1-millivolt, increments.

If our computer needs to know the temperature within one degree, it must respond to sensor voltage changes of 0.020 volt (20 millivolts). Most automotive computers can do this. If 0 voltage equals 0-degree temperature and 5 volts equals 250 degrees, then:

1.0 volt	= 50 degrees
0.2 volt	= 10 degrees
0.1 volt	= 5 degrees
0.02 volt	= 1 degree

If the temperature is 150 degrees, the sensor signal is 3.00 volts. If temperature rises to 151 degrees, sensor voltage rises to 3.02 volts.

Of course, the temperature passes through fractions of a degree as it changes from 150 degrees to 151 degrees, and the sensor signal passes through smaller fractions of a volt as it changes from 3.00 to 3.02 volts. These are true analog changes. Figure 5-6 shows a changing curve for any analog variable. It could be temperature; it could be voltage. It doesn't matter. The analog curve traces a continuous line from low to high and back to low. You can mark an infinite number of points along such an analog curve.

Our computer, however, is a digital computer. It only needs to process signals that equal one degree temperature changes. The computer converts the analog voltage from the sensor to a series of 0.020-volt (20-millivolt) changes for each degree. The computer does this through analog-to-digital (AD) conversion circuits. Engineers refer to this process as "digitizing" an analog signal. The result is a stairstep graph of digital signals that approximates the true analog signal, figure 5-7. The smaller and closer together the digital increments, the more closely the digital inputs resemble the actual analog measurement.

The process of analog-to-digital conversion takes us beyond the scope

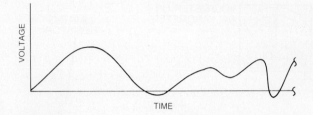

Figure 5-6. A continuously variable analog signal.

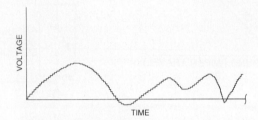

Figure 5-7. A digitized representation of the analog signal in figure 5-6.

of an automobile service text, but it does bring us back to the binary number system. Transistors can be built to switch on and off at different voltage levels or with different combinations of voltage signals. In our sample computer, groups of transistors must switch from no conduction (off) to full conduction (on, or saturation) at 20-millivolt increments. Remember also that we can convert any decimal number to a binary number. We can display that binary number, or create an input signal, by varying combinations of transistors that are on or off. Our 150-degree temperature in binary numbers is:

10010110

When the temperature changes to 151 degrees, the binary number changes to:

10010111

We can represent these binary combinations of 1's and 0's by switching different groups of transistors on and off. The computer reads the resulting combinations of voltage signals as the binary numbers and does its calculations. Because electrons of current travel at the speed of light through miniature computer circuits, all of these actions happen faster than you can read the decimal number 150.

Number System Conversion

Digital computers do all their processing in binary digits (bits) of 1's and 0's. Binary equivalents of decimal numbers can get quite awkward for people to work with, however. The binary number 10010110, which equals decimal 150, is quite long enough. Consider the binary equivalent of an engine speed of 2,500 rpm: 100111000100. To simplify these awkward binary numbers, computer engineers use other number systems: the octal system (base 8), the hexadecimal system (base 16), and the binary coded decimal (BCD) system.

These other number systems allow engineers to load programming information into computers with simpler number combinations than they could with binary numbers. The computer then changes the octal, hexadecimal, or BCD numbers into binary numbers. The octal and hexadecimal systems work well for this because they are based on numbers that are powers of 2: $8 = 2^3$, $16 = 2^4$. Conversions between binary numbers and base 8 or base 16 numbers are relatively easy for a digital computer.

Conversions between decimal (base 10) and binary numbers are not as easy for the computer because decimal 10 is not a power of 2. Extra circuits are needed and the calculations are more complicated. Engineers do use binary coded decimal (BCD) numbers for some operations, however. BCD numbers use groups of four binary numbers to represent each digit of a decimal number.

Again, octal, hexadecimal, and BCD mathematics takes us beyond the scope of an automotive service text. We won't go into these number systems because they are subjects for several complete texts in themselves. Different number systems are important, however, as examples of various ways in which information can be coded and processed. Any number system can be used to represent any measurable value. Similarly, any number can be converted to binary 1's and 0's for digital processing as on-off voltage signals. And this brings us to the subject of digital logic.

DIGITAL LOGIC

How does a computer compute or decide to turn an output signal on and off? You can spend years studying digital logic, but all digital computers manipulate data bits with three basic logic circuits, or **logic gates**: the NOT, AND, and OR gates. These terms describe the switching functions of the circuits, not the electronic construction. We call them "gates" because the circuits act as gates for output voltage signals in response to different combinations of input signals. Each gate accepts a voltage signal at its input terminals and transforms it according to the switching arrangements of its internal circuits. The transformed signal appears at the output terminal of the logic gate. Inside each logic gate is one or more active switching elements. These are controlled by the input voltage and, in turn, control the output voltage.

Just as atoms are the fundamental building blocks of matter, logic gates are the fundamental building blocks of all digital computer operations. Logic gates are the thousands of field-effect transistors (FET's) in a microprocessor. The symbols in figures 5-8

through 5-12 represent logic functions, not electronic construction. The tables next to the symbols are called "truth tables." They indicate the logical (truthful) combinations of input and output signals for each logic gate.

A digital microprocessor computes by switching output voltage on and off in response to one or more input voltage signals. The absence or presence of input voltage changes the transistors of the logic gate from cutoff to full saturation. This equals an *off* (low) or an *on* (high) signal (a binary 0 or 1). Input and output signals can be combined in logical combinations to equal binary numbers.

Just as there are two current flow theories (conventional and electron flow) and two rules for determining electromagnetic current direction (right-hand and left-hand), there are two rules for explaining digital logic.

1. Positive logic defines the most positive (highest) voltage as a logical 1 (on). Therefore, negative (low) voltage is a logical 0 (off).

2. Negative logic defines the most negative (lowest) voltage as a logical 1 (on). Therefore, positive (high) voltage is a logical 0 (off).

Additionally, high or low voltage can result from closing a circuit and allowing current to flow to a switching point. It also can result from leaving a circuit open with high voltage applied to a switching point. When the circuit is closed, voltage drops low at that point as current flows through the complete circuit. The following examples are based on positive logic and the simple application of voltage to logic gate inputs.

Basic Logic Gates

The simplest logic gate is a NOT gate, figure 5-8, which inverts the signal. If voltage to its single input terminal is high, or on (logic 1), output voltage is low, or off (logic 0). If input logic is logic 0, output logic is logic 1. A NOT gate simply changes binary 1's to 0's and vice versa. Figure 5-8 also shows the truth table for a NOT gate and the logic symbol: an A with a bar over

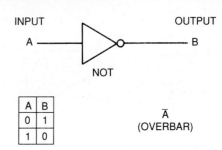

Figure 5-8. A NOT gate, logic symbol, and truth table.

A	B
0	1
1	0

$\overline{A}$
(OVERBAR)

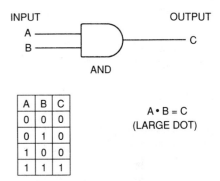

Figure 5-9. An AND gate, logic symbol, and truth table.

A	B	C
0	0	0
0	1	0
1	0	0
1	1	1

$A \cdot B = C$
(LARGE DOT)

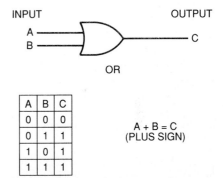

Figure 5-10. An OR gate, logic symbol, and truth table.

A	B	C
0	0	0
0	1	1
1	0	1
1	1	1

$A + B = C$
(PLUS SIGN)

the top. (The overbar represents an inverted output signal in any logic symbol.)

An AND gate has at least two inputs; it may have more. Figure 5-9 shows a simple AND gate with two inputs. Output is high (1) only when both inputs are high (1). If either or both of the inputs are low (0), output is low (0).

An OR gate, figure 5-10, also has two or more inputs and one output. The output is high (1) when any one or more of the inputs are high (1). Output

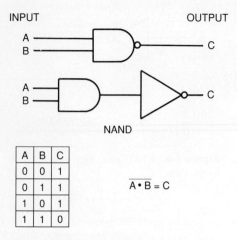

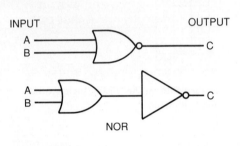

A	B	C
0	0	1
0	1	1
1	0	1
1	1	0

$$\overline{A \cdot B} = C$$

Figure 5-11. A NAND gate, logic symbol, and truth table.

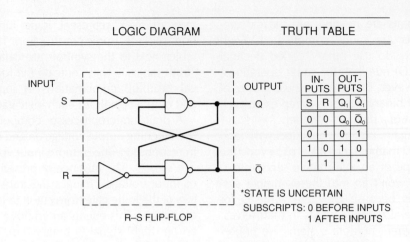

R–S FLIP-FLOP

LOGIC DIAGRAM	TRUTH TABLE

IN-PUTS		OUT-PUTS	
S	R	Q_1	$\overline{Q}_1$
0	0	Q_0	$\overline{Q}_0$
0	1	0	1
1	0	1	0
1	1	*	*

*STATE IS UNCERTAIN
SUBSCRIPTS: 0 BEFORE INPUTS
1 AFTER INPUTS

A	B	C
0	0	1
0	1	0
1	0	0
1	1	0

$$\overline{A + B} = C$$

Figure 5-12. A NOR gate, logic symbol, and truth table.

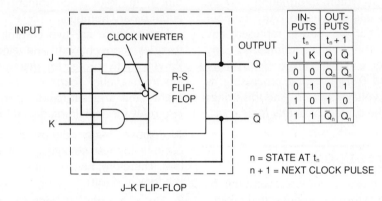

J–K FLIP-FLOP

IN-PUTS		OUT-PUTS	
t_n		$t_n + 1$	
J	K	Q	$\overline{Q}$
0	0	Q_n	$\overline{Q}_n$
0	1	0	1
1	0	1	0
1	1	$\overline{Q}_n$	Q_n

n = STATE AT t_n
n + 1 = NEXT CLOCK PULSE

Figure 5-13. Flip-flop circuits (R-S and J-K types) are the basis of computer memory. They "remember" their output settings until they receive new input signals.

is low (0) only when all inputs are low (0). Figures 5-9 and 5-10 also show the logic gate truth tables and symbols.

Other logic functions can occur when these basic gates are combined. An inverter (NOT gate) placed after an AND or an OR gate inverts the output signal and creates a NAND (not AND), figure 5-11, or a NOR (not OR) gate, figure 5-12. Notice that the NAND and NOR gates can be drawn as an AND or an OR gate followed by a NOT gate, or as the basic AND and OR gates with a small circle on the output. The circle represents an inverted output on any logic gate symbol.

Other Logic Circuits. A combination of OR, AND, and NOR gates can create an "exclusive OR," or XOR circuit in which the output is high only when one or the other input is high, but not both. XOR and AND gates can be combined into adder circuits, which are the basis of electronic calculators.

All of these logic gates are combinational logic circuits whose outputs are determined only by the present inputs. They have no memory. Other logic circuits can be built from these basic gates that remember previous inputs and do not change their outputs until they receive new input signals. These are called sequential logic circuits, and they are the basis of computer memory circuits. Flip-flop circuits, such as those in figure 5-13, hold their output signals when input signals are removed. They generate new outputs only when they receive new combinations of inputs.

Additionally, a computer engineer can build any arrangement of logic gates for any processing function by combining transistors in various circuit combinations. Fortunately, the engineer does not have to collect thousands of separate resistors, diodes, capacitors, and transistors and then wire them together on a circuit board to build his or her computer. Thirty years ago, before integrated circuits were invented, engineers did just that. Even earlier, engineers had to wire together thousands of vacuum tube amplifiers to perform digital logic operations. Today, all of the transistors needed for different logic gates are built into IC chips. IC devices are available with different combinations of gates per circuit and different input and output connections for various gates.

Also fortunately, you don't have to be a computer engineer to troubleshoot an automobile onboard com-

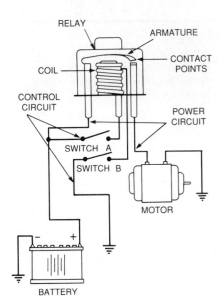

Figure 5-14. Switches A and B work like an AND gate in the control circuit to energize (close) the power circuit.

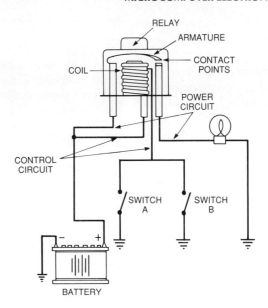

Figure 5-15. Switches A and B work like an OR gate in the control circuit to energize (close) the power circuit.

puter. Understanding these fundamentals of computer logic circuits and the way they operate on the electrical principles of voltage and current will help you understand computer operation as you study it in this and later chapters.

Relay Logic

It's often difficult to visualize computer logic operations because the processing takes place so fast and on circuits so small that you can't see the parts without a microscope. We can, however, build a simple computer with some relays and switches.

Suppose that we take one relay and connect the voltage supply terminal of its control circuit to the battery. Then we put a switch in that wire, figure 5-14. Next, we connect the other control circuit terminal to ground, also through a switch. The relay will be actuated and complete the power circuit only when both switches are closed. We have just built an AND gate. We have also built a common starter relay circuit to switch voltage for a starter motor. Even though we drop voltage across the relay coil and the voltage level is different at each switch, both switches must be closed

(high) to produce an output voltage through the relay. This makes it a basic logic gate with the AND function.

Suppose we take another relay and connect two switches in parallel to one terminal of the control circuit. Each switch can complete a circuit to ground. The other control circuit terminal is connected to the battery, figure 5-15. We can actuate the relay and provide an output signal in the power circuit by closing either or both of the control switches. This is a basic OR gate. We can take this relay and these switches and install them in a dome lamp circuit to turn on the interior lights when either or both doors of a car are open.

These are only two examples of "relay logic" circuits that have been used on automobiles for decades. Individual computer logic gates are also this simple. In fact, you may hear computer technicians talk about computer "relay logic."

If you look at the input switch connections in figures 5-14 and 5-15, you can see that different combinations of series and parallel connections can produce different logic functions. Semiconductor engineers do the same thing on IC chips by arranging thousands of transistors in various series

and parallel combinations to produce thousands of logic gates.

COMPUTER PROGRAMS

Earlier in this chapter, we mentioned that any computer needs instructions to do its job. These instructions are the computer program. Computer designers use programming languages to translate instructions into binary numbers (or octal or hexadecimal or BCD numbers). The numbers are then translated into voltage signals that a computer can "read" to understand its program instructions.

The program instructions that a computer uses to understand its input data, do its calculations, and send its output commands consist of:

• The mathematical instructions, in binary form, for processing data.

• Information on engine and vehicle constant values, such as number of cylinders, displacement, compression ratio, gear ratios, type of fuel system, emission devices, vehicle weight, and accessories.

• Information on variable values, such as engine and vehicle speed combinations, temperature, airflow, fuel flow, timing, EGR flow, air injection operation, transmission gear position, vehicle load, braking effort, and other factors.

The first two elements are fixed values and can be loaded into computer memory rather easily. To load the variable values into memory, engineers must simulate the vehicle, or a vehicle system, in operation. They load programs with all of the possible variable conditions for any system into a large mainframe computer. Then they let the mainframe computer calculate all the combinations of those variables and determine the control program for the vehicle onboard computer.

One example of this system simulation is the process called **engine mapping**. Engineers operate a vehicle on a dynamometer and manually adjust speed, load, spark timing, fuel metering, airflow, and other variables. Using a larger computer with the dynamometer, they determine the optimum fuel, ignition, exhaust gas recirculation (EGR), and other output settings for best performance, economy, and emission control. This information becomes part of the program for the onboard computer. It is stored in the programmable read-only memory (PROM) chip for the computer on that particular model of car.

Engine mapping creates a 3-dimensional performance graph for a particular engine, vehicle, and accessory combination, figure 5-16. When the PROM is installed in a computer, it "remembers" the settings for timing, EGR, fuel metering, and other adjustable variables. Then, based on speed, temperature, airflow, and other information from its sensors, the computer adjusts timing, fuel, EGR, and other conditions for best performance, economy, and emission control.

By storing this information on one PROM, carmakers can use one basic computer for many vehicle models. To make the engine control system work for a specific model, they install the correct PROM. Some carmakers use a single PROM chip plugged into the computer, figure 5-17. Others use a larger calibration module, figure

COMPUTERS PLUS

When you get into troubleshooting, replacing parts, and otherwise servicing onboard computer systems, you will probably feel overwhelmed with thousands of part numbers and other variations. Don't worry about it. Don't try to memorize all the part numbers. You're not alone. Here are some statistics to show you what the world's largest corporation has to deal with in terms of electronic variations.

In 1986, General Motors introduced its Computerized Automotive Maintenance System (CAMS). CAMS is a computer-based diagnostic system that lets a technician plug into a GM car and troubleshoot electronic problems. CAMS provides online test procedures, specifications, and service bulletins for all GM vehicles from about 1980 to the present.

As of the 1988 model year (the last year for which complete figures are available), CAMS represented the following volume of data "crunched" into a computer database:

• Over 7,000 part numbers for ECM PROM's from 1980 to 1988

• 60,000 unique part numbers for the CAMS system, its parts, and its software

• 3,000 part numbers for different electrical connectors on all GM vehicles

• 6.2 million lines of computer code to make the CAMS system operate

• 37 dedicated service bays at the GM technical center to test the CAMS application software

Do you think that the proliferation of electronic systems for vehicle operation and vehicle troubleshooting represents another application of Moore's Law? Looks like it, doesn't it?

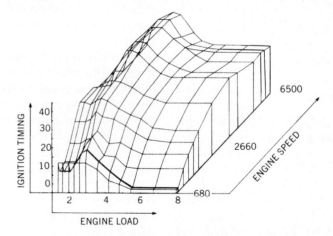

Figure 5-16. This engine map calculates the optimum ignition point for each combination of speed and load. Similar maps are computed for fuel metering and other operating variables. (Porsche)

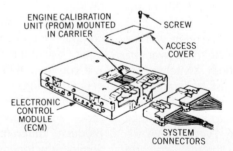

Figure 5-17. The General Motors CCC computer uses a single removable PROM. (Chevrolet)

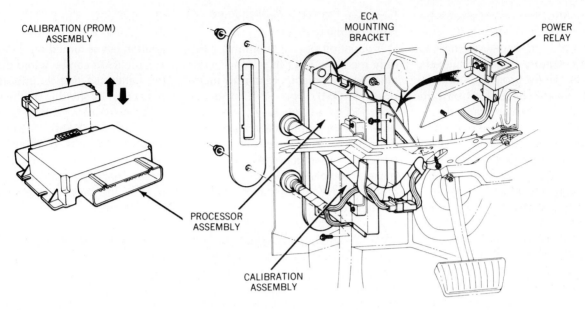

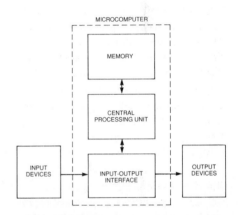

Figure 5-18. The calibration assembly (module) of this Ford EEC computer contains the system PROM. (Ford)

5-18. Engine computers have become economical and versatile because engineers can use a single **computer hardware** assembly with interchangeable PROM's to change the **software**. When you service engine control systems, you will learn that checking for the correct PROM installation is an important service step.

PARTS OF A COMPUTER

Up to this point, our discussion of computers has concentrated on computer functions, computer logic, and software. The software is the programs and logic functions stored in the electronic circuits of the computer. You can't see it and touch it; you can only see the results of its operation. You can see and touch the computer hardware, however. The hardware is the mechanical, magnetic, electrical, and electronic parts that make up the physical structure of a computer. Although the sizes, arrangements, and quantity of computer hardware vary from mainframes to microcomputers, you can understand the basic structure of a digital computer from the block diagram in figure 5-19.

Central Processing Unit (CPU)

The microprocessor, which we discussed earlier, is the **central processing unit (CPU)** of the computer. All of the mathematical operations and logical decisions occur in its integrated circuits. (Some microcomputers have more than one microprocessor.) You can consider the microprocessor as the heart of the computer because it performs the essential processing function (along with the microcomputer memory). It is only part of the complete hardware structure, however.

Computer Memory

Other electronic IC devices provide the computer storage, or memory, function. These are not processing circuits; they simply store data for the CPU. Memory circuits can store three basic kinds of data:

1. The computer operating program
2. Input data from system sensors
3. Output data to system actuators

Often a computer will receive an input signal or send an output signal, but it also must remember the signal data for later reference. Because an

Figure 5-19. The basic structure of a digital computer.

automobile computer operates with complex programs and large amounts of input and output data, the memory circuits often are as large and sophisticated as the microprocessor circuits.

Read-Only Memory (ROM). Computers use different memories for different purposes. Memory can be divided into two different types: memory that can be changed, and memory that can't be changed. In an automotive onboard computer, both kinds are stored in the computer's IC chips. For any computer to do its job properly, its program instructions must be stored in memory and remain unchanged. Also, the program can't be lost when power is turned off. This kind of stored, permanent memory is **read-only memory (ROM)**. Engineers sometimes call the programs stored in ROM "firmware" instead of software because they cannot be changed.

The operating program is a series of instructions organized into a given sequence to perform a given task. The operating program includes system strategy and lookup tables. The system strategy is a blueprint used by the computer to control engine operation under a wide variety of operating conditions and includes all of the decision-making logic and equations necessary to accomplish its job. The lookup tables contain specifications and calibrations required to make the engine perform as it should. For example, when a cold engine is started and the temperature sensor sends its signal to the computer, the microprocessor determines the engine operating condition and selects the most appropriate system strategy for it. The exact duration of engine warmup time is then determined by comparing the sensor temperature reading to the warmup time code in the lookup tables.

For most automotive computers, the operating program is loaded into an IC chip called a **programmable read-only memory (PROM)**. Computer engineers do this by applying a series of voltage pulses to a PROM chip that sets the switching positions of the transistors in prescribed on and off conditions. The small amount of current that flows with each voltage pulse blows a fuse on each circuit path after the transistor is set. The switching positions, therefore, become permanent memory and cannot be changed. Input signal voltages to be processed by the program are applied across parallel circuits and don't affect the program memory. The programming process is called "burning a PROM." A PROM differs from ROM because it can be removed from the computer and replaced with a different PROM containing new design in-

formation. ROM is permanently installed in the computer.

A variation of programmable read-only memory (PROM) is called **erasable, programmable, read-only memory (EPROM)**. The EPROM differs from PROM in two ways: the computer can write information into it for permanent storage, and it can be erased and reprogrammed by the carmaker (other PROM's are programmed by the chipmaker and have a 1-time use).

This first feature makes the EPROM ideal for handling important automotive functions such as storage of odometer information. General Motors uses EPROM's to store the option content of a vehicle equipped with a body computer module (BCM).

The erasable feature allows EPROM memory to be changed either by electrically altering the memory one byte at a time **(an electrically erasable programmable read-only memory— EEPROM)** or by exposing the memory to ultraviolet light through a small window in the top of the chip for 15 to 20 minutes. Intel, a leading chipmaker, has developed a "flash" memory that can be electrically erased in less than one second. The blank chip memory then can be reprogrammed with new information in less than four seconds. Chrysler uses EEPROM's to record engine fault codes on late-model cars. This type of chip memory allows a dealership to electrically update or change a module memory instead of replacing the entire module.

Random-Access Memory (RAM).

Input and output signals that are stored temporarily are held in computer memory circuits called **random-access memory (RAM)**. Actually, "read-write memory" would be a better name because information can be written into and read from RAM circuits. They can be changed, while ROM circuits cannot (except for EEPROM).

Two types of RAM memory are used in automobile computers: vola-

tile and nonvolatile. Information in the volatile RAM is erased when the ignition key is turned off. However, a volatile RAM can be wired directly to the battery so that its information is not erased by shutting off the ignition. This type of RAM is often called **keep-alive memory (KAM)**. However, RAM and KAM circuits lose their memory when power is disconnected from them. That's the reason why disconnecting the battery in a car with a "programmable" radio results in the loss of all the station settings, which have to be reset when the battery is reconnected. All those settings were stored in RAM, not ROM.

The nonvolatile RAM memory retains its information even when power is disconnected. This type of RAM is often used for storing odometer information in an electronic speedometer. The memory chip retains the accumulated mileage of the vehicle. If the speedometer is replaced, the odometer chip must be removed and installed in the new speedometer.

Adaptive Learning Strategy. Computer programs now in use contain many backup or fail-safe modes and are sophisticated enough to compensate for such things as sensor failure. For example, turning on the fuel pump in an electronically controlled fuel injection system is done through a relay. If the relay fails, however, the computer will take its signal from the oil pressure switch. In most cases, the driver will never realize that the fuel pump relay has failed.

A variety of other factors (such as variations in production, fuel quality, and engine wear) may gradually move the real needs of the engine away from the ideal values designed into the computer program. In addition to failure, sensors may gradually shift their response range, providing a signal that the computer questions. To compensate for such problems, an **adaptive learning strategy** is incorporated in many computer programs. If a controlled value falls outside the original design parameters, the adaptive learning strategy modifies the original program to restore proper operation.

Program modifications made by the adaptive learning strategy are stored in RAM that is connected directly to the battery. The modifications remain intact when the ignition is shut off. When the battery is disconnected, however, the modifications are lost and vehicle driveability becomes unsatisfactory.

Vehicle driveability will also be unsatisfactory if a malfunctioning sensor is replaced, since the program has compensated for signals from the unreliable sensor and is now receiving signals that conflict with its adapted program. If you are unaware of the presence of an adaptive learning strategy, you may question your diagnosis, because the vehicle will not perform any better immediately after replacing the sensor.

After the vehicle in question has been driven about 15 to 20 miles under varying driving conditions, the adaptive learning strategy will correct the program, and vehicle driveability will return to normal.

General Motors uses a pair of functions within its electronic control module (ECM) on fuel-injected engines called integrator (short-term) and block learn (long-term). They control fuel delivery by changing the injector duty cycle, just as the mixture control solenoid dwell (duty cycle) does on carbureted engines. The two functions interact with a base fuel calculation stored in the ECM's memory to make minor adjustments in the air-fuel mixture of the injection system. The ECM adds or subtracts fuel from the base calculation according to the feedback signal received from the exhaust gas oxygen (EGO) sensor.

The integrator function is a short-term, temporary change in fuel delivery that functions only in closed-loop mode. It monitors the EGO sensor voltage and adds or subtracts fuel according to the sensor data. Integrator uses a value of 128 as neutral, figure 5-20. When integrator reads 128, the

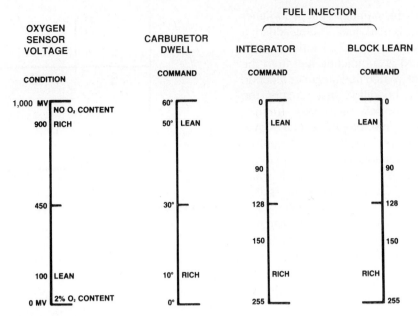

Figure 5-20. The relationship between oxygen sensor voltage, carburetor dwell, integrator, and block learn. (General Motors)

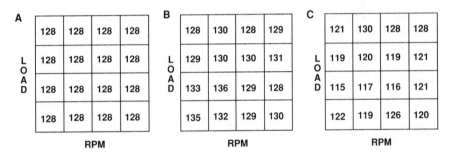

Figure 5-21. Computer memory dealing with block learn divides engine operating range for a given combination of load and speed conditions into 16 blocks. In **A**, all blocks are operating at a 14.7:1 air-fuel ratio under all engine load and speed conditions. **B** shows examples of block learn readings when the oxygen sensor reads a slightly lean exhaust. Similar examples are shown in **C** for a slightly rich exhaust. (General Motors)

EGO sensor is reporting the results of a 14.7:1 air-fuel mixture burning in the engine cylinder. Block learn continually watches the integrator and makes the same correction in its own values.

Block learn cannot make as great a correction in fuel delivery, but its correction remains for a longer time. The name comes from the concept that divides the operating range of the engine for any given combination of load and speed into 16 cells or blocks, figure 5-21. (Block learn also uses the number 128 as representing a 14.7:1 air-fuel ratio.) A given fuel delivery is

stored in each block in the computer memory. As the operating range moves into a particular block, the fuel delivery is based on the value stored in that memory block. Each time that block learn makes a correction, the integrator makes the same correction in its values.

A scan tool is used to obtain integrator and block learn data from the ECM. Properly connected to the car's test connector, the scan tool taps into the ECM serial data transmission link and reads the inputs and outputs that the ECM receives and sends. The base fuel calculation appears to the scan tool as the number 128. If a higher number is read, fuel is being added; a number less than 128 indicates that the ECM is subtracting fuel from the mixture. When the integrator function notes a condition that remains too high or too low for a predetermined length of time, block learn takes over and makes a long-term correction.

Integrator and block learn are forms of adaptive memory but with some limitations. An example is the result of a vehicle in stop-and-go traffic for a long period of time. Much of that time is spent at idle, with occasional minor accelerations and stops. The integrator function compensates for this operating condition, and after a period of time, block learn takes over. By the time that the traffic condition suddenly clears and the vehicle is ready to resume cruise speeds, block learn has revised the air-fuel mixture as a long-term correction. This can cause a driveability problem. To solve the problem, GM has resorted to a technique of imposing predetermined limits on the integrator and block learn function called "clamping."

Input and Output Circuits

Computer processing and memory circuits can't do anything without receiving input signals and sending output signals. The microprocessor, however, is not connected directly to every input and output device in the system. Other IC devices receive and send the signals. Most of these provide parallel connections for the microprocessor so that it can read several input signals and send several output signals simultaneously.

Converter or Conditioning Circuits

A microprocessor is limited in the types of voltage signals with which it can work. In many cases, voltage signals provided by sensors must be converted or conditioned before the microprocessor can use them. Earlier in this chapter, we said that many sensors in vehicle computer systems send

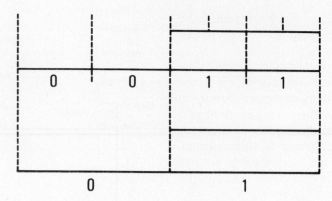

Figure 5-22. Computers use clock pulses to distinguish between these two signals. (General Motors)

analog voltage signals to the computer. The analog signals must be changed to digital data, or "digitized," for the microprocessor. The conversion is done by analog-to-digital (AD) converter circuits. These are generally housed on separate IC devices, connected to the microprocessor. A few sensors, however, contain their own input conditioning circuitry.

Other sensor voltage signals may be too small or not have the correct voltage range for use by the microprocessor circuits. Such voltage signals must be amplified before they are digitized. Amplification is performed; then the signals are sent through the AD converter circuitry.

Although most vehicle system actuators and instrument displays (the output devices) are digital components, some are analog devices. This means that the digital output signals from the microprocessor must be converted to analog values. Digital-to-analog (DA) converter circuits do this. Suppose a computer must control radio volume at a preselected level as the radio signal strength changes. This requires a changing analog voltage to be applied to a radio amplifier transistor. The DA converter circuits produce the analog signal from the microprocessor digital signals. Actually, the analog output is still a "digitized" signal that changes in discrete stairsteps. The digitized curve, however, is close enough to the analog curve that it produces the desired response.

Computer Clock Rates and Timing

To this point, we know that a computer receives input data in the form of voltage signals from various sensors. It processes the input data and sends output voltage signals to various actuators. The processing of the data is done by a microprocessor, which acts as the "brain" by communicating with various memories.

All of this communication, from input to output, is accomplished using the binary code, consisting of lengthy strings of 0's and 1's that pulse through the computer from input to output. Have you wondered yet how the computer components are able to tell when one pulse ends and another starts? Or, put another way, how does a computer tell the difference between a 01 and a 0011, figure 5-22?

Clock Pulses. Computers contain a crystal oscillator or clock generator, figure 5-23. This clock delivers a constant stream of steady pulses one bit in length. The microprocessor and memories both watch the clock pulses while they are interfacing, figure 5-24. In this way, they are able to distinguish between a 01 and a 0011 since they know how long each voltage pulse is supposed to last. The process is extended to include the input and output circuits, figure 5-25.

Computer Speeds (MHz). Some computers operate faster than others. Computer speed is measured in the

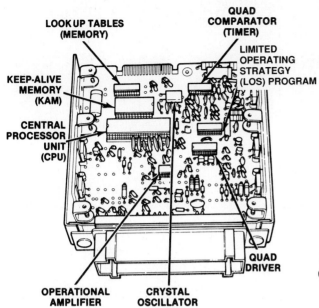

Figure 5-23. A computer contains a clock generator, which provides constant voltage pulses the length of one bit. (Ford)

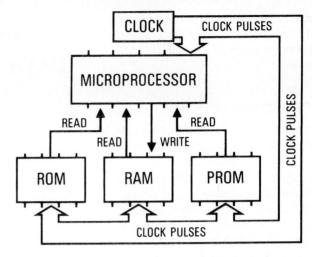

Figure 5-24. The microprocessor and memories watch the clock pulses. (General Motors)

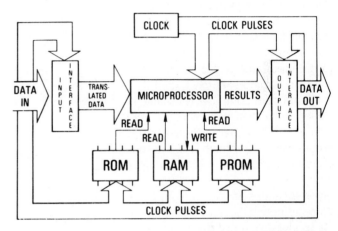

Figure 5-25. Input and output circuits also watch the clock pulses. (General Motors)

cycle time, or clock speed, in hertz (4.7 MHz, 8.0 MHz, etc.) required to perform certain measurements such as adding two 10-digit numbers.

The clock speed in hertz is difficult to relate to the real world in terms of actual speed, since many other factors besides processor speed enter into the rate at which a computer functions. A computer that operates at 8.0 MHz may actually work more slowly than one that operates at 4.7 MHz because of an inefficient program, a slower data transfer rate, or an inferior operating system.

Baud Rate. All manufacturers use the **baud rate**, or bits per second, as a standard measure of how quickly a computer transmits data. Baud rate is most useful in estimating the length of time one computer requires to transmit a specific amount of data to another computer. The standard storage of a single alphabetic or numeric character uses 8 bits per byte. Adding one start bit and one stop bit brings the transmission requirement of one character to 10 bits. To determine the maximum number of words per minute that can be transmitted electronically, the baud rate is divided by 10. Thus, a baud rate of 300 means that

about 30 words can be sent or received per minute. A baud rate of 1200 will transmit about 120 words per minute.

When you study electronic engine control systems and body electronic systems later in this text, you will study examples of vehicles with high-baud and low-baud computers. As Chrysler, GM, Ford, and foreign carmakers have developed their computer systems, they have gone from low baud rates on computers of the early 1980's to high baud rates on computers of the later 1980's and 1990's. Baud rate, or data transmission speed, is important in computer system operation and troubleshooting. Generally, higher baud rates are necessary for advanced, more precise

control operations and communication on late-model vehicles.

Processor Bit Size. Microprocessor bit size is another factor that determines the speed of a computer. The early microprocessors were capable of transmitting 4 bits at a time and thus were called 4-bit processors. Since a byte contains 8 bits, the 4-bit processor had to make two passes to process or transmit a byte. The 4-bit processor was superseded by an 8-bit processor, which could process or transmit a byte in a single pass. However, since some data requires more than a single byte, even 8-bit processors must make more than one pass to process or transmit such data. Processors may be designed to handle 16 bits, 32 bits, or more. Automotive processors generally use 4-, 8- or 16-bit processors, depending upon their particular application.

Computer Installations

Automotive onboard computers are called electronic control units, modules, and assemblies. Some are even called computers. All have the basic features of input, processing, storage, and output. All of the computer hardware is mounted on one, or a few, small circuit boards and installed in a metal case. The metal case helps to shield it from radiofrequency interference (RFI) and other sources of signal interference. Multipin connectors or edge connectors on the circuit boards join the computer to wiring harnesses. The harnesses connect the computer to the input and output devices (sensors and actuators) of the system.

An onboard computer is usually installed under the instrument panel or behind a kick panel in the passenger compartment, although a few engine computers are located in the engine compartment. Carmakers usually favor locations inside the passenger compartment to keep the computer as far as possible from the extremes of temperature, dirt, and vibration found elsewhere on the vehicle.

Some onboard computers are single-function units that control just one operation. Others are multifunction units that regulate all engine systems, for example. Even a simple ignition module can "compute" timing based on an input signal from a distributor. A more complex computer can use other input signals from speed, temperature, and vacuum sensors (besides distributor signals) to vary the timing for different temperatures, speeds, and loads.

BODY COMPUTER MODULES

A body computer module (BCM) is just like any other computer we've discussed thus far. It contains a microprocessor and memories in ROM and RAM, and it interfaces with input and

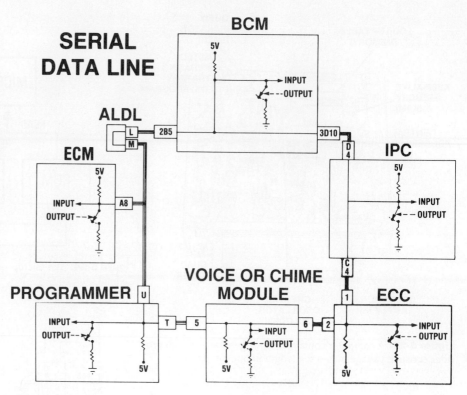

Figure 5-26. The serial data line allows computer communication. (General Motors)

output devices. Perhaps the simplest way to describe the BCM is to call it a master computer, since it receives inputs from, and sends output to, other computers in the vehicle. In fact, it may receive inputs from various sensors as well as one or more computers. How does all this information reach the BCM?

Sequential Sampling

The BCM cannot look at all of the inputs from all the components at the same time. To introduce the required order, the computer contains a **multiplexer (MUX)** for inputs and a **demultiplexer (DEMUX)** for outputs. The MUX and DEMUX connect the microprocessor with the input and output devices using a complex switching method called **sequential sampling**.

To understand how the MUX and DEMUX handle input and output data, think of them as a series of ganged rotary switches connecting the input and output devices with the microprocessor. The switches turn together, allowing the input sensor and

its output device to be connected to the microprocessor. This lets the microprocessor receive and process the input from a sensor and then signal the necessary actuator. When this is completed, the rotary switch turns, giving the next sensor and actuator access to the microprocessor. In this way, the microprocessor is able to deal with all the sensors and actuators one at a time, or sequentially, rather than being bombarded by inputs from them all at the same time.

Data Transmission

Since the BCM acts as the master computer, it must communicate with other computers in the vehicle. The other computers become slaves; that is, they respond at the command of the master computer. Communication takes place on a **serial data line**, figure 5-26. In serial data transmission, all of the data words are transmitted one after the other.

There are two types of serial data lines. The simplest is shown in figure 5-27. This type allows one computer to communicate with the other. Both

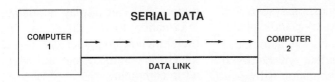

Figure 5-27. Serial data transmission takes place on a data link between computers. (General Motors)

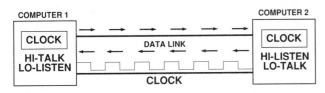

Figure 5-28. A duplex serial data line uses a clock line to permit 2-way transmission over the data link. (General Motors)

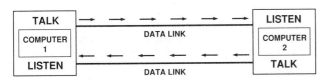

Figure 5-29. A peripheral serial bus uses two data links, one for talking and one for listening. (General Motors)

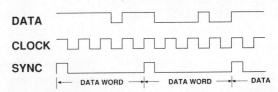

Figure 5-30. In synchronous data transmission, data flows continuously with uniform clock pulse intervals to signal the start of a new word. (General Motors)

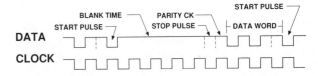

Figure 5-31. In asynchronous data transmission, data flows when required with a uniform tone indicating dead space between transmission. Start and stop pulses indicate the beginning and end of a word and the computer performs a parity check to ensure that the entire word was properly received. (General Motors)

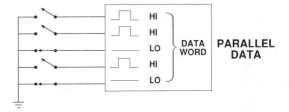

Figure 5-32. In parallel transmission, all components of the data are sent at the same time over their own lines. (General Motors)

computers are clocked together and are synchronized to the data being transmitted. Communication is possible because it takes place extremely fast—the serial data line might be turned on and off more than 8,000 times per second. This type of data transmission is commonly used in automotive systems.

The other type is a **duplex serial data line**, figure 5-28. The BCM communicates with other components in the system by sending and receiving data on the single circuit. This makes the serial data line an input-output or two-way circuit; thus its name. To control which computer sends and which one receives, an external clock line is provided between the two computers.

Communication between the BCM and other components takes the form of turning the circuit on with high voltage (5 volts) and off with low voltage (0 volts). When the clock pulse is high, computer 1 talks and computer

2 receives. When the clock pulse is low, computer 2 talks and computer 1 receives. Grounding either the link or the clock line, however, causes a loss of communication between the computers.

Another method of communication uses a **peripheral serial bus**, figure 5-29. In this form of transmission, one link is used for talking and the other link is reserved for listening. Its advantage over a duplex serial data line is that if one link is grounded, the other will continue to function.

Serial data transmission can be **synchronous** or **asynchronous**. Synchronous transmission is a constant flow of data with uniform clock pulse intervals, figure 5-30. Since the clock pulses are generated at consistent intervals, the computer recognizes the synchronous pulse as the beginning of a new piece of data.

Asynchronous transmission means that data is not continuous, but sent when required. A constant, uniform

tone indicating dead time fills the intervals between the sending and receiving of data. When new data is to be transmitted, it is preceded by a start pulse, figure 5-31. When the word has been sent completely, the final pulse in the series is a stop pulse, which tells the computer to stop data processing. The computer then performs a parity check to assure that the total word has been transmitted completely. The constant tone then reoccurs until the next word transmission, which begins with a start pulse.

A **parallel transmission** method can also be used to send data. Each element composing the data to be transmitted is sent at the same time over its own line, figure 5-32. Switches can be turned on and off as required to indicate various forms of data.

BCM Operation

To see how a typical BCM system works, let's consider the system to be at rest. This means that all components in the system are holding the serial data output line at 5 volts—telling the BCM that the serial data system is idle. Each component in the system has a code number. When the BCM requires communication with a particular component, it pulses the serial data circuit with the code number for that component. All the components in the system "hear" the code number, but only the component to which the code has been assigned is allowed to respond. Other components in the system can only communicate with the BCM when it requests them to do so. Furthermore, the BCM cannot communicate with more than one device at a time.

Suppose that the BCM has called the electronic control module (ECM). It transmits its instructions to the ECM in a data stream. When the BCM has finished transmitting, the ECM holds the serial data line high (5 volts) long enough for the system to return to idle, and then it signals the BCM with its code. This lets the BCM know that the ECM is about to answer. As the ECM sends its data to the BCM, other components in the system can "hear" what is being said, and some may need to process the data for their own purposes. For example, the instrument panel cluster (IPC) may be "listening" for engine temperature so that it can display the information for the driver.

When the ECM has finished transmitting its data, it holds the circuit high (5 volts) again to idle the system. At this point, the BCM can signal another component and go through the same process. We will look at specific BCM functions in greater detail in later chapters.

INSTRUMENTATION SYSTEMS AND CONTROL SYSTEMS

We have looked at two different ways to classify computers and computer systems:

• By size—mainframe, minicomputer, and microcomputer

• By type of processing system and kinds of signals—analog and digital

Another way to classify automotive computer systems that will help you understand their operation is by purpose. Generally, automotive computer systems have two basic purposes: instrumentation and control.

Basically, an instrumentation system measures some variable quantities and displays the output information to the driver. Speedometers, odometers, tachometers, fuel gauges, and warning lamps are all instrumentation devices. A trip computer is an obvious example of a computerized instrumentation system. The computer receives input data on vehicle speed, clock time, elapsed time of travel, fuel flow, and other factors. The processed information is displayed to the driver on the instrument panel. By depressing a series of buttons, the driver can read the car speed (in miles or kilometers per hour), the total travel time, the estimated time of arrival, average fuel mileage, current fuel mileage, and anything else he or she might like to know.

A control system uses a computer to regulate the operation of another system, or even a variety of systems. You have already learned how a body computer module communicates with other computers such as those controlling ignition timing, antilock brakes, electronic suspension, and even instrument panel displays. We have many computer control systems on late-model cars, but the most common example is the engine control computer. This computer receives input data on engine speed and load, vehicle speed, ignition timing, airflow, exhaust gas composition, and many other factors. The processed information is sent as output signals to actuators that control ignition timing, fuel flow, and emission control operation.

The basic purposes of instrumentation and control are not exclusive, however. Many computer systems do both jobs. An automatic temperature control system regulates heating and air conditioning through system ac-

tuators and can display temperature information to the driver. A single multifunction computer can regulate the cruise control system and serve as a trip computer.

The instrumentation and control functions may be apparent, and the examples may seem obvious. The importance of the distinction lies in understanding the system output devices. The same basic microprocessor can receive and process a similar input signal in two different systems for two different purposes. Let's go back to our earlier example of a temperature signal. A computer can receive a signal that indicates engine temperature or passenger compartment air temperature. The signals could be identical. In one system, the computer can process the signal to change engine operation or turn on an air conditioner. The computer also can light up an instrument panel display with the same processed information. Similarly, a single vehicle speed sensor can send a signal to two computer systems:

• One computer processess the signal and displays vehicle speed on a digital speedometer

• The second computer processes the signal and controls transmission shifting or emission systems.

Input signals can be identical. Processing operations are basically the same. But a system can produce several different output signals for different instrumentation and control purposes. These examples show that there are more similarities than differences among the dozen or more computer systems on late-model automobiles.

CONTROL SYSTEM OPERATING MODES—OPEN LOOP AND CLOSED LOOP

Any computer control system can have different operating modes. The computer does not respond to information from its sensors in exactly the same way all the time. It can ignore sensors under some conditions, or it can respond to one signal in several ways, depending on what several other sensors tell it. Because a computer can be selective, engineers can design control systems with two basic operating conditions, or modes: **open loop** and **closed loop**.

Open-Loop Control

Open-loop control means that a computer—or any control device—adjusts a system to operate in a certain way. If there is an error or a deviation in the results of the operation, a signal of the error or deviation does not get sent back to the computer or controller. Figure 5-33 shows a simple block diagram of open-loop system control.

Open-loop control is not unique to computer systems. You exercise open-loop control over your car radio when you set the volume for a certain level. The volume control switch signals the amplifier for a certain power output, and that's where it stays. If you drive through a tunnel, the volume weakens because the input signal gets weaker. But the amplifier power output doesn't change until you readjust the volume control. The radio system itself didn't receive an error **feedback** signal that the volume was too low. It relied on an outside force for adjustment. Similarly, a manually operated car heater works in an open-loop control mode. You turn it on and set it for maximum heating. The system stays in that operating mode until you readjust it or turn it off.

Closed-Loop Control

Closed loop means that the computer, or controller, is reading and responding to an output error signal, or feedback signal, figure 5-34. Again, closed-loop control is not limited to computer systems. We use closed-loop control systems every day. A temperature-control thermostat is a good example.

You can set an oven thermostat for a cooking temperature of 350° F or a furnace thermostat for 75° F. If the oven or the room temperature is

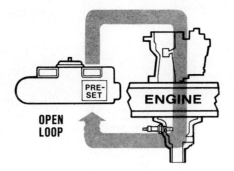

Figure 5-33. When a system is in open loop, it operates according to preset values and ignores any feedback messages sent by a sensor. (Chrysler)

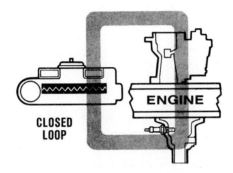

Figure 5-34. Once a system moves into closed loop, it adjusts its operation according to feedback messages from a sensor. (Chrysler)

below the setting, the controller turns on the oven or furnace. When temperature rises above the setting, the controller turns off the heat. This is a simple kind of closed-loop control, and it is an example of **limit-cycle control**. Limit-cycle control is a control system that monitors the system output and responds only when output goes above or below selected limits. The system tries to maintain an average operating condition. For a simple temperature-control system, the limits may be ±5° or ±25° or whatever the system designer chooses. A furnace controller may turn the heat on at 70° F and off at 80° F. The result is an average room temperature of 75° F.

A limit-cycle controller can be a simple thermostatic switch, or it can be a computer. A simple automotive air conditioner thermostat is a closed-

loop, limit-cycle controller. It turns the air conditioning compressor on and off, depending on evaporator cooling temperature. A speed governor for an industrial engine is another kind of limit-cycle controller. You can set the throttle for a steady 2,000 rpm with no engine load. If engine load increases, speed will decrease. Centrifugal weights in the governor respond to the speed change and move the throttle to regain the 2,000-rpm setting.

The same principle works in an engine control system that uses a computer as a controller. The computer PROM can be programmed with the desired idle speed (plus or minus upper and lower limits) for a particular vehicle and engine. If idle speed rises or falls from the upper and lower limits of the setpoint for any reason, input from a speed sensor tells the computer to send an output signal to an idle speed control motor or other actuator. Figure 5-35 shows a computer-controlled idle air control (IAC) valve in a fuel injection throttle body. In response to engine speed signals, the computer controls the motor that moves the IAC valve in and out of the air passage. This changes the idle airflow and thus regulates idle speed.

Proportional control is another kind of closed-loop control. A proportional control system uses a feedback signal just as a limit-cycle system does. The control electronic devices subtract the feedback signal from the output signal to get an error signal. The controller, or computer, then changes its output signal in proportion to the error signal. If the error signal shows that output is 10 percent higher than it should be, the computer reduces the output by 10 percent.

Engine control computers use proportional closed-loop control for many output signals. For closed-loop fuel control, the error sensor is the exhaust gas oxygen sensor. The sensor signal tells the computer whether the air-fuel mixture passing through the engine is too rich or too lean. (You will learn how it does this later.) The computer can use the signal to read-

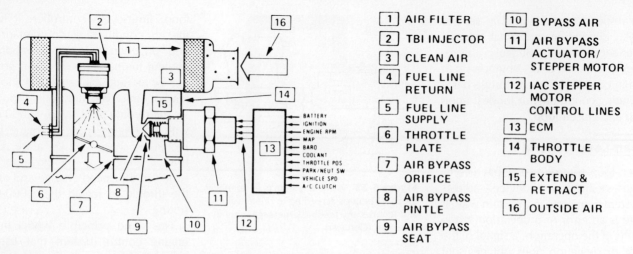

1	AIR FILTER	10	BYPASS AIR
2	TBI INJECTOR	11	AIR BYPASS ACTUATOR/ STEPPER MOTOR
3	CLEAN AIR		
4	FUEL LINE RETURN	12	IAC STEPPER MOTOR CONTROL LINES
5	FUEL LINE SUPPLY	13	ECM
6	THROTTLE PLATE	14	THROTTLE BODY
7	AIR BYPASS ORIFICE	15	EXTEND & RETRACT
8	AIR BYPASS PINTLE	16	OUTSIDE AIR
9	AIR BYPASS SEAT		

Figure 5-35. The computer (ECM) adjusts the idle air control (IAC) stepper motor to control airflow and idle speed. (Chevrolet)

just fuel metering, or it can ignore the signal. When it ignores the signal, the computer is operating the fuel system in open loop. When the computer responds to the signal, it is exercising proportional closed-loop control. If the oxygen sensor says the mixture is too lean, the computer adjusts the variable fuel actuator to enrich the mixture. If the computer calculates that the mixture is 10 percent too lean, it enriches the mixture by 10 percent, figure 5-36.

Fuel metering is not the only proportional closed-loop function performed by an engine computer. Many systems have knock sensors to detect detonation (pinging). Spark timing is a major factor that affects detonation. When the knock sensor detects detonation, it sends a signal to the computer, which then retards timing until detonation stops. That's another kind of proportional output control.

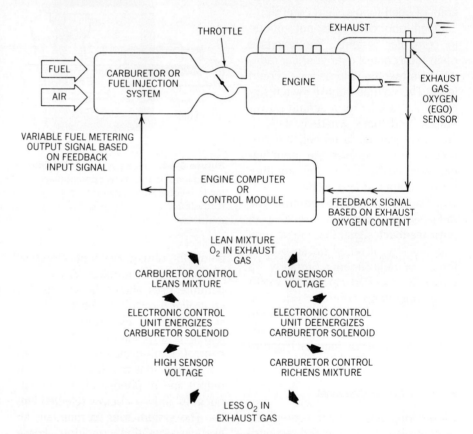

Figure 5-36. In closed-loop operation, the computer responds to the output error feedback signal and readjusts the input.

SUMMARY

Every computer—large mainframe or small microcomputer—works on the four principal functions of input, processing, storage, and output. Personal microcomputers and automotive on-board computers use the same digital microprocessors for their operation.

Computers, as well as input and output devices, can operate on analog or digital signals. An analog signal is infinitely variable. A digital signal, or processing operation, varies in discrete on-off or high-low increments. Most variable measurements on an automobile produce analog signals, but computers change these to digital signals for processing.

Most automotive computer systems are digital systems. These systems convert measurements to binary numbers (combinations of 0's and 1's) that are represented by on-off or high-low voltage signals. These voltage signals are switching pulses for thousands of transistor logic gates. The basic NOT, AND, and OR logic gates are the building blocks of all digital computers.

Computer programs are the instructions, in numerical form, that a computer follows to do its job. Programs are part of computer software. The physical structure of any computer is the hardware. Computer hardware consists of the central processing unit (CPU) and other circuit devices for computer memory, input and output signals, and signal conversion.

Computer programs are stored in ROM and RAM. ROM is permanent stored memory; RAM can be changed and is not permanent. Adaptive learning strategies allow the computer program to alter its program and accommodate small deviations from the norm caused by engine wear, poor fuel quality, sensor values that have shifted, and other factors.

When more than one onboard computer is used on a vehicle, a body computer module (BCM) may be used as a master computer. It receives input data from the other computers and sends output data back.

Automotive computers are used in instrumentation and control systems. An instrumentation system measures some variable quantities and displays its output information to the driver. A control system regulates the operation of another system.

A control system can operate in open-loop or closed-loop modes. In an open-loop mode, the system does not respond to an output feedback, or error, signal. In a closed-loop mode, the computer responds to a feedback error signal and readjusts the output to a selected value. Closed-loop operation can provide limit-cycle control or proportional control.

Although the computer and its microprocessor are the heart of an onboard computer system, the system cannot operate without its sensors and actuators (input and output devices). These are the subjects of the next chapter.

REVIEW QUESTIONS

Multiple Choice

1. The operating program for a specific engine and vehicle is stored in the computer:

a. random access memory (RAM)

b. programmable read-only memory (PROM)

c. keep-alive memory (KAM)

d. relay logic

2. Student A says that an engine computer receives input information, processes data, stores data, and sends output information. Student B says that late-model engine computers are based on digital microprocessors. Who is right?

a. A only

b. B only

c. both A and B

d. neither A nor B

3. Student A says that the computer can read but not change the information stored in RAM. Student B says that the computer can read and change the information stored in ROM. Who is right?

a. A only

b. B only

c. both A and B

d. neither A nor B

4. A digital computer uses the binary number system. This consists of:

a. 2 numbers

b. 4 numbers

c. 6 numbers

d. 8 numbers

5. Student A says that digital computer switching circuits are called NOT, AND, and OR gates. Student B says that NOT gates can be added to AND gates and OR gates to create NAND and NOR gates. Who is right?

a. A only

b. B only

c. both A and B

d. neither A nor B

6. Engine mapping is used by automotive engineers to:

a. increase horsepower and torque

b. produce a 3-dimensional performance graph

c. provide more space in the engine compartment

d. all of these

7. Student A says that onboard computers work with binary numbers. Student B says that onboard computers work with voltage signals. Who is right?

a. A only

b. B only

c. both A and B

d. neither A nor B

8. The microprocessor can do all of the following except:

  a. ignore its system strategy under specified conditions

  b. respond in two or more ways to the same input signal

  c. receive and accept an input signal from other computers

  d. ignore input from its sensors under specified conditions

9. Student A says that a digital signal is either on or off. Student B says that an analog signal changes proportionally to the quantity measured. Who is right?

  a. A only

  b. B only

  c. both A and B

  d. neither A nor B

10. Student A says that a volatile RAM will retain its information even when power is removed. Student B says that a nonvolatile RAM will be erased when power is removed. Who is right?

  a. A only

  b. B only

  c. both A and B

  d. neither A nor B

11. Student A says that the microprocessors used in onboard automotive computers are the same as those used in personal minicomputers. Student B says that a minicomputer is "a computer in a box." Who is right?

  a. A only

  b. B only

  c. both A and B

  d. neither A nor B

12. Student A says that a transistor working as a relay is the basis for a digital computer. Student B says that a transistor working as an amplifier is the basis for an analog computer. Who is right?

  a. A only

  b. B only

  c. both A and B

  d. neither A nor B

13. Digital computers convert analog input signals from sensors to digital bits through:

  a. a DA circuit

  b. an AD circuit

  c. a MOSFET transistor

  d. binary numbers

14. Student A says that an onboard computer can act as an instrumentation system. Student B says that an onboard computer can act as a control system. Who is right?

  a. A only

  b. B only

  c. both A and B

  d. neither A nor B

15. Student A says that when the computer ignores the EGO sensor signal, it is exercising limit-cycle control. Student B says that when the computer responds to the EGO sensor, it is exercising proportional closed-loop control. Who is right?

  a. A only

  b. B only

  c. both A and B

  d. neither A nor B

16. Student A says that computers send and receive digital signals through data links. Student B says that computer speed is a function of MHz, baud rate, and processor bit size. Who is right?

  a. A only

  b. B only

  c. both A and B

  d. neither A nor B

17. Computers distinguish the length of each voltage pulse representing a bit by watching a:

  a. clock

  b. data link

  c. serial bus

  d. nonvolatile memory

18. Student A says that RAM is used for permanent storage because it can be written into. Student B says that a volatile RAM retains its information when power is removed. Who is right?

  a. A only

  b. B only

  c. both A and B

  d. neither A nor B

Fill in the Blank

19. A digital computer processes information in binary digits called _____ .

20. An AD converter circuit changes _____ signals into _____ signals.

21. An input or output signal that is either high-low or on-off is a _____ signal.

22. The engineering process of measuring the best combinations of timing, air-fuel ratio, and other variables for various operating conditions is called _____ .

23. The two basic operating modes for all late-model engine control systems are _____ and _____ .

24. In closed-loop operation, the computer receives an output error, or _____ signal from the EGO sensor.

25. The _____ in a computer keeps all the components going at the same pace and tells the microprocessor the length of one bit.

26. A signal whose value constantly varies is called (a/an) _____ signal.

27. The instructions used by a computer are called its _____ .

28. Sensor voltage signals may have to be _____ before being digitized by the converter circuit.

29. _____ serial data transmission permits 2-way communication between computers by using a data link and clock line.

30. When each component of the data is sent over its own line at the same time, the computer is using _____ transmission.

6 INTRODUCTION TO SENSORS, ACTUATORS, AND DISPLAYS

WHAT

Input and output are two of the four basic computer system functions. The computer processing and storage circuits can do nothing without an input signal from a sensor or without sending an output to an actuator or display device. Input and output signals connect the computer system to another system being controlled or monitored. Chapter 5 summarized the operation of computer instrumentation and control systems. This chapter examines the design and function of common sensors, actuators, and display devices.

WHY

A single computer system can have a dozen or more input and output devices. If any one does not send a correct input signal or respond properly to an output signal, the entire system can malfunction. Most of your electronic service work will deal with the system sensors, actuators, and display devices.

The operating principles and design technology of input and output devices are based on the electrical and electronic principles you have already learned. Sensors used in different systems have many common features. The same is true of actuators and displays. If you understand the general way in which a specific sensor, actuator, or display works and the operating condition that it measures or controls, you can test it quickly and accurately. Therefore, it is a good idea to examine the principles of sensors, actuators, and display devices before working with them in individual systems.

GOALS

After studying this chapter, you should be able to:

1. Explain what a transducer does.

2. List five of the seven variable conditions and quantities sensed by an automotive sensor and give an example of a correct sensor to be used for each condition or quantity.

3. List and explain the four major characteristics required of an automotive sensor.

4. Explain the difference between a generating and nongenerating sensor.

5. Identify five different types of resistive sensors and explain their use in an automotive control system.

6. Explain how solenoids, relays, and stepper motors are used as actuators.

7. Differentiate between light-emitting diodes (LED's), liquid crystal displays (LCD's), and vacuum fluorescent displays (VFD's) used in instrument control displays.

TRANSDUCERS

All sensors and actuators are **transducers**. A transducer is any device that converts (transduces) one form of energy to another. Sensors transduce motion, temperature, light, and other kinds of energy to electrical energy in the form of voltage signals. Actuators transduce electrical energy (voltage and current) into mechanical work. Some carmakers refer to specific sensors as transducers, such as a throttle position transducer. This particular kind of transducer senses the position of an engine throttle and produces a corresponding input signal to a computer.

We can also classify display devices in the broad category of transducers. An instrument panel gauge converts an electrical signal to mechanical work as the analog movement of a needle across a dial. A digital instrument transduces electrical energy to light energy in an illuminated display. Whether a sensor, an actuator, or a display device is called a transducer or not, each one performs the function of a transducer—which allows them to produce computer input signals or put output signals to work.

Transducer functions are not limited to electrical and electronic devices. Automotive systems also use many mechanical transducers. A simple vacuum diaphragm on an ignition distributor, figure 6-1, is a mechanical transducer. It transduces air-pressure fluctuations on a movable diaphragm into mechanical work to move a breaker plate and advance or retard ignition timing. Similar vacuum transducers use air-pressure signals to

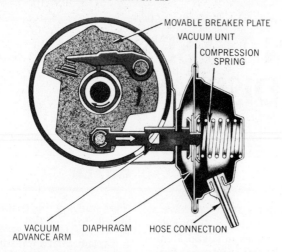

Figure 6-1. A distributor vacuum advance diaphragm changes air pressure fluctuations into mechanical work, moving a breaker plate to advance or retard ignition timing. (Chrysler) (Bosch)

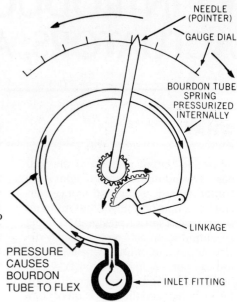

Figure 6-2. A direct reading pressure gauge changes pressure to move a needle around a dial.

open and close air conditioning doors and to increase the force applied to a brake master cylinder. Many exhaust gas recirculation (EGR) systems have similar diaphragm-type transducers to control EGR flow. A direct reading pressure gauge, figure 6-2, transduces pneumatic or hydraulic pressure to the movement of a needle around a dial.

It's helpful to compare the operation of mechanical and electrical or electronic transducers to recognize common purposes. Many sensors and actuators on modern automotive computer systems do the same jobs that mechanical transducers did on earlier vehicles. If you recognize the input and output signals or functions with which a system operates and the system's overall purpose, you can understand the similarities between electrical, electronic, and mechanical sensors and actuators.

Also, many automotive computer systems use combinations of electrical and electronic sensors and actuators and mechanical transducers to achieve their goals. Electrical solenoids and vacuum diaphragms often are combined to produce a required analog output action. Some sensors are solid-state electronic devices, but many are electromechanical trans-

ducers that use a mechanical transducer to produce an electrical signal.

SENSORS

Because a computer can only read voltage signals, an automotive sensor must convert motion, pressure, temperature, light, and other energy to voltage. Automotive sensors are switches, timers, resistors, transformers, and generators, figure 6-3. They can send either analog or digital signals. The computer converts analog signals to digital form for processing. It may also have to amplify certain voltage signals before converting them. Automotive sensors send their input signals to the computer in one of the following ways:

1. *By generating a voltage*—Only a generator sensor can produce a signal voltage on its own. Various means are used to create the voltage signal, depending upon the type of sensor involved. Some sensors use a specific type of quartz crystal (piezoelectric sensor). Others use electrically conductive materials, such as zirconium dioxide, or operate on electromagnetic principles. Generator sensors are explained in more detail later in this chapter.

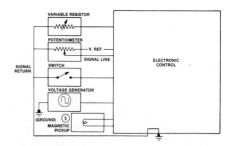

Figure 6-3. Various types of sensors are used in an automotive control system. (Ford)

2. *By modifying a reference voltage*—Most automotive sensors are switches, resistors, and transformers. These sensors cannot generate a voltage; they can only modify a voltage applied to them. Therefore, switches and resistive sensors must operate with a reference voltage (V_{ref}) from the computer. This is a fixed voltage supplied to the sensor by a voltage regulator within the computer. Most computer control systems operate with a 5-volt reference voltage. Some use a 9-volt reference voltage. In any case, reference voltage must be less than minimum battery voltage to prevent inaccurate sensor signals. The computer sends the reference voltage to the sensor. As the sensor changes, the return voltage is altered and relayed to the input conditioners for conversion, then transmitted to the microprocessor for use.

Physical Qualities and Operating Conditions

The best way to start examining sensors is to look at the physical qualities or operating conditions that they sense. Whether a computer system controls engine operation, instrument panel displays, antilock braking, or any other vehicle operation, its sensors measure some or all of the following variable conditions and qualities:

1. Motion and position
   a. linear (straight line)
   b. angular (rotation)
2. Speed
   a. engine rpm (angular)
   b. vehicle speed (linear)
   c. transmission and driveline speed (angular)
   d. rate of change (acceleration and deceleration of the engine, the vehicle, or the wheels)
3. Physical mass or volume
   a. airflow
   b. fuel flow
   c. exhaust oxygen content
4. Temperature
   a. air
   b. liquid (coolant, oil, and other fluids)
5. Pressure
   a. hydraulic (fuel, oil, refrigerant, and transmission and brake fluid)
   b. pneumatic (barometric pressure, boost pressure, and engine vacuum)
   c. physical pressure (engine detonation or knock)
6. Light
7. Sound or noise

Most of these conditions and quantities are analog variables, but current vehicle computers use digital microprocessors. Some computer programs require only a digital, high-or-low, signal for some of the conditions listed above. Other programs require an analog input signal. Therefore, a system can use either a digital or an analog sensor to monitor many of these variables. The choice of a sensor depends upon the system program and the control or instrumentation requirements.

Sensor Characteristics

Whether a sensor sends a digital or an analog signal, the following characteristics, or operating features, affect the selection of a sensor for a particular system. These features also establish the specifications for troubleshooting and service.

Repeatability. A simple digital sensor must switch from a low to a high signal at a specific point in the range of values that it senses. A temperature switch may close at 160° F. It may open again at 160° or 180° F. The opening and closing switching points are design considerations for the system engineer. Once they are determined, the switch must close and open consistently at the required points. This is the necessary repeatability required of a sensor.

An analog sensor produces a signal that varies in proportion to the quantity or condition being measured. It, too, must deliver a repeatable signal for each increment of change. If an analog temperature sensor must provide a 20-millivolt signal change for each degree of temperature change, it must do so throughout its operating range. Moreover, the signal increments must be repeatable both upwards and downwards.

Accuracy. We expect sensors to be accurate, but accuracy is not a simple matter of right or wrong. All sensor signals have tolerances, or limits, on their accuracy. The degree of accu-

racy also is a design consideration. Once the accuracy requirements are determined, however, the sensor must operate consistently within those tolerances.

A digital temperature switch may close at 160° F, but it need not always switch at exactly 160° F. Its required accuracy may be 160° ± 1° F or 160° ± 10° F. These design tolerances establish the test specifications that are used to check the sensor operation.

Similarly, an analog sensor may provide a signal change of 20 ± 2 millivolts for each 1 degree ± 0.1 degree of temperature change. These tolerances are based on the accuracy requirements of the computer system and also help to determine the test specifications for the sensor.

Operating Range. A digital temperature switch closes at a specific temperature: 160° ± 5° F, for example. It may open again at the same point, or at another point: 180 degrees ± 5° F, for example. Simple throttle position switches that sense idle and wide-open positions operate similarly. So do simple pressure switches. The operating range of a digital sensor is just one or two switching points.

The operating range of an analog sensor is broader. An analog temperature sensor may be required to provide accurate, proportional signals through a range from 0° to 250° F, or from 100° to 300° F. An analog pressure sensor's range may be from 5 to 50 psi, or from 0 to 30 inches of mercury. An analog throttle position sensor may deliver signals that are proportional to throttle positions from 0 degrees to 90 degrees. The operating range is called the **dynamic range** of the sensor, and it is also reflected in test specifications. Outside of the upper and lower limits of the dynamic range, the sensor signal is not proportional to the variable value being measured. Most computers are programmed to ignore a signal outside of the dynamic range.

Linearity. Within the dynamic range, an analog sensor signal must be as consistently proportional to the measured value as possible. This is an expression of signal **linearity**. Linearity is an expression of sensor accuracy throughout its dynamic range. If a temperature sensor signal varies in 20-millivolt increments for each 1 degree of temperature change, it should do so ideally from the lower to the upper limits of its dynamic range. A perfect linearity signal curve is a straight diagonal line, figure 6-4.

In practice, no sensor has perfect linearity. The signal curve of a typical sensor is S shaped, figure 6-5, varying more or less from a perfectly linear straight line. Linearity is usually most accurate near the center of the dynamic range. Computer programs often contain memory data to compensate for nonlinear signals in a sensor's range. Signal processing circuits adjust the input signal to give the computer a true indication of the variable measured by the sensor.

Other Sensor Features. Repeatability, accuracy, operating range, and linearity are the requirements that define sensor design. They also are features that will help you recognize different kinds of sensors and test their operation.

All automotive sensors are built for long-term, reliable operation in a harsh environment. They must provide reliable signals in extremes of temperature, vibration, and dirt. Simplicity aids reliability, and thus many sensors are simple, general-purpose items. The same pressure sensor, for example, may be used in a throttle-body fuel injection system and in a multiport injection system. A single common temperature sensor may also have different uses in different systems.

Sensors provide low-voltage, low-current signals. Low-power operation means that they do not put a large load on the vehicle's electrical system, but it also makes them susceptible to electromagnetic interference

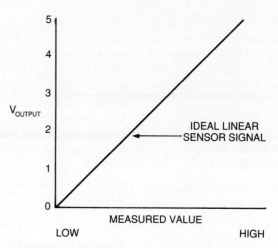

Figure 6-4. A perfectly linear sensor signal represents a straight line, with output voltage proportional to the changes in the measured value.

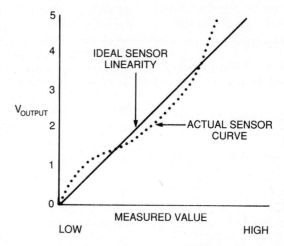

Figure 6-5. Actual linearity of a sensor varies from the ideal proportional signal.

(EMI). Therefore, sensor design and installation often include EMI suppression and shielding devices. Wiring location and low-resistance connections are critical for proper sensor signal transmission. All of these sensor characteristics are important points for correct testing and service. With these facts in mind, we can continue with an examination of specific sensor types.

Switches and Timers

A switch is the simplest digital sensor. A switch opens or closes a circuit and delivers a high or a low voltage signal, figure 6-6. One switch terminal receives input voltage from the electri-

cal system, often through the computer. The other terminal returns a high-voltage signal when the switch closes and a low-voltage signal when it opens. The computer can respond to either a high or low signal, or both, depending upon its program.

Switches. All switches are mechanical devices, but they can be operated by mechanical linkage or contacts, by pressure, or by temperature. A simple throttle-position switch, figure 6-7, is closed by linkage or by a contact stop when the throttle is closed at idle or wide open, or both.

Pressure switches, figure 6-8, sense hydraulic or pneumatic pressure. Engine oil pressure switches and trans-

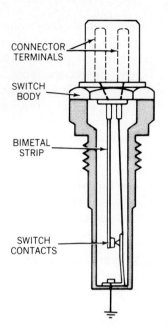

Figure 6-6. When this temperature switch closes a ground connection, signal voltage is high. When it opens the circuit, voltage is low.

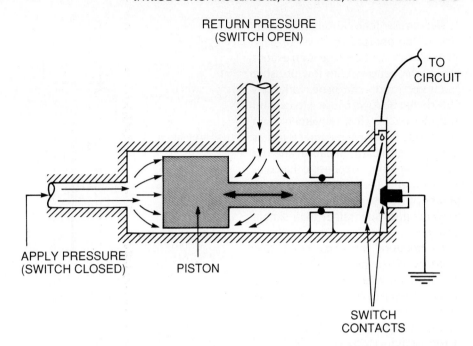

Figure 6-8. This hydraulic pressure switch is similar to one that you might find in a transmission. Applying pressure from fluid in one direction moves the piston to close the switch contacts. Return pressure moves the piston in the other direction, and the spring-loaded switch contacts open.

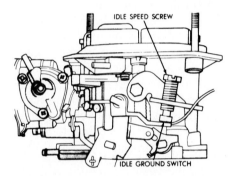

Figure 6-7. This throttle position (idle ground) switch sends a simple on-off signal to the computer. (Chrysler)

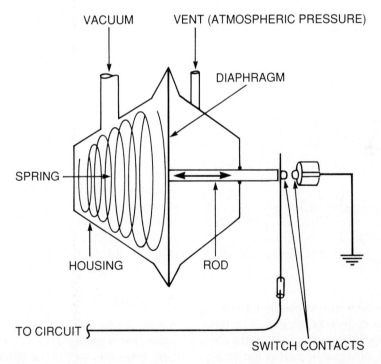

Figure 6-9. The combination of atmospheric pressure and vacuum (low pressure) move the diaphragm against spring pressure to open the switch contacts. When vacuum is cut off, spring pressure moves the diaphragm to close the switch.

mission pressure switches are older than computers, but many are used with modern electronic control systems. Fluid pressure acting on a movable piston or diaphragm causes the switch contacts to open and close. Most air conditioning systems have similar switches to sense high and low refrigerant pressure. Simple pneumatic pressure switches also have movable diaphragms that open and close the switch contacts, figure 6-9. The diaphragm can be actuated by positive air pressure or by negative pressure (vacuum).

Pressure switches also can be actuated by an **aneroid** bellows, or capsule. The aneroid capsule is an evacuated metal bellows with low pressure (vacuum) inside. Pressure variations outside the bellows cause it to expand and contract. This movement can open and close switch contacts just as a diaphragm can. Because aneroid capsules are more expensive than diaphragms and their movements more precise, their use is generally reserved for analog sensors rather than simple switches.

Temperature switches open and close as temperature rises and falls past a specified switching point. The simplest temperature switch is a **bimetal** element that forms part of the circuit conductor. The element is made of two strips of metal joined together, figure 6-6. Each metal strip expands and contracts at a different rate when exposed to changing temperature. These different expansion rates cause the bimetal element to bend as it heats and cools. Most bimetal switches are closed when cold. As surrounding temperature heats the element, it bends to open the switch contacts. The switch closes again when the element cools and bends back.

Bimetal switches also can be heated by current flowing through the element. Because most computer system sensors are low-power devices, however, current for an electrically heated bimetal switch usually is provided by a separate circuit. This leads to the design of a common timer, or timed switch.

Timers. A timer combined with a switch can delay a signal. The timer can be electronic circuitry in the computer, or it can be part of the switch. Many switch and timer combinations are thermo-time switches, as used with Bosch gasoline fuel injection systems, figure 6-10. The switch delivers the signal that controls the cold-start injector. Closing the switch depends on temperature from the engine or from current passing through the

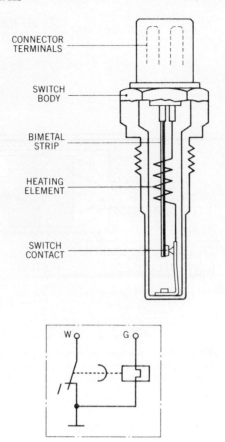

CONNECTOR TERMINALS

SWITCH BODY

BIMETAL STRIP

HEATING ELEMENT

SWITCH CONTACT

W   G

Figure 6-10. This thermo-time switch limits the operating time of the cold-start injector according to engine temperature. (Bosch)

switch. When the engine is cold, current passes through the heating winding. After a specified time, the current heats the bimetal thermostat and opens the circuit to turn off the cold-start injector.

Resistors

A resistor can send an analog voltage signal that is proportional to temperature, pressure, motion, or other variables. A resistor, like a switch, cannot generate a voltage. It can only modify a voltage applied to it. Therefore, automotive resistive sensors operate with a reference voltage from the computer.

Chapter 3 introduced two kinds of variable resistors that are used as sensors: rheostats and potentiometers. These typically are used to sense motion, position, and pressure. Of the two, potentiometers are more common as computer input sensors. A potentiometer changes mechanical motion to a voltage signal and often is used to indicate the position of a specific component, such as a valve. Thermistors, piezoresistive strain gauges, and hot-wire or hot-film sensors are other resistive sensors used to measure temperature and pressure.

Potentiometers. A potentiometer is a variable resistor with three terminals. Reference voltage is applied to one end of the resistor, and the other end is grounded, figure 6-11. The third terminal is connected to a movable wiper or contact that slides across the resistor. Depending on whether the contact is near the supply end or the ground end of the resistor, return voltage will be high or low. Constant current through the resistor maintains constant temperature. Therefore, resistance does not change due to temperature variations. This ensures a constant voltage drop across the resistance so that return voltage changes only in relation to sliding contact movement.

Rheostats. A rheostat is a 2-terminal variable resistor. Reference voltage is applied to a fixed terminal at one end of the resistor. The other terminal is connected to a movable contact and provides the return voltage signal, figure 6-12. Voltage drop across the resistor varies with the position of the movable contact. Resistor temperature also varies because current flows through varying amounts of resistance as the contact moves. Therefore, the return voltage signal is not as consistent as that of a potentiometer. Nevertheless, rheostats are used as system sensors where the repeatability of the signal is not extremely critical. Rheostats require fewer circuit connections and are simpler to build.

The movable contact of a potenti-

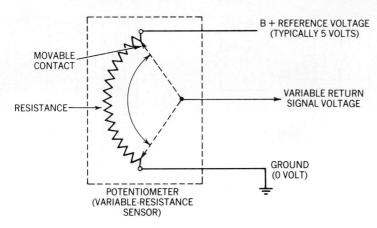

Figure 6-11. A potentiometer is a variable resistor with three terminals. Signal voltage is taken from the movable contact.

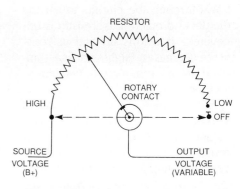

Figure 6-12. A rheostat is a 2-wire variable resistor. Rheostats were often used in older heater motor controls.

ometer or a rheostat can move in a straight line or in an arc. Thus, these devices can sense linear motion and position or rotary motion and angular position. Coupled to a movable diaphragm or other mechanical transducer, they also can sense pressure variations.

A rheostat is sensitive to the current in a circuit. A potentiometer delivers a governed voltage to another resistance in a circuit (the computer).

Thermistors. A **thermistor** is a solid-state variable resistor with two connector terminals, figure 6-13. The resistance of any resistor changes as temperature changes, but the resistance variations throughout the operating range of a thermistor make it very accurate as an analog temperature sensor.

Thermistors are divided into two groups: **positive temperature coefficient (PTC) resistors** and **negative temperature coefficient (NTC) resistors**. These names simply mean that:

• The resistance of a PTC thermistor increases as temperature increases.

• The resistance of an NTC thermistor decreases as temperature increases.

Figure 6-14 shows the operating characteristics of PTC and NTC thermistors. Both kinds are used in automotive systems, but the NTC thermistor is more common. Heat can come from

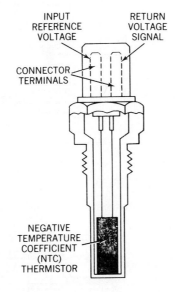

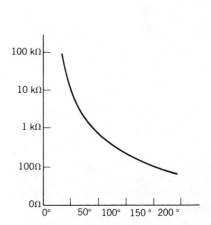

Figure 6-13. The graph shows that the resistance of a thermistor decreases as temperature increases. (Bosch)

an external source or from current through the resistor. Self-heated PTC thermistors can be used as current limiters and timers in electronic systems. Externally heated NTC thermistors are the most common analog sensors for engine coolant temperature and intake air temperature.

NTC thermistors can also be used in indicator circuits, figure 6-15. In this case, the thermistor controls voltage applied to a low-fuel warning lamp. When fuel covers the thermistor in the tank, its temperature is low and its

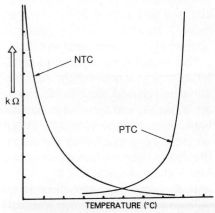

Figure 6-14. Temperature characteristics of PTC and NTC thermistors. (Toyota)

resistance is high. Voltage applied to the lamp is low, and little current flows through the circuit. When the fuel level drops, the thermistor is uncovered. It warms up and its resistance decreases. Higher voltage is applied to the lamp, more current flows, and the lamp lights.

NTC thermistor sensors are made of semiconductor material with high resistance at low temperature and low resistance at high temperature. The computer applies the reference voltage to one thermistor terminal and takes the return voltage from the other, figure 6-13. As the thermistor warms up, return voltage increases.

Piezoresistive Sensors. In chapter 2 you learned that a piezoelectric crystal develops voltage across its surfaces when pressure is applied to it. Similar crystals change their resistance when pressure is applied to them. This feature makes piezoresistive sensors excellent devices for analog pressure measurement.

A typical piezoresistive sensor is made of a small silicon diaphragm sealed to a quartz plate, figure 6-16. The chamber in the middle is evacuated to create a vacuum. Four resistors are formed around the edge of the diaphragm by doping the silicon. Pressure applied to the diaphragm causes it to deflect, which changes the resistance of the resistors. The resistors are connected to an external circuit in a **Wheatstone bridge** arrangement. A constant reference voltage is applied to the sensor input terminal.

This bridge circuit is a series-parallel arrangement between the input terminal and ground. Resistors R_1 and R_2 are in series, and they are in parallel with series resistors R_3 and R_4. When no pressure is applied to the sensor diaphragm, the resistances are equal. The voltage drops across R_1, R_2, R_3, and R_4 are equal; and there is no voltage difference between terminals A and B, which are the output connections. The bridge circuit is balanced.

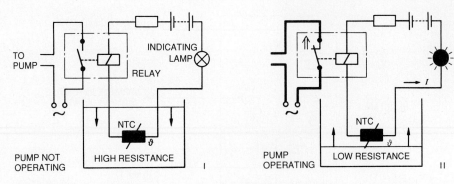

Figure 6-15. The application of an NTC thermistor in an indicator circuit. (Bosch)

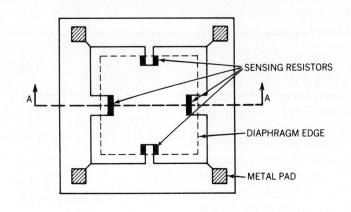

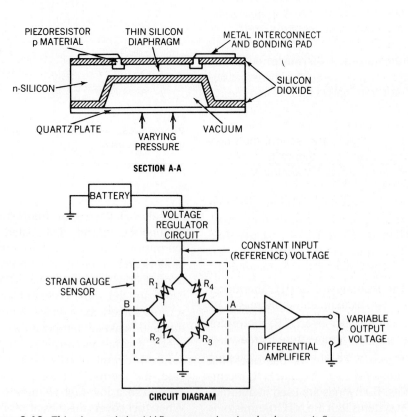

Figure 6-16. This piezoresistive MAP sensor varies signal voltage as it flexes.

When pressure on the sensor changes, it causes the resistances to change proportionally to the pressure on the diaphragm. R_1 and R_3 increase, and R_2 and R_4 decrease. This unbalances the bridge circuit and creates a voltage difference between terminals A and B. This is the sensor output voltage, which is also proportional to the pressure applied to the silicon diaphragm.

Piezoresistive sensors are commonly used to measure engine intake manifold absolute pressure (MAP). They can also be used as mechanical strain gauges to measure physical force.

Magnetoresistive Sensors. Some magnetic materials change their resistance in a rotating magnetic field. Magnetoresistors can be connected in a bridge circuit similar to the piezoresistors in figure 6-16. The computer supplies the constant reference voltage. A rotating magnetic field changes the resistance of the resistors and unbalances the bridge circuit. This produces a variable output voltage proportional to the rate of change of the magnetic field.

Heated Resistive Sensors. The application of electric current to a platinum wire or metal-foil sensing screen as part of a bridge circuit can be controlled by the computer to maintain the wire at a constant temperature regardless of the ambient air temperature. The current required to maintain the wire or screen temperature is then changed into a voltage signal at a resistor.

This type of sensor is most useful in measuring mass airflow and is found in some fuel injection systems, figure 6-17. Air flowing past the hot wire or screen tends to cool it, according to the temperature and velocity of the airflow. As this occurs, the computer applies more current to maintain the wire at a constant temperature. The amount of current required to maintain the wire temperature is inter-

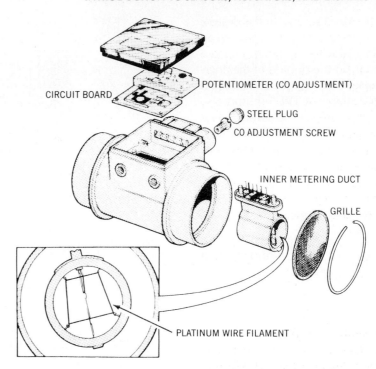

Figure 6-17. This hot-wire air mass sensor is used on Bosch LH-Jetronic EFI systems. (Volvo)

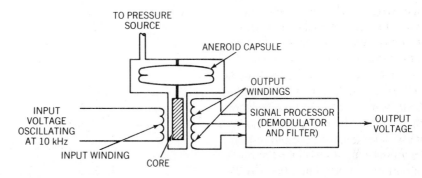

Figure 6-18. This MAP sensor is a transformer that creates a voltage differential between two output windings.

preted by the computer as the amount of air mass taken into the engine.

Transformers. Like resistors, transformer sensors send an analog return signal to the computer in response to a reference voltage. The transformer is a set of induction coils with a movable core, figure 6-18. This kind of device is called a **linear variable differential transformer (LVDT) sensor**. The electromagnetic coupling between the input and output windings varies with core position. An oscillating reference

voltage (usually 10 kHz) is applied to the input winding. Two output windings are balanced so that output voltage of each is the same with the core in the center position. When the core moves, the output voltage of one winding exceeds that of the other winding. The two output winding voltages are processed to produce a single sensor signal voltage that is proportional to amount and direction of movement.

This kind of transformer sensor is used as one type of manifold absolute pressure (MAP) sensor. In this design, core movement is controlled by an aneroid bellows or capsule. Pressure variations on the outside of the aneroid cause it to expand and contract and move the core. LVDT sensors also have been used to measure linear movement, such as throttle position. In these designs, the core is moved by mechanical linkage.

Voltage Generators

Every sensor we have seen thus far sends an input signal in response to a reference voltage. A few sensors, however, can generate a signal voltage. When you study electronic ignitions in chapter 12, you will learn about distributor pulse generators. These use a rotating trigger wheel to vary the reluctance around a magnetic pole piece and pickup coil, figure 6-19. Some carmakers call them **reluctance sensors**. Engine computers can use these signals as a reference for basic timing. Signal frequency also indicates engine speed.

Pulse generators also can be used to indicate crankshaft position, engine speed, and firing order. Some systems use a pulse generator or reluctance sensor in the engine block to respond to a tooth or a cutout on the harmonic balancer or the flywheel, figure 6-20. Bosch, Ford EEC-I & II, and GM distributorless ignition systems use these sensors. Some engines have two separate sensors of this kind to indicate crankshaft speed and position. Other systems use a Hall-effect switch in the distributor, figure 6-21, to indicate crankshaft position and basic timing.

Exhaust Gas Oxygen Sensor

The exhaust gas oxygen (EGO) sensor is a unique voltage generator of zirconium dioxide that measures exhaust oxygen content. It generates analog signals from 0 to 1 volt by comparing the difference between oxygen in the exhaust and oxygen in the ambient air.

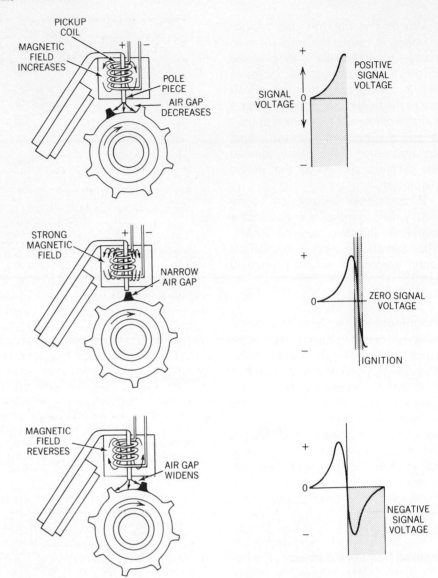

Figure 6-19. The rotating trigger wheel varies the reluctance around a pole piece and pickup coil to generate voltage.

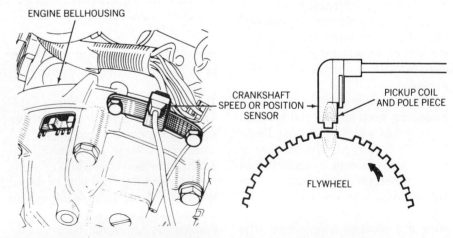

Figure 6-20. Some GM, Ford, Renault, and other Bosch systems use crankshaft position sensors in the engine block. (AMC-Renault)

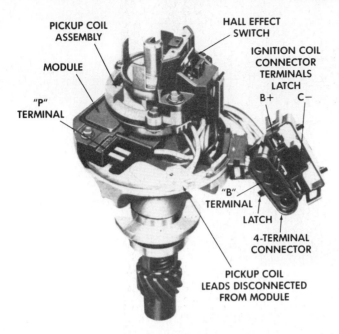

PICKUP COIL
ASSEMBLY

HALL EFFECT
SWITCH

MODULE

IGNITION COIL
CONNECTOR
TERMINALS
LATCH
B+   C−

"P"
TERMINAL

"B"
TERMINAL

LATCH

4-TERMINAL
CONNECTOR

PICKUP COIL
LEADS DISCONNECTED
FROM MODULE

Figure 6-21. This Hall-effect switch in a Delco HEI distributor indicates crankshaft position and basic timing. (Delco-Remy)

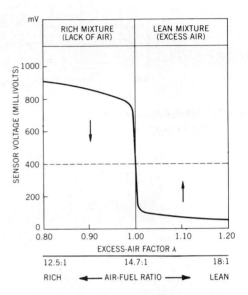

Figure 6-22. Lambda (EGO) sensor voltage at 800° C (1,472° F). (Bosch)

HOW SENSITIVE ARE PRESSURE SENSORS?

One of the first electronic pressure sensors for automotive use was designed by Delco Electronics in 1976. Delco made more than 32 million manifold absolute pressure (MAP) and barometric or BMAP sensors for automobiles in the decade following that first one. Today's MAP and BMAP sensors continue to shrink in size while increasing in sensitivity. Today's sensor uses a silicon membrane only 0.001 inch thick, (see photo). That's pretty thin for a piece of silicon strong enough to survive both the corrosive gases and extreme heat found in an engine compartment, yet sensitive enough to tell whether it's mounted right side up or upside down. The next generation of MAP sensors is right around the corner and will combine the sensor with its signal circuitry on a single silicon membrane.

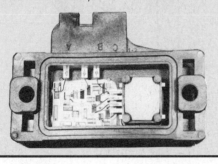

The EGO sensor is based on the **lambda** concept. Lambda is the Greek symbol engineers use to indicate the ratio of one number to another. For air-fuel control, lambda indicates the ratio of excess air to stoichiometric air quantity. That's why Bosch calls EGO sensors lambda sensors.

At an air-fuel ratio of 14.7:1, as much air as possible combines with fuel. There is no excess air, and there is no shortage of air. Lambda, there-fore, equals 1. With a lean mixture ratio of 15, 16, or 17:1, there is excess air left after combustion. The lambda ratio of excess air to desired air is greater than 1. It may be 1.03, 1.07, 1.15, or some other number. With a rich mixture of 12, 13, or 14:1, there is a shortage of air and the lambda ratio is less than 1. It may be 0.97, 0.93, 0.89, etc. With lambda (excess air) ratios less than 0.8 or greater than 1.20, the engine will not run. These roughly equal air-fuel ratios of 11.7:1 and 18:1.

The EGO sensor works as a **galvanic battery** to generate voltage up to about 1 volt. Its effective signal range is from about 0.1 to 0.9 volt (100 to 900 millivolts). When exhaust oxygen content is low (rich mixture), sensor voltage is high (450 to 900 millivolts). When exhaust oxygen content is high (lean mixture), sensor voltage is low (100 to 450 millivolts). Figure 6-22 shows the operating range of the sensor at a temperature of about 800° C (1,472° F). Notice that sensor voltage changes most rapidly near a lambda ratio of 1 (air-fuel ratio of 14.7:1), which makes it ideal for

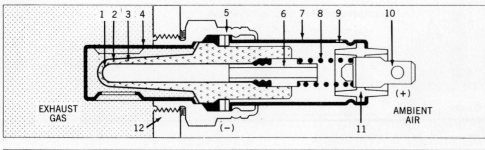

1 ELECTRODE (+)
2 ELECTRODE (−)
3 CERAMIC BODY
4 PROTECTIVE TUBE (EXHAUST—GAS SIDE)
5 HOUSING (−)
6 CONTACT BUSHING
7 PROTECTIVE SLEEVE (AIR SIDE)
8 CONTACT SPRING
9 VENTILATION OPENING
10 ELECTRICAL CONNECTION
11 INSULATING PART
12 EXHAUST PIPE WALL

Figure 6-23. The EGO sensor is installed in the exhaust manifold and is exposed to ambient air as well as to exhaust. (Bosch)

maintaining a stoichiometric ratio. The sensor must warm up to at least 300° C (572° F) before it will generate an accurate signal, and it provides the fastest switching times at about 800° C. That is the major reason for open-loop fuel control with a cold engine.

The EGO sensor is installed in the exhaust manifold or headpipe, figure 6-23, and consists of two platinum electrodes separated by a zirconium dioxide (ZrO_2) ceramic electrolyte. ZrO_2 attracts free oxygen ions, which are negatively charged. One electrode is exposed to ambient (outside) air through vents in the sensor shell, figure 6-24, and collects many O_2 ions. It becoms a more negative electrode. The other electrode is exposed to exhaust gas and also collects O_2 ions. However, it collects fewer ions and becomes more positive. When there is a large difference between oxygen in the exhaust and oxygen in the air (rich mixture), the negative oxygen ions on the outer electrode move to the positive inner electrode. This is simple electric current (electron flow). The sensor then develops a voltage between the two electrodes. When there is more oxygen in the exhaust (lean mixture), there is less difference between O_2 ions on the electrodes and a lower voltage. Figure

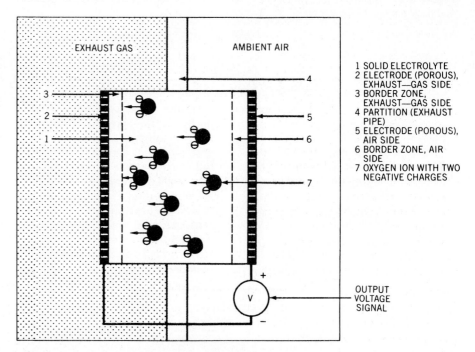

1 SOLID ELECTROLYTE
2 ELECTRODE (POROUS), EXHAUST—GAS SIDE
3 BORDER ZONE, EXHAUST—GAS SIDE
4 PARTITION (EXHAUST PIPE)
5 ELECTRODE (POROUS), AIR SIDE
6 BORDER ZONE, AIR SIDE
7 OXYGEN ION WITH TWO NEGATIVE CHARGES

Figure 6-24. The ZrO_2 ceramic electrolyte attracts O_2 ions to the electrodes and thus generates a voltage. (Bosch)

6-25 summarizes the relationships of engine air-fuel mixture, exhaust oxygen content, sensor voltage, and computer response.

An important point to remember about an EGO sensor is that it measures oxygen; it does not measure air-fuel ratio. If the engine misfires, no oxygen is consumed in combustion. There is a large amount of oxygen in the unburned exhaust mixture, and the sensor will deliver a false "lean mixture" signal. This is one reason why computer control of ignition timing and EGR is essential for effective fuel metering control.

All EGO sensors work on the principles explained above, but construction details differ. Some sensors have a single-wire connector for the output signal. The ground connection exists between the sensor shell and the exhaust manifold or pipe, figure 6-23. Other sensors have a 2-wire connector that provides a ground connection through the computer, figure 6-26. Single-wire and 2-wire sensors are not interchangeable. Figure 6-26 also shows a silicone boot that protects the sensor and provides a vent opening for ambient air circulation. The boot position is important for such a sensor. If it is pushed down too far on the body, it will block the air vent and create an inaccurate signal voltage.

There is a growing trend toward the use of heated EGO sensors. These sensors have a third wire that delivers battery current of 1 ampere or less to the sensor electrodes whenever the ignition switch is on. This current warms the sensor faster with a cold engine and helps to maintain sensor temperature for accurate voltage signals at all times. Heated EGO sensors often are used on turbocharged engines where the sensor is installed downstream from the turbo. The turbo absorbs much of the heat energy in the exhaust, which delays sensor warmup on a cold engine and can cause the sensor to cool during long periods of idling and low-speed operation. A heated EGO sensor overcomes these problems. Some heated EGO sensors have an additional pair of wires to supply heating current to a PTC thermistor in the sensor.

EGO sensors are always installed in the exhaust manifolds or headpipes, but exact locations vary for different engines. Some V-type engines have separate sensors in each manifold, figure 6-27. Other V-type engines have only a single sensor. Sensors are often located low in the engine compartment and access can be difficult. Other sensors are installed in the center of the exhaust manifold and access is easy, figure 6-28. Some Toyota engines have two EGO sensors: one be-

Air-Fuel Mixture	Exhaust Oxygen Content	Oxygen Sensor Voltage	Computer Output Signal	Fuel Metering Change To	Idle Airflow
Rich	Low	High	Decrease Fuel Metering	To Lean	Increase
Lean	High	Low	Increase Fuel Metering	To Rich	Decrease

Figure 6-25. This table shows the relationships of air-fuel mixture, exhaust O_2, sensor voltage, and computer response.

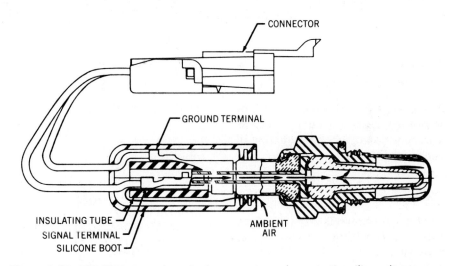

Figure 6-26. This EGO sensor has a 2-wire connector and a protective silicone boot. (AC-Delco)

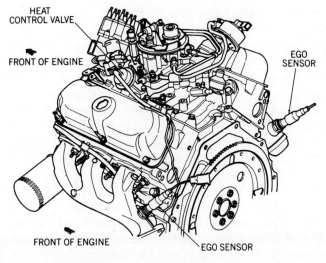

Figure 6-27. Some V-type engines have two EGO sensors, one in each exhaust manifold. (Ford)

Figure 6-28. This EGO sensor is easily accessible in the center of the manifold, at the front of the engine.

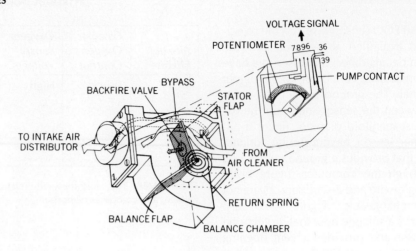

fore and one after the catalytic converter. Engineers determine the best sensor location for accurate O_2 measurement during laboratory testing of each engine design.

Other Sensors

Here is a brief summary of other sensors used in electronic engine control systems.

1. *Airflow sensors*—Airflow sensors are usually analog devices that use a potentiometer to vary a return voltage signal in proportion to airflow volume, figure 6-29. They provide information to regulate fuel flow in relation to airflow as a venturi does in a carburetor.

2. *Manifold pressure, vacuum, and barometric pressure sensors*—These can be load sensors, air volume sensors, or both. Most are analog devices that use a peizoresistive sensor, figure 6-30, or a transformer or potentiometer operated by a vacuum diaphragm or aneroid bellows, figure 6-18. These sensors allow the computer to adjust fuel metering in relation to air volume and engine load. They also allow the computer to simultaneously adjust timing and EGR in relation to load. Remember that vacuum is engine negative pressure; barometric pressure is atmospheric pressure; and

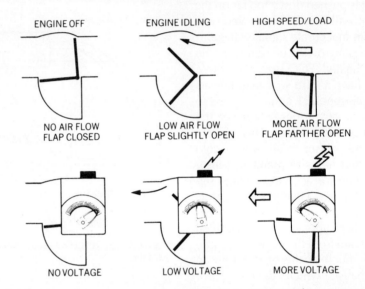

Figure 6-29. This airflow sensor uses a potentiometer to change analog movement into a variable voltage signal. (Volkswagen)

manifold absolute pressure is barometric pressure minus vacuum. A combination of this information allows more precise engine control than manifold vacuum can provide directly.

3. *Temperature sensors*—If a computer only needs to know whether coolant or air temperature is above or below a single point, a simple bimetal switch will do the job, figure 6-6. If a computer needs to know any temperature within a range, a thermistor is necessary, figure 6-13. For fuel metering, coolant and air temperature sensors do the jobs of a carburetor

choke coil and supplement the control of a thermostatic air cleaner. They also allow the computer to fine tune ignition timing and EGR flow.

4. *Throttle position sensors*—A throttle position sensor indicates whether an engine is at idle, wide open throttle, or a point in between. It is both a load and a speed sensor. A throttle position sensor can be a simple wide-open throttle switch or idle position switch, figure 6-31, to indicate the extremes of throttle travel with a high or low voltage. Many systems use potentiometers as throttle sensors, figure 6-32. The throttle moves a slid-

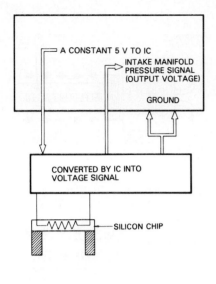

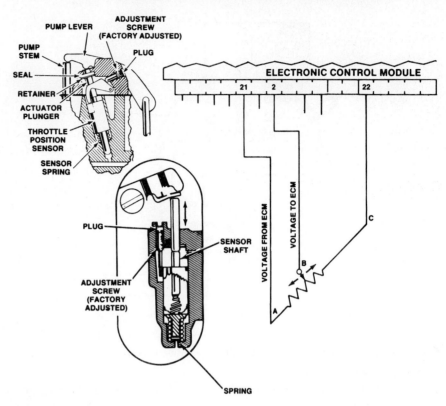

Figure 6-32. This GM throttle position sensor is a potentiometer, mounted in the carburetor fuel bowl. (GM)

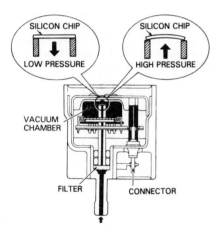

Figure 6-30. Operation of a piezoresistive MAP sensor. (Toyota)

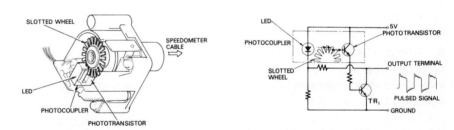

Figure 6-33. This speed sensor uses an LED and a photocell in the speedometer. (Toyota)

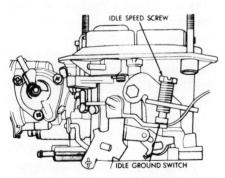

Figure 6-31. A simple wide-open throttle switch or idle position switch indicates the extremes of throttle travel with a high or low voltage. (Chrysler)

ing contact across a resistor to send an analog signal that indicates the position and speed of throttle movement.

5. *Ignition timing, crankshaft position, and engine speed sensors*—We looked at these sensors at the beginning of this section. They send the computer both analog and digital signals to control timing, fuel metering, and EGR.

6. *Vehicle speed sensors*—Some control systems need to know vehicle speed to control torque converter lockup and transmission gear selec-

tion. Speed sensors are usually pulse generators or optical sensors in the speedometer, figure 6-33.

7. *EGR sensors*—Knowing the EGR flow rate at any time is important for controlling timing and fuel metering, as well as EGR valve operation. Many EGR valves have a transducer that consists of a sliding-contact potentiometer on the top of the valve stem, figure 6-34. Through engine mapping, the computer knows that a certain return voltage signal equals a certain valve position, which equals a

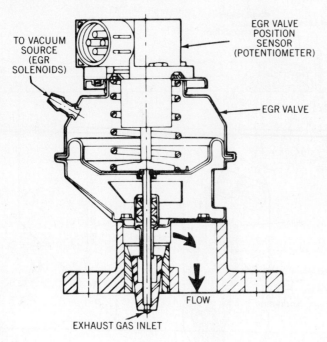

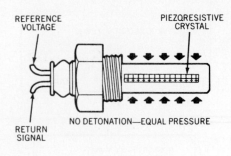

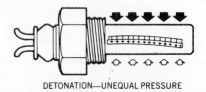

Figure 6-34. This potentiometer senses EGR valve position. (Ford)

Figure 6-35. Detonation (knock) sensors have a piezoresistive crystal that flexes when detonation occurs. (Audi)

specific EGR flow rate. When combined with speed, load, and temperature signals, the computer uses this information to adjust timing, EGR, and fuel metering.

8. *Air conditioning sensors*—Most air conditioning sensors are switches that indicate when the compressor clutch is engaged. The A/C compressor can use 5 to 10 extra horsepower, which increases engine load. When the computer knows that the compressor is engaged, it can adjust timing, fuel flow, idle speed, and other variables to compensate for the extra load.

9. *Detonation sensors*—Most detonation sensors contain a piezoresistive crystal that changes resistance when pressure is applied to it. When detonation does not exist, pressure is uniform across the crystal, figure 6-35. Reference voltage is applied to the sensor and the return signal voltage remains at its programmed value. When detonation occurs, it changes the pressure applied to the sensor crystal. This changes the sensor resistance and, thus, the return signal voltage.

ACTUATORS (CONTROL SYSTEMS)

An actuator is an output device that changes voltage signals to mechanical action. Most engine control actuators are solenoids or relays. Some, however, are stepper motors. As you know:

- A solenoid is an electromechanical device that uses magnetism to move a metal core, thus changing an electrical voltage into mechanical movement.
- A relay uses one electric current to control another electric current.
- A stepper motor is a dc motor that moves in incremental steps from deenergized (no voltage) to fully energized (full voltage).

Solenoids

A computer controls voltage to a solenoid, but it usually does not switch the system voltage. Battery voltage is applied to one solenoid terminal, and the computer opens and closes a

ground switch connected to the other terminal, figure 6-36. Thus, most actuators are grounded through the computer, and a secure computer ground connection is essential for proper system operation. The solenoid can be energized for a random length of time, or it can vibrate on and off at a certain number of cycles per second.

Pulse Width and Pulse Width Modulation. Computer control of solenoid-operated metering devices uses a concept called **pulse width modulation (PWM)**. This is a term you will hear in relation to many solenoid-operated metering devices. If a solenoid, such as a canister purge solenoid or an EGR vacuum solenoid, stays energized indefinitely, we don't concern ourselves with pulse width modulation. The complete operating cycle of any other solenoid-operated metering device is the sequence from on to off to back on again. A device can operate at any number of cycles per second, depending upon its design: 10, 20, 60, and so on.

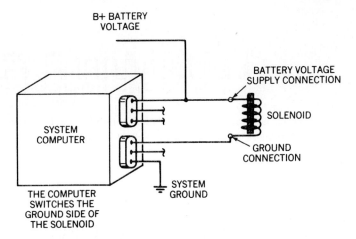

Figure 6-36. Most engine control system solenoids are grounded through the computer so the computer does not have to switch system voltage.

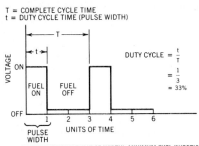

SHORT DUTY CYCLE (PULSE WIDTH), MINIMUM FUEL INJECTION

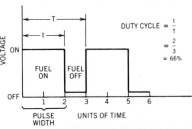

LONG DUTY CYCLE (PULSE WIDTH), MAXIMUM FUEL INJECTION

Figure 6-37. Pulse width is the duration of solenoid on-time. Duty cycle is the percentage of on-time during one complete cycle.

For a fast-acting, on-off solenoid, however, **pulse width** is the amount of time that the device is energized, measured in milliseconds. An electronic injection nozzle used in a fuel injection system provides a good example of pulse width. The computer varies injector pulse width in relation to the amount of fuel a particular engine requires at any given time. A short pulse width delivers little fuel; a longer pulse width delivers more fuel, figure 6-37. The computer modulates, or varies, the pulse width to establish the duty cycle, which will achieve the required solenoid output.

MULTIFUNCTION SENSORS

Wouldn't it be nice if one sensor could do everything? Nice but not likely. How about one type of sensor that can do several different things? Also nice, and quite probable. A piezoelectric level switch has been developed that allows a given sensor to function differently in different fluids. An oscillator drives the piezo element, transferring the mechanical vibrations it creates to the sensor diaphragm, which has an inherent frequency. Submerging the diaphragm in a fluid dampens the sensor, shifting the resonating frequency to a different range. The resonating frequency is transmitted to a control module that uses a sweep generator and resonance discriminator for signal processing. The piezo oscillator frequency is swept between a lower and upper frequency limit. The module circuitry processes the frequency range and amplitude transmitted by the sensor and compares it to a value in memory to determine the level of the fluid being measured. If the fluid level is low, the module circuit activates a display. The illustration shows how several sensors of this type could function with different fluids and a single control unit.

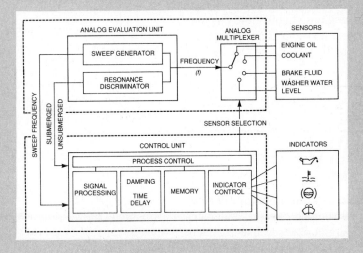

Duty Cycle. The **duty cycle** is the percentage of the complete cycle during which the solenoid is on (energized). Another way to say it is that the duty cycle is the ratio of pulse width to complete cycle width. Pulse width is measured in absolute time; duty cycle is measured as a percentage. A timed voltage pulse from the computer determines the duty cycle. Figure 6-38 shows the relationship of pulse width, variable duty cycle, and fixed cycle time for a feedback carburetor mixture-control solenoid.

Relays. The computer output driver opens and closes the control circuit of a relay on command from the microprocessor. When the control circuit is open, the power circuit stays open and no power is delivered through the relay to the device being controlled, figure 6-39A. When the control circuit is closed, the energized coil generates a magnetic field that causes the relay switch to close. This allows current to flow through the relay, operating the control device, figure 6-39B.

Stepper Motors

Stepper motors are also digital actuators. A typical stepper motor can have 100 to 120 steps of movement from deenergized to fully energized, depending on voltage. Stepper motors are commonly used as idle speed controls. The dc motor generally acts directly on the throttle linkage of carbureted engines, figure 6-40. In fuel injection systems, it usually controls an idle air bypass inside the throttle body.

DISPLAYS (INSTRUMENTATION SYSTEMS)

Electronic displays are found in electronic instrument clusters and electronic readout devices like scanners and other test instruments. Like conventional analog instruments, digital

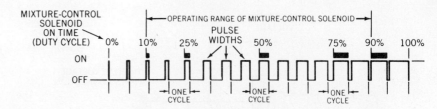

Figure 6-38. Duty cycle is the percentage of solenoid on-time and can be changed to control fuel metering. Total cycle time remains constant, but duty cycle and pulse width can vary. (GM)

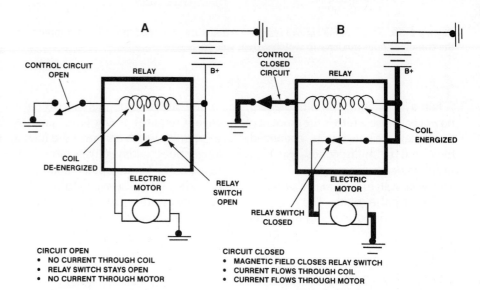

Figure 6-39. A relay used as an actuator is controlled by the computer output driver on command from the microprocessor. (Ford)

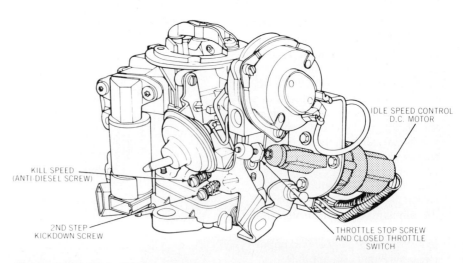

Figure 6-40. Idle speed is controlled by the engine computer through a stepper motor called an idle speed control motor. (Ford)

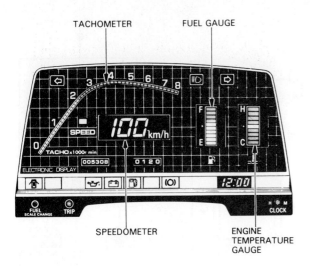

Figure 6-41. A typical digital instrumentation cluster. (Toyota)

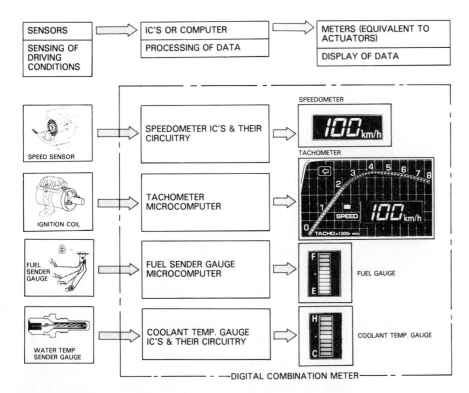

Figure 6-42. The sensors and circuitry involved in displaying information electronically. (Toyota)

displays provide a variety of operating information for the driver. They differ from analog instruments in the way in which the information is displayed. A typical digital instrument cluster is shown in figure 6-41. Individual sensors, computer circuitry, and data display for each display function on the instrument panel are shown in figure 6-42.

Many electronic displays are dimmed in intensity when the headlamp switch is turned on. On such units, the display intensity also can be controlled by the headlamp switch rheostat. On some units, the information can be displayed in either U.S. or metric units by depressing a switch.

There are three major types of displays currently used with electronic instruments. These are described below.

Light-Emitting Diodes (LED's)

As you learned in chapter 4, an LED is a semiconductor diode that will transmit light whenever electric current passes through it. An LED is generally used in one of three ways:

1. As a single indicator light to indicate an on-off status

2. Arranged in a line to form a bar graph, figure 6-43

3. Combined to display an alphabetic or numeric character

When combined, the LED display

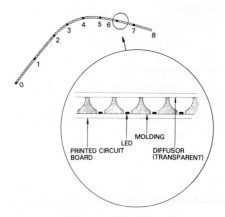

Figure 6-43. Light-emitting diodes can be arranged in linear fashion to create a bar-type graph. (Toyota)

consists of seven segments that will form any letter or number as selected segments are turned on, figure 6-44.

LED's are generally green, yellow, or red. They are easily seen in the dark but are difficult to read in bright sunlight. They also are inefficient compared to other types of displays because they require a large amount of power in relation to their brightness.

Liquid Crystal Displays (LCD's)

A **liquid crystal display (LCD)** consists of electrodes and polarized fluid sandwiched between special glass. Polarized fluid must be used because the random arrangement of its light slots makes the fluid opaque; no light can pass through it when voltage is absent. However, when voltage is applied to the electrodes, it causes a rearrangement of the light slots in the fluid and allows light to be transmitted. The crystal display sandwich is very dense, and the filters placed in front of the display to create various colors increase this density. This requires back lighting from a bright lamp, such as a halogen bulb, to illuminate the display, figure 6-45.

Because an LCD does not need high current to operate, it can be driven by the microprocessor through an interfacing output circuit. However, cold temperatures slow down the rearrangement of the light slots in the fluid, and the driver circuits must be programmed to compensate for this factor. An LCD display consumes very little power in relation to its brightness, but it is also very delicate and must be properly aligned. The LCD display can be very spectacular in its visual effect, as was demonstrated on the 1984 Corvette, but it is the least frequently used type of display.

Vacuum Fluorescent Displays (VFD's)

Durability and the brightness of its display makes the **vacuum fluorescent display (VFD)** the most often

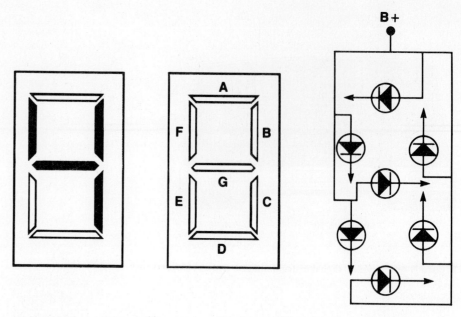

Figure 6-44. An alphanumeric display can be created by selectively applying voltage through 7-segment light-emitting diodes (LED's). (General Motors)

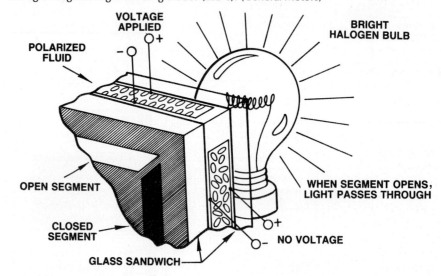

Figure 6-45. A liquid crystal display (LCD) is created by transmitting light through a polarized fluid. (General Motors)

used display. The technology involved dates back to the days of vacuum tubes. The VFD generates light in a manner similar to a television picture tube. Free electrons from a heated filament strike phosphor material and results in a blue-green light, figure 6-46.

The VFD consists of three components: a cathode of tungsten filaments, an anode of alphanumerical segments, and a grid between the anode and cathode, figure 6-47. All are sealed into an evacuated chamber of flat glass, figure 6-48, that is filled with either argon or neon gas. When current passes through the cathode, tungsten electrons literally fly off the wires. Passing a high positive voltage through the anode segments to be illuminated draws the electrons to the anode segments to form the characters to be displayed, figure 6-49. When the positive voltage is turned off, the electrons flow to ground, then return to the filaments to complete the circuit. The fine grid placed between the anode and cathode ensures that the electrons will strike the anode uniformly.

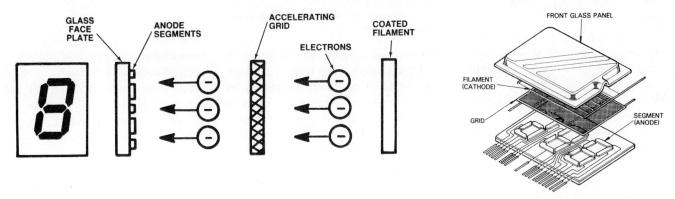

Figure 6-46. Selectively applying voltage to anode segments causes phosphors to glow in a vacuum fluorescent display (VFD). (Chrysler)

Figure 6-47. The major components of a vacuum fluorescent display (VFD). (Toyota)

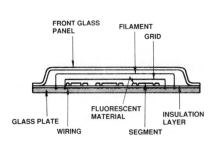

Figure 6-48. The VFD display is sealed, evacuated, and filled with argon or neon gas. (Toyota)

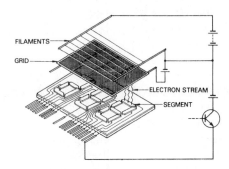

Figure 6-49. Heating the cathode filaments and applying a positive voltage to the anode segments causes electrons to flow through the grid and strike the segments, illuminating the phosphors. (Toyota)

CATHODE RAY TUBES AND MENU-DRIVEN INSTRUMENTATION

The instrumentation display in the 1986 and later Buick Riviera and other late-model luxury automobiles uses a cathode ray tube (CRT), which is very similar to the tube used in an oscilloscope or a television picture tube. A CRT contains a cathode to emit electrons and an anode to attract them. Electrons generated by an electron gun at the rear of the tube are emitted in a thin beam. This beam is shaped by permanent magnets arranged around the outer neck of the tube and by control plates grouped around the beam on the inside of the tube. A tube-shaped anode surrounds the beam. As the beam leaves the electron gun, it is accelerated by the anode. The resulting momentum of the beam is so great that its electrons pass through the anode and strike a phosphorus coating on the screen of the tube. This causes the screen to glow at the points hit by the electrons. The control plates can

move the position of the beam on the screen. This causes different parts of the screen to illuminate, resulting in a display on an oscilloscope or a picture on a television set. This type of display combines two attributes of a personal computer; it is menu driven and has touch-screen control.

Menu-driven instrumentation means that the CRT operational program allows the driver several options from a list or "menu" provided by the program. Each option on the list or menu concerns a particular area of vehicle operation. For example, suppose the driver selects TRIP MONITOR. Depressing the proper key brings up a display of instantaneous fuel economy, average fuel economy, and range in miles. If the driver desires more information, he can depress either the TRIP DATA or TRIP COMPUTER key to bring up another menu, or "page," which will provide

further information. The TRIP DATA page provides average speed, fuel used, and elapsed time; the TRIP COMPUTER page will display estimated time of arrival, as well as time and distance to destination.

The various functions of such a display are accessed by touching the face of the CRT, which has a touch-sensitive mylar screen over it. The mylar screen is actually a switch panel containing minute wires that are coded by column and row. Touching the screen in certain places blocks a light beam, triggering a configuration of switches in the panel. The switches signal the CRT controller circuitry, which has all of the display pages stored in its memory. The controller responds by sending a picture of the desired page to the CRT. The body computer module (BCM) provides the information to the displayed page through the CRT controller.

When the electrons strike the anode segments to which the positive voltage has been applied, they cause the phosphors to glow brightly. Electrons striking segments with no voltage have no effect, and the phosphors on those segments do not glow. Voltage supply circuits controlled by the microprocessor determine which anode segments receive the positive charge and in what sequence.

Because VFD displays are extremely bright, their intensity is controlled for night viewing by varying the voltage on the accelerating grid. Their intensity also can be controlled by pulse width dimming—turning the display on and off rapidly while controlling the on-time duration. This is similar to the pulse width modulation discussed under solenoids and takes place so fast that the human eye does not detect what is happening.

SUMMARY

All sensors, actuators, and displays are transducers. That is, they convert or transduce one form of energy to another. Sensors are input devices used to convert light, motion, temperature, and other forms of energy into voltage signals (electrical energy) for processing by the computer. Actuators are output devices that change the voltage signals of the computer into mechanical work. Displays are solid-state devices that change voltage signals into visual representations.

Automotive sensors are switches, timers, resistors, transformers, and voltage generators. Their input to the computer may take the form of analog or digital signals. Analog signals are converted into digital signals by special circuits in the computer for use by the microprocessor. Sensors must have certain characteristics. These are repeatability, accuracy, a specific operating range, and linearity.

Sensors relay voltage signals to the computer either by controlling a reference voltage or by generating voltage. Sensors that operate with a reference voltage receive a 5-volt or a 9-volt signal from the computer. This voltage is modified by the sensor and returned to the computer, which is able to interpret the returned voltage to indicate the engine condition being sensed. Sensors that generate their own voltage convert the condition they are sensing into a specific voltage according to the degree of the condition.

Automotive actuators are generally solenoids or relays, but may also be stepper motors. They translate voltage signals from the computer into mechanical motion to change an engine operating condition according to the input from the sensors.

Electronic display systems use light-emitting diodes (LED's), liquid crystal displays (LCD's), or vacuum fluorescent displays (VFD's) controlled by the microprocessor to transmit a variety of operating information to the driver.

REVIEW QUESTIONS

Multiple Choice

1. Digital computer switching circuits are known as:

a. logic gates

b. logic relays

c. the binary system

d. AD converters

2. An exhaust gas oxygen sensor is an example of a:

a. thermistor

b. potentiometer

c. generator

d. voltage divider pickup

3. An engine detonation sensor uses a:

a. reference voltage

b. piezoresistive crystal

c. bimetal element

d. Wheatstone bridge

4. A stepper motor:

a. is a type of relay

b. is either on or off

c. is a less complicated solenoid

d. moves in discrete steps

5. The reference voltage sent to a sensor by the computer:

a. must exceed battery voltage

b. must equal battery voltage

c. must be less than minimum battery voltage

d. has no relation to battery voltage

6. The simplest of all digital sensors is a:

a. switch

b. potentiometer

c. relay

d. none of these

7. Student A says that a variable resistor with three terminals is called a resistor. Student B says that a variable resistor with two terminals is called a potentiometer. Who is right?

a. A only

b. B only

c. both A and B

d. neither A nor B

8. The percentage of time a solenoid is energized in relation to its total cycle time is called the:

a. frequency

b. duty cycle

c. pulse width modulation

d. linear variation factor

9. Student A says that the resistance of a PTC thermistor increases as temperature increases. Student B says that the resistance of an NTC thermistor decreases as temperature decreases. Who is right?

a. A only
b. B only
c. both A and B
d. neither A nor B

10. Student A says that piezoresistive sensors are excellent devices for digital pressure measurement. Student B says that piezoresistive sensors are used to measure engine intake manifold absolute pressure (MAP). Who is right?

a. A only
b. B only
c. both A and B
d. neither A nor B

11. Student A says that an exhaust gas oxygen (EGO) sensor measures oxygen, not air-fuel ratio. Student B says that the EGO sensor is based on the lambda concept. Who is right?

a. A only
b. B only
c. both A and B
d. neither A nor B

12. Student A says that pulse width is the amount of time that a solenoid is energized. Student B says that duty cycle is the percentage of the complete cycle during which the solenoid is off (deenergized).

Who is right?

a. A only
b. B only
c. both A and B
d. neither A nor B

13. Which solid-state display device requires a large amount of power relative to its brightness?

a. liquid crystal display (LCD)
b. vacuum fluorescent display (VFD)
c. light-emitting diode (LED)
d. cathode ray tube (CRT)

14. Which of the following does not act as an actuator?

a. solenoid
b. relay
c. stepper motor
d. linear variable differential transformer (LVDT)

15. Student A says that overly bright VFD displays can be dimmed with a form of pulse width modulation. Student B says that the intensity of VFD display is controlled by varying the voltage on the accelerating grid. Who is right?

a. A only
b. B only
c. both A and B
d. neither A nor B

Fill in the Blank

16. The time of solenoid pulse width is measured in _____ .

17. A thermistor is a variable resistor whose resistance _____ as it is heated.

18. A distributor pulse generator is sometimes called a _____ sensor.

19. An exhaust gas oxygen (EGO) sensor functions as a _____ battery.

20. The duty cycle of a solenoid is the _____ of pulse width to complete cycle width.

21. A semiconductor diode that will transmit light whenever electrical current passes through it is called an _____ .

22. A sensor that converts the condition it is sensing into a specific voltage according to the degree of the condition is called a

_____ .

23. The density of an _____ is so great that it requires back lighting from a bright lamp such as a halogen bulb to illuminate the display.

24. The four characteristics required of all sensors are repeatability, accuracy, operating range, and _____ .

25. The most often used solid-state instrumentation display is called a _____ .

PART TWO
BATTERIES AND ENGINE ELECTRICAL SYSTEMS

INTRODUCTION

The battery has traditionally been considered the heart of the automobile electrical system, and that is a very good concept. Every electrical and electronic device on a vehicle draws its power from the battery.

Chapter 7 explains the construction and operation of lead-acid "storage" batteries. As you study battery operation, you will see many of the principles that you learned in Part One at work in this major component of automobile electrical systems.

Chapters 8 and 9 explain the roles of the starting system and the charging system in overall vehicle performance. Working on these systems has always been a major part of automobile electrical service. They are as important today as they were 50 or 60 years ago.

The battery could not act as a reservoir of electrical power if the charging system did not keep it operating at full capacity. A car engine could not start and run if the starting system did not provide the cranking power. In chapters 8 and 9 you will learn the operating principles of these important systems, including the latest applications of solid-state electronic controls.

7 BATTERIES

WHAT

Early automobiles did not have batteries. They also didn't have much in the way of electrical systems. Ignition was accomplished by a magneto of some kind, and it took muscle power to crank and start the engine. Headlamps (if a car had them) were fired by acetylene gas, and early cars had *no* electrical accessories. In these respects, our modern cars would be similar to those of 80 years ago if it were not for storage batteries. If our cars did not have batteries, they would not have self-starters; they would not have inductive ignition systems or safe lighting; and they would not have the reservoir of steady electrical power for accessories such as radios, air conditioners, and other systems.

This chapter explains the electrochemical principles of the batteries that make modern automobile electrical systems possible.

WHY

None of the combustion control systems or accessories on a modern car can operate right if the battery is discharged or defective. These are the jobs of a battery:

1. To operate the starter motor—the primary function

2. To provide ignition current and power for the engine computer and combustion control systems during cranking

3. To act as a voltage stabilizer, or electrical reservoir, for the entire electrical system of the vehicle

4. To provide power for lights and accessories when the engine is off

5. To provide reserve power when the electrical demands of the car exceed the output of the charging system

6. To provide reserve electrical power in case of charging system failure

This list also outlines the vehicle systems that you *can't* test or service if the battery is defective. *Every* service procedure that you follow for ignition, starting, charging, lighting, accessory, and other electrical and electronic systems will begin with instructions to *check the battery voltage and state of charge.* Understanding the principles of battery construction and operation is the first step in automobile electrical service.

GOALS

After studying this chapter, you should be able to:

1. Explain the electrochemical action of a lead-acid automotive battery.

2. Identify the parts of a battery and explain battery construction.

3. Explain battery charging voltage and the effects of temperature and the state of charge on charging voltage.

4. Define various battery rating methods.

5. Explain the factors that affect battery life.

BATTERY TYPES

Every battery is either a **primary battery** or a **secondary battery**. In a primary battery, the electrochemical action is not reversible. Eventually, one or both of the **electrode** materials are destroyed. The chemical structure of the electrode changes so that it no longer reacts to create voltage and deliver current. Most dry-cell batteries in flashlights and portable radios are primary batteries. Rechargeable nickel-cadmium batteries, however, are secondary batteries.

The electrochemical action in a secondary battery is reversible. The chemical state of the electrolyte and the electronic state of the electrode materials in any battery (primary or secondary) change as the battery applies voltage and delivers current to a circuit. This is the discharging action of a battery, but it can be reversed. A secondary battery can be recharged, which is important for a car battery.

If we apply sufficiently high voltage

and current from an outside source (an alternator) to the battery terminals, we can force current through the battery. This charging current flows in the direction opposite to the battery's discharge current, figure 7-1. In a secondary battery, this charging current reverses the electrochemical action and eventually restores the battery materials to their original conditions. In other words, the battery again stores chemical energy, which can be converted to electrical energy. The battery then can produce more current and once again supply power to an outside circuit. The electrochemical condition of battery electrolyte and plate materials of any given time is the battery's **state of charge**.

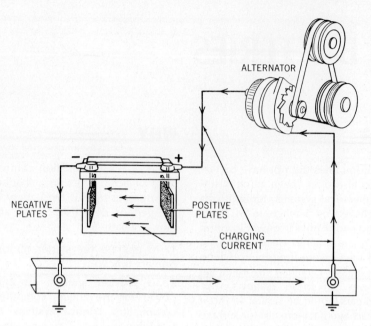

Figure 7-1. Charging current flows into the battery in the direction opposite discharge current flow.

BATTERY ELECTRO-CHEMICAL ACTION

We call automobile batteries "storage" batteries, but they do more than store electricity. The **electrochemical** action of a battery:

- Changes chemical energy to electrical energy
- Changes electrical energy to chemical energy

The battery stores energy in chemical form until it is connected to an external circuit. The stored energy then changes to electrical energy that flows from one battery terminal, through the circuit, and back to the other terminal, figure 7-2. The electrochemistry of a battery works on the reaction that occurs when two dissimilar materials, or electrodes, are placed in a conductive and reactive solution called an **electrolyte**.

The chemical reaction causes the battery terminals to become oppositely charged—positive and negative. This creates a difference in potential, or voltage, between the two terminals of the battery.

The battery electrolyte is the medium through which the dissimilar materials react. These materials are lead (Pb) and lead dioxide (PbO_2) on

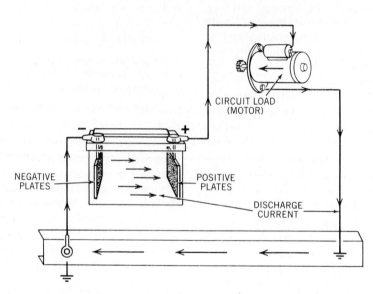

Figure 7-2. A storage battery does not simply store electricity. It stores chemical energy that it changes to electrical voltage and current, which it delivers to a circuit.

the battery plates. Battery electrochemistry is an application of oxidation and reduction reactions.

In a fully charged battery, the lead (Pb) plates have surplus electrons and a negative (−) potential. When a battery is connected to an external circuit, oxidation occurs at the negative plates, which are joined to form a negative (−) electrode terminal, or cathode. Reduction occurs at the positive plates, which are joined to

form a positive (+) electrode terminal, or anode, which has a deficiency of electrons. You can think of it in these terms:

- Oxidation at the negative (−) plates, or cathode, releases electrons and drives them through the external circuit.
- Reduction at the positive (+) plates, or anode, collects electrons that travel through the circuit.

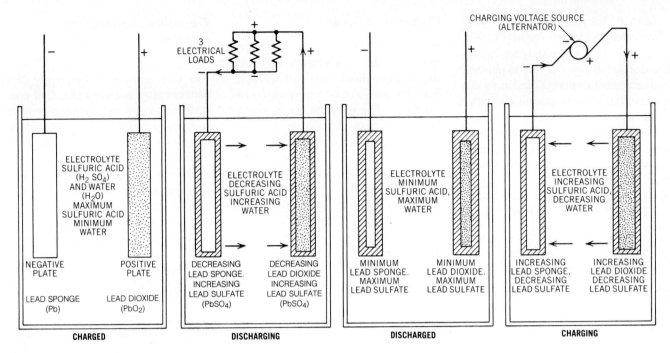

Figure 7-3. Battery electrochemical action is reversed as a battery changes from charged to discharged and back to charged.

As the negative plates give up electrons and the positive plates acquire electrons, their charges change. The negative plates become less negative, and the positive plates become less positive. The voltage difference between the battery terminals decreases, and the battery becomes discharged.

Remember that automobile electrical systems operate on the conventional current flow theory. Current flow is opposite to electron flow. So, if electrons flow from negative to positive during discharge, *current flows from the positive battery terminal, through the external circuit, to the negative terminal.* That is the way we view all electric current in an automobile.

During the discharge reaction, the chemical structures of the electrolyte and the plates change. The reaction is an example of the chemical principles of electron transfer and compound formation that you learned in chapter 2. As you will learn later, charging the battery reverses the electrochemical discharge reaction. The electrochemical properties of the battery materials allow a battery to do more than store

energy. The battery creates voltage and provides current when connected to a circuit.

If we connect a conductor and a load (a motor, a lamp, or some other electrical device) across the battery terminals, we complete an external circuit. Current flows from the positive (+) battery terminal, through the circuit, and back to the negative (−) terminal, figure 7-2. Because the internal parts are part of the *total* circuit, conventional current theory also assumes that discharge current flows from negative to positive *inside* the battery.

Electrochemical Discharge and Recharge

An automobile battery has negative plates of lead (Pb) in a spongy metallic form. The positive plates are lead dioxide (PbO_2). When the battery is fully charged, the electrolyte is a mixture of sulfuric acid (H_2SO_4) and water (H_2O).

As the battery discharges, figure 7-3, electrochemical action reduces the acid percentage in the electrolyte and increases the water percentage.

Sulfate (SO_4) ions from the electrolyte combine with lead ions generated in both plates to form lead sulfate ($PbSO_4$). The plates then become similar, not dissimilar, materials, and the electrolyte contains less acid and more water. Two similar electrodes in an electrolyte cannot produce voltage (an electrical difference) or current between two terminals. The battery is then discharged. Because all the plates in a discharged battery contain sulfate, we often say that a completely discharged lead-acid battery is "sulfated."

A discharged battery, figure 7-3, has a weak acid solution for electrolyte, and the plates are mostly lead sulfate. Recharging reverses this condition. The lead sulfate in the positive plates changes back to lead dioxide (PbO_2), and the lead sulfate in the negative plates changes back to spongy lead (Pb). The sulfate ions recombine in the electrolyte, and hydrogen ions are generated, which increase the sulfuric acid (H_2SO_4) percentage. The battery then returns to a fully charged state, figure 7-3. The process of discharging and recharging a battery is called **cycling**.

During charging, a vented, lead-acid battery releases oxygen (O_2) and hydrogen (H_2) gases as part of the reaction. Hydrogen is very explosive, and any spark or open flame around a battery, particularly during charging, can cause an explosion.

Always keep sparks and open flame away from a battery. To be safe, treat a battery as if hydrogen were present at all times.

BATTERY CONSTRUCTION

We have talked about battery plates, terminals, and electrolyte, which are a few parts of a battery. The following sections outline features of complete battery construction.

Plates and Grids

Plates are made of grids of conductive metal, figure 7-4, which are frames for the reactive lead and lead dioxide. The Pb and PbO_2 are spread uniformly on different grids in paste form. When the paste dries, it is solid but porous so the electrolyte can penetrate the plates. The grids are the conductors for the current generated by the plate materials.

Groups of similar all-positive or all-negative plates, figure 7-4, are welded to a plate strap by "lead burning." Each plate strap has a connector or post to join similar positive or negative plate groups together in the battery.

Elements, Separators, and Cells

You will hear the active units of a battery called **battery cells**. Cell construction begins by placing a positive and a negative plate group together so their plates alternate. The negative group has one more plate than the positive group. Two plate groups form a battery element, not yet a complete cell. To finish the cell, we first must add separators, figure 7-5.

The separators are thin sheets of inert material that prevent short circuits between the positive and negative plates. Separators in older batteries were often wood, rubber, or coated paper. Modern batteries have fiberglass separators. Most separators have ribs on the sides near the positive plates to keep electrolyte near these plates for an efficient reaction. Many late-model batteries have porous plastic envelopes that surround the plates and act as separators, figure 7-6. The most recent Delco batteries use separators of polyvinyl chloride and are sealed on the bottom with a plastic border.

Such envelopes offer more resistance to damage from vibration or high temperatures. They also help to minimize internal "treeing" between plates. This defect arises when active material transfers between plates through a hole in the separator or around the ends of plates. When treeing occurs, it tests as a short. The envelope construction also catches active material that flakes off the positive plates during discharging. The envelopes hold the material closer to the plates so that it is redeposited more completely during charging.

When we put the assembled plate groups and separators into a battery case and add electrolyte, the battery cell is complete. Whether an automobile battery cell has 3 or 23 or any other number of plates, the lead and sulfuric acid compounds cause the cell to develop about 2.1 volts when fully charged. Compounds used in other kinds of batteries develop differ-

TWO IMPORTANT KINDS OF REACTIONS

Oxygen is an example of a common element that combines easily with other elements. Water (H_2O) is the most obvious oxygen compound. When oxygen combines with iron (Fe), we have iron oxide (FeO_2), or rust. When oxygen combines with silicon, we have SiO_2, or sand. Because reactions that form oxygen compounds are so common, they are called oxidation reactions. Oxidation reactions are basic to the operation of your automobile. Gasoline, a very complex mixture of compounds, is mixed with air that contains oxygen and is drawn into the engine cylinders where it is ignited and burns. The heat causes the oxygen to recombine with some of the gasoline molecules and form new compounds. Thus, combustion in an engine is an oxidation reaction.

If oxygen can be combined easily with other elements and compounds, it also can be separated from them. This is the opposite of an oxidation reaction. It is called a reduction reaction, which also is important in your automobile. You know that

some of the new compounds formed when oxygen reacts with gasoline are harmful air pollutants. If some harmful pollutants are formed by oxidation, it stands to reason that it will take a reduction reaction to get rid of them. Other pollutants are formed by incomplete oxidation, and it takes further oxidation to eliminate them.

These examples of oxidation and reduction reactions in engine combustion are the ones that people usually remember regarding automobile operation. But these basic chemical reactions also affect automobile electrical systems. Oxidation and reduction reactions are fundamental to the electrochemistry that allows a battery to develop voltage and deliver current. Additionally, electronic systems on modern automobiles control the oxidation and reduction reactions that reduce emissions. All of these facts further demonstrate that automobiles are some of the best examples of basic science applied to solving human needs.

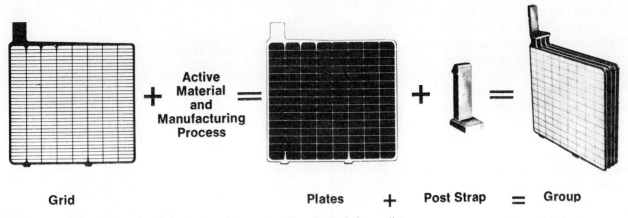

Grid   **Plates** + **Post Strap** = **Group**

Figure 7-4. The grid is the framework for battery plate construction. Several plates, all + or −, are joined in a plate group.

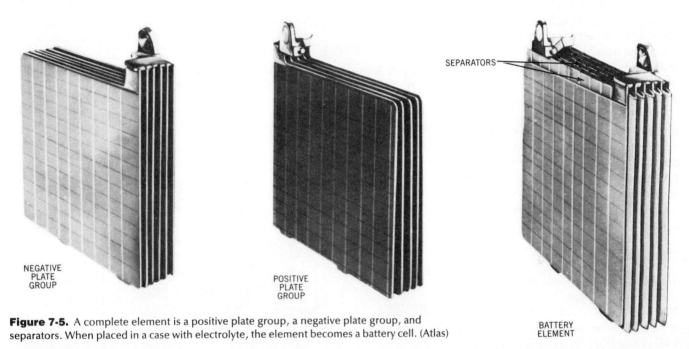

NEGATIVE
PLATE
GROUP

POSITIVE
PLATE
GROUP

SEPARATORS

BATTERY
ELEMENT

Figure 7-5. A complete element is a positive plate group, a negative plate group, and separators. When placed in a case with electrolyte, the element becomes a battery cell. (Atlas)

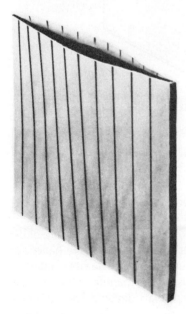

Figure 7-6. Many late-model batteries have envelope-type separators that retain active materials near the plates.

ent voltages. An electronic camera battery, for comparison, is very small and has only one cell, yet it develops 6 volts. Its current capacity, however, is very small.

While the number and size of the plates in an automobile battery do not determine fully charged, open-circuit voltage, they do determine current capacity. The ampere rating of a battery is based on the total plate area in the battery. Batteries with high current capacity have more or larger plates than batteries with low capacity, figure 7-7.

Because each battery cell produces 2.1 volts, a 12-volt battery has six cells. The cells are connected in series inside the battery (+ to −) so that their voltages add together. The fully charged open-circuit voltage, then, of a 12-volt battery is actually 12.6 volts.

Although plate area and current capacity do not determine fully charged, open-circuit voltage, they do affect the rate of discharge. A large-capacity battery maintains high voltage longer than a small-capacity battery.

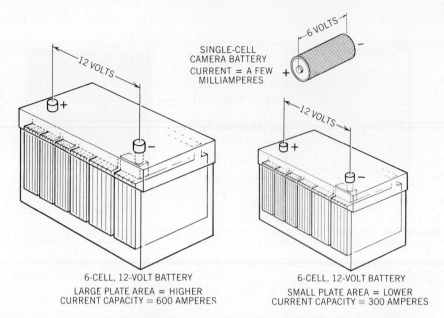

Figure 7-7. Total plate area of a battery determines current capacity. Different kinds of batteries can develop higher voltage per cell but very low current capacity.

Cases and Terminals

The cases of late-model batteries are made of lightweight, but strong, plastic, figure 7-8. Cells are separated from each other by plastic partitions. Cell-connecting straps pass over or through the partitions. Short connectors, passed through the partitions, reduce the internal resistance. Plate groups in many batteries sit on raised supports in the case. The supports form chambers at the bottom of the battery where sediment that flakes off the plates can collect without shorting across the plates. In batteries with envelope separators, the plates may rest on the bottom of the case because the envelopes retain sediment and prevent short circuits.

On modern batteries, the case is closed with a hard plastic cover to form a liquid-tight container. Older batteries had hard rubber cases, and the tops were sealed with a soft compound. Cell-connecting straps were

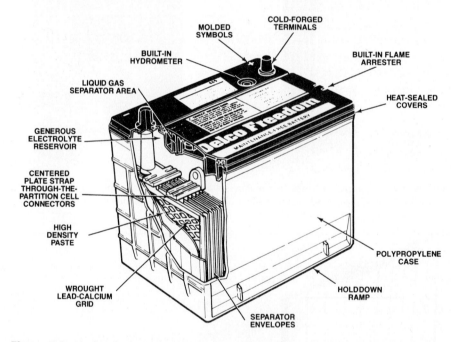

Figure 7-8. Modern batteries have one-piece plastic cases and plastic tops. (Delco-Remy)

exposed on the top of the battery. Some industrial batteries are still made this way, but few automobile batteries are.

Every battery has two terminals (one + and one −) to connect it to an external circuit. The terminals are

connected to either end of the plate group connectors inside the battery, figure 7-8. Battery terminals are either tapered posts on top of the battery or side terminals with female (internal) threads. Some manufacturers say that side terminals develop less corrosion than top terminals because vapors from gassing and evaporation do not collect as easily on side terminals.

To ensure correct installation in a car's electrical system (to be sure battery polarity isn't reversed), the positive and negative terminals are slightly different. The positive post is slightly larger than the negative post. Battery cables have terminals that match either the positive or the negative terminal of a battery.

Battery Vents and Cell Caps

Because a traditional battery releases hydrogen (H_2) gas during charging, the case cannot be completely sealed. Every automobile battery has one or more vent openings. In a vent-cap battery (not maintenance-free), the vents are in the cell caps, figure 7-9. The cell caps of a vent-cap battery are removable so that you can inspect and test the electrolyte and add water to compensate for evaporation.

In a maintenance-free battery (which you will learn more about later), the vent is one or more small openings in the edge of the cover, figure 7-10. A series of passages is molded into the top of the battery case. The passages act as a liquid-gas separator. When the battery gases, the gas must pass through the passages to reach the vent in the side of the top cover. Any liquid that reaches the passages when the battery is tipped less than 45 degrees will be trapped and drain back into the battery case. Figure 7-11 shows how the most current Delco design differs from other batteries: the flame arrestor ramp angle has been increased from 2 degrees to 6 degrees to minimize electrolyte loss during a minor overcharge. Large antiairlock slots are provided to reduce the possibility of trapped air pressurizing the battery.

Electrolyte

Electrolyte is a solution (a mixture) of water and sulfuric acid. The acid is the chemically active part of the solution that reacts with the lead compounds to generate voltage.

Acid is about 35 to 39 percent of the electrolyte solution in a fully charged battery. As a battery discharges, sulfate ions (SO_4) combine with lead ions formed at the plates. This reduces the H_2SO_4 percentage in the electrolyte. Some of the freed hydrogen ions combine with oxygen from the lead dioxide (PbO_2) to increase the water percentage. The percentages of water and acid in the electrolyte cycle back and forth as the battery cycles from charged to discharged. The volume of electrolyte stays relatively constant. A battery always loses some electrolyte volume, however, through water evaporation and hydrogen release during charging.

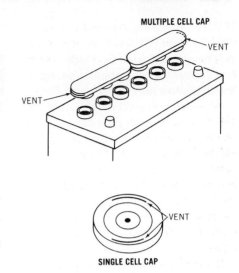

Figure 7-9. Vent-cap batteries have removable cell caps with gas vents.

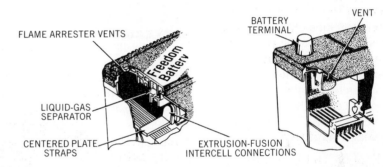

Figure 7-10. Maintenance-free batteries have closed covers with one or two small gas vents in the edges.

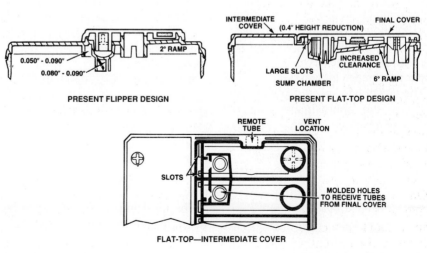

Figure 7-11. Delco Freedom batteries have an increased flame arrestor ramp angle and large antiairlock slots. (Delco-Remy)

We won't go any farther into battery chemistry except to point out that 35- to 39-percent acid in the electrolyte is the proper molecular volume for a complete reaction with Pb and PbO_2. Any higher acid percentage would not increase voltage or current capacity. It would simply corrode the plate grid and connector metals. Over the life of a battery, the acid concentration decreases very slowly because of small, irreversible reactions. The ratio of acid to lead compounds stays relatively constant, however. That is why we add only water, not acid, to replenish electrolyte and compensate for water evaporation.

Specific Gravity. The **specific gravity** is the measurement of the density of any material to that of water. We usually use it to compare another liquid to water. Specific gravity also directly indicates the percentage of any liquid mixed in a solution with water. If we know what the specific gravity *should be* and then measure what it *is*, we can determine the percentage concentration of another liquid mixed with water. We use specific gravity measurements to determine acid concentration in battery electrolyte and antifreeze concentration in engine coolant.

The specific gravity of pure water is always 1.000. The specific gravity of electrolyte in a fully charged battery should be 1.260 to 1.280. This is equivalent to the 35- to 39-percent acid solution. As a battery discharges, the specific gravity decreases because the acid percentage decreases and the water percentage increases.

The electrolyte specific gravity can tell you the approximate state of charge of a battery:

Specific Gravity	Charge Percentage
1.265	100
1.225	75
1.190	50
1.155	25
1.120 or lower = discharged	

Specific gravity measurements are based on a standard temperature of 80° F (26.7° C). Specific gravity is lower at higher temperature and higher at lower temperature. Every 10° F above or below 80° F changes the specific gravity by 4 points (0.004), as follows:

• Every 10° above 80° F—*add* 0.004 to the specific gravity measurement.

• Every 10° below 80° F—*subtract* 0.004 from the specific gravity measurement.

You can measure electrolyte specific gravity of a vent-cap battery with a **hydrometer**. When you study battery service, you will learn to do this and to correct specific gravity measurements for different temperatures.

MAINTENANCE-FREE BATTERIES

Manufacturers call maintenance-free batteries such things as "sealed batteries" or "lifetime batteries." Most are not truly sealed; most have vents. While they usually last longer than older style vent-cap batteries in comparable service, they are not truly lifetime items. They are not even truly maintenance free because they do need occasional cleaning, testing, and possible recharging. Since their introduction in the mid-1970's, however, maintenance-free batteries have become standard original equipment on most late-model cars. They also are the most common kind sold for replacements.

Most maintenance-free batteries do not have removable cell caps to test specific gravity and add water. Most also have a large electrolyte capacity to eliminate the need to add water during the battery lifetime. Large electrolyte volume alone does not make a maintenance-free battery, however.

The most important difference between maintenance-free batteries and older vent-cap batteries is in the plate grid material. Older batteries used 6-

to 12-percent antimony alloyed with lead as the grid metal. Antimony is a good conductor, easy to manufacture, and supports the lead materials well. But it also generates heat from the flow of charging current. Heat adds internal resistance to the battery and is the major cause of water evaporation.

Maintenance-free batteries have grids made of a calcium alloy, which has less resistance to charging current and generates less heat. Reducing heat reduces water loss so that electrolyte does not need water added to it. The heat reduction and better conductivity of calcium grid alloys also allow a maintenance-free battery to have a current capacity about 20 percent higher than an antimony-grid battery.

Battery heat and water loss, along with the charging reactions, are major causes of battery gassing. As hydrogen escapes from a battery and water evaporates, they carry a small amount of sulfuric acid vapors. These vapors condense on the outside of the battery and corrode the terminals, cables, and holddown fasteners. Heat, water loss, and gassing are all reduced in a maintenance-free battery. This, in turn, reduces corrosion.

Also, as an antimony-grid battery ages, the antimony moves from the grids to the active lead material of the negative plates. This causes two problems. Antimony reacting with the negative plates causes a slow self-discharge action. It also makes the battery less able to resist overcharging, which creates more heat. Calcium-grid batteries eliminate these problems.

While you can't add water or check the specific gravity of a maintenance-free battery, you can test it accurately with a load test. You will learn to do this when you study battery service. Delco and some other maintenance-free batteries have built-in state-of-charge indicators that work like a simple hydrometer, figure 7-12. The indicator is a plastic rod inserted in the battery top. The rod has a small cage on the bottom that holds a small green

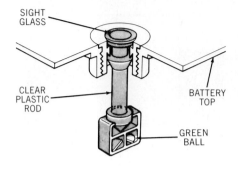

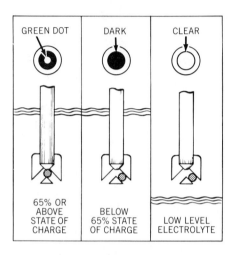

Figure 7-12. Delco and other maintenance-free batteries have small, built-in hydrometers to show the general state of charge. (Chrysler)(Delco-Remy)

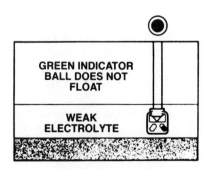

Figure 7-13. The state-of-charge indicator will not give a correct reading if the sulfuric acid separates from the electrolyte. (Delco-Remy)

ball. When the specific gravity is high (about 1.255 to 1.265), the ball floats in the electrolyte and touches the end of the rod. This makes the indicator appear green, which means that the battery is fully, or almost fully, charged. When the specific gravity is lower, the ball drops in the electrolyte and does not touch the rod. The indicator then appears black, which means that the battery should be tested and possibly charged. The bottom of the indicator rod is the minimum level for battery electrolyte. If electrolyte level falls below this point because of age or overcharging, the indicator appears clear. The battery then must be replaced.

Two problems can arise in using this state-of-charge indicator:

1. A battery that is left on charge too long or one that has been overcharged by the alternator may percolate, giving a false reading. The battery should be shaken gently or left to stand long enough for the bubbles to disperse before reading the indicator.

2. Stratification may take place if a battery has been deeply discharged, as in cranking the engine for a long period of time. Stratification is a condition in which the heavier sulfuric acid rests in a separate layer at the bottom of the case, with only the weak electrolyte surrounding the indicator, figure 7-13. This condition can be corrected by shaking the battery gently or by tilting it a few degrees back and forth several times before reading the indicator.

Second-Generation Maintenance-Free Batteries

In the mid-1980's several manufacturers introduced new maintenance-free batteries that are truly sealed. Envelope-type separators in these batteries retain free hydrogen ions near the plates for recombination with the electrolyte during charging. While hydrogen is generated during charging, none is released from the battery. Additionally, improved grid materials allow many such batteries to develop about 2.2 volts per cell for total open-circuit voltage of about 13.2 volts. Although these new batteries are an advancement in battery technology, test and service requirements are generally the same as for other maintenance-free batteries. However, fast

---

BATTERY SERVICE TIPS

Do the terminal clamps on the battery charger in your shop get corroded? Do you have to clean them regularly and perhaps replace them every year

or so? You can reduce corrosion on the terminal clamps by always connecting them horizontally on batteries with removable vent caps. It's often easier to attach the clamps to the battery terminals in a vertical position, but this places them closer to the vents. Hydrogen gas that escapes from the vents during charging promotes the corrosion on the terminal clamps, so attach the charger clamps horizontally with the handles pointing away from the battery top.

Here's another point to remember about using a wire brush to clean battery terminals. When you are cleaning a battery in a car, you may have only a couple inches of clearance between the positive terminal and the body, frame, or engine. If your wire brush accidentally strikes the battery positive terminal and part of the car body or engine, a short-circuit spark can occur. This spark may burn you or, worse, ignite hydrogen fumes from the battery. If you can't remove the battery from the car to clean it, at least disconnect both cables from the terminals before going at them with your wire brush.

charging at a high current rate may damage some of these batteries. Check the manufacturer's test and service instructions.

BATTERY CHARGING VOLTAGE

Charging current flows into a battery in the direction opposite to the battery discharge current, figures 7-1 and 7-2. When a battery supplies power to a circuit, current flows *out* of the battery + terminal, through the circuit, and back to the − terminal. Charging current flows *into* the battery + terminal and through the battery to the − terminal. To do this, charging current must overcome the battery's own resistance, which exists in two forms:

1. The physical resistance of the battery parts: the electrolyte, the plate metals, and the internal connectors

2. The countervoltage, or **counter-electromotive force (CEMF)**, of the battery.

Charging current enters the battery only when charging voltage is higher than the battery CEMF *plus* the voltage drop created by the battery internal resistance. When a battery is fully charged, CEMF is high; and very little charging current flows through the battery. When a battery is discharged, CEMF is low; and more charging current flows through the battery. Figure 7-14 is a graph that shows the relationships of charging voltage, charging current, and battery CEMF.

Understanding the relationship of CEMF to battery state of charge will help you understand battery charging methods. A discharged battery needs and will accept high charging current. A fully charged battery with high CEMF resists charging current. High charging current applied to a fully charged battery will overheat and damage the battery.

Battery temperature also affects battery resistance to charging current. A

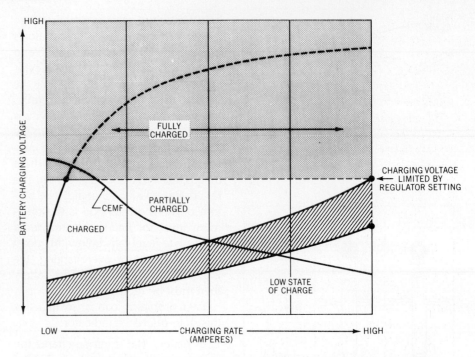

Figure 7-14. This graph shows the relationships of battery charging voltage, charging current, and CEMF.

cold battery has higher resistance than a warm battery, largely because of the resistance of the electrolyte. When you learn to service batteries and charging systems, you will learn to consider the effects of temperature. Very high charging current applied to a cold battery, even if it is completely discharged, may damage the battery as the current tries to overcome the high resistance of cold electrolyte. Similarly, high charging system voltage in very hot weather may overheat a battery, and low charging system voltage in cold weather may not keep a battery fully charged.

BATTERY SELECTION AND REPLACEMENT

Engineers select batteries as original equipment for a vehicle to supply the current requirements of a particular car or truck with specific electrical loads. As a professional mechanic,

you must select a replacement on the same basis. The major factors that influence battery selection are:

1. Battery type
2. Battery current capacity rating
3. Battery size and group number

Battery Type

All modern automobile batteries are 12-volt, lead-acid, wet-cell batteries. They come in different sizes and shapes and with different current ratings. Yet, battery companies also make 12-volt automotive-type batteries that are not intended for automobile use.

Batteries are designed for one or the other of two uses:

1. To start an automobile or truck engine
2. To be the power source for an electric vehicle or an electrical accessory system without continual recharging

The two basic types of batteries, therefore, are starting batteries and cycling batteries. Automobile batteries are starting batteries, designed principally to deliver large power output for a short time to start an engine. The vehicle charging system then supplies most of the current. The battery stabilizes the system and provides current when electrical loads exceed charging current output at any time or engine speed.

Cycling batteries deliver low, steady current for long periods of time. They are designed for electric vehicles such as industrial trucks (fork-lifts), golf carts, electric wheelchairs, and electric outboard motors. They also are used for marine and recreational vehicle (RV) electrical accessory systems. Most of the current capacity is depleted in each cycle before the battery is recharged. Figure 7-15 shows the differences between the current requirements of starting and cycling batteries.

The current capacity of a battery used to start a car engine is a small percent of its rated capacity, but actual current is very high for a few seconds. It may be as high as 600 amperes to crank an automotive diesel engine. This high current for a few seconds is obtained by using thinner plates in a starting battery than in a cycling battery. The battery can be subjected to high current drain many times, followed by recharging, and still maintain its rated capacity.

A cycling battery has thicker plates to sustain a steady current drain for several hours. If an automobile starting battery is subjected to such deep cycle use, the plates wear out rapidly. The positive plates get soft and shed active material. Conversely, a cycling battery used to start an automobile engine will get hot from the momentary high current draw and take longer to recharge. Its overall life probably will be shorter than that of a starting battery in this application.

An automobile battery is not the best choice to power an electric vehicle, and a cycling battery may not have the expected service life if used for automobile starting applications. Understanding these basic differences in battery types makes it easier to understand why there are different ways to rate battery current capacity. A single battery can be, and often is, rated by more than one method. To ensure adequate electrical power for any application, a replacement battery should have the same or higher current-capacity rating as the OEM battery, but never a lower rating.

Battery Current-Capacity Ratings

A battery's current-capacity rating indicates its ability to provide cranking power for an engine, reserve power for an electrical system, or both. The following sections explain test standards and rating methods developed by the Battery Council International (BCI) and the Society of Automotive Engineers (SAE), as well as the types of batteries for which they are used.

Ampere-Hour Rating. Also called the 20-hour discharge rating, the **ampere-hour rating** is the oldest current-capacity rating method. It also is the

Starting Battery
Typical starting current = 300 amperes
Typical starting time = 4 seconds
Typical current drain from the battery =
  300 amperes × 4 seconds = 1200 ampere-seconds or 0.33 ampere-hour

Nominal ampere-hour capacity = 62 ampere-hours

Cycling Battery
Typical steady current drain of
  an electric outboard motor = 10 amperes

Typical running (battery discharge)
  time for a fishing trip = 3 hours
Typical current drain from the battery =
  10 amperes × 3 hours = 30 ampere-hours

Nominal ampere-hour capacity = 80 ampere-hours

Figure 7-15. These comparison figures show the different requirements for a starting battery and a cycling battery.

best way to rate a cycling battery. This rating indicates the steady current flow that a battery will deliver for 20 hours at 80° F (26.7° C) before cell voltage drops below 1.75 volts. This equals 10.5 volts for a 12-volt battery. For example, a battery that continuously delivers 4 amperes for 20 hours is an 80-ampere-hour battery (4 amperes × 20 hours = 80 ampere-hours).

Cold-Cranking Rating. The **cold-cranking rating** is the newest and most common way to rate the current capacity of a modern automobile battery. This rating indicates the power that a battery can supply to start an engine at low temperature. Cold-cranking ratings are given in total amperes, such as 300, 375, 425, or 500. This represents the current a battery can deliver for 30 seconds at 0° F (−17.8° C) before cell voltage drops below 1.2 volts (7.2 volts, total, for a 12-volt battery).

Reserve-Capacity Rating. The **reserve-capacity rating** indicates the number of minutes that a fully charged battery can deliver 25 amperes before cell voltage drops below 1.75 volts (10.5 volts for a 12-volt battery). These ratings are listed in minutes, such as 60, 110, 120, and so on. The reserve capacity indicates the time that a vehicle can be driven if the charging system fails.

Battery Size and Group Numbers

A battery must fit the space available for it in a vehicle and connect to the cables. Batteries of various current-capacity ratings and both types (starting and cycling) are built in different sizes and shapes. **BCI group numbers** indicate the length, width, height, terminal design, holddown locations, and other physical features of a battery, figure 7-16. The group number indicates only the size, shape, and voltage of a battery, not the current capacity.

BATTERY INSTALLATIONS

Most automobiles have a single 6-cell, 12-volt battery mounted in the engine compartment. Several factors determine battery location:

1. The battery should be close to the engine and the alternator so that long cables do not increase electrical system resistance.

2. The battery should be located away from exhaust system parts in a place where air can flow over it to cool it.

3. The battery should be mounted securely to protect it from vibration that can damage the plates.

4. The battery must be accessible for service and located so that its weight does not upset the balance of the vehicle.

The need to reduce weight and increase fuel mileage in late-model cars has led engineers to design lighter and smaller batteries with current capacity equal to the larger batteries of the past. Lightweight plastic case materi-

als and designs have made this possible.

Some older cars and some race cars have the battery in the trunk or under the floor to keep it away from engine heat and put its weight over the rear driving axle. These installations require long cables, which usually are heavier gauge wire than cables used for engine compartment installations. The heavier cables reduce resistance but add cost and weight to vehicle design.

Many late-model GM diesel automobiles have two 12-volt batteries connected in parallel, figure 7-17. The + terminals of both batteries are connected to each other and to the + battery cable attached to the starter motor. Similarly, the − terminals are

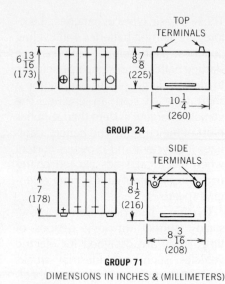

Figure 7-16. Battery group numbers indicate battery dimensions and terminal types and locations.

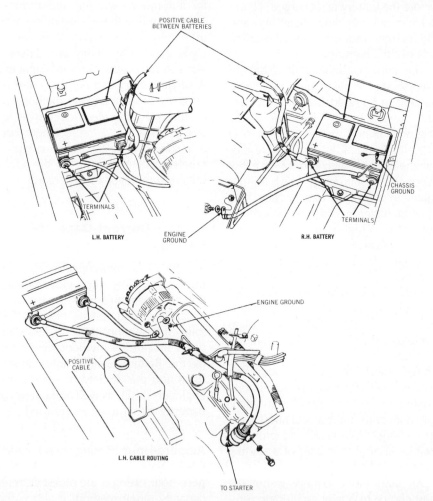

Figure 7-17. Many GM diesel automobiles have two 12-volt batteries for increased cranking current with a 12-volt starter. (Oldsmobile)

connected to each other and to the battery ground cable. This parallel connection doubles the available current for starting a high-compression diesel, but the two batteries still provide just 12 volts to the electrical system. The alternator charges both batteries simultaneously.

Remember that if two or more similar batteries are connected in series, the voltages add together. If two or more similar batteries are connected in parallel, the total system is the same as with a single battery, but current capacity increases.

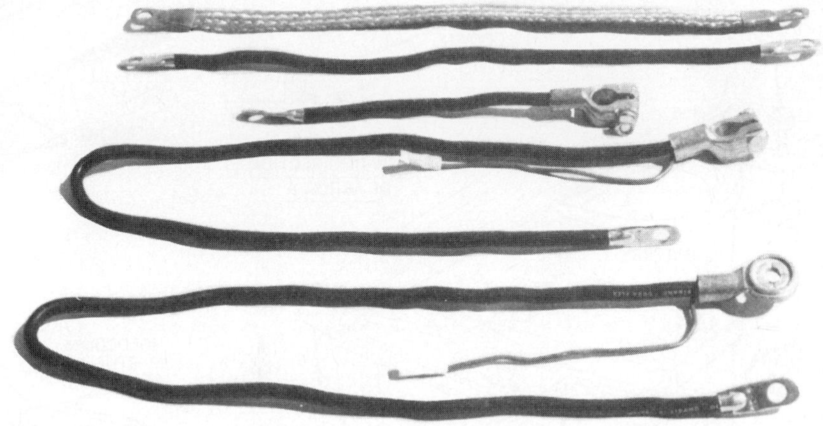

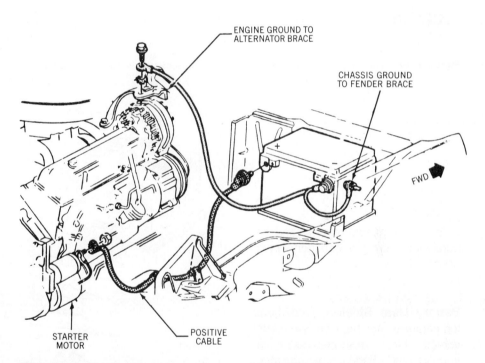

Figure 7-18. Typical battery cables for top-post and side-terminal batteries.

Battery Installation Parts

Correct design and selection of battery installation parts and their proper maintenance are essential for good battery service life and operation.

Battery Cables. Battery cables are large-diameter, multistrand wire to carry the high current needed by the starter motor. Twelve-volt electrical systems usually have number 4 or number 6 gauge battery cables. You can install a larger gauge cable than the original equipment manufacturer (OEM) cable on a vehicle, but not a smaller one. A smaller gauge cable will increase the voltage drop in the starter circuit and may cause poor starting operation.

The cables must have connectors that match the posts or the side terminals of the battery on which they are used, figure 7-18. Some cables have smaller gauge wire pigtails soldered into the battery connectors for specific circuits that get power directly from the battery on some cars. The ground cable on a battery installation may be a flat braided cable without insulation. These have the same resistance and electrical characteristics as insulated cables. Insulation is not required for the low-voltage ground side of the system.

The battery ground cable is connected to *either* the engine or the vehicle chassis. To ensure a low-resis-

Figure 7-19. This bonding strap ensures a good ground between the battery, the engine, and the vehicle chassis.

tance ground connection *between* the engine and chassis, some vehicles have a braided strap or a small cable between the engine and frame, figure 7-19. While not actually a battery cable, this ground "bonding" strap is necessary on some cars for a complete electrical system ground path.

Battery Carriers and Holddown Parts. A battery is usually mounted on a shelf or tray, called a carrier, in the engine compartment. The battery must be held securely to protect it from vibration and to keep it from spilling acid. Various kinds of holddown clamps and brackets are used

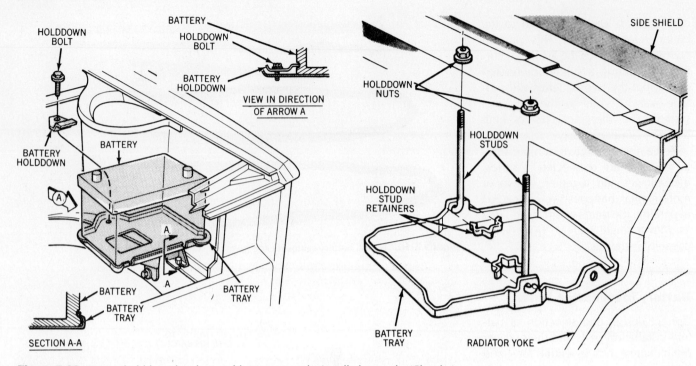

Figure 7-20. Battery holddown brackets and fasteners must be installed securely. (Chrysler)

on different vehicles, figure 7-20. Regardless of design, all holddown parts must be installed correctly and securely to ensure proper battery operation.

Battery Heat Shields. Underhood temperatures are high on late-model vehicles. Heat can shorten battery life and reduce battery performance. Therefore, most vehicles have shields to protect the battery from engine heat or to direct cooling airflow from the front of the car around the battery, figure 7-21. Most shields are made of heat-resistant plastic. Some are part of the holddown components; others are separate ducts to direct airflow around the battery. Like correctly installed holddown brackets, heat shields are necessary for proper battery performance and life. Heat shields must be reinstalled whenever a battery is removed and replaced.

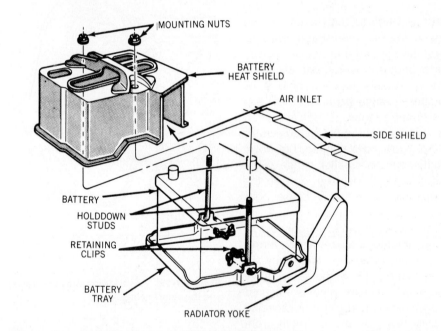

Figure 7-21. Many late-model cars have heat shields to protect batteries from underhood heat.

FACTORS OF BATTERY LIFE AND PERFORMANCE

A well-maintained modern battery, operating with a charging system in good condition, will last 4, 5, 6, or more years. Yet, even the finest maintenance-free "lifetime" batteries wear out eventually. Several factors (operating conditions) can extend or shorten battery life and affect performance.

Overcharging

A battery can be overcharged by the vehicle charging system or by a shop battery charger. Overcharging results from continually high charging voltage or high charging current rates, or both. In any case, excess current is forced through the battery, which creates heat. Heat can buckle plates and oxidize the positive plate material. Overcharging also causes the electrolyte to break down and release hydrogen and oxygen gases. The released gases can wash active material off the plates, decrease electrolyte level, and increase battery corrosion.

Undercharging and Sulfation

If a charging system does not deliver enough voltage and current to a battery, the battery will not be fully charged. Undercharging may be due to a fault in the charging system, continually high electrical loads from accessories, or a battery with lower current capacity than the vehicle needs. The undercharged condition can range from 70 or 80 percent charged to fully discharged.

When a battery is less than fully charged, lead sulfate remains on the plates. The amount of sulfation varies with the state of charge. If a battery is constantly undercharged, the sulfate can crystalize and will not recombine with the electrolyte. Eventually, a constantly undercharged battery can never reach a state of full charge. A completely sulfated battery cannot be effectively recharged.

Cycling

Automobile batteries are not designed for continual deep-cycle use. If a car battery is cycled repeatedly from fully charged to almost discharged, the positive plates will shed active material. The material cannot be restored to the plates, and battery current capacity and life will be reduced.

Temperature

High and low temperatures affect battery life and performance in several ways. High temperature caused by engine heat, overcharging, or ambient air temperature will increase electrolyte loss and shorten battery life. Low temperature also can damage a battery.

If electrolyte freezes, it can expand and crack the battery case. The freezing point of electrolyte depends on specific gravity and, therefore, on the battery state of charge. A fully charged battery with specific gravity of 1.265 to 1.280 will not freeze until temperature is below −60° F (−51° C). A discharged battery with electrolyte specific gravity around 1.120 to 1.150 can freeze at 18° F (−7.7° C).

Low temperature also increases electrolyte resistance, which reduces battery cranking power. But, an engine needs *increased* cranking power to start at low temperatures. Figure 7-22 is a chart that compares the cranking power available from a battery and the cranking power needed by an engine at 80°, 32°, and 0° F (26.7°, 0°, and −17.8° C).

Electrolyte resistance also means that a cold battery is harder to recharge than a warm battery.

Electrolyte Level

Calcium-grid maintenance-free batteries have reduced electrolyte water loss to the point that battery cases can be closed. Additional water is not needed during the normal use and life of the battery. You know, however, that high temperature, overcharging, and deep cycling and recharging all create heat that can cause battery gassing and water loss. Even maintenance-free batteries lose some water. Electrolyte inspection, testing, and replenishment are parts of regular battery care for vent-cap batteries.

If electrolyte level drops below the tops of the plates, the plate materials are exposed to the air and harden.

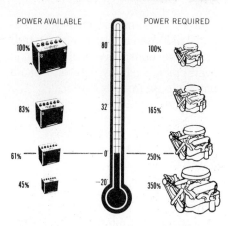

POWER AVAILABLE | POWER REQUIRED

Figure 7-22. A battery delivers less cranking power at low temperature than at high temperature, but an engine needs more power to start. (Delco-Remy)

They do not take part in the electrochemical reaction. Even when water is added, hardened plate materials are not restored to a fully active condition. Additionally, electrolyte that has lost water has a higher acid concentration, which increases plate corrosion.

Overfilling a battery also is harmful. Too much water reduces the acid concentration and lowers specific gravity. It also raises electrolyte level closer to the vents, which increases battery corrosion due to gassing.

Corrosion

Battery corrosion is caused by spilled electrolyte and by normal battery gassing. Sulfuric acid destroys metal connectors, terminals, holddown brackets, and carriers. Corroded terminals and connectors increase circuit resistance. Corrosion also weakens holddown brackets and damages sheet metal of the car body.

Vibration

We have mentioned several times that vibration can shake active materials off battery plates. Vibration also can loosen internal connections between cells and plate groups, which increases resistance. Similarly, vibration can loosen external battery terminal connections. Severe vibration can even crack a battery case or shake a battery loose from its carrier.

Parasitic Loads and Phantom Drains

Once a battery has been installed in a vehicle, it is constantly being discharged by the minute current loads required to power the memory circuits of various electrical devices, such as digital clocks. The problem is greater in vehicles with electronic circuits and devices simply because the number of circuits and devices requiring power is greater. Such minute current loads are called parasitic loads because their circuits are constantly connected to the battery and thus drain small amounts of current even when the ignition is off.

Parasitic loads can completely discharge a battery over a period of time. Once a battery has been discharged in this way and allowed to stand for a long period of time, it may not accept a charge easily. Parasitic loads are generally measured in milliamps and can be determined by connecting an ammeter with a milliamp scale in series with the battery. Normal parasitic current drains are usually between 10 and 30 mA. Figure 7-23 gives examples of typical parasitic loads.

Most 1988 and later Chrysler vehicles have an "ignition-off draw" connector installed in the main headlamp and dash wiring harness between the battery and the fuse links. This black 2-blade terminal connector opens the circuits to prevent parasitic loads from draining the battery while the vehicle is in transit from the factory. It is connected by the dealer during new car preparation before sale of the vehicle. It also may be disconnected to prevent battery drain if the vehicle is stored for a period of time.

Phantom drains may also discharge a battery in the same way as parasitic loads, but the current drain is generally greater (more than 30 mA). A

Component	Milliamp Draw
Voltage regulator	1
Digital clock	3–4.5
Quartz clock	7
ECM	6.5–8
ETR radio and clock	7
Load leveling	4
Memory seat	3
Twilight sentinel	3

Figure 7-23. Typical examples of parasitic loads. (Delco-Remy)

phantom drain is caused by a component such as a glove box or trunk light switch that is malfunctioning or misadjusted. The defective switch allows a light to remain on when the ignition switch is off, but there is no way of knowing this, since the light is supposed to be on when the glove box door or trunk lid is opened.

Before the advent of electrical components that cause parasitic loads, the usual test for a phantom drain was to connect a test lamp in series between the battery terminal and cable. On late-model vehicles, however, parasitic loads are normal and the test is no longer a valid one. The best way to locate a phantom drain on such vehicles is to check total current drain with a multimeter that reads in milliamps, and then distinguish between a normal parasitic load (10 to 30 mA) and a phantom drain (more than 30 mA).

SUMMARY

Automobile batteries are lead-acid secondary batteries, which can be recharged after discharging. Batteries do more than store electrical power. They generate voltage and current through electrochemical action between the dissimilar plates (Pb and PbO_2) and sulfuric acid (H_2SO_4) in the electrolyte.

Each cell of a battery contains groups of positive (+) and negative

(−) plates with separators between them. Each cell produces about 2.1 volts regardless of the number of plates. Cells are connected in series (+ or −) so that six cells produce about 12.6 volts in a fully charged 12-volt battery. Current capacity depends on the total surface area of all plates in all cells.

Electrolyte specific gravity indicates the battery state of charge. Electrolyte in a fully charged battery should have specific gravity of 1.265 to 1.280. Maintenance-free batteries have calcium-alloy grids that reduce battery heat and water loss. Electrolyte cannot be checked, and water cannot be added to a maintenance-free battery.

Automobile batteries are designed principally for engine-starting service, not for continual deep cycling. Cycling is the operation of a battery from fully charged to discharged and back to fully charged. Battery current capacity can be rated by several methods, such as the ampere-hour rating, the cold-cranking rating, and the reserve-capacity rating. Ampere-hour ratings are most appropriate for cycling batteries. Cold-cranking ratings are most appropriate for starting-type batteries.

Battery charging rate and charging current are affected by the battery state of charge and CEMF. Overcharging, undercharging, cycling, temperature, vibration, corrosion, and electrolyte level all affect battery service life and performance.

WORD TO THE WISE

When you are servicing a battery with removable cell caps, don't take the caps off and set them on any painted surface of a car. Moisture that collects on the caps as the battery gases contains sulfuric acid. If it contacts a car's paint, it will leave a mark and probably leave you with an angry customer. When you remove a cell cap to check or add water or test specific gravity, set the cap on the top of the battery case or away from the car on your workbench.

REVIEW QUESTIONS

Multiple Choice

1. An automobile battery:
a. stores energy in chemical form
b. changes chemical energy to electrical energy
c. changes electrical energy to chemical energy
d. all of the above

2. Student A says that the positive (+) plates of a battery are lead (Pb). Student B says that oxidation occurs at the positive plates when the battery delivers current to a circuit. Who is right?
a. A only
b. B only
c. both A and B
d. neither A nor B

3. Open-circuit voltage of a fully charged 12-volt battery is usually:
a. 11.8 volts
b. 12 volts
c. 12.6 volts
d. 13.3 volts

4. Student A says the plate area in a battery cell determines cell voltage. Student B says that the plate area in a battery cell determines current capacity. Who is right?
a. A only
b. B only
c. both A and B
d. neither A nor B

5. Battery electrolyte is approximately:
a. one-third sulfuric acid and two-thirds water
b. two-thirds sulfuric acid and one third water
c. half water and half sulfuric acid
d. one-quarter sulfuric acid and three-quarters water.

6. Specific gravity of the electrolyte in a fully charged battery should be approximately:
a. 1.235 to 1.255
b. 1.260 to 1.280
c. 1.275 to 1.290
d. 1.290 to 1.310

7. Specific gravity measurements must always be corrected to which of the following temperatures:
a. 60° F
b. 32° F
c. 80° F
d. 100° F

8. The grid material of a maintenance-free battery is alloyed with
a. antimony
b. silicon
c. cadmium
d. calcium

9. Student A says that maintenance-free batteries are completely sealed. Student B says that specific gravity cannot be checked in a maintenance-free battery. Who is right?
a. A only
b. B only
c. both A and B
d. neither A nor B

10. When selecting a replacement battery, you must consider all of the following, except:
a. charging voltage rating
b. battery type
c. current capacity rating
d. battery size and group number

11. A battery cold-cranking rating is based on:
a. steady current that the battery will deliver for 20 hours before cell voltage drops below 1.75 volts.
b. current that a battery can deliver for 30 seconds at 0° F before cell voltage drops below 1.2 volts.
c. current required to crank a 300-cid engine at 0° F for 6 seconds, or one-tenth of a minute.
d. the number of minutes that a battery can deliver 25 amperes before cell voltage drops below 1.75 volts.

12. A battery ampere-hour rating is based on:
a. steady current that the battery can deliver for 20 hours before cell voltage drops below 1.75 volts.

b. current that a battery can deliver for 30 seconds at 0° F before cell voltage drops below 1.2 volts.
c. current required to crank a 300-cid engine at 0° F for 6 seconds, or one-tenth of a minute.
d. the number of minutes that a battery can deliver 25 amperes before cell voltage drops below 1.75 volts.

13. A battery reserve-capacity rating is based on:
a. steady current that the battery will deliver for 20 hours before cell voltage drops below 1.75 volts.
b. current that a battery can deliver for 30 seconds at 0° F before cell voltage drops below 1.2 volts.
c. current required to crank a 300-cid engine at 0° F for 6 seconds, or one-tenth of a minute.
d. the number of minutes that a battery can deliver 25 amperes before cell voltage drops below 1.75 volts.

14. Student A says that a parasitic load is a normal battery drain. Student B says that a phantom drain is an abnormal battery drain. Who is right?
a. A only
b. B only
c. both A and B
d. neither A nor B

Fill in the Blank

15. A battery in which one or both of the electrode materials are destroyed is called a _____ battery.

16. The electrochemical action in a secondary battery is _____ .

17. A car battery is recharged by high voltage and current delivered by the _____ .

18. In a battery, the medium through which the positive and negative terminals react is called an _____ .

19. The negative terminal in a battery is the _____ .

20. The positive terminal in a battery is the _____ .

21. Current always flows from the _____ battery terminal.

22. Battery electrolyte is a mixture of _____ and water.

23. When both plates in a battery become similar, the battery is _____ .

24. The process of discharging and recharging a battery is called _____ .

25. During charging, a vented, lead-acid battery releases _____ which is explosive.

26. The active units of a battery are called _____ .

27. To replenish electrolyte, we add _____ to a battery.

28. The measurement of the density of any material to that of water is called its _____ .

29. The _____ is the instrument used to measure the specific gravity in a vent-cap battery.

30. Maintenance-free batteries use a calcium alloy because of its conductive properties and because it produces less _____ .

31. The two basic types of batteries are charging batteries and _____ batteries.

32. _____ is a condition that tests as a short and occurs when active material transfers between plates through a hole in the separator or around the ends of plates.

8 STARTING SYSTEMS

WHAT

In chapter 7, you learned that automobile batteries are designed primarily to provide high current for the starting system. The starting system is one of the simplest electrical systems on an automobile. It consists of one or two switches, a relay or a solenoid, and a high-torque motor. It also is one of the most important automobile systems.

Obviously, if the starting system cannot crank an engine, the engine cannot start and run. Problems in the starting system also can affect the battery state of charge and battery life. Additionally, starting system problems can reduce ignition voltage so that the engine may not fire and run even if it cranks. This chapter explains the design and operation of starter motors and other parts of this vital electrical system.

WHY

Hard-starting complaints are among the most common engine performance problems. The cause of an engine starting problem may be in the parts of the starter system; it may be a high-resistance fault in the circuit; or it may be a discharged battery. Starting problems also may be due to the effects of the starting circuit on other vehicle systems. In any case, a thorough knowledge of starting system operation and how it relates to other vehicle systems is essential for complete engine performance service.

GOALS

After studying this chapter, you should be able to:

1. Explain the operation of starting control circuits and motor circuits and identify the parts of each.

2. Explain the operation of various starter motors and identify principal motor parts.

3. Identify and explain the operation of various starter devices.

STARTING SYSTEM CIRCUITS

The starting system, figure 8-1, consists of two related circuits: the motor circuit and the control circuit. The starter motor draws very high current for a few seconds to crank the engine. Cranking speed for most engines is about 200 rpm. If the starter cannot crank the engine at this speed, a hard-start or a no-start problem will probably result.

The amount of starter current varies from 150 or 200 amperes for small 4- and 6-cylinder engines to more than 300 amperes for large gasoline V-8 and diesel engines. Some diesels may require 500 or 600 amperes of cranking current to start in very cold weather. The starter motor draws this high current for only a few seconds. A well-running gasoline engine should start with 2 to 3 seconds of cranking time.

The high-current requirement of the starter motor is the reason that battery cables are made of heavy-gauge wire. Compare the several hundred amperes of starting current to the 10, 20, or 30 amperes needed by other circuits. If it were not for the starter motor, the battery could be connected to the rest of the electrical system with 10- or 12-gauge primary wiring.

The high-current requirement of the starter also is the reason that the starting system has two circuits. Heavy cables connect the motor to the battery as directly as possible. The motor circuit uses a relay, or the relay action of a solenoid, to connect the motor to the battery momentarily. The relay or solenoid is mounted on or near the motor and connected directly to the battery. The ignition switch energizes the relay or solenoid to operate the starter. If the battery were connected to the motor through the ignition

switch, the cables would be excessively long and expensive. Moreover, the extra cable length would add resistance to the circuit, which could cause excessive voltage drop to the starter. The ignition switch also would have to be large and cumbersome to hold the heavy contacts needed to conduct high current to the starter.

Figure 8-2 shows the basic arrangement of the starting system motor and control circuits. The motor circuit carries high current from the battery, through the magnetic switch (relay or solenoid), to the motor. The control circuit energizes the relay or solenoid through the ignition switch and the starting safety switch. The battery ground connection is part of both the motor and the control circuits. You have already studied the battery, which is the power source for the starting system and all other electrical circuits. The following sections out-

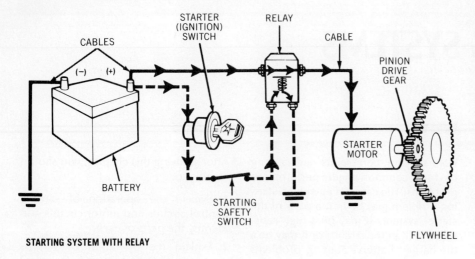

STARTING SYSTEM WITH RELAY

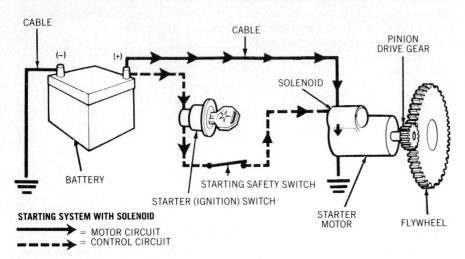

STARTING SYSTEM WITH SOLENOID

= MOTOR CIRCUIT
= CONTROL CIRCUIT

Figure 8-1. All starting systems have a motor circuit and a control circuit. (Chrysler)

line the operation of the starting circuits and their major parts.

The Starter Control Circuit

The starter control circuit contains:

• The ignition switch
• The starting safety (neutral start) switch
• The control side of the relay or solenoid

These components are connected to the battery by primary wiring. The ignition switch usually receives battery voltage from the terminal on the relay or solenoid to which the positive (+) battery cable is connected. The

ignition switch and the starting safety switch are in series. When both switches close, current flows through the relay or solenoid coil. Electromagnetic action closes the heavy contacts in the relay or solenoid and connects the motor to the battery through the heavy cables.

The Ignition Switch. Late-model ignition switches have multiple switch contacts and five positions.

1. Accessories
2. Lock
3. Off
4. On (Run)
5. Start

The ignition switch is the power distribution point for many circuits. In the accessories position, it supplies power to accessory circuits but not to ignition and engine control circuits. In the lock and the off positions, all circuits are open at the switch. Additionally, the lock position mechanically locks the steering and, on many cars, the transmission gear selector. In the run position, the switch provides power to the ignition and the engine control circuits, as well as other circuits. In the start position, the switch provides power only to the starter control circuit, the ignition, and other engine control circuits.

The switch start position is a **momentary contact** position. It is spring loaded so that when the driver releases the key, the switch automatically moves to the on (run) position. All other switch positions are **detented**. The switch stays in one selected position until turned to another.

With few exceptions, late-model ignition switches are mounted on the steering column. There are two basic designs:

1. Most switches are mounted remotely from the key and operated by linkage, figure 8-3.
2. Some switches are attached directly to the key at the upper end of the steering column, figure 8-4.

All ignition switches connect battery voltage to the ignition system in the start and the run positions. For ignition systems with a ballast resistor and a starting bypass circuit, the switch connects full battery voltage to the ignition when starting and lower voltage (through a resistor) when running. For ignitions without a ballast resistor, the switch delivers full battery or charging system voltage during both starting and running. The actual starting circuit to the ignition may be connected through the switch or through the starter relay. The ignition system chapters in Part Four of this book explain more about ignition ballast resistor and starting bypass circuits.

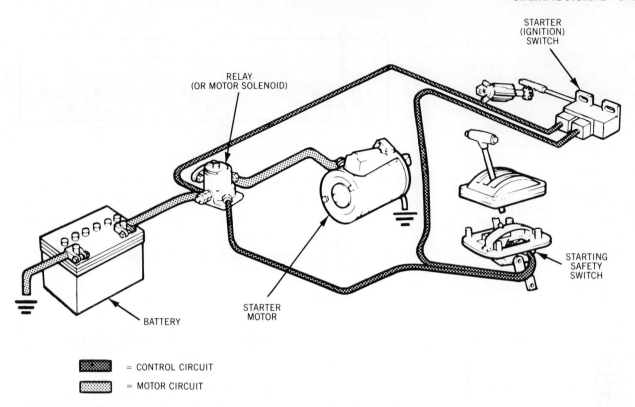

Figure 8-2. This is the basic arrangement of starting system motor circuits and control circuits. (Chrysler)

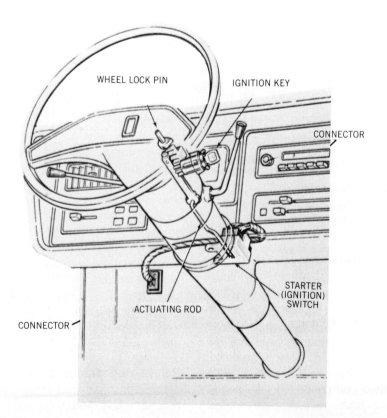

Figure 8-3. Most ignition switches are mounted away from the key lock and operated by linkage. (Ford)

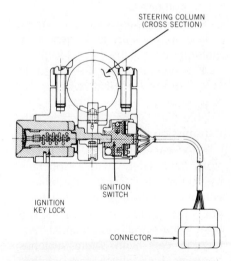

Figure 8-4. Some ignition switches are mounted in the steering column and attached directly to the key lock. (Chrysler)

Figure 8-5 shows a typical ignition switch symbol that you will see on electrical diagrams.

The Starting Safety Switch. Once used only with automatic transmissions, the starting safety switch is now used on many cars with manual transmissions as well. The starting safety switch, or neutral start switch, closes the control circuit only when the automatic transmission is in park or neutral or the manual transmission is in neutral or the clutch is disengaged. This normally open switch is in series with the start position of the ignition switch but can be connected to the circuit in two ways:

1. The safety switch can be between the ignition switch and the relay or solenoid, figure 8-6.

2. The switch can be on the ground side of the relay or solenoid coil, figure 8-7.

In either case, the safety switch must be closed before current can flow through the relay or solenoid coil and close the motor circuit.

The physical location of the starting safety switch depends on the kind of transmission and the location of the shift lever. Switches for automatic transmissions can be on the steering column or on a floor-mounted shift console, figure 8-8, or on the transmission, figure 8-7.

Some installations use mechanical linkage to block the movement of the ignition key until the gear selector is in park or neutral, figure 8-9. These devices are not electrical switches, but they serve the same purpose. They disable the starting switch unless the transmission is disengaged.

Some cars with manual transmissions have safety switches operated by shift linkage. These are similar to automatic transmission installations. The switch closes only when the shift lever is in neutral. Most manual transmission cars with safety switches, however, have clutch-start switches. The clutch linkage closes the switch when the pedal is depressed, figure 8-10.

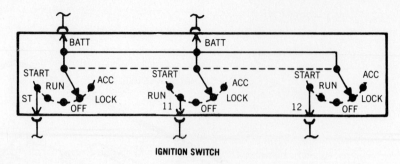

IGNITION SWITCH

Figure 8-5. This is a typical ignition switch symbol you will see on wiring diagrams. (Ford)

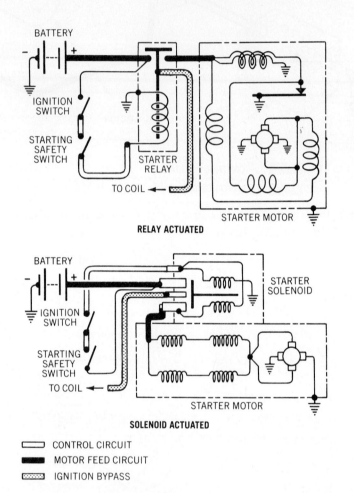

RELAY ACTUATED

SOLENOID ACTUATED

☐ CONTROL CIRCUIT
■ MOTOR FEED CIRCUIT
▨ IGNITION BYPASS

Figure 8-6. The starting safety switch can be in series between the ignition switch and the starter relay or solenoid. (Ford)

Regardless of the design and location of the starting safety switch, it is always in series with the start position of the ignition switch. The relay or solenoid coil cannot receive current unless *both* switches are closed. Many safety switches are adjustable to allow for shift linkage or clutch pedal adjustment. Often, you can fix a no-

start problem by checking and adjusting the safety switch.

Relays and Solenoids. Chapter 3 outlined the basic electromagnetic action of relays and solenoids. Both kinds of devices use current through an electromagnetic coil to move an armature or a movable iron core. The

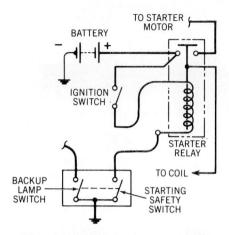

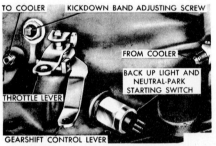

Figure 8-7. This Chrysler transmission-mounted safety switch is in series on the ground side of the relay. (Ford) (Chrysler)

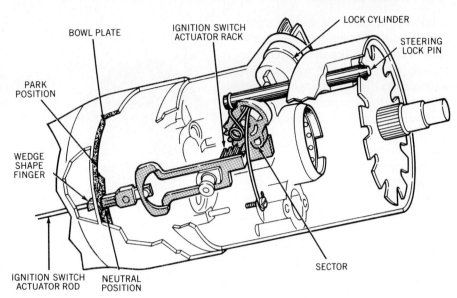

Figure 8-9. Many GM vehicles and other cars have mechanical linkage to disable the ignition key unless the transmission is in park or neutral. (Cadillac)

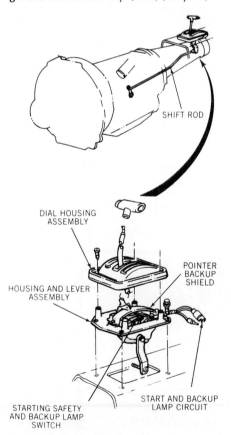

Figure 8-8. Most safety switches for floor-shift automatic transmissions are on the shift console. (Ford)

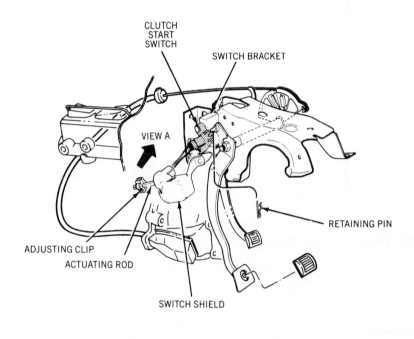

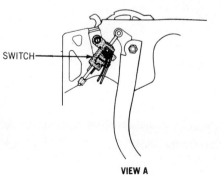

VIEW A

Figure 8-10. Typical clutch-start safety switch installation for a manual transmission. (Ford)

ignition switch and the starting safety switch control current through the coil. When the control circuit is closed, current in the relay or the solenoid coil forms a magnetic field that moves the armature or the core. This movement closes the heavy contacts of the starter motor circuit. In this way, both relays and solenoids can act as magnetic switches for the starter motor, figure 8-11.

The solenoids used in many starting systems also have a second function. The movement of the core operates linkage that engages the starter drive mechanism with the ring gear on the engine flywheel. The terms used to describe switching functions in starter motor circuits can be confusing. A simple solenoid-controlled circuit can use the solenoid as a relay to operate the magnetic switch for the motor and as a mechanical device to engage the starter drive. With slightly different connections, a separate relay can be added to the circuit. The solenoid may or may not switch the motor current. Ford starter relays, for example, are actually solenoid-type magnetic switches. They act as a relay, but they open and close the motor circuit. Chrysler relays switch the control circuit for a motor solenoid. We will examine starter motor circuits more fully in the next section.

The Starter Motor Circuit

The motor circuit is a simple circuit that contains just the starter relay or solenoid and the motor. As explained previously, this circuit provides the most direct path possible for the momentary high-current needs of the motor.

Solenoid-Actuated Circuit. In a solenoid-actuated motor circuit, the solenoid engages the starter drive with the engine and closes the high-current motor circuit. Delco-Remy starting systems on GM vehicles are the most common examples, figure 8-12. Similar systems are used on most Japanese and European cars as well.

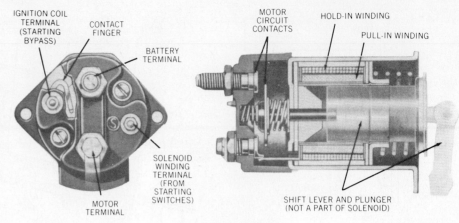

TYPICAL STARTER SOLENOID

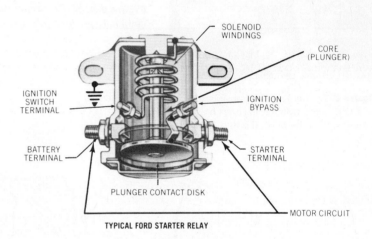

TYPICAL FORD STARTER RELAY

Figure 8-11. Relays and solenoids both can act as magnetic switches for the motor circuit. (Delco-Remy) (Ford)

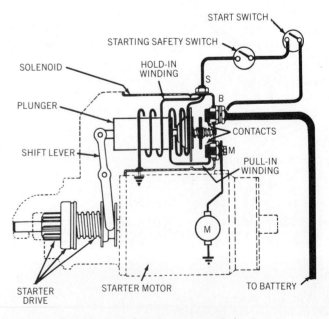

Figure 8-12. Typical solenoid-actuated starting system. (Delco-Remy)

In a basic solenoid-actuated circuit, the battery positive (+) cable is connected to the solenoid battery terminal. The control circuit energizes the solenoid windings through the ignition switch and the safety switch. The electromagnetic field of the windings moves the solenoid core, or plunger, which does two things. The solenoid plunger moves the starter drive pinion gear to engage the flywheel ring gear. It also closes the heavy contacts for the motor circuit, figures 8-11 and 8-12.

Starter solenoids have separate pull-in windings and hold-in windings. The hold-in winding has many turns of light-gauge wire. The pull-in winding has fewer turns of heavier wire. Both windings are energized when the control circuit closes. Together they create the strong magnetic field needed to move the heavy plunger and starter drive mechanism.

The pull-in winding is grounded through the motor terminal and the armature and field windings, figure 8-12. When the plunger disc contacts the solenoid motor terminals, battery voltage is applied to both ends of the pull-in winding. This deactivates the pull-in winding. The lighter hold-in winding is grounded through the solenoid case and remains activated. Less current is needed to hold the plunger engaged than is needed to move it. The double-winding construction reduces solenoid current draw when the starter motor and the ignition are both drawing current during cranking.

The solenoid plunger disc completes the high-current motor circuit through the heavy terminals at the end of the solenoid. A large motor feed strap, or connector link, connects the solenoid motor terminal to the motor field coils and armature. We will look at the mechanical action of starter solenoids further in a later section of this chapter.

Relay-Actuated Circuit. There are two basic kinds of relay-actuated starter motor circuits. A Ford starter circuit uses a large solenoid-type relay

THE STARTERLESS ENGINE

If it weren't for permanent-magnet starter motors, you might be learning to service engines without starter motors today. In the early 1980's, General Motors engineers were struggling with the problem of getting weight out of the new, smaller cars. Starter motors and high-capacity batteries account for 30 or 40 pounds of total car weight. Some engineers thought that if they could eliminate the starter completely, along with a large battery that provided several hundred amperes of cranking current, they could reach a substantial weight-reduction goal.

The method they tried required the use of a direct ignition system, electronic port fuel injection, and a sophisticated engine control computer. Direct ignition eliminated the mechanical distributor and allowed a spark plug in any given cylinder to be fired by computer control. Electronic port fuel injection allowed fuel to be directed to any cylinder by computer control. The idea was to apply spark and fuel to a cylinder that was in position to start a power stroke. The resulting combustion would crank the engine and allow the other cylinders to fire up.

GM engineers did have some success with the project. They got a few engines to start (and may have blown up a few others). To make the system truly reliable, however, would have required sensors to detect piston position in each cylinder and auxiliary startup injectors inside each cylinder.

The availability of powerful permanent magnets put the starterless engine on the shelf. Today's permanent magnet starters weigh much less than motors with field coils, and elimination of field current requirements allows the use of smaller, lighter batteries.

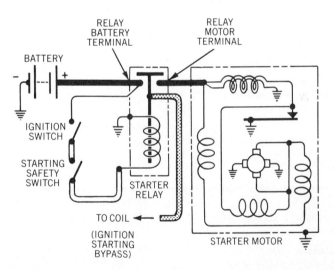

Figure 8-13. Typical Ford relay-actuated starter system with the relay in the motor circuit. (Ford)

to conduct high starting current to the motor, figure 8-11. Full motor current flows through the relay when it is energized.

Most Ford vehicles have movable pole shoe starter motors, which require this kind of relay for operation.

The battery + cable is connected to the battery terminal of the relay, figure 8-13. A similar heavy cable connects the relay motor terminal to the motor. The control circuit from the ignition and safety switches energizes the relay. Some Ford relays have a fourth terminal that provides the starting by-pass connection for the ignition. Systems without the fourth terminal on the relay provide the starting by-pass connection through the ignition switch.

Some Ford products with large V-8 or diesel engines have solenoid-operated starter motors. For manufacturing simplicity, these vehicles have the same kind of starter relay used with movable pole shoe starters. The control circuit actuates the relay, rather than the solenoid. The solenoid engages the starter drive and completes the motor circuit. To energize the solenoid, a connector link is installed between the battery and switch terminals of the solenoid, figure 8-14.

The second kind of relay-actuated motor circuit has a relay in the control circuit to actuate a solenoid-operated starter. Chrysler systems are the most common examples, figure 8-15, but this arrangement also is used on many imported vehicles. The relay does not conduct full starting current to the motor as in a Ford system. Rather, the control circuit through the ignition and safety switches energizes the relay, which completes the control circuit from the battery to the motor solenoid. The solenoid motor circuit is connected to the battery as in a Delco-Remy system. The relay simply provides a simple, low-current connection from the battery directly to the

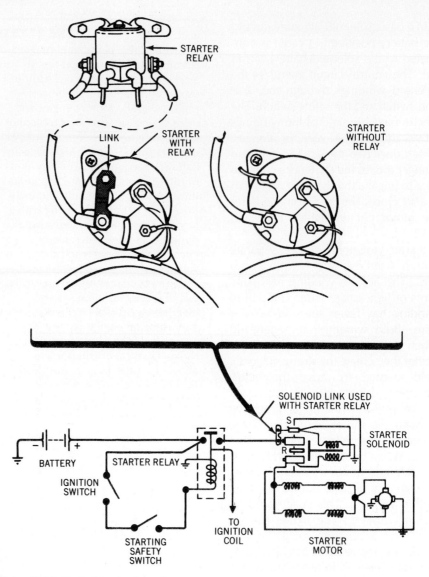

Figure 8-14. Typical Ford solenoid-actuated starter motor with a relay in the motor circuit. (Ford)

IT'S A 350, BUT WHICH ONE?

Many carmakers, domestic and foreign alike, have a long tradition of using a single "corporate engine" in several different car models made by different divisions of the company. Ford did this when it introduced the first Mercury in 1939 and powered it with the proven Ford flathead V-8. In England, Morris and Austin build several family sedans and sports cars, all powered with essentially one or two basic engines.

General Motors began using engines made by one division in cars built by another division during the 1960's. In 1977, the interchanging of

V-8 engines among GM divisions reached a high point. Chevrolet, Pontiac, Oldsmobile, and Buick were all building 350-cid V-8's, and it was quite common to find a Chevrolet-built engine in an Oldsmobile or a Buick-built engine in a Pontiac. Confusion arose with a lot of car owners because as far as they were concerned, their cars had 350 V-8's, period.

If you service a 1977 GM car with a 350 V-8, you need to know *which* 350 because many of the engine specs are different for the engines built by each division. You can tell the difference

by checking the fifth character on the vehicle identification number (VIN) plate on the instrument panel near the base of the windshield. Here are the codes for 1977 GM 350-cid V-8's:

Code	Engine Manufacturer
H	Buick
J	Buick
L	Chevrolet
R	Oldsmobile
P	Pontiac

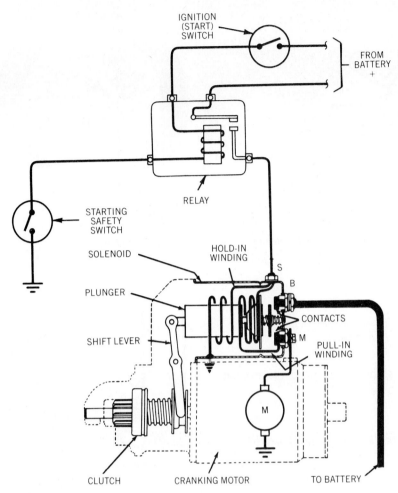

Figure 8-15. Typical relay-actuated starting system with the relay in the control circuit. (Delco-Remy)

solenoid control windings. The solenoid engages the starter drive and completes the motor circuit as in other solenoid-operated motor circuits.

STARTER MOTORS

All electric motors operate on the principles of electromagnetism that you learned in chapter 2. A current-carrying conductor develops a magnetic field around itself. The strength of the field depends on the amount of current, and the magnetic polarity depends on the direction of current flow. If you bring two current-carrying conductors close together, their magnetic fields will interact. Opposite poles will attract each other; like poles will repel each other, figure 8-16. This interaction of magnetic fields can change electrical energy to mechanical energy. This is the basis for all electric motors.

The Motor Principle

If we place a current-carrying conductor in a strong magnetic field, the field created by conductor current tries to

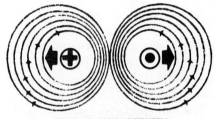

STRONG FIELD BETWEEN CONDUCTORS

CONDUCTORS TEND TO MOVE APART

Figure 8-16. Two conductors with current in opposite directions form magnetic fields that repel each other. (Delco-Remy)

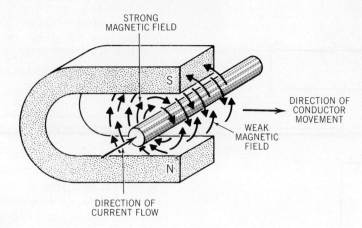

Figure 8-17. A current-carrying conductor in a magnetic field tries to move from the strong field to the weak field.

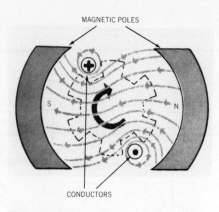

Figure 8-18. The interaction of magnetic fields causes electric motors to operate. (Delco-Remy)

move the conductor out of the surrounding field. The conductor tries to move from the stronger field to a weaker field, figure 8-17. If we place two conductors with current in opposite directions between strong north and south poles, the conductor magnetic fields will interact with the surrounding field, figure 8-18. The clockwise field of the top conductor adds to the field of the poles. This creates a strong field beneath the conductor, which forces it upward. The counterclockwise field of the lower conductor also adds to the field of the poles and creates a stronger field above the conductor. This forces the lower conductor downward.

The two conductors in figure 8-18 can be opposite sides of a single loop. Each side carries current in an opposite direction. If the loop conductor is mounted on a shaft, figure 8-19, we have constructed a simple motor **armature**. An actual motor armature has many conductors to react with the stationary magnetic poles. Continuous interaction of the fields causes the armature shaft to rotate, figure 8-20.

The magnetic poles surrounding the current-carrying conductors can be permanent magnets or electromagnets. Many small motors are made with permanent magnet poles. Starter

motors, however, have electromagnetic poles.

Starter Motor Construction

A typical starter motor, figure 8-21, contains:

• A field frame with pole shoes and electromagnetic field windings

• A rotating armature and shaft with current-carrying conductors

• A commutator end, or brush end, housing that holds the motor electrical terminals, and the brushes that conduct current to the armature

• A drive end housing that supports the starter drive gear, which engages the engine flywheel

• A solenoid, or a movable pole shoe, to close the motor circuit and engage the starter drive

Both end housings have bearings, or bushings, to support the armature shaft.

The motor field frame is an iron housing that holds the iron pole shoes and the field windings, figure 8-22. Iron of the frame and pole shoes increases and concentrates the field strength of the poles. Most starter motors have four pole shoes and four sets of field windings. The pole shoes are

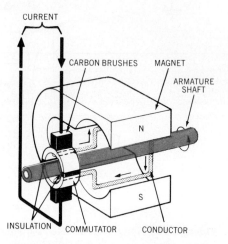

Figure 8-19. A loop conductor on a shaft within a magnetic field is a simple electric motor. (Bosch)

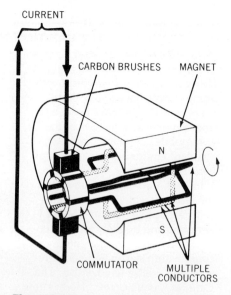

Figure 8-20. An actual motor has many loop conductors on the armature. (Bosch)

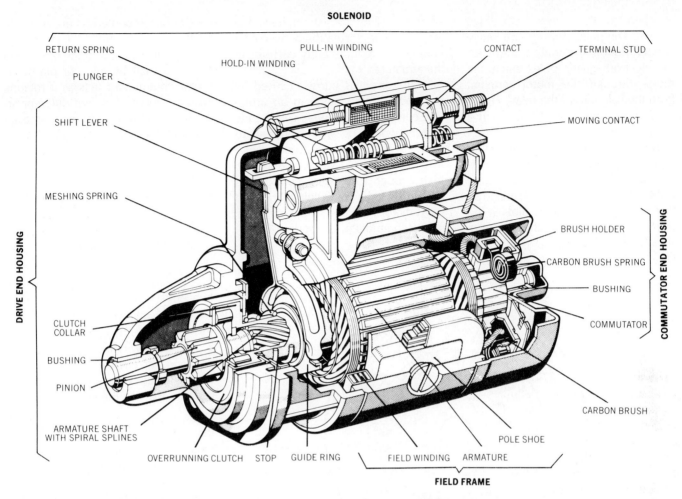

Figure 8-21. This Bosch starter motor is typical of most solenoid-operated starters. (Bosch)

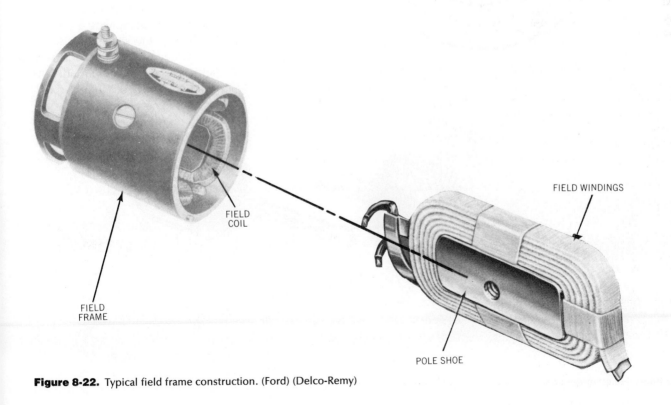

Figure 8-22. Typical field frame construction. (Ford) (Delco-Remy)

attached to the frame with large screws. The field windings are heavy copper ribbon material. Current for the electromagnetic poles enters the motor through the motor terminal from the solenoid or the relay. Figure 8-23 shows the magnetic fields in a 4-pole motor.

The armature holds the armature windings (conductors), the **commutator**, and the armature core, figure 8-24. The armature core is made of thin laminated iron discs. Slots in the iron laminations hold the armature windings. The iron strengthens the armature field. Insulation between the laminations reduces **eddy currents** in the armature.

Eddy current is current caused by induced countervoltage in an armature core. If the core were solid, eddy current would be strong enough to overheat the armature. Counterelectromotive force (CEMF) would also be high enough to develop current and an opposing magnetic field that would resist motor rotation.

The commutator is a series of small copper bars mounted on the armature shaft. Each commutator bar, or segment, is insulated from the others and from the shaft by mica or plastic. A motor commutator acts as a rotating switch. One end of two different armature windings is soldered to each commutator segment, figures 8-18 and 8-20. The opposite end of each winding is connected to a different segment. This arrangement connects the windings in a long series of loop conductors.

Armature windings can be connected to the commutator in two ways:

1. In a lap winding, figure 8-25, the two ends of each winding are connected to adjacent commutator segments.

2. In a wave winding, figure 8-26, the two ends of each winding are connected to segments that are 90 or 180 degrees apart on the commutator.

Wave windings have less resistance than lap windings and are used in most starter motors.

Carbon brushes conduct current to the commutator segments and the armature windings, figure 8-27. Four-pole motors must have four brushes to carry current to the commutator. Each pair of brushes completes a parallel circuit through the armature. Each of the two armature circuits reacts with the field poles to rotate the shaft. One

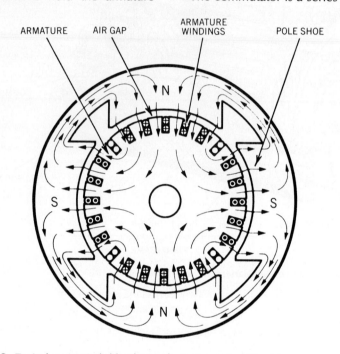

ARMATURE   AIR GAP   ARMATURE WINDINGS   POLE SHOE

Figure 8-23. Typical magnetic fields of a 4-pole starter motor. (Bosch)

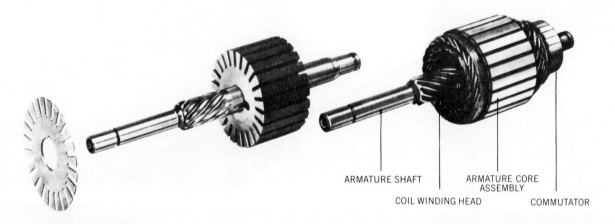

ARMATURE SHAFT   ARMATURE CORE ASSEMBLY

COIL WINDING HEAD   COMMUTATOR

ARMATURE LAMINATION   ARMATURE CORE   ASSEMBLED ARMATURE

Figure 8-24. Typical motor armature construction. (Bosch)

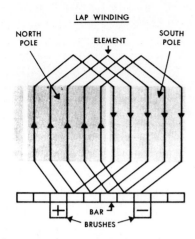

Figure 8-25. This diagram represents a lap-wound armature. (Delco-Remy)

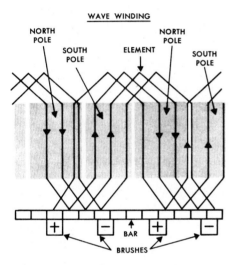

Figure 8-26. This diagram represents a wave-wound armature. (Delco-Remy)

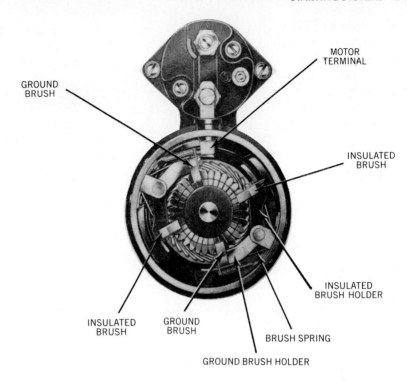

brush of each pair is connected in parallel to the motor battery terminal. The other brush of each pair is grounded to the motor frame.

The brushes are held against the commutator by springs in the brush holders of the commutator end frame. The commutator end frame of most motors also holds the terminals that connect the insulated brushes and the field windings to battery voltage. Commutator end frames on most motors are made of aluminum to reduce weight.

The drive end frame supports the armature shaft and the starter drive. It also provides the mounting flange where the motor is bolted to the engine.

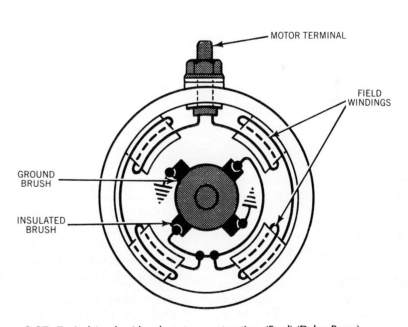

Figure 8-27. Typical 4-pole, 4-brush motor construction. (Ford) (Delco-Remy)

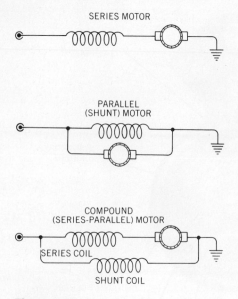

Figure 8-28. Three basic kinds of dc motor circuits. (Ford)

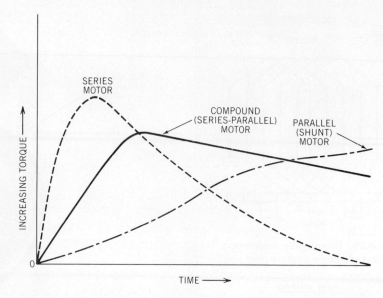

Figure 8-29. Typical torque and speed relationships of different dc electric motors.

Motor Field and Armature Circuits

Field current and armature current enter the motor through a single terminal. Therefore, the field windings and the armature windings must be connected in a single complete circuit. There are three ways to do this in any dc electric motor, figure 8-28.

1. Series connection
2. Parallel (shunt) connection
3. Compound (series-parallel) connection

The field and armature connections affect the torque and speed relationship of the motor, figure 8-29.

Series Motor. A series-connected motor develops maximum torque at startup speed—zero rpm, figures 8-28 and 8-29. This is because induced CEMF in the armature and field windings is low when the motor is not rotating. CEMF generates current that opposes battery current and a magnetic field that opposes motor rotation. Because CEMF is low at low motor speed, however, it produces little opposition to armature and field current. A series motor, therefore, develops maximum torque as it starts to rotate. Torque then decreases as motor speed and CEMF increase. This high starting torque characteristic makes series motors ideal for many engine starting applications.

Parallel (Shunt) Motors. In this kind of motor, the field coils are in parallel with the armature, figure 8-28. Torque is low at startup speed and increases as motor speed increases, figure 8-29. Changing the load on the motor changes the CEMF in the armature but not in the field. The motor adjusts its torque output to the load and operates at a relatively constant speed. Parallel motors are ideal for applications such as power windows and power seats, but not for engine cranking. Combining the features of a series motor and a parallel motor produces a compound motor, which can be used to crank an engine.

Compound (Series-Parallel) Motors.

A compound motor has one or more field coils in series with the armature and one or more coils in parallel, figure 8-28. A compound motor develops high torque soon after startup and maintains comparatively high torque as speed increases, figure 8-29. Many starter motors for large engines are the compound type.

Typical Field and Armature Circuits. We could go farther into the electrical theory of starter motor construction, but that isn't necessary for starter system service. Recognizing the different kinds of field and armature connections is important, however, when testing motors for open or short circuits. If you can recognize the connections for different series and compound motors, you can trace the circuits with an ohmmeter or self-powered test lamp.

Remember that most automobile starter motors are 4-pole, 4-brush motors. A simple series motor can be connected with all four field windings in series and then with parallel connections to the two insulated brushes, figure 8-30. A series motor also can be connected with two field windings in series with each insulated brush. These two circuits then can be connected in parallel with a common connection, figure 8-31. A compound motor typically will have three field coils in series with two parallel brushes and a shunt coil connected to a third insulated brush, figure 8-32.

Engineers select starter motors to meet the cranking speed and torque needs of different engines. Electrical diagrams for starting systems will show motor field and armature connections to help you troubleshoot motor problems.

STARTER MOTOR AND DRIVE DESIGNS

We have examined starting motor circuits and the electrical design and construction of starter motors. The final major feature of starting systems is the kind of drive mechanism that engages the motor with the engine flywheel.

For any motor to apply enough torque to crank the engine at starting speed, the torque must be increased through gear reduction. The motor turns a pinion gear that engines a ring gear on the flywheel. A typical flywheel ring gear has approximately

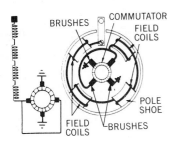

Figure 8-30. This motor has four field coils in series with two parallel brushes. (Oldsmobile)

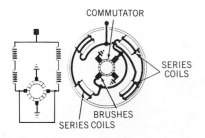

Figure 8-31. This motor has four field coils. Two are in series with each other and one brush. (Oldsmobile)

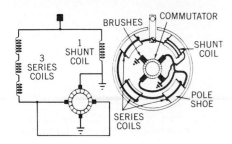

Figure 8-32. This compound motor has three field coils in series and one in parallel. (Oldsmobile)

150 to 200 teeth. A typical starter drive pinion has about 10 teeth. The ratio between the pinion and the flywheel gear, then, is approximately 15 : 1 to 20 : 1. The motor turns at 3,000 to 4,000 rpm to crank the engine at about 200 rpm.

Remember that the motor turns for only a few seconds. The starter drive is a mechanism that moves the motor pinion to engage the flywheel. Just as importantly, the starter drive disengages the pinion from the flywheel when the engine starts and turns faster than cranking speed. At an idle speed of 600 rpm, a starter motor would be turned at 9,000 to 12,000 rpm if it stayed engaged with the flywheel. At 3,000 engine rpm, the starter would turn at 45,000 to 60,000 rpm if it were engaged with the engine. These speeds would literally tear the motor apart. Occasionally, a starter drive may fail and leave the pinion engaged with the flywheel. The results will be a destroyed motor.

Starter motors on almost all late-model automobiles are the **positive-engagement** type. They use mechanical leverage provided by a solenoid or

a movable pole shoe on the motor to engage the starter drive pinion with the engine flywheel. Older domestic cars and a few late-model European cars use **inertia-engagement** starters. These use what is commonly called a Bendix-drive mechanism. Positive-engagement starters are far more common on current vehicles than Bendix-drive starters. Positive-engagement starter drives are divided into three major groups:

1. Solenoid-operated, direct drive
2. Solenoid-operated, reduction drive
3. Movable pole shoe

The following paragraphs explain their design and operation.

Solenoid-Operated, Direct Drive

The most common solenoid-operated, direct-drive starter motors are made by the Delco-Remy Division of General Motors. The Delco-Remy MT series of starter motors, figure 8-33, has been used on almost all GM cars and light trucks for decades. These motors vary in size, as well as in field

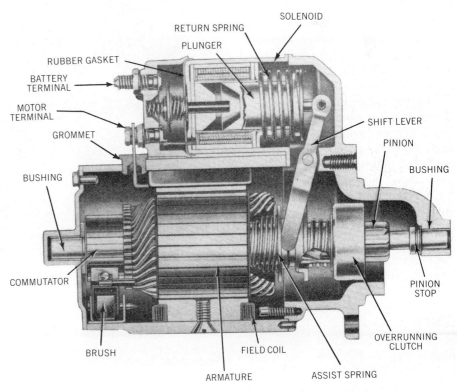

Figure 8-33. Delco MT series starter motors have been used on GM cars for 30 years. (Delco-Remy)

and armature connections, for different sizes of engines. They may be either series or compound motors. However, all have a solenoid-operated, positive-engagement drive mechanism. Although construction details vary, operating principles are the same for all of these motors.

Some large Ford engines also have solenoid-operated, direct-drive engagement. Most Bosch starter motors, figure 8-21, and Japanese motors from Nippondenso and other manufacturers work on the same principles. A few Chrysler engines also have similar direct-drive starters. We examined the solenoid action earlier as part of the starter motor electrical circuit. Now, let's look at the mechanical part of the solenoid-operated starter drive.

When the control circuit energizes the pull-in and hold-in windings of the solenoid, the plunger moves to close the high-current motor circuit. The plunger also moves a shift lever that slides the drive pinion assembly along the armature shaft, figure 8-34.

The pinion must engage the flywheel *before* the solenoid completes the motor circuit. To do this, the shift lever may have a mechanical leverage ratio that will engage the pinion before the solenoid closes the motor circuit. The solenoid plunger also may have two parts. The first part engages the drive pinion and then forces the second part to close the motor circuit. This is the common design used in Delco-Remy starters.

If the pinion teeth hit the flywheel teeth and do not engage fully, a spring on the starter drive compresses so that the solenoid plunger can complete its stroke. The spring forces the pinion to engage with the flywheel as soon as the armature shaft moves. This positive engagement prevents damage to the pinion or the flywheel ring gear when the starter motor applies cranking torque.

When the engine starts and runs faster than cranking speed, a 1-way, or overrunning, clutch disengages the pinion from the flywheel. The 1-way clutch has rollers held between a col-

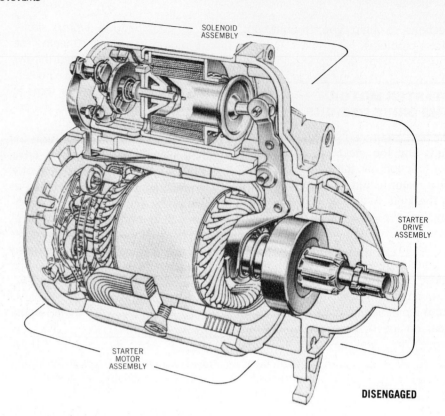

DISENGAGED

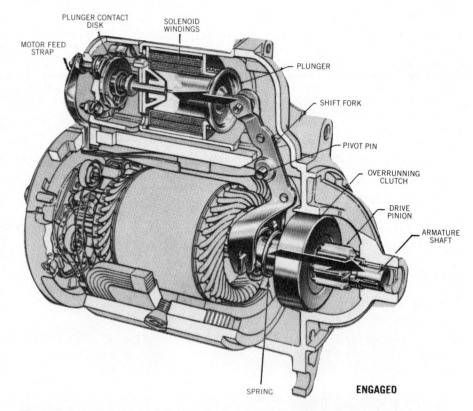

ENGAGED

Figure 8-34. Solenoid action closes the motor circuit and mechanically engages the starter drive. (Ford)

lar on the pinion and an outer clutch housing and shell. Motor torque is transferred through the shell to the rollers and the pinion. The shell has tapered slots in which the rollers can ride freely or wedge between the collar and the shell, figure 8-35. When the motor armature turns to crank the engine, the rollers are wedged against spring pressure into the narrow ends of the slots. When the engine starts and turns faster than the motor, the armature accelerates and releases pressure on the rollers. The springs then force the rollers into the wider areas of the slots. This uncouples the motor from the pinion and lets the pinion spin freely.

When the driver releases the ignition switch from the start position, the solenoid is deenergized. A return spring in the solenoid moves the plunger and the shift lever to withdraw the starter drive from the flywheel.

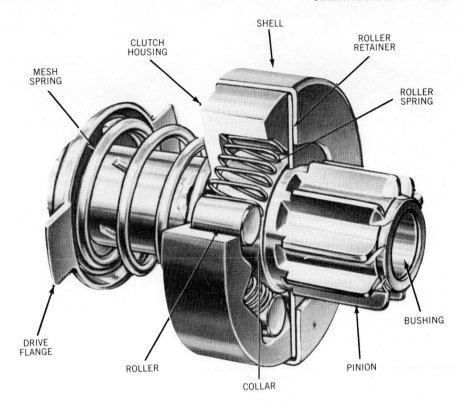

Figure 8-35. Most starter drives have a 1-way (overrunning) clutch. (Ford)

Solenoid-Operated, Reduction Drive

A reduction-drive starter also uses a solenoid to engage the pinion with the flywheel and to complete the motor circuit. The motor armature, however, does not drive the pinion directly. Instead, it turns a small drive gear that meshes with a larger gear, figure 8-36. This provides a reduction ratio of about 2 : 1 to 3.5 : 1. The exact ratio depends on motor design and engine cranking requirements.

The armature gear and the reduction gear are permanently meshed. The reduction gear turns the shaft for the starter drive pinion, which is engaged by the solenoid shift lever. The pinion drive mechanism works exactly like a solenoid-operated, direct-drive starter. A 1-way clutch releases the pinion when the engine starts. A solenoid return spring withdraws the drive from the flywheel when the solenoid is deenergized.

Reduction-drive starters allow a small, lightweight, high-speed motor to develop enough torque to crank a

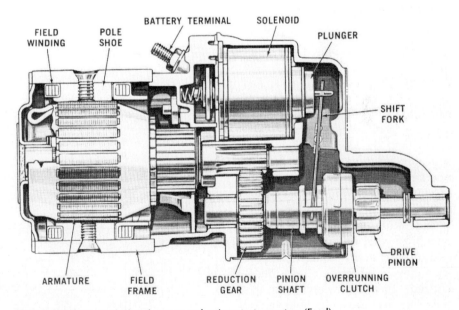

Figure 8-36. Typical Chrysler gear-reduction starter motor. (Ford)

large or high-compression engine. For years, Chrysler was the major user of reduction-drive starters. Today, reduction-drive starters are used for small, high-compression engines and diesel engines in many imported and domestic vehicles. Reduction-drive starters are usually compound motors.

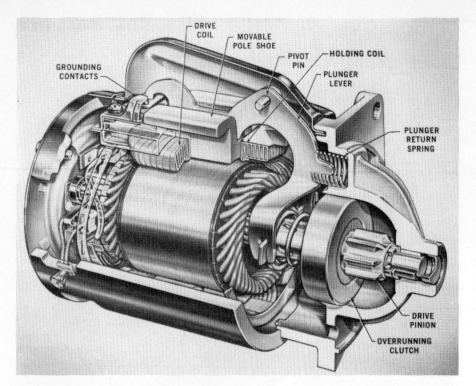

Figure 8-37. Ford calls the movable pole shoe starter a "positive engagement" starter. (Ford)

Movable Pole Shoe

Ford Motor Company is the only maker of movable pole shoe starter motors, figure 8-37. Ford has used these motors for over 25 years, and they are the most common Ford starters. Ford calls the movable pole shoe starter a "positive-engagement" starter. In fact, the drive mechanism is similar to the drive used on solenoid-operated, direct-drive starters. It is engaged, however, by movement of one of the pole shoes in the motor.

One of the pole shoes is mounted on a pivot in the drive end housing. A return spring holds the movable pole shoe upward when the relay is deenergized. The field winding for this pole shoe has a parallel holding coil that is independently grounded. All four field windings also have a normally closed ground contact.

When the Ford starter relay closes, current flows through all four field windings and the holding coil to ground, figure 8-38. This creates a strong magnetic field that pulls the pole shoe toward the motor armature. The movable pole shoe is linked to the

160

Figure 8-38. Typical circuit diagram for a Ford movable pole shoe starter system.

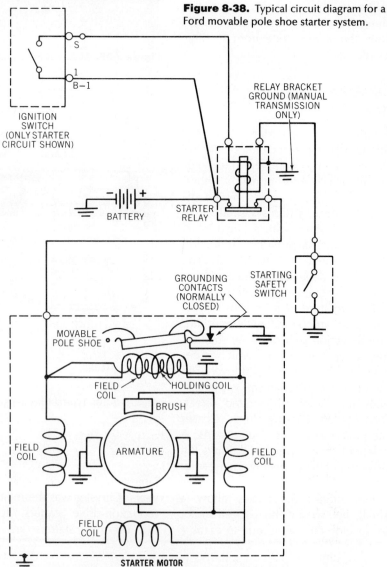

starter drive by a shift lever, or yoke. Movement of the pole shoe shifts the drive pinion to engage the flywheel. When the pole shoe moves to operating position, it opens the normally closed grounding contacts. The motor field circuit is then completed through the armature and the ground brushes, and the motor rotates. The holding coil remains independently grounded to hold the movable pole shoe in operating position.

When the engine starts, a 1-way clutch in the starter drive allows the pinion to freewheel. When the driver releases the key, the motor circuit opens. The return spring then moves the pole shoe and shift lever to withdraw the drive from the flywheel.

The movable pole shoe starter requires a separate relay to provide motor current. These motors, made by Ford's Motorcraft Division, are used on many AMC vehicles, as well as Ford products.

Permanent Magnet Gear Reduction (PMGR) Starters

Permanent magnet (PM) starter motors were introduced on some 1986 Chrysler and AMC models and on 1988 Chevrolet and GMC light trucks. This type of starter motor has no electromagnetic field coils or pole shoes. The magnetic field is provided by four or six small permanent magnets, depending upon the size of the motor, figure 8-39. As a result, there is no motor field circuit and thus there are no potential field wire-to-frame shorts or other electrical problems related to the field. The motor uses only an armature circuit. The permanent magnets, figure 8-40, are made from an alloy of iron and rare-earth materials that delivers a magnetic field strong enough to operate the motor with the same cranking performance as a comparable starter motor with electromagnetic fields.

A planetary gear train transmits power between the armature and the pinion shaft, resulting in a high-speed, low-torque starter motor. (The armature revolves at speeds up to 7,000 rpm). Figure 8-41 shows the Bosch

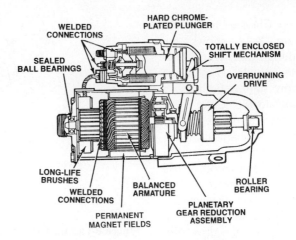

Figure 8-39. The PMGR starter motor uses permanent magnets to create a magnetic field instead of the field coils and pole pieces of a conventional starter design. (Delco-Remy)

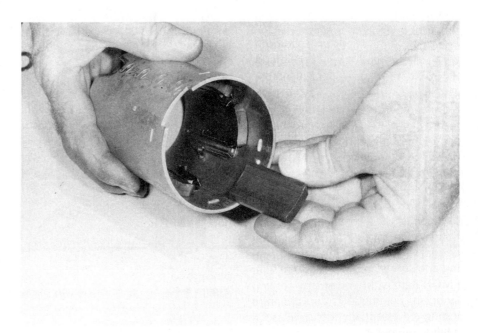

Figure 8-40. The magnets used in PMGR starter motors are made of a new alloy of iron and rare-earth materials, but are brittle and require careful handling.

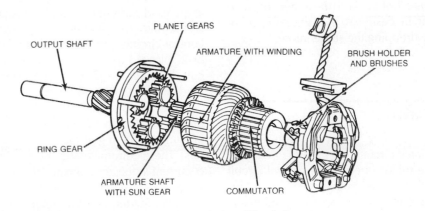

Figure 8-41. The Bosch planetary gearset design. (Chrysler)

design used on Chrysler and AMC vehicles; figure 8-42 shows the Delco-Remy design used with Chevrolet and GMC vehicles. The Bosch and Delco-Remy starters both use a solenoid to operate the starter drive and close the motor armature circuit. While the drive mechanism is the same as that used on other solenoid-actuated starters, some models use lightweight plastic shift levers.

The planetary gearset installed between the armature and starter drive increases the torque at the drive pinion while reducing the speed. The gearset is quite compact, measuring only 1/2- to 3/4-inch deep. It is mounted inline with the drive pinion and armature. By keying the internal ring gear to the field frame, it remains stationary in the motor. The armature shaft drives the sun gear, which meshes with three planetary pinions. The pinions drive the pinion carrier in reduction during their rotation around the ring gear. Because the starter drive shaft is mounted on the carrier, it is driven at a reduced speed with increased torque.

Although the Bosch and Delco-Remy PMGR starters are mechanically different, their electrical operation is identical to that of a field coil design, figure 8-43. Field circuit testing and service are not required with PMGR starters, but other service such as brush, commutator, and armature testing are essentially the same as for a field coil motor.

Like any other permanent magnet motor, PMGR starters require care in handling. The permanent magnets are quite brittle, and the magnetic field can be destroyed by a sharp impact or by dropping the starter motor.

SUMMARY

The starting system consists of two related circuits: the control circuit and the motor circuit. The control circuit contains the ignition switch, the starting safety switch, and the control side (coil) of the starter relay or solenoid.

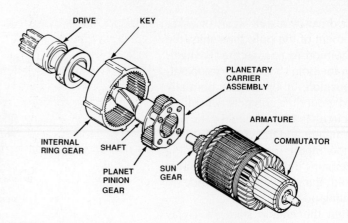

Figure 8-42. The Delco-Remy planetary gearset design. (Delco-Remy)

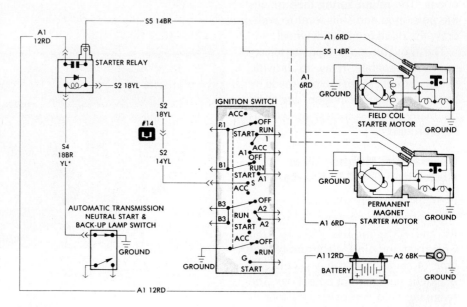

Figure 8-43. The electrical circuitry of PMGR and conventional starter motors is the same. (Chrysler)

The motor circuit is a high-current circuit that conducts several hundred amperes of current to the high-torque starter motor for a few seconds. Starter control circuits can use either a relay or a solenoid to close the motor circuit. In either case, the relay or solenoid acts as a magnetic switch.

Starter motors, like all dc motors, operate on the electromagnetic action of current flowing through conductors. The electromagnetic interaction of current in the armature and the field windings causes the motor armature to rotate. Starter motor armatures and fields draw current from a common

source—the battery. The field and armature windings can be connected in series or in a compound (series-parallel) arrangement.

Permanent magnet gear reduction (PMGR) starter motors have no field coils or pole shoes. They rely on small permanent magnets to create a magnetic field. A planetary gearset couples the armature with the drive to provide gear reduction with high torque at the pinion. They are smaller, lighter, and less prone to electrical problems than conventional field coil designs.

Almost all late-model starters use a

positive-engagement drive mechanism to engage the motor pinion with the flywheel ring gear. There are three common kinds of starter drives:

1. Solenoid-operated, direct drive
2. Solenoid-operated, reduction drive
3. Movable pole shoe

All of these starter drives use a 1-way (overrunning) clutch to release the starter drive pinion from the flywheel when the engine starts.

Hard-starting complaints are common engine performance problems. The cause of an engine starting problem may be in the parts of the starting system, or the problem may be due to the effects of the starting circuits on other vehicle systems. Because of the high current draw of the starter motor, starting system problems also can affect battery performance and ignition operation.

REVIEW QUESTIONS

Multiple Choice

1. Automobile batteries are designed primarily to provide high current to:
   a. the distributor
   b. the ignition switch
   c. the starter
   d. the voltage regulator

2. The starting system consists of two related electrical circuits. They are:
   a. the motor circuit and the ignition circuit
   b. the motor circuit and the cranking circuit
   c. the control circuit and the ignition circuit
   d. the control circuit and the motor circuit

3. Cranking speed for most engines is approximately:
   a. 200 rpm
   b. 100 rpm
   c. 600 rpm
   d. 700 rpm

4. Battery cables are made of heavy guage wire because:
   a. they must withstand engine heat
   b. they must carry high electrical current
   c. they must provide a good electrical contact
   d. smaller gauge wire breaks too easily

5. The ignition switch usually receives battery voltage from a terminal on the:
   a. relay or solenoid
   b. voltage regulator
   c. distributor
   d. starter safety switch

6. The starter control circuit contains:
   a. the ignition switch
   b. the starting safety switch and the control side of a relay or solenoid
   c. the battery
   d. all of the above

7. The ignition switch start position is:
   a. a momentary contact position
   b. a detented position
   c. a spring-loaded switch position
   d. none of the above

8. Ballast resistors are used to:
   a. increase the voltage to the ignition after the engine has started
   b. decrease the voltage to the ignition after the engine has started
   c. connect the battery to a starter solenoid
   d. reduce the voltage supplied to the starting circuit

9. A starting safety switch:
   a. controls transmission operation
   b. is a neutral start switch
   c. is a normally open switch
   d. both b and c

10. A solenoid uses current through an electromagnetic field to move an armature or a movable iron core. In a starter control circuit it can be used to:
   a. cause the starter drive to engage the ring gear
   b. control safety bypass voltage
   c. close the contacts in a starter motor circuit
   d. all of the above

11. A basic starter control circuit energizes the solenoid windings through the ignition switch and the:
   a. solenoid core
   b. starting safety switch
   c. electromagnetic field
   d. pinion gear

12. Starter solenoids have separate:
   a. pull-in windings and pull-out windings
   b. pull-out windings and hold-in windings
   c. pull-in windings and hold-in windings
   d. pull-out windings and hold-out windings

13. A motor armature has many conductors designed to react with stationary magnetic poles. This interaction causes the armature shaft to:
   a. remain stationary
   b. move from one direction to another
   c. turn in 90 degree increments
   d. rotate

Fill in the Blank

14. The starter motor field frame is an iron housing that holds the _____ and the _____ .

15. Insulation between the laminations of the armature core reduces _____ in the armature.

16. CEMF means _____ .

17. The _____ is a series of small copper bars mounted on the armature shaft.

18. _____ are used to conduct current to the commutator segments and the armature windings.

19. A series motor develops maximum _____ at startup speed.

20. _____ motors are ideal for use with power windows and power seats.

21. Most automobile starter motors are _____ motors.

22. Starter motors are mostly of the _____ type.

23. General Motors makes heavy use of the _____ starter.

24. Chrysler has been the major user of the _____ starter.

25. Ford Motor company is the only maker of the _____ starter.

26. All starter types use a _____ to release the starter drive pinion from the flywheel ring gear.

27. _____ is one of the most common engine performance problems.

28. The starter control circuit contains the _____ , the _____ , and a _____ .

29. All electric motors operate on the principle of _____ .

30. Armature windings can be connected to the commutator by _____ or _____ .

31. Series motors are ideal for engine starting applications because they develop _____ at startup speed.

32. PMGR starter motors use _____ instead of field coils and pole shoes to create a magnetic field.

9 CHARGING SYSTEMS

WHAT

The battery is the source of electric power for all circuits on an automobile. But a battery can't supply the vehicle's voltage and current needs indefinitely. As it delivers current, it cycles from a charged to a discharged condition. Eventually, it would discharge completely if the vehicle did not have a charging system.

The alternator is the principal part of the charging system. It generates current through electromagnetic induction and delivers current to the battery at about 12.6 to 14.5 volts. Whenever the alternator is operating, it also delivers current and applies charging voltage to the rest of the electrical system.

The entire electrical system depends on correct alternator operation. This chapter describes the construction and operation of alternators and other charging system parts.

WHY

The battery and the alternator rely on each other for proper operation. Obviously, the alternator must maintain the battery state of charge. The alternator can't operate, however, without initial field current from the battery. The charging system also affects other vehicle circuits. The alternator must deliver enough output current and steady system voltage for lights, air conditioning, power accessories, ignition, and engine control systems. The charging voltage must be held within regulated limits. If charging voltage is lower than battery voltage, the alternator can't charge the battery or deliver adequate current to other circuits. If charging voltage is too high, it can damage the battery, ignition parts, and solid-state electronic components. These are a few basic reasons why charging system testing and service are part of total engine performance service.

GOALS

After studying this chapter, you should be able to:

1. Identify the major parts of a charging system and their relationships: the battery, the alternator, the regulator, and indicators.

2. Explain current generation and rectification in an alternator. Describe the functions of the rotor, stator, brushes, sliprings, and diodes.

3. Explain the operation of solid-state and electromechanical voltage regulators. Explain field relay operation.

4. Explain the operation of vehicle ammeters, voltmeters, and indicator lamps.

CHARGING VOLTAGE

Remember that each battery cell produces about 2.1 volts. The open-circuit voltage of a 12-volt, 6-cell battery is about 12.6 volts. Even though the vehicle electrical system is nominally a 12-volt system, the charging system must produce more than 12 volts. If the alternator were regulated at 12 volts, it could not charge the battery until system voltage fell below 12 volts. This would not allow an adequate voltage reserve for the rest of the electrical system. Charging voltage also must be above 12 volts to overcome the battery's internal resistance and CEMF.

Most charging systems are regulated to develop about 14.5 volts,

maximum. This voltage will deliver adequate charging current to the battery as well as current to other electrical loads. Some systems may be regulated as low as 13.5 volts. Lower voltage slightly reduces heat from high current and may prolong the life of lamp bulbs and other parts. Some systems are regulated at 15 to 15.5 volts maximum. Higher voltage ensures adequate current under all operating conditions. Expensive electronic parts of some vehicles, however, can be damaged by excess current if voltage exceeds 15.5 or 16 volts.

If charging voltage is below the carmaker's specifications, the battery gradually will become sulfated. If charging voltage is above specifications, the battery may overheat with

excessive gassing. In either case, battery life will be shortened.

All of these factors are reasons why the carmaker's maximum charging system voltage specification is important for engine performance service.

CHARGING SYSTEM CIRCUITS

The charging system, figure 9-1, consists of:

• The battery, which is charged by the alternator and which provides initial field current to the alternator

• The alternator, which is turned by an engine drive belt and which is the charging voltage and current source

• The regulator, which limits maximum charging voltage

• An ammeter, a voltmeter, or an indicator lamp, which indicates charging system operation

Like the ignition, starting, and other electrical systems, the charging system has more than one major circuit. The two circuits of the charging system, figure 9-2 are:

• The output circuit, which delivers voltage and current to the battery and other electrical loads

• The field circuit, which delivers current to the alternator field

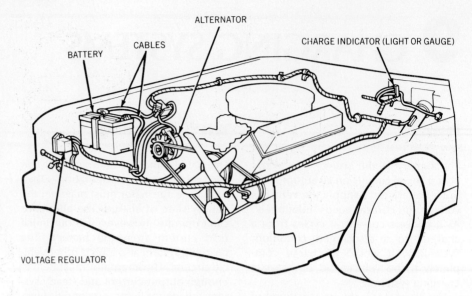

Figure 9-1. The charging system contains these major parts. (Chrysler)

ALTERNATORS

Alternators generate current and voltage by the principles of electromagnetic induction introduced in chapter 2. One way to induce voltage and generate current is to rotate a magnet inside a stationary looped conductor, figure 9-3. That is an alternator.

As the magnet rotates, its field induces a varying voltage and alternating current in the conductor. The amount of current and the voltage polarity (current direction) depend on:

1. The direction of magnetic polarity
2. The strength of the magnetic field
3. The number of conductors
4. The number of magnetic flux lines cut by each conductor
5. The speed of relative motion between the magnetic field and the conductors

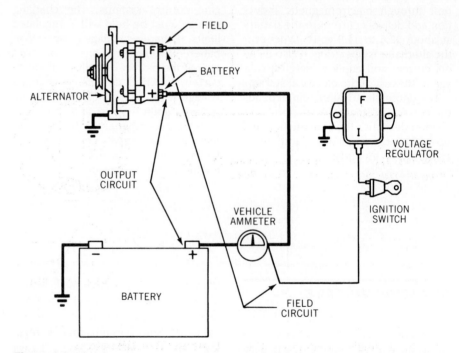

Figure 9-2. The charging system contains the output circuit and the field circuit. (Prestolite)

Alternating Current Generation

Figure 9-4 shows the voltage polarity and alternating current induced in the top half of a single looped conductor during one rotor revolution. Look at these points in the drawing:

A. The conductor is parallel with the magnetic field. The conductor is not cut by any flux lines. Voltage and current are at zero.

B. The rotor has turned 90 degrees, and the magnetic field is at a right angle to the conductor. The maximum number of flux lines cut the conductor at the north pole. Voltage and current are at maximum positive values.

C. The rotor has turned another 90 degrees, and the field is again parallel with the conductor. No flux lines cut the conductor, and voltage and current return to zero.

D. The rotor has turned another 90 degrees, but the magnetic field has reversed at the top conductor. The maximum number of flux lines cut the conductor at the south pole. Voltage and current increase to maximum negative values.

E. Voltage and current return to zero as the rotor completes one revolution and returns to its starting point.

One rotor revolution produces one ac

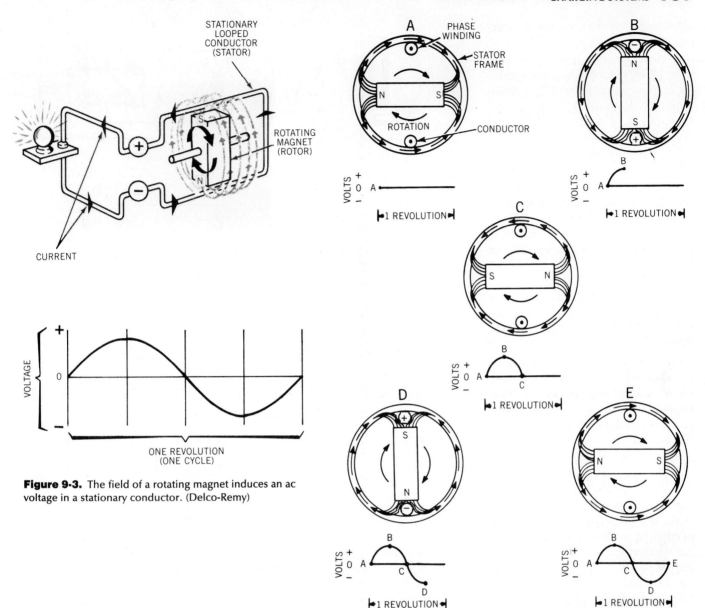

Figure 9-3. The field of a rotating magnet induces an ac voltage in a stationary conductor. (Delco-Remy)

Figure 9-4. Positive and negative voltage induced in the upper half of one conductor during one rotor revolution. (Prestolite)

cycle in a single conductor. The changing voltage polarity between positive and negative is called **sine wave voltage,** figure 9-5. The angle between the magnetic field and the conductor determines the sine wave shape. This is based on the trigonometry sine function of angles. The sine wave voltage induced in one conductor during one rotor revolution is **single-phase voltage**.

We could build a simple alternator as described here, using a bar magnet and a length of wire. It wouldn't have any practical use in a charging system, however.

Current Rectification

Automobile electrical devices are dc devices because the battery is a dc voltage source. Automobile devices require a steady supply of direct current at a relatively steady voltage of constant polarity. Most importantly, you can't charge a battery with alternating current. The ac output of an alternator must be rectified to direct current. There are several ways to **rectify** ac to dc, but the only practical way to do it in an alternator is with diodes.

Chapter 4 introduced a diode as a

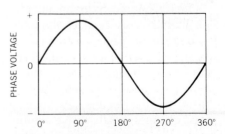

Figure 9-5. Sine wave voltage, + to −, generated during one rotor revolution. (Bosch)

semiconductor electrical check valve, figure 9-6. It allows current flow in one direction but blocks it in the other. If we put a diode in the alternator output circuit, figure 9-7, it allows current to flow from A (+) to B (−) but not from B to A. This is **half-wave rectification**. A single diode can rectify current with positive or negative potential, but not both. A single diode produces intermittent pulsating dc. This is not useful to charge a battery or power other dc devices.

If we add more diodes to the circuit, we can rectify the negative half of the ac sine wave voltage, figure 9-8. Here, diodes 2 and 3 allow current to flow in one direction (positive polarity) from A, through the outside circuit, and back to B. When alternator polarity reverses, diodes 1 and 4 allow current to flow from B, through the circuit, and back to A. Polarity remains positive in the outside circuit because of diode action. The result is pulsating, full-wave direct current. Current fluctuates from zero to maximum positive and back to zero. This is steadier than half-wave rectified current but still not good enough for an automobile electrical system.

To get the steady direct current needed by an automobile dc system we must add more conductors to the alternator. Alternators have three output conductors, coiled in multiple loops, figure 9-9. The conductors are placed at different angles to the rotating field so that the ac voltage cycles overlap. These are the **phase angles** of the conductors. The result is **three-phase voltage**. Adding additional diodes, figure 9-9, allows us to rectify 3-phase voltage into steadier dc output.

A final requirement for an automobile alternator is to replace the rotating permanent magnet with an electromagnet. Alternator induced voltage varies with field strength and rotating speed. Because the alternator is driven by the engine, its rotating speed changes greatly. If the alternator field were a permanent magnet, induced voltage could not be controlled within the limits needed by the

electrical system. Using an electromagnet for the field allows us to regulate field current and the strength of the field. This produces voltage within controlled limits and generates current for the load requirements of the electrical system. Also, an electromagnet can produce a stronger magnetic field, when needed, than a comparably sized permanent magnet.

We will return to alternator current generation and voltage regulation later in this chapter. To understand alternator operation completely, however, we should look at alternator construction.

Alternator Construction

All alternators have these major parts, figure 9-10:

• A housing that supports the stationary output conductor windings and the rotating field

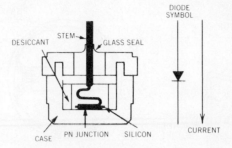

Figure 9-6. A diode is an electrical check valve. (Delco-Remy)

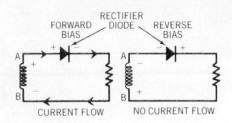

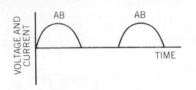

Figure 9-7. One diode provides half-wave rectification from one output winding. (Delco-Remy)

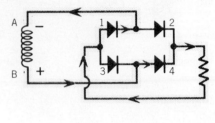

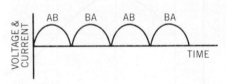

Figure 9-8. Four diodes provide full-wave rectification from one output winding. (Delco-Remy)

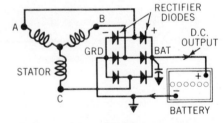

Figure 9-9. Six diodes provide full-wave rectification from three output windings (3-phase rectification). (Delco-Remy)

• A rotor, which is the rotating magnetic field

• Sliprings and brushes that conduct field current to the rotor

• A stator, which contains the output windings

• Rectifying diodes or 1-piece rectifier bridges to change ac to dc output

Most late-model alternators have solid-state electronic voltage regulators. Many are mounted on, or inside, the alternator housing. Earlier alternators used electromechanical regulators, similar to those used with older dc generators. These are mounted away from the alternator. We will examine regulator operation later in this chapter.

The Alternator Housing. Most automobile alternators have 2-piece housings made of cast aluminum, figure 9-11. Heavy-duty alternators used on large trucks, buses, and industrial equipment often have separate center housings to hold larger stators and rotors.

The drive end housing, or end frame, holds a bearing for the rotor shaft. The shaft extends through the housing and holds the drive pulley and the cooling fan. The fan draws air through openings in the opposite end of the alternator. Cooling air leaves the alternator through openings behind the fan in the drive end housing.

The other housing is the slipring end housing (end frame), or rear end housing. It, too, holds a bearing for the shaft. It contains the brushes that carry field current to the rotor sliprings, and it has all electrical terminals for alternator connections. The slipring end housing also holds the regulator for an alternator with a built-in solid-state regulator.

Three or more through bolts hold the end housings together and provide a rigid mounting for the stator core. On some alternators, the stator core is exposed. On others, it is inside the housing.

The alternator housing is bolted directly to the engine so that it is part of the electrical ground path. Anything that is attached to the housing, and not insulated from it, is grounded. Checking ground connections through the housing is an important part of alternator troubleshooting. Some parts must be insulated; others specifically must be grounded.

The Rotor. The rotor is the alternator's magnetic field. It contains two magnetic pole pieces, a field winding, an iron core, and a pair of sliprings,

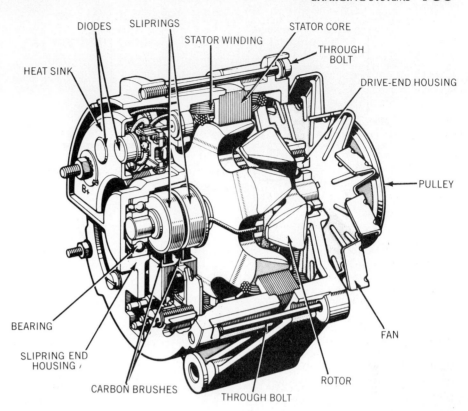

Figure 9-10. Typical automobile alternator construction. (Bosch)

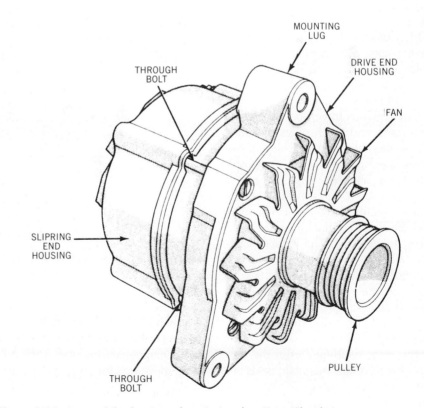

Figure 9-11. Automobile alternators have 2-piece housings. (Chrysler)

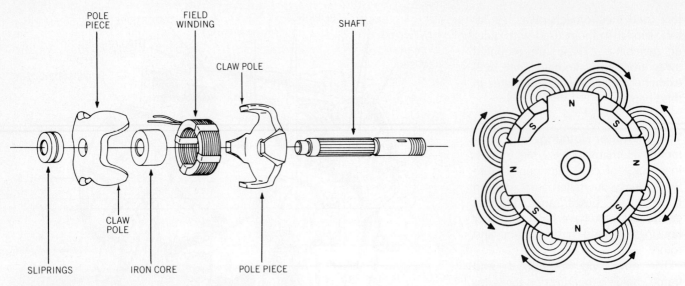

POLE PIECE FIELD WINDING SHAFT

CLAW POLE

CLAW POLE

SLIPRINGS IRON CORE POLE PIECE

Figure 9-12. Typical alternator rotor construction. (Prestolite)

Figure 9-13. Rotor field north and south poles alternate. (Prestolite)

figure 9-12. All of these are mounted on the rotor shaft. The opposite pole pieces have fingers, or **claw poles**, that fit together, or interlace with each other. The fingers are the magnetic poles of the field. One pole piece has all north poles; the other has all south poles. When the pole pieces are assembled on the shaft, the poles alternate: N–S, N–S, and so on, figure 9-13. Automobile alternators usually have rotors with 8, 10, 12, or 14 poles. Each of the pole pieces thus has 4, 5, 6, or 7 fingers. Most rotors have 12 or 14 poles.

Magnetic flux travels between adjacent north and south poles. Because of the alternating arrangement of the poles, the flux lines move in opposite directions between adjacent poles. Rotors are built this way so that several alternating magnetic fields intersect the stator conductors as the rotor turns, figure 9-14. The induced voltages alternate as in our example of a 1-conductor alternator. But, the voltages alternate at different, closely spaced phase angles in many conductors. This helps to produce uniform, rectified dc voltage.

The rotor winding carries the current that develops magnetic fields between the rotor poles. The iron core inside the winding concentrates and strengthens the field. One pole piece

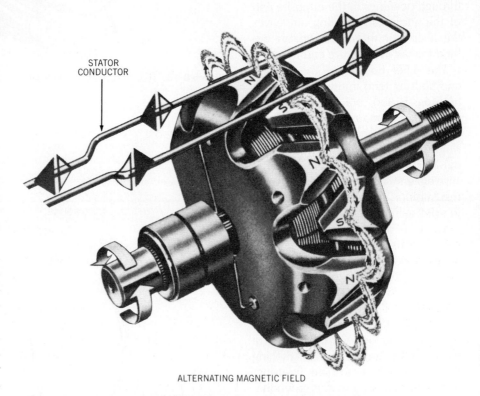

STATOR CONDUCTOR

ALTERNATING MAGNETIC FIELD

Figure 9-14. Alternating N fields intersect the stator conductors as the rotor turns.

is attached to either end of this core. When current flows through the winding, it magnetizes the core. Each pole piece develops the magnetic polarity of the end of the core to which it is mounted.

Changing the amount of current

through the field winding changes the magnetic strength of the alternator field. When the alternator is not turning, the poles retain a little magnetism, but not enough to induce any voltage in the stator. Therefore, the field winding must receive field cur-

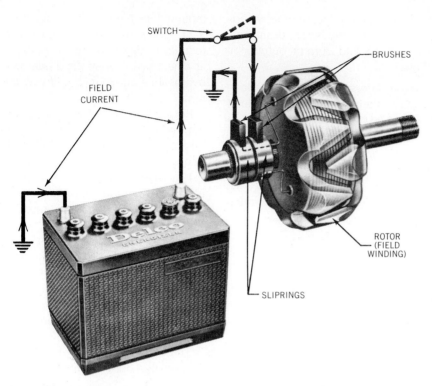

Figure 9-15. The field winding receives current from the battery when the alternator starts. (Delco-Remy)

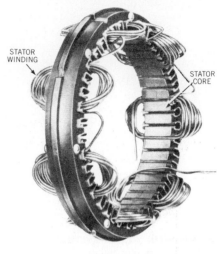

Figure 9-16. The coils of one stator winding are 120 degrees apart, electrically. (Delco-Remy)

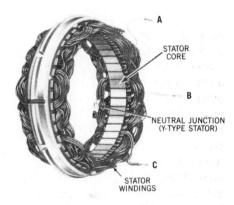

Figure 9-17. A complete stator has three overlapping windings. (Delco-Remy)

rent and voltage from the battery when the alternator starts to turn, figure 9-15.

Field current often is called **excitation current**, and the field winding may be called the excitation winding. After the alternator starts to generate, field current usually comes from the output connections of the stator. Voltage that delivers field current, from the battery or from the stator output, is **excitation voltage**. We will examine this in more detail later.

The Sliprings and Brushes. The field winding receives current through a pair of sliprings on the rotor shaft, figure 9-15. One end of the winding is connected to each of the sliprings. The sliprings are insulated from each other and from the shaft.

The sliprings receive current through a pair of brushes. The insulated brush is connected to the current source—the battery or the stator. The other brush is grounded to the alternator housing or through the regulator to complete the field circuit.

The sliprings are smooth (not segmented like a commutator), and the brushes conduct field current of only 1.5 to 3.0 amperes. Therefore, alternator brushes do not suffer the wear and high-current arcing of motor or generator brushes.

The Stator. An automobile alternator has three separate output conductors in multiple windings on the stator core. The core is made of laminated sections to reduce unwanted eddy currents in the stator. Eddy currents would oppose induced voltage and current.

Each of the three conductors has the same number of coils as the rotor has pairs of north and south poles. For example, an alternator with 7 pairs of N–S poles (a 14-pole rotor) has a stator with 7 coils in each winding. The coils of each conductor are evenly spaced around the core, figure 9-16. The three conductors, or sets of windings, alternate and overlap, figure 9-17, to produce the required phase angles.

The three stator windings are connected to each other and to the rectifying diodes in one of two ways:

1. In a **Y-type stator**, one end of each winding is connected to a **neutral junction**, figure 9-18. The other end of each winding is connected between a positive and a negative diode.

2. In a **delta stator**, the three windings are connected end to end, figure 9-19. Each connection point is also connected to a pair of positive and negative diodes. There is no neutral junction. The circuit diagram for this arrangement looks like the Greek letter "delta," or a triangle.

Delta-type and Y-type alternators both produce 3-phase current, which is rectified for dc output. Both kinds of

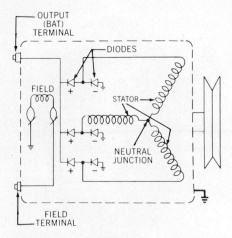

Figure 9-18. Y-type stator electrical schematic diagram. (Prestolite)

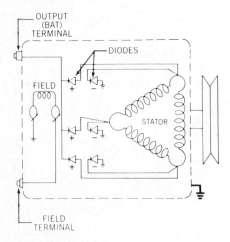

Figure 9-19. Delta stator electrical schematic diagram. (Prestolite)

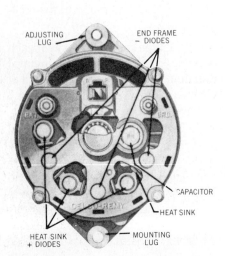

Figure 9-20. Early alternators had six diodes in the end housing and a heat sink. (Delco-Remy)

alternators are used in automotive applications, and the stator design affects voltage and current output, as follows:

• Y-type stators produce high voltage at lower alternator speed than delta stators. Most passenger cars have Y-type alternators.

• Delta stators produce higher maximum current than Y-type stators. They are used on large vehicles with high current loads. Most alternators rated at 100 amperes or more have delta stators.

The Diodes or the Rectifier Bridge.
Three-phase alternators use three pairs of diodes to rectify output current. Figures 9-18 and 9-19 show the basic diode circuits for Y-type and delta-type stators. Each conductor is attached to one positive and one negative diode.

Early alternators had six separate diodes pressed into the slipring end housing and an insulated **heat sink**, figure 9-20. Because of improved semiconductor manufacturing, many late-model alternators have all six diodes in a small **rectifier bridge**,

mounted in the end housing, figure 9-21. Either the end housing or the rectifier bridge housing, or both, act as a heat sink to keep the diodes from overheating due to high charging current.

Regardless of the physical construction of the diodes or the rectifier bridge, the circuit connections are basically as shown in figures 9-18 and 9-19. Three positive (+) diodes are insulated from the alternator housing and connected to the output terminal. The terminal is connected to the battery + terminal and the rest of the electrical system. The battery can't discharge through the alternator connection because diode bias blocks discharge current. The positive diodes conduct current only from the alternator to the battery.

Three negative (−) diodes are grounded in one of three ways:

1. They may be pressed or threaded into the alternator housing.

2. They may be grounded to the housing through the rectifier bridge.

3. They may be grounded through the regulator.

The negative diodes are a ground connection for the alternator output cir-

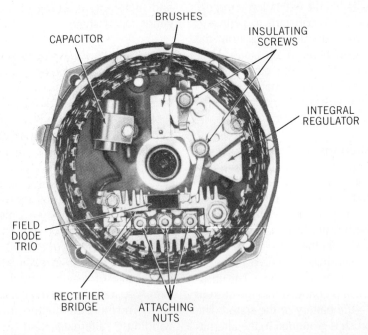

Figure 9-21. Most late-model alternators have the diodes in one or two rectifier bridge assemblies. (Delco-Remy)

cuit. Their bias allows them to conduct current only from the ground side of the alternator into the circuit.

Three-Phase Current Generation

The coils of the three stator windings are spaced evenly around the stator core. Separate voltages are induced in each winding at different phase angles, figure 9-22. The alternator produces three overlapping, evenly spaced, single-phase sine waves. Because the windings are connected to each other, the result is **three-phase alternating current**. Here is how current is generated and rectified in the two kinds of alternators.

Y-Type Stator Current. In a Y-type stator, two windings are always in series between a + and − diode. The position of the rotor at any point determines current direction through the two windings. It also determines the voltage level in each winding. Current flows from ground (−), through the − diode, through the two windings, to the + diode, and to the output terminal, figure 9-23. Induced voltages across the two series windings add together to produce total output voltage. Because the series voltages add together, the Y-type stator can produce high regulated voltage at startup and low engine speeds.

The neutral junction of a Y-type stator is connected to a "center tap" terminal on some alternators, figure 9-24. The center tap voltage is lower than output voltage, but it can be used to control field current, light an indicator lamp, power an electric choke heater, or do other jobs.

Delta-Type Stator Current. The windings of a delta stator always form two parallel circuits between a + and a − diode, figure 9-25. Again, the rotor position at any instant determines current direction through the windings and voltage level in each winding. Because there are always two parallel circuits, however, more

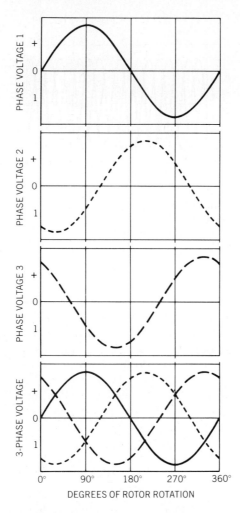

Figure 9-22. The sine wave voltages of the three stator windings are 120 degrees apart. (Bosch)

current can flow in a delta stator than in a Y-type stator.

Three-Phase Rectification

The 3-phase ac voltage in figure 9-22 is the sine wave voltage of three stator windings, generated by a rotor with only one pole. Real rotors have several pairs of north and south poles. Each *pair* of poles produces one complete sine wave in each winding during each revolution. Figure 9-26 compares the single sine wave produced in one winding by one pair of poles with multiple sine waves produced by multiple poles. During one revolution, a 12-pole rotor (6 pairs of poles) produces 6 sine waves.

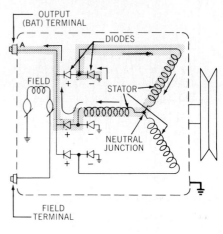

Figure 9-23. Current generation in a Y-type stator. (Prestolite)

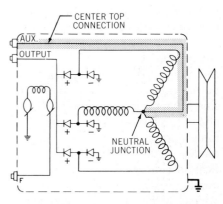

Figure 9-24. The neutral junction of a Y-type stator can be connected to a center tap. (Prestolite)

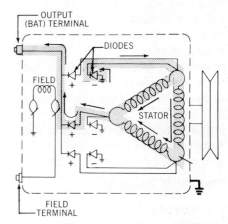

Figure 9-25. Current generation in a delta stator. (Prestolite)

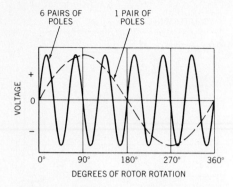

Figure 9-26. Sine wave voltage produced in one stator winding by one pair of poles and six pair of poles. (Bosch)

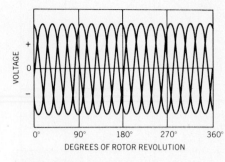

Figure 9-27. Overlapping sine wave voltages from three windings and six pair of poles (12 poles). (Bosch)

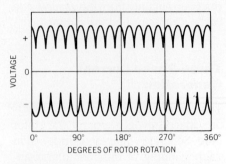

Figure 9-28. Rectifier diodes receive maximum positive and negative voltage. (Bosch)

Remember that the stator has three windings, equally spaced at overlapping phase angles. The 12-pole rotor generates three overlapping sine wave voltage cycles in the stator. In one revolution, the 3-winding stator output from 6 pairs of rotor poles is 18 sine wave cycles, figure 9-27. The + and − voltage peaks of each cycle force current through the + and − diodes, figure 9-28. Diode rectification changes the − current to + output. The final rectified dc voltage appears at the alternator output terminal as shown in figure 9-29.

A common test of alternator operation is to observe the output voltage on an oscilloscope. The scope pattern of a good alternator is similar to figure 9-29. The small waves at the top are called an **ac ripple.** They are the peaks of the ac voltage sine waves. Any dc voltage from a rectified ac source always has a slight ac ripple. Dc voltage from a dc source, such as a battery, does not. You will learn to recognize the causes of abnormal alternator scope patterns when you study alternator testing.

The Field Circuit

The magnetic field of the rotor is produced by current from a source outside the rotor. When the engine and the alternator start, the source is the battery, figure 9-15. The field circuit connects the battery to the rotor through the alternator output termi-

nal. When the engine is off, the battery must be disconnected from the field circuit, or it would discharge through the rotor. Some systems use a field relay to do this. Others use diodes to block discharge current. The regulator or the ignition switch also can be connected to open the field circuit when the engine is off.

When the alternator starts, field current comes from the stator output. In some alternators, the field is connected to rectified dc output. In others it is connected to separately rectified voltage from the stator. In this latter design, three more diodes are connected to the three stator windings to provide direct current for the field, figure 9-30. These three diodes may be called "field diodes," "exciter diodes," or a "diode trio" if they are joined in a single assembly. Field current is fully rectified because the three negative output diodes also are in the circuit with the field diodes.

Every alternator field circuit includes the regulator. As an introduction to regulator operation in the next section, we will look at three basic field circuit designs.

A-Circuit. An A-circuit alternator has an externally grounded field, figure 9-31. One insulated brush is connected to the output circuit inside the alternator to draw field current. The other brush also is insulated from the alternator housing and connected to the regulator through the alternator

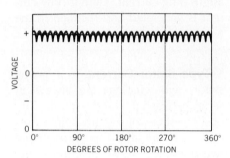

Figure 9-29. Rectified alternator output is pulsating dc with a slight ac ripple. (Bosch)

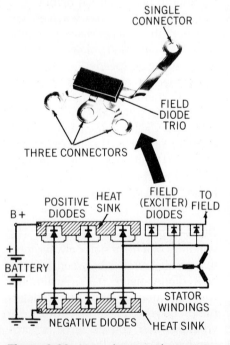

Figure 9-30. Many alternators have separate field diodes. (Bosch) (Delco-Remy)

field terminal. The regulator is between the field and ground. The field is grounded through the regulator.

B-Circuit. A B-circuit alternator has an internally grounded field, figure 9-32. One insulated brush is connected to the output circuit *through the regulator* to draw field current. The other brush is grounded to the alternator housing. The regulator is between the current source and the field. The field is grounded inside the alternator housing.

A good way to remember the difference between these two circuit designs is:

• An A-circuit regulator is located *after* the stator.

• A B-circuit regulator is located *before* the stator.

Isolated-Field Circuit. The isolated-field circuit is a variation of the A-circuit. It is most commonly used in some Chrysler alternators. The field is grounded through the regulator, figure 9-33. Field current comes from the output circuit outside the alternator. It enters through a third terminal on the housing. Field current is switched by a field relay or a switch. Both brushes are insulated from the alternator housing.

ALTERNATOR REGULATORS

An alternator regulator regulates field current and the magnetic strength of the field. This produces output voltage within controlled limits, while allowing the alternator to generate current for the load requirements of the electrical system.

Current Regulation

Direct current generators used on most cars until the early 1960's needed separate current regulators. Alternators do not. Alternator design limits maximum current output. You learned in chapter 2 that induced voltage and current in a conductor create

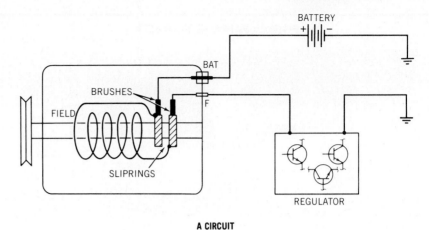

Figure 9-31. Typical A-circuit regulator installation.

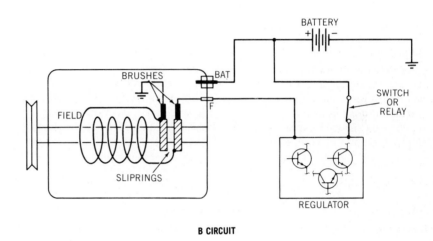

Figure 9-32. Typical B-circuit regulator installation.

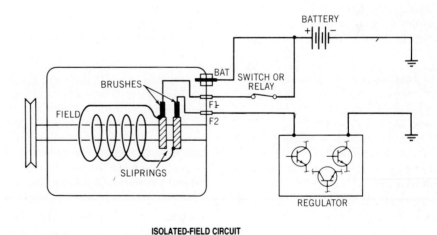

Figure 9-33. Typical isolated-field regulator installation.

a countervoltage, or counterelectromotive force (CEMF). The CEMF produces current that opposes the induced current in the conductor. This is what happens in an alternator stator.

As induced current generated by the alternator increases, CEMF increases. At some point, current produced by the CEMF is high enough to block further output current. This point varies for different alternators

FORD'S FAMOUS FLIVVER

The Ford Model T, symbol of low-cost reliable transportation, chugged into our lives and history over 80 years ago on October 1, 1908. Designed to be simple to operate, easy to repair, inexpensive, and durable, the Model T retired the horse to pasture. The first year's production of 10,660 units broke all industry records.

From the first, Ford conceived of his T as a car for everyone, but it wasn't until 1913 that Ford began building the T chassis on a moving assembly line. From that point on, Ford perfected his mass production methods that eventually brought the price for a basic T as low as $450.00. By 1914, Model T's were rolling out of Ford's Highland Park, Michigan, plant at the rate of one every 40 seconds.

The Model T not only was the first mass-produced affordable automobile, it was the first mass production car to have its engine

block and crankcase cast as a single unit. It was the first production car to popularize the steering wheel on the left side and the first to have a removable cylinder head for easy engine service. But it was a no-frills car. The fuel level was checked with a stick, and standard equipment did *not* include a spare tire, a water pump, an oil pump, a horn, windshield wipers, a radio, rear-view mirrors, a trunk, or bumpers. Its simplicity challenged inventors who developed more than 5,000 separate accessories for the Model T during its 19-year production run.

The official farewell for the Model T came on May 26, 1927, with the production of the 15-millionth car at Highland Park. That Ford plant then was retooled for the Model A, but many more T's were built during the summer of 1927 at other Ford factories. Official production records say that Ford built 15,458,781 Model T's from 1908 through 1927.

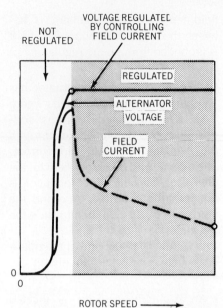

Figure 9-34. The regulator reduces field current as rotor speed increases to maintain a regulated voltage. (Bosch)

according to the design of the stator and the rotor. In any alternator, however, the point where CEMF blocks further output current is the design limit of the alternator. It may occur at 30 amperes, 60 amperes, 100 amperes, or any other point.

Although alternator design limits maximum current, output voltage could continue to rise as alternator speed increases. Rotor speed is governed by engine speed and can't be changed to control alternator voltage. Field current can be controlled electrically to regulate output voltage.

Voltage Regulation

Alternator voltage depends on field current and rotor speed. At low speed,

the regulator allows full current to the field, and voltage rises quickly to its regulated level, figure 9-34. As speed increases, the regulator reduces field current to keep output voltage at a regulated maximum, even as rotor speed increases.

Raising the output current load on an alternator will cause output voltage to drop. This happens, for example, when you turn on the headlamps or the air conditioner. In this case, the regulator allows field current to increase, which raises output voltage to its regulated maximum, figure 9-35.

At low speeds, the regulator lets field current flow for relatively long periods and reduces it for short periods, figure 9-36. This produces high average field current. At high speeds, the regulator lets field current flow for shorter periods and reduces it for longer periods. This produces low average field current.

Regulator Design

Early alternators used electromechanical, vibrating-contact regulators, similar to those used with dc generators. Since the early 1970's, most charging

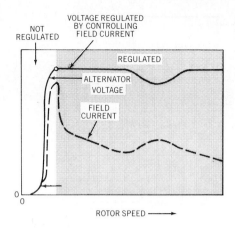

Figure 9-35. Increasing vehicle current loads cause field current to increase to maintain regulated voltage. (Bosch)

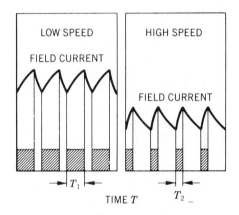

Figure 9-36. Field current flows for less time at low speed than at high speed to reduce average current. (Bosch)

systems have used solid-state electronic voltage regulators. Solid-state regulators have no moving parts; they are compact and not affected much by extreme temperatures. These electronic regulators control field current and output voltage with diodes, transistors, capacitors, and other electronic devices you learned about in chapter 4.

Regulator shapes and sizes vary from manufacturer to manufacturer, figure 9-37. Some small units are installed in the alternator housing. Some regulators are attached to the outside of the alternator, and others are mounted away from the alternator and connected by a wiring harness.

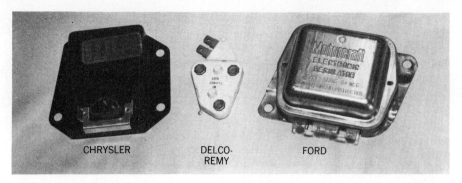

Figure 9-37. Solid-state regulators can be built into the alternator or mounted remotely.

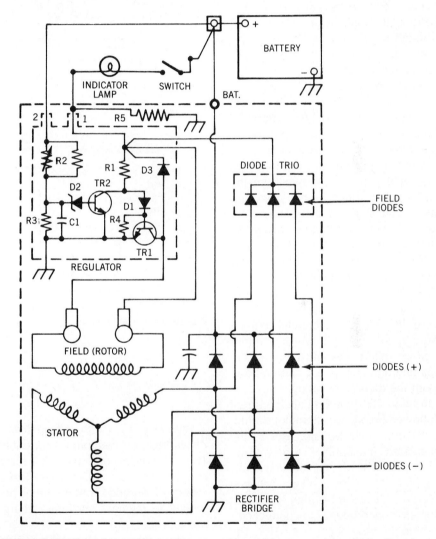

Figure 9-38. Typical circuit for an alternator with a solid-state regulator. (Delco-Remy)

Electronic Regulator Circuit Operation. We will use the integral regulator of a Delco-Remy 10-SI alternator to explain the general operation of electronic voltage regulators. These alternators are an A-circuit design (regulation between the field and ground) and have been standard equipment on GM vehicles for more than a decade.

The circuit diagram in figure 9-38 shows the alternator output, or BAT, terminal connected to the battery. The regulator number 2 terminal also is connected to the battery. The regulator number 1 terminal is connected to the dashboard indicator lamp and the ignition switch.

When the engine and the alternator are off, the battery can't discharge through the field because resistors R2 and R3 restrict current. The resistors (R) and diodes (D) in the regulator are arranged to let the regulator sense voltage of the battery and the charging system.

When the ignition switch closes, figure 9-39, current flows from the battery, through the indicator lamp, through terminal 1 of the regulator, and to transistor TR1. The base-emitter circuit of TR1 conducts current to ground. This biases TR1 so the emitter-collector circuit conducts current through the alternator field. This magnetizes the field to start generation and turns on the indicator lamp.

When the alternator starts to generate, field current is drawn from the stator and rectified by the diode trio (field diodes), figure 9-40. Stator voltage is higher than battery voltage, so no current flows from the battery to the regulator. The indicator lamp goes out because system voltage is applied to both ends of the lamp circuit. Voltage across the lamp is essentially zero. Resistor R5 is a parallel connection to ground that prevents minor voltage differences and current from lighting the lamp. Field current flows from the diode trio through the same circuit to TR1 that the battery current followed before the alternator started.

When system voltage rises to the regulated maximum, current flows through terminal 2 of the regulator, figure 9-41. When voltage between resistors R2 and R3 is high enough, it forces zener diode D2 to conduct current to the base of transistor TR2. The base-emitter circuit of TR2 conducts current to ground and biases TR2 to complete the emitter-collector circuit. The emitter-collector circuit of TR2 is in parallel with TR1. It provides a shunt path to ground for field current. TR1 turns off so that no current reaches the field.

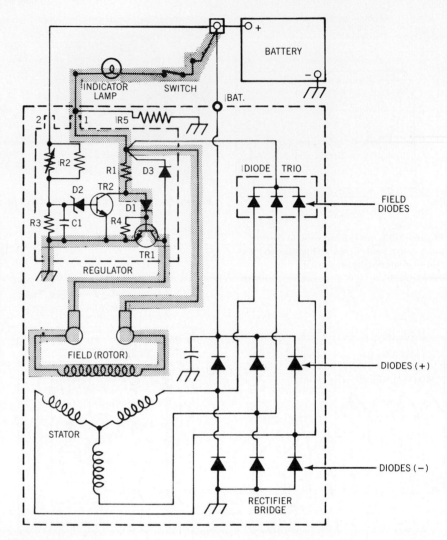

Figure 9-39. Field current through a solid-state regulator when starting. (Delco-Remy)

With TR1 off, system voltage drops. Zener diode D2 then blocks current to TR2. TR2 turns off, and TR1 turns back on. The two transistors TR1 and TR2 cycle on and off many times per second to regulate maximum charging voltage.

Among the other electronic parts of the regulator:

• Capacitor C1 absorbs voltage surges to maintain uniform voltage across R3 and TR2.

• Resistor R3 shunts high current past TR1 at high temperature.

• Diode D3 bypasses high induced voltage in the field when TR1 turns off.

• Resistor R2 in the regulation circuit is a thermistor that changes regulated voltage as temperature changes.

Since the mid-1970's many Delco-Remy 10-SI alternators have used regulators with three, instead of two, transistors. Circuit operation is a bit more complicated, but the principles of regulation are essentially the same as those explained above. Test procedures are basically similar for all 10-SI regulators and alternators.

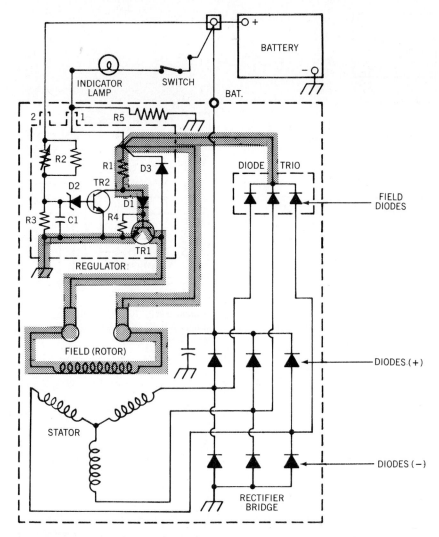

Figure 9-40. Field current through a solid-state regulator from the alternator output. (Delco-Remy)

Electromechanical Regulator Operation.

Older electromechanical regulators are usually connected for a B-circuit field design. The regulator is between the current source and the field. It regulates field current by adding resistance to the field or by providing a shunt path to ground.

An electromechanical regulator is built like a relay. Current flow through a coil creates a magnetic field that moves the regulator armature. Figure 9-42 shows a simple electromechanical field circuit. The alternator field is connected to the battery through the regulator and the ignition switch.

When the ignition switch closes, current flows through regulator terminal 3, through the closed lower contacts of the regulator, and to the alternator rotor. Current also flows through the regulator coil winding and a resistor to ground. The resistor limits coil current until system voltage rises to a regulated level.

When the alternator starts, field current continues through terminal 3, and system voltage starts to rise. When voltage rises high enough, current through the regulator coil and resistor produces a strong enough magnetic field to move the regulator

armature. The lower contacts open as the armature moves toward the coil. Field current then flows through the resistor between terminals 3 and F. This reduces current to the alternator rotor.

At high engine and alternator speeds, field current may be high enough, even with the series resistor, to raise system voltage too high. However, current through the regulator coil also increases and moves the regulator armature farther. This closes the upper set of contacts and grounds the field current, figure 9-43.

Electromagnetic regulators are more

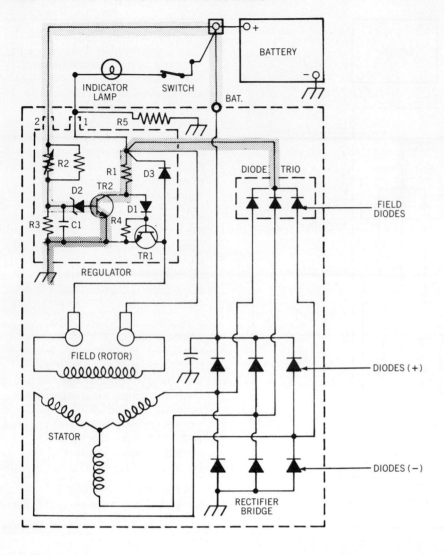

= CHARGING CURRENT
= FIELD CURRENT

Figure 9-41. Field current through a solid-state regulator during regulation. (Delco-Remy)

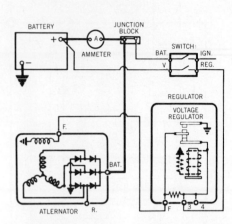

Figure 9-42. Typical wiring diagram for a single-unit electromechanical voltage regulator. (Delco-Remy)

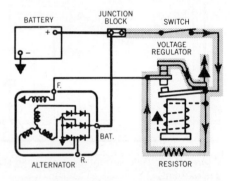

Figure 9-43. At high speed, with high field current, a double-contact regulator grounds the field. (Delco-Remy)

sensitive to temperature change than electronic regulators. To control field current through a changing temperature range, these older regulators include one or more of the following devices, figure 9-44:

• A *bimetallic hinge* for the armature. Spring tension is high when the hinge is cold and requires higher coil current to open the regulator contacts. At higher temperature, hinge spring tension decreases, and lower current will open the contacts.

• A *magnetic shunt* is a piece of nickel steel on top of the regulator coil. At low temperature, its permeability is high, and coil magnetism concentrates in the shunt. A stronger field is needed to open the regulator contacts. At higher temperature, shunt permeability decreases. The magnetic field of the coil increases with less current and opens the contacts.

• A *ballast resistor,* similar to an ignition resistor, can be placed in series with the regulator coil. The ballast resistor provides almost constant resistance at all temperatures. The regulator coil can then be designed with low resistance. Temperature changes

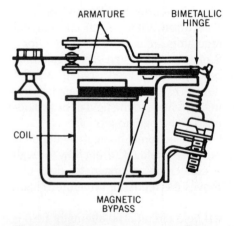

Figure 9-44. Electromechanical regulators use magnetic shunts and bimetallic hinges to compensate for temperature changes. (Delco-Remy)

in the coil will change the total resistance very little so that field current remains relatively constant.

Field Relays

Several charging systems use a field relay along with either an electronic or an electromechanical regulator. The relay reduces the wiring in the field circuit and the voltage drop across the field. In a system with an ammeter, the field relay opens and closes the field circuit. In a system with an indicator lamp, the relay also controls the lamp circuit.

In a system with an ammeter and a relay, field current flows from the battery, through the ammeter, through the ignition switch, to the relay coil, figure 9-45. The relay closes the contacts, and field current flows through the relay and the regulator to the field. The relay stays closed as long as the ignition switch is closed. Field current comes from the battery during starting and from the alternator output when running.

In a system with an indicator lamp and a relay, field current flows from the battery, through the lamp, through the regulator, to the field, figure 9-46. Current lights the lamp and excites the alternator field. When the alternator starts to supply voltage, this voltage is applied to the relay coil. The coil closes the relay contacts, which complete a circuit to supply voltage directly to the regulator. The relay also applies voltage to the opposite side of the indicator lamp. The voltage difference across the lamp is then zero, and the lamp goes out. The field relay stays closed as long as the alternator is operating.

INDICATORS

Every vehicle charging system includes an indicator for the driver to monitor system operation. The indicator may be an ammeter, a voltmeter, a warning lamp, or a combination of these devices.

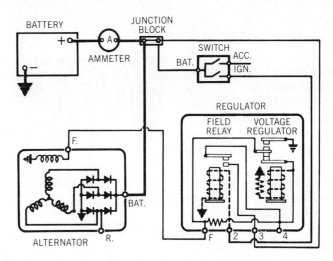

Figure 9-45. Typical wiring diagram for a 2-unit electromechanical voltage regulator with a field relay and ammeter. (Delco-Remy)

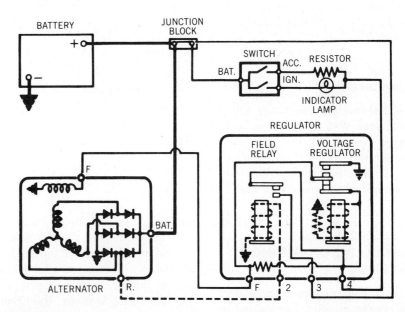

Figure 9-46. Typical wiring diagram for a 2-unit electromechanical voltage regulator with a field relay and indicator lamp. (Delco-Remy)

Ammeters

An instrument panel ammeter measures charging system current into and out of the battery and other parts of the electrical system. As with all ammeters, it is in series with the vehicle electrical system, figures 9-42 and 9-45. When battery current flows to the alternator field or any other part of the electrical system, the ammeter shows a discharge (negative current). When the alternator generates cur-

rent, the alternator shows a charge (positive current).

Although the ammeter may indicate charging current flow, the amount of current may not be high enough to recharge the battery if vehicle electrical loads are heavy and the battery is discharged.

Indicator Lamps

Most charging systems have an indicator lamp, or warning lamp, to indicate general charging system operation. The previous descriptions of regulator operation explained how battery voltage and system voltage are applied to the lamp circuit.

The lamp lights when field current flows through it from the battery. When the alternator produces output voltage, this voltage is applied to the opposite side of the lamp circuit. The lamp goes out because there is no voltage difference across it. The lamp will not warn the driver of an overcharged battery or high charging voltage, but it indicates low voltage from the alternator. Low charging voltage will lead to an undercharged battery.

An indicator lamp often has a parallel resistor, figure 9-46, to carry field current to the alternator if the lamp bulb fails.

Voltmeters

Many late-model cars have instrument panel voltmeters to indicate charging system voltage. Most such systems also include an indicator lamp. Voltage is applied to the voltmeter through the ignition switch.

CARMAKERS' CHARGING SYSTEMS

Although all alternators and regulators work on the principles explained in this chapter, carmakers' charging systems vary for different vehicle applications. Different manufacturers also approach alternator and charging circuit design differently to achieve common goals. Recognizing the major alternator makers and their charging systems will help you to service charging systems efficiently.

The Delco-Remy Division of General Motors supplies charging system components and parts for other electrical systems of GM cars and trucks. Delco-Remy refers to its alternators as Delcotron generators.

CS Series. The Delco CS alternator series, figure 9-47, was introduced on

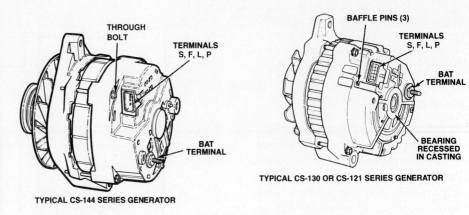

Figure 9-47. Delco-Remy CS series alternators are used on late-model GM vehicles. (GM)

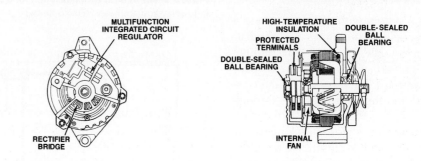

Figure 9-48. The Delco-Remy CS alternator uses a multifunction integrated circuit regulator and has an internal fan for cooling on some models. (GM)

some car lines in 1986. These downsized alternators use a totally different integral regulator than other Delco alternators and produce a higher amperage output for their size than previous Delco SI series. The CS designation number indicates the outer diameter of the stator laminations in millimeters and can be used to compare relative sizes and ampere output of different CS models.

All CS series alternators take their field current directly from the delta-type stator. This eliminates the need for a diode trio. An internal cooling fan mounted on the rotor of CS-121 and CS-130 models, figure 9-48, is used to pull air through one end frame. After cooling the rectifier bridge and regulator assembly, the air passes out through openings in the other end frame. Sealed and lifetime-lubricated bearings are used in both end frames.

A conventional BAT output terminal is used on all CS series alternators, but the regulator may have either a 1-or 2-wire connector, depending upon its application. Figure 9-49 and figure 9-50 show the two basic circuits used with CS alternators, but the vehicle wiring diagram must be consulted for the complete charging system circuits. Use of the P, F, and S terminals, figure 9-49, is optional:

• The P terminal connects to the stator, and may be externally connected to a tachometer or comparable device.

• The F terminal is connected internally to field positive. It is used as a fault indicator on vehicles with a body computer module (BCM).

• The S terminal may be connected to battery voltage as a means of sensing the voltage to be controlled.

• The L terminal connects the regulator with an indicator lamp and battery voltage.

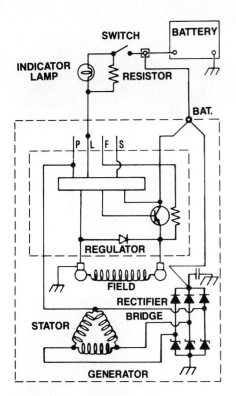

Figure 9-49. The basic circuit configuration for a CS series alternator using an L terminal. (GM)

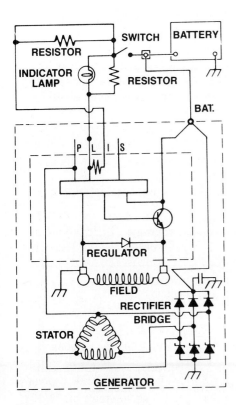

Figure 9-50. The basic circuit configuration for a CS series alternator using L and I terminals. (GM)

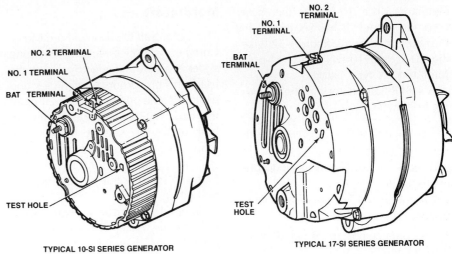

TYPICAL 10-SI SERIES GENERATOR

TYPICAL 17-SI SERIES GENERATOR

Figure 9-51. The Delco-Remy SI series alternators appeared in the early 1970's and are still used on some vehicles. (GM)

Full battery voltage should never be applied to the L terminal or the voltage regulator will be destroyed. Full battery voltage can be applied to the I terminal, however, because of the resistor in the regulator circuit, figure 9-50.

The I terminal on regulators so equipped, figure 9-50, turns the regulator on and supplies field current (in addition to that applied internally), either through a resistor or directly from the switch. Figure 9-50 shows the alternate circuit connections. The I circuit can be used alone or with the L circuit. On vehicles with a body computer module (BCM), such as the Cadillac Allanté, the BCM uses the I circuit to shut the alternator off during wide-open throttle conditions to improve performance, if battery voltage is above a calibrated value.

BCM-equipped vehicles also have a fault detection capability built into the alternator regulator. Whenever the ignition is on, the BCM sends 12-volts to the I terminal. This causes the alternator to start operation and regulate system voltage. The alternator sends a pulse-width-modulated (PWM) signal back to the BCM on the F terminal circuit. This signal keeps the BCM informed of the regulator duty cycle.

Vehicles with a BCM can set trouble codes, which light warning lamps in the instrument cluster. The trouble codes and their use are de-scribed in the test procedures in chapter 8 of Volume 2.

SI Series. The Delco SI alternator series, figure 9-51, was standard equipment on GM vehicles for over 15 years, and is still used on vehicles not yet equipped with CS series alternators. All SI series alternators have integral voltage regulators in the slipring end housing. The 10- and 12-SI alternators use a Y-type stator; 15-, 17-, and 27-SI models use delta-type stators. A 14-pole rotor is used in most SI alternators. The 27-SI alternator is primarily used on commercial vehicles and has an adjustable voltage regulator located under an adjustment cap on the rear end frame.

Early 10-SI alternators had six separate diodes in the slipring end housing and a separate ground (GRD) terminal. The 10-SI alternators used for the past 10 years have six diodes in a small rectifier bridge to replace the six large diodes of early models, figure 9-21. Regulator connections and circuit operation are explained earlier in this chapter. All Delco-Remy SI alternators have capacitors in the rear housing to protect the rectifier bridge from sudden voltage surges and to reduce radiofrequency interferences.

DN Series. GM vehicles built before about 1970 have Delco-Remy DN alternators with electromechanical regulators. The 10-DN is the most common model. It has six diodes in the rear end housing, figure 9-52. Like the 10-SI, the 10-DN has a 14-pole rotor and a Y-type stator.

A 10-DN alternator has the following terminals:

• BAT is the output terminal, connected to the battery.

• GRD is an additional ground connection.

• R is connected to a field relay for an indicator lamp.

• F is connected to the B-circuit electromechanical regulator.

Delco-Remy electromechanical regulators are built with and without field relays. Regulator terminals are marked F, 2, 3, and 4, figure 9-53. Single-unit regulators, without a field relay, do not have a 2 terminal. Terminal connections are as follows:

• F connects the regulator to the alternator field.

• 2 connects the alternator output to the field relay, if a relay is installed.

• 3 connects the battery to the contacts of the regulator and the relay.

• 4 connects the ignition switch to the contacts of the regulator and the relay.

Motorcraft

The Motorcraft Division of Ford Motor Company supplies parts for charging systems and other electrical systems used on Ford-produced vehicles and those of some other carmakers. Before the early 1970's, components were built under the Autolite name. Late-model Motorcraft alternators use a color code stamped on the front end frame to identify the model and current rating.

Before 1985, all Motorcraft charging systems, except one, used either an electromechanical voltage regulator (through 1978) or a remotely mounted, solid-state regulator (1978 and later). The 1969-71 charging system with a 55-ampere alternator had a solid-state regulator mounted on the rear end frame, figure 9-54. This Motorcraft alternator used an A-circuit; all others have a B-circuit.

IAR Series. The Motorcraft integral alternator regulator (IAR) charging system was introduced on some 1984 Ford Motor Company vehicles. Its name comes from the solid-state regulator assembly, figure 9-55, mounted on the alternator rear housing. The rectifier assembly is sealed and se-

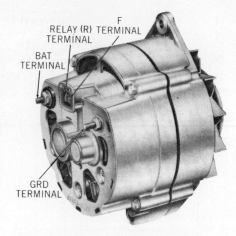

Figure 9-52. Typical Delco 10-DN alternator. (Delco-Remy)

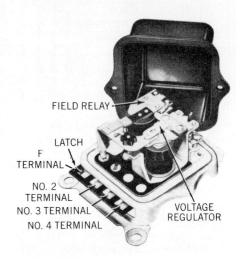

Figure 9-53. Typical Delco electromechanical regulator. Units without a field relay have no number 2 terminal. (Delco-Remy)

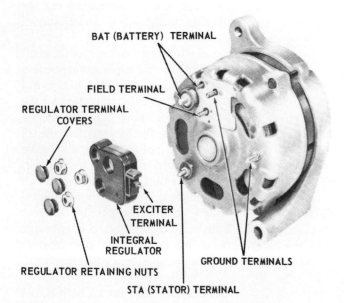

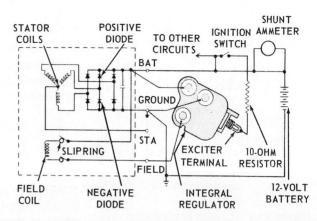

Figure 9-54. This Ford Motorcraft 55-ampere alternator has a solid-state regulator attached to the outside of the rear housing. (Ford)

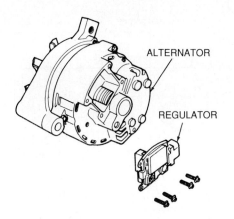

Figure 9-55. A solid-state regulator assembly is mounted on the rear housing of the Motorcraft IAR alternator. (Ford)

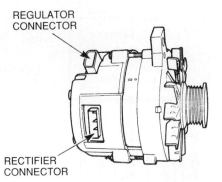

Figure 9-56. The Motorcraft IAR regulator connector protrudes from the rear of the unit; the rectifier connector extends through the end frame. (Ford)

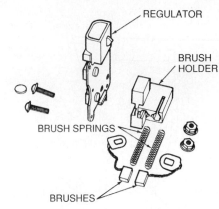

Figure 9-57. The IAR regulator and brushes form a single assembly. (Ford)

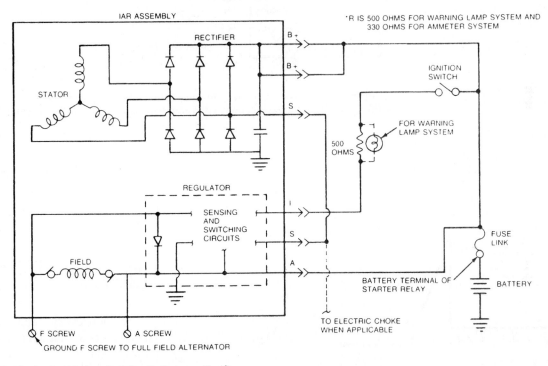

Figure 9-58. The basic IAR charging circuit diagram. (Ford)

cured to the slipring end frame. Its BAT and STA terminals are enclosed in a plastic housing that extends through the side of the end frame, figure 9-56. The brushes are attached to the regulator, requiring that both assemblies be removed if either requires service, figure 9-57. A 12-pole rotor is used with the Y-type stator.

When the ignition is turned on, voltage is sent to the regulator I terminal through a resistor in the I circuit. As long as the ignition is on, system voltage is sensed and field current is drawn through the regulator A terminal. Field current is supplied from the regulator to the rotor through the brushes riding on the sliprings. When the ignition is turned off, the control circuit is shut down. Figure 9-58 shows the basic IAR alternator circuit.

EVR Series. Motorcraft charging systems using an external solid-state regulator are now known as external voltage regulator (EVR) systems. They may use either a side-terminal or a rear-terminal alternator, figure 9-59.

The rear-terminal alternator is built in 40- to 65-ampere ratings. The same housing is used for all models, with the higher ampere ratings obtained by using more wire in the stator and rotor windings. The side-terminal alternator is built in 70- to 100-ampere ratings. Output at lower engine speeds is greater than the rear-terminal models. High-current 90- and 100-ampere models have delta stators. All others have Y-type stators. All use a 12-pole rotor.

Motorcraft alternators with external

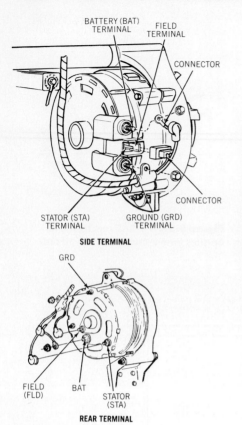

SIDE TERMINAL

REAR TERMINAL

Figure 9-59. Motorcraft builds rear-terminal and side-terminal alternators of various current ratings. (Ford)

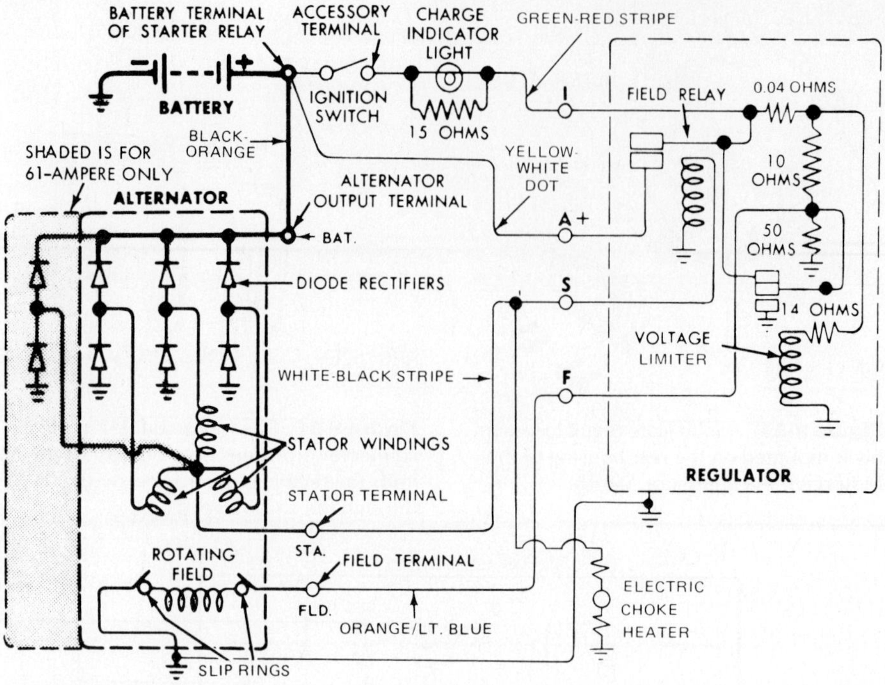

Figure 9-60. Typical Motorcraft charging system diagram. The center tap of the 61-ampere alternator (shaded area) is connected to another pair of rectifying diodes. (Ford)

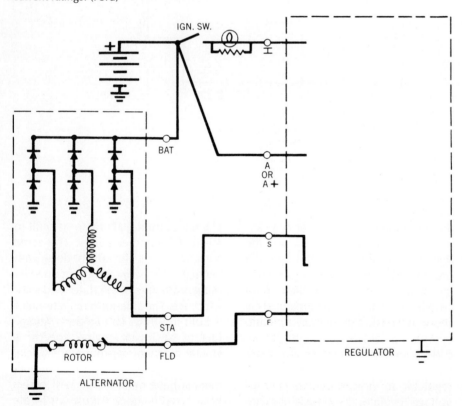

Figure 9-61. Ford regulator terminals are the same for solid-state and electromechanical units. (Ford)

voltage regulators or electromechanical regulators have the following terminals:

• BAT is the output terminal, connected to the battery.

• GRD is a ground connection.

• STA connects the center tap (neutral junction) of a Y-type stator to different units, such as a field relay and lamp and the electric choke heater.

• FLD connects the rotor field winding to the regulator.

The 61-ampere Motorcraft rear-terminal alternator has the stator center tap connected to two more diodes, figure 9-60. This creates a parallel output circuit to increase current at low speed. The STA terminal on a 90-ampere, side-terminal alternator connects to rectified output because the delta stator has no center tap.

Motorcraft regulator terminals are marked as follows, figure 9-61:

• I is used only without an ammeter to connect the ignition switch to the field relay contacts and the regulator contacts.

• A+ or A connects the battery to the field relay contacts.

• S connects the alternator output to the field relay coil.

• F connects the field to the regulator contacts or to the regulator transistors.

Chrysler

In the late 1950's, Chrysler was the first domestic carmaker to use ac charging systems as standard equipment on its passenger cars. In 1985, Chrysler introduced a dual-output 40- or 90-ampere alternator with computer-regulated voltage regulation on some models. Other models use dual-output Bosch or Mitsubishi alternators with external or integral solid-state regulators. The output of the new design exceeds the previous Chrysler alternator by 56 percent at idle and 35 percent during cruising. The Chrysler dual-output alternator has a delta-type stator; Bosch and Mitsubishi dual-output alternators use a Y-type stator.

Computer-controlled Alternator.

The regulator circuitry used with the computer-controlled Chrysler alternator is an isolated-field type, but integrated circuitry in the logic and power modules controls field current, figure 9-62. The logic module senses battery temperature according to system resistance and switches field current on and off in a duty cycle to regulate charging voltage.

The Chrysler computer-controlled charging system has two unique capabilities:

• It can vary charging voltage according to ambient temperature, as well as in response to the system's voltage needs.

• The computer can detect problems in the charging system and set fault codes.

Whenever the ignition is turned on, the logic module checks battery temperature, figure 9-63. This determines

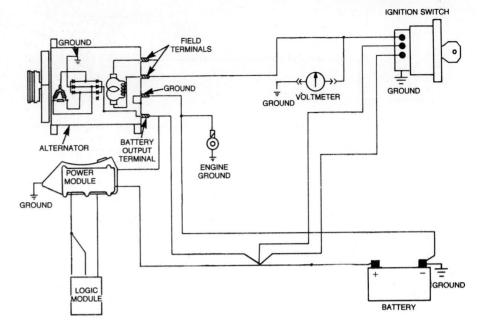

Figure 9-62. A typical Chrysler dual-output alternator charging circuit with computer-controlled voltage regulation. (Chrysler)

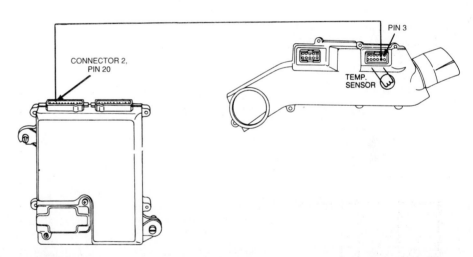

Figure 9-63. The Chrysler charging system with computer-controlled voltage regulation. (Chrysler)

the control voltage. A predriver transistor in the logic module signals the power module driver translator to turn on the alternator field current, figure 9-64. System voltage and battery temperature are continually monitored by the logic module, which uses this data to inform the power module driver when field current adjustment is required to maintain output voltage be-

tween 13.6 and 14.8 volts, ± 0.3 volt, figure 9-65.

On vehicles with computer-controlled voltage regulation, charging system problems can be detected by the computer, which records fault codes in the system memory. Some codes light a POWER LIMITED, POWER LOSS, or CHECK ENGINE lamp on the instrument cluster; others do not. The fault codes

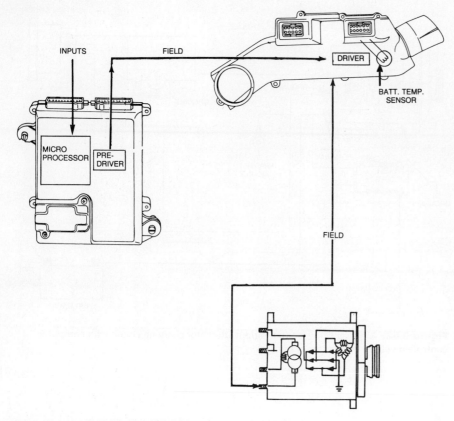

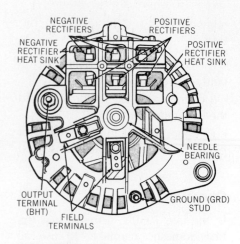

Figure 9-66. Typical late-model Chrysler alternator. (Chrysler)

Figure 9-64. A predriver in the logic module activates a driver in the power module to turn on the alternator field. (Chrysler)

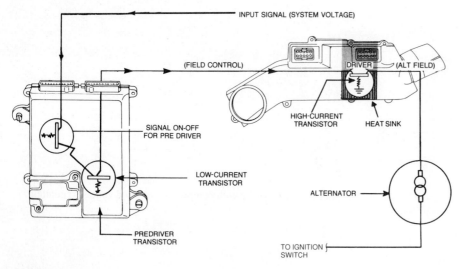

Figure 9-65. Internal field control of the Chrysler charging system with computer-controlled voltage regulation. (Chrysler)

tors. Six diodes are mounted on positive and negative heat sinks in the rear housing of standard-duty alternators, figure 9-66. The heavy-duty 100-ampere model has each stator winding attached to two positive and two negative diodes. The 12 diodes provide extra rectification circuits for high-current output.

Chrysler alternator terminals are marked as follows:

• BAT is the output terminal.

• GRD is a ground connection.

• Two FLD terminals connect the regulator to the field brushes.

Except for the computer-controlled alternator, Chrysler products have used a remotely mounted, solid-state regulator, figure 9-67, since 1972. Most systems have a field relay to open and close the field circuit. Before 1972, Chrysler used an alternator with six separate diodes pressed into a heat sink and into the rear housing. These alternators used a single-unit electromechanical regulator in a B-circuit arrangement.

Imported Vehicle Charging Systems

Alternators and charging systems on imported vehicles follow the same design and operating principles as domestic equipment, even though physical construction may vary somewhat.

and how to use them are described in the test procedures in chapter 8 of Volume 2.

1972–1984 Systems.
Between 1972 and 1984, Chrysler built single-output alternators of two basic designs. Models rated at less than 100 amperes have an exposed stator core. Heavy-duty 100- and 117-ampere alternators have an enclosed stator. All Chrysler alternators have 12-pole rotors. All have Y-type stators, except the heavy-duty models, which have delta sta-

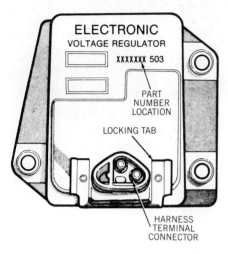

Figure 9-67. Typical Chrysler solid-state regulator. (Chrysler)

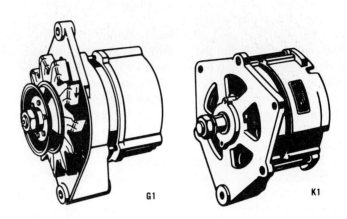

Figure 9-68. Bosch G1 and K1 alternators. (Bosch)

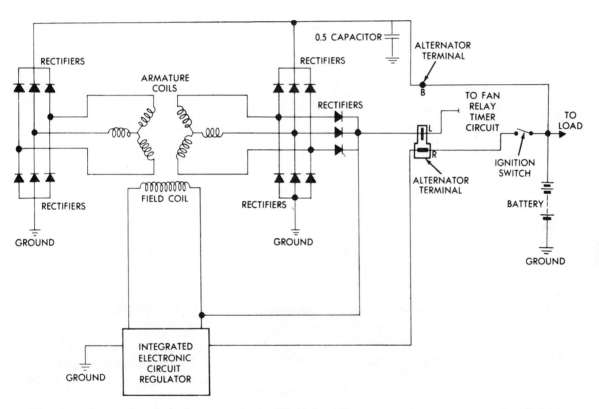

Figure 9-69. Mitsubishi alternator charging system. (Chrysler)

Robert Bosch is a major European maker of electrical equipment. Most Bosch alternators on passenger cars are the type G1 and K1 designs, figure 9-68. These have Y-type stators and are used with either solid-state or electromechanical regulators.

Japanese carmakers use alternators from several manufacturers, such as Nippondenso, Hitachi, Mitsubishi,

and others. Some feature unique construction but operate on the principles explained here. One Mitsubishi alternator with an integral regulator, for example, has a double-Y stator and 12 diodes in two rectifier assemblies, figure 9-69. This design provides high current, along with high voltage at low speed.

SUMMARY

Charging systems contain the battery, the alternator, the regulator, and an indicator. The output circuit and the field circuit are the two major circuits of the charging system.

The alternator uses a rotating magnetic field (the rotor) to generate alternating current (ac) in stationary conductors (the stator). Diodes rectify the ac sine wave voltage to direct current (dc). Most alternators have 12- or 14-pole rotors (6 or 7 pairs of N–S magnetic poles) and three sets of windings in the stator. Stator windings are installed at overlapping phase angles to generate multiple sine wave voltage output. Stator windings are connected to each other in two ways:

1. A high-voltage Y-type connection
2. A high-current delta connection

Field current flows to the rotor through two brushes and sliprings on the rotor shaft. Alternator design regulates maximum current output, but a voltage regulator is placed in the field circuit to control maximum output voltage. The regulator controls field current and thus limits maximum voltage.

Although charging systems with computer-controlled voltage regulation are beginning to appear, most late-model vehicles have internal or external solid-state regulators that control field current through a pair of parallel transistors. Earlier systems used electromechanical regulators that controlled field current through a vibrating armature and an electromagnetic coil. Regulators can be connected to the field in three ways:

1. *A-circuit*—The field is externally grounded through the regulator.
2. *B-circuit*—The field is internally grounded, with the regulator between the current source and the field.
3. *Isolated field*—The field is isolated and externally grounded through the regulator.

The charging system indicator lets the driver monitor system operation. The indicator may be an ammeter, a voltmeter, or a warning lamp. Some systems use a combination of two, or all three, kinds of indicators.

REVIEW QUESTIONS

Multiple Choice

1. An alternator generates current through:

  a. voltage drop
  b. electromagnetic induction
  c. CEMF
  d. the field and relay circuits

2. A battery cell in a normal state of charge produces:

  a. about 3 volts
  b. about 2.5 volts
  c. about 2.1 volts
  d. about 2.9 volts

3. Most charging systems are regulated to develop:

  a. about 14.5 volts
  b. about 12 volts
  c. about 12.6 volts
  d. about 13 volts

4. Battery life can be shortened by:

  a. sulfation caused by charging voltage that is below specifications
  b. excessive gassing caused by charging voltage that is above specifications
  c. unregulated charging voltage
  d. all of the above

5. The two circuits of the charging system are:

  a. the motor circuit and the control circuit
  b. the input circuit and the output circuit
  c. the output circuit and the field circuit
  d. the field circuit and the input circuit

6. The simplest form of an alternator is:

  a. a rotating magnet in a stationary looped conductor
  b. a fixed magnet in a stationary looped conductor
  c. a stator in a stationary looped conductor
  d. a rotor

7. Voltage polarity means:

  a. magnetic polarity
  b. current direction
  c. the direction of sine wave voltage
  d. voltage cycle

8. When a rotor revolves in an alternator, and no flux lines cut the conductor:

  a. voltage and current increase
  b. voltage increases and current decreases

  c. voltage and current return to zero
  d. voltage increases and current returns to zero

9. When an alternator rotor makes one revolution and the voltage polarity changes from positive to negative, it is called:

  a. the sine function of angles
  b. sine wave voltage
  c. rectified voltage
  d. dc voltage

10. An alternator uses diodes to:

  a. increase voltage to the battery
  b. rectify alternating current to direct current
  c. allow current to flow in two directions
  d. reduce current flow

11. Alternators have three output conductors in order to produce:

  a. three-phase voltage
  b. two-phase voltage
  c. single-phase voltage
  d. sine-wave voltage

12. Field current is often called:

  a. flux current
  b. excitation current

c. polarity current

d. stator current

13. A voltage regulator controls output voltage by regulating:

a. CEMF

b. battery voltage

c. field current

d. output current

14. Student A says that the Chrysler charging system with computer-controlled voltage regulation can set fault codes. Student B says that its control voltage is determined by battery temperature. Who is right?

a. A only

b. B only

c. both A and B

d. neither A nor B

Fill in the Blank

15. Most passenger car alternators use _____ stators.

16. Most alternators rated at 100 amperes or more use _____ stators.

17. A rectifier bridge is used to keep diodes from _____ .

18. An _____ can be used to view alternator output voltage waveforms.

19. In an alternator, the field current connects the battery to the _____ through the alternator output terminal.

20. After an alternator starts working, field current comes from the _____ output.

21. An A-circuit alternator has an _____ grounded field.

22. A B-circuit alternator has an _____ grounded field.

23. Turning on the headlamps of a vehicle will cause alternator _____ to drop.

24. The charging system consists of the _____ , the _____ , the _____ , and a _____ .

25. An alternator can't operate without initial _____ from the battery.

26. Field current in the Chrysler charging system with computer-controlled voltage regulation is adjusted according to voltage and _____ temperature.

PART THREE

IGNITION AND ELECTRONIC ENGINE CONTROL SYSTEMS

INTRODUCTION

The four chapters in Part Three explain the principles of electrical spark ignition systems for gasoline engines. The ignition system is essential to ignite the air-fuel mixture for combustion in a gasoline engine. It is equally important as an emission control system to reduce the formation of harmful combustion byproducts.

The principles of timed, inductive-discharge ignition systems have not changed for more than 75 years. The applications of the principles, however, have continuously evolved and improved. For generations, engineers relied on mechanical breaker points to control ignition operation. Breaker-point ignitions have been obsolescent in new-car design for almost 20 years. They are not yet obsolete, however, in automobile service. There are still millions of breaker-point ignitions in vehicles on the road that require regular service.

Chapter 10 reviews the principles of 4-stroke gasoline engine operation. You must understand the fundamentals of engine performance in order to understand the role of the ignition system in overall engine operation.

Chapter 11 explains the principles of ignition operation. It also covers the fundamentals of ignition primary and secondary circuits, dwell, timing, and emission control that are common to breaker-point and electronic ignitions alike. Understanding the electromechanical fundamentals of breaker-point ignitions and engine operation provides the background for understanding electronic ignition control.

Chapter 12 continues the explanation of ignition systems by outlining the principles of electronic ignition control used by most carmakers. It also summarizes the ignition system development of major domestic and foreign manufacturers. This information will give you the foundation to understand and service late-model ignition systems. It also provides an introduction to fully integrated electronic engine control systems.

Chapter 13 explains the electronic engine control systems developed by major carmakers. It covers the principles of engine computers, system sensors and actuators, and engine-operating modes. If you understand these fundamentals, you can recognize their applications in different systems. You also can follow the continuing development of engine combustion control systems throughout your career. This chapter is really a summary of all previous chapters in Part Three. It also is an introduction to the future of automobile electronic service.

Electronic engine control systems on late-model cars integrate the operation of fuel, ignition, emission control, and other vehicle systems. Electronic engine controls are the state-of-the-art in automobile engineering.

10 ENGINE OPERATING PRINCIPLES—A REVIEW

WHAT

This chapter summarizes the design and operation of automobile engines. It begins with engine operating cycles and the structure of an engine from its block and crankshaft to its manifolds and accessory covers. This chapter also explains engine specifications and introduces the relationships among the fuel, ignition, and electrical systems. Understanding basic engine operation is the starting point for understanding combustion control systems.

WHY

To understand engine combustion controls, you have to begin with engine operation. If you know about the 4-stroke cycle, basic engine design, fuel delivery, and ignition, you then can study various systems in detail and understand how they work together.

Efficient engine operation depends on the individual parts of seven separate but interrelated systems:

1. The engine mechanical parts
2. The engine lubrication system
3. The engine cooling system
4. The fuel system
5. The ignition system
6. Related emission controls
7. The engine electrical system (the battery and the starting and charging systems).

A breakdown in any one of these systems can reduce overall engine performance. A professional mechanic must know how one part in any of these systems can affect other systems.

GOALS

After studying this chapter, you should be able to:

1. Explain 4-stroke operation of a reciprocating engine.

2. Explain the ignition methods and differences between spark-ignition (ottocycle) and compression-ignition (diesel) engines.

3. Illustrate various multicylinder engine designs.

4. Explain the operating relationships of engine blocks, heads, and reciprocating and rotating parts.

5. Define the following terms: bore, stroke, displacement, compression ratio, torque, horsepower and kilowatts, and engine pressure and efficiency.

ENGINE OPERATION

All engines burn fuel to change chemical energy to heat energy to kinetic energy and develop mechanical power. An engine that burns its fuel in a closed chamber and uses the heat energy directly to produce mechanical power is an **internal-combustion engine**. All automobile engines are internal-combustion engines. An engine, such as a steam engine, that burns its fuel outside of the working chamber where mechanical power is developed is an external combustion engine.

A mixture of fuel and air is compressed, ignited, and burned to develop pressure and force in an internal-combustion engine. The pressure and force produce mechanical power. To get the most energy from a burning liquid fuel, it must be **atomized**, vaporized, and compressed into a small area before it is burned. Without compression, the burning air-fuel mixture would not produce any force, pressure, and power.

Other than the Wankel rotary engine, automobile engines are **reciprocating engines** in which a piston moves up and down or back and forth in a cylinder and compresses the air-fuel mixture in the cylinder. When this mixture ignites and burns, it produces the high pressure that moves the piston. To drive an automobile, the inline reciprocating, or **linear** power of the moving piston must be changed to rotary power by the crankshaft figure 10-1.

Basic Engine Design and Parts

Engines are classified by the number of cylinders and the arrangement of the cylinders in the block, such as V-6, V-8, inline-4, or flat-4. Most

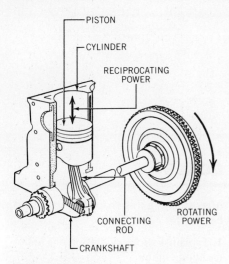

Figure 10-1. Power from the reciprocating motion of the piston is changed to rotary motion by the crankshaft. This rotating power ultimately drives the wheels of the car.

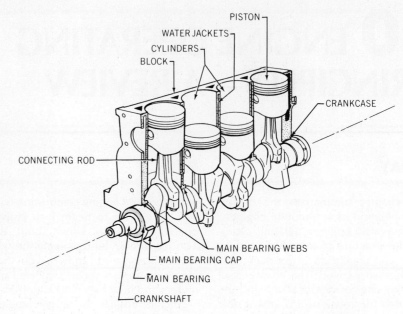

Figure 10-3. Most engines are built from a cast, 1-piece block that contains the cylinders, water jackets, and crankcase.

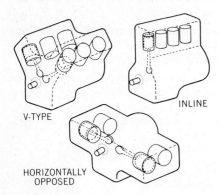

Figure 10-2. Most automobile engines are built with inline, V-type, or horizontally opposed cylinder arrangements.

automotive engines have 4, 6, or 8 cylinders, although there are engines with 2, 3, 5, 12, and 16 cylinders. Figure 10-2 shows the most common cylinder arrangements for automotive engines:

1. *Inline engine*—All cylinders are in a straight line or single bank. Most 4-and 6-cylinder engines are built like this, as are 3- and 5-cylinder engines.

2. *V-type*—Cylinders are in two equal banks, separated by an angle of 60 or 90 degrees. Most V-type engines have 6 or 8 cylinders, but V-4 engines have also been built. Engines with 8 or more cylinders are usually V-type engines.

3. *Horizontally opposed*—Cylinders are in two equal banks 180 degrees

apart. Volkswagen and Porsche 4- and 6-cylinder engines are the best known "flat" or "pancake" engines. Subaru also builds a flat 4-cylinder engine.

Regardless of the number of cylinders, all pistons are connected to a single crankshaft. Engines with more cylinders produce more power strokes for each rotation of the crankshaft and run more smoothly than engines with few cylinders. For example, an 8-cylinder engine has twice as many power strokes as a 4-cylinder engine for each crankshaft revolution. The 8-cylinder engine runs more smoothly because its power strokes are closer together in time and in degrees of crankshaft revolution.

Most gasoline and diesel engines are built with a 1-piece block and crankcase of cast iron or aluminum that contains the cylinders. The block also contains coolant passages, or water jackets, for cooling, figure 10-3. The block casting forms the cylinders and water jackets. The lower part of the block forms the upper portion of the crankcase, which supports the crankshaft in main bearings. The oil pan forms the lower portion of the crankcase.

Horizontally opposed engines usually are built with a crankcase in two pieces that join at the centerline of the crankshaft, figure 10-4. Half of each main bearing is in each half of the crankcase. The cylinders, particularly in flat air-cooled engines, often are separate detachable castings that are bolted to the crankcase.

The cylinder head covers the top of the block and cylinders and forms the combustion chambers. Modern engines have the intake and exhaust valves in the head and are called **overhead-valve (ohv) engines**, figure 10-5. The cylinder head also contains the fuel intake and exhaust passages (ports) and the intake and exhaust valves.

The main bearing journals of the crankshaft are arranged in a straight line on the center of the shaft. The crankshaft rotates around this centerline in the block, figure 10-6. The **crankshaft throws** are offset from the centerline. Each throw has a journal to which one or two connecting rods are bolted. The crankshaft throws provide the leverage for the force of the moving piston to develop rotating power. In most multicylinder engines, the rod journals are offset equally

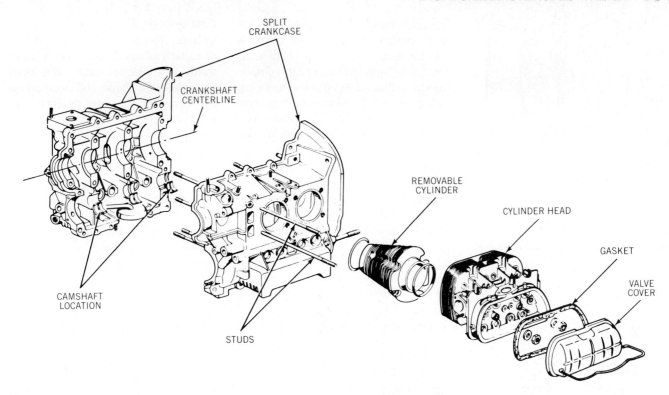

Figure 10-4. Most horizontally opposed engines are built up from a 2-piece split crankcase and separate, detachable cylinder barrels.

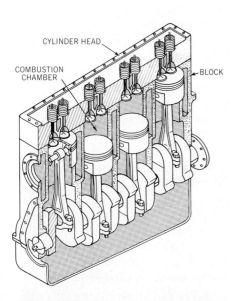

Figure 10-5. The cylinder head covers the top of the cylinders and contains the combustion chamber and valves.

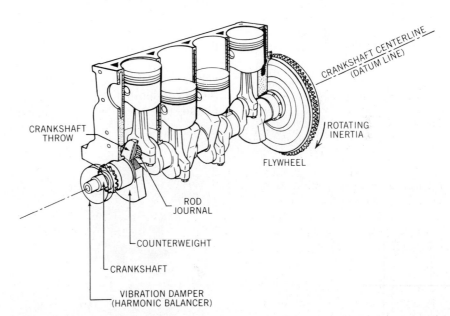

Figure 10-6. The crankshaft rotates in main bearings in the block. A flywheel at one end of the crankshaft provides rotating inertia.

around the crankshaft centerline so that the firing impulses of the power strokes are evenly spaced.

All engines have a flywheel on one end of the crankshaft, figure 10-6. The weight of the flywheel provides rotating inertia to the crankshaft that carries it smoothly through the periods between firing impulses. A smaller rotating weight, called a vibration damper, or harmonic balancer, is located at the opposite end of the crankshaft, figure 10-6. The vibration damper further smooths out the engine's firing impulses and other vibrations. Some 4-cylinder engines also use counterrotating shafts in the engine block or underneath the crankshaft to reduce vibrations.

Most crankshafts are solid, 1-piece units. The rods that connect the pistons to the crankshaft have removable caps on their big ends. The bottom of each connecting rod and its cap are

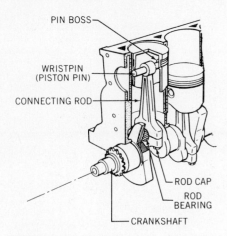

Figure 10-7. Connecting rods attach the pistons to the crankshaft.

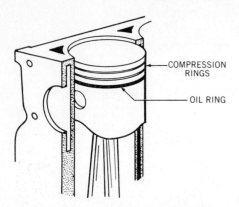

Figure 10-8. Piston rings seal the piston in the cylinder and control the amount of oil on the cylinder walls.

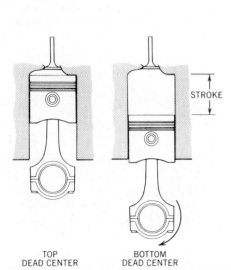

Figure 10-9. One piston stroke from top to bottom or from bottom to top of the cylinder equals one-half crankshaft revolution, or 180 degrees.

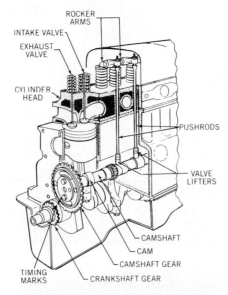

Figure 10-10. The camshaft is driven by the crankshaft through gears as shown here or by a chain or belt. Timing marks synchronize camshaft and crankshaft rotation.

bolted around a crankshaft journal and contain a split bearing called a rod bearing. At its top or small end, the connecting rod has a piston pin, or wristpin, that allows the rod to swing sideways as the piston moves up and down, figure 10-7. The piston has three or four grooves around its circumference that hold piston rings, figure 10-8. The rings seal the piston in the cylinder so compression is not lost through the clearance between the piston and cylinder. The rings also control the amount of oil on the cylinder walls for piston lubrication.

The movement of the piston from the top of the cylinder to the bottom, or from bottom to top, is called a **stroke**. The top of a stroke is **top dead center (tdc)**. The bottom of a stroke is **bottom dead center (bdc)**. Each stroke of the piston turns the crankshaft one-half revolution, or 180 degrees, figure 10-9. Two piston strokes turn the crankshaft 360 degrees through one complete revolution. The term **revolutions per minute (rpm)** indicates the number of revolutions the crankshaft makes in one minute.

Automotive engines use **poppet valves**, which open and close in linear motion against fixed seats. When closed, the valves are sealed against their seats by the compression of coil springs. The valves are opened by irregularly shaped lobes on a **camshaft**. The lobe for each valve must have the right shape and position on the camshaft to open its intake or exhaust valve at the desired point in the 4-stroke cycle. Similarly, each lobe must allow its valve to close at another precise point in the cycle. Each valve opens and closes once for each revolution of its lobe. The camshaft is driven by the crankshaft through timing gears, figure 10-10, chains, or belts to synchronize valve operation with piston position during the 4-stroke cycle. The camshaft rotates at a 2 : 1 reduction ratio, or at one-half crankshaft speed.

Every engine design is a compromise. While it is simple to locate the camshaft in the block, the valve train necessary to get the cam motion to the valve is complicated, figure 10-10. Many engines are built with the camshaft in the head. This design allows higher engine speeds and placement of the valves for more efficient engine breathing. A **single overhead-cam (ohc) engine** uses one camshaft to operate intake and exhaust valves; a **double overhead-cam (dohc) engine** uses separate camshafts to operate the intake and exhaust valves. Figure 10-11 shows both designs.

Every multicylinder engine (unless it has a separate carburetor or fuel injector bolted to each intake port) needs an intake manifold. The intake manifold is a metal casting with passages that route the intake air or air-fuel mixture from a central inlet to the individual cylinders. Similarly, every engine needs an exhaust manifold to route the exhaust away from the cylinders to a central exhaust systems. Figure 10-12 (inline) and figure 10-13 (V-type) show the positioning of the intake and exhaust manifolds.

The oil pan closes the bottom of the crankcase and acts as a reservoir for the engine's lubricating oil, figure 10-14. The top of each cylinder head above the valves is enclosed by a valve cover or cam cover, figure 10-14. Some form of cover is also used over the timing gears or camshaft

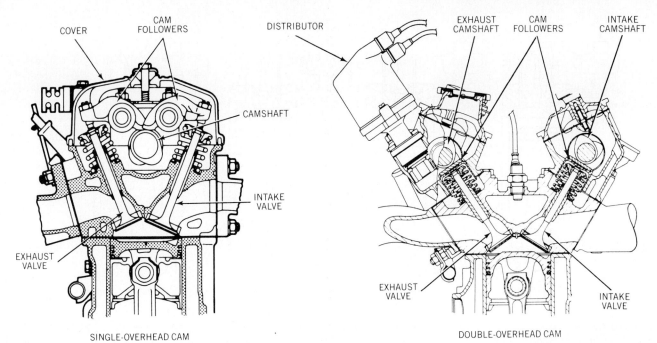

Figure 10-11. Typical single- and double-overhead-cam engines. (Chrysler)/(Clymer Publications)

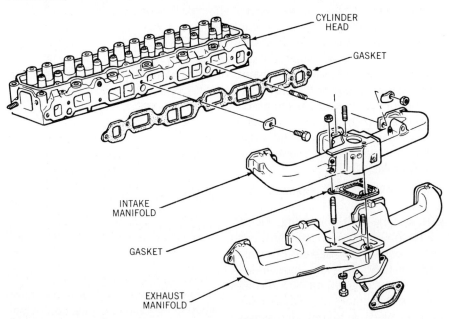

Figure 10-12. Inline engines have the intake manifold on the side of the head. The exhaust manifold can be on the same side or the opposite side.

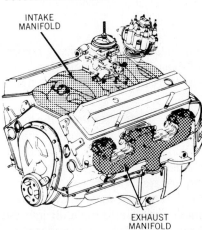

Figure 10-13. V-type engines have the intake manifold between the cylinder banks and exhaust manifolds bolted to the outside of each head.

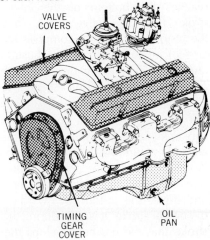

Figure 10-14. The oil pan, the valve covers or cam covers, and the timing cover are the most visible of an engine's covers.

drive mechanism on the front of the engine, figure 10-14.

ENGINE OPERATING CYCLES

An engine operating cycle is the process of drawing air and fuel into a cylinder, compressing it, burning it to develop power, and exhausting the burned mixture. In a reciprocating en-gine, an operating cycle is measured in the number of piston strokes needed for one complete cycle. Most gasoline and diesel engines operate on a **four-stroke cycle**.

The 4-Stroke Cycle

The 4-stroke cycle consists of two piston strokes up and two down. Each stroke is named after its principal ac-

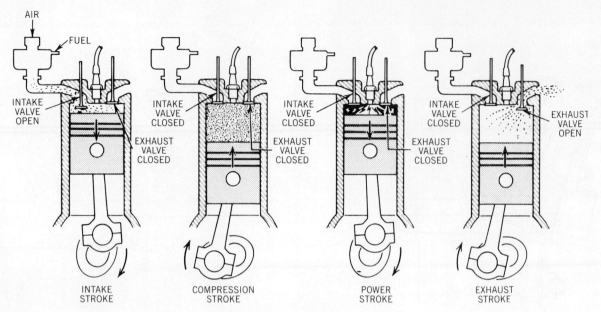

Figure 10-15. The 4-stroke cycle of intake, compression, power, and exhaust is repeated continuously in every cylinder as long as the engine is running.

tion: intake, compression, power, and exhaust. Here is how they work in a 4-stroke gasoline engine, figure 10-15.

1. *Intake stroke*—Starting at the top of its stroke (tdc), the piston moves down. This increases the available cylinder volume and creates a low-pressure area, or vacuum, in the cylinder. The vacuum allows atmospheric pressure to force air into the engine. This draws a vaporized air-fuel mixture into the cylinder through an open intake valve.

2. *Compression stroke*—As the piston reaches the bottom of the intake stroke, the intake valve closes. Then the piston moves up to compress the air-fuel mixture into the combustion chamber. Compression develops high potential energy in a small space.

3. *Power stroke*—As the piston nears top dead center of the compression stroke, the spark plug fires to ignite the air-fuel mixture. As the mixture burns in the confined space of the combustion chamber, it releases its energy and drives the piston downward on the power stroke. It is only during this stroke that the engine develops mechanical power.

4. *Exhaust stroke*—Near the bottom of the power stroke, the exhaust valve

opens. The exhaust valve opens slightly before bdc so that pressure in the cylinder will help to expel exhaust gases. At bottom dead center, the piston starts back up on the exhaust stroke to force the burned air-fuel mixture out of the cylinder. As the piston nears the top of the exhaust stroke, the exhaust valve closes and the cycle starts over with another downward intake stroke.

The 4-stroke cycle is repeated continuously in every cylinder of an engine as long as it is running. Figure 10-16 shows that each stroke for one piston requires 180 degrees of crankshaft rotation. Therefore, four strokes require 720 degrees, or two revolutions of the crankshaft. Four-stroke-cycle engines often are called simply "4-stroke" engines. They also are called "ottocycle" engines, after Dr. Nikolaus Otto, the German inventor who perfected their operation in 1876.

Air-Fuel Mixture Ignition

The principal difference between gasoline and diesel engines is the method used to ignite the air-fuel mixture. Gasoline engines use a timed electric spark. Diesel engines rely on the heat

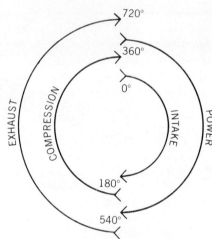

Figure 10-16. Each piston stroke—intake, compression, power, and exhaust—requires 180 degrees of crankshaft rotation. Four strokes equal 720 degrees of rotation.

of highly compressed air and control ignition by timing the injection of fuel into the combustion chamber. Ignition timing must be controlled in either type of engine so that combustion occurs when the piston is in a position to develop maximum power.

In a gasoline engine, air and fuel are mixed in the carburetor or in the intake manifold by the fuel injection system. The air-fuel mixture is compressed in the cylinder to a pressure of 100 to 200 pounds per square inch (psi), or 700 to 1,400 kilopascals (kPa), before ignition. This raises the temperature of the mixture to 750° to

1,100° F (400° to 600° C), which is not high enough to ingite it spontaneously. Ignition is provided by the spark plug in the combustion chamber, figure 10-17. Speed and power of a gasoline engine are controlled by regulating the amount of air-fuel mixture that enters the cylinders. This is done by **throttling** the mixture. A throttle valve in the carburetor or manifold inlet varies the size of the opening through which air enters the engine. Fuel is mixed with the incoming air, and the throttling process regulates the volume of the combined air-fuel mixture.

In a diesel engine, only air is drawn into the cylinder through an intake valve. The piston compresses the air volume in the cylinder to a pressure of 450 to 800 psi (3,000 to 5,600 kPa). This raises the air temperature to 1,300° to 1,650° F (700° to 900° C), which is high enough to ignite any fuel that might be present. Fuel must be kept out of this hot compressed air until the time when combustion will develop the most useful power. If fuel were present in the highly compressed air, the mixture would ignite before the piston reached the desired point on the power stroke. Therefore, ignition timing in a diesel is controlled by injecting fuel into the combustion chamber at the exact time of maximum combustion efficiency, figure 10-18.

Diesel engines run with an unthrottled air intake. Air volume in a diesel cylinder on the intake stroke is relatively constant at any engine speed. It must be to maintain uniform combustion temperatures at all speeds because only air volume and compression pressure cause ignition. Diesel engine speed and power are regulated by varying the amount of fuel injected into the compressed air in the cylinder.

Gasoline engines operate with a ratio of air to fuel by weight that can vary from 8:1 at the richest to 18.5:1 at the leanest. However, engine throttling varies the *volume* of the mixture greatly from idle to full power. Diesel engines operate with a constant volume of air but air-fuel ratios that vary

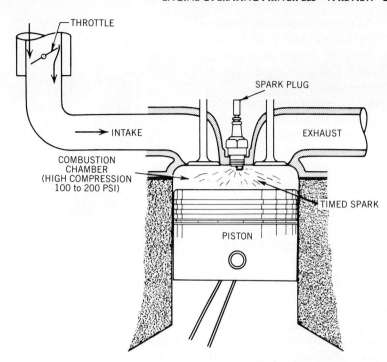

Figure 10-17. Ignition in a gasoline engine occurs when a timed spark ignites the air-fuel mixture.

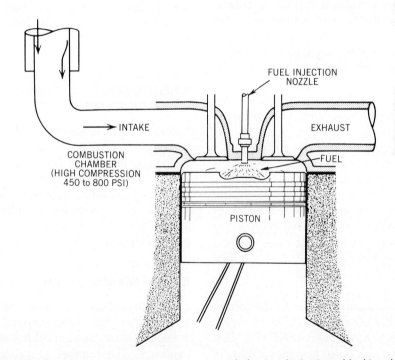

Figure 10-18. Ignition in a diesel engine occurs with the timed injection of fuel into highly compressed air in the cylinder.

from as rich as 20:1 at full power to as lean as 85:1 at idle.

Engine Cooling

Not all of the chemical energy of fuel is changed to mechanical energy during combustion. As much as 40 percent of the fuel energy is lost as heat energy that does no mechanical work. Peak combustion temperatures range from 3,500° to 6,000° F (2,000° to 3,330° C), and engine temperatures average from 1,200° to 1,700° F (650°

to 925° C) during a complete operating cycle. Excess heat must be removed from the engine or it would literally melt down. This is the job of the cooling system.

Actually, "temperature regulation system" would be a better name because an engine cannot operate efficiently if it is too cold. Engine temperature must be high enough for complete combustion but not so high that it will damage the engine. The cooling system carries excess heat away from the engine *and* maintains uniform temperatures throughout the engine. Two methods are used for engine cooling, or temperature regulation.

The most common engine cooling system is a liquid cooling system. Liquid is circulated through passages in the engine called water jackets, and heat is transferred from the metal to the liquid, figure 10-19. The liquid then is circulated through a radiator where the heat is transferred to the surrounding air. Although parts of the cooling system are called the "water pump" and "water jackets," the liquid coolant really is a mixture of approximately half water and half ethylene glycol compound, with oxidation inhibitors.

The other method used to cool an engine is air cooling, in which air is circulated directly around the surfaces of the engine block, cylinders, and heads. The cylinders and heads of air-cooled engines have cooling fins that increase the surface area exposed to the circulating air and aid heat transfer from the metal to the air.

Air-cooled engines have been used in some automobiles since the earliest days but not as much as liquid-cooled engines have been used. The best known air-cooled engines are those of the Type 1 Volkswagen "Beetle" and many Porsches. Air cooling does not provide the uniform heat transfer and temperature control that liquid cooling does. Air-cooled engines rely on the incoming air-fuel mixture for a large part of combustion chamber cooling and therefore run with richer mixtures than liquid-cooled engines. This is the main reason that air-cooled

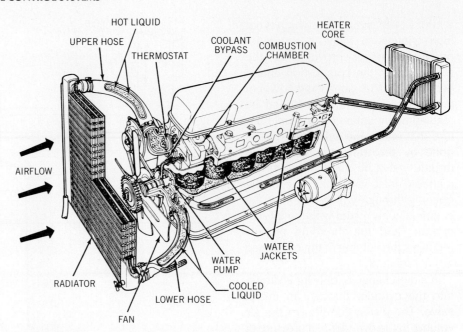

Figure 10-19. Liquid cooling systems are the most common cooling systems for automobile engines. (Chrysler)

engines are impractical for the emission control and fuel economy requirements of late-model automobiles.

ENGINE DISPLACEMENT AND COMPRESSION RATIO

Everything you have read in the last few pages has dealt with the mechanical parts of an engine. There are some basic specifications for all engines that you must know about to understand engine operation completely. Two of these are engine **displacement** and **compression ratio**.

Engine Displacement

Engine displacement is often referred to as "engine size." Displacement is a measurement of the total volume of all cylinders. The number of cylinders partly determines displacement, but the arrangement of the cylinders does not.

To calculate total engine displacement, you start with one cylinder. You know that the distance each piston travels from the bottom to the top of a cylinder is its stroke, figure 10-20, which is measured in inches or millimeters. The displacement of a single

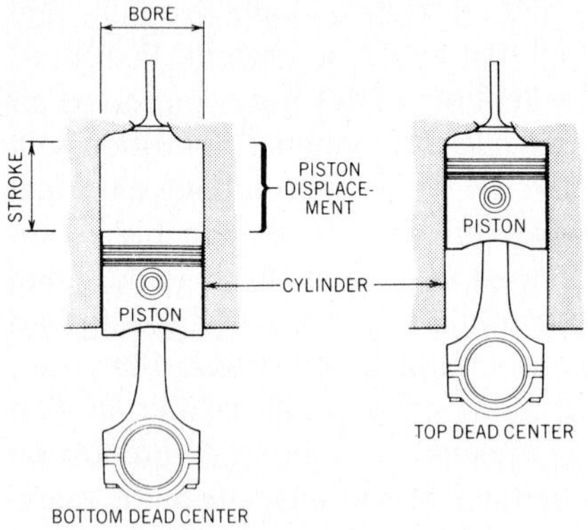

Figure 10-20. The bore is the diameter of the cylinder, and the stroke is the distance that the top of the piston travels from bottom dead center to top dead center.

cylinder is the volume of gas or air displaced by the top surface of the piston as it travels from bottom dead center (maximum cylinder volume) to top dead center (minimum cylinder volume) during its stroke.

The diameter of the cylinder is the **bore**. To calculate cylinder displacement, use the following formula with a bore of 3.000 inches and a stroke of 3.000 inches, figure 10-21:

1. Divide the bore (cylinder diameter) by 2 to determine the radius of the cylinder: 3 ÷ 2 = 1.5.

TWO STROKES = FOUR

Like a 4-stroke engine, a 2-stroke engine can be either a spark-ignition or a compression-ignition type. A two-stroke engine produces a power stroke for each revolution of the crankshaft, while a 4-stroke engine produces one power stroke for every two revolutions. Gasoline 2-stroke, spark-ignition engines don't have poppet valves as 4-stroke engines do. Instead, the piston uncovers intake and exhaust ports in the side of the cylinder as it nears the bottom of its stroke. Here is how a 2-stroke engine combines intake and compression into one single stroke, and power and exhaust into a second stroke.

1. *Intake and compression stroke*— As the piston moves up in the cylinder, it creates a low-pressure area in the crankcase. A reed valve or rotary valve opens in the side of the crankcase, and the air-fuel mixture is drawn in. At the same time, the piston compresses a previous air-fuel charge in the cylinder. As the piston nears top dead center, the spark plug fires to ignite this mixture.

2. *Power and exhaust stroke*—As the piston is forced down by the burning air-fuel mixture on the power stroke, it uncovers exhaust ports in the side of the cylinder, toward the bottom. By the time the ports are uncovered, the mixture is almost completely burned, and the exhaust flows out through the ports.

As the piston continues down, it compresses the air-fuel charge in the crankcase. The reed valve or rotary valve closes to hold the charge in the crankcase. Crankcase compression forces this mixture through a transfer passage to intake ports in the side of the cylinder. The force of the incoming mixture helps drive the remaining exhaust out the exhaust ports on the opposite side of the cylinder, but a ridge on the piston top deflects the incoming mixture upward so that it doesn't flow out the exhaust ports. As the piston moves upward, it covers both the intake and the exhaust ports and compresses the new air-fuel charge in the cylinder to repeat the cycle.

Because the crankcase of a 2-stroke gasoline engine is used as a "precompression chamber" for the air-fuel mixture, it can't serve as a lubricating oil reservoir. Therefore, oil must be mixed with the fuel or injected intermittently into the engine.

The most common 2-stroke diesel engines are truck engines build by the Detroit Diesel Allison Division of GM. Detroit Diesels have cam-operated exhaust valves rather than exhaust ports in the cylinder walls. A Roots blower supplies the intake air charge through cylinder-wall intake ports. Timed diesel injection controls fuel delivery and ignition timing. Because the crankcase does not have to serve as an intake precompression chamber, Detroit Diesels use a conventional oil pan and lubricating oil supply.

The accompanying diagrams show the differences—and similarities—beween 4-stroke and 2-stroke operating cycles.

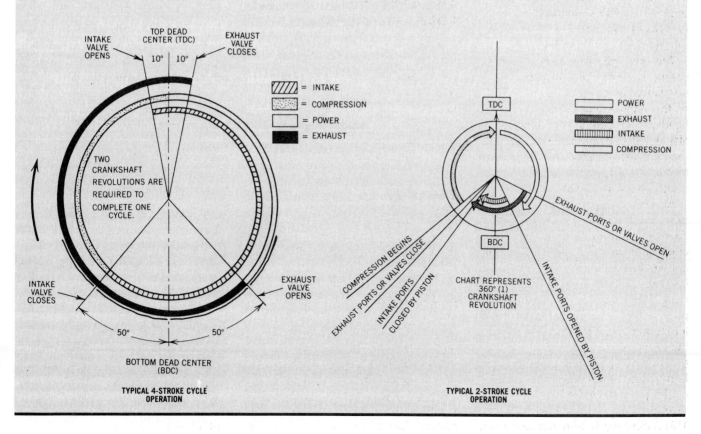

TYPICAL 4-STROKE CYCLE OPERATION

TYPICAL 2-STROKE CYCLE OPERATION

2. Square the radius (multiply it by itself): $1.5 \times 1.5 = 2.25$.

3. Multiply the square of the radius, 2.25, by pi (π), or 3.1416, to find the area of the cylinder cross section: $2.25 \times 3.1416 = 7.069$.

4. Multiply the area of the cylinder cross section by the stroke (3.000 inches) to determine the displacement of one cylinder: $7.069 \times 3.000 = 21.207$ cubic inches.

5. Multiply the displacement of one cylinder by the total number of engine cylinders to determine engine displacement. If the engine has four cylinders, its displacement is: $4 \times 21.207 = 84.828$ cubic inches. In practice, this would be rounded off to an even 85-cubic-inch displacement. This often is abbreviated "85 cid."

If an engine with the same bore and stroke dimensions had six cylinders, its displacement would be $6 \times 21.207 = 127.242$ cubic inches, or simply 127 cubic inches. An 8-cylinder engine with the same bore and stroke would have a displacement of $8 \times 21.207 = 169.656$ cubic inches. Rounded off, we would say it was a 170-cid engine.

You can use a simplified formula, based on the same calculations:

bore^2 × 0.7854 × stroke × cylinders

Here's how it works for the same 3-inch bore and stroke measurements:

$$3^2 \times 0.7854 \times 3 \times 8 \text{ cylinders}$$
$$9 \times 0.7854 \times 3 \times 8$$
$$= 169.6 \text{ cubic inches.}$$

Metric Displacement Specifications. In the example above, we used measurements in customary inch units. The same formula works with bore and stroke measurements in millimeters. Let's say that the bore is 75 millimeters, and the stroke is 70 millimeters, figure 10-22. Displacement is expressed in cubic centimeters, so change the millimeter dimensions to centimeters by moving the decimal one place to the left (75 mm = 7.5 cm and 70 mm = 7.0 cm). Then proceed as follows:

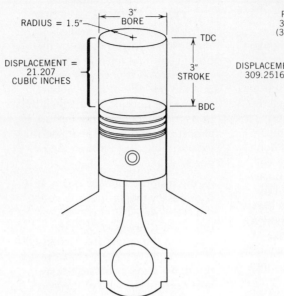

Figure 10-21. Calculate total cylinder displacement by multiplying the surface area of the cylinder cross section, or piston top, times the stroke.

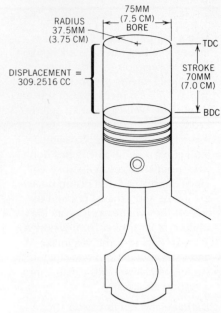

Figure 10-22. Use the same formula to calculate cylinder displacement with either metric or customary dimensions.

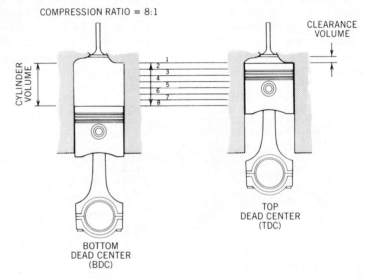

Figure 10-23. The compression ratio is total cylinder volume divided by combustion chamber, or clearance, volume.

1. The bore, 7.5 cm, divided by 2, equals a radius of 3.75 cm.

2. $3.75 \times 3.75 = 14.0625$.

3. $14.0625 \times 3.1416\,(\pi) = 44.1788$ cm^2 cylinder cross-sectional area.

4. 44.1788×7.0 cm (stroke) $= 309.2516$ cm^3, or cc, cylinder displacement.

If the engine has four cylinders, the total displacement is 4×309.3516 cc $= 1,237.406$ cc. We would nor-

mally round this off to 1,237 cc or 1.2 liters. (Actually, if you were a carmaker, you would probably advertise it as a 1.3-liter engine.)

Using the simplified formula:

Bore^2 × 0.7854 × stroke × cylinders
$7.5^2 \times 0.7854 \times 7.0 \times 4$ cylinders
$56.25 \times 0.7854 \times 7.0 \times 4 = 1,237$ cc

Remember that you can convert metric to customary displacement measurements with the following factors:

• To change cubic centimeters to cubic inches, multiply by 0.061 (1,237 cc × 0.061 = 75.457 cubic inches).

• To change liters to cubic inches, multiply by 61.02 (1.2 liters × 61.02 = 73.224 cubic inches).

• To change cubic inches to cubic centimeters, multiply by 16.39 (75 cubic inches × 16.39 = 1,229.25 cc).

You can see that conversion accuracy depends on where you round off the numbers. To maintain best accuracy, work in one system, customary or metric, and use conversions only for approximate measurements.

Compression Ratio

Engine compression ratio is the ratio of total cylinder volume (piston at bdc) to combustion chamber volume (piston at tdc), figure 10-23. Total cylinder volume is piston displacement *plus* combustion chamber volume. Combustion chamber volume also is called **clearance volume**. Therefore, the compression ratio is total cylinder volume divided by clearance volume. If the clearance volume is 1/8 of the total, the compression ratio is 8:1. Here is the simple formula:

$$\frac{\text{total cylinder volume}}{\text{clearance volume}} = \frac{\text{compression}}{\text{ratio}}$$

Here is an example of a compression ratio calculation. First, calculate cylinder displacement from the bore and stroke dimensions. Let's say it is 21.207 cubic inches as in our earlier example. Let's also say that the combustion chamber volume is 3.0 cubic inches. Now, add the two volumes:

$$21.207 + 3.0$$
$$= 24.207 \text{ (total cylinder volume)}$$

Then, divide total volume by clearance volume:

$$\frac{24.207}{3.0} = 8.069$$

The compression ratio is 8.069:1, which would be rounded off and listed as an 8:1 compression ratio.

Theoretically, a high compression ratio improves the efficiency of an engine and allows it to develop more power from a given amount of fuel. Combustion occurs faster with higher compression because fuel molecules are packed more tightly and the combustion flame travels fast.

Most gasoline engines, however, are limited to compression ratios of about 11.5:1 or less. If compression is too high, the air-fuel mixture will overheat and ignite before the spark plug fires, which can damage an engine. Compression ratios as high as 10:1 or 11:1 were common in the 1960's, but the higher octane fuel available then burned more evenly than today's gasoline. Higher compression also raises combustion temperatures and increases emission of oxides of nitrogen (NO_x). In the 1970's, carmakers lowered compression, and oil companies introduced lower octane unleaded fuel to meet stricter emission limits. Compression ratios on today's gasoline engines range from 8:1 to 9:1.

Diesel engines have higher compression ratios than gasoline engines because they rely on high compression to create heat for fuel ignition. Diesel compression ratios range from about 16:1 to 22:1.

ENGINE TORQUE AND POWER

You know that torque is rotating work measured in foot-pounds, inch-pounds, or newton-meters. You also know that power is the rate, or speed, of doing work and can be measured in horsepower or watts. Engines produce both torque and power. They are related to each other and are common specifications given for almost all automobiles.

Engine Torque

The engine crankshaft changes reciprocating work into rotary torque, so engine torque is measured at the end of the crankshaft. To measure torque with the engine running, we can install a friction clutch, or adjustable

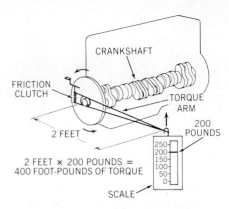

Figure 10-24. This engine applies 200 pounds of force through a 2-foot arm and therefore develops 2 × 200, or 400 foot-pounds of torque.

clamp, on the end of the crankshaft. We can connect an arm to this clutch, and we can connect the other end of the arm to a scale, figure 10-24. When we tighten the clutch, the rotating crankshaft starts to exert force on the scale. Let's say the force is 200 pounds.

To know what this represents in foot-pounds (ft-lb) of torque, we must consider the length of the arm. If it is 2 feet, the 200 pounds of force represent 2 feet times 200 pounds, or 400 foot-pounds of torque, figure 10-24. If the engine is running at 2,000 rpm and we tighten the clutch so that the engine almost stalls at full throttle as it develops 400 foot-pounds of torque, we can say that this is its maximum torque at 2,000 rpm.

Engine Horsepower

To develop power, an engine must move some weight, not simply exert force on a scale. To determine what the power is, we have to know the weight, the distance, and the speed of movement. Let's allow our engine to rotate a 200-pound weight on the end of the 2-foot arm at a speed of 2,000 rpm. To calculate torque now, we must consider the distance through which the weight moves, not just the force on the end of a 2-foot arm. The distance is the circumference of a circle formed by the arm as it turns

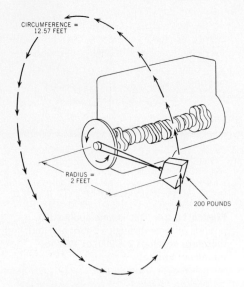

Figure 10-25. If the engine moves 200 pounds through a 12.57-foot-diameter circle, it does 2,514 foot-pounds of work.

through a complete revolution, figure 10-25. That distance is

2 × radius (2 feet) × 3.1416

= 12.57 feet

Now, multiply 12.57 feet by 200 pounds to determine the work done during one engine revolution:

12.57 feet × 200 pounds

= 2,514 foot-pounds

The engine is running at 2,000 rpm, so multiply 2,514 by 2,000 to determine the amount of work done per minute:

2,000 rpm × 2,514 ft-lb

= 5,028,000 ft-lb/min

Remember that 1 horsepower equals 33,000 foot-pounds per minute, so divide 5,028,000 by 33,000 to determine horsepower:

$$\frac{5,028,000}{33,000} = 152.36 \text{ horsepower}$$

If you know engine torque at any rpm, you can calculate horsepower with this formula:

$$\text{horsepower} = \frac{\text{torque} \times 2\pi \times \text{rpm}}{33,000}$$

If you divide 33,000 by 2π (6.2832), you have the shorter formula:

$$\text{horsepower} = \frac{\text{torque} \times \text{rpm}}{5,252}$$

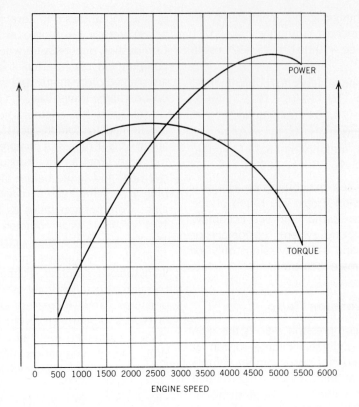

Figure 10-26. Most engines develop maximum torque at a lower speed than maximum power.

Metric Torque And Power. The previous examples of torque and power calculations used customary units of foot-pounds and horsepower. Most carmakers now list the torque and power of their engines in both customary units and the metric units of newton-meters (Nm) and kilowatts (kW). Remember, there are direct relationships between foot-pounds and newton-meters and between horsepower and kilowatts. For review, here are the conversion factors to change from one specification to another:

foot-pounds × 0.7376

= newton-meters

newton-meters × 1.356

= foot-pounds

horsepower × 0.746

= kilowatts

kilowatts × 1.3405

= horsepower

Torque and Power Relationships

The arm and scale that we used to measure torque and power are a simple **dynamometer**. All dynamometers

work by applying a load to an engine and measuring torque at different speeds.

Torque can be measured at any rpm, usually at wide-open throttle to determine maximum torque at a given engine speed. Most automobile gasoline engines develop maximum torque at about 2,500 rpm and maximum power at 3,500 to 5,000 rpm. Above 2,500 rpm, torque decreases because an engine takes in less air at higher speeds and combustion efficiency drops. There is less compression pressure and therefore less force on the piston to develop torque. Power, however, continues to increase as speed increases because speed goes up faster than torque drops off. As long as the torque decrease is less than the speed increase, power continues to rise. In the upper part of an engine's speed range, torque drops faster, and power similarly drops off. Figure 10-26 shows typical power and torque curves for an automobile gasoline engine. Most diesel engines develop maximum torque and power at lower speeds than gasoline engines.

Brake Horsepower

The horsepower measured at an engine's crankshaft is called **brake horsepower (bhp)** because early engine dynamometers used a friction brake, called a prony brake, to apply a load to the engine. Brake horsepower is the horsepower available at the flywheel. **Gross brake horsepower** is the maximum power output with only the fuel, oil, and water pumps and built-in emission controls as accessory loads on the engine. **Net brake horsepower** is the power output of a fully equipped engine with all accessories such as the cooling system, exhaust system, air filter, charging system, and add-on emission controls installed. Before 1970, carmakers advertised the gross bhp ratings of engines. Since the early 1970's, they have advertised net bhp ratings, which are lower.

Indicated Horsepower and Friction Horsepower

The difference between gross and net bhp shows that not all of an engine's power is available to drive the car. Some is used to power various accessories. Energy that otherwise would be mechanical power also is lost as heat energy in the cooling and exhaust systems.

Remember, too, that friction is heat energy, and a lot of engine power is used to overcome the friction of its own moving parts. This lost horsepower is **friction horsepower**. We can't measure friction horsepower with simple equipment, but we can calculate it if we know the **indicated horsepower** of an engine.

Indicated horsepower is the theoretical maximum power that could be produced inside the cylinders of a particular engine. Engineers measure indicated horsepower with instruments that measure gas pressures in the cylinders through all four strokes of an operating cycle. The simple engineering comparisons of indicated friction, and brake horsepower are:

brake hp = indicated hp
 − friction hp
friction hp = indicated hp
 − brake hp

Brake horsepower (the power an engine *does* produce) divided by indicated horsepower (the power it *could* produce) is a measure of an engine's mechanical efficiency. For example, if brake hp is 100 and indicated hp is 125, the mechanical efficiency is: 100 ÷ 125 = 0.8, or 80% efficiency.

By now, you can see that all of the potential energy in an engine's gasoline or diesel fuel is not changed to useful mechanical energy or power. Figure 10-27 shows that only about 25 percent of the potential energy in a gallon of fuel is available as mechanical power at the engine crankshaft.

ENGINE PRESSURE

An engine is basically an air pump that draws in air, compresses it, and then exhausts it. Engine cylinder pressure varies during the 4-stroke cycle, and it varies according to the compression ratio and combustion efficiency of an engine.

The simplest pressure measurement is the **compression pressure**. This is the pressure that the piston creates as it moves from bottom dead center to top dead center on the compression stroke *without having the air-fuel mixture ignited*. In a gasoline engine it ranges from 100 to 200 psi (700 to 1,400 kPa). In a diesel engine, it ranges 450 to 800 psi (3,000 to 5,600 kPa), figure 10-28. Compression pressure is a useful tuneup specification that you can test with a pressure gauge to see if the cylinder is properly sealed. It is not, however, the operating pressure of the engine.

Operating pressures in a gasoline engine are as high as 700 psi during the power stroke because the heat of combustion raises the pressure of the compressed air and fuel. This pressure increase is what develops force on the piston and torque and power in an engine. If the mixture doesn't burn on one power stroke (the cylinder misfires), there is no pressure rise, and that power stroke produces no power.

During the 4-stroke cycle, cylinder pressure varies from less than atmospheric pressure (14.7 psi) during the intake stroke to about 700 psi during combustion, figure 10-29. Engineers use the average pressure during all four strokes to calculate indicated horsepower. This is the **mean effective pressure**. Engineers also use **brake mean effective pressure (bmep)** to

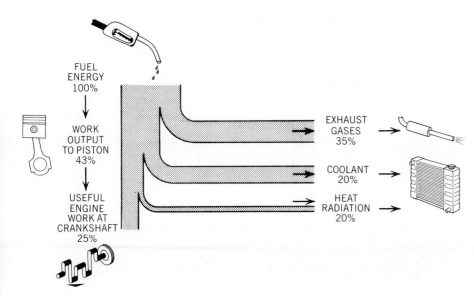

Figure 10-27. Only about 25 percent of an engine's potential fuel energy is available as mechanical power at the crankshaft.

indicate engine efficiency. This is calculated from the brake horsepower measured on a dynamometer, as follows for a 4-stroke gasoline engine:

$$bmep = \frac{792,000 \times bhp}{rpm \times cid}$$

SUMMARY

All gasoline and diesel automotive engines are internal-combustion engines that operate on the 4-stroke cycle of intake, compression, power, and exhaust. Engines are commonly identified by the number of cylinders and cylinder arrangement. Engine size is measured by displacement, which is the total volume of all cylinders.

Engine torque is the amount of rotating work that an engine can perform, measured in foot-pounds or newton-meters. Power is the amount of torque delivered in a given amount of time. An engine develops power and torque as pressures rise in the cylinders during combustion.

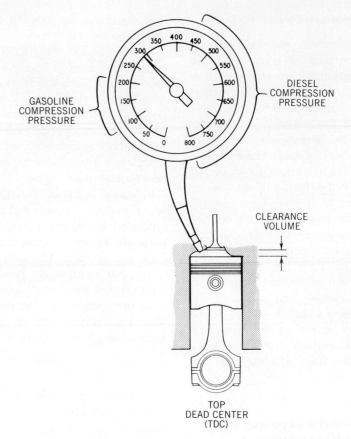

Figure 10-28. Compression pressure is the pressure created by the piston on the compression stroke without having the air-fuel mixture ignited.

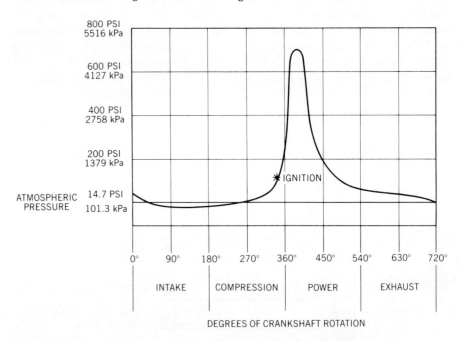

Figure 10-29. Cylinder pressures vary widely during the 4-stroke cycle.

REVIEW QUESTIONS

Multiple Choice

1. Mechanic A says that gasoline and diesel engines are both internal-combustion engines. Mechanic B says that steam engines are also internal-combustion engines. Who is right?

a. A only
b. B only
c. both A and B
d. neither A nor B

2. Piston travel from the top to the bottom of a cylinder is called a:

a. cycle
b. revolution
c. rotation
d. stroke

3. An engine block casting contains all of the following, except the:

a. cylinders
b. flywheel
c. water jackets
d. upper part of the crankcase

4. Mechanic A says ignition in a gasoline engine is controlled by a timed electric spark. Mechanic B says ignition in a diesel engine is controlled by air-fuel ratio. Who is right?

a. A only
b. B only
c. both A and B
d. neither A nor B

5. Speed and power of a diesel engine are controlled by:

a. varying the amount of fuel mixed with a constant volume of air
b. varying the amount of air mixed with a constant volume of fuel
c. advancing or retarding ignition timing
d. throttling the air-fuel mixture

6. The 4-stroke cycle for each cylinder requires which of the following number of degrees of cylinder rotation:

a. 180
b. 270
c. 360
d. 720

7. A simplified formula to calculate engine displacement is:

a. bore $\times$ 0.7854 $\times$ stroke $\times$ no. cylinders
b. bore $\times$ 0.7854 $\times$ stroke^2 $\times$ no. cylinders
c. bore^2 $\times$ 0.7854 $\times$ 1/2 stroke $\times$ no. cylinders
d. bore^2 $\times$ 0.7854 $\times$ stroke $\times$ no. cylinders

8. To change cubic inches to cubic centimeters, multiply by:

a. 0.016
b. 61.39
c. 0.061
d. 16.39

9. The total cylinder volume of one engine cylinder is 27 cubic inches. The clearance volume is 3 cubic inches. The compression ratio, therefore, is:

a. 8.5:1
b. 8:1
c. 9:1
d. 9.2:1

10. Torque (in foot-pounds) $\times$ rpm $\div$ 5,252 is the formula for:

a. engine kilowatts
b. torque in newton-meters
c. engine horsepower
d. torque rise in relation to engine speed

11. In an overhead cam (ohc) engine, the camshaft is located:

a. above the engine
b. in the cylinder head
c. in the engine block
d. below the engine

12. In an overhead valve (ohv) engine, the camshaft is located:

a. above the engine
b. in the cylinder head
c. in the engine block
d. below the engine

13. The camshaft and crankshaft are connected by:

a. the flywheel
b. a vibration damper
c. the valve train
d. timing gears, chains, or belts

14. The valves in an automotive engine are opened and closed by:

a. camshaft lobes
b. crankshaft throws
c. wristpins
d. fixed seats

Fill in the Blank

15. The exact top of a piston stroke is called _____ .

16. Diesel ignition air temperatures are approximately _____ to _____ .

17. Diesel air-fuel ratios vary from as rich as _____ at full power to as lean as _____ at idle.

18. The range of gasoline air-fuel ratios varies from approximately _____ at the richest to approximately _____ at the leanest.

19. To change liters to cubic inches, multiply by _____ .

20. Compression ratio is the ratio of total cylinder volume to _____ volume.

21. The piston is attached to the _____ by a piston pin.

22. The _____ provides rotating inertia to the crankshaft to smooth out the intervals between firing impulses.

23. A closed valve is sealed against its seat by a _____ .

24. An engine that uses separate camshafts for intake and exhaust valves is called a _____ engine.

11 IGNITION, FUEL SYSTEM, AND EMISSION CONTROL REVIEW

WHAT

Since Charles Kettering invented the inductive-discharge battery ignition system in 1908, it has been almost the only spark ignition system used on automotive engines. For about 70 years, ignition systems used breaker points as an electromechanical switch to open and close a low-voltage primary circuit and to time high-voltage ignition in the engine cylinders. Since the mid-1970's, almost all ignition systems have used solid-state electronic switching devices to control the primary circuit and ignition timing. Whether an ignition system uses breaker points or electronic devices, however, the principles of producing high voltage through electromagnetic induction are exactly the same.

This chapter introduces the relationships between the fuel, ignition, and electrical systems. It explains the components and operation of the low-voltage primary and the high-voltage secondary ignition circuits. It describes a simple breaker-point system and the functions of high-voltage induction, ignition dwell, spark timing, and advance. It concludes with a discussion of the problem of combustion byproducts that pollute our air and the use of spark-timing controls as one major means of reducing pollution.

WHY

A spark-ignition, gasoline engine requires an air-fuel mixture compressed and ignited in the cylinders at the exact moment when it will burn to produce the most power. If either fuel or spark is missing, or is not timed properly, the engine will not run. The fuel and ignition systems are the most important combustion controls on any engine. One cannot work without the other. To understand engine performance and to service an engine professionally, you must know how the fuel and ignition systems work—separately and together.

Although breaker-point ignitions are not used on late-model automobiles, there are still millions of vehicles on the road that have these systems and that require service. There are other equally important reasons to study breaker-point ignitions as an introduction to breakerless electronic ignitions. All inductive-discharge ignitions operate on the principles of magnetic induction. The principles of ignition dwell, timing, and spark advance are the same, whether they are controlled mechanically or electronically. Ignition secondary circuits from the coil to the spark plugs operate the same way whether the primary circuit has an electronic switch or electromechanical breaker points. This chapter explains the basic operating requirements of ignition primary and secondary circuits. When you understand these principles in the context of simple breaker-point operation, you can understand breakerless electronic systems more easily.

GOALS

After studying this chapter, you should be able to:

1. Explain basic fuel system operation for spark-ignition and diesel engines.

2. Explain how ignition secondary voltage is produced in an induction coil.

3. Illustrate a simple ignition circuit and identify the primary and secondary components.

4. Explain voltage and current action in primary and secondary circuits.

5. Explain ignition dwell angle and point gap.

6. Explain spark plug firing action and the following design features: reach, heat range, diameter and seat type, and gap.

7. Explain the operation of centrifugal and vacuum advance mechanisms and the principles of spark advance and initial timing.

8. Explain the purposes and operation of various spark-timing emission control devices.

FUEL SYSTEM FUNDAMENTALS

Now that you have a fundamental understanding of engine design and operation, we can look at the basics of fuel delivery. The fuel system, which is a major combustion control system, has the following major parts, figure 11-1:

- A fuel storage tank
- Fuel lines
- A fuel pump
- Fuel filters
- Air inlet and air filter
- Fuel delivery components (carburetor or fuel injectors)
- Evaporative emission controls
- Other related emission controls

The fuel tank stores the gasoline or diesel fuel. Steel lines and rubber hoses connect the tank to the fuel delivery parts on the engine. One or more fuel pumps move fuel from the tank to the carburetor or fuel injection system. One or more fuel filters remove water, dirt, and other impurities from the fuel before it enters the engine. Another filter at the engine air inlet removes dirt from the incoming air. Evaporative emission controls keep fuel vapors from escaping to the atmosphere from the tank, the carburetor, and other fuel system parts.

The carburetor or the fuel injection system atomizes and vaporizes the fuel and mixes it with air in ratios that satisfy an engine's operating needs from light load to full load.

Air and Fuel Mixing

Traditionally, the carburetor has been the standard device to mix air and fuel for a gasoline engine, but fuel injection systems are now as common as carburetors. With either a carburetor or fuel injection, gasoline is atomized, vaporized, and mixed with air outside the combustion chamber, figure 11-2.

When an intake valve opens, engine vacuum draws air into the engine's air intake and a mixture of air and fuel into the combustion chamber. Actually, atmospheric pressure forces air into the low-pressure area in the manifold and cylinders that is created as the pistons move down on their intake strokes. Air passing through a carburetor draws gasoline from a fuel bowl, or float bowl. As gasoline enters the intake airstream, it is atomized and then vaporized. Gasoline flow is precisely metered through jets so that it mixes with air in controlled ratios.

Air-Fuel Ratios

Air-fuel ratios are measurements of the amount of air, *by weight*, mixed with an amount of fuel, *by weight*. An air-fuel ratio of 15:1 means that the mixture contains 15 pounds of air for every 1 pound of gasoline. In volume measurements, rather than weight, that equals approximately 9,000 gallons of air for every 1 gallon of gasoline, figure 11-3.

The air-fuel ratios for a gasoline engine range from 8:1 at the richest (most fuel) to 18.5:1 at the leanest (least fuel), figure 11-4. With more or less fuel, the mixture would not be combustible. The best ratios for maximum power are approximately 12:1 to 13.5:1. The best ratios for fuel economy are about 15:1 to 16:1. The most efficient ratio that provides almost complete combustion is approximately 14.7:1. This is called a **stoichiometric ratio** and is important for emission control.

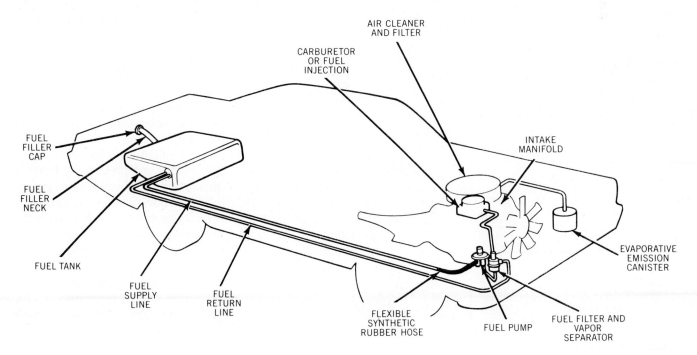

Figure 11-1. These are the major parts of a gasoline fuel system.

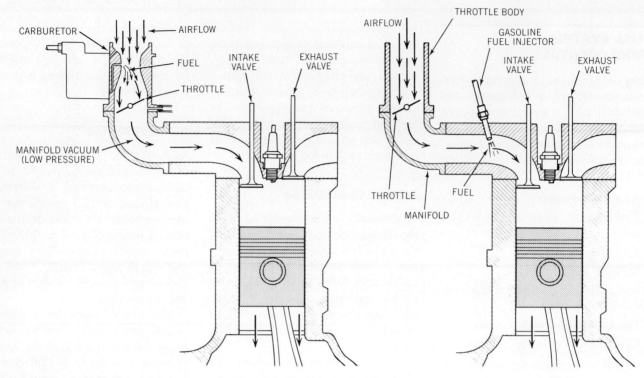

Figure 11-2. In a gasoline engine, fuel is vaporized and mixed with air outside of the combustion chamber.

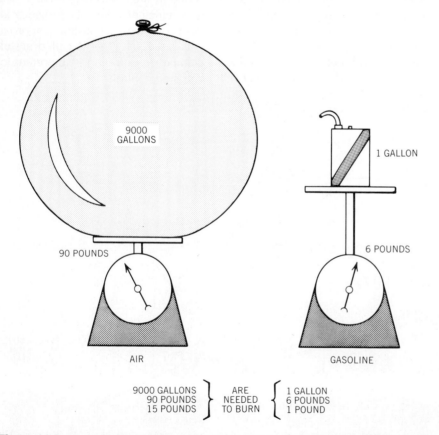

9000 GALLONS		1 GALLON
90 POUNDS	ARE NEEDED TO BURN	6 POUNDS
15 POUNDS		1 POUND

Figure 11-3. An air-fuel ratio of 15 : 1 means that 15 pounds of air are mixed with every 1 pound of gasoline. That equals 9,000 gallons of air for every one gallon of gasoline.

Fuel Distribution

Carburetors, fuel injectors, and intake manifolds do not provide perfect air-fuel distribution. For example, if one carburetor mixes air and fuel for several cylinders, it is hard to locate the carburetor an equal distance from all cylinders so that each gets an equal mixture. Long passages and sharp turns in the manifold slow down the airflow and cause liquid fuel to drop out of the mixture. Multiple carburetors and fuel injection eliminate some of these problems.

Electronic fuel injection (EFI) on late-model cars provides precise air-fuel ratio control with the best combination of power, economy, and emission control. EFI systems are either throttle body injection systems or direct port or manifold injection systems.

Throttle body injection systems have one or two electronically controlled injection nozzles on a throttle body that is mounted on a manifold similarly to a carburetor, figure 11-5. Gasoline is injected into the airflow

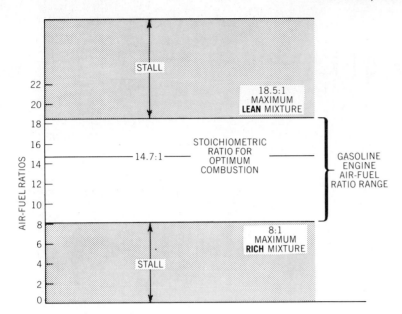

Figure 11-4. Air-fuel ratios for a 4-stroke gasoline engine can range from 8 : 1 at the richest to about 18.5 : 1 at the leanest.

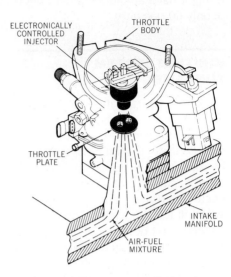

Figure 11-5. The injectors of a throttle body fuel injection system are mounted on the throttle body.

before it passes through the throttle opening. Fuel vaporization starts in the throttle body, and air-fuel mixing continues through the manifold to the intake valves. Injecting the fuel under pressure provides better atomization and vaporization than a carburetor does, and electronic control provides faster and more precise fuel metering changes.

Direct port, or manifold, injection systems have separate injectors in each manifold passage, near the intake ports of the cylinder head, figure 11-6. Only air passes through the intake throttle and the manifold up to where the injectors are located. Air-fuel mixing takes place immediately before the mixture enters the cylinder.

Volumetric Efficiency

This discussion of the volume and ratios of air and fuel taken in by an engine leads us to the principle of **volumetric efficiency**. This is a concept that compares the airflow volume actually entering an engine to maximum volume that *could* enter, which is the same as the displacement. Volumetric efficiency is stated as a percentage, and it changes with engine speed.

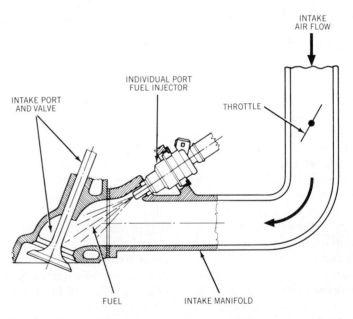

Figure 11-6. This direct port injection system has separate injectors for each cylinder, near the cylinder head intake ports.

To determine volumetric efficiency, engineers measure airflow volume in units such as cubic feet per minute (cfm) at standard temperature and pressure. Standard pressure is atmospheric pressure of 14.7 psi (101.28 kPa) or 760 millimeters of mercury (mm Hg). Standard temperature is 32° F (0° C). If intake airflow is equivalent to engine displacement, volumetric efficiency is 100 percent. We often determine carburetor airflow capacity for an engine based on 100 percent volumetric efficiency, but few engines ever reach complete efficiency. Volumetric efficiency for a stock passenger car engine also will vary under different operating conditions. At 2,000 rpm, an engine might be 85-percent efficient. At 1,000 rpm, it might be rated at 75 percent, and at 4,000 rpm, it might have a volumetric efficiency of only 60 percent.

IGNITION SYSTEM FUNDAMENTALS

After the air-fuel mixture is compressed in the cylinders, it must be ignited. For either a gasoline or a diesel engine, the timing of ignition—by spark or by fuel injection—is critical to engine operation. Ignition must occur near the start of the power stroke. If it is too early or too late, the engine won't develop full power and may even be damaged. The principles of ignition timing are the same for gasoline and diesel engines, but since gasoline engines are more common in passenger cars, we concentrate on spark ignition in the following sections.

Ignition Intervals

Remember that every piston stroke rotates the crankshaft 180 degrees, and there are 720 degrees in a complete 4-stroke cycle. During each cycle, the spark plug in each cylinder fires once. Therefore, ignition occurs in a 1-cylinder engine once every 720 degrees. The 720 degrees are the **ignition interval** for a 1-cylinder engine. The ignition interval is the number of degrees of crankshaft rotation between ignition, or power strokes, for each cylinder of an engine.

A 4-cylinder engine has four power strokes in every 720 degrees of crankshaft rotation, so the ignition interval of a 4-cylinder engine is 180 degrees (720 ÷ 4 = 180), figure 11-7. An inline 6-cylinder engine has six power strokes every 720 degrees, so its ignition interval is 120 degrees (720 ÷ 6 = 120), figure 11-8. An 8-cylinder engine has eight power strokes in 720 degrees of rotation for an ignition interval of 90 degrees (720 ÷ 8 = 90), figure 11-9. Three-cylinder engines, such as the Suzuki-Chevrolet Sprint engine, have 240-degree ignition intervals; 5-cylinder VW, Audi, and Mercedes-Benz engines have 144-degree intervals.

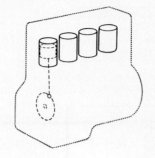
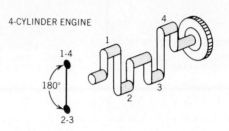

Figure 11-7. Inline 4-cylinder engines fire 1-3-2-4 or 1-2-4-3.

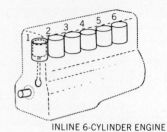

INLINE 6-CYLINDER ENGINE

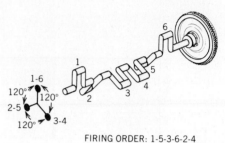

FIRING ORDER: 1-5-3-6-2-4

Figure 11-8. All inline 6-cylinder engines fire 1-5-3-6-2-4.

Most 4-, 6-, and 8-cylinder engines have the ignition intervals listed above. V-6 engines can have several different intervals. A V-6 engine with a 60-degree angle between cylinder banks has a 120-degree ignition interval, the same as an inline 6-cylinder engine. A 90-degree V-6 can have 120-degree ignition intervals if the crankshaft rod journals are split, such as on 1978 and later Buick-built V-6's. Buick 90-degree V-6's built before 1978 did not have split journals and fired alternately at 90- and 150-degree intervals. Chevrolet 90-degree V-6's have split rod journals that create alternate 108- and 132-degree intervals. V-12 engines usually have 60-degree blocks and 60-degree ignition intervals.

Firing Order and Cylinder Numbering

Ignition interval is the amount of crankshaft rotation between ignition in each cylinder. **Firing order** is the sequence in which ignition occurs in the various cylinders. So that the cylinders fire at regular intervals and each cylinder fires once every 720 degrees, the crankshaft throws are arranged in a particular order. This crank throw arrangement creates the firing order, and it varies depending

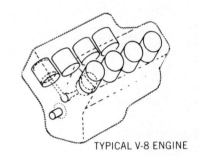

TYPICAL V-8 ENGINE

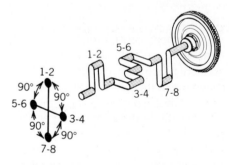

Figure 11-9. V-8 firing orders vary according to the cylinder number sequence.

on the number of cylinders and the block design.

Engine cylinders are numbered for identification, but they usually don't fire in cylinder number order. Inline engine cylinders are numbered from front, or the end opposite the flywheel, to rear. For an inline 4-cylinder engine, the crankshaft rod journals are offset and the cylinders are numbered as shown in figure 11-7.

The cylinders must fire at 180-degree intervals, so the firing order must be 1-3-4-2 (most common) or 1-2-4-3. For an inline 6-cylinder engine, the rod journals are arranged and the cylinders are numbered as shown in figure 11-8. All inline 6-cylinder engines fire 1-5-3-6-2-4.

Except for Ford products and a few older GM engines, most domestic V-type engines have the cylinder number patterns and firing orders shown in figure 11-10. Odd-numbered cylinders are on the left bank viewed from the flywheel end; even-numbered cylinders are on the right. The one major exception to the firing order shown for V-6 engines is the GM-Chevrolet 60-degree, 2.8-liter (170-cid) V-6. It fires 1-2-3-4-5-6.

Ford V-type engines have the number 1 cylinder at the right front. Cylinder numbers follow in order down the right bank and then continue from front to rear on the left. Figure 11-11 shows Ford V-6 and V-8 cylinder numbering and firing orders. Fortunately, most carmakers cast the firing order of an engine on the intake manifold to avoid confusion during engine service.

Cylinder Running Mates

Notice in figure 11-7 that the crankshaft throws for cylinders 1 and 4 of a 4-cylinder engine are in the same position, as are the throws for cylinders 2 and 3. In an inline 6-cylinder engine, figure 11-8, the throws for cylinders 1 and 6, 3 and 4, and 2 and 5 share common positions. Cylinders with crank throws in the same positions in relation to firing order are called **running mates**. Although the pistons are at tdc simultaneously, they are 360 degrees apart in firing order. When piston 1 of a 4-cylinder engine is at tdc at the start of the power stroke, piston 4 is at tdc at the start of its intake stroke.

Visualizing cylinders that are running mates in a V-type engine is a bit more difficult because you must account for the angle between cylinder banks. In the V-8 engine in figure 11-9, cylinders 1 and 6, 8 and 5, 4

and 7, and 3 and 2 are running mates because you must add the 90-degree cylinder angle to the crankshaft angle.

You can determine cylinder running mates in any engine from its firing order. Simply take the first half of the firing order and write it above the second half of the firing order, like this:

$$\frac{1 - 8 - 4 - 3}{6 - 5 - 7 - 2}$$

This establishes the running mates for the V-8 engine in figure 11-9. It works the same way for an inline 6-cylinder engine:

$$\frac{1 - 5 - 3}{6 - 2 - 4}$$

and for an inline-4:

$$\frac{1 - 3}{4 - 2} \text{ or } \frac{1 - 2}{4 - 3}$$

Knowing the cylinder running mates is useful when you adjust mechanical valve lifters and for ignition timing on some engines, as you will learn when you study these subjects.

Engine and Ignition Sychronization

During each 4-stroke cycle, the intake and exhaust valves of each cylinder open and close at precise times in relation to piston and crankshaft position. Ignition must be similarly synchronized with piston and crankshaft position at the end of the compression stroke and the start of the power stroke. The ignition distributor delivers one spark to each cylinder in each 4-stroke cycle. Distributors are built so that one revolution of the distributor shaft delivers ignition voltage once to each cylinder; that is, every 360 degrees of distributor rotation. But, each cylinder fires once for every *two* revolutions of the crankshaft: 720 degrees. Therefore, the distributor turns at one-half crankshaft speed. Because the camshaft also turns at one-half crankshaft speed, most distributors are driven by the camshaft. In this way, crankshaft position, valve timing, and ignition timing are all synchronized, figure 11-12.

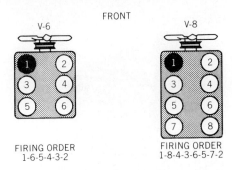

FRONT

FIRING ORDER 1-6-5-4-3-2

FIRING ORDER 1-8-4-3-6-5-7-2

Figure 11-10. These are the most common cylinder numbering patterns and firing orders for V-type engines.

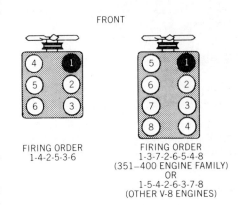

FRONT

FIRING ORDER 1-4-2-5-3-6

FIRING ORDER 1-3-7-2-6-5-4-8 (351–400 ENGINE FAMILY) OR 1-5-4-2-6-3-7-8 (OTHER V-8 ENGINES)

Figure 11-11. Ford numbers the cylinders of its V-type engines like this.

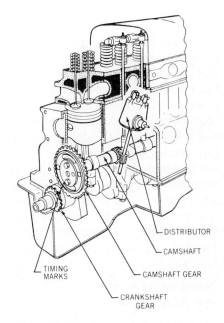

DISTRIBUTOR

CAMSHAFT

CAMSHAFT GEAR

TIMING MARKS

CRANKSHAFT GEAR

Figure 11-12. The camshaft and the ignition distributor rotate at one-half engine speed, so that crankshaft position, valve timing, and ignition timing are synchronized.

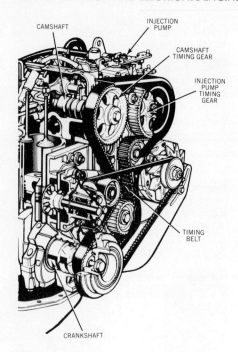

Figure 11-13. Diesel injection pumps operate at one-half engine speed to time fuel injection similarly to spark ignition in a gasoline engine. (AMC-Jeep)

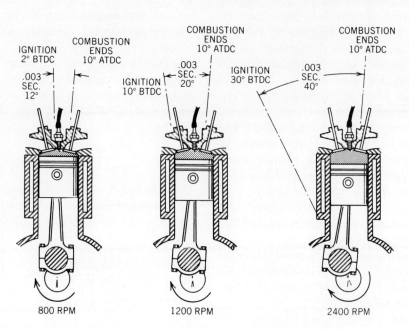

Figure 11-14. Ignition timing must be advanced as engine speed increases.

Diesel fuel injection must be timed similarly to the spark ignition of a gasoline engine, and each cylinder must receive fuel once for every two crankshaft revolutions. Diesel fuel injection pumps distribute fuel to each cylinder in firing-order sequence and time the injection the way a distributor delivers and times spark ignition. In fact, some diesel pumps are called "distributor pumps." Because diesel fuel injection pumps operate at one-half engine speed, some are driven and synchronized by the camshaft. In other diesel engines, the pumps are driven by separate gears or belts but synchronized to time injection with crankshaft and valve position, figure 11-13.

Crankshaft Position and Burn Time

Combustion is not an instantaneous explosion, but a controlled burning, although the **burn time** is extremely short. It takes about 3 milliseconds (0.003 second) from the time of ignition until combustion is complete in a gasoline engine. In a diesel engine, a

similar, but shorter, amount of **ignition lag** occurs from the time fuel is injected until it mixes with the hot compressed air and burns.

Burn time or ignition lag is strictly a function of time, not of piston or crankshaft position. Ignition must occur early enough so that maximum combustion pressure develops when the piston is starting down on its power stroke. Combustion should be finished about 10 degrees **after top dead center (atdc)**. If ignition occurs too early when the piston is **before top dead center (btdc)** on the compression stroke, the rising piston is opposed by combustion pressure. If ignition occurs too late atdc, combustion force is reduced as the piston is farther down the power stroke. In either case, the combustion process doesn't develop full power, and the engine may be damaged.

As engine speed increases, the piston and crankshaft travel farther (rotate through more degrees) in a given amount of time. Burn time or ignition lag, however, remains relatively constant. Therefore, ignition timing must vary with engine speed so that maxi-

mum combustion pressure occurs at the correct piston position.

Consider, for example, an engine that needs a 3-millisecond burn time and is most efficient with combustion ending at 10° atdc. Let's say that at 800 rpm, the crankshaft rotates 12 degrees in 3 milliseconds. So, ignition must occur 2° btdc for proper burn time in relation to piston and crankshaft position, figure 11-14. At 1,200 rpm, the crankshaft rotates 20 degrees in 3 milliseconds, so ignition must occur 10° btdc for combustion to end 10° atdc. At 2,400 rpm, the crankshaft rotates 40 degrees in 3 milliseconds. Now ignition must be at 30° btdc for combustion to end at 10° atdc, figure 11-14.

Ignition Timing and Advance

The point where ignition occurs is called ignition timing, or spark timing, and it is measured in terms of crankshaft degrees before or after top dead center. The ignition timing of an engine at idle speed is called **basic, or initial, timing**. It is usually a few degrees before or after tdc. As engine speed increases, ignition must occur sooner before top dead center. This is called **timing, or spark, advance**. As engine speed decreases from high rpm to idle, timing must be retarded from its advanced condition back to its basic setting. In some operating conditions (principally for some emission control needs), it is necessary to retard the timing to several degrees atdc.

Spark ignition systems have devices to advance and retard timing automatically as engine speed changes. Older distributors used centrifugal flyweights and vacuum diaphragms connected to intake vacuum to control timing for varying engine speeds and loads. Late-model electronic ignitions control timing electronically by sensing engine speed and other conditions and processing the sensor signals in a computer.

Diesel injection pumps have devices that advance and retard injection timing as engine speed and load change.

Ignition Voltage

Ignition in a gasoline engine requires that an electrical circuit be completed across an air gap to create a spark. This requires very high voltage because such a circuit contains very high resistance. Resistance exists because:

• The air gap between the spark plug electrodes is an open-circuit condition that creates several thousand ohms of resistance.

• High pressure and high temperature in the engine cylinders create high resistance.

• The air-fuel mixture is a high-resistance conductor.

To complete a circuit through these conditions and create a spark requires 5,000 to 25,000 volts, or more. However, the electrical system of an automobile receives voltage from a 12-volt battery and an alternator. System voltage ranges from 10 to 15 volts under various operating conditions, about one-thousandth of the voltage needed for ignition.

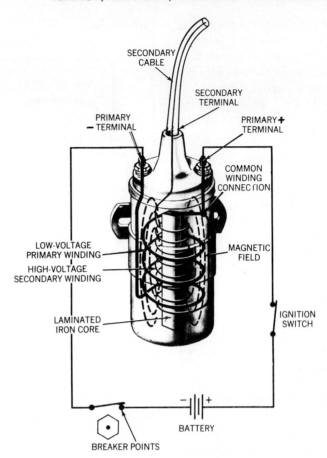

Figure 11-15. The coil primary winding receives low-voltage current from the primary circuit and induces high voltage in the secondary winding. (Bosch)

High-voltage Induction. High voltage for ignition is provided by an induction coil. To begin to understand ignition voltage, you should review what you learned about electromagnetic induction in chapter 2.

An ignition coil uses mutual induction to transform, or increase, low battery voltage to high ignition voltage. The coil contains two windings of copper wire around an iron core. The primary winding has a few hundred turns of heavy wire and is connected to the low-voltage primary circuit, figure 11-15. The **primary circuit** receives low-voltage current from the battery and uses it to induce higher voltage in the coil secondary winding.

The secondary winding has several thousand turns of fine wire and is connected to the high-voltage **secondary circuit** of the ignition system. We will look at the primary and sec-

ondary ignition circuits in detail later. First, we will review high-voltage induction in the ignition coil.

Remember from chapter 2 that one way to induce voltage in a coil is to place it near another primary coil, through which current flows. Current in the primary coil creates magnetic flux lines that cut the windings of both the primary and secondary coils. If you designed a circuit so that you could switch primary current on and off rapidly, the flux lines would expand and contract with each *change* in current flow. Each rapid expansion and contraction of the magnetic field would induce voltage in the primary and secondary coils. This is how an **inductive-discharge ignition system** works. An important point to remember is that induction occurs when primary current flow *changes* and the magnetic field expands and collapses.

The changing current flow creates the relative motion between the field and the coil windings. When current flow is steady, the magnetic field does not move, and no voltage is induced.

Several factors determine the amount of voltage induced in the coil secondary winding.

1. The ratio of the number of turns in the secondary winding to the number of turns in the primary winding. This is fixed by the design and manufacture of the coil and is between 100 : 1 and 200 : 1. The **turns ratio** is a voltage multiplier. The voltage induced in the secondary winding is 100 to 200 times higher than the voltage applied to the primary winding.

2. The amount of current in the primary winding and the strength of its magnetic field. More current creates a stronger magnetic field with more flux lines to cut the secondary winding.

3. The speed with which primary current flow stops and the magnetic field collapses. Fast collapse of the primary field creates fast relative motion between the field and the turns of the secondary winding.

Under most conditions, 9 to 10 volts are applied to the coil primary winding. At high engine speeds, voltage may rise to 12 volts. This voltage produces 1 to 4 amperes of current in the primary winding. Primary current increases gradually and builds up a magnetic field around both the primary and secondary windings. When this field reaches full magnetic strength, it is called **magnetic saturation**.

When the primary circuit opens, current stops abruptly, and the magnetic field collapses rapidly. The fast collapse of the field induces a higher voltage of 250 to 400 volts in the primary winding through self-induction. The turns ratio of the coil multiplies this voltage to produce several thousand volts, or kilovolts (kV), in the secondary winding. For example if the self-induced voltage in the primary winding is 300 volts and the turns ratio is 150 : 1, the induced voltage in the secondary winding is 45,000 volts (45 kV). We now have

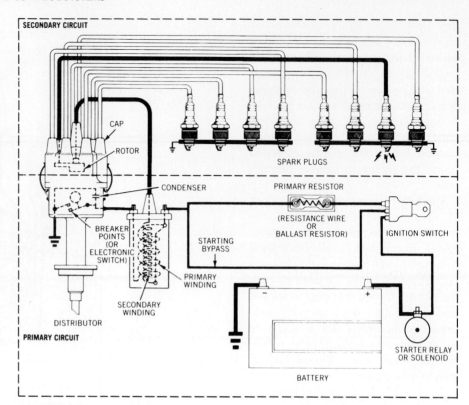

Figure 11-16. The ignition system consists of the low-voltage primary and the high-voltage secondary circuits. (Prestolite)

voltage high enough to ignite the air-fuel mixture for all conditions.

Although a modern ignition coil can produce 30,000 to 50,000 volts (30 to 50 kV), it delivers only enough voltage to jump the air gap and create an arc (spark) at the spark plug. This voltage requirement changes with changing resistance conditions in the cylinder. At idle, only 5,000 volts may be needed to create an ignition spark. At high speed or heavy load, 25,000 volts or more may be needed. Electrical resistance increases in a cylinder with:

• A wider spark plug gap
• Higher temperatures and compression pressures
• A leaner air-fuel mixture

As soon as the spark is created, the remaining coil energy is expended as current flow in the secondary circuit. A coil must have the capability to produce more than the voltage required for an ignition spark. You will

learn more about required voltage, available voltage, and voltage reserve when you study coils in more detail as part of the ignition secondary circuit.

Ignition Circuits and Current Flow

We have reviewed the principles used to induce high ignition voltage and seen where the primary and secondary circuits come together in the coil. We can now examine the primary and secondary circuits and their major parts. The low-voltage primary circuit, figure 11-16, is basically a series circuit with a couple of parallel branches. It contains:

1. The battery
2. The ignition switch
3. The primary (ballast) resistor
4. The starting (ballast) bypass
5. The coil primary winding
6. The breaker points
7. The condenser (capacitor)

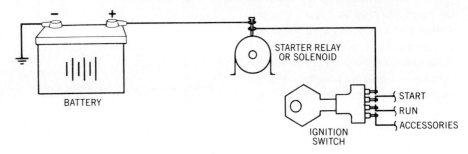

Figure 11-17. The ignition primary circuit starts and ends at the battery.

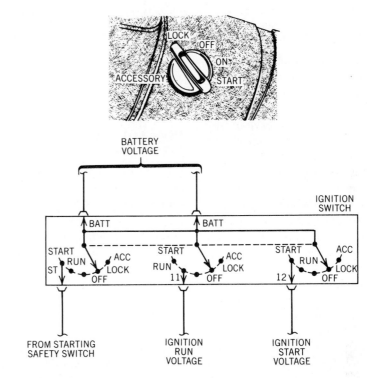

Figure 11-18. The ignition switch controls primary ignition current for starting and running, and it controls other electrical circuits on the car. (Ford)

When the driver turns on (closes) the ignition switch, current flows:

• From the battery through the ignition switch

• Through the primary wiring and primary (ballast) resistor

• Through the coil primary winding

• Through the breaker points, which are an automatic switch

• To ground and back to the grounded terminal of the battery

The breaker points turn low-voltage primary current on and off. As current starts and stops in the coil primary winding, it creates the expanding and contracting magnetic field that induces high secondary voltage. The high voltage from the coil secondary causes high-voltage current to flow from the coil:

• Through a cable to the distributor cap

• To and through the distributor rotor, the rotor air gap, and another terminal in the distributor cap

• Through another cable to one spark plug

• Across a spark plug gap, where it creates an arc, and back to ground

IGNITION PRIMARY CIRCUIT COMPONENTS

The following sections explain the purposes of the major parts of the primary circuit.

The Battery

The battery is the source of low-voltage current for all electrical systems on the car, including the ignition. Current flows to the ignition system, figure 11-17, when the ignition switch is turned to start or run.

The Ignition Switch

The ignition switch, figure 11-18, is the driver's control switch for the ignition and other electrical circuits on the car. Current flows through the ignition primary circuit when the driver turns the switch to start or run. The switch also has other positions to deliver current to accessory circuits when the ignition circuit is open (off). On most cars, the ignition switch also mechanically locks the steering wheel, and it also may lock automatic transmission shift linkage.

All carmakers are basically similar switches. General Motors vehicles receive ignition current from a connection on the starter solenoid. Ford vehicles receive current from a connection on the starter relay. Chrysler vehicles receive ignition current from a connection between the battery and the alternator.

The Primary (Ballast) Resistor

All 12-volt breaker-point ignition systems have a **primary, or ballast, resistor** to provide stable voltage and current flow to the coil primary winding, figure 11-16. For a coil to have consistent secondary voltage capabilities under all engine operating conditions, it must have uniform and complete saturation of its magnetic field under all conditions. Magnetic saturation depends on the amount of voltage applied to the coil and the amount and time of current flow through the primary winding.

However, the primary circuit does not have uniform voltage and current at all times. During cranking, the starter motor draws several hundred amperes of current, and battery voltage drops to about 10 or 11 volts. The ignition coil must produce enough secondary voltage to start the engine with this low primary voltage. When the engine starts, system voltage rises above 12 volts. At high speed, system voltage reaches 14 or 15 volts.

Additionally, the amount of time that current flows through the primary circuit affects coil saturation. At high speed, there is less current because there is less time, and magnetic field strength decreases. At low speed there is more current because there is more time, and field strength increases. But too much current can overheat the coil and burn the breaker points.

An ignition coil must produce satisfactory secondary voltage with varying primary voltage and current. Most coils are designed to operate with a voltage of 9 or 10 volts under most conditions. To provide this stable volt-

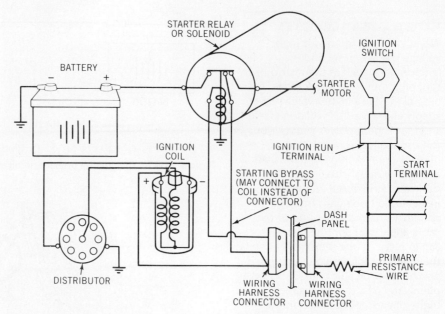

Figure 11-19. Most GM, Ford, and other breaker-point ignitions have a length of resistance wire as the ballast resistor.

age, the primary circuit must have a device to compensate for changing system voltage. Moreover, this device must compensate for varying amounts of current at different engine speeds. These are the jobs of the ballast resistor.

At low engine speed, current flows through the resistor longer than at high speeds. This heats the resistor and increases its resistance, which decreases voltage applied to the coil. At high speeds, current flows through the resistor for less time, and it cools. This decreases its resistance and allows more voltage to the coil. The higher voltage but shorter current flow time produces about the same secondary voltage capabilities as the lower voltage and longer current flow that the resistor allows at low speeds. The ballast resistor simply *stabilizes* primary voltage and current for uniform secondary voltage capabilities at all speeds.

Most ballast resistors have about 1.5 ± 0.25 ohms of resistance at 75° F (24° C) with no current flow. However, Chrysler breaker-point ignitions have ballast resistors rated at about 0.5 ohm. The ballast resistor provides about half of the ignition primary circuit resistance. The coil primary winding provides the other half. In most GM, Ford, AMC, and other pri-

mary circuits, the ballast resistor is a length of resistance wire between the ignition switch and the coil, figure 11-19. In Chrysler primary circuits, and a few others, the ballast resistor is a coil of wire in a ceramic block, mounted on the firewall, figure 11-20. These resistors, too, are connected between the run contacts of the ignition switch and the coil.

The Starting (Ballast) Bypass

The current draw of the starter motor drops primary voltage to about 10 volts, so the ballast resistor is bypassed during starting. A low-resistance bypass circuit branch, in parallel with the ballast resistor, does this. The **starting bypass** is closed by the start contacts of the ignition switch. When the engine starts, and the ignition switch moves to the run position, the bypass opens, and primary current flows through the ballast resistor. Figure 11-19 shows a starting bypass between the starter relay or solenoid and the ignition coil. When the ignition switch closes the relay or solenoid, the bypass applies battery voltage to the coil. Figure 11-20 shows a starting bypass connected from the start contacts of the ignition switch to the coil.

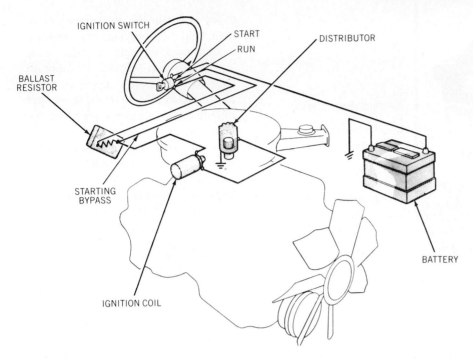

Figure 11-20. Chrysler and a few other carmakers use a ballast resistor in a ceramic block. It is connected to the circuit in the same way a resistance wire is. (Chrysler)

The Coil Primary Winding

The coil primary winding contains 100 to 150 turns of heavy copper wire, figure 11-21, with a resistance of about 1.5 to 2.0 ohms. The turns of the winding are insulated from each other by a coating of enamel. If they were not insulated, the winding would develop a short circuit, and the primary magnetic field would not develop.

The two ends of the primary winding are connected to the coil positive (+) and negative (−) primary terminals, figure 11-21. In a **negative-ground electrical system**, the coil + terminal is connected to the battery through the ballast resistor and the ignition switch. The coil − terminal is connected to ground through the breaker points. These connections are reversed in a **positive-ground electrical system**.

The Breaker Points

The coil primary magnetic field must collapse quickly and completely to induce high secondary voltage. After the secondary voltage has discharged

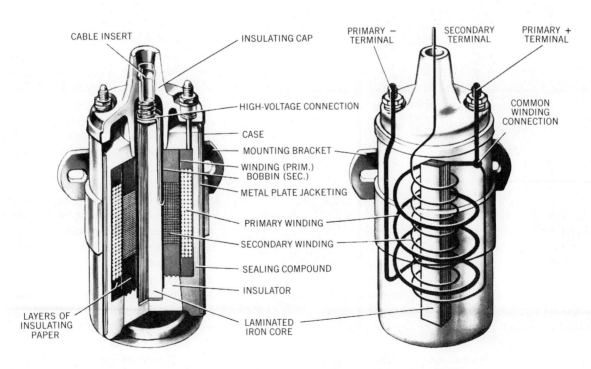

Figure 11-21. The coil primary and secondary windings are both wound around a soft iron core. (Bosch)

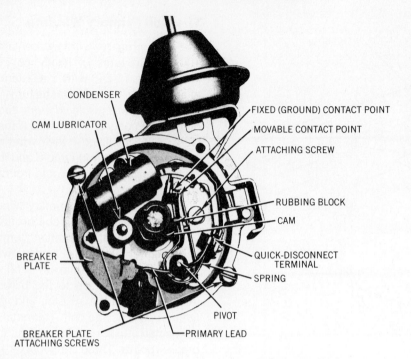

Figure 11-22. Individual designs may vary somewhat, but all breaker-point assemblies have these parts. (Delco-Remy)

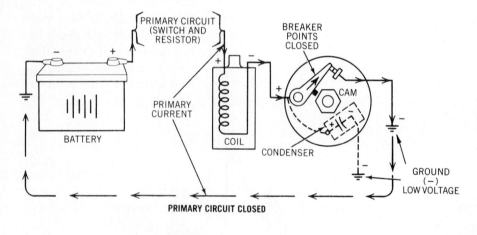

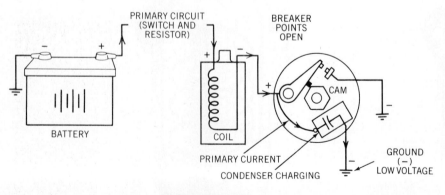

Figure 11-23. The breaker points are a switch on the ground side of the coil to open and close the primary circuit. The condenser absorbs a voltage charge when the points open.

to fire one cylinder, the primary magnetic field must build up again quickly to start inducing high secondary voltage for the next cylinder. Because an ignition system must supply as many as 15,000 to 25,000 timed sparks per minute, it must have a precise automatic switch to open and close the primary circuit synchronized in time with the engine firing order.

Until the mid-1970's ignition systems used breaker points as a mechanical switch to open and close the primary circuit. Even though breaker points have been replaced by electronic switching devices on late-model ignition systems, there are still millions of breaker-point-equipped automobiles on the road. Because of their simplicity, breaker points are a good starting point to learn the principles of ignition timing control.

A complete breaker-point assembly, figure 11-22, contains:

- A fixed contact point
- A movable contact point and arm
- A pivot point for the movable arm
- A spring
- A rubbing block
- A breaker plate

Both contact points are made of tungsten for hardness and good conductivity. The point spring is the connector that joins the movable contact and its arm to the primary terminal of the distributor. The movable contact, the arm, the spring, and the primary terminal are insulated from the distributor housing and connected to the coil negative (−) terminal, which is at a higher voltage potential than the fixed contact point. The fixed contact is grounded through the breaker plate to the distributor housing and completes the primary circuit back to the engine ground and the battery, figure 11-23. When the points are closed, current flows from the movable contact at + potential to the fixed contact at − potential in a negative-ground system.

The distributor shaft has a cam with as many lobes as the engine has cylinders, figures 11-22 and 11-23. As the distributor shaft rotates, its cam pushes the rubbing block on the mov-

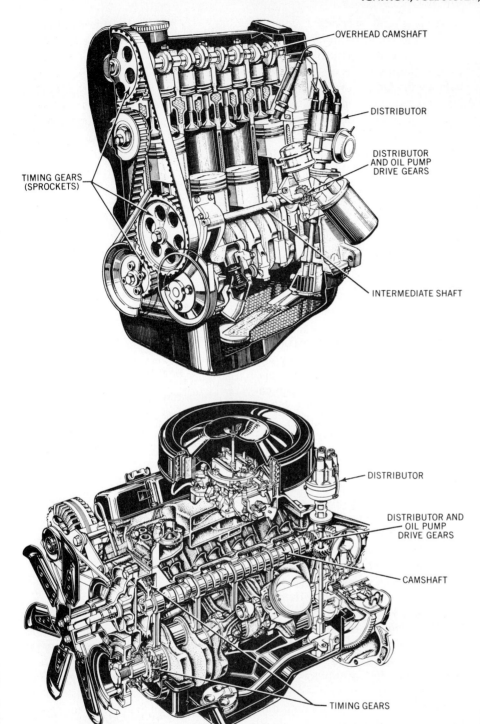

OVERHEAD CAMSHAFT

DISTRIBUTOR

DISTRIBUTOR AND OIL PUMP DRIVE GEARS

TIMING GEARS (SPROCKETS)

INTERMEDIATE SHAFT

DISTRIBUTOR

DISTRIBUTOR AND OIL PUMP DRIVE GEARS

CAMSHAFT

TIMING GEARS

Figure 11-24. The distributor turns at camshaft speed (one-half crankshaft speed). It is driven by the camshaft or by an auxiliary shaft. (Chrysler)

able arm to open the points. As the cam lobe rotates away from the rubbing block, the spring closes the points. This is the automatic switching action for the primary circuit. Because opening and closing the primary circuit must be synchronized with engine speed and firing order, the dis-

tributor turns at engine camshaft speed (one-half crankshaft speed). Distributors on overhead-valve engines are driven by the camshaft. The distributor on an overhead-cam engine can be driven by the camshaft or by an auxiliary shaft that turns at camshaft speed, figure 11-24.

DUAL POINTS

In the days before electronic ignitions, short dwell time was a problem for high-performance engines at high rpm. A 32-degree dwell angle on a V-8 engine at 6,000 rpm, for example, simply did not allow enough time for complete coil saturation. The result was usually a high-speed misfire as available voltage fell below required voltage. If a mechanic tried to adjust the points for a longer dwell angle, they would arc and burn at low speeds because of the insufficient gap.

A common solution to the problem was to build a distributor with two sets of breaker points in parallel. The points are offset in relation to the distributor cam. One set opens the primary circuit; the other set closes the circuit. The dwell on each set of points can be 27 to 31 degrees, for example, with sufficient gap to minimize arcing. The combined dwell of both sets, however, can be 36 to 40 degrees to provide adequate coil saturation and voltage at high speed.

Because the point sets are in parallel, the primary circuit is closed whenever either or both of the point sets are closed. The first set to open is the "closing" point set because the other set maintains primary current flow. The second set to open is the "opening" point set. Dual-point distributors like this were common on high-performance engines before electronic ignitions became common.

Ignition Dwell Angle. Each time the breaker points open, the coil secondary winding discharges high voltage to a spark plug. In this way, the points control ignition timing. When the points are closed, they control the amount of magnetic saturation that develops in the coil. The distributor, or ignition, **dwell angle** is the number of degrees of distributor rotation during which the points are closed.

In figure 11-25, the points close at line A and open again at line B. The number of degrees between A and B is the dwell angle. This is the period when current flows through the coil primary winding to build up the magnetic field.

Remember that magnetic field strength is proportional to the *time* that current flows. The dwell angle actually controls this time, but we measure it in degrees of distributor rotation because this is the easiest way to measure and adjust it. At a slow rotation speed, a dwell angle of 30 degrees allows more current time than the same dwell angle allows at high speed. However, at high speed, the ballast resistor allows a higher primary voltage than it does at low speed. Short current time at higher voltage produces about the same magnetic field strength as longer current time at lower voltage.

In chapter 2, you learned that current in any coil induces a countervoltage that opposes original current direction. This means that current flow and the magnetic field in a coil do not reach full strength instantly. It takes about 10 to 15 milliseconds (0.010 to 0.015 second) for an ignition coil to develop complete magnetic saturation from primary current, figure 11-26.

At idle speed, an ignition dwell angle of 30 degrees allows about 15 milliseconds of primary current flow. At higher speeds, the dwell angle may not change, but the dwell *time* decreases. At 1,000 rpm, a 30-degree dwell angle allows about 9 milliseconds of current. At 2,000 rpm, the same dwell angle allows only 4.5 milliseconds of dwell time.

If current time were the only factor

controlling coil secondary voltage, the voltage could be too low at high speed to fire the spark plugs. However, ignition systems are designed to balance the factors of current amperage, current time, primary voltage, and the turns ratios of the primary and secondary coil windings. Careful design ensures that the system will provide the secondary voltage needed for ignition under all conditions. As you understand all the factors of correct ignition operation, you can appreciate why correct maintenance of all parts of the system is essential for proper engine operation.

Now that you have learned about ignition dwell, you should have a better idea how the breaker points and the ballast resistor work together to control primary voltage and current. These combined actions allow the coil secondary winding to have relatively constant secondary voltage capabilities at all engine speeds. When you study electronic ignitions, you will see other interesting ways that electronic devices accomplish the same thing.

Ignition dwell angle is related to an engine's firing intervals and crankshaft and camshaft rotation. Remember that in an 8-cylinder engine, there are 90 degrees of crankshaft rotation between cylinder firing intervals. This is the same as 45 degrees of camshaft and distributor rotation. Theoretically, an 8-cylinder engine could have 45 degrees of ignition dwell. But, the points must open and close during several of those 45 degrees. Most 8-cylinder distributors rotate about 15 degrees from the time the points open (break contact) until they close again. Therefore, the dwell angle is about 30 degrees.

In an even-firing 6-cylinder engine, the crankshaft rotates 120 degrees between cylinder firing intervals (60 degrees of camshaft and distributor rotation). In a 4-cylinder engine, the crankshaft rotates 180 degrees, and the camshaft rotates 90 degrees between firing intervals. For a 6-cylinder engine, the dwell angle could be about 45 degrees, and it could be about 75 degrees for a 4-cylinder en-

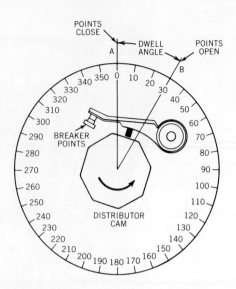

Figure 11-25. The dwell angle is the number of degrees during which the points are closed.

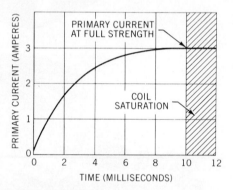

Figure 11-26. Primary current requires about 10 to 15 milliseconds to reach full strength. (Bosch)

gine. However, a larger dwell angle would allow longer current flow time at low speed. This is not necessary for complete coil saturation and could overheat the primary winding. Therefore, 4- and 6-cylinder distributors have less dwell than they theoretically could have, about 45 to 50 degrees for a 4-cylinder distributor and about 35 to 40 degrees for a 6-cylinder distributor.

Point Gap. The **point gap** is the maximum distance between the point contact surfaces when the rubbing block is on the high point of the distributor cam and the points are fully open. The points in any distributor must open far enough to avoid primary current arcing between them. Point gap is a com-

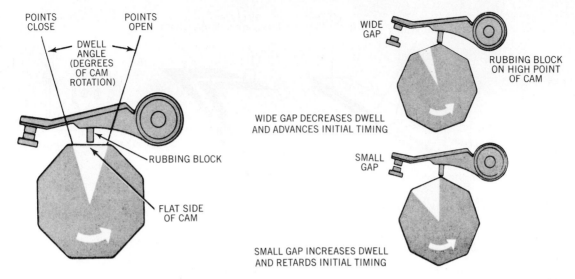

Figure 11-27. A close point gap creates a long dwell angle. A wide gap creates a short dwell angle. (Ford)

mon distributor specification and is inversely related to the dwell angle, figure 11-27. A large point gap provides a small dwell angle. A small point gap provides a large dwell angle. Point gap is measured in thousandths of an inch or hundredths of a millimeter. For an 8-cylinder engine, a gap of about 0.020 inch (0.50 mm) provides a dwell angle of about 30 degrees. A gap of 0.018 inch (0.46 mm) for the same set of points may provide a dwell angle of 34 degrees.

The Condenser

As breaker points start to open, current tries to keep flowing across the gap. Moreover, the countervoltage induced in the primary winding increases the force that tries to move current across the point gap. This would create an arc between the points that would have two harmful effects. It would burn the points, and it would delay the collapse of the primary magnetic field.

All breaker-point ignitions have a capacitor, or condenser, to minimize point arcing and to help cut off primary current quickly. Recall from your study of electrical principles that a capacitor is a device that will store a voltage charge when it is connected between two points of different volt-

VISUAL POLARITY TEST

Modern ignition system design makes the probability of reversed coil polarity unlikely. Moreover, modern test equipment makes the condition easy to detect when it does occur. An upside-down oscilloscope pattern, for example, is an immediate clue to possible reversed system polarity.

Old-time mechanics had simpler ways to check for engine problems, such as reversed polarity, however. Here's an easy test that you can use on any breaker-point ignition.

CAUTION

Do not use this test on a Delco HEI or similar high-voltage electronic ignition. A high-voltage arc may damage system components. Do not use a metal mechanical pencil or you will get shocked.

You can use a common lead pencil to check coil polarity on a breaker-point ignition, as follows:

1. Disconnect one spark plug cable from its plug.

2. Hold the cable terminal about 1/4 inch from the plug, with the tip of a wooden pencil about halfway between the cable and plug terminals, as shown in the illustration.

3. Crank the engine briefly and watch the spark flare at the pencil tip. If the flare goes toward the plug, polarity is correct. If the flare goes toward the cable, polarity is reversed.

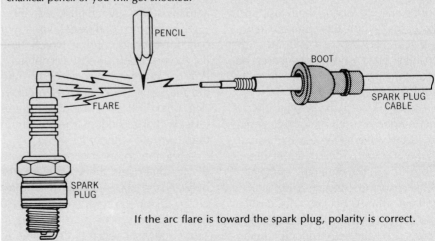

If the arc flare is toward the spark plug, polarity is correct.

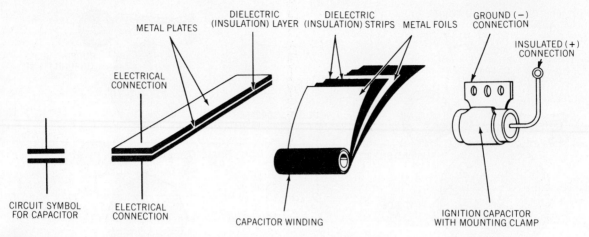

Figure 11-28. An ignition condenser is a capacitor made of two foil strips installed in a canister. (Bosch)

age potential. A capacitor has two conductive plates, or surfaces, separated by a dielectric insulating material. An ignition condenser is a capacitor made of two thin foil strips separated by insulating paper, figure 11-28. The two strips are installed in a small metal canister. One strip is connected to a small wire lead. The other is connected to the canister shell, which provides a ground connection for the capacitor.

The condenser wire lead is connected to a positive voltage source at the breaker points. The canister shell is grounded to a negative potential by connecting it to the distributor housing, figures 11-22 and 11-23. The condenser is in parallel with the breaker points. When the points are closed, they offer less resistance than the condenser, so current flows through the points to ground. As the points start to open, their resistance increases. At this time, the condenser is discharged, so current flows to the positive plate of the condenser because it has less resistance than the point gap.

Current flows to the positive plate of the condenser until its voltage potential is the same as the positive voltage of the primary circuit. Current cannot pass through the dielectric of the condenser, so the condenser develops a voltage charge between its positive and negative plates. The condenser is charged by the self-induced counter-

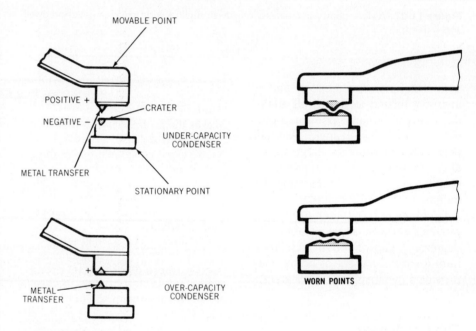

Figure 11-29. A low-capacity condenser causes pitting on the ground point. An over-capacity condenser causes opposite metal transfer. (Chrysler)

voltage of the primary winding, so it actually stores several hundred volts.

Charging the condenser takes about 0.1 millisecond, during which time the points open almost completely. Primary current stops abruptly, and the magnetic field collapses quickly. The field collapses about 20 times faster with the condenser in the circuit than it would without it.

While the points are open, the condenser maintains the voltage charge between its plates. When the points close, primary current is at zero, and there is no magnetic field in the coil. The condenser releases its charge to

the primary circuit and helps to start current flow. The condenser energy then **oscillates** between the condenser and the coil primary winding.

The charge capacity of any capacitor is rated in farads. A typical ignition condenser has a capacity of 0.18 to 0.32 microfarad. If a condenser with too little capacity is used in a circuit, primary current will charge the condenser and still be able to arc across the points. This causes burning and metal transfer from the − to the + contact point, figure 11-29. If a condenser capacity is too large, metal transfer occurs in the opposite direction. The **minus rule** will help you remember how condenser capacity affects point burning:

Minus metal on the minus (−) point means a minus-capacity condenser.

Badly worn points often have metal transfer and erosion on both surfaces, figure 11-29.

IGNITION SECONDARY CIRCUIT COMPONENTS

Figure 11-16 shows the relationships of the primary and secondary circuit components. The ignition secondary circuit, figure 11-30, consists of:

- The coil secondary winding
- The distributor cap
- The distributor rotor
- The ignition cables
- The spark plugs

The Coil Secondary Winding

The ignition secondary circuit begins at the coil secondary winding. The secondary winding has 15,000 to 30,000 turns of fine copper wire, figure 11-21, insulated from each other by a coating of enamel. Remember that the turns ratio between the secondary and the primary windings is 100 : 1 to 200 : 1 and acts as a voltage multiplier. To further increase the coil's magnetic field strength, both windings are installed around a soft iron core. The primary and secondary windings are insulated from each other, and the coil case is filled with wax or oil for more insulation. Most coils are contained in a metal cylinder. The coil top is made of an insulating material and has terminals for primary and secondary connections.

Coil Polarity. The primary and secondary circuit connections to the coil determine coil polarity and the polarity of the secondary circuit. One end of the secondary winding is connected to the primary + terminal in a negative-ground electrical system. The other end of the secondary winding is connected to the high-tension

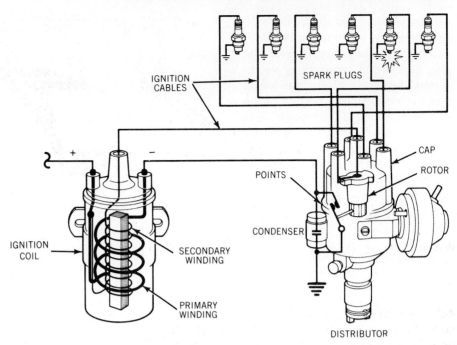

Figure 11-30. The high-voltage secondary circuit includes the coil secondary winding, the distributor cap and rotor, the spark plugs, and cables. (Bosch)

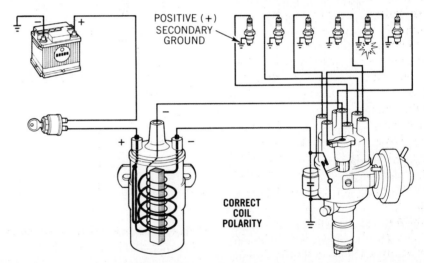

Figure 11-31. Correct (negative) secondary polarity exists when the coil is connected so that the spark plug center electrode is negative and the ground electrode is positive. (Bosch)

terminal of the coil. In this way, the secondary circuit is grounded through the primary circuit. The ground side of the secondary circuit is electrically positive. The other side of the circuit—the center electrode of the spark plug—is negative, figure 11-31.

The polarity of the secondary circuit is opposite to that of the primary circuit in most vehicles. Regardless of whether the primary circuit has negative or positive polarity, the secondary circuit must have negative polarity (positive ground) because:

1. Electrons (current) flow more easily from a negative point to a positive point than they do in the opposite direction.

2. High temperature of the spark plug center electrode increases the rate of electron movement (current).

The center electrode of a spark plug is hotter than the side electrode because it can't transfer heat to the cylinder head as easily. If the center electrode is at a negative potential, electrons will move more easily to the side electrode. Less secondary voltage will be required to force current across the plug gap. If coil connections are reversed, figure 11-32, or the wrong coil is installed, the direction of the coil magnetic field is reversed. This reverses the secondary voltage polarity and forces electrons to move from the side electrode to the center electrode of the spark plug. This **reverse polarity** increases the required secondary voltage 20 to 40 percent, figure 11-33.

Coil Secondary Voltage. Earlier you learned that a coil delivers only the secondary voltage required to jump the spark plug gap at any given instant. This is the **required voltage** of the ignition system, and it changes with varying engine conditions. You also learned that the coil must be *able* to deliver more secondary voltage than the engine requires so that it will always have enough voltage capability for *all* conditions. The maximum, or peak, voltage that a coil can deliver is its **available voltage**. The difference between the required voltage and the available voltage under any condition is the coil's **voltage reserve**.

Available voltage is determined by a coil's secondary-to-primary turns ratio and other factors of its design. Available voltage also is affected by primary circuit voltage, current, and resistance. Required voltage is determined by conditions in the engine cylinders and in the secondary circuit. You know that engine compression pressure and temperature and the spark plug gap create high resistance in the secondary circuit. The air-fuel mixture, too, is a high-resistance conductor. Here are some conditions that will *increase* the secondary circuit resistance and the required voltage:

1. A wider spark plug gap or an overheated plug

2. A leaner air-fuel mixture (fewer conductive gasoline molecules)

3. An overheated engine

4. Faster engine speeds and heavier engine loads, which increase temperature and pressure

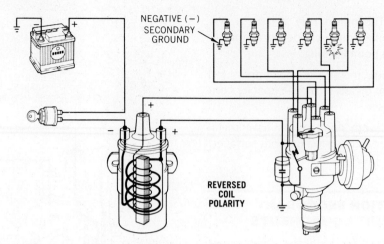

Figure 11-32. Reverse (positive) polarity exists when the coil is connected so that the spark plug center electrode is positive. (Bosch)

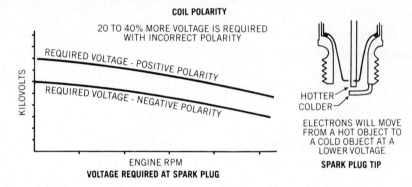

Figure 11-33. Reversed polarity requires 20 to 40 percent more secondary voltage to fire the plugs. (Prestolite)

5. Loose or corroded connections or other high-resistance conditions in the secondary cables from the coil to the distributor and the distributor to the spark plugs

A few conditions *decrease* secondary resistance and required voltage:

1. A narrower spark plug gap or a fouled plug that provides a low-resistance path for secondary current

2. A richer air-fuel mixture (more gasoline molecules)

3. Slow engine speeds and light loads, which decrease temperature and pressure

These last three conditions can occur *inside* the cylinders. Secondary circuit resistance also can be reduced by a short circuit *outside* the cylinders, such as a conductive path on the outside of the coil, a spark plug, a cable, or in the distributor cap. This kind of lower resistance short circuit

still requires secondary voltage from the coil, but the voltage jumps to ground outside the cylinder. It never gets near the spark plug gap, and the engine misfires.

Conditions in an engine and in an ignition system can affect both available voltage and required voltage. Low voltage or high resistance in the primary circuit decreases available secondary voltage because either will reduce primary field strength. If available voltage decreases when secondary voltage requirements are high, the coil may not have enough voltage reserve to fire the spark plugs. Figure 11-34 compares available and required voltage under good and bad circuit conditions. To ensure correct engine operation, a well-tuned ignition system should have a 60-percent voltage reserve under most conditions.

We can get a picture of the changing secondary voltage conditions by

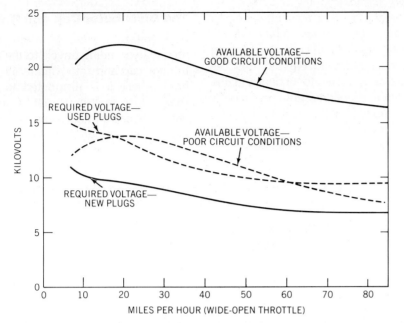

Figure 11-34. A well-tuned ignition system should maintain a 60-percent voltage reserve. (Prestolite)

Figure 11-35. Open-circuit (no-load) voltage is the coil's maximum available voltage. (Bosch)

looking at a series of graphs that plot voltage levels over a period of time. These graphs are similar to voltage waveforms displayed on an **oscilloscope**, which you will use for ignition service.

If the secondary circuit were open—that is, if there were no spark plug or cable between the coil and ground—the maximum available voltage of the coil could not complete a circuit. The voltage would oscillate through the coil windings, and between the coil and condenser, and dissipate its energy as heat. Figure 11-35 shows the pattern of this **open-circuit (no-load) voltage**. This is the same as the coil's available voltage and ranges from 20 kV to 50 kV for different coils. Figure 11-35 also shows primary current and voltage during the same time periods.

With a spark plug in the circuit, coil voltage completes the circuit by creating an arc across the gap. When the secondary winding discharges, voltage rises to the level needed to jump the gap. The high voltage ionizes the air and fuel molecules at the plug gap and makes them more conductive. When voltage overcomes resistance at the plug gap, the plug fires. Figure 11-36 shows this **firing (ionization) voltage**, which is the same as the

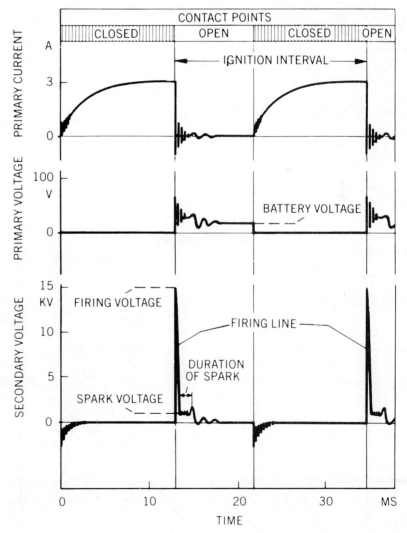

Figure 11-36. Firing voltage is the voltage required to create a spark at the plug. It is lower than open-circuit voltage. (Bosch)

required voltage. Engineers also call this the capacitive portion of the secondary voltage discharge because the spark gap acts as a capacitor in the circuit. Secondary voltage charges the capacitive terminals formed by the plug electrodes until the voltage overcomes the dielectric resistance of the gap.

Once the plug fires, less voltage is needed to sustain the spark across the gap. Voltage drops almost instantly to a much lower level, called the **spark voltage**, figure 11-36. This is the inductive portion of the secondary discharge because the coil now discharges the rest of its voltage as an induction coil in a closed circuit. Figure 11-37 shows an enlarged view of the secondary voltage trace from the point at which the plug fires until voltage drops too low to sustain the spark across the gap. This figure also shows the time in microseconds for each part of the plug-firing sequence. The final part of the secondary voltage oscillates in the coil windings and between the coil and condenser. It dissipates its energy as heat and is called the voltage decay.

We have taken quite a bit of time to examine ignition secondary voltage before looking at the other parts of the secondary circuit. We did this because it is easier to understand the design and operation of these parts if you know something about the voltage requirements of the circuit and how the high voltage originates.

The Distributor Cap and Rotor

High-voltage current from the coil secondary winding travels to the distributor cap and rotor, figure 11-38, from where it is distributed to the spark plugs in firing order. Current enters the cap through a central terminal, passes through the rotor, crosses an air gap from the rotor tip to a

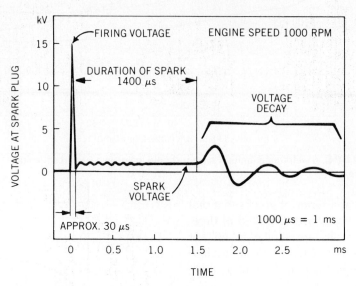

Figure 11-37. This complete secondary voltage pattern shows the lower spark plug voltage that maintains the spark after the plug fires. (Bosch)

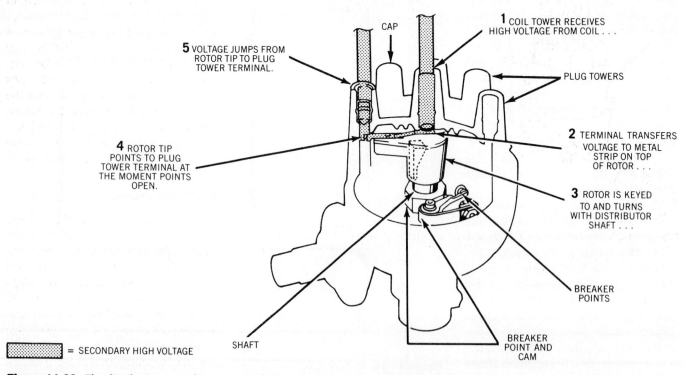

= SECONDARY HIGH VOLTAGE

Figure 11-38. The distributor cap and rotor receive high-voltage current from the coil and distribute it to the spark plugs. (Ford)

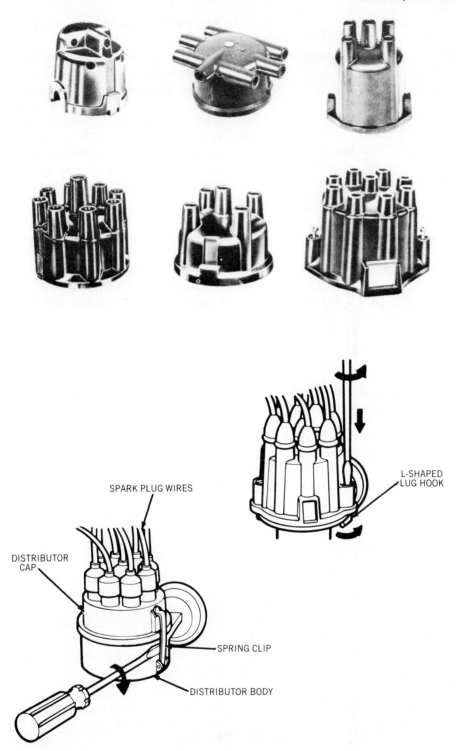

SPARK PLUG WIRES

L-SHAPED LUG HOOK

DISTRIBUTOR CAP

SPRING CLIP

DISTRIBUTOR BODY

Figure 11-39. Regardless of the shape, every distributor cap serves the same purpose. (Chrysler)

terminal in the cap, and travels through another cable to a spark plug.

Distributor Cap. The distributor cap, figure 11-39, is made of bakelite, silicone plastic, or a similar insulating material. The central terminal for the coil cable and metal inserts in the spark plug towers are circuit connections for the cables and the rotor. The coil terminal inside the cap may be a carbon insert of a spring-loaded metal button that contacts the rotor. The cap is keyed to the distributor body and held in place by spring clips, spring-loaded latches, or screws.

Distributor Rotor. The rotor is attached to the distributor shaft and rotates with it to distribute secondary voltage to the spark plug terminals in the cap. The rotor may simply press onto the shaft and be located by a key, or it may be mounted with screws, figure 11-40. The rotor is made of an insulating plastic material, similar to the cap. The metal electrode on the rotor conducts current from the coil terminal of the cap to the spark plug terminals.

The rotor tip cannot touch the plug terminals in the cap, or the rotor and cap would be damaged. An air gap of 0.003 to 0.009 inch exists between the rotor tip and the plug terminals of the cap, figure 11-41. The air gap adds resistance to the secondary circuit that requires 3,000 to 9,000 volts to create a small arc and complete the circuit. The voltage needed to bridge the rotor air gap is an important service specification, as you will learn when you service ignition systems.

Ignition Cables

Ignition cables, or spark plug cables, carry high-voltage current from the coil to the distributor and from the distributor to the plugs. They are heavily insulated so that the high-voltage current will not jump to ground before reaching the plugs. Cables for breaker-point ignitions have 7-mm-diameter insulation around a conductive core. Many electronic ignitions use 8-mm cables.

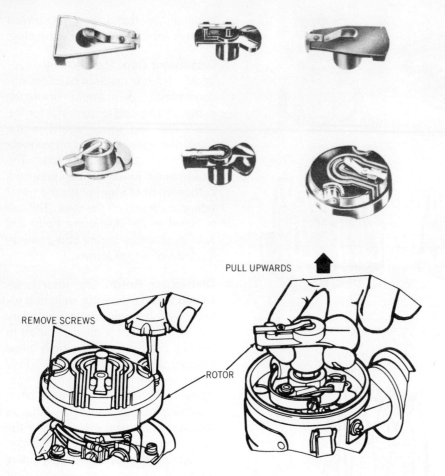

Figure 11-40. Most rotors press onto the top of the distributor shaft. Some Delco-Remy rotors are secured by screws. (Chrysler)

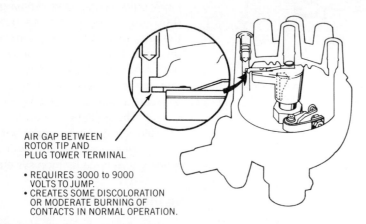

Figure 11-41. The rotor air gap adds resistance to the secondary circuit. (Ford)

Years ago, most ignition cables were made of copper or steel wire. Although this kind of cable is still made, most cars for over 30 years have used cables with high-resistance, nometallic conductors. Figure 11-42 shows both kinds of cable construction. The nonmetallic conductor is made of carbon or from linen or fiberglass strands impregnated with graphite. High-resistance cables are used for two basic reasons:

1. High-voltage discharge from the coil causes **radiofrequency interference (RFI)**, which interferes with radio and television transmission. High resistance in the cables reduces this RFI, and the cables are often called **television-radio-suppression (TVRS) cables**.

2. High resistance in the cables reduces current, which would burn spark plug and distributor cap electrodes. This resistance also raises the voltage applied to the spark plug, which improves plug firing in the high-resistance conditions in the cylinder.

Resistance in the cables and in the spark plugs affects secondary voltage and current after the plug fires. Before that time, the circuit is not complete. TVRS cables and resistor spark plugs suppress radio interference, and they lower secondary current that would erode spark plug electrodes.

Ignition cables have insulating boots around the terminals that connect them to the distributor cap and the spark plugs, figure 11-43. The boots keep dirt and water away from the cable connections and help insulate the secondary circuit.

Spark Plugs

The spark plugs complete the secondary ignition circuit. They cause high-voltage current to arc across a gap and ignite the air-fuel mixture. Spark plugs have always been critical parts of the ignition system. When you service ignition systems, you will learn that spark plugs are also good indicators of engine operating condition.

The major parts of a spark plug, figure 11-44, are:

1. The center electrode that carries high-voltage current to the plug gap and becomes the negative terminal of the plug

2. The ceramic insulator (core) that insulates the center electrode and its high voltage

3. The side, or ground electrode, which is attached to the shell and becomes the positive electrode

4. The steel shell that holds the other parts in a gas-tight assembly and has threads so that the plug can be installed in the cylinder head

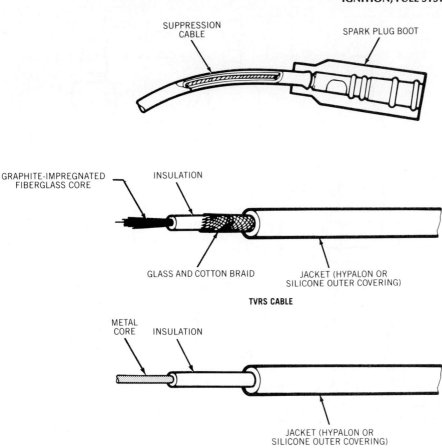

TVRS CABLE

METALLIC-CONDUCTOR CABLE

Figure 11-42. Modern automobile ignition systems use nonmetallic, high-resistance spark plug cables. Metallic cables are used for special applications. (Chrysler)

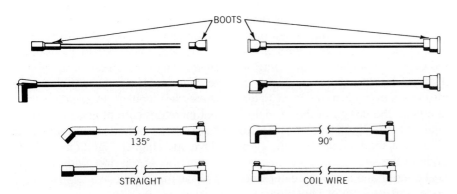

Figure 11-43. Insulating boots on the ends of spark plugs and coil cables keep out dirt and moisture and help keep high voltage from short circuiting to ground.

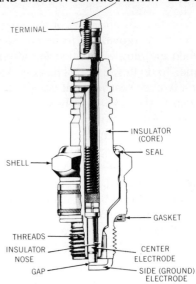

Figure 11-44. These are the basic parts of all spark plugs. (Bosch)

You already have learned something about the high-voltage spark when you read about coil voltage. Remember that the firing voltage develops because of a capacitive charge across the plug electrodes, negative at the center and positive at the side (ground) electrode. When voltage becomes high enough, it ionizes the gases in the plug gap, which makes them more conductive. The resistance of the gap breaks down, and the plug fires. Ignition systems are designed to have a high firing, or ionization, voltage at the plug gap. This is the voltage that ignites the mixture.

The current that continues to flow across the gap after ignition provides the visible part of the spark. This current contributes nothing to combustion, but it does create electrical interference and burns the plug electrodes. A high firing voltage reduces this current after the spark is established because more of the secondary voltage is discharged for initial firing. Modern ignition systems—including spark plugs—are designed to have high firing voltages, but not higher than the available voltage from the coil. These high voltages also improve ignition of lean air-fuel mixtures.

While all spark plugs have the same purposes, plugs have different design features for different engine requirements. The most important for spark plug selection and service are:

- Thread diameter and seat design
- Reach
- Heat range
- Gap

Thread Diameter and Seat Design.
All modern spark plug threads are made to metric dimensions. Most plugs today have a thread diameter of 14 millimeters, but some older Ford engines use 18-mm plugs. Forty years ago, some GM engines used 10-mm plugs, and even older plugs had pipe threads.

The threads and shell of any spark plug must provide a leakproof seal when the plug is installed in the engine. To do this, the shell has a gasket or a tapered seat where it compresses against the cylinder head, figure 11-45. All 18-mm plugs, and many 14-mm plugs, have tapered seats. Most 14-mm plugs have gaskets that compress between the plug seat and the cylinder head.

The steel shell has a hexagonal section that fits a wrench used for plug installation and removal. Standard sizes for spark plugs and wrenches are:

• 14-mm gasketed plug—13/16-inch wrench

• 14-mm taper-seat plug—5/8-inch wrench

• 18-mm taper-seat plug—13/16-inch wrench.

Reach. The **spark plug reach** is the distance from the plug seat to the end of the threads, figure 11-46. This includes threaded and unthreaded portions because some plugs have threads for only part of their reach. The reach dimension must match the depth of the tapped hole in the cylinder head, figure 11-47. If the plug reach is too short for the cylinder head hole, the plug will be shrouded in a pocket, and the spark will not ignite the air-fuel mixture completely. If plug reach is too long, the plug will extend into the combustion chamber. In this case, several problems can occur:

1. The plug will overheat and ignite the mixture prematurely.

2. Carbon deposits will form on the exposed threads and make plug removal difficult.

3. The piston may strike the plug and damage both the plug and the piston.

Mixing up a 3/4-inch reach plug with a 3/8-inch reach plug doesn't happen too often because the dimensions are obviously different. However, it is not hard to interchange 3/8-, 7/16-, and 1/2-inch plugs because they look al-

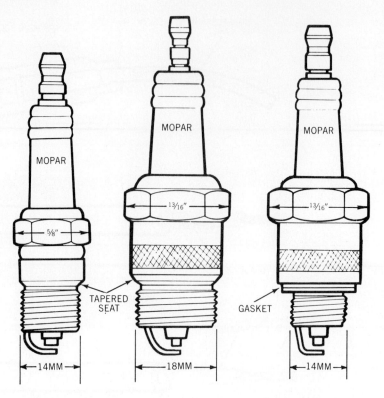

Figure 11-45. Common spark plug thread diameters are 14 and 18 millimeters, with gasketed or tapered seats. (Chrysler)

most the same at first glance. Always check the carmaker's specifications for plug part numbers and reach before installing new plugs.

Heat Range. Spark plug **heat range** does not include ignition temperature, or the temperature of the spark. It indicates the ability of the plug to dissipate heat from its firing end, or insulator core. Heat range is determined by the design of the insulator, figure 11-48. The insulator of a cold plug has a short length from the electrode to the shell. This promotes fast heat transfer and a cooler center electrode. The insulator of a hot plug has a longer length from electrode tip to shell, which promotes slower heat transfer and a hotter tip.

Heat range is related to expected engine operating temperature. A cold-running engine used for short trips or easy driving requires a hotter plug to burn deposits off the end of the plug. A hot-running engine requires a colder plug so that the electrodes will not overheat. An overheated plug can create high resistance and a misfire,

or it can ignite the mixture prematurely.

Spark Plug Gap. The spark plug gap is one of the most important engine service specifications. It is the distance between the center and ground electrodes, measured in thousandths of an inch or hundredths of a millimeter, figure 11-49. A narrow gap requires less voltage to create a spark but increases current flow, which can burn the electrodes. A wide gap develops higher ignition voltage, but if the gap is too wide, enough voltage may not be available to create a spark.

Spark plug gaps for breaker-point ignitions range from 0.030 to 0.040 inch (0.75 to 1.0 mm). Some electronic ignitions require plug gaps of 0.045 to 0.080 inch (1.0 to 2.0 mm), figure 11-49. All spark plugs are made with a gap between the electrodes, but that does not mean that the gap is exactly what is required for a specific engine. Plug gaps must always be checked and adjusted before installation.

Figure 11-46. Spark plug reach is the distance from the seat to the tip of the threads, or end of the shell. (Champion)

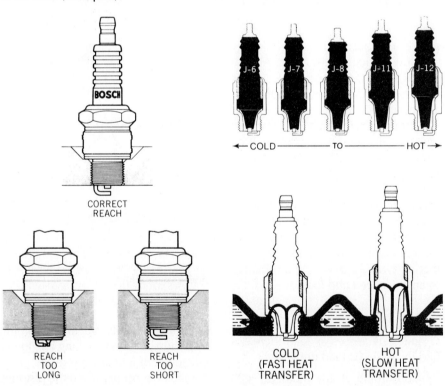

Figure 11-47. Spark plug reach must match the depth of the tapped hole in the cylinder head. (Bosch)

Figure 11-48. The distance of the heat path from the center electrode through the insulator to the shell determines the heat range.

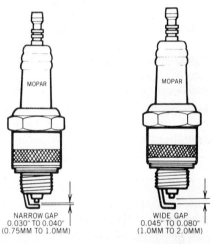

Figure 11-49. Narrow-gap and wide-gap plugs are made differently. Do not substitute one for the other. (Chrysler)

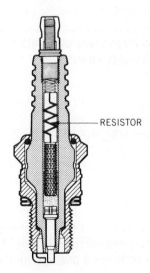

Figure 11-50. The resistor in the plug electrode reduces radio interference and plug erosion. (Bosch)

Other Spark Plug Design Features.

Thread diameter, seat design, reach, heat range, and gap are the most common features you must consider when you install spark plugs. There are other features, or special-purpose spark plugs that you must be aware of, however.

Resistor spark plugs have a resistor of about 5,000 to 10,000 ohms in the center electrode, figure 11-50. This resistor reduces the inductive portion

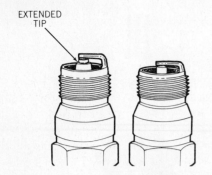

Figure 11-51. The insulators and electrodes of extended-core spark plugs extends farther into the combustion chamber. (Chrysler)

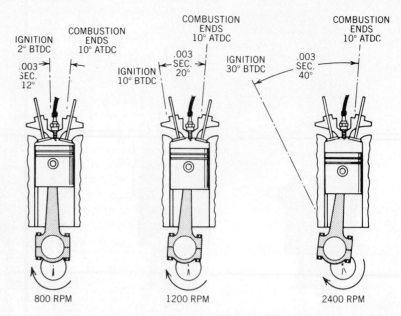

Figure 11-52. Ignition timing must advance as engine speed increases.

of the spark that causes radio interference and plug erosion.

Extended-core spark plugs have insulators and electrodes that extend farther into the combustion chamber, figure 11-51. Part numbers for many extended-core plugs indicate the same heat range as a standard plug. Most extended-core plugs, however, operate efficiently over a wider temperature range than standard plugs. They operate hotter at slow speeds to help burn off plug deposits. They also operate slightly colder at high speeds, which prevents overheating.

Other special-purpose plugs are made for 2-stroke engines, Wankel rotary engines, racing engines, and marine and motorcyle engines.

IGNITION TIMING AND SPARK ADVANCE

Earlier in this chapter, you learned about ignition intervals and how ignition is synchronized with crankshaft rotation and firing order. You also learned that ignition timing must change as engine speeds and loads change. This is called advancing and retarding the timing.

Remember that the air-fuel mixture has a relatively constant burn time of about 3 milliseconds, figure 11-52. Peak combustion pressure must occur when the piston, connecting rod, and crankshaft are in the position to develop the most power. At high engine

speeds, combustion must start sooner to allow enough burn time. At low engine speeds, less spark advance is needed in relation to crankshaft speed and position.

Although burn time is *relatively* constant, it does vary slightly with engine load. The lean air-fuel mixtures provided by the carburetor under light load take longer to ignite and burn. Rich mixtures under heavy load ignite and burn slightly faster.

The first principle of ignition timing for any internal combustion engine is that *all changes in timing are related to engine speed and load.*

• Timing advances as speed increases and retards as speed decreases.

• Timing decreases as load increases and increases as load decreases.

Ignition timing at any moment, with any combination of speed and load, is a combination of these actions. Ideal ignition timing also varies for different engine designs. Ideal timing for any engine under any combination of speed and load produces optimum cylinder pressure to deliver the most power with best fuel economy and emission control.

If ignition occurs too early, combustion pressure acts as a brake on the piston. Increased combustion pres-

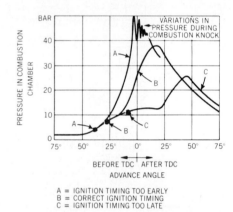

A = IGNITION TIMING TOO EARLY
B = CORRECT IGNITION TIMING
C = IGNITION TIMING TOO LATE

Figure 11-53. These graphs show the relationship of ignition timing and combustion pressure. (Bosch)

sures with overly advanced timing also cause engine knocking and lower efficiency. If ignition is too late, peak combustion occurs when the piston is farther down on the power stroke. This reduces cylinder pressure and overall efficiency. Figure 11-53 shows different cylinder pressures with different amounts of spark advance.

Breaker-point distributors use simple mechanical devices—centrifugal weights and vacuum diaphragms—to control timing. Many electronic distributors use the same devices, but late-model computer-controlled engine systems alter timing electroni-

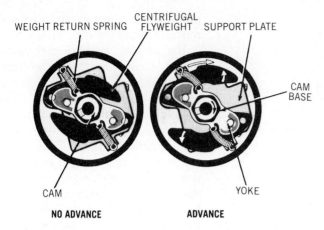

Figure 11-54. As the centrifugal weights move outward, they rotate the distributor cam ahead of shaft rotation. (Bosch)

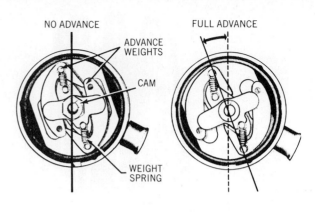

Figure 11-55. No-advance and full-advance positions of a typical centrifugal advance mechanism. (Delco-Remy)

cally. Whether timing is controlled by weights, vacuum diaphragms, or computers, it is controlled in relation to engine speed and load.

We will begin the study of ignition timing with the devices used on breaker-point distributors and simple electronic distributors. In later chapters, you will learn about variations on these systems that have been used to help control exhaust emissions. You also will learn about electronic systems that control timing more precisely than mechanical devices can.

Speed Control— Centrifugal Advance

The distributor shaft rotates at camshaft speed, or one-half crankshaft speed. Its speed increases and decreases directly with engine speed. If we could rotate the distributor cam around the center of the shaft so that it opens the points sooner as speed increases and later as speed decreases, we could control timing in relation to engine speed. Centrifugal advance weights provide this kind of control.

The distributor cam and rotor are on a separate shaft that fits over the distributor main drive shaft and pivots around it. The **centrifugal (mechanical) advance** mechanism consists of two centrifugal weights that pivot at the edge of a weight base on the drive shaft. A spring connects each weight to the shaft of the distributor cam, figure 11-54.

As distributor speed increases, the weights swing outward through centrifugal force and rotate the cam and rotor ahead of the main drive shaft. Higher speed creates more centrifugal force, which advances the timing. The springs control the movement of the weights and pull them back inward as speed decreases. A lug or pin on the advance mechanism limits the movement for maximum advance and acts as a stop for the no-advance position. Figure 11-55 shows the positions of a centrifugal advance mechanism with no advance and with full advance.

The amount and rate of advance for any distributor are determined by the size and shape of the weights and the tension of the springs. Engineers select springs and weights to design distributor advance "curves" for different engines. Figure 11-56 shows centrifugal advance curves for different engines. Notice that advance does not occur suddenly, but increases gradually over a specific speed range.

The centrifugal weights in most distributors are below the cam and breaker plate, figure 11-57. Delco distributors for V-8 and V-6 engines, as well as some Japanese distributors, have the weights above the cam and breaker plate, figure 11-58.

Centrifugal advance curves are usually designed for full-load conditions. This assumes a constant air-fuel mixture and engine load so that timing can be regulated only in relation to

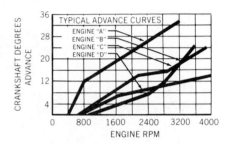

Figure 11-56. Centrifugal advance varies for different engines. It occurs gradually over a wide speed range. (Delco-Remy)

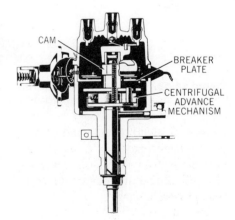

Figure 11-57. Most distributors have the centrifugal advance weights below the breaker plate. (Prestolite)

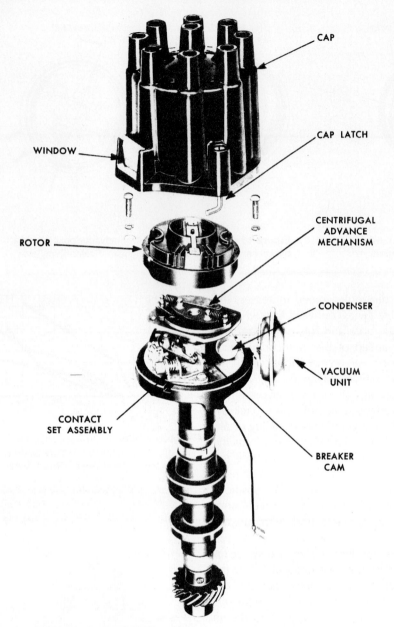

Figure 11-58. Delco-Remy V-8 and V-6 distributors have the centrifugal advance weights above the cam and breaker plate. (Delco-Remy)

increasing speed. In operation, however, engine loads can change independently of speed. Vacuum advance changes timing in relation to additional load changes.

Load Control—
Vacuum Advance

Centrifugal force varies directly with engine speed and provides a way to control timing in relation to speed. Engine vacuum varies directly with engine load and provides a way to control timing in relation to load.

Under light load, vacuum is high. Under heavy load, vacuum is low.

If we connect a vacuum diaphragm to a ported vacuum outlet just above the carburetor throttle, we can get a vacuum signal that is proportional to engine load and throttle position:

• High vacuum at part throttle (light load)

• Low vacuum at full throttle (heavy load) or closed throttle

Then, if we link that diaphragm to a movable breaker plate in the distributor, we can rotate the plate so that the

points open sooner to ignite the lean mixtures at part throttle and light load.

The **vacuum advance** mechanism uses a vacuum diaphragm to rotate the breaker plate in the direction opposite distributor rotation, figure 11-59. That is, if the distributor rotates clockwise, the diaphragm moves the plate counterclockwise. This causes the point rubbing block to contact the cam lobes sooner, which advances the timing. A spring in the diaphragm housing forces the plate in the opposite direction as vacuum decreases. This retards the timing slightly for increased load and reduces the detonation ping that would result with too much advance.

Ignition Advance
and Initial Timing

Up to this point, we have looked at centrifugal and vacuum advance separately, but they don't operate separately. Under any combination of speed and load, total ignition advance is determined by combined centrifugal and vacuum action, figure 11-60. This graph also shows that total ignition advance for any engine is affected by *initial timing*.

Remember from chapter 4 that initial (basic) timing is usually set at engine idle speed. It could be set at top dead center (tdc) of the compression stroke, or it could be set a few degrees before or after tdc. The centrifugal and vacuum advance devices for most breaker-point ignitions do not operate at idle. They add nothing to initial timing, and the engine runs at its basic timing setting. When engine speed moves off idle and speed and load change, the advance mechanisms start to operate.

To determine total spark advance from this point, you must add initial timing to the combined centrifugal and vacuum advance. For example, if the centrifugal and vacuum combination provides 20 degrees of spark advance at 2,000 rpm with light load and initial timing is 8° btdc, total advance is 28° btdc. Suppose, on the other hand, that initial timing is 4°

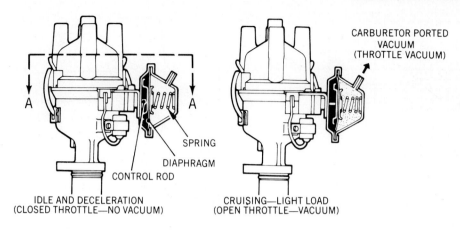

IDLE AND DECELERATION
(CLOSED THROTTLE—NO VACUUM)

CRUISING—LIGHT LOAD
(OPEN THROTTLE—VACUUM)

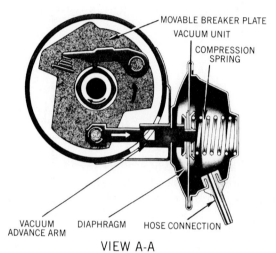

VIEW A-A

Figure 11-59. The vacuum advance mechanism moves the breaker plate opposite to distributor rotation to advance timing. (Chrysler) (Bosch)

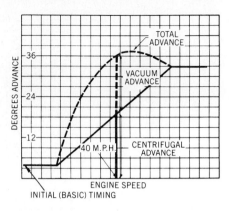

Figure 11-60. Total advance equals initial timing plus centrifugal and vacuum advance at any combination of speed and load. (Delco-Remy)

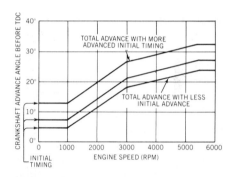

Figure 11-61. The same distributor can provide different amounts of spark advance, depending on initial timing.

atdc. The same 20 degrees of centrifugal and vacuum advance then provides only 16 degrees of total spark advance. Figure 11-61 shows the spark advance curves for the same distributor with two different initial timing settings.

Spark Advance Specifications

When you service ignition systems, you will find spark advance specifications given in several ways:

• Degrees of crankshaft advance at engine rpm
• Degrees of distributor advance at distributor rpm
• Degrees of vacuum advance with different amounts of vacuum

Remember that the distributor rotates at one-half engine speed. Therefore, the point where the primary circuit

opens advances only half as far in distributor degrees as spark timing advances in crankshaft degrees. Remember also that vacuum advance is independent of distributor and engine speed. At any speed, you can have high or low vacuum with light or heavy load.

Centrifugal advance can be measured out of the engine in a distributor test machine. For this, you need advance specifications in distributor degrees at distributor speed. Centrifugal advance also can be measured with the distributor running in the engine. For this, you need advance specifications in crankshaft degrees at engine speed. *Both* of these are double the distributor specifications and must be added to the initial timing setting when testing a distributor in an engine.

Vacuum advance can be tested

with the distributor in or out of the engine. Vacuum advance specifications are given in distributor degrees or crankshaft degrees at various vacuum levels, such as 4, 8, 12, 16, and 20 inches of mercury (in. Hg), figure 11-62. Some curves also include specifications for vacuum retard.

All of these specifications do relate to each other and to the specific ignition requirements of any engine. As you learn more about ignition system service, you will learn how to use these specifications for professional engine service.

INTRODUCTION TO EMISSION CONTROL

Twenty years ago, automobiles were a major source of pollution. Today, automobile emissions are greatly re-

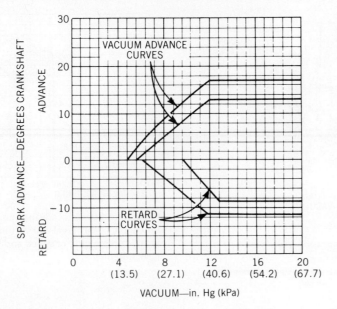

Figure 11-62. Typical vacuum advance and retard curves. (Chrysler)

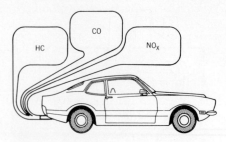

Figure 11-63. The major pollutants emitted by automobiles are hydrocarbons (HC), carbon monoxide (CO), and oxides of nitrogen (NO_x).

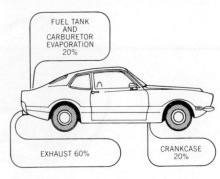

Figure 11-64. Hydrocarbon (HC) emissions come from the engine crankcase and fuel system evaporation, as well as from the exhaust.

duced because of government regulations and the engineering efforts of carmakers.

Air pollution is the presence of enough contamination in the atmosphere to injure human, animal, or plant life. Pollution is either natural or manmade. Natural air pollution comes from dust storms, volcanic eruptions, forest fires, and the cyles of plant and animal life. Manmade pollution comes from industrial plants, synthetic chemicals, transportation systems—and automobiles.

An automobile and its internal combustion engine emit three major pollutants: hydrocarbons (HC), carbon monoxide (CO), and oxides of nitrogen (NO_x), figure 11-63. These are all gaseous compounds. Additionally, an engine produces some solid emissions of lead, sulfur, carbon, and other particulates, as well as some sulfur oxides. Diesel engines emit less HC and CO but more particulates and sulfur oxides than gasoline engines. NO_x emissions are slightly less from a diesel but still enough to require controls on late-model automobiles.

Hydrocarbons (HC)

Gasoline, diesel fuel, and motor oil are all hydrocarbons. HC emissions from an automobile are largely unburned fuel in the exhaust, but hydrocarbons are the only major pollutant that come from areas of a car *other than* the exhaust, figure 11-64. The three major sources of HC emissions from a car are:

1. Engine exhaust—60 percent

2. Crankcase vapors (blowby and oil fumes)—20 percent

3. Gasoline fuel system evaporation—20 percent

Even paint and tires emit traces of hydrocarbons. The film that often clouds the insides of car windows comes from hydrocarbons emitted by vinyl upholstery.

There are more than 200 kinds of hydrocarbons emitted by automobile sources, but hydrocarbons of all kinds can be broken down by complete combustion. If an engine burned its fuel completely, there would be no HC in the exhaust, only water vapor and carbon dioxide (CO_2). But combustion is seldom *complete*. Fuel near the edges of the combustion chamber often cools before it can burn and passes out with the exhaust. If the air-fuel mixture is too rich, not all of the fuel burns. If a cylinder misfires, the complete air-fuel charge passes out the exhaust unburned. A car with-

out emission controls produces approximately 200 pounds of HC emissions for every 1,000 gallons of gasoline it uses, figure 11-65.

Carbon Monoxide (CO)

Carbon monoxide (CO) also results from incomplete combustion. The amount of CO produced depends on how hydrocarbon fuel burns. If the air-fuel mixture is rich, there is not enough oxygen to combine with carbon to form harmless CO_2. The air-fuel mixture must be extremely lean to have enough oxygen to form CO_2 with no CO. In fact, CO formation can't be eliminated completely from the combustion process in an engine. The same car without emission controls that produces 200 pounts of HC, produces 2,300 pounds of CO from every 1,000 gallons of gasoline, figure 11-65.

CO is an incomplete compound that lacks oxygen. CO is a poisonous

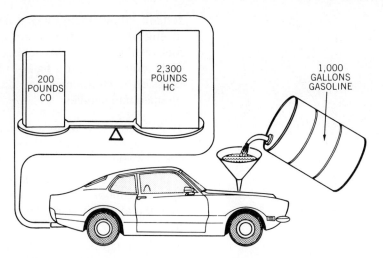

Figure 11-65. A car without emission controls emits 200 pounds of HC and 2,300 pounds of CO for every 1,000 gallons of gasoline that it burns.

gas because it is heavier than oxygen or air and displaces oxygen from the atmosphere. In small amounts, CO causes headaches, dizziness, and nausea. In large amounts, it kills because it deprives the body of oxygen.

Oxides of Nitrogen (NO$_x$)

High temperatures and pressures of combustion are what produce good performance and fuel economy in an engine. They also produce oxides of nitrogen (NO$_x$). Air is about 21-percent oxygen and 78-percent nitrogen. When combustion temperature exceeds about 2,500° F (1,370° C), oxygen and nitrogen combine in large quantities to form NO$_x$. NO$_x$ is not a single compound, but a family of compounds that includes nitrous oxide (NO), nitrogen dioxide (NO$_2$), and nitrogen trioxide (NO$_3$). By themselves, NO$_x$ emissions are no great hazard. When the amounts of NO$_x$ and HC in the air reach the right ratio, however, they combine in the presence of sunlight to form smog.

Automobile NO$_x$ emissions can be reduced by lowering combustion temperatures and pressures. This, however, lowers combustion efficiency, which increases HC and CO emissions. Modern electronic engine controls and 3-way catalysts are the most effective devices for the opposing requirements of HC, CO, and NO$_x$ control.

Particulates

Solid particulate exhaust emissions are so small that they stay in the atmosphere for a long time before settling. Lead particulates in the air can cause lead poisoning if a person is constantly exposed to them for several years. Carbon and soot particulates can damage people's lungs and respiratory systems. Automobile particulate emissions are controlled mostly be eliminating lead and other additives from gasoline and changing the formulation of fuels, rather than by systems on the car.

Sulfur Oxides

Some of the sulfur in automobile fuels, especially diesel fuel, combines with oxygen to form **sulfur oxides** in the exhaust. Some of these oxides combine with water vapor in the air to form sulfuric acid. Large amounts of sulfuric acid can be a health hazard in polluted urban air, and it can mix with water and fall as "acid rain." Sulfur oxide pollution from industrial sources is a larger problem than it is from automobiles. But, the large number of diesel vehicles on the road has in-

creased the interest in sulfur oxide automobile emission controls.

Smog

Not all air pollution is smog. CO, for example, pollutes the air, but it does not form smog. Smog forms when HC and NO$_x$ combine in the presence of sunlight and quiet air. Scientists still don't understand the nature of smog completely, but they call its formation a **photochemical reaction**.

Smog is worse when a layer of warm air forms in the upper atmosphere and holds the smog close to the ground, figure 11-66. This **temperature inversion** keeps cooler air from rising from the ground and carrying smog with it. Certain geographic and climatic conditions can create a temperature inversion within a thousand feet of the ground and act as a lid to trap smog. Temperature inversions were first noted and studied in Los Angeles, which suffered some of the worst smog pollution in the country.

Automobile Emission Controls

A single car emits only a small amount of pollution in daily use, but there are almost 150 million motor vehicles in the United States. Without emission controls, all of these vehicles would produce almost half of the air pollution in the country.

The automobile industry has done much to reduce motor vehicle air pollution since 1966 when exhaust emission controls were introduced. HC emissions from the engine crankcase and from fuel evaporation (about 40 percent of total HC emissions) have almost been eliminated. HC emissions from the exhaust of late-model cars are less than 1/10 the HC emissions from pre-1966 cars. Total HC emissions from all vehicle sources have been reduced more than 98 percent, and CO emissions have been reduced about 95 percent. Since 1973, NO$_x$ emissions have been reduced about 65 percent, figure 11-67.

Emission controls on modern automobiles are not a separate system, or

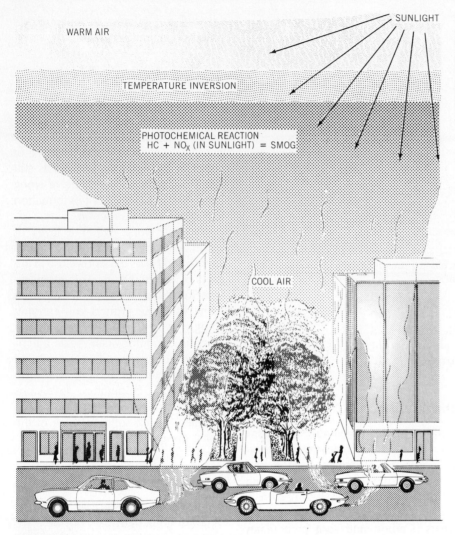

Figure 11-66. Smog forms from a photochemical reaction between HC and NO_x. A temperature inversion traps the smog at ground level.

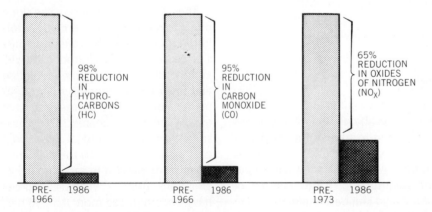

Figure 11-67. Automobile NO_x emissions have been reduced more than half, and HC and CO emissions almost eliminated in less than 20 years.

systems. They are an integral part of an engine's combustion controls—the fuel, ignition, exhaust, lubrication, and cooling systems, figure 11-68. Emission controls, however, can be grouped into families:

1. *Positive crankcase ventilation* (PCV) systems control HC emissions from the crankcase.

2. *Evaporative emission control* (EEC) systems control HC vapor emission from the fuel tank, pump, and carburetor

3. *Exhaust emission controls* are parts of the fuel, ignition, and exhaust systems and other devices that control HC, CO, and NO_x. The principal methods used to control exhaust emissions are:

    a. *Air injection*—Injecting extra air into the exhaust helps oxidize HC and CO to H_2O and CO_2, figure 11-69.

    b. *Engine modifications*—Redesigned combustion chambers and valve timing have helped reduce all three major pollutants.

    c. *Spark timing*—Early emission systems used retarded timing to reduce HC and NO_x. Late-model cars have electronically controlled timing that provides the best ignition timing for emission control, economy, and performance.

    d. *Exhaust gas recirculation*—One effective way to reduce NO_x is to recirculate some exhaust to the intake air-fuel mixture, figure 11-70. Because the recirculated exhaust doesn't aid combustion, it lowers the combustion temperature, which reduces NO_x.

    e. *Catalytic converters*—The first catalytic converters on 1975–76 cars helped to oxidize HC and CO. Second-generation converters, introduced in 1977—78, chemically reduce NO_x emissions.

    f. *Electronic engine controls and closed-loop fuel systems*—On late-model cars, controls for igni-

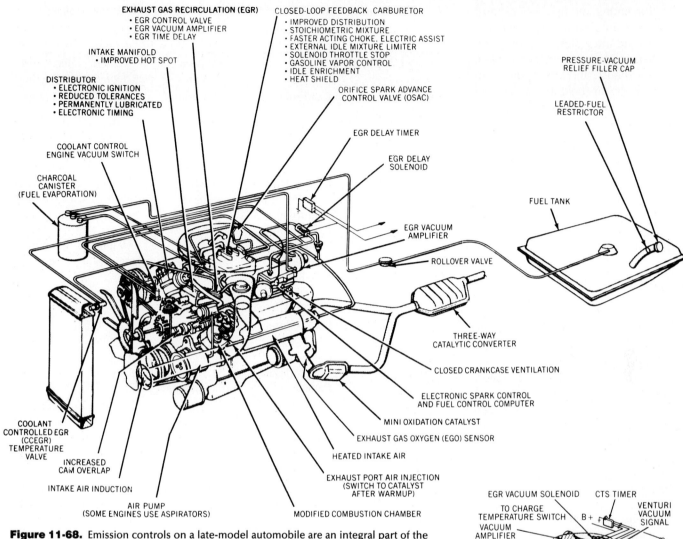

EXHAUST GAS RECIRCULATION (EGR)
• EGR CONTROL VALVE
• EGR VACUUM AMPLIFIER
• EGR TIME DELAY

INTAKE MANIFOLD
• IMPROVED HOT SPOT

DISTRIBUTOR
• ELECTRONIC IGNITION
• REDUCED TOLERANCES
• PERMANENTLY LUBRICATED
• ELECTRONIC TIMING

COOLANT CONTROL
ENGINE VACUUM SWITCH

CHARCOAL
CANISTER
(FUEL EVAPORATION)

CLOSED-LOOP FEEDBACK CARBURETOR
• IMPROVED DISTRIBUTION
• STOICHIOMETRIC MIXTURE
• FASTER ACTING CHOKE, ELECTRIC ASSIST
• EXTERNAL IDLE MIXTURE LIMITER
• SOLENOID THROTTLE STOP
• GASOLINE VAPOR CONTROL
• IDLE ENRICHMENT
• HEAT SHIELD

ORIFICE SPARK ADVANCE
CONTROL VALVE (OSAC)

EGR DELAY TIMER

EGR DELAY
SOLENOID

EGR VACUUM
AMPLIFIER

ROLLOVER VALVE

THREE-WAY
CATALYTIC CONVERTER

CLOSED CRANKCASE VENTILATION

ELECTRONIC SPARK CONTROL
AND FUEL CONTROL COMPUTER

MINI OXIDATION CATALYST

EXHAUST GAS OXYGEN (EGO) SENSOR

HEATED INTAKE AIR

EXHAUST PORT AIR INJECTION
(SWITCH TO CATALYST
AFTER WARMUP)

MODIFIED COMBUSTION CHAMBER

COOLANT
CONTROLLED EGR
(CCEGR)
TEMPERATURE
VALVE

INCREASED
CAM OVERLAP

INTAKE AIR INDUCTION

AIR PUMP
(SOME ENGINES USE ASPIRATORS)

PRESSURE-VACUUM
RELIEF FILLER CAP

LEADED-FUEL
RESTRICTOR

FUEL TANK

Figure 11-68. Emission controls on a late-model automobile are an integral part of the combustion control systems. (Chrysler)

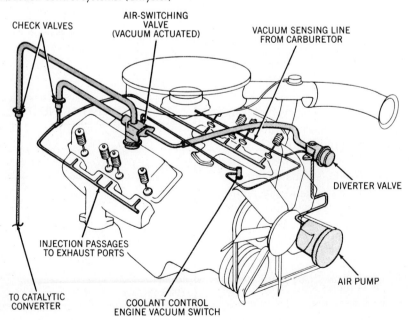

CHECK VALVES

AIR-SWITCHING
VALVE
(VACUUM ACTUATED)

VACUUM SENSING LINE
FROM CARBURETOR

DIVERTER VALVE

INJECTION PASSAGES
TO EXHAUST PORTS

AIR PUMP

TO CATALYTIC
CONVERTER

COOLANT CONTROL
ENGINE VACUUM SWITCH

Figure 11-69. Air injection systems were among the first HC and CO emission controls. (Chrysler)

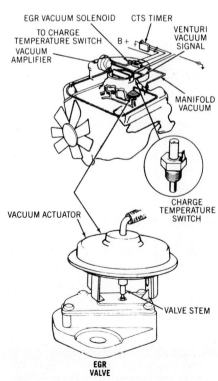

EGR VACUUM SOLENOID   CTS TIMER

TO CHARGE
TEMPERATURE SWITCH   B + F   VENTURI
VACUUM   VACUUM
AMPLIFIER   SIGNAL

MANIFOLD
VACUUM

VACUUM ACTUATOR

CHARGE
TEMPERATURE
SWITCH

VALVE STEM

EGR
VALVE

Figure 11-70. Exhaust gas recirculation (EGR) is one of the most effective ways to reduce NO$_x$ emissions. (Chrysler)

tion timing, air injection, exhaust gas recirculation, and fuel delivery are integrated electronically. Sensors measure oxygen content in exhaust, and a computer controls the air-fuel ratio for efficient combustion.

Emission and Fuel Economy Regulations

The engineering advances that have almost eliminated automobile air pollution did not happen without a lot of scientific research. While air pollution and smog have existed in many parts of the world for generations, they were first studied extensively in Southern California in the late 1940's and early 1950's. By the early 1950's scientists proved that automobile emissions and photochemical reactions were major causes of smog.

In 1961, California required control of crankcase emissions on new cars sold in that state. Carmakers began installing PCV systems on all 1963 cars nationwide. California required the first exhaust emission controls on new 1966 cars, and these systems appeared nationwide on 1967–68 models.

Congress passed the Clean Air Act in 1963, which gave money to states for air pollution control programs. The amended Clean Air Act of 1965 required the Federal government to set standards for automobile emissions, figure 11-71. This law was supplemented by the Air Quality Act of 1967 and its amendments of 1970, 1974, and 1977. The Canadian Ministry of Transport established vehicle emission requirements, beginning with 1971 models.

The U.S. Federal Environmental Protection Agency (EPA) sets standards for all air quality control, including vehicle emissions. The California Air Resources Board (ARB) operates under authority of the EPA to set standards for that state. For many model years, California emission limits have been more stringent than Federal requirements.

The oil shortages of 1973 and 1979 focused government and industry at-

tention on improving vehicle fuel economy, as well as emission control. The Federal Energy Act of 1975 established the Corporate Average Fuel Economy (CAFE) standards for fuel mileage. These standards are administered by the EPA and the Department of Transportation (DOT).

Engineers then had two, often conflicting, goals to reach: reduced emissions and increased economy. The 1978 vehicles sold by each carmaker had to average 18 miles per gallon. The mileage standards increased steadily to a 27.5-mpg average for 1985 models, figure 11-72.

Fifty-Thousand-Mile Emission Standards, Gasoline-Powered Automobiles

Year	Regulations	HC	CO	NO$_x$
Before Controls[a]		850 ppm[b] (16.8 g/mi)[c]	3.4% (125.0 g/mi)	1000 ppm (4.0 g/mi)
1966-69	California	275 ppm	1.5%	none
1968-69	U.S. Federal			
1970	California and U.S. Federal	4.6 g/mi	46.0 g/mi	none
1971	California	4.6 g/mi	46.0 g/mi	4.0 g/mi
	U.S. Federal	4.6 g/mi	46.0 g/mi	none
	Canada	2.2 g/mi[d]	23.0 g/mi[d]	none
1972	California	3.2 g/mi	39.0 g/mi	3.2 g/mi
	U.S. Federal and Canada	3.4 g/mi	39.0 g/mi	none
1973	California	3.2 g/mi	39.0 g/mi	3.0 g/mi
	U.S. Federal and Canada	3.4 g/mi	39.0 g/mi	3.0 g/mi
1974	California	3.2 g/mi	39.0 g/mi	2.0 g/mi
	U.S. Federal and Canada	3.4 g/mi	39.0 g/mi	3.0 g/mi
1975-76	California	0.9 g/mi	9.0 g/mi	2.0 g/mi
	U.S. Federal	1.5 g/mi	15.0 g/mi	3.1 g/mi
	Canada	2.0 g/mi	25.0 g/mi	3.0 g/mi
1977-79	California	0.41 g/mi	9.0 g/mi	1.5 g/mi
	U.S. Federal	1.5 g/mi	15.0 g/mi	2.0 g/mi
	Canada	2.0 g/mi	25.0 g/mi	3.0 g/mi
1980	California	0.39 g/mi	9.0 g/mi	1.0 g/mi
	U.S. Federal	0.41 g/mi	7.0 g/mi	2.0 g/mi
1981	California	0.41 g/mi	3.4 g/mi	1.0 g/mi
1981 and later	U.S. Federal	0.41 g/mi	3.4 g/mi	1.0 g/mi
1982 and later	California	0.39 g/mi	7.0 g/mi	0.7 g/mi

[a] approximate estimates   [c] g/mi = grams per mile
[b] ppm = parts per million   [d] theoretical flow rate

Figure 11-71. Exhaust emission limits for new gasoline-powered automobiles from 1966 to the present.

FUEL ECONOMY STANDARDS

Model Year	MPG	Improvement Over 1974 (%)
1978	18.0	50
1979	19.0	58
1980	20.0	67
1981	22.0	83
1982	24.0	100
1983	26.0	116
1984	27.0	125
1985	27.5	129

Figure 11-72. Carmakers improved fleet average fuel economy 129 percent in 10 years.

IGNITION TIMING AND EMISSION CONTROL

Some engineers say that the ignition system is the major emission control system on an engine. It is certainly one of the most important. You have already studied the principles of ignition timing and the relationship of timing to emission control. For a better understanding of why ignition timing must be modified to control emissions, we should review the basic reasons for spark advance. Then we will look at spark timing modifications in the larger context of emission controls.

Timing must be advanced as engine speed increases to allow enough burn time for combustion pressure to develop full power. Timing can be advanced more at high speed under light load to allow the engine to burn a lean mixture. Lean mixtures take longer to burn, but they improve fuel economy. As engine load increases, speed decreases slightly and mixtures become richer. Timing should be retarded slightly from a highly advanced position. Centrifugal and vacuum advance mechanisms can adjust timing as speed and load change so that combustion occurs with the greatest heat and pressure. Maximum timing advance for a given speed and load allows the engine to get the most energy possible from its fuel. Unfortunately, it also has harmful side effects.

With maximum advance, the fuel is completely burned as the piston starts its exhaust stroke. Although peak combustion temperatures are hotter, final exhaust gases are cooler and do not heat the exhaust ports and manifold as much as they would if timing were later. Any unburned fuel left in the cylinder is carried out as hydrocarbon (HC) emissions. Exhaust temperatures are not high enough to cause this fuel to combine with any remaining oxygen. Also, maximum spark advance and high temperatures and pressures increase the formation of oxides of nitrogen (NO_x) early in the combustion process.

If timing is retarded, combustion is less efficient, and performance and economy will suffer. However, NO_x emissions decrease because combustion temperatures are lower. Also with retarded timing, high temperatures occur later in the combustion process. This increases exhaust gas temperature and helps to oxidize any unburned fuel in the exhaust system. Originally, the principal reasons for spark timing control modifications were to reduce HC and NO_x emissions.

You might ask, "Why not just run the ignition system with later initial timing and less overall advance?" If engineers did this, performance and economy would suffer at all times. This isn't necessary because HC and NO_x emissions are highest under certain conditions and not under others. HC emissions are high when a spark plug misfires and fuel does not burn. They also are high with a rich mixture and during deceleration and gear shifting with a manual transmission when high manifold vacuum draws extra fuel through the carburetor. NO_x emissions are high when combustion temperatures and pressures are high and mixtures are lean. By modifying timing only when necessary, engineers were able to maintain reasonable performance and economy while reducing emissions.

Spark Timing Controls of the 1970's

As emission limits become more strict, carmakers adopted two general methods to modify vacuum advance:

- Vacuum delay valves
- Speed- and transmission-controlled timing

Most automobiles of the 1970's used one or both of these spark advance modifications. You also can find some of these devices (and their principles) in later model electronic engine control systems.

Vacuum-Delay Valves. A vacuum-delay valve delays the application of engine vacuum to the distributor advance unit for about 15 to 30 seconds to help decrease HC and NO_x emis-

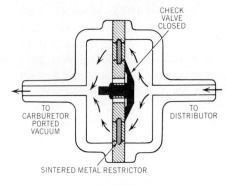

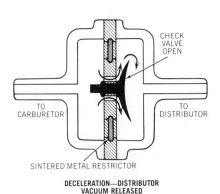

Figure 11-73. A spark delay valve "filters" vacuum to the distributor to delay advance. The check valve releases trapped vacuum on deceleration.

sions. This holds timing in a less advanced condition at low and intermediate speeds than it would be with full vacuum advance. The results are lower overall combustion temperatures, with peak temperature occurring later in the cycle.

The spark delay valve (SDV) used by Ford, GM, and some other carmakers is a small plastic housing with a sintered metal disc, figure 11-73. One side of the valve is connected to ported vacuum; the other is connected to the distributor advance unit. Vacuum must "filter" through the sintered metal disc to reach the distributor. This delays spark advance. When ported vacuum drops under load, deceleration, or idle, a check valve in the SDV opens to release vacuum from the distributor. This prevents too much advance when it isn't needed. Spark delay valves usually are color coded to indicate the amount of delay the valve provides.

Before mid-1973, some Ford engines had delay valve bypass systems that allowed immediate vacuum advance when the engine was cold. These systems had a solenoid vacuum valve in a bypass line around the SDV, figure 11-74. At low temperature, an ambient temperature switch energized the solenoid to open the vacuum bypass valve. Since combustion temperatures are low with a cold engine, full advance could be allowed to aid warmup and driveability. Some post-1973 systems from Ford and other carmakers have high-temperature bypass features. Typically, a thermostatic vacuum valve, controlled by coolant temperature is in a manifold vacuum line to the distributor. If engine temperature rises above normal, the valve opens and applies manifold vacuum to the distributor. This advances timing to prevent overheating. Similar systems have been built with an ambient air temperature switch that energizes a solenoid to allow vacuum advance at high temperature.

Chrysler's orifice spark advance control (OSAC) valve is another form of spark delay valve. Instead of a sintered metal disc, the OSAC valve has an orifice in the vacuum line to the distributor, figure 11-75. This delays vacuum advance just as an SDV does. Chrysler used the OSAC valve from 1973 through the late 1970's. Some early installations had a low-temperature bypass system that allowed full vacuum at low temperatures. Later installations have a thermostatic vacuum valve in the vacuum line to the distributor. This valve is installed in the engine water jacket and opens the vacuum line at high coolant temperature. The valve allows manifold vacuum to the distributor to advance timing and prevent overheating, figure 11-76.

Although the needs of different engines vary, and engineers have used different methods to reach similar goals, all temperature bypass systems have common purposes. They override the vacuum advance control systems to provide vacuum advance at high or low temperatures, or both. A bypass system can provide smoother

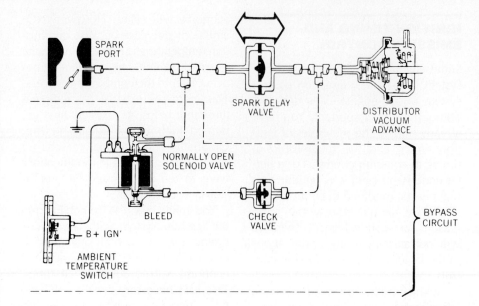

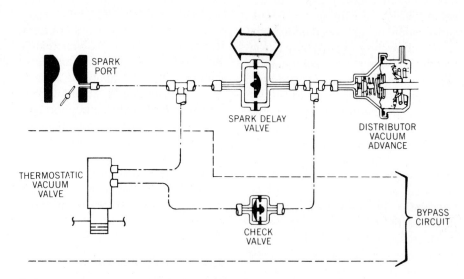

Figure 11-74. A vacuum-delay system can have either a thermostatic valve or a solenoid-controlled bypass. The vacuum bypass can occur at high or low temperature, depending on engine requirements. (Ford)

warmup or prevent engine overheating.

When catalytic converters appeared on 1975 cars, most carmakers reduced the use of vacuum delay valves. They still appeared, however, on many cars through the late 1970's and early 1980's.

Speed- and Transmission-Controlled Timing. Many cars of the late 1960's and early 1970's had systems that sensed vehicle speed or transmission gear range and cut off vacuum advance at low and intermediate speeds. Carmakers used various names for these systems, such as:

- Transmission-controlled spark (TCS)
- Speed-controlled spark (SCS)
- NO_x spark control
- Electronic distributor modulator (EDM)
- Electronic spark control (ESC)
- Transmission-regulated spark (TRS)

Regardless of the name, all of these systems work on the same principles and have similar parts. All systems

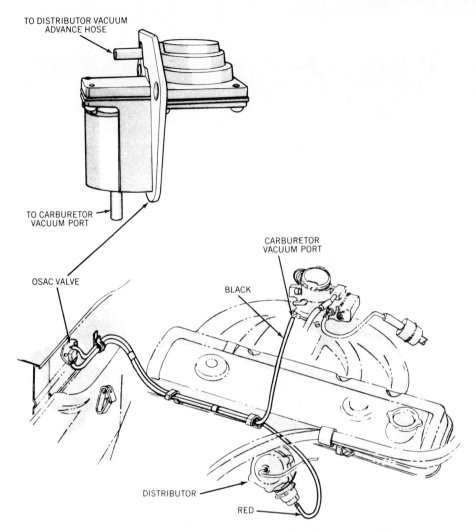

Figure 11-75. Chrysler's OSAC valve is another kind of vacuum advance delay valve. (Chrysler)

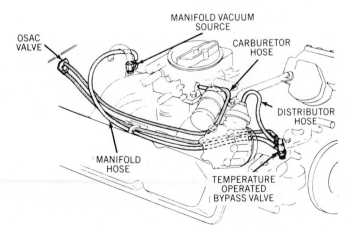

Figure 11-76. Chrysler's high-temperature bypass for the OSAC valve uses a coolant-controlled vacuum valve. (Chrysler)

DISTRIBUTOR ROTOR QUICK TEST

It's possible for a distributor rotor to develop a short-circuit path to ground in the form of a crack or a carbon track that allows high voltage from the coil to go directly to ground in the distributor shaft. Sometimes the short is a small hole that often is called "punch through." Whatever the cause of the short, it keeps the coil voltage from ever reaching the plug cable terminals in the cap, and usually the car won't start.

If you're trying to cure a no-start condition, you might put in a new rotor just to see if that solves the problem. That's really shooting in the dark; it's not the kind of logical troubleshooting a professional mechanic does. If the car still doesn't start, you don't know if the first rotor or the second, or both, was bad. There is, however, a quick and accurate way to check for a shorted rotor on a breaker-point distributor.

Disconnect the coil center cable from the cap but leave it connected to the coil. Remove the cap and move it out of your way. Then, put a small insulator, such as a cardboard match, between the points to block them open. Connect one end of a jumper wire to the insulated breaker-point arm (that's the hot connection to the ignition primary circuit) and turn the ignition switch on. Using insulated pliers, hold the disconnected end of the coil cable about 1/8 to 1/4 inch above the center terminal of the rotor on the distributor shaft. Finally, touch the other end of your jumper wire to ground several times to open and close the primary circuit.

Each time you open the primary circuit, the coil will discharge. If the rotor is shorted, a healthy spark will jump from the coil cable to the rotor and straight through to ground. If the rotor is properly insulated, the secondary circuit from the coil will remain open. No spark will jump to the rotor, but you may see a yellowish-blue corona around the end of the coil cable.

have a solenoid-operated vacuum valve that shuts off vacuum advance at low speeds. All systems also have a speed-sensing switch or a transmission switch to energize or deenergize the solenoid. All systems also have one or more switches that sense **ambient air temperature** or engine coolant temperature. These are override switches that allow full vacuum advance at high or low engine or air temperatures. Full advance is allowable at low temperatures because combustion temperatures are not at their maximum, and NO_x formation is low. Full advance is necessary at high temperatures to prevent overheating.

Speed-controlled spark systems, such as Cadillac's SCS and Ford's EDM and ESC systems, have speed-sensing switches in the speedometer cables, figure 11-77. These are rotating magnets that turn inside a stationary winding. Above a certain speed, the magnet induces enough voltage in the winding to activate an electronic module or energize the solenoid.

Transmission-controlled spark systems were more common than speed-controlled systems. They use switches activated by shift linkage position on manual transmissions or by hydraulic pressure on automatic transmissions, figure 11-78. The switches are wired to deny vacuum advance at low speeds and allow it at high speeds.

A solenoid vacuum valve can be **normally energized**, which means that when the ignition is on, voltage is applied to the solenoid windings. Or, the valve can be **normally deenergized**, which means that when the ignition is on, voltage is *not* applied to the windings until a switch closes. Further, the valve can be built to open or close a vacuum line in either the energized or deenergized condition. Therefore, a solenoid-operated vacuum valve can be wired in one of four ways, as shown in figure 11-79.

All of this may sound confusing, and it can be. We haven't the room in this book to detail all of the combinations of speed and transmission switches and solenoids used by carmakers over a 10- or 12-year period.

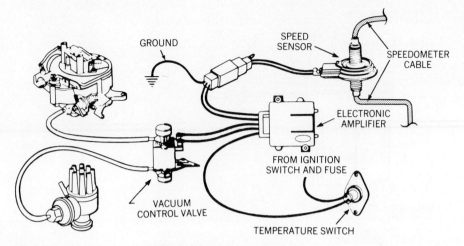

Figure 11-77. Speed-controlled spark systems have speed-sensing switches in the speedometer cable. (AC-Delco)

When you service or troubleshoot a spark control system, you will need the electrical and vacuum diagrams for *that specific year and model of car*. There are some principles, however, that you can use to help sort out different systems:

- A **normally open switch** will energize a solenoid when it closes.

- A **normally closed switch** will deenergize a solenoid when it opens.

GM violated this rule of thumb, however, when it used **reversing relays** on some TCS and combination emission control (CEC) systems in 1971 and '72 to energize a solenoid when a normally closed switch opens, figure 11-80.

Many early systems were built so that if a switch, relay, or solenoid failed, vacuum advance would be available at all times. This was fine for driveability and fuel economy, but not for emission control. In mid-1973, the Environmental Protection Agency (EPA) required all carmakers to build their speed- and transmission-controlled spark systems so that *if a part failed, vacuum advance would be shut off at all times*. Therefore, most systems built after March 1973 follow the model shown in the fourth diagram of figure 11-79. A normally open transmission or speed-sensing switch closes at high speed or in high gear. This energizes a normally deenergized solenoid to open a normally

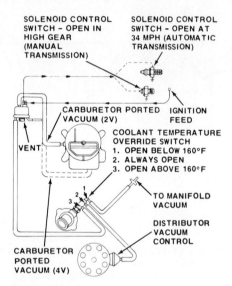

Figure 11-78. Transmission-controlled spark systems have switches activated by gear lever position or by automatic transmission hydraulic pressure. (AMC)

closed vacuum line and allow vacuum spark advance. High- and low-temperature override switches were still used in most systems.

While this became the most common speed- or transmission-controlled spark system after 1973, it was not universal. We went through the preceding summary of switch, solenoid, and valve combinations to emphasize the point that you must check vacuum and electrical diagrams to accurately service any specific system.

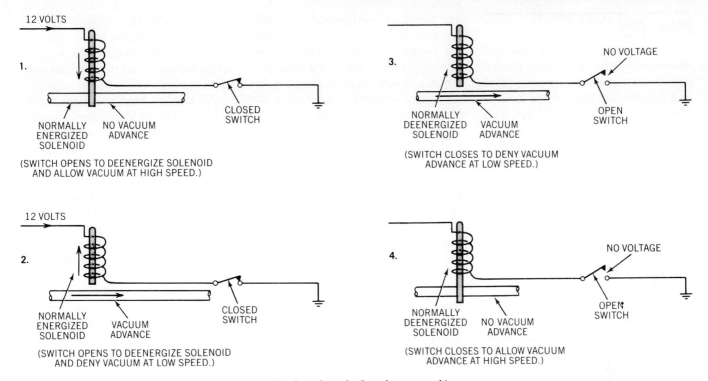

Figure 11-79. Vacuum advance solenoids and switches have been built and connected in four different ways. The fourth method shown is the most common.

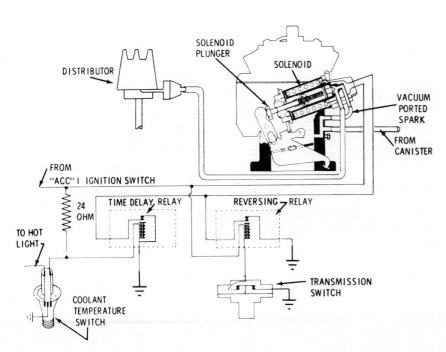

Figure 11-80. This diagram of a GM TCS-CEC system shows that you can't take switch and solenoid positions for granted in any system. (Oldsmobile)

The Demise of Spark-Timing Controls

All of the spark-timing control systems of the 1970's used vacuum and electromechanical devices to delay or retard vacuum advance. As carmakers developed exhaust gas recirculation (EGR) in the mid-1970's, EGR became more effective for reducing NO_x emissions. Many carmakers, therefore, dropped or simplified the spark control systems. Vacuum delay valve and vacuum-retard distributors continued into the late 1970's to assist HC and NO_x control.

By the late 1970's, most carmakers had introduced the first electronic engine control systems, and the earlier timing control systems disappeared. Electronic engine controls use the same principles of delaying timing under certain speed and load conditions to control emissions, but they do it more precisely. Electronic systems use vacuum, speed, and temperature sensors to send information to a central computer, which calculates the best timing for performance, economy, and emission control. You will learn more about these systems in chapter 13.

SUMMARY

The fuel system delivers a measured amount of fuel to the engine, where it is mixed with air before combustion. In a gasoline engine, air and fuel are mixed outside of the cylinders. In a diesel engine, fuel is mixed with air when it is injected into the combustion chamber at the time of ignition.

Ignition in a gasoline engine is provided by a timed electric spark from an electrical ignition system. Ignition in a diesel is controlled by timing fuel injection to the cylinders. Ignition timing for any engine must be advanced as engine speed increases to allow adequate burn time and develop full power.

Almost all ignitions for gasoline engines are the inductive-discharge type. Electromagnetic induction in the ignition coil uses low-voltage current from the battery to develop high voltage necessary for ignition. Low-voltage current in the coil primary winding creates a magnetic field. When primary current stops, the field collapses and induces high voltage in the secondary winding. Secondary available voltage can be as high as 20 to 50 kV, but the coil delivers only the voltage required to fire the plugs. The difference between required voltage and available voltage is the voltage reserve, which should be about 60 percent in a well-tuned engine.

The high-voltage secondary circuit contains the coil secondary winding, the distributor cap and rotor, the ignition (high-tension) cables, and the spark plugs. Secondary voltage always has negative potential (positive ground) for efficient firing action. Delco-Remy direct ignition systems are the exception to this rule, as you will learn in a later chapter.

Important specifications of a spark plug are its thread diameter and seat design, the reach, the heat range, and the gap. Some special-purpose spark plugs have resistors in the center electrode. Others have extended tips.

All breaker-point and many breakerless electronic distributors use centrifugal weights to advance ignition timing in relation to engine speed. These distributors also have vacuum advance mechanisms to advance timing in relation to engine load.

Motor vehicles have been a major cause of air pollution, largely from the fuel they burn. The major automotive air pollutants are HC, CO, and NO_x.

Fuel economy regulations of the mid-1970's created the doubly difficult goals of increasing mileage while reducing emissions.

REVIEW QUESTIONS

Multiple Choice

1. All of the following create resistance in the ignition primary or secondary circuit, EXCEPT:

- **a.** the spark plug gap
- **b.** the rotor air gap
- **c.** the condenser
- **d.** the coil primary winding

2. Mechanic A says that ignition secondary voltage is created by electromagnetic induction. Mechanic B says that secondary voltage is created by primary current. Who is right?

- **a.** A only
- **b.** B only
- **c.** both A and B
- **d.** neither A nor B

3. All of the following determine ignition secondary voltage levels, EXCEPT:

- **a.** the direction of primary current
- **b.** the coil turns ratio
- **c.** the amount of primary current
- **d.** the speed at which primary current stops or changes

4. Mechanic A says that high compression pressures increase ignition resistance. Mechanic B says that lean air-fuel mixtures decrease ignition resistance. Who is right?

- **a.** A only
- **b.** B only
- **c.** both A and B
- **d.** neither A nor B

5. The ignition primary circuit includes all of the following EXCEPT the:

- **a.** ignition switch
- **b.** rotor air gap
- **c.** battery
- **d.** starting bypass circuit

6. An ignition primary (ballast) resistor limits maximum primary voltage to approximately:

- **a.** 6 volts
- **b.** 9 volts
- **c.** 5 volts
- **d.** 12 volts

7. For a breaker-point ignition on any engine, the dwell angle is usually between:

- **a.** 15 and 25 degrees
- **b.** 20 and 30 degrees
- **c.** 30 and 45 degrees
- **d.** 45 and 60 degrees

8. Mechanic A says that as breaker-point gap decreases, dwell increases. Mechanic B says that as breaker-point gap decreases, timing retards. Who is right?

- **a.** A only
- **b.** B only
- **c.** both A and B
- **d.** neither A nor B

9. A typical ignition condenser has a capacity of:

- **a.** 0.02 to 0.03 microfarad
- **b.** 0.18 to 0.32 microfarad
- **c.** 1.8 to 3.2 microfarad
- **d.** 2.0 to 3.0 microfarad

10. Mechanic A says that a spark plug center electrode should always have positive polarity. Mechanic B says that reverse polarity increases voltage reserve. Who is right?

- **a.** A only
- **b.** B only

c. both A and B

d. neither A nor B

11. All of the following are measurements of ignition voltage, EXCEPT:

a. reference voltage

b. required voltage

c. available voltage

d. reserve voltage

12. Ignition secondary circuit resistance is increased by:

a. a narrow spark plug gap

b. a rich air-fuel mixture

c. low engine temperature

d. high engine speeds

13. Coil open-circuit (no-load) secondary voltage is the same as:

a. reference voltage

b. required voltage

c. available voltage

d. ionization voltage

14. Mechanic A says that spark voltage is higher than firing voltage. Mechanic B says that firing voltage is affected by resistance in the cylinder. Who is right?

a. A only

b. B only

c. both A and B

d. neither A nor B

15. The voltage required to jump the rotor air gap is approximately:

a. 12 to 14 volts

b. 500 to 1,000 volts

c. 10 kV to 20 kV

d. 3 kV to 9 kV

16. Ignition (spark plug) cables are made with nonmetallic conductors primarily to:

a. reduce required voltage

b. suppress radiofrequency interference

c. increase spark voltage

d. reduce secondary resistance

17. The thread diameter of most spark plugs for late-model engines is:

a. 10 mm

b. 12 mm

c. 14 mm

d. 18 mm

18. Mechanic A says that plugs with 3/8-inch and 1/2-inch reach are interchangeable. Mechanic B says that 14-mm plugs

with gaskets and tapered seats are not interchangeable. Who is right?

a. A only

b. B only

c. both A and B

d. neither A nor B

19. Mechanic A says that ignition timing advances as speed increases to maintain a relatively constant burn time. Mechanic B says that timing advances under light load because lean mixtures take longer to burn. Who is right?

a. A only

b. B only

c. both A and B

d. neither A nor B

20. Centrifugal advance controls timing in relation to:

a. engine load

b. engine speed

c. air-fuel ratio

d. ignition lag

21. Vacuum advance controls ignition timing in relation to:

a. ignition firing voltage

b. engine speed

c. required voltage

d. engine load

22. Mechanic A says that timing should advance as speed increases. Mechanic B says that timing should advance as load increases. Who is right?

a. A only

b. B only

c. both A and B

d. neither A nor B

23. Mechanic A says that initial timing affects total centrifugal advance for any engine. Mechanic B says that initial timing affects total vacuum advance for any engine. Who is right?

a. A only

b. B only

c. both A and B

d. neither A nor B

24. Originally, the principal reasons for spark timing control modifications were to control:

a. CO emissions

b. CO and HC emissions

c. NO_x and HC emissions

d. particulate and CO emissions

25. Mechanic A says that high HC emissions can be caused by a misfiring spark plug. Mechanic B says that HC emissions are high during deceleration. Who is right?

a. A only

b. B only

c. both A and B

d. neither A nor B

26. Mechanic A says that CO emissions are high with a lean mixture. Mechanic B says that NO_x emissions are high with a lean mixture and high temperature. Who is right?

a. A only

b. B only

c. both A and B

d. neither A nor B

27. Mechanic A says that early spark timing control systems modified vacuum advance. Mechanic B says that early spark timing controls worked to control CO emissions. Who is right?

a. A only

b. B only

c. both A and B

d. neither A nor B

28. The stoichiometric air-fuel ratio for a gasoline engine is approximately:

a. 12.5 : 1

b. 13.6 : 1

c. 14.7 : 1

d. 16 : 1

29. The 4-stroke cycle for each cylinder requires which of the following number of degrees of crankshaft rotation:

a. 180

b. 270

c. 360

d. 720

30. Most 8-cylinder engines produce a power stroke every:

a. 60 degrees of crankshaft rotation

b. 90 degrees of crankshaft rotation

c. 120 degrees of crankshaft rotation

d. 180 degrees of crankshaft rotation

31. Even-firing 6-cylinder engines produce a power stroke every:

a. 60 degrees of crankshaft rotation

b. 90 degrees of crankshaft rotation

c. 120 degrees of crankshaft rotation

d. 180 degrees of crankshaft rotation

32. Four-cylinder engines produce a power stroke every:

a. 60 degrees of crankshaft rotation

b. 90 degrees of crankshaft rotation

c. 120 degrees of crankshaft rotation

d. 180 degrees of crankshaft rotation

Fill in the Blank

33. The _____ circuit receives low voltage from the battery and uses it to induce higher voltage in the coil secondary winding.

34. The coil secondary winding has several thousand turns of fine wire and is connected to the high-voltage _____ circuit of the ignition system.

35. In an inductive-discharge ignition system, voltage is induced in the primary and secondary coils with each _____ in current flow.

36. If the turns ratio between the primary and secondary winding is 200 : 1, then the voltage in the secondary winding would be _____ times greater than the voltage in the primary winding.

37. When the magnetic field produced in the coil primary and secondary windings is at full strength, it is called _____ .

38. An ignition coil produces only enough voltage to create an _____ .

39. With retarded, or delayed, ignition timing, high temperatures occur _____ in the combustion process.

40. Spark timing controls of the early 1970's delayed vacuum advance at _____ and _____ speeds and allowed vacuum advance at _____ speeds.

41. Most transmission-controlled spark systems use a normally _____ transmission switch and a normally _____ vacuum solenoid.

42. If a part fails in a transmission-controlled spark system built after mid-1973, vacuum advance is usually _____ at all times.

43. The exact top of a piston stroke is called _____ .

44. The firing order of *most* inline 4-cylinder engines is _____ .

45. In a gasoline engine, an air-fuel ratio of approximately 14.7 : 1 is called a _____ ratio.

12 BASIC ELECTRONIC IGNITION SYSTEMS

WHAT

This chapter continues with ignition systems by examining the solid-state electronic ignitions that have become the "standard," or "conventional," systems used by almost all carmakers. There are several reasons for the wholesale changeover from breaker-point ignitions that occurred in the mid-1970's:

• By the 1970's electronic technology had advanced to the point that economical and reliable solid-state devices could be mass produced by the millions.

• Increasingly more stringent emission control and fuel economy requirements demanded more accurate and uniform control of ignition and spark timing.

• Engineers found that electronic systems allowed them to control engine operation more precisely and with fewer compromises than electromechanical devices did.

Even though the 1970's are considered the decade when the "electronic revolution" started in the auto industry, electronic ignitions were not a radical change. A basic electronic ignition simply has the breaker points replaced by an electronic switch. Most original equipment electronic ignitions are inductive-discharge systems that generate and distribute high ignition voltage in the same way that breaker-point systems have done since 1912. You will find that all the principles of current flow, dwell, coils, distributors, spark plugs, and spark advance are present in both electronic ignitions and breaker-point systems.

WHY

For the past decade, automobile service has been going through a transition. Nowhere is the transition more apparent than in ignition service. Modern ignition service has become a field of electronic testing and diagnosis. You will find it easier to master electronic skills if you understand how electronic principles are similar to electrical principles that have always been used in automobiles. Basic electronic ignition systems are a good place to learn these similarities. Today, a professional mechanic must be able to service both breaker-point and electronic ignitions. If you understand how the systems are similar, you can do your job faster and better.

GOALS

After studying this chapter, you should be able to:

1. Explain the similarities between inductive-discharge electronic ignition and breaker-point ignition.

2. Explain the operation of magnetic-pulse, metal-detection, and Hall-effect ignition trigger circuits.

3. Explain dwell and current regulation in electronic ignitions.

4. Explain the differences between capacitive-discharge and inductive-discharge ignitions.

5. Identify various original equipment electronic ignition systems and the principal parts of each.

6. Recognize ignition timing and spark advance devices for electronic ignitions.

PRIMARY CIRCUIT CONTROL

Breaker points are simple, cheap, and (within limits) reliable devices for switching primary current. They have disadvantages, however, that make them less than ideal for the precise ignition control needed on modern engines:

1. Mechanical wear of the point rubbing block on the distributor cam decreases the gap and increases the dwell angle. This retards basic ignition timing and reduces performance and fuel economy.

2. Force applied by the point spring to the rubbing block increases wear on the distributor cam and shaft bushings. This too causes timing and dwell to vary, not only over a period of time, but also from cylinder to cylinder.

3. At high speeds, the points open and close so fast that the spring can't maintain uniform pressure on the movable arm. The points can actually bounce, which upsets both dwell and timing and creates a high-speed misfire.

4. Even with a condenser of required capacitance and with perfect point alignment and spring tension, some arcing always occurs across the points as they open. This causes burning and pitting, and upsets timing and dwell.

5. Because of their small size and an opening gap of a few thousandths of an inch, points can only switch current of 4 to 6 amperes, maximum. Even with a coil that could produce 50 kV of available voltage, breaker points cannot handle the current needed for full magnetic saturation.

6. Breaker points rely on physical movement to control primary current time, and this time changes with engine speed. Therefore coil saturation and available voltage are always a compromise between high and low engine speeds.

Electronic Primary Circuit Advantages

Electronic ignitions do not rely on mechanical switching devices to control primary current.

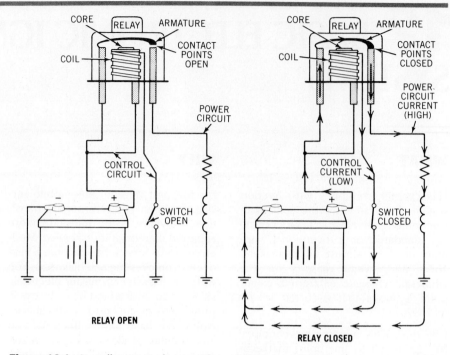

Figure 12-1. A small amount of current through the relay coil closes the contacts and allows the relay power circuit to carry a large amount of current.

1. Electronic ignitions have no moving parts that bear against each other to cause mechanical wear. Distributor shaft bushings can still wear from rotational forces, but there is no sideways force from a spring and rubbing block to accelerate the wear.

2. Dwell and timing do not change during several thousand miles of operation because there is no rubbing block to wear down.

3. Electronic switching devices cannot "bounce" at high speeds. Switching operation is uniform from idle to maximum rpm.

4. The triggering devices in electronic distributors do not carry primary current. Therefore, current is not limited by the physical capacity of breaker points. Engineers can provide any amount of primary current based on the design of the coil and the capacity of the transistors in the electronic system.

Ignition Transistor Operation

Primary current control in an electronic ignition is based on the ability of a transistor to control a high current flow in response to a very small current. The small current is created by a small voltage applied to its base. Chapter 4 explains basic transistor operation. An important feature of a transistor for ignition control is its ability to act as a solid-state relay.

Figure 12-1 shows an electromagnetic relay of the kind used to control a starter motor, a horn, or a headlamp circuit. When the control switch is closed, a small amount of current flows through the relay coil. This sets up a magnetic field that attracts the relay armature, closes the relay contacts, and completes the power circuit. When the relay control switch is open, the electromagnetic field collapses, and the armature spring opens the contacts of the power circuit. Current through the relay coil and control circuit may be only 1 or 2 amperes. Current through the power circuit may be 10 or 20 amperes, or more. (A starter motor can draw several hundred amperes through a starter relay.)

If we replace the relay with a power transistor, we can achieve the same kind of switching. In figure 12-2A, the switch to the transistor base is open. No voltage is applied to the base, and no current flows through the emitter-to-base circuit. Also, the transistor emitter-to-base junction acts as a

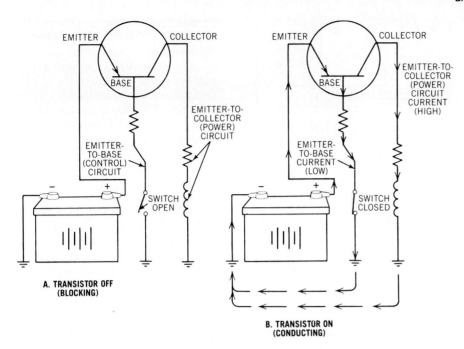

Figure 12-2. In this circuit, a transistor has replaced the relay for the same kind of current control.

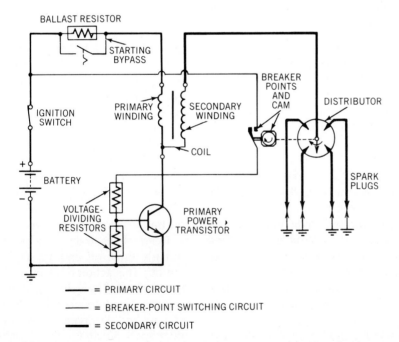

— = PRIMARY CIRCUIT

— = BREAKER-POINT SWITCHING CIRCUIT

— = SECONDARY CIRCUIT

Figure 12-3. In this transistorized ignition, breaker points are the trigger for the power transistor, but they do not carry full primary current.

BURNED TO A CRISP

Usually when we think of something that's burned to a crisp, we visualize it as blackened like charcoal. So it is with burned toast, a well-done steak, or the ashes of a bonfire. It's not that way with spark plugs, however; it's just the opposite.

The ceramic insulator tip of a spark plug that's badly overheated, "fried," or "burned up" isn't black; it's almost pure white. This condition reflects overly high operating temperatures of the plug that completely burn away any residue or "ash" that might collect on the tip. The plug is literally operating "white hot." A blackened plug, on the other hand, isn't burned to a crisp. It's operating too cold. Black deposits on a plug tip may be gasoline residue from an overly rich air-fuel mixture. You can think of it as "gasoline ash." Black deposits also can be from oil that has gotten into the combustion chamber past leaky piston rings or valve guides and hasn't been completely burned. In either case the plug wasn't operating hot enough to burn itself clean.

You can't solve engine air-fuel ratio problems or oiling problems by changing spark plugs, but you can tell a lot about engine conditions by learning to recognize a plug that's burned to a crisp and one that isn't.

diode, and no current flows through the emitter-to-collector circuit. If we close the switch and apply a small voltage to the base, we cause a small amount of current to flow through the emitter-to-base circuit. This creates a forward bias on the emitter-to-base junction and allows a larger amount of current to flow through the emitter-to-collector power circuit, figure 12-2B.

This is basically how an electronic ignition system uses transistors to turn primary current on and off. The early transistorized ignitions of 20 or 25 years ago used distributor breaker points as a mechanical switch to control voltage applied to a transistor

base, figure 12-3. Full primary current did not flow through the points; it flowed through the transistor. The breaker points carried less than 1 ampere of current. Pitting and burning of the points due to arcing were greatly reduced. But the points still bounced at high speed and suffered mechanical wear.

The electronic ignitions that became standard replaced the points with an electronic signal generator that has no rubbing parts. Modern electronic ignitions provide uniform timing, dwell, and secondary voltage at all engine speeds and loads for tens of thousands of miles. Before we go on to look at the signal generators in electronic distributors, you should un-

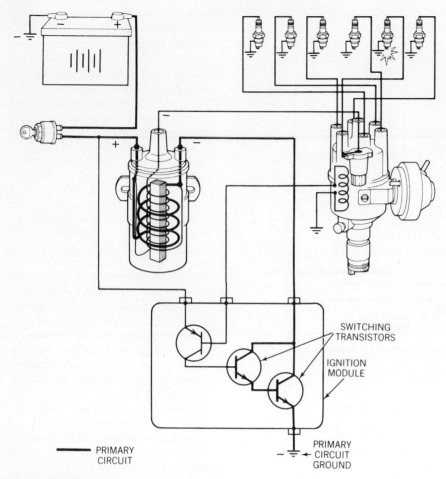

SWITCHING
TRANSISTORS

IGNITION
MODULE

PRIMARY
CIRCUIT

PRIMARY
CIRCUIT
GROUND

Figure 12-4. The ignition control module switches primary current on and off on the ground side of the coil, just as breaker points do in a breaker-point system.

derstand a couple more things about transistor control of primary current.

In an electronic ignition, *no primary current passes through the distributor.* All primary current passes through an **ignition control module**, which is an assembly of transistors, resistors, capacitors, and other electronic devices. The ignition coil positive (+) terminal is connected to battery voltage through the ignition switch and receives primary current similarly to a coil in a breaker-point system, figure 12-4. The coil negative (−) terminal is connected to ground through the ignition module. Primary current is thus switched on and off on the ground side of the coil by the transistors in the module.

Most ignition modules use one or more large power transistors to switch primary current. The **power transistors** can reliably handle current up to

10 amperes, much more than breaker points can handle. These are the **switching transistors** of the primary circuit. The switching transistor, or transistors, are controlled by another **driver transistor** that receives timing voltage signals from the signal generator in the distributor. Figure 12-5 is a simplified ignition module circuit. Here is how it works.

When the ignition switch is turned on, a low base current flows through the driver transistor, T1. The driver transistor turns on, and its emitter-to-collector current flows to the base of transistor T2. Transistor T1 requires only very low base current and voltage (a few millivolts and milliamperes), but it produces enough collector current to turn on T2. Voltage applied to the base of T2 turns it on. Emitter-to-collector current from T2 is applied to the base of transistor T3 to

switch it on. Transistors T2 and T3 are connected in a current-amplifying arrangement, called a **Darlington circuit**. Ignition primary current flows through the ignition coil and builds up the magnetic field as long as all three transistors are switched on.

As the engine starts and runs, the signal generator in the distributor changes the voltage on the base of transistor T1 each time a piston nears tdc on the compression stroke. The voltage change on the base of T1 turns this transistor off. Its collector current no longer flows to the base of T2. T2 similarly turns off and causes T3 to turn off. This action turns off coil primary current. The coil magnetic field collapses, and secondary voltage is induced and distributed to the appropriate spark plug.

Electronic ignition control modules have several forms, but all work on these principles. Some modules are large assemblies, figure 12-6. Other modules are small integrated circuit assemblies, mounted in the distributor, figure 12-7. Some modules, like the original Chrysler design, use a single large power transistor to switch primary current. Others use several power transistors in a Darlington arrangement.

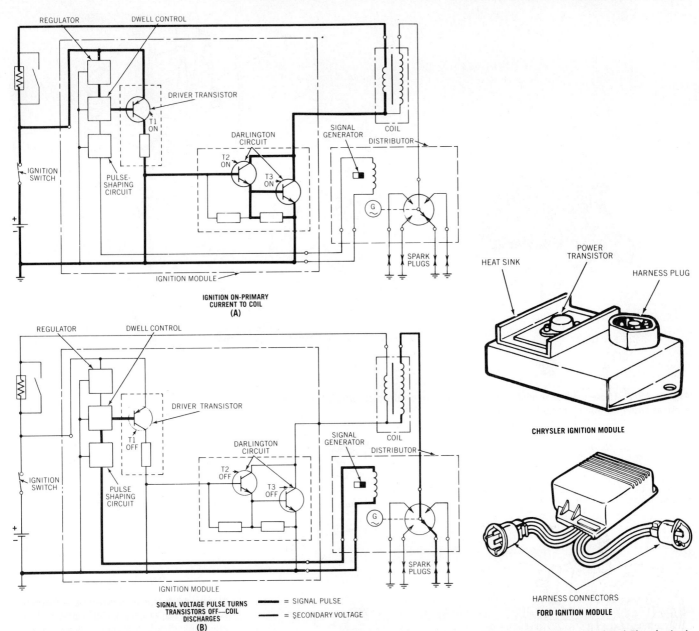

Figure 12-5. (A) With the ignition switch on, current flows through the switching transistors to charge the coil. (B) A trigger signal from the distributor turns off the driver and switching transistors to discharge the coil.

Figure 12-6. These Ford and Chrysler ignition modules are mounted in the engine compartment, separately from the distributor. (Champion Spark Plug)

ELECTRONIC DISTRIBUTOR TRIGGER DEVICES

You have seen how primary current is switched on and off by transistors in the ignition control module. Timing of the switching is controlled by a trigger device in the distributor. We have called this device a "signal generator" because it generates a voltage signal that changes the bias on the base of the driver transistor.

The signal generator is a device that triggers ignition much as the cam and breaker points do in a breaker-point ignition. Remember, though, that the signal generator, or trigger device, does not carry ignition primary current. All electronic distributor trigger devices create or alter a voltage signal on the base of the driver transistor. Depending on the driver transistor design, this voltage may be only a few millivolts (thousandths of a volt), and

its current may be only a few milliamperes. There are several ways to create such a voltage signal in an electronic distributor:

1. Magnetic-pulse generator
2. Hall-effect switch
3. Metal-detection circuit
4. Optical (light-detection) circuit

All trigger devices consist of a trigger wheel that rotates with the distributor shaft and a stationary sensor, figure

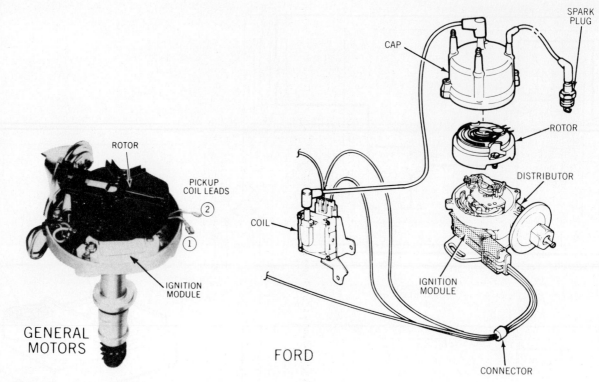

ROTOR

PICKUP COIL LEADS

② ①

IGNITION MODULE

GENERAL MOTORS

CAP

SPARK PLUG

ROTOR

DISTRIBUTOR

COIL

IGNITION MODULE

CONNECTOR

FORD

Figure 12-7. These ignition modules are mounted in or on the distributor. They work the same as larger modules. (Ford) (Champion Spark Plug)

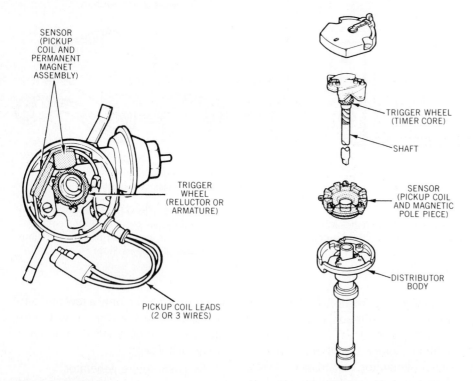

SENSOR (PICKUP COIL AND PERMANENT MAGNET ASSEMBLY)

TRIGGER WHEEL (RELUCTOR OR ARMATURE)

PICKUP COIL LEADS (2 OR 3 WIRES)

TRIGGER WHEEL (TIMER CORE)

SHAFT

SENSOR (PICKUP COIL AND MAGNETIC POLE PIECE)

DISTRIBUTOR BODY

Figure 12-8. These magnetic pulse-generators all use a low-reluctance trigger wheel to induce a voltage signal in a pickup coil. (Chrysler) (Chevrolet)

Manufacturer	Sensor	Trigger Wheel
AMC	Sensor	Trigger wheel
Bosch	Pickup coil & pole piece	Trigger wheel
Chrysler	Pickup coil	Reluctor
Ford	Stator	Armature
General Motors	Pole piece & magnetic pickup	Timer core

Figure 12-9. Manufacturers have different names for the sensors and trigger wheels in electronic distributors, but all devices serve the same purpose.

12-8. Figure 12-9 lists the names that manufacturers have given to these devices. We will generally use the terms "trigger wheel" and "sensor" or "pickup coil" to describe their operation.

Magnetic-Pulse Generator

Magnetic-pulse generators are the most common trigger devices in electronic distributors. The original Chrysler, Ford, and GM electronic ignitions used them, and still do today. So do most European and Japanese ignitions. These devices have a stationary sensor with a permanent magnet and a pole piece. Fine wire is wrapped around the pole piece to form a pickup coil, figure 12-10. The permanent magnet establishes a field around the pickup coil. If the strength (magnetic flux) of this field changes, it will induce a small voltage in the pickup coil.

Whether the pickup coil has one pole piece or several, it works the same way. If the pickup has several pole pieces, the coil winding is wound around each in series so that the voltages at each pole piece add together for a single signal voltage, figure 12-10.

The trigger wheel for a magnetic-pulse generator is attached to the distributor shaft and usually has as many teeth, or spokes, as the engine has cylinders. The trigger wheel is made of steel that is nonmagnetic but that has low magnetic reluctance (high permeability). As a tooth of the trigger wheel enters the magnetic field around the pole piece and pickup coil, magnetic flux concentrates in the tooth. This changes the magnetic field

strength and induces a voltage in the pickup coil. This voltage is proportional to the *rate of change of the magnetic flux.*

Pickup coil voltage is low when a trigger wheel tooth is farthest from the pole piece in degrees of rotation. As a tooth rotates closer to the pole piece, the magnetic field starts to increase, and voltage starts to increase in the pickup coil. Voltage in the pickup coil is an ac voltage, figure 12-11, that develops as follows:

1. Voltage increases with positive polarity as a tooth approaches the pole piece.

2. Voltage falls to zero when the tooth is directly aligned with the pole piece.

3. The magnetic field reverses, and voltage then increases with opposite polarity as the tooth moves away from the pole piece.

Even though magnetic field strength is strongest when the tooth is aligned with the pole piece, the *rate of change of the flux density* is zero at this point. That is why the voltage drops to zero. This point corresponds with the ignition timing point for one cylinder. It is the same as the point where breaker points open. The distributor pickup

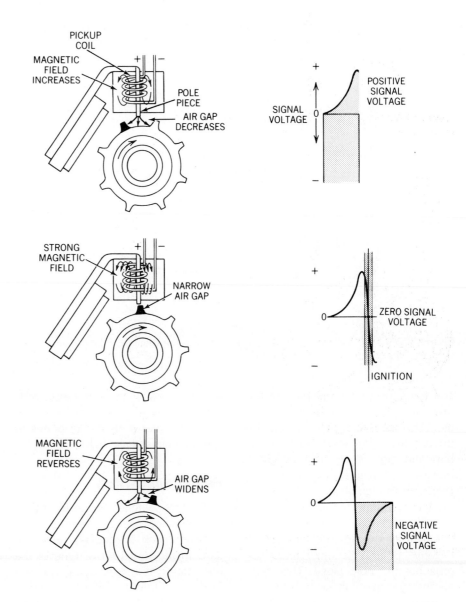

Figure 12-10. Whether the pickup coil has a single pole piece or multiple pole pieces, it generates a signal voltage the same way. (Bosch)

Figure 12-11. The pickup coil generates an ac voltage as the trigger wheel moves in and out of the magnetic field.

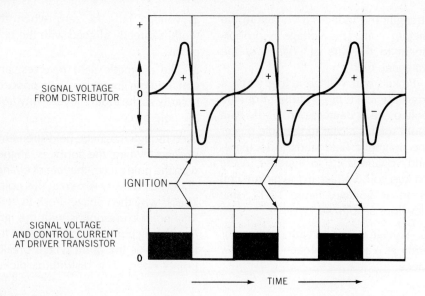

Figure 12-12. A circuit in the ignition module converts continuous ac voltage pulses from the pickup coil to dc square-wave pulses that signal the driver transistor. (Bosch)

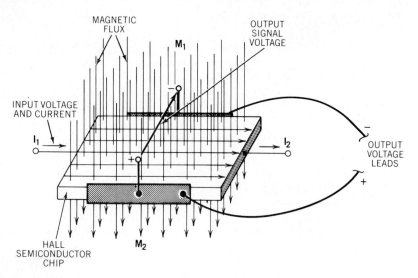

Figure 12-13. The Hall-effect output voltage changes as the strength of the magnetic field changes. Input current must stay constant.

coil is connected to the base of the driver transistor in the ignition module. The zero-voltage signal on the driver transistor changes the transistor bias and turns it off. The switching transistors then turn off primary current, and the ignition coil discharges secondary voltage to the plug.

As the pickup coil voltage induced by one trigger wheel tooth changes to negative polarity, another tooth approaches the pole piece. This starts another positive voltage pulse in the pickup coil. The ignition module receives continuous sine wave ac voltage from the pickup coil. A pulse-shaping circuit in the module converts these signals to dc voltage pulses so that the driver transistor responds to zero-voltage signals, figure 12-12.

Hall-Effect Switch

Hall-effect switches began to appear in production ignition systems in the 1970's. Bosch introduced such systems in the mid-1970's. One of the first major domestic uses was on Chrysler's Omni and Horizon models in 1978. Their use has increased with other carmakers since.

Like a magnetic-pulse generator, a **Hall-effect switch** has a stationary sensor and a rotating trigger wheel. However, it does not generate a signal voltage in the same way. In fact, it requires a small input voltage to generate an output voltage.

The Hall effect is the ability to generate a small voltage in semiconductor material by passing current through it in one direction and applying a magnetic field to it at a right angle to its surface, figure 12-13. When current flows through a semiconductor chip from I_1 to I_2 and magnetic flux crosses the chip at a right angle from M_1 to M_2, voltage develops across the chip at a right angle to the input current. If we hold the input current steady and vary the magnetic field, the output voltage will change in proportion to field strength.

A typical Hall-effect switch in a distributor has a Hall element, a permanent magnet, and a ring of metal blades, or shutters, similar to a trigger wheel. The blades may hang down from the rotor, as on Bosch and Chrysler distributors, figure 12-14. Or, they may be on a separate ring on the shaft, as on the Ford and GM distributors, figure 12-15.

When a shutter blade enters the gap between the magnet and the Hall element, it creates a magnetic shunt that changes the field strength through the Hall element. This causes the Hall output voltage to change, which changes the bias on the ignition driver transistor just as the signal from a magnetic-pulse generator does.

The Hall element is a complex integrated circuit with the Hall-effect semiconductor and an output voltage generator. The generator receives the signal voltage from the Hall chip, processes it, and sends a square-wave voltage pulse to the ignition module. Figure 12-16 summarizes the relationships of the Hall-effect switch and the complete ignition circuit. A key point to remember is that ignition occurs when the rotating vane *leaves* the window between the Hall-effect switch and the magnet.

Although a Hall-effect switch requires connections for input voltage, its output voltage does not depend on

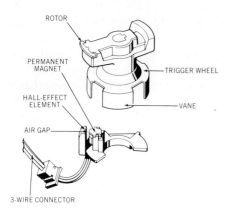

Figure 12-14. This Hall-effect distributor has the trigger wheel vanes on the bottom of the rotor. (Bosch)

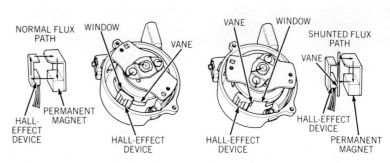

Figure 12-15. The Hall-effect wheel of this distributor is on the shaft rotor base. These views show how the vanes and windows change the magnetic field around the Hall-effect device. (Ford)

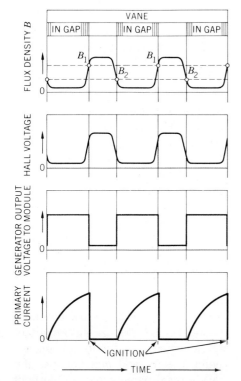

Vane	Magnetic field (B)	Hall voltage	Generator Output Signal Voltage to Module	Ignition Module Transistors
not in the air gap	permeates the Hall layer	maximum	minimum	switched off
enters the air gap	is deflected away from the Hall layer	drops	increases abruptly	switch *on*
in the air gap	very weak at the Hall layer	minimum	maximum	switched *on* (energy storage)
leaves the air gap	permeates the Hall layer increasingly	increases	drops abruptly	switch *off* (**ignition point**)

Figure 12-16. The table and graphs explain the relationships of Hall-effect signal voltage and ignition discharge. (Bosch)

the speed of the rotating trigger wheel. Therefore, it generates a full-strength output voltage even at slow cranking speeds.

Metal-Detection Circuit

The metal-detection circuit creates an output signal voltage similarly to a magnetic-pulse generator and a Hall-effect switch. This kind of signal generator does not have a permanent magnet, however. It receives an input voltage from the ignition control module to an electromagnet in the distributor sensor. The rotating metal teeth of the trigger wheel affect the strength of the electromagnetic field and cause voltage pulses in the sensor. The ignition control module senses these voltage pulses as signals to open the ignition primary circuit. The module provides primary switching action similar to the action of other ignition modules. Like a Hall-effect switch, a metal-detection cir-

cuit provides full-strength voltage signals at slow speeds.

Prestolite is the major manufacturer of metal-detection electronic ignition systems. American Motors cars from 1975 through 1977 used a Prestolite electronic ignition called "Breaker-less Inductive Discharge (BID)" ignition. International Harvester light-duty gasoline engines of the late 1970's have a variation of the same system. In the AMC-Prestolite distributor, the trigger wheel has teeth

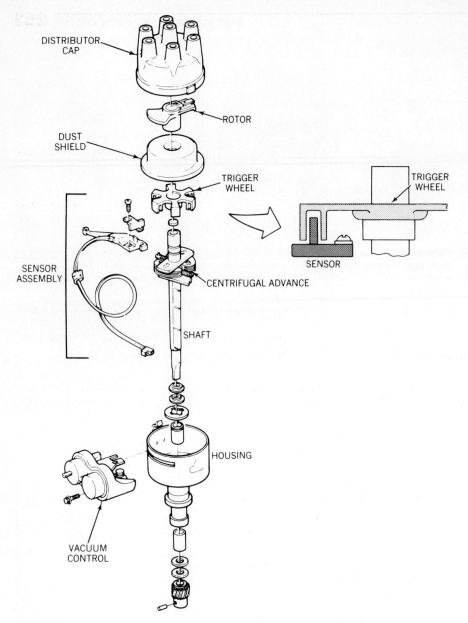

DISTRIBUTOR
CAP

ROTOR

DUST
SHIELD

TRIGGER
WHEEL

TRIGGER
WHEEL

SENSOR
ASSEMBLY

SENSOR

CENTRIFUGAL ADVANCE

SHAFT

HOUSING

VACUUM
CONTROL

Figure 12-17. This Prestolite distributor used by American Motors has a metal-detection triggering device. (AMC)

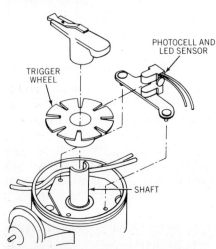

PHOTOCELL AND
LED SENSOR

TRIGGER
WHEEL

SHAFT

Figure 12-18. Light-detection triggering devices have been used in some aftermarket ignition conversions.

with an inverted U shape, figure 12-17, that pass over the sensor. The International-Prestolite distributor has a trigger wheel and sensor similar to the trigger wheel and pickup coil in Chrysler and Ford magnetic-pulse distributors.

Optical (Light-Detection) Circuit

An optical signal generator uses the light from a light-emitting diode (LED) to strike a phototransistor and generate a voltage signal. The trigger wheel is a slotted disc that passes between the LED and the phototransistor,

figure 12-18. When a slot is between the LED and the transistor, the light beam creates a voltage signal that triggers the ignition module.

Several aftermarket systems have been made to convert breaker-point distributors to optically triggered electronic distributors. Chrysler is the first major carmaker to use an optical signal generator as original equipment.

DWELL IN ELECTRONIC IGNITIONS

In chapter 11, you learned that dwell is the period when the primary circuit is on (closed) and the coil magnetic field is increasing. In a breaker-point ignition, dwell is always measured in degrees of distributor rotation, but it really represents coil charging time. Because electronic ignitions are inductive-discharge systems, they also have a dwell period to charge the coil. However, the start of the dwell period is not controlled by a signal from the distributor as it is when the points close in a breaker-point system.

The ignition control module controls the start of the dwell period through a timing or a current-sensing circuit. When you service ignition systems, you will learn that you can measure dwell in degrees of distributor rotation, using an oscilloscope, figure 12-19. This is an important service measurement for a breaker-point system, and you can use the dwell measurement to troubleshoot several parts of the distributor.

You can use an oscilloscope to observe the dwell period for an electronic ignition, and you can identify some mechanical problems in electronic distributors from the dwell portion of the pattern. However, dwell is not adjustable in most electronic distributors, and you normally do not use the dwell measurement as a service specification. There are two kinds of electronic ignitions in terms of dwell control:

1. Fixed-dwell systems
2. Variable-dwell systems

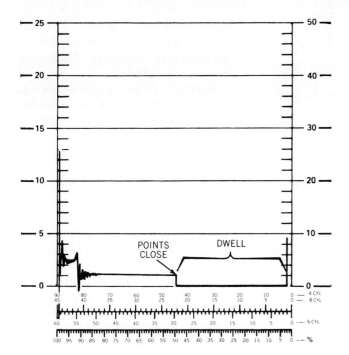

Figure 12-19. This primary circuit scope pattern for a breaker-point ignition shows that dwell starts when the points close and stays relatively constant at all speeds. (Coats Diagnostic)

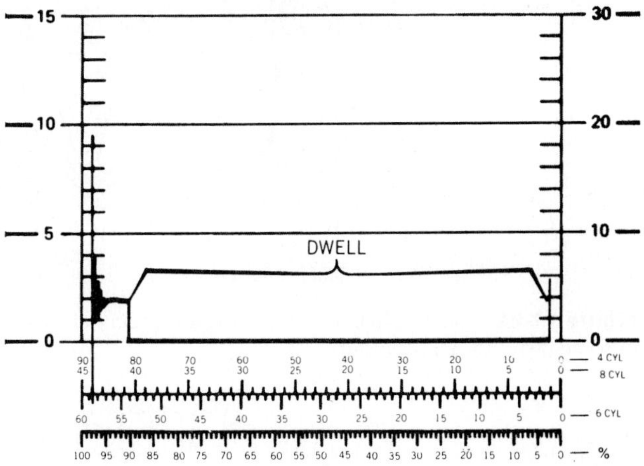

Figure 12-20. In a fixed-dwell electronic ignition, dwell starts when the transistor turns on and stays relatively constant at all speeds. (Coats Diagnostic)

Fixed-Dwell Electronic Ignitions

A **fixed-dwell electronic ignition** has a ballast resistor in the primary circuit to limit current and voltage. Dwell starts when secondary voltage and current fall below specific levels. The ballast resistor controls primary voltage and current as it does in a breaker-point system. Dwell is the same in distributor degrees at all engine speeds. Figure 12-20 shows a typical fixed-dwell electronic ignition primary circuit oscilloscope pattern.

The original Chrysler electronic ignition is a fixed-dwell system and continues in use on some engines today. The original Ford solid-state ignitions and Dura-Spark II systems are fixed-dwell systems with ballast resistors, as are many Bosch and Japanese electronic ignitions.

Variable-Dwell Electronic Ignitions

In a **variable-dwell electronic ignition**, the dwell period varies in distributor degrees at different engine speeds but stays relatively constant in actual time. Figure 12-21 shows the

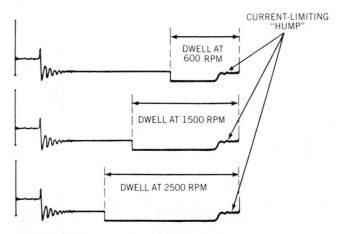

Figure 12-21. In a variable-dwell ignition, dwell measured in degrees changes with speed, but dwell *time* stays relatively constant. (Delco-Remy)

primary circuit oscilloscope pattern for a variable-dwell electronic ignition. Notice that the dwell period in distributor degrees is relatively short at idle and increases at higher rpm.

A circuit in the ignition control module senses primary current to the coil and reduces the current when the magnetic field is fully saturated. Notice the small hump toward the end of the dwell periods in figure 12-21. This is the point where current is reduced. Primary current is not shut off, how-

ever, and voltage remains applied to the primary until the module receives a trigger signal from the distributor.

Variable-dwell systems do not use a ballast resistor as fixed-dwell and breaker-point ignitions do. The coil and the ignition module receive full battery or charging system voltage at all times when the engine is cranking or running. The variable-dwell feature allows the coil to receive the right amount of current for full magnetic saturation because the dwell *time* re-

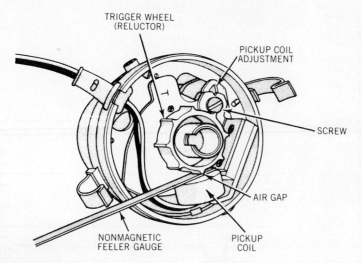

Figure 12-22. The air gap between the trigger wheel (reluctor) and pickup coil is adjustable in some distributors. (Chrysler)

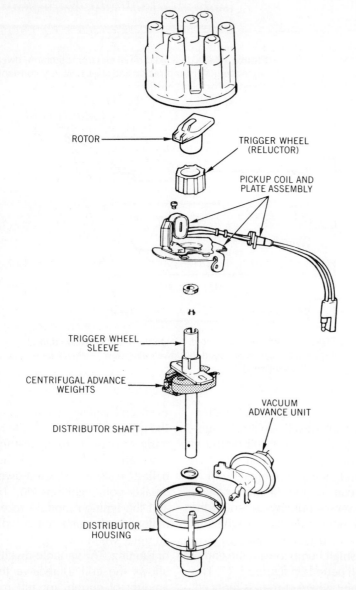

Figure 12-23. Early electronic distributors have centrifugal advance mechanisms similar to those in breaker-point distributors. (Chrysler)

mains relatively constant. This ensures enough coil secondary voltage for ignition under the most demanding operating conditions.

Ignition coils for variable-dwell systems generally have higher available voltage capabilities than the coils for fixed-dwell systems. These coils usually have lower primary resistance and a higher turns ratio.

The GM Delco-Remy high-energy ignition (HEI) systems are all variable-dwell systems, as are Ford Motorcraft Dura-Spark I and thick-film integrated (TFI) systems. Other variable-dwell systems include the AMC and International Prestolite ignitions, most Chrysler Hall-effect ignitions, some VW Bosch systems, Marelli systems, and several Japanese ignitions.

Dwell And Trigger Wheel Gap

The clearance, or gap, between the rotating trigger wheel and the sensor or pickup coil is adjustable on some electronic distributors, figure 12-22. This gap affects the strength of the magnetic field in the pickup coil and thus the strength of the trigger signal. In most distributors, however, it does not affect dwell or timing as the point gap does in a breaker-point distributor. Only in the International Prestolite distributor does the trigger wheel and sensor gap affect dwell.

SPARK ADVANCE IN ELECTRONIC IGNITIONS

Spark advance in a basic electronic ignition system (on an engine without electronic engine controls) is controlled in the same way it is in a breaker-point system. The trigger wheel is mounted on a sleeve that rotates on the distributor drive shaft, figure 12-23. Centrifugal advance weights rotate the trigger wheel position a few degrees ahead of distributor shaft rotation as engine speed increases. This advances the trigger signal to advance the timing. In a Delco HEI distributor, the advance weights are above the trigger wheel and pickup coil, figure 12-24, as in a

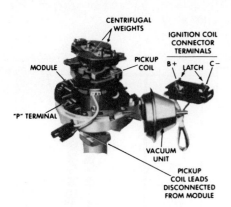

Figure 12-24. Centrifugal advance weights in Delco HEI distributors are above the trigger wheel. (Delco-Remy)

Delco V-8 breaker-point distributor. In most other distributors, the weights are below the "breaker plate."

Basic electronic distributors also have vacuum advance mechanisms to change timing in response to engine load. The vacuum advance works as it does in a breaker-point distributor. The vacuum diaphragm linkage is attached to the plate that holds the sensor or pickup coil, figure 12-25. (We can call it the "breaker plate" or the "baseplate.") High vacuum at light load rotates the plate opposite to distributor rotation. This causes the pickup coil or sensor to align with the trigger wheel tooth sooner and advance the timing.

The first generation of electronic ignitions in the early and mid-1970's used the simple centrifugal and vacuum advance mechanisms that breaker-point distributors have. In the late 1970's, carmakers began to equip engines with control systems that perform spark timing and fuel-metering functions electronically. A central computer receives signals from sensors that measure engine temperature, speed, manifold pressure (vacuum), airflow, exhaust oxygen content, and other operating factors. The computer then changes ignition timing more accurately than simple centrifugal and vacuum controls can. Electronic engine controls are commonplace today, and you will learn more about them in a later chapter.

The ignition systems used with electronic engine controls have trigger devices and primary circuit controls of

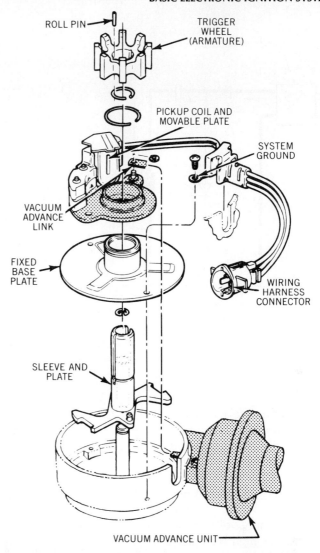

Figure 12-25. Early electronic distributors also have vacuum advance mechanisms similar to those in breaker-point distributors. (Ford)

the kind you have studied here. The distributors do not have centrifugal and vacuum advance mechanisms. They are principally secondary voltage distributors. Most have magnetic-pulse or Hall-effect triggering devices for basic timing. The triggering devices also act as engine speed sensors or crankshaft position sensors in electronic engine control systems.

CAPACITIVE-DISCHARGE ELECTRONIC IGNITIONS

Almost all original equipment ignition systems—breaker point and electronic—are inductive-discharge systems. There is another kind of ignition system, however, that you may find

on a few engines. This is a **capacitive-discharge (CD) ignition**.

In a capacitive-discharge (CD) ignition, primary current and voltage charge a large capacitor in the ignition module. The time when the ignition module circuit is on and the capacitor is charging corresponds to dwell in an inductive-discharge system. In a CD system, current does not flow through the coil during this time. Instead, it flows to the storage capacitor. A charging circuit in the module has a transformer that increases battery voltage to charge the capacitor to about 300 to 400 volts. While the capacitor is charging, a silicon-controlled rectifier (SCR) in the module acts as an open switch to prevent capacitor discharge, figure 12-26.

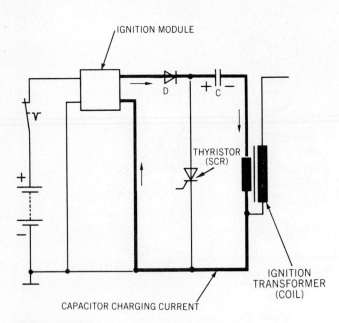

Figure 12-26. A CD ignition stores energy by charging the capacitor. The thyristor, or SCR, blocks the discharge circuit. (Bosch)

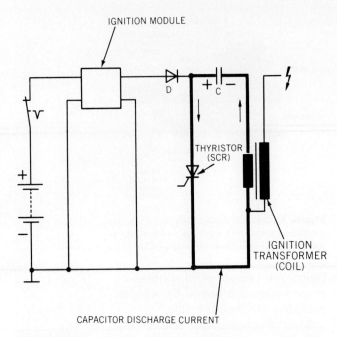

Figure 12-27. When the thyristor, or SCR, receives a trigger voltage from the distributor, it allows the capacitor to discharge energy to the coil primary winding. (Bosch)

When a triggering device—electronic signal generator or breaker points—sends a signal pulse to the gate of the SCR, it closes the capacitor discharge circuit. The capacitor then discharges its voltage to the coil primary winding, figure 12-27. The sudden increase in primary voltage and current flow induces high secondary voltage in the coil. Secondary voltage is then distributed to a spark plug as in any other ignition system.

In an inductive-discharge ignition, primary current flows through the coil during a dwell period and is turned *off* to induce high secondary voltage. In a capacitive-discharge ignition, primary current and voltage charge a capacitor. The capacitor is then switched *on* to the coil to induce high secondary voltage.

In either kind of system, secondary voltage is induced by the relative motion of a collapsing or expanding magnetic field. The speed at which the capacitor discharges and the coil field expands is faster than the speed at which the field collapses in an inductive-discharge system. A CD ignition, therefore, can produce a higher and faster firing voltage, figure 12-28. This can be an advantage in high-performance engines or in engines with lean

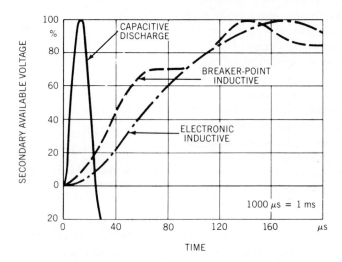

Figure 12-28. Secondary voltage can be higher and rise faster in a CD ignition, but ignition duration may not be long enough for many engines. (Bosch)

mixtures and other high ignition resistance. The CD spark duration may be too short, however, for reliable ignition in many passenger car engines.

ORIGINAL EQUIPMENT ELECTRONIC IGNITIONS

The following sections briefly describe the major electronic ignitions used by domestic carmakers, as well as some imported systems. While all are inductive-discharge systems, trigger devices and ignition module

circuits vary slightly from one manufacturer to another. The secondary components of these systems do the same job of high-voltage distribution as the secondary components of breaker-point systems. Because they often handle higher voltages, however, many have unique shapes.

All carmakers have modified their ignition systems slightly from year to year and model to model. We can't give you all the details, but we will summarize the basic changes. When you service an electronic ignition on a

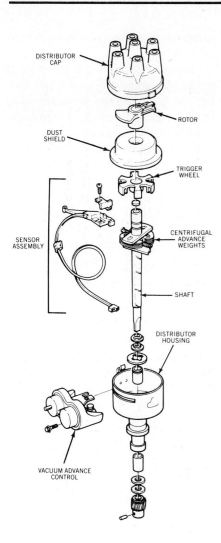

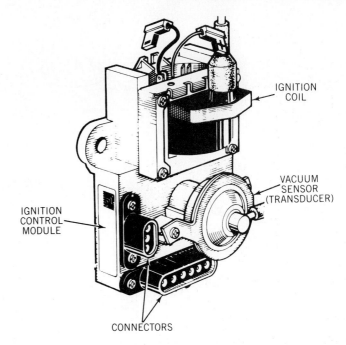

Figure 12-30. The coil for the Renix ignition system is mounted above the module. (AMC-Renault)

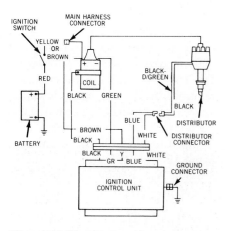

Figure 12-29. This Prestolite ignition system and BID distributor were used on 1975–77 AMC engines. (AMC)

specific car, refer to the carmaker's shop manual or an independent repair manual for exact specifications.

American Motors Corporation (1975–1987)

The first AMC electronic ignition was the Prestolite breakerless inductive-discharge (BID) system. AMC used the Prestolite system on 6- and 8-cylinder engines from 1975 through 1977. This is a variable-dwell system with a metal-detection triggering device. The ignition control module is mounted remotely from the distributor. Figure 12-29 shows a typical AMC-Prestolite distributor with its unique trigger wheel, as well as its centrifugal and vacuum advance mechanisms. This figure also includes a basic ignition circuit diagram. The BID system uses a conventional-appearing distributor cap, rotor, and ignition coil and 7-mm spark plug cables. Because no ballast resistor is used, full battery voltage is present at the coil and module whenever the system is on. The module provides a steady input voltage for the electromagnet in the distributor sensor.

In 1978, AMC discontinued the Prestolite ignition. AMC uses the Ford

Motorcraft solid-state ignition (or Dura-Spark II) on 1978 and later AMC-built 4-, 6-, and 8-cylinder engines. AMC uses the Delco-Remy HEI system in 1980–87 AMC vehicles with GM 4-cylinder and V-6 engines. These systems are described below in the Ford and General Motors sections.

AMC-Renault vehicles use a Renix electronic ignition, built as a joint venture between Renault and Bendix. These inductive-discharge systems are used with electronic engine controls. The distributor simply distributes secondary voltage. The engine computer controls spark timing. The Renix system has a unique-looking coil, mounted on the ignition control module, figure 12-30.

Chrysler Corporation

Chrysler introduced its electronic ignition on some engines in 1971, and made it standard on all 6- and 8-cylinder engines in 1973. Chrysler's basic electronic ignition uses a distributor with a magnetic pulse generator, figure 12-31. Chrysler calls the rotating trigger wheel a "reluctor" and the stationary sensor a "pickup coil." The basic Chrysler distributor has simple centrifugal and vacuum

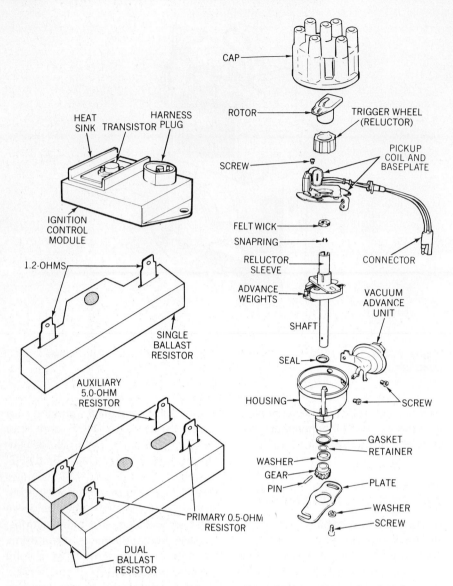

Figure 12-31. Typical distributor, ignition module, and ballast resistors for Chrysler's electronic ignition system. (Chrysler)

computer regulates primary current to the coil.

Chrysler has modified its original electronic ignition several times during the past decade to adapt it to various electronic engine control systems. The distributors for some electronic lean-burn (ELB) and electronic spark control (ESC) systems have two pickup coils, figure 12-33. One provides a fixed timing signal for engine starting only. The other provides a timing signal for all conditions when the engine is running. Distributors for early ELB systems had centrifugal advance but no vacuum advance mechanisms. Distributors for later ESC systems have neither centrifugal nor vacuum advance. All spark advance is controlled by the system computer. The air gap between the reluctor and pickup coil, or coils, is adjustable in Chrysler distributors. Specifications vary for different years.

In 1978, Chrysler introduced its first front-wheel drive (FWD) cars, the Dodge Omni and Plymouth Horizon. The electronic ignitions for these cars have a Hall-effect distributor switch, figure 12-34. The original Omni and Horizon ignitions were fixed-dwell types and used a ballast resistor to control primary current and voltage. The original Chrysler Hall-effect distributors also had centrifugal and vacuum advance mechanisms.

Late-model Chrysler 4-cylinder engines use Hall-effect distributors in ignition systems with no ballast resistor. The ESC spark control computer controls dwell and spark advance. The distributors have no centrifugal or vacuum advance mechanisms.

The Chrysler optical distributor, figure 12-35, was introduced with the 3.0-liter V-6 engine in some 1987 models. A thin timing disc in the distributor contains two sets of chemically etched slots, figure 12-36, to provide crankshaft angle and tdc signals.

• *Crankshaft angle slots*—Also called the high-data-rate slots, these are located on the outer edge of the plate and occur at crankshaft rotation intervals of 2 degrees. They generate a

advance mechanisms to control spark advance.

The rest of the system consists of a conventional coil, distributor cap, rotor, and 7-mm spark plug cables. The ignition control module is mounted on the firewall or fender panel and has a single power switching transistor to control the primary circuit, figure 12-31. The transistor is on top of the module and has enough voltage across it when the system is on to produce a shock. Figure 12-32 is a diagram of the basic Chrysler ignition.

The basic Chrysler electronic ignition is a fixed-dwell system with a ballast resistor to limit primary voltage and current. Most Chrysler systems built through the late 1970's have a dual-ballast resistor. The 0.5-ohm resistor is the conventional ballast resistor that regulates primary voltage and current. It is bypassed during starting. The 5.0-ohm resistor protects the electronic circuitry against high-voltage surges and current flow. Most late-model versions of this ignition used with electronic engine controls have a single ballast resistor. Some late-model Chrysler electronic spark control (ESC) systems with the magnetic-pulse distributor do not have a ballast resistor. The spark control

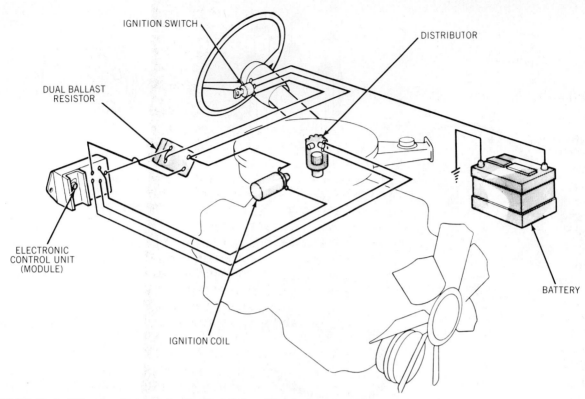

Figure 12-32. Typical Chrysler electronic ignition installation. (Chrysler)

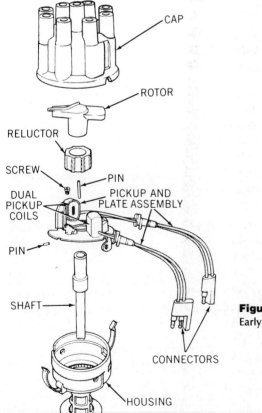

Figure 12-33. Many late-model Chrysler distributors have dual START and RUN pickup coils. (Chrysler)

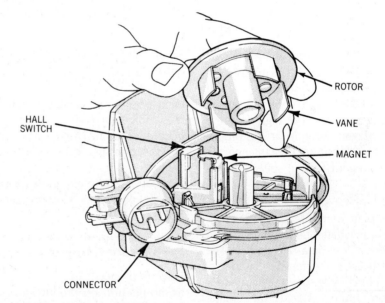

Figure 12-34. Chrysler uses a Hall-effect distributor with electronic spark control systems. Early models have centrifugal and vacuum advance. (Chrysler)

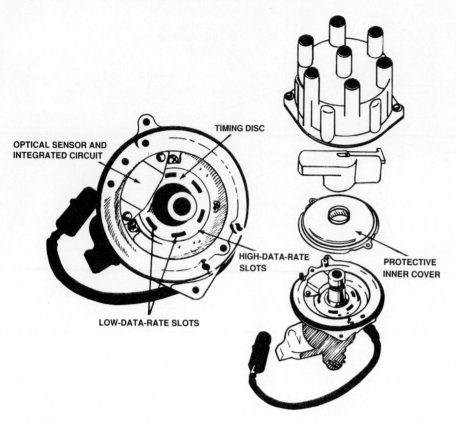

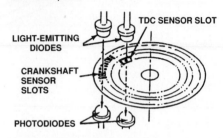

Figure 12-36. The outer slots in this timing disc provide crankshaft angle data; the inner slots identify top-dead-center position. (Chrysler)

Figure 12-37. The timing disc slots interrupt light beams sent to photodiodes by light-emitting diodes (LED'S), creating ac voltage in each diode that is converted into on-off pulses and sent to the logic module. (Chrysler)

Figure 12-35. Chrysler's optical distributor is the first use of a light-detection triggering device to be used in production automobiles. (Chrysler)

signal used to increase ignition timing accuracy at engine speeds up to 1,200 rpm. Engine speed oscillates with the firing pulses of each cylinder during cranking and idle. The high-data-rate signal triggers ignition at the proper crankshaft position instantaneously without regard for the speed oscillations.

• *TDC sensor slots*—The inner slots on the plate correlate to the tdc angle of the crankshaft for each cylinder and provide a low-data-rate signal. The signal triggers the fuel injection system, controls idle speed, and provides ignition timing signals at engine speeds above 1,200 rpm.

The disc revolves between a set of LED's and photodiodes positioned in line with each series of slots, figure 12-37. One set picks up the high-data-rate signal; the other set picks up the low-data-rate signal. The light beam from each LED is focused on its respective photodiode by a mask. As the disc rotates, its two series of slots interrupt the light beams, creating an ac voltage in each photodiode. A hybrid integrated circuit inside the dis-

tributor converts the ac voltage into on-off pulses, which are transmitted to the logic module or the single module engine controller (SMEC).

A protective cover is installed between the timing disc (optical sensor) and the rotor, figure 12-35. This cover protects the optical system from contamination and prevents actuation errors that could be caused by electrical noise or EMI.

Ford Motor Company

Ford introduced its first fully electronic ignition on production cars in mid-1973. It was available on all 6- and 8-cylinder domestic engines in 1974 and became standard in 1975. Looking back on more than a decade of Ford electronic ignitions, it seems that there have been several different systems. The changes, however, have been steady improvements in the original system. Most changes have been in the shape of distributor parts. We can identify Ford ignitions as:

1. Original solid-state ignition (SSI)— 1973–76 (cars) and 1974–79 (trucks)

2. Dura-Spark II and III—electrically similar to SSI but with high-dielectric distributor cap, rotor, and cables; 1977 and later cars and trucks

   a. Dual-mode timing—timing control subsystem of Dura-Spark II, 1978 and later

   b. Cranking retard—timing control subsystem of Durak-Spark II, 1979 and later

3. Dura-Spark I—high secondary voltage system; 1977–79 passenger cars

4. Thick-film integrated (TFI) ignition—electrically similar to Dura-Spark I, but with miniature ignition control module installed in the distributor; 1982 and later cars and trucks

Ford Solid-State Ignition. Figure 12-38 is an installation drawing of the basic Ford SSI system. Figure 12-39 is a wiring diagram for the primary circuit. The original Ford electronic distributor used a magnetic-pulse generator, as have all Ford distributors except some TFI units. Ford calls the trigger wheel an "armature" and the pickup coil a "stator."

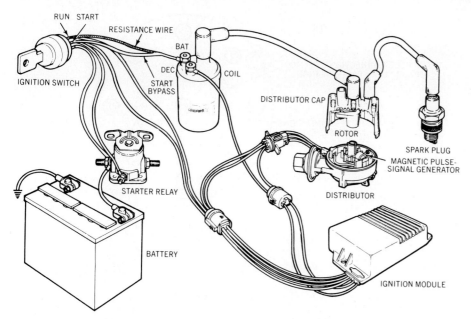

Figure 12-38. Ford has modified the original SSI system over the years, but it still has these basic parts. (Ford)

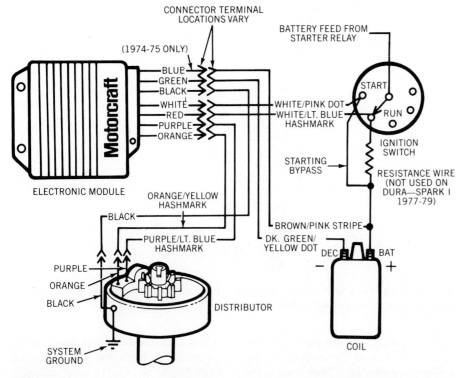

Figure 12-39. This basic wiring arrangement is used on all Ford SSI and Dura-Spark systems. (Ford)

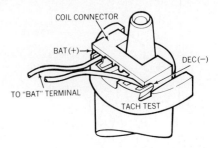

Figure 12-40. This connector for the primary terminals of a Ford coil prevents reversed connections. (Ford)

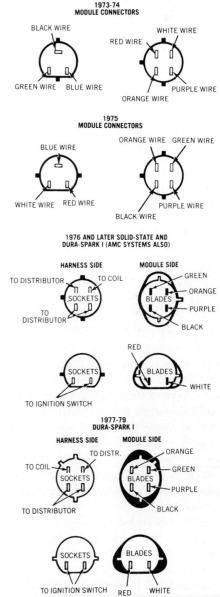

COLOR CODES ARE FOR MODULE CONNECTORS, NOT HARNESS CONNECTORS

Figure 12-41. Ford has changed the ignition module connectors from system to system to prevent misconnection. Wire color codes are the same. (Ford)

The SSI system has a distributor with centrifugal and vaccum advance mechanisms, a conventional-appearing ignition coil, and 7-mm spark plug cables. The SSI system also is a fixed-dwell system with a ballast resistor, as is the later Dura-Spark II system. In 1975, Ford changed the ignition coil connector to a design that prevents reversed primary connections at the coil, figure 12-40.

As Ford refined all of its electronic ignitions over the years, engineers changed the shape and wire arrangement of ignition module connectors so that modules can't be interchanged from one system to another, figure 12-41. In 1976, Ford eliminated the

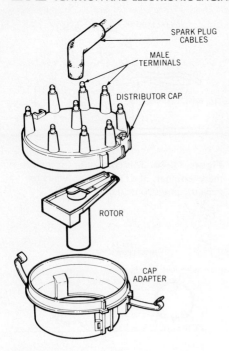

Figure 12-42. Typical Dura-Spark distributor cap, rotor, and adapter. (Ford)

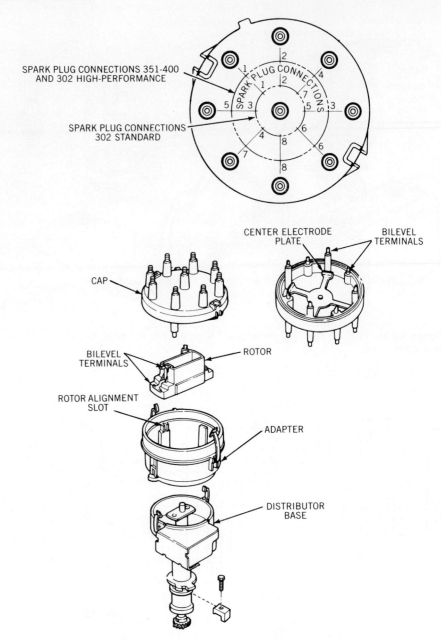

Figure 12-43. Dura-Spark I and III distributors have bilevel caps and rotors. Spark plug cables are not in firing order. (Ford)

blue overload shunt wire to the ignition module. All other wire connections and color codes are basically the same for all SSI and Dura-Spark systems, figure 12-39.

Dura-Spark II and III Ignition. The primary circuits of Dura-Spark II and III are almost identical to Ford's original SSI system. The resistance of the coil primary and the ballast resistor were lowered slightly to provide higher secondary available voltage. For this reason, the distributor cap and rotor were redesigned to provide more space between the secondary terminals to prevent arcing, figure 12-42. Ford has used a variety of cap and rotor styles on its Dura-Spark systems. All of these designs, along with the plastic materials of the cap and rotor, provide high-dielectric resistance to prevent crossfiring, secondary voltage leakage, and radio interference. These systems also use 8-mm spark plug cables.

Dura-Spark II and III are fixed-dwell systems and use the original magnetic-pulse distributor. Dura-Spark II distributors have centrifugal and vacuum advance mechanisms. Dura-Spark III ignitions are used with elec-

tronic engine control systems, and all spark advance is controlled by the system computer. Therefore, the Dura-Spark II and III ignition modules are not identical. Dura-Spark III distributors have caps and rotors with the secondary terminals on two levels, figure 12-43. The greater distance between the terminals prevents secondary voltage arcing. Spark plug cables do not connect to the caps in firing-order sequence, but the cap terminals are numbered by cylinder, figure 12-43.

The dual-mode timing and cranking-retard systems are subsystems of Dura-Spark II. Dual-mode systems have ignition modules with three, rather than two connectors, figure 12-44. The "altitude" version uses a signal from a barometric pressure switch to retard timing at low altitudes. The "economy" version uses a signal from a manifold vacuum switch to retard timing under heavy load. The cranking-retard ignition module senses slow engine speed from the distributor signals during cranking.

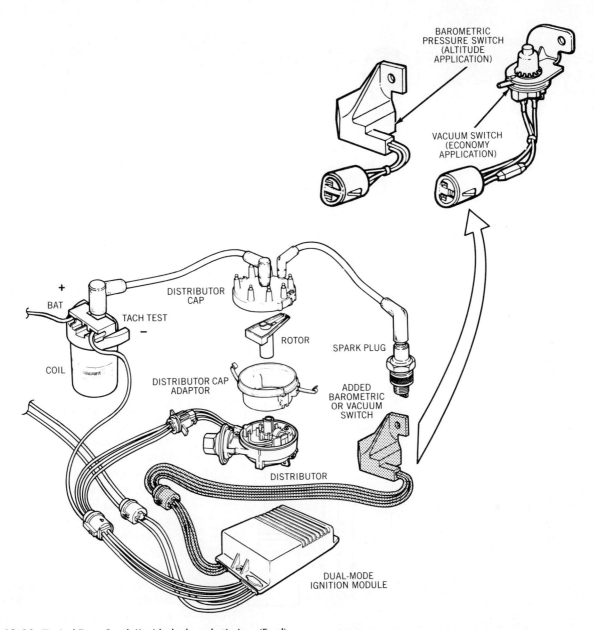

Figure 12-44. Typical Dura-Spark II with dual-mode timing. (Ford)

The module electronically retards timing about 18 degrees for easier starting.

Dura-Spark I Ignition. Ford's Dura-Spark I system is a high secondary voltage system used with electronic engine controls on some 1977–79 V-8 engines. It uses a magnetic-pulse distributor with centrifugal and vacuum advance. It is a variable-dwell system, however, with no ballast resistor. The ignition module has a current-limiting circuit to control coil saturation.

Thick-Film Integrated (TFI) Ignition. Ford introduced its TFI ignition on 1982 1.6-liter 4-cylinder engines in Escort and Lynx models and has expanded its use since. The system is named for the semiconductor manufacturing process used to make the ignition module. Figure 12-45 shows a typical TFI ignition installation, and figure 12-46 is a simplified wiring diagram. The TFI module is a miniature design, mounted on the distributor body, figure 12-47. Like Dura-Spark I, the TFI ignition is a high-voltage, variable-dwell system with no ballast resistor.

The first thick-film ignition ignitions used a magnetic-pulse generator in the distributor and had centrifugal and vacuum advance mechanisms. Later TFI systems for electronic engine controls have Hall-effect switching devices that supply crankshaft position signals. Spark advance is controlled electronically by the EEC-IV engine control computer.

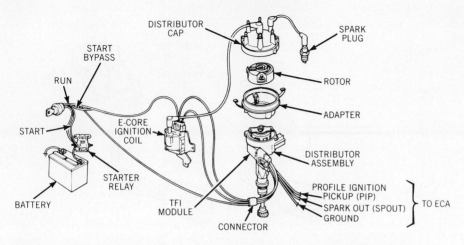

Figure 12-45. Typical thick-film integrated (TFI) ignition system installation. (Ford)

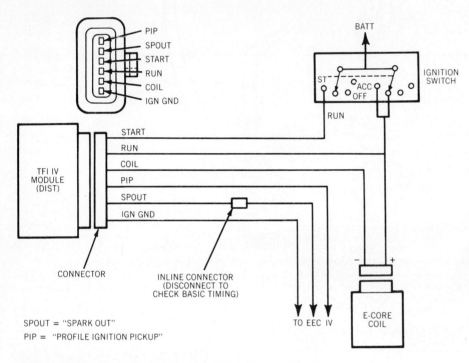

SPOUT = "SPARK OUT"
PIP = "PROFILE IGNITION PICKUP"

Figure 12-46. Typical Ford TFI ignition wiring diagram. (Ford)

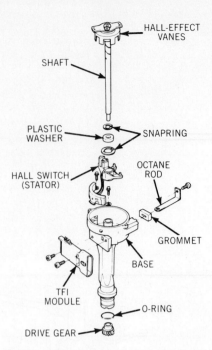

Figure 12-47. Typical Ford TFI distributor. (Ford)

General Motors

The Delco-Remy high-energy ignition (HEI) system was introduced on some GM V-8 engines in 1974. It became standard on all GM engines in 1975. The HEI system was the first major electronic ignition to use a variable-dwell primary circuit with no ballast resistor. In its first decade of use, the HEI system appeared in several versions. But, as with Ford ignitions, the changes were steady improvements and adaptations of the basic HEI design.

Basic HEI. The HEI system was the first major system to have all components built into the distributor. A miniature ignition control module is installed in the distributor, and the most common HEI design has the coil mounted in the top of the distributor cap. Figure 12-48 shows a complete HEI distributor. Some systems for in-line 4- and 6-cylinder engines have a coil separate from the distributor for clearance on some engines, figure 12-49. All HEI systems operate alike, however.

The HEI distributor has a magnetic pulse generator, with a trigger wheel called a "timer core." The trigger wheel and the pickup coil pole piece have as many equally spaced teeth as the engine has cylinders, figure 12-50, with one exception. Uneven-firing Buick-built V-6's have three teeth on the trigger wheel and six unevenly spaced teeth on the pole piece. The basic HEI distributor has centrifugal and vacuum advance mechanisms similar to a Delco V-8 breaker-point distributor. HEI distributors contain an RFI suppression capacitor that is not part of the primary circuit. All HEI systems use 8-mm spark plug cables, and many engines use wide-gap spark plugs to take advantage of the system's high-voltage capabilities.

HEI with C-3. The basic HEI system has an ignition module with four terminals: two for pickup coil signals, one for battery voltage (B+), and one for the coil ground, figure 12-51. Figure 12-52 is a circuit diagram of the basic HEI system. GM has used six other HEI versions over the years with electronic engine controls and for certain spark timing requirements.

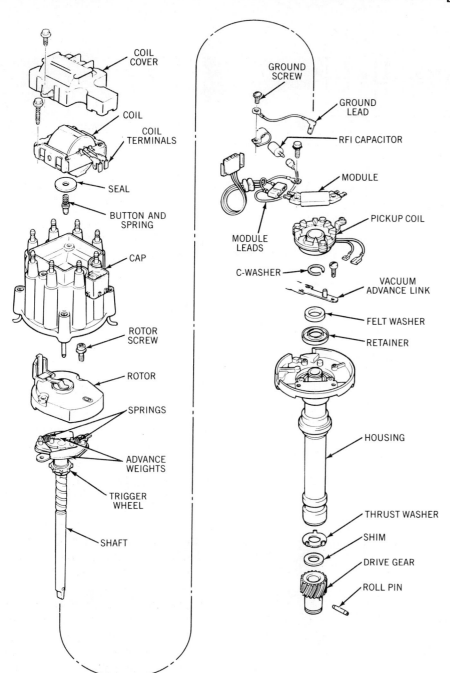

Figure 12-48. The complete HEI distributor contains the coil and the ignition module. (Chevrolet)

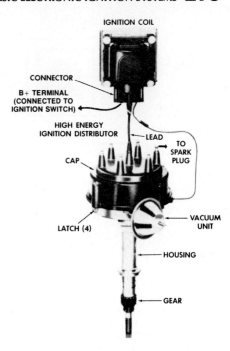

Figure 12-49. HEI system with separate coil. (Delco-Remy)

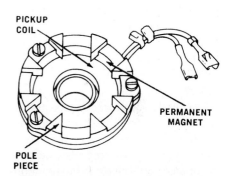

Figure 12-50. The HEI pickup coil has multiple pole pieces. (Delco-Remy)

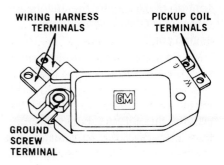

Figure 12-51. Basic Delco-Remy HEI control module. (Delco-Remy)

• HEI with electronic spark control (ESC)—This system uses a 5-terminal module and a detonation sensor in the manifold or block. When the sensor detects detonation, it signals the module to retard timing until the detonation stops.

• HEI with electronic spark selection (ESS)—This system uses a 5-terminal module, along with a signal decoder. The decoder monitors signals from the distributor pickup coil, a manifold vacuum switch, and a coolant temperature switch. The decoder signals the ignition module to retard timing for low-temperature starting and to prevent too much advance at cruising speeds.

• HEI with electronic module retard (EMR)—This system uses a 5-terminal ignition module and a manifold vacuum switch or another electronic

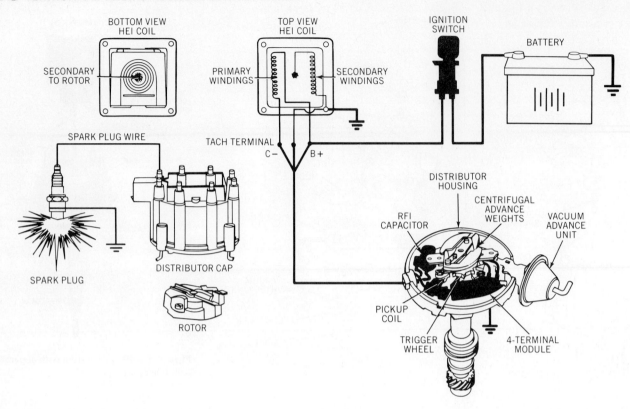

Figure 12-52. This is the basic circuit for the Delco-Remy HEI system. (Sun Electric)

module. Under certain conditions of vacuum, temperature, and engine speed, the vacuum switch or EMR module grounds the EMR lead to the HEI module to retard timing about 10 degrees.

• HEI with electronic spark timing (EST)—This system uses a 7-terminal ignition module. EST is used with electronic engine controls, such as computer-controlled catalytic converter (C-4) and computer command control (C-3) systems. The engine control computer controls all spark timing.

• HEI with EST and ESC—This system combines the fully electronic spark control of EST with the detonation sensor of ESC. It is used with some C-3 engine control systems.

• HEI with EST and a Hall-effect switch—This system also is used with C-3 engine controls. It has a Hall-effect switch added to the HEI distributor, figure 12-53, but the distributor also has the magnetic-pulse generator. During cranking, the pickup coil sends timing signals to the HEI module. When the engine starts, the Hall-effect switch takes over and

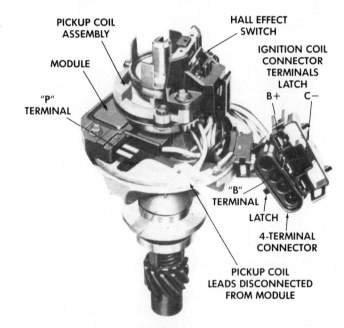

Figure 12-53. The Hall-effect switch is a crankshaft position sensor in HEI-EST distributors. (Delco-Remy)

sends crankshaft position signals to the C-3 computer, which then controls all timing electronically.

HEI distributors for ESC, ESS, and EMR have centrifugal and vacuum advance. All EST distributors do not.

Distributorless Ignition (DIS)

The first of several distributorless ignitions from General Motors was introduced on some fuel-injected, turbocharged, 3.8-liter Buick V-6 engines in 1984. Nissan and Saab followed

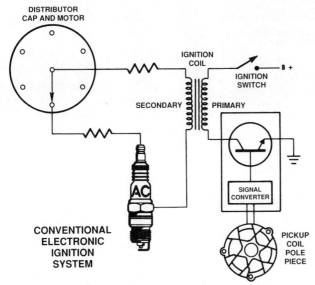

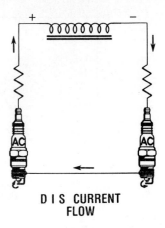

D I S CURRENT FLOW

Figure 12-55. In a distributorless ignition system, the coil is connected to two spark plugs. It fires one plug forward and one plug backwards. The forward-firing plug ignites the mixture, while the spark of the backward-firing plug is "wasted." (General Motors)

Figure 12-54. Electrons flow from a spark plug's center electrode to its outer electrode and then to ground in a conventional electronic ignition system. (General Motors)

with their own versions of a distributorless ignition. Ford introduced its version on the 1989 Thunderbird supercharged V-6, Taurus V-6, and 2.3-liter 4-cylinder OHC engine in the Ranger pickup truck.

The acronym DIS is used to describe any ignition system without a distributor. It also is used in reference to the specific system used on GM 2.0-liter and 2.5-liter 4-cylinder engines and 2.8-liter V-6 engines; this system is referred to as a direct ignition system.

DIS uses the **waste spark** theory, similar to the ignitions used for years in motorcycles and outboard engines. Each end of a coil secondary is connected to a spark plug. These two spark plugs are in cylinders that are both at top dead center at the same time. When the coil fires, the spark going to the cylinder on compression ignites the mixture. The spark to the other cylinder is "wasted" at the top of the exhaust stroke.

With distributor-type ignition systems, all spark plugs are connected to the coil and fired in a forward direction; that is, from the center to the side electrode, figure 12-54. In a DIS ignition, one spark plug connected to a coil is fired forward; the other is fired backwards, or from the side to the center electrode, figure 12-55. In other words, one plug in each pair always fires with reverse polarity.

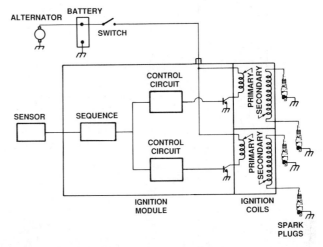

Figure 12-56. The ignition module in a direct ignition system contains circuits to control primary current and dwell time limiting. (General Motors)

Since it requires about 30 percent more energy to fire a spark plug backwards, the coils used in a DIS system have a different saturation time and primary current flow than a conventional coil. This results in more than 40 kilovolts of available energy, or between 10 and 20 percent more energy than a conventional coil produces.

The coil firing order is determined and maintained by the ignition module. When a coil fires, one spark plug fires forward and the other fires backwards at the same time. Polarity and cylinder pressure determines the voltage dropped across each plug. Obviously, the plug in the cylinder on compression will need more voltage to create an arc between the elec-

trodes than will the cylinder on exhaust.

A control circuit inside the module handles primary current flow and limits dwell time. The primary coil winding has very low resistance (under 1 ohm). When combined with an applied voltage of 14 volts, this low resistance produces a theoretical current flow in excess of 14 amperes, which helps to decrease saturation time. However, to prevent damage to system components, the maximum current flow must be kept between 8.5 and 10 amperes. To achieve this, the circuit current is monitored by the module, which modifies the control transistor's base current to limit the collector-emitter current within a

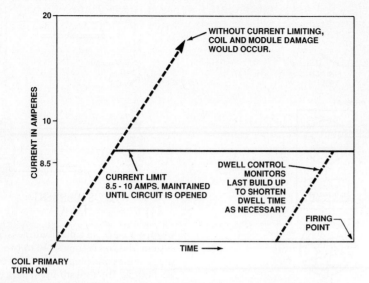

Figure 12-57. The closed-loop dwell control feature of a DIS ignition module increases or decreases dwell time to permit full saturation of the ignition coil. (General Motors)

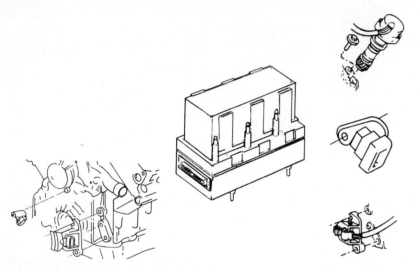

Figure 12-58. A computer-controlled coil ignition system uses a module, coil pack, and crankshaft and camshaft sensors. (General Motors)

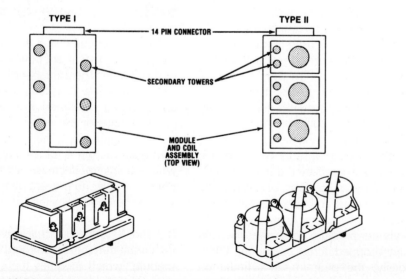

Figure 12-59. Type I and type II C3I systems can be identified by the type of coil pack used. (General Motors)

range of 8.5 to 10 amperes, figure 12-56.

A form of **closed loop dwell control**, figure 12-57, is used by the module. The previous coil buildup is monitored for maximum current. If maximum current was not achieved, the module increases dwell time to permit full saturation of the coil. If maximum current was achieved, the module decreases dwell time to reduce the wattage consumed by the system. If current limiting takes place before discharge, the module increases dwell for the next firing sequence.

DIS was designed to replace the mechanical HEI system in controlling and distributing secondary coil voltage. There are currently three versions of DIS in use on GM vehicles and two versions used by Ford.

GM Computer-controlled Coil Ignition (C3I). The C3I system is used on V-6 engines built by Buick. The basic system contains a coil pack, an ignition module, and Hall-effect sensors to determine crankshaft and camshaft position, figure 12-58. There are three different versions of C3I, each of which can be identified visually.

1. *Type 1*—This version has all three coils molded into a single pack, figure 12-59. If one coil malfunctions, the entire coil pack must be replaced. This system is used with all 1984 and later turbocharged 3.8-liter V-6 engines, and 1985 and later 3.0-liter V-6 engines. Type 1 coil modules are built by Magnavox.

2. *Type 2*—This is the same as type 1, except that the coils can be replaced individually, figure 12-59. The system is used with 1985–87 3.8-liter V-6 engines with sequential fuel injection (SFI).

3. *Type 3*—The coil pack is similar in appearance to, and can be interchanged with, a type 1 pack. The module, however, differs electronically and the connector plugs are not compatible with components from other systems. The type 3 system is used on 1988 and later Buick 3800 V-6 engines.

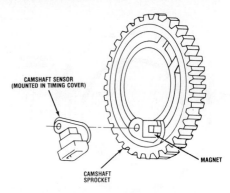

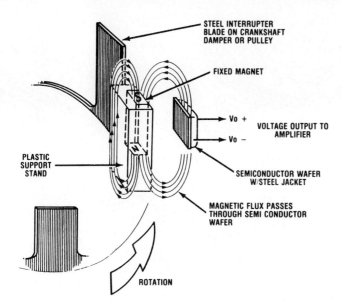

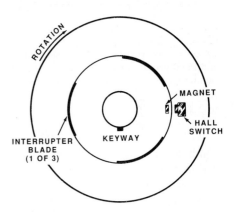

Figure 12-60. Alternating interrupter blades and air gaps passing through a Hall-effect switch create a voltage signal to indicate crankshaft position. (General Motors)

Hall-effect switch sensors are used to synchronize and fire the coils at the correct time. The ignition module supplies a reference voltage, which is pulled down or dropped by the Hall-effect switch whenever a ferrous metal comes between the semiconductor material and permanent magnet in the switch, figure 12-60. The change in reference voltage tells the module the exact position of the device being monitored. A variation of this is used with the 3.8-liter V-6 camshaft sensor, wherein a moving magnet is rotated past the Hall-effect switch to turn it on and pull down the voltage, figure 12-61.

Three equally positioned metal interrupters pass between the permanent magnet and Hall-effect switch as the crankshaft rotates, figure 12-62. The on-off action of the transistor switches the module reference voltage from high (6 to 8 volts) to low (0 to 0.5 volt). Because each signal is identical in time and amplitude, the module cannot determine which signal it should send to which coil.

The 3.8-liter V-6 camshaft sensor signal is used by the module to identify the correct crankshaft signal and its corresponding coil. Like the crank sensor, the cam sensor also switches the reference voltage from the module. The initial cam sensor signal is synchronized with one of the crankshaft sensor signals during cranking.

This synchronization is maintained by the module, which remembers the sequence of the crankshaft sensor until the ignition is turned off. The cam sensor serves no other purpose once the initial ignition setup routine is established.

The 3.0-liter V-6 differs from the 3.8-liter somewhat in signal generation and processing. The combination crankshaft sensor contains a separate Hall-effect switch on each side of the permanent magnet. Two concentric rings on the rear of the harmonic balancer pass between the magnet and the Hall-effect switches. The three inner interrupter rings provide three sensor switches to indicate crankshaft position. The outer ring with a single open area provides one signal per crankshaft revolution, which acts as the synchronization signal to the module, figure 12-63. As with the 3.8-liter V-6, the synchronization signal is required only during engine cranking and coil sequence setup.

Both engines will run without a camshaft or synchronization signal if the engine is running before the sensor failure. However, neither engine will start without the signal. Some 3.0-liter engines may start if the synchronization signal is pulled low during cranking; but if the circuit is pulled low with the engine running, the module resynchronizes the crankshaft signal, often resulting in a stall.

Figure 12-61. The camshaft sensor on Buick's 3.8-liter SFI V-6 engine rotates a magnet past the Hall-effect switch to turn it on and pull down the reference voltage. (General Motors)

Figure 12-62. The Hall-effect transistor switches the ignition module's reference voltage from high to low as the interrupter blades and air gaps pass through the switch. (General Motors)

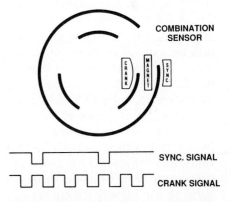

Figure 12-63. Dual Hall-effect switches using one magnet provide two sets of signals in the Buick 3.0-liter V-6 design. (General Motors)

The type 3 system used with the 1988 and later 3800 V-6 engine is slightly different and more sophisticated electronically. It is sometimes referred to as "fast start 1" because it provides a faster startup. The system

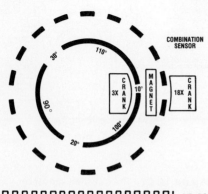

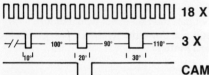

Figure 12-64. The type 3 or "fast start 1" C3I system uses dual Hall-effect switches and 18 interrupter blades to provide a more accurate measurement of the crankshaft sensor signals. (General Motors)

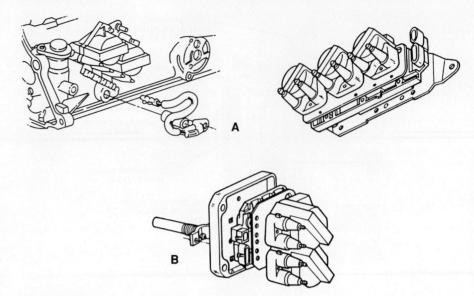

Figure 12-65. The direct ignition system (DIS) used with 1987 and later GM 4-cylinder and V-6 engines uses a block-mounted crankshaft sensor instead of Hall-effect switches to provide a crankshaft position signal. (General Motors)

combines a dual crank sensor (much like that on the 3.0-liter V-6) with a separate camshaft sensor in the front cover (like the 3.8-liter SFI V-6). The crank 1 signal is provided by 18 interrupter rings evenly spaced around the outside of the harmonic balancer, figure 12-64. The signal is called the "18× crank signal" because it delivers 18 pulses per crankshaft revolution. A crank 2 signal comes from the inside ring, which contains three rings with air gaps or windows of 10 degrees, 20 degrees, and 30 degrees spaced 110 degrees, 100 degrees, and 90 degrees apart, figure 12-64. This is called the "3× crank signal."

The module can energize the proper coil without waiting for the cam signal or the synchronization signal because of the variations in the 3× signal. It can identify the correct coil within 120 degrees of crank rotation and will start firing on whatever coil it identifies first. The 18× pulse is used by the module as a "clock" pulse to determine the length of each 3× pulse. The 18× signal changes once during the 3× 10-degree air gap, twice during the 20-degree gap, and three times during the 3× 30-degree window. The module uses this infor-

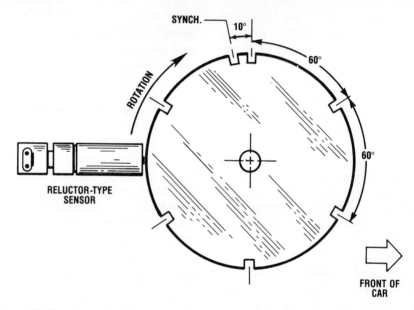

Figure 12-66. The crankshaft sensor in a DIS is mounted 0.050 ± 0.020 inch from a rotating reluctor machined in the crankshaft. Notches in the reluctor modulate the sensor signal, with one notch providing the signal used to synchronize the coil firing sequence to crankshaft position. (General Motors)

mation to identify which 3× pulse it is reading and then energizes the proper coil.

The module equalizes and buffers the 3× crank signal, sending it to the electronic control module (ECM) on one circuit. This is followed by a buffering of the 18× signal, which is then sent to the ECM on a separate circuit as a more accurate engine speed signal. The camshaft signal is buffered and sent to the ECM on a third circuit

to control fuel injection. Since the module requires no camshaft signal to set up or synchronize the coil firing, the engine will start and run even with a malfunctioning cam sensor.

GM Direct Ignition System. The direct ignition system (DIS) is used on Chevrolet 2.0-liter 4-cylinder and 2.8-liter V-6 engines, as well as the Pontiac-built 2.5-liter 4-cylinder engine. System operation is similar to that of the C3I system, with the major difference in the method of sensing the position of the crankshaft. A magnetic sensor installed in the side of the engine block performs the function of the Hall-effect switches. In the 2.0-liter and V-6 applications, the magnetic sensor is mounted below the module and connects to it externally, figure 12-65A. In the 2.5-liter application, the sensor is mounted on the rear of the module, figure 12-65B.

A reluctor or special wheel cast into the crankshaft has seven machined slots or notches and performs the interrupter function. The sensor contains a permanent magnet with a wire winding and is installed 0.050 ± 0.020 inch from the crankshaft reluctor, figure 12-66. When the crankshaft rotates, the reluctor notches modulate the intensity of the sensor's magnetic field, inducing a small ac, or push-pull, voltage in the wire winding around the sensor, figure 12-67. Since the reluctor is a machined part of the crankshaft and the sensor is installed in a fixed position on the engine block, ignition timing adjustment is not possible, nor required, for DIS.

Six of the seven notches on the crankshaft are spaced at 60-degree intervals around the reluctor surface. The seventh notch is 10 degrees away from one of the evenly spaced notches and provides the signal used by the module to synchronize the coil sequence to the crankshaft position, figure 12-68.

Since one coil fires two spark plugs at a time, the DIS is mainly concerned with coil order and the position of crankshaft rotation in which to fire the coils. The 4-cylinder engines make this determination in a slightly different way from the V-6 engine.

On a 4-cylinder engine, the ignition module monitors the seventh notch to start the firing sequence. Below a specified engine speed, the module controls ignition timing by firing each coil at a preset interval based only on engine speed. This is called **bypass** or **module timing**. The synchronization notch notifies the module to omit the first notch and use the second notch to establish 10° btdc for cylinders 2 and

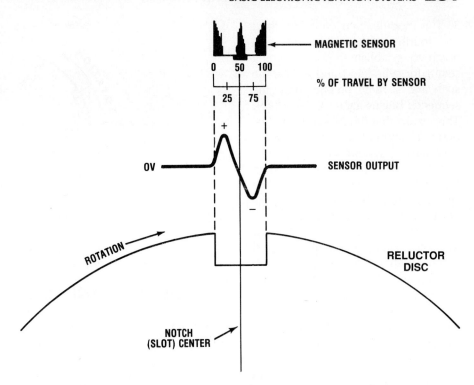

Figure 12-67. Interruption of the sensor's magnetic field induces a small ac voltage in the wire wound around the permanent magnet sensor. This voltage change tells the ignition module when to fire each coil. (General Motors)

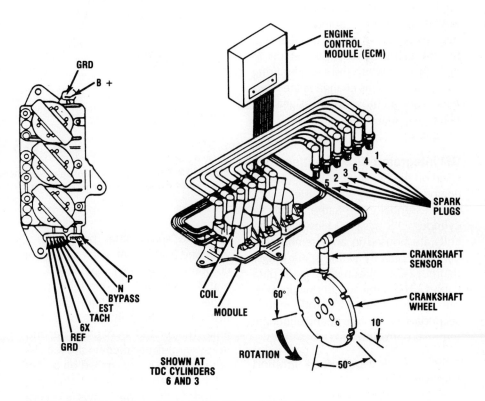

Figure 12-68. Operation of the V-6 DIS. (General Motors)

3. The module then omits the third and fourth notches, using the fifth notch to establish the same timing setting for cylinders 1 and 4. After the sixth and seventh notches pass, the sequence begins again, figure 12-69. This means that the 2/3 coil fires first on initial setup. (Except for the type 3 "fast start 1" system, all DIS and C3I systems start up the second cylinder in the firing order first.) Once engine speed exceeds the specified rpm, the ECM takes over ignition timing.

The V-6 engine system functions much the same, except that the synchronization notch notifies the module to omit the first notch and use the second notch to establish base timing for cylinders 2 and 5. The module then omits the third notch, using the fourth notch to establish the same timing setting for cylinders 3 and 6. Finally, the module omits the fifth notch and uses the sixth notch for cylinders 1 and 4. After the seventh notch passes, the sequence begins again. The firing order in the first crankshaft revolution is 1-2-3 and 4-5-6 in the second crank revolution, figure 12-70.

In both the 4- and 6-cylinder DIS applications, the reference pulse is pulled low by the notch that is 60 degrees ahead of the notch that will fire the cylinder, and then returns to its high state when the cylinder firing notch passes. This change in the reference voltage provides the signal for electronic spark timing (EST) and fuel injection.

GM Integrated Direct Ignition (IDI). Used on the Oldsmobile-built Quad 4 engine, figure 12-71, this system functions essentially the same as the 4-cylinder DIS system. However, the coils are housed in an assembly that connects directly to the spark plugs, figure 12-72, eliminating spark plug cables. The 1-piece conductors permit precise routing control, reduce secondary capacitance, and eliminate terminal corrosion.

Ford 4-2 Distributorless Ignition System (DIS). This DIS is unique in that the 2.3-liter 4-cylinder engine

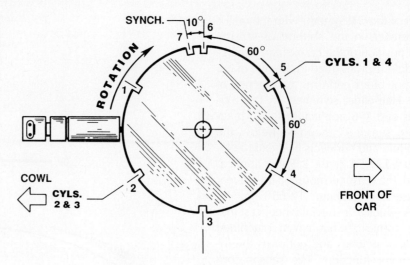

2.0L, 2.3L, AND 2.5L 4-CYLINDER ENGINES

Figure 12-69. In the 4-cylinder DIS, reluctor notch 2 fires the ignition coil for cylinders 2 and 3. Reluctor notch 5 fires the cylinder 1 and 4 coil. (General Motors)

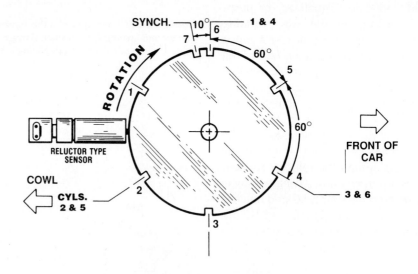

2.8L V-6 ENGINE

Figure 12-70. The V-6 DIS uses reluctor notches 2, 4, and 6 to fire cylinders 2 and 5, 3 and 6, and 1 and 4 respectively. (General Motors)

uses two spark plugs per cylinder, with one installed on each side of the combustion chamber. The engine operates at all times on one set of plugs called the primary system. These are installed on the right side of the engine. The second set of plugs (secondary system) is installed on the left side of the engine and switched on and off by the EEC-IV computer. A dual plug inhibit (DPI) circuit allows the computer to switch the ignition system from single- to dual-plug operation according to engine load and speed requirements. During the cranking mode, only the primary plugs fire. When the engine is running, the EEC-IV computer signals the DIS module to switch to the dual-plug mode. The EEC-IV system also controls spark timing and dwell for the ignition system.

The DIS 4-2 ignition also contains

IGNITION COIL AND
MODULE ASSEMBLY

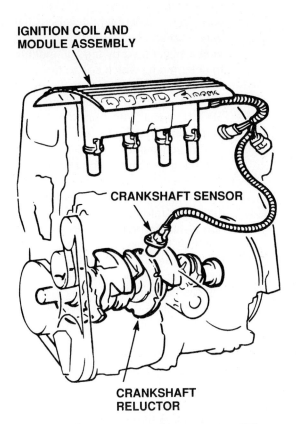

CRANKSHAFT SENSOR

CRANKSHAFT
RELUCTOR

Figure 12-71. The integrated direct ignition (IDI) system uses an integral coil and module assembly that connects directly to the spark plugs without secondary wiring. (Oldsmobile)

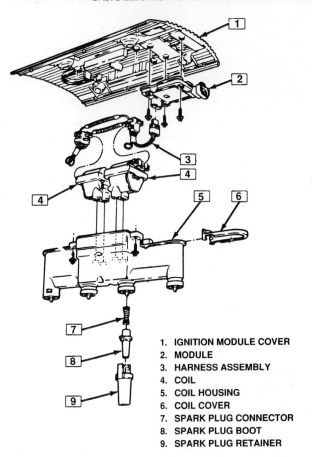

1. IGNITION MODULE COVER
2. MODULE
3. HARNESS ASSEMBLY
4. COIL
5. COIL HOUSING
6. COIL COVER
7. SPARK PLUG CONNECTOR
8. SPARK PLUG BOOT
9. SPARK PLUG RETAINER

Figure 12-72. An exploded view showing placement of the components in the IDI system. (Oldsmobile)

two 4-tower DIS coil packs, figure 12-73, and a crankshaft-mounted dual Hall-effect switch sensor. Two coil packs are required because of the dual set of plugs. One coil pack fires the primary set during normal engine operation; the other coil pack fires the secondary set when directed to do so by the EEC-IV computer and DIS module. Figure 12-74 is a block diagram of the Ford DIS 4-2 ignition.

A bracket-mounted, dual-digital-output Hall-effect switch acts as the crankshaft sensor and responds to two rotating metal shutters, or rotary vane cups, mounted on the crankshaft damper in the same way as other Hall-effect switches you have studied. The dual-digital-sensor operation is similar to that in the GM C3I ignition. The profile ignition pickup (PIP) vane cup and Hall-effect switch provide

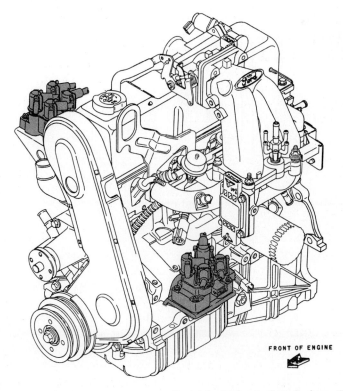

FRONT OF ENGINE

Figure 12-73. The Ford 4-2 DIS uses one coil pack for each set of spark plugs. (Ford)

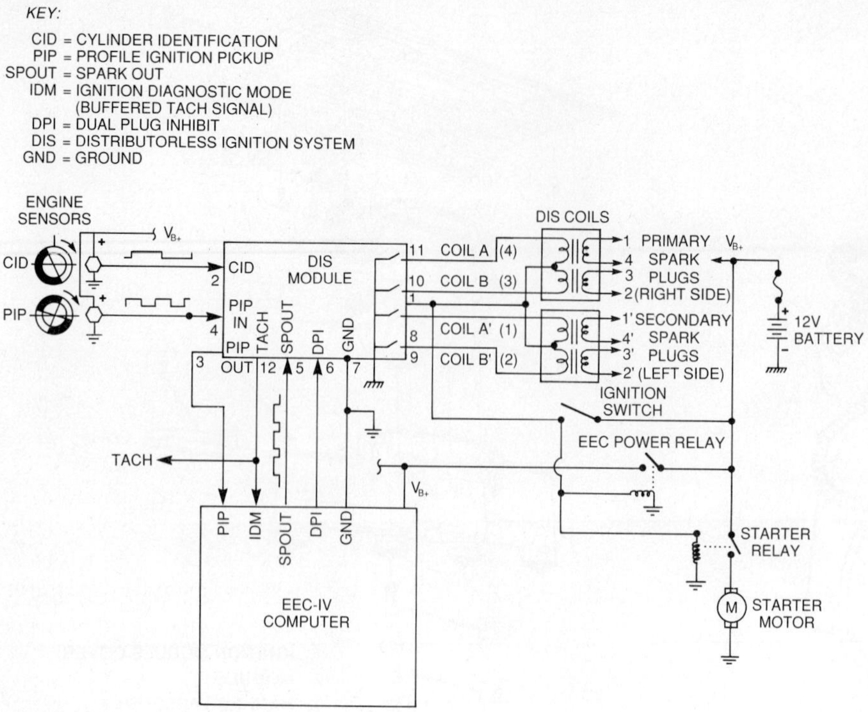

KEY:
CID = CYLINDER IDENTIFICATION
PIP = PROFILE IGNITION PICKUP
SPOUT = SPARK OUT
IDM = IGNITION DIAGNOSTIC MODE
(BUFFERED TACH SIGNAL)
DPI = DUAL PLUG INHIBIT
DIS = DISTRIBUTORLESS IGNITION SYSTEM
GND = GROUND

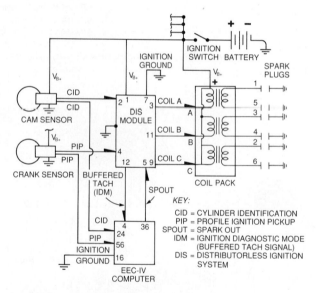

Figure 12-74. A block diagram of the Ford 4-2 DIS.

Figure 12-75. A block diagram of the Ford V-6 DIS.

crankshaft position signals (basic spark timing data) to the EEC-IV system. The cylinder identification (CID) vane cup and Hall-effect switch provide a signal used by the DIS module in determining which coil to fire.

The computer-controlled dwell (CCD) feature uses a spark output, or SPOUT, signal sent from the EEC-IV computer to the DIS module. The leading edge fires the coil, and the trailing edge controls the dwell time. A buffered tach signal from the DIS module to the EEC-IV system provides diagnostic information about the ignition system for self-test purposes.

If the CID sensor or circuit fails, the DIS module will randomly select and fire one of the two coils. The engine still can be started by turning the ignition key off and on until the DIS selects the correct firing sequence.

A failure effects management (FEM) program allows the vehicle to run when an ignition failure prevents a SPOUT signal. The EEC-IV computer opens the SPOUT line, and the DIS module fires the coils directly from the PIP output, resulting in a fixed spark timing of 10° btdc with fixed dwell.

Ford V-6 Distributorless Ignition System. This system operates in the same way as the Ford 4-2 DIS system just discussed but the components differ, figure 12-75.

• Three coils are mounted together to form a 6-tower coil pack with an individual tach wire for each coil.

• The camshaft sensor on the 3.0-liter V-6 is mounted at the end of one camshaft.

• The camshaft sensor on the 3.8-liter supercharged V-6 is mounted in the normal distributor location.

Ford's DIS installations on V-6 engines operated with only one spark plug per cylinder. All Ford distributorless ignition systems work on the same principles as the GM DIS versions. In all systems, each coil fires a pair of spark plugs. One spark ignites the air-fuel mixture at the top of the compression stroke. The other spark of the pair is wasted at the top of the exhaust stroke. The secondary circuit for each coil is a series circuit; one plug of each pair has positive (+) polarity, the other has negative (−) polarity.

Imported-Car Electronic Ignitions

Imported-car manufacturers began to use electronic ignitions about the same time as domestic carmakers, and there is nothing "foreign" about their systems. All major imported-car ignitions are inductive-discharge systems. Most have magnetic-pulse generators in the distributor to send timing signals to the ignition module. Bosch, however, makes a Hall-effect distributor used on many Volkswagen engines. Most Japanese ignitions are variable-dwell systems with no ballast resistor and full battery voltage applied to the system at all times.

SUMMARY

Almost all original equipment electronic ignitions are inductive-discharge systems. They produce high secondary voltage in the same way a breaker-point ignition does. Electronic ignitions, however, use electronic switching circuits rather than breaker points.

Primary current control in an electronic ignition is based on the ability of a transistor to act as a solid-state relay. Transistors turn primary current on and off in response to voltage signals from a triggering device in the distributor. All primary current flows through the switching transistors, not through the distributor.

Distributor triggering devices can be magnetic-pulse generators, Hall-effect switches, metal-detection circuits, or optical circuits. Magnetic-pulse generators and Hall-effect switches are most common. A magnetic-pulse generator uses a low-reluctance trigger wheel to change the field strength of a magnet. Changing magnetic flux induces a voltage in a pickup coil, which switches the driver transistor off. A Hall-effect switch uses a rotating series of blades to change magnetic flux through a semiconductor chip. This varies the output voltage, which switches the driver transistor. A Hall-effect switch requires an input voltage; a magnetic-pulse generator does not.

Basic electronic ignition systems use centrifugal and vacuum advance mechanisms in the distributors to advance and retard timing. These work just like the advance mechanisms in breaker-point distributors. Late-model electronic ignitions used with electronic engine control systems do not have centrifugal and vacuum advance. Spark advance is controlled electronically by the system computer.

All carmakers have changed their electronic ignitions from year to year. These have not been radical changes, however, but steady improvements in basic designs. Electronic ignitions eliminate the problems of mechanical wear and varying timing and dwell that exist in breaker-point ignitions.

The introduction of distributorless ignition systems (DIS) points the way to the future. The mechanical distributor will soon go the way of the carburetor. Increased reliance on electronics and elimination of moving mechanical parts results in more precise ignition control with fewer potential problems.

REVIEW QUESTIONS

Multiple Choice

1. Most late-model electronic ignitions are:

  a. point-controlled systems
  b. capacitive-discharge systems
  c. optically triggered systems
  d. inductive-discharge systems

2. Mechanic A says that ignition power transistors generate the basic ignition timing signal. Mechanic B says that ignition primary current flows through the distributor generator to control timing. Who is right?

  a. A only
  b. B only
  c. both A and B
  d. neither A nor B

3. Mechanic A says that ignition transistors can act as solid-state relays. Mechanic B says that ignition transistors can act as current amplifiers. Who is right?

  a. A only
  b. B only
  c. both A and B
  d. neither A nor B

4. All the following are kinds of distributor signal generators, EXCEPT:

  a. a Hall-effect switch
  b. an acoustic coupler
  c. a magnetic-pulse generator
  d. a metal-detection circuit

5. The pickup coil of a magnetic-pulse generator contains:

  a. a ferromagnetic armature
  b. a permanent magnet and a pole piece
  c. a nonmagnetic sensor
  d. a magnetic reluctor

6. "Armature" and "reluctor" are names for the _____ in a magnetic-pulse distributor.

  a. stator
  b. pickup coil
  c. sensor
  d. trigger wheel

7. To generate an output voltage signal, a Hall-effect switch requires:

  a. an input voltage
  b. no magnetic field
  c. a shunt transistor
  d. a crankshaft position sensor

8. Mechanic A says that a Hall-effect switch is an optical signal generator. Mechanic B says that a Hall-effect switch generates full-strength signal voltage at all engine speeds. Who is right?

  a. A only
  b. B only

c. both A and B

d. neither A nor B

9. Mechanic A says that electronic ignitions can have a fixed dwell angle or a variable dwell angle. Mechanic B says that coil saturation varies directly with a change in the dwell angle in electronic ignitions. Who is right?

a. A only

b. B only

c. both A and B

d. neither A nor B

10. Mechanic A says that a variable-dwell ignition requires a larger ballast resistor than a fixed dwell ignition. Mechanic B says that the dwell angle usually increases at high speed in a variable-dwell system. Who is right?

a. A only

b. B only

c. both A and B

d. neither A nor B

11. Centrifugal advance weights in an electronic distributor move the:

a. baseplate (breaker plate)

b. pickup coil (sensor)

c. trigger wheel

d. stator

12. The only original-equipment ignition with metal-detection triggering used by a domestic carmaker was used by AMC and made by:

a. Delco-Remy

b. Motorcraft

c. Robert Bosch

d. Prestolite

13. The first domestic carmaker to use electronic ignition as standard equipment was:

a. AMC

b. Chrysler

c. Ford

d. General Motors

14. Mechanic A says that the Delco-Remy HEI system is a variable-dwell ignition. Mechanic B says that the Ford Solid-State and Dura-Spark II systems are fixed-dwell systems. Who is right?

a. A only

b. B only

c. both A and B

d. neither A nor B

15. Dual-mode timing is a feature of:

a. HEI systems

b. Chrysler ignitions

c. Bosch ignitions

d. Ford Dura-Spark systems

16. Thick-film integrated (TFI) ignition systems are used by:

a. AMC

b. Chrysler

c. Ford

d. General Motors

17. Which of the following is NOT used in a direct ignition system?

a. ignition coil

b. ignition module

c. distributor

d. crankshaft and camshaft sensors

18. Student A says that the ignition coil in a direct ignition system is connected to two spark plugs. Student B says that the ignition module controls primary current flow and dwell time limiting. Who is right?

a. A only

b. B only

c. both A and B

d. neither A nor B

19. Student A says that one spark plug in a direct ignition system fires forward and the other fires backwards. Student B says that all spark plugs in a DIS system fire forward. Who is right?

a. A only

b. B only

c. both A and B

d. neither A nor B

20. Student A says that a spark plug fired backwards in a direct ignition system requires 30 percent less voltage to create the arc. Student B says that a direct ignition system may use a Hall-effect sensor or a magnetic sensor. Who is right?

a. A only

b. B only

c. both A and B

d. neither A nor B

21. Student A says that a C3I system can be identified by the appearance of the coil pack. Student B says that the coil packs in all C3I systems are interchangeable. Who is right?

a. A only

b. B only

c. both A and B

d. neither A nor B

Fill in the Blank

22. In modern electronic ignitions, breaker points have been replaced by an _____ .

23. In an electronic ignition, all primary current passes through an ignition control _____ .

24. The most common trigger devices in electronic distributors are _____ generators.

25. The Hall effect works by passing current through semiconductor material and then applying a _____ to it at a right angle to its surface.

26. In a metal-detection circuit, an input voltage is transmitted to an _____ in the distributor sensor.

27. For either a breaker-point ignition or an electronic ignition, the best test instrument for determining problems with dwell is an _____ .

28. The type of electronic ignition in which dwell is the same in distributor degrees at all engine speeds is called a _____ ignition.

29. In a variable-dwell electronic ignition, the dwell period varies in distributor degrees at different engine speeds but dwell _____ remains relatively constant.

30. If an ignition system uses primary current and voltage to charge a capacitor, it is called a _____ system.

31. In many ignition modules, two power transistors are arranged in a _____ circuit.

32. Ignition switching transistors control primary current. The switching transistors are usually controlled by another _____ transistor.

33. A direct ignition system uses the _____ spark theory.

34. When an engine with a direct ignition system is first cranked, ignition timing signals are provided by the _____ .

35. The direct ignition system requires a _____ pulse to set up the crankshaft signal and ignition coil sequence.

36. The ignition module in a direct ignition system allows full coil saturation by a process called _____ .

37. In some direct ignition systems, crankshaft position is sensed by the use of a magnetic sensor and crankshaft _____ .

13 ELECTRONIC ENGINE CONTROL SYSTEMS

WHAT

In previous chapters, you learned about some engine sensors, actuators, and electronic control devices. Since electronic ignitions were introduced in the early 1970's, carmakers have continually brought more engine functions under electronic control. Today, fully integrated electronic control systems are state-of-the-art, standard equipment on most cars. Current systems use a central computer to monitor and control all ignition, fuel metering, and emission control functions. Many systems also regulate automatic transmission operation. This chapter explains the common principles of electronic engine control systems now used by all carmakers.

WHY

Chapter 4 in Part One of this book introduced the basic facts of automotive electronics. To begin studying electronic engine controls, it may be helpful to review the basics of analog and digital voltage signals, sensors and actuators, and computer memory and operation in that chapter. Chapter 4 also introduced the term, "system integration," to describe the function of an engine control computer. You will practice "service integration" when you work on these systems. You know that when you troubleshoot and repair a late-model car, you must look at the complete combustion control system. You can't service *just* the ignition, the fuel system, or the emission controls. A single temperature sensor signal to a central computer can affect ignition timing, fuel metering, EGR, and air injection. To service such a system professionally, you must know what the input and output signals mean, what they should be, and how to recognize them when they are wrong. This chapter will help you to understand the principles of engine control systems so you can service them accurately.

GOALS

After studying this chapter, you should be able to:

1. Identify the engine control systems used by various carmakers and list and explain the functions they monitor and control.

2. Identify and explain the differences between the following fuel injection features:

   a. port injection and throttle body injection

   b. continuous and intermittent injection

   c. mechanical and electronic injection

3. Identify and explain the operation of engine sensors, actuators, and auxiliary systems in gasoline injection systems.

4. Identify various analog and digital inputs from engine sensors and outputs to different control devices (actuators). Explain how each is used to monitor or control ignition timing, fuel metering (air-fuel ratio), idle speed, and other engine functions.

5. Explain the operation of an exhaust gas oxygen sensor.

6. Identify various air-fuel ratio control devices in different carburetors and fuel injection systems and explain how they work.

HISTORY OF ENGINE CONTROL SYSTEMS

Electronic engine controls first appeared in the 1977 model year. Early versions were partial-function systems that regulated ignition timing *or* fuel metering, but not both. Some were introduced with 3-way catalysts to provide a constant stoichiometric ratio. Carmakers quickly expanded their systems to control many engine functions. All systems have one or more of the following features. Most late-model systems have all:

• Electronic timing control instead of vacuum and centrifugal advance

• A 3-way catalytic converter and an exhaust gas oxygen (EGO) sensor for stoichiometric air-fuel ratio control

• Electronic control of fuel metering in the carburetor or fuel injection system

• Electronic control of EGR, air injection switching, vapor canister purging

• Open- and closed-loop operating modes for exhaust sensor feedback, fuel metering, and other control functions

• Electronic control of automatic transmission shifting and torque converter lockup

The exhaust gas oxygen (EGO) sensor is a key part of fully integrated engine control systems. Some carmakers call it simply an oxygen (O_2) sensor.

In the late 1970's Nissan (Datsun) introduced a twin-ignition system on some 4-cylinder engines. Called the NAPS-Z system, it features two spark plugs per cylinder. The electronic distributor and single ignition coil fire both plugs in each cylinder simultaneously. This provides more uniform flame front propagation to burn the mixture completely in a high-swirl combustion chamber.

Nissan adopted the twin-ignition system on selected engines for more efficient performance, economy, and emission control. It was not, however, a revolutionary new idea. Rather, it was a modern rebirth of an old idea.

In the late 1930's and early 1940's, the Electric Auto-Lite Company built several kinds of twin ignition systems that had two sets of breaker points, two ignition coils, and two spark plugs per cylinder. Each set of points, coil, and plugs was a completely separate ignition system that provided two sparks per cylinder simultaneously. Nash automobiles of

REBIRTH OF AN OLD IDEA

the late 1930's used 6- and 8-cylinder versions of this system, and some versions were adapted for use on Ford flathead V-8 racing engines.

The early twin-ignition systems were complicated and expensive to build and service. Improved combustion chamber design, higher octane gasoline, and other ignition advancements made the early systems obsolete after World War II. Nissan, however, saw that an old idea can have a modern application in the NAPS-Z system.

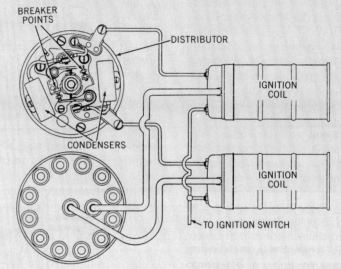

This breaker-point twin-ignition system was used on some engines of the late 1930's and early 1940's.

Chrysler Corporation

Introduced in late 1976, Chrysler's electronic lean-burn (ELB) system was the first system from a domestic carmaker to replace mechanical spark advance controls with electronic devices. The ELB system, figure 13-1, used sensors for vacuum, throttle position, coolant temperature, and air temperature to send input signals to the spark control computer. Engine speed and basic timing signals came from the electronic distributor pickup coil. Chrysler systems have used distributors with one or two pickup coils. The two pickup coils send different timing signals for starting and running conditions. Chrysler 4-cylinder engines have Hall-effect distributors.

The sensors simply convert the information on engine speed and vacuum to voltage signals for the computer. The computer adjusts timing fast and precisely by processing the input signals and regulating the output signal to the ignition module. Chrysler distributors for electronic control systems have never had vacuum advance

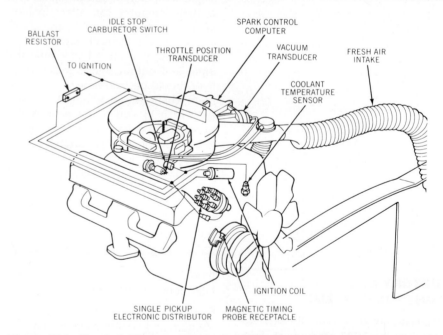

Figure 13-1. Chrysler's ELB system was the first system from a domestic carmaker to replace centrifugal and vacuum advance mechanisms with electronic timing control. (Chrysler)

devices. The 1976 distributors had centrifugal advance, but this was eliminated in 1977. The computer also controls timing in relation to temperature because it gets input signals

from the coolant and air temperature sensors.

The ELB system had a standard carburetor, calibrated for air-fuel ratios as lean as 16:1 to 18:1. The lean

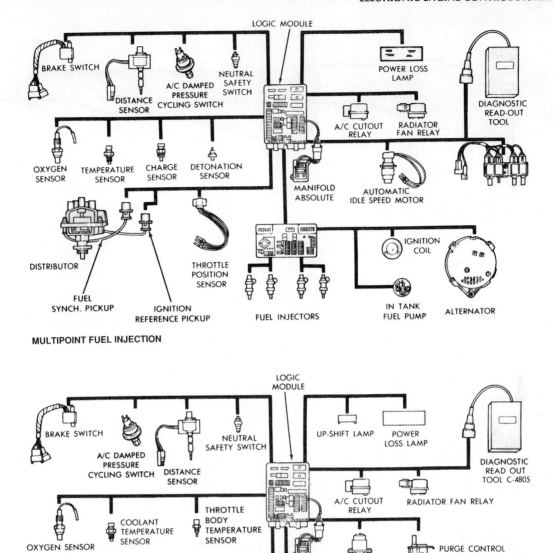

MULTIPOINT FUEL INJECTION

THROTTLE BODY FUEL INJECTION

Figure 13-2. Chrysler's late-model engine control systems regulate fuel metering, ignition timing, and emission control with port and throttle body injection, as well as with feedback carburetors. (Chrysler)

mixtures could be ignited and burned efficiently with electronically controlled timing, while they could not be with traditional mechanical controls. This system improved mileage and was fine for emission requirements of 1976–78. It did not include a 3-way catalyst, an EGO sensor, or feedback-controlled fuel metering.

In 1979, Chrysler renamed the ELB

system, electronic spark control (ESC) and recalibrated carburetors for air-fuel ratios closer to 14.7 : 1. In the same year, Chrysler introduced its first 3-way catalysts, EGO sensors, and feedback-controlled carburetors. In later years, Chrysler added a detonation sensor and other devices, and put more functions under electronic control. Chrysler calls its systems elec-

tronic spark advance (ESA) and electronic feedback carburetor or electronic fuel control (EFC), in addition to ESC. Since the early 1980's Chrysler has used fully integrated systems on 4-, 6-, and 8-cylinder engines with injection, carburetors, and turbocharging, figure 13-2. In 1983, Chrysler added self-diagnostic capabilities to its ECS systems.

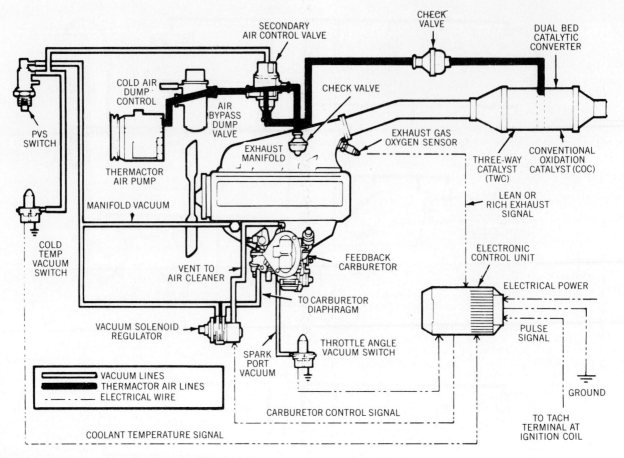

Figure 13-3. Ford's first electronic control, feedback carburetor system regulated only fuel metering, not ignition timing. (Ford)

Ford Motor Company

In 1978, Ford introduced an electronically controlled feedback carburetor system with a "three-way catalyst and conventional oxidation catalyst" (TWC-COC). Used only on 2.3-liter 4-cylinder engines, figure 13-3, this system had an EGO sensor, an analog computer, and a vacuum control solenoid. It controlled only fuel metering for a 14.7 : 1 air-fuel ratio as needed by the 3-way catalyst. Ignition was controlled by the standard ignition module, and distributors had centrifugal and vacuum advance. The fuel electronic control unit, however, received an engine speed signal from the ignition module. In 1980, Ford renamed this system the microprocessor control unit (MCU) system, figure 13-4, to reflect a change from an analog to a digital computer. System function remained the same on many engines through the 1980's.

Also in 1978, Ford introduced the first of its electronic engine control (EEC) systems. EEC-I, figure 13-5, was used on 302-cid (5-liter) V-8's in Lincoln Versailles to control spark timing, EGR, and air injection. It did *not* have a 3-way catalyst, an EGO sensor, or feedback fuel control.

EEC-I has Ford's 2700 VV variable-venturi carburetor and Dura-Spark II ignition with no centrifugal or vacuum advance. The computer controls timing signals to the ignition module and receives input signals from manifold pressure and barometric sensors, coolant and air temperature sensors, a crankshaft position sensor, an EGR valve position sensor, and a throttle position sensor. The computer also controls a solenoid that regulates vacuum to the air injection diverter valve and two solenoids that control air pressure to the EGR valve. The EGR valve works on air pressure from the

air injection pump rather than on vacuum, figure 13-6. The EGR system also includes an EGR cooler, through which engine coolant circulates to lower recirculated exhaust temperature. Dura-Spark distributors used with EEC systems have unique bilevel rotors and cap terminals, figure 13-7, to prevent crossfiring within the distributor.

In 1979, Ford added feedback fuel control for the 3-way catalyst, vapor canister purging, and air injection switching to the EEC system and called it EEC-II. Used on 351-cid (5.8-liter) V-8's, figure 13-8, EEC-II has an EGO sensor and a 7200 VV carburetor with a fuel control stepper motor. The EGR valve is vacuum operated, but vacuum is regulated by two solenoids similar to those of EEC-I. In 1980, Ford added self-diagnostic capabilities to the computer and modified the system to operate with throttle body injec-

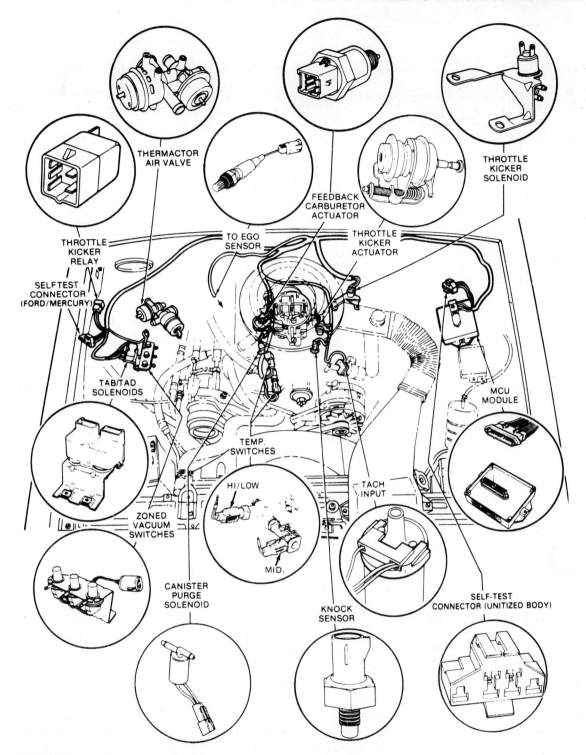

Figure 13-4. Ford renamed the electronic feedback carburetor system the MCU system in 1980 to reflect a change from analog to digital electronics. (Ford)

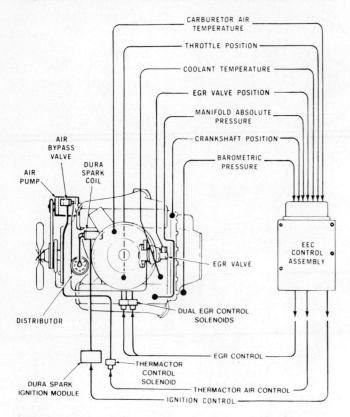

Figure 13-5. Ford's EEC-I system was used only on 1978 Lincoln Versailles models to control ignition timing, EGR, and air injection. (Ford)

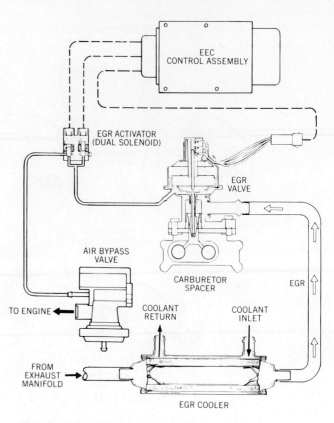

Figure 13-6. Ford's EEC-I system had an air-pressure-operated EGR valve. Ford used an EGR cooler on this and some later EGR systems. (Ford)

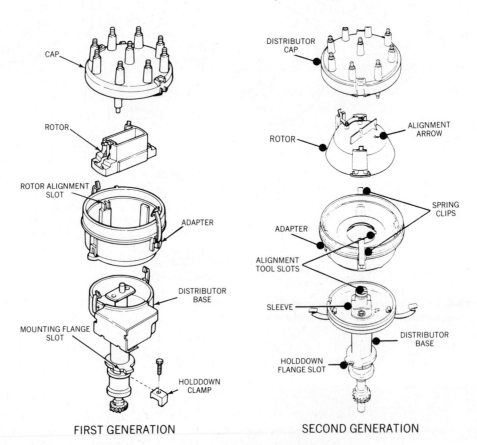

FIRST GENERATION

SECOND GENERATION

Figure 13-7. Dura-Spark distributors used with EEC systems have unique bilevel rotors and terminals in the cap. Numbers on the caps are cylinder numbers, not firing order. (Ford)

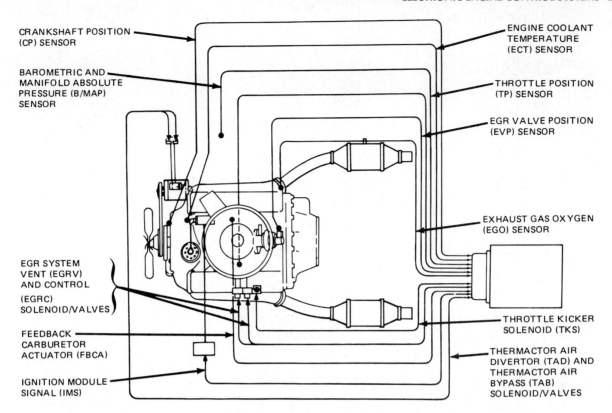

Figure 13-8. EEC-II was Ford's first fully integrated system to control timing, fuel metering, and emission devices. (Ford)

tion, figure 13-9, as well as the 7200 VV carburetor. This system is called EEC-III and is used on many 302- and 351-cid (5.0- and 5.8-liter) V-8's.

Ford continued EEC-III through 1983 and MCU systems through the late 1980's. Also in 1983, Ford introduced EEC-IV on 1.6-liter 4-cylinder engines. This system, figure 13-10, features a redesigned computer, Ford's thick-film-integrated (TFI) ignition, and port fuel injection. EEC-IV regulates all timing, fuel, and emission control functions. In 1984 and later models, Ford extended EEC-IV to most 4-, 6-, and 8-cylinder engines with both carburetors and injection, including Festiva, Tracer, and other captive-import models. After 1985, the only carbureted engines in Ford automobile EEC systems were some 1.9- and 2.3-liter engines.

General Motors

Like other carmakers, GM has developed its systems since the late 1970's. In 1977–78, Oldsmobile Toronados had a system called microprocessor sensing and automatic regulation

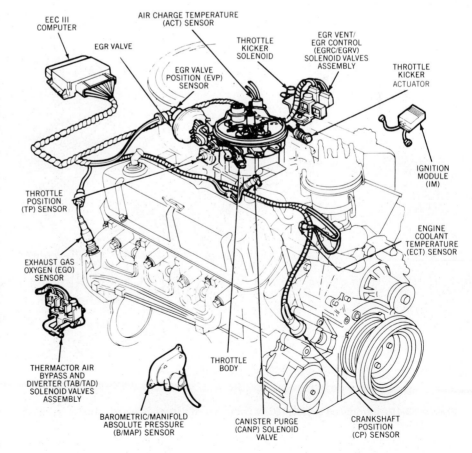

Figure 13-9. EEC-III is similar to EEC-II but used with throttle body injection on some engines. (Ford)

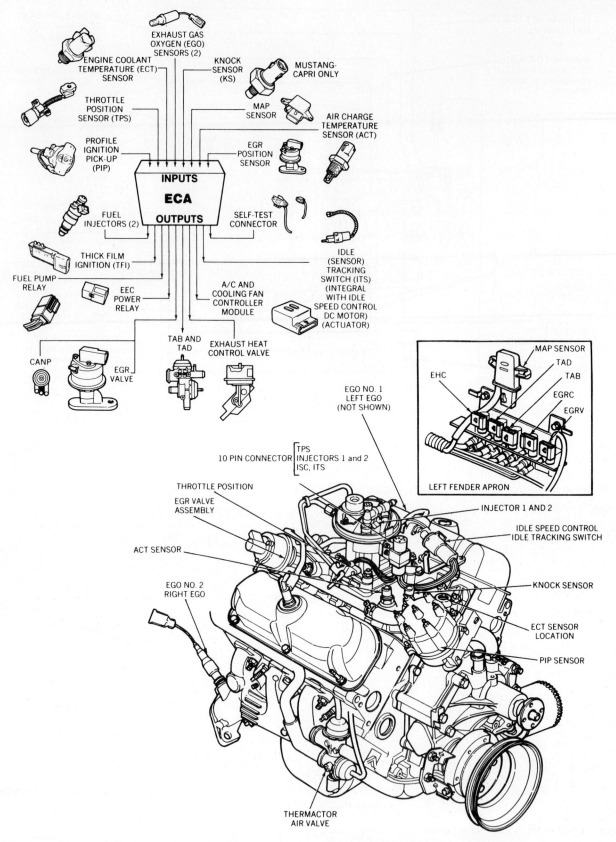

Figure 13-10. Introduced in 1983, EEC-IV became Ford's standard engine control system in the mid-1980's. (Ford)

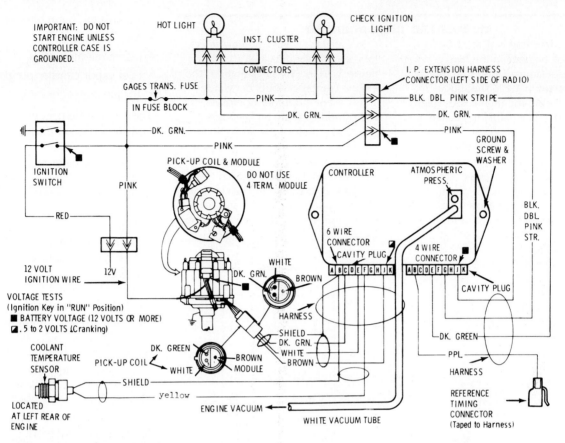

Figure 13-11. Oldsmobile's MISAR system of 1977–78 was GM's first electronically controlled timing system. (Oldsmobile)

(MISAR) that controlled only timing, figure 13-11. It was discontinued after 1978. In 1978, Cadillac began using electronic spark selection (ESS) that retards timing during cranking and cold operation. The electronic ignition chapter of this text summarizes the electronic timing modifications used with GM high-energy ignition (HEI) systems. Some of these systems are used with independent electronic injection systems, such as the early Seville EFI, and some are used with fully integrated engine systems.

Also in 1978, GM introduced an electronic fuel control (EFC) system on some 4-cylinder engines, figure 13-12. Like Ford's TWC-COC and MCU systems, it had a 3-way catalyst, an EGO sensor, and a feedback carburetor. While this 1978–79 system provided electronic fuel control, it did not have electronic ignition timing. In 1979, GM installed its first fully integrated computer-controlled catalytic

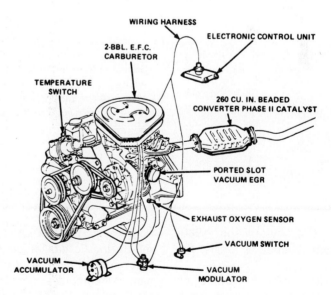

Figure 13-12. GM's first electronic fuel control system was used on 1978–79 4-cylinder California engines. (GM)

MODULATED DISPLACEMENT

Ford experimented with it on 6-cylinder truck engines in the late 1970's. Cadillac marketed it as the V8-6-4 system in 1981. The modulated-displacement engine uses solenoid-operated actuators to change the valve rocker arm pivot points. The solenoid moves a blocking plate that slides over the top of the spring-loaded valve selector. This releases spring force on the normal rocker arm pivot and allows the rocker to pivot on the tip of the valve, figure 1. The valve springs hold the valves closed. The pistons continue up and down, but the cylinders receive no intake charge and produce no exhaust. They are effectively shut off. Air in the cylinder is compressed and expanded. No power is produced, and no fuel is consumed.

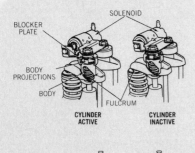

CYLINDER ACTIVE   CYLINDER INACTIVE

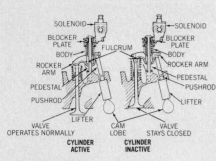

CYLINDER ACTIVE   CYLINDER INACTIVE

In Cadillac's V8-6-4 system, selectors are on cylinders 1, 4, 6, and 7, figure 2. In 6-cylinder operation, the engine computer shuts of cylinders 1 and 4. For 4-cylinder operation, the computer shuts off cylinders 1, 4, 6, and 7. Before the engine is allowed to run on 4 or 6 cylinders, it must be at normal temperature, the transmission in high gear, and the fuel injection system in closed loop. The computer deactivates and reactivates cylinders according to engine load.

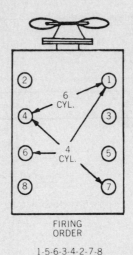

FIRING ORDER

1-5-6-3-4-2-7-8

Cadillac's V8-6-4 system did not provide the long-term reliability and driveability the manufacturer wanted. It was discontinued after 1982, but the modulated-displacement concept may return on future engine systems.

converter (C-4) system on 1980-model front-wheel-drive X-cars, figure 13-13.

Used with feedback carburetors, the C-4 system receives input signals from engine speed and crankshaft position sensors, manifold and barometric pressure sensors, coolant and air temperature sensors, throttle position sensors, and an EGO sensor. The computer controls fuel metering, EGR, air injection switching, and igni-

tion timing. The C-4 system also has self-diagnostic capabilities. In 1981, GM modified the C-4 system and renamed it computer command control (CCC or C-3). The CCC system, figure 13-14, can monitor up to 15 vehicle functions and can control the following operations:

• Electronic spark timing (EST)
• Fuel metering—feedback carburetor or fuel injection
• Idle speed

• Exhaust gas recirculation
• Air injection
• Intake manifold heat
• Fuel vapor canister purging
• Torque converter lockup

The CCC system is now used by all GM divisions on most cars and light trucks. The CCC self-diagnostic capabilities are greater than those of C-4, and the CCC system is used on carbureted and fuel-injected engines, with and without turbochargers.

Throughout the 1980's, the CCC control system and GM onboard computers have developed steadily and acquired more capabilities. In 1981 and 1982, most CCC systems were used with carbureted engines and were known as "minimum function" and "full-function" systems. Minimum-function systems were used on T-cars (Chevettes and Pontiac 1000 models) and some Oldsmobile V-8's. They had fewer sensors and did not provide the control sophistication of full-function systems. Today, the terms "minimum-function" and "full-function" are often used to refer to carbureted CCC systems. In fact, carbureted engines sometimes are distinguished from fuel-injected engines by calling them CCC, or C-3, engines.

All late-model GM fuel injection systems use the basic CCC system introduced in the early 1980's but often referred to by the names given the various injection systems. Since 1986, systems with high-speed computers are often called "P-4" systems. Regardless of the popular names for GM engine control systems, all are evolutionary developments of the original systems introduced on 1980–81 models. Later sections of this chapter explain GM injection systems in detail and outline the continuing development of the onboard computers.

Bosch Lambda and Motronic Systems

Historically, many European carmakers have used ignition, fuel injection, and electronic systems made by the Robert Bosch company. Bosch was a pioneer in diesel and gasoline fuel in-

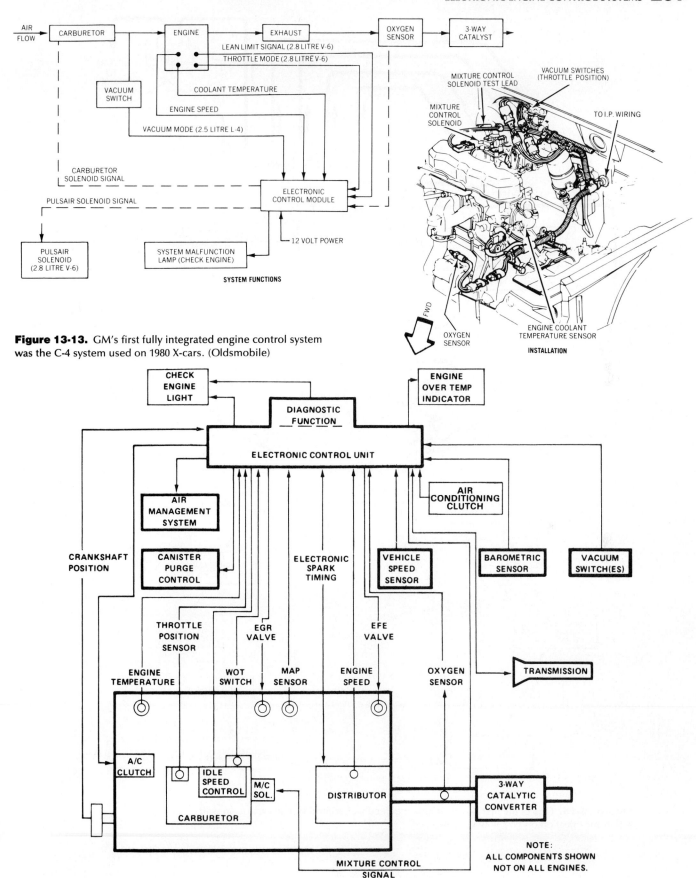

Figure 13-13. GM's first fully integrated engine control system was the C-4 system used on 1980 X-cars. (Oldsmobile)

Figure 13-14. The CCC system became the standard GM engine control system in the early 1980's. (Chevrolet)

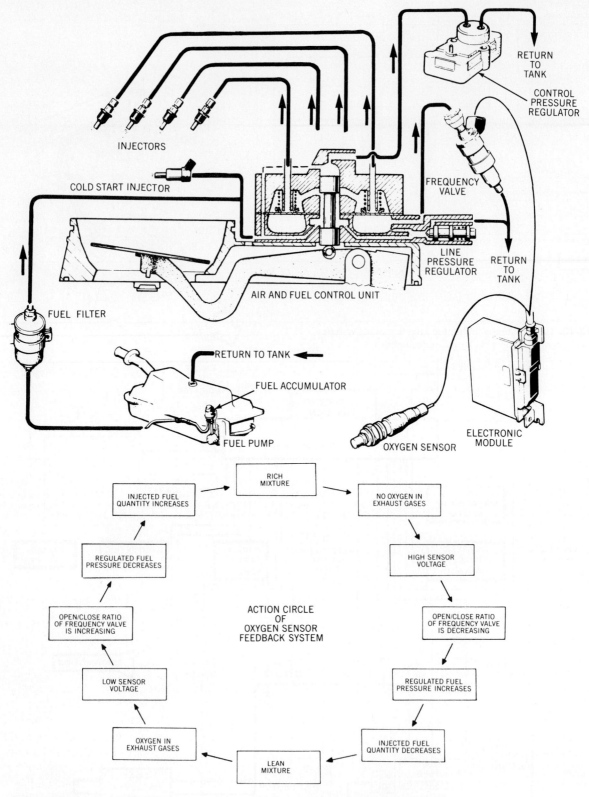

Figure 13-15. One of the first Bosch lambda fuel feedback control systems was used with K-Jetronic injection on 1977 Volvos. (Volvo)

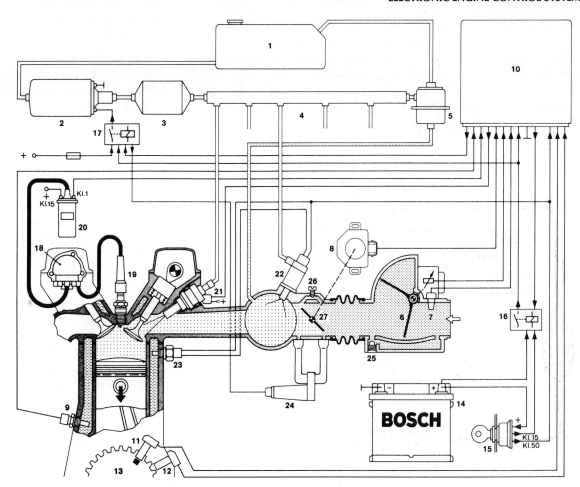

1 FUEL TANK, 2 FUEL PUMP, 3 FUEL FILTER, 4 DISTRIBUTOR TUBE, 5 PRESSURE REGULATOR, 6 AIR-FLOW SENSOR, 7 INTAKE-AIR TEMPERATURE-SENSOR, 8 THROTTLE-VALVE SWITCH. 9 ENGINE-TEMPERATURE SENSOR, 10 CONTROL UNIT, 11 REFERENCE-MARK SENSOR, 12 SPEED SENSOR, 13 FLYWHEEL, 14 BATTERY, 15 IGNITION AND STARTER SWITCH, 16 MAIN RELAY. 17 PUMP RELAY, 18 HIGH-VOLTAGE DISTRIBUTOR, 19 SPARK PLUG, 20 IGNITION COIL, 21 INJECTION VALVE, 22 START VALVE, 23 THERMO-TIME SWITCH, 24 AUXILIARY-AIR DEVICE. 25 IDLE-MIXTURE ADJUSTMENT SCREW, 26 IDLE-SPEED ADJUSTMENT SCREW, 27 THROTTLE VALVE.

Figure 13-16. The Bosch Motronic system combines lambda fuel control and electronic timing with L-Jetronic injection. (Bosch)

jection and holds many basic patents for injection and electronic systems.

In 1977, Volvo installed an electronically controlled fuel-metering system on cars sold in the U.S. Volvo's lambda-sond system was made by Bosch and used with K-Jetronic injection, figure 13-15. Later adopted by other carmakers, the lambda-sond system was the first with a 3-way catalyst and EGO sensor. The electronic unit receives an input signal from the EGO sensor and sends an output signal to a timing valve in the K-Jetronic system. The valve varies injection control pressure and regulates the fuel delivered by the continuous injection nozzles. The original

lambda-sond system does not regulate ignition timing or other emission functions. These came later with the Motronic system.

The Bosch Motronic system, or digital motor electronics (DME), combines L-Jetronic injection with lambda feedback fuel control and electronic spark timing, figure 13-16. Besides a 3-way catalyst and EGO sensor, the Motronic system uses input signals from crankshaft speed and position sensors, the pulse generator in the ignition distributor, and the L-Jetronic sensors. The computer regulates the injector pulse width for air-fuel ratio control and adjusts ignition timing for combined speed and load conditions.

The system also shuts injection off completely during closed-throttle deceleration.

The Motronic system is a full-function control system based on the Bosch L-Jetronic injection system, but late-model versions of the mechanical K-Jetronic injection system have some of the same control capabilities. The KE-Jetronic system includes fuel cutoff on deceleration, altitude compensation, and engine speed limiting functions. All of these are regulated by the system computer, or electronic control unit. The KE-Jetronic system, however, does not include ignition timing control and other management functions in its computer. These are handled by other electronic control units. A later section of this chapter explains Bosch gasoline injection systems in more detail.

Control System Development

From these summaries of engine control systems used by various carmakers, you probably have the idea that there has been a lot of experimentation and continuous development. You're right. We haven't the room in this book to give you all the specifications for each manufacturer for every year and model. Consider these trends during the 1980's, however:

• The earliest control systems used analog computers with limited control functions and slow processing speed. In the early 1980's digital computers replaced earlier analog units, and processing speed increased.

• The earliest systems were designed primarily to control feedback fuel metering. A few were designed as spark timing control systems. Carmakers quickly combined these functions in fully integrated systems.

• Computer size has decreased as speed and processing capability has increased. The earliest onboard computers were relatively large units with many discrete components soldered to several circuit boards. Chrysler's first computers had separate circuit boards for power components and for computer logic devices. The latest Chrysler systems have all devices integrated into a single-module engine controller (SMEC) or single-board engine controller (SBEC) computer. GM's first CCC computers communicated with sensors and actuators at a 160-baud data transmission speed. The latest CCC computers communicate at 8192 baud.

• Computer networks have appeared as the latest generation of control systems. On GM cars, the engine control module (ECM) shares sensor signals with the body computer module (BCM). Late-model Chrysler systems and some imported systems work similarly. Ford and other manufacturers introduced similar computer networks in the early 1990's.

All of these trends illustrate the fact that when you service a particular system, you will need the manufacturer's system description, procedures, and specifications from a shop manual or an independent service manual. Control systems will continue to evolve and grow during the next decade, and you must always work with the latest service procedures for a specific year and model of vehicle.

Remember, though, that the laws of electricity, physics, and chemistry don't change from one engine to another. All systems operate on the same principles, and all engineers have the same goals of best performance, driveability, emission control, and economy for the cars they design. The rest of this chapter outlines engine control principles and will help you recognize more similarities than differences among systems.

GASOLINE FUEL INJECTION REQUIREMENTS

Air volume, air pressure, and airflow into the engine are the factors that control fuel metering with a carburetor *and* with an injection system. A fuel injection system must provide the same kinds of air-fuel ratios that a carburetor does for these basic operating conditions:

• *Starting*—Low intake vacuum, low airflow, a cold engine, and poor fuel vaporization require a slightly rich air-fuel ratio.

• *Idle*—Low airflow, high manifold vacuum, low carburetor vacuum, and poor vaporization still require a slightly rich mixture.

• *Low speed*—Increasing engine speed, airflow, and carburetor vacuum allow the air-fuel ratio to become leaner.

• *Cruising economy*—With light engine loads and high, relatively constant, vacuum and airflow, the engine provides best economy with lean air-fuel ratios.

• *Extra power requirements*—An engine needs slightly rich air-fuel ratios for heavy loads and acceleration (low vacuum and low airflow) and for full-throttle operation (low vacuum and high airflow).

A carburetor provides rich air-fuel ratios of 12.5:1 to 13.5:1 and lean ratios of 15:1 to 16:1. A fuel injection system does exactly the same things for exactly the same engine needs. Late-model injection systems and carburetors used with electronic engine controls have fuel-metering devices to maintain the stoichiometric air-fuel ratio of 14.7:1 for most operating conditions. The rich and lean limits stay much closer to the ideal 14.7:1 ratio than they did on earlier engines.

Fuel injection and carburetors have a lot in common in their operating requirements. The parts that carburetors and injection systems use to meet these needs look different, but every system of a carburetor has a fuel injection counterpart. Whether mechanical or electronic, port or throttle body, all systems have these basic groups of parts:

• Fuel delivery system
• Air control system
• Engine sensors and auxiliary systems

GASOLINE FUEL INJECTION SYSTEMS

For many years, gasoline fuel injection was used on high-performance engines. In the 1970's, however, engineers took a fresh look at gasoline injection, combined with electronic engine control, as a way to reach the conflicting goals of good performance, fuel economy, and emission control. Today, all major carmakers offer fuel injection on most of their vehicles.

Fuel injection is steadily forcing the carburetor into obsolescence. Today, fuel injection is a major feature of most fully integrated engine control

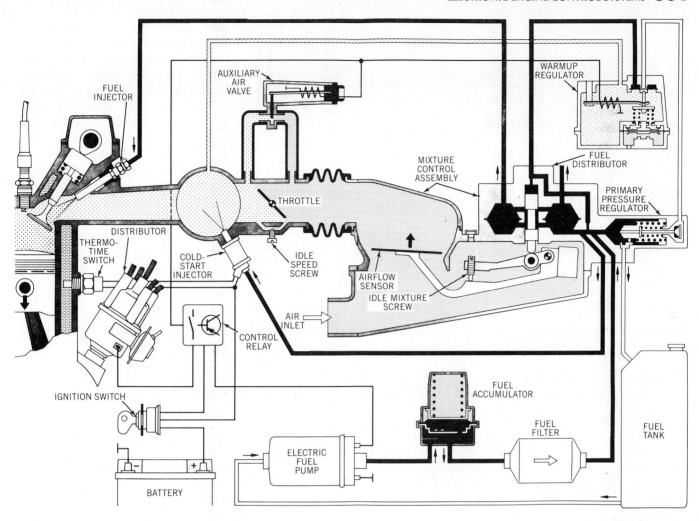

Figure 13-17. Bosch K-Jetronic fuel injection is a mechanical continuous injection system. (Bosch)

systems. The following sections explain the various kinds of injection systems and their common principles. Gasoline injection can be classified as:

- Mechanical or electronic injection
- Port (or manifold) injection or throttle body injection
- Continuous or intermittent injection

Mechanical injection systems inject fuel by using the pressure of gasoline in the injector lines to open the injector valves. They are usually continuous, which means that they inject fuel constantly while the engine is running. Most electronic systems use solenoid-operated injectors to spray fuel intermittently (in timed pulses) into the manifold or intake ports. Port,

or manifold, systems have individual injectors for each cylinder. Throttle body systems have one or two injectors to spray fuel into the intake manifold inlet, above the throttle. These distinctions are not clear-cut. All electronic systems are not exclusively port or throttle body systems. All mechanical systems have some electronic parts. When you study a specific injection system, you must ask yourself how it is controlled, how the injection nozzles are located, and how it operates.

Before we examine the principles of all systems, we will look at some of the most common specific systems. This introduction will help you recognize the different devices that do similar jobs.

Bosch K-Jetronic

Introduced in the early 1970's on many European cars, the Bosch K-Jetronic is a mechanical continuous injection system (CIS), figure 13-17. The individual port injectors inject fuel by gasoline pressure at the nozzles. The system regulates this pressure in relation to air volume, which is measured by sensing airflow.

Bosch KE-Jetronic

The Bosch KE-Jetronic system is a development of the basic K-Jetronic system with increased electronic control capabilities. KE-Jetronic systems have additional sensors for throttle position, airflow sensor position, and en-

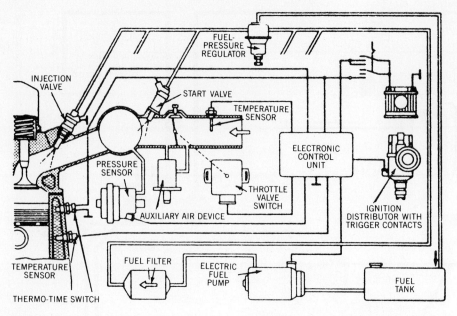

gine coolant temperature. KE systems have a more powerful computer than basic K-Jetronic systems and use input signals from the ignition distributor and a heated EGO sensor (in most installations). The electrohydraulic pressure actuator built into the KE-Jetronic fuel distributor controls fuel pressure, and thus fuel quantity, in response to signals from the system computer. Idle speed is programmed into the computer and cannot be adjusted in service.

Bosch D-Jetronic

This electronic fuel injection (EFI) system uses individual solenoid-operated port injectors, figure 13-18. Fuel is metered in relation to manifold air

Figure 13-18. Bosch D-Jetronic fuel injection is an electronic intermittent injection system, controlled by manifold pressure. (Bosch)

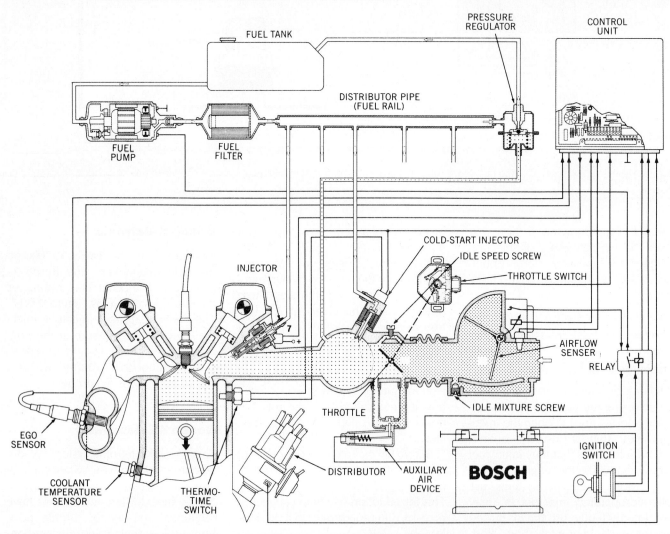

Figure 13-19. Bosch L-Jetronic fuel injection is an electronic intermittent injection system, controlled by airflow measurement and engine speed. (Bosch)

pressure and engine speed. Injection is in intermittent pulses. D-Jetronic injection was used on 1968–73 Volkswagens and other European cars.

Bosch L-Jetronic

Introduced in 1974, the Bosch L-Jetronic system uses solenoid-operated intermittent injectors for each port. As with the mechanical K-Jetronic system, fuel metering is controlled in relation to airflow. The L-Jetronic system does this, however, with an electronic module that responds to a voltage signal from an airflow sensor, figure 13-19. The module also regulates fuel metering in relation to engine speed and temperature. This system often is called airflow-controlled (AFC) injection.

Bosch LH-Jetronic

Introduced in the 1980's, the LH-Jetronic system, figure 13-20, is similar to the L-Jetronic system. Air volume, however, is measured by a hot-wire air mass sensor rather than an airflow sensor. This provides more precise measurement of the molecular volume of combustible air entering the engine.

Bendix Electronic Port Injection System

The Bendix EFI system used on 1976–79 Cadillac Sevilles, figure 13-21, was the first modern port injection system in widespread use on domestic cars. This system has individual port injectors that deliver fuel intermittently. The electronic module controls injection in relation to manifold pressure, throttle position, engine speed, and air and coolant temperature. The last versions of this system included an exhaust gas oxygen (EGO) sensor and feedback control of fuel metering.

The Bosch D-Jetronic and Cadillac-Bendix systems were very similar in design and operation. In fact, Bosch D-Jetronic design was based on earlier engineering work by Bendix.

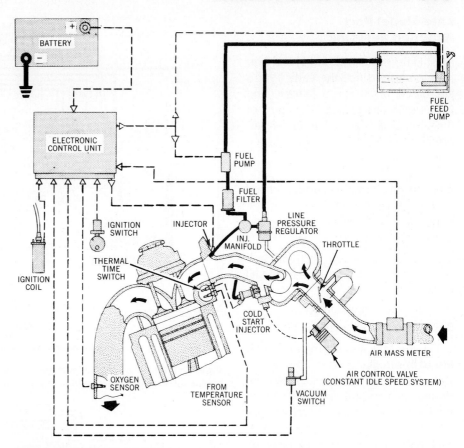

Figure 13-20. Bosch LH-Jetronic fuel injection is similar to L-Jetronic but controlled by an air mass sensor. (Volvo)

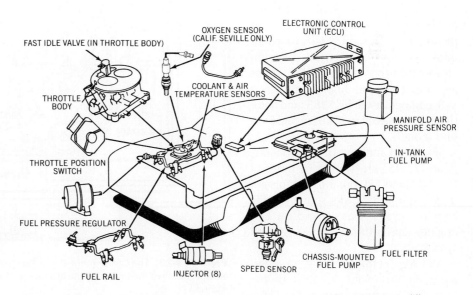

Figure 13-21. The Bendix EFI system with port injectors was used on 1976–79 Cadillac Sevilles. (Cadillac)

Late-Model Port Injection Systems

Most EFI systems with individual port injectors used since the early 1980's are based on Bosch L-Jetronic and LH-Jetronic designs. In fact, many of the components are made under patent license from the Robert Bosch Corporation.

General Motors Systems. General Motors introduced port injection systems on its 1984 models and now uses three different types:

1. Port fuel injection (PFI) or multiport (multipoint) fuel injection (MFI or MPFI)

2. Tuned port injection (TPI)

3. Sequential fuel injection (SFI)

PFI and MFI systems, figure 13-22, are both simultaneous double-fire injection systems. All injectors fire once during each revolution of the engine, mixing two injections of fuel with intake air for each combustion cycle. MFI systems were used on 1984–85 engines. PFI systems are used on 4-cylinder and small V-6 engines with conventional HEI distributors.

TPI operates essentially the same as PFI and MFI, but uses an intake air plenum that has individually tuned air intake runners to provide optimum airflow for each cylinder. TPI systems are found on the high-performance V-8 engines used in 1985 and later Corvettes, as well as Camaro and Firebird models.

SFI design and system components, figure 13-23, are similar to those of PFI, MFI, and TPI, but the injectors are triggered in firing order sequence. SFI injection systems are found on GM engines with a distributorless ignition system (DIS).

All GM port injection systems operate with advanced versions of the basic CCC system introduced in 1981.

Ford Systems. Ford's port injection systems are called electronic fuel injection (EFI). The 4-cylinder EFI systems are based on the Bosch L-Jetronic design with simultaneous double-fire injector triggering. The first

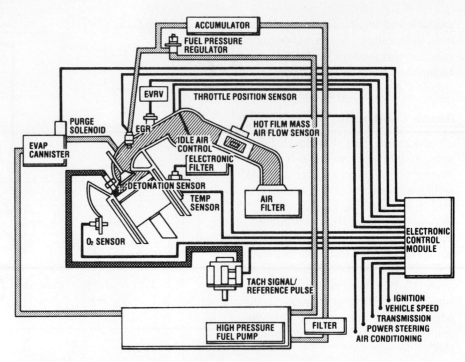

Figure 13-22. The GM multiport fuel injection (MFI) system uses a hot film mass airflow sensor and fires the injectors once every crankshaft revolution. (General Motors)

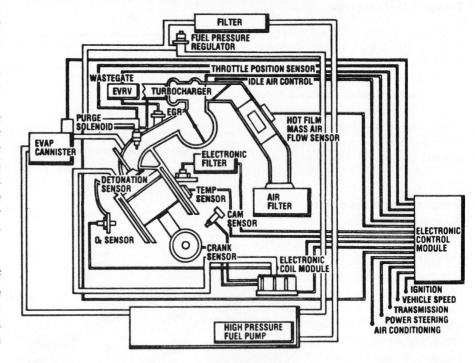

Figure 13-23. The GM sequential fuel injection (SFI) system also uses a hot film mass airflow sensor, but fires the injectors one at a time according to engine cylinder firing order. (General Motors)

Ford EFI system appeared on the 1.6-liter 4-cylinder engine in 1983 Escort and Lynx vehicles and is used essentially unchanged on certain 1.6- and 1.9-liter engines in other models. A variation of the system is found on 1984 and later 1.6- and 2.3-liter turbocharged engines. Figure 13-24 shows a port injection system installation on a Ford 4-cylinder engine.

A simultaneous injection system also is used on the 183-cid (3.0-liter)

V-6 engine introduced in the 1986 Taurus and Sable vehicles. The system is similar to those used on 4-cylinder engines. A sequential fuel injection (SFI) system is used on 1986 and later 302-cid (5.0-liter) V-8 engines. Injectors are triggered in firing order sequence by the EEC-IV computer, with each injector firing once every two crankshaft revolutions.

Chrysler Systems. The Chrysler grouped double-fire port injection system, figure 13-25, is similar to a Bosch D-Jetronic system. It uses Bosch-designed injectors with Chrysler-engineered electronics and is found on 1984 and later 2.2-liter 4-cylinder engines.

Japanese Systems. Most port injection systems used by major Japanese carmakers were derived from the Bosch L-Jetronic system. Nissan was the first to introduce EFI in 1975; Toyota's system first appeared in 1979. These applications controlled

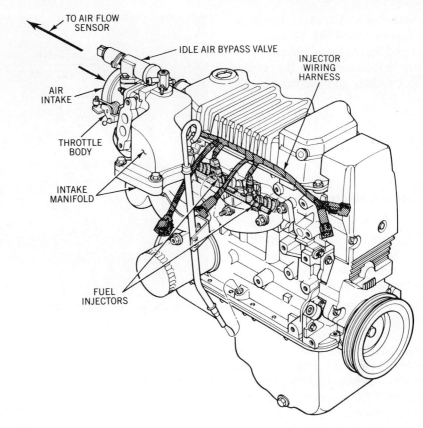

Figure 13-24. Ford port EFI systems are similar to Bosch L-Jetronic systems. (Ford)

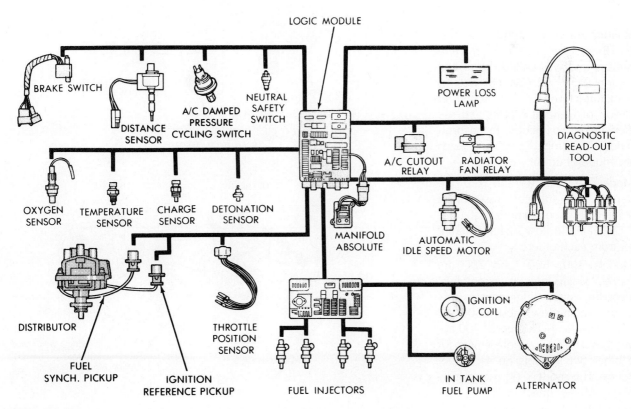

Figure 13-25. Chrysler uses a grouped, double-fire port injection system based on Bosch D-Jetronic system principles.

only fuel injector duration. However, the systems used by Nissan since 1981 and Toyota since 1983 are completely integrated with the engine control system and incorporate idle speed, EGR, and ignition timing control according to injection system requirements. Figure 13-26 shows a late-model Toyota injection system, based on Bosch designs.

Throttle Body Injection

Throttle body injection (TBI) systems first appeared on domestic engines in the early 1980's. Today, gasoline injection systems are about equally divided between individual port injection and TBI systems.

Except for the Chrysler V-8 system, all TBI systems have similar parts. One or two solenoid-operated injectors are located in a throttle body assembly that resembles the base of a carburetor. The injectors deliver fuel intermittently to the intake air charge. A manifold pressure sensor measures intake air volume, and the electronic module controls fuel injection volume proportionally.

GM-Rochester Systems. The first GM TBI system appeared on 1980 Cadillacs and was called digital fuel injection (DFI). All GM TBI systems are manufactured by the Rochester Division of General Motors and use either one or two injectors in the throttle body housing. There are seven basic models currently in use:

• Models 100, 200, and 220 are 2-barrel, dual-injector assemblies. The injectors in some model 220 units are calibrated to flow fuel at different rates from each other.

• Models 300, 500, and 700 are 1-barrel, single-injector assemblies. Except for minor differences in fuel metering and airflow, models 300 and 500 are identical. The model 700 appeared in 1987 as a replacement for the other two models on 4-cylinder engines. The model 700 uses a low-pressure Multec injector.

• Model 400 is an assembly of two single-barrel, single-injector TBI units

Figure 13-26. The Nippondenso injection system on this Toyota is similar to the Bosch L-Jetronic system.

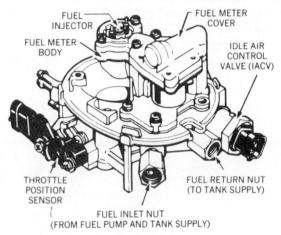

MODEL 300 TBI ASSEMBLY

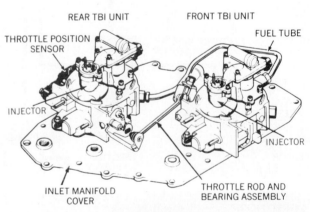

MODEL 400 TBI ASSEMBLY

Figure 13-27. First used on 1980 Cadillacs, Rochester TBI systems are now used by all GM car divisions. (Rochester)

on a single intake manifold. It is also known as crossfire injection, because the electronic control module (ECM) is programmed to fire the TBI units in an alternating, or crossfire, sequence. The model 400 is found on some 1982–83 305-cid (5.0-liter) V-8 engines used in Camaros and Firebirds.

Rochester TBI systems are now used on many 4-, 6-, and 8-cylinder GM engines. Figure 13-27 shows typical Rochester model 300 and model 400 TBI assemblies. Because these systems are used with electronic engine controls, the TBI units include throttle position sensors and idle air control valves or idle speed motors.

Ford Systems. Ford also introduced a TBI system on some 1980 V-8 engines. Now called central fuel injection (CFI), the high-pressure Ford TBI system has been used mostly on V-6 and V-8 engines through the early 1980's. A single-injector low-pressure TBI unit is used on the 1985 and later 2.3-liter HSC and some 2.5-liter HSC 4-cylinder engines.

Figure 13-28 shows a typical Ford 2-barrel, dual-injector TBI assembly, which Ford calls a fuel charging assembly. Because Ford's TBI systems are used with electronic engine controls, they also include throttle position sensors and idle speed control motors.

Chrysler Systems. Chrysler introduced its first TBI system on 1981 V-8 engines in Imperials and now uses other TBI systems on 4-cylinder engines. Like GM's crossfire injection, the Chrysler continuous flow system proved to be a technological dead end. The Chrysler V-8 system, figure 13-29, uses dual injectors to deliver fuel continuously in response to varying pressure from a control pump. This system measures air volume with a unique airflow sensor in the air cleaner inlet.

Chrysler's 4-cylinder TBI systems are similar to other TBI systems for small engines. From 1981 through 1985, Chrysler used a single-injector, high-pressure system with a Bendix

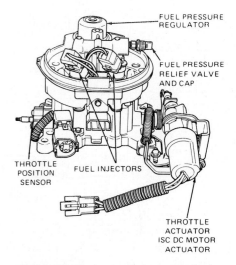

Figure 13-28. Ford calls its throttle body injection "central fuel injection (CFI)," but it works similarly to other systems. (Ford)

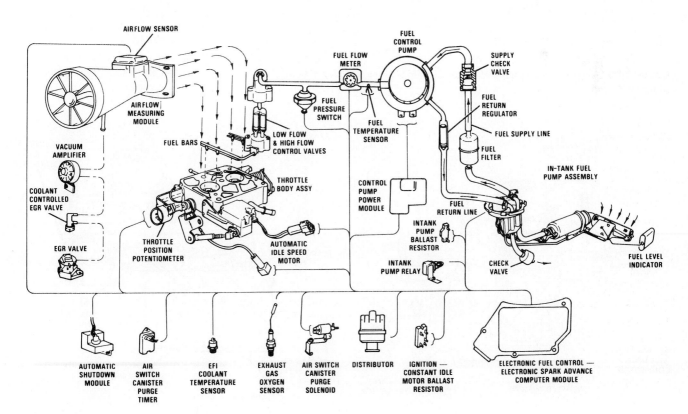

Figure 13-29. Chrysler's V-8 TBI system uses continuously operating injectors, regulated by control pump pressure. (Chrysler)

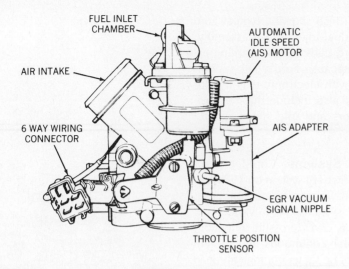

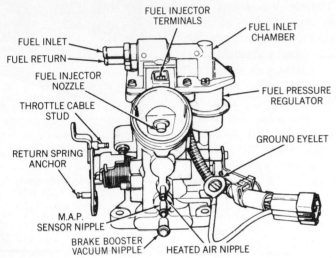

Figure 13-30. Chrysler's high-pressure throttle body injection assembly for 4-cylinder engines. (Chrysler)

fuel injector, figure 13-30. The system was redesigned for 1986 and later models to operate at low pressure using a Bosch fuel injector, figure 13-31. All late-model Chrysler TBI systems are part of fully integrated electronic engine control systems.

Imported Car TBI Systems. Several imported cars use TBI systems that are similar to those on domestic vehicles. Figure 13-32 shows the major components of an AMC-Renault TBI system. Although built in North America, these vehicles use a typical example of one type of imported TBI system.

An atypical example is the TBI system used on turbocharged Japanese vehicles built by Mitsubishi and sold under both the Mitsubishi and Chrysler nameplates in the United States. This system uses a Karman vortex airflow sensor in the air cleaner, figure 13-33, to measure intake airflow rate. The dual injectors mounted in the injection mixer or throttle body inlet port, figure 13-34, work like other solenoid-operated injectors and are fired in an alternating sequence. The electronics of this system, however, are considerably more complex than the other TBI systems discussed.

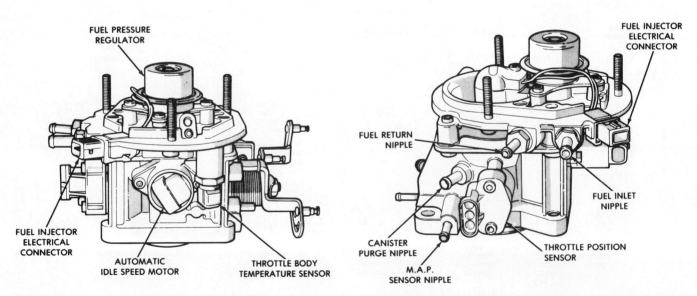

Figure 13-31. Chrysler's low-pressure throttle body assembly for 4-cylinder engines. (Chrysler)

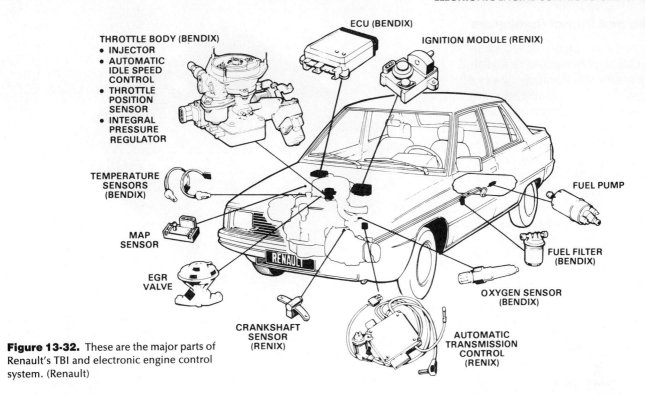

Figure 13-32. These are the major parts of Renault's TBI and electronic engine control system. (Renault)

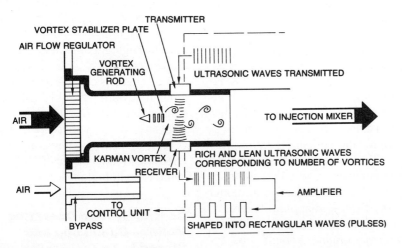

Figure 13-33. The Mitsubishi TBI system measures intake airflow by passing it through a vortex generator to create ultrasonic waves. The ultrasonic waves are amplified, shaped into rectangular waves, and sent to the control unit. (Chrysler)

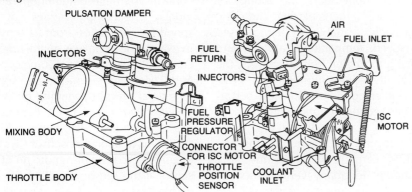

Figure 13-34. The Mitsubishi ECI throttle body assembly used on turbocharged 4-cylinder engines. (Chrysler)

ENGINE COMPUTERS

As you learned in chapter 5, automotive engine computers may be called electronic control units, modules, or assemblies. Some are single-function units that control just ignition or fuel injection. Others are multi-function units that regulate all engine systems.

Computer Functions

Every computer, regardless of its use, performs four basic functions:

1. *Input*—Receives input information in the form of voltage signals from sensors.

2. *Processing*—Processes, or "computes," the input data to make decisions and perform output functions.

3. *Storage*—Along with processing, the computer can store an input signal for later reference, or store and delay an output signal. It also can "remember," or store, a previous operating condition or other information.

4. *Output*—After receiving and processing input data, the computer sends output information or commands to display devices or actuators.

Analog and Digital Computers

Like input and output signals, computers can be either analog or digital. Analog means that a voltage signal or a processing function is infinitely variable relative to something being measured or an adjustment to be made. Digital means that an input or output signal or a processing decision is either yes-no, high-low, or on-off.

Since most engine operating conditions are analog variables, some early engine computers were analog devices that received and delivered analog input and output signals. Analog computers, however, are expensive and susceptible to changes in temperature, supply voltage, and signal interference.

All current engine computers are based on digital microprocessors, figure 13-35. These are the same microprocessors used in small personal and business computers. Digital computers change analog input signals to digital bits of information through converter circuits. The microprocessor processes data as high-low, on-off voltage signals through digital logic networks and sends an output voltage to the appropriate actuator to change an operating condition.

Computer Programs

The program instructions that a computer uses to understand its input data, do its calculations, and send its output commands consist of:

• The mathematical instructions, in binary form, for processing data.
• Information on engine and vehicle constant values, such as number of cylinders, displacement, compression ratio, gear ratios, type of fuel system, emission devices, vehicle weight, and accessories.
• Information on variable values, such as engine and vehicle speed combinations, temperature, airflow, fuel flow, timing, EGR flow, and air injection.

The first two elements are fixed values and can be loaded into computer memory rather easily. To load the

Figure 13-35. This engine control computer uses the same microprocessors that are used in small personal computers. (AMC-Renault)

variable values into memory, engineers use a process called **engine mapping**. They operate a vehicle on a dynamometer and manually adjust speed, load, spark timing, fuel metering, airflow, and other variables. Using a larger computer with the dynamometer, they determine the optimum fuel, ignition, EGR, and other output settings for best performance, economy, and emission control. This information is then burned into the programmable read-only memory (PROM) chip for that particular model of car. Engine mapping creates a 3-dimensional performance graph for a particular engine, vehicle, and accessory combination, figure 13-36. When the PROM is installed in a computer, it "remembers" the settings for timing, EGR, fuel metering, and other adjustable variables. Then, based on speed, temperature, airflow, and other information from its sensors, the computer adjusts timing, fuel, EGR, and other conditions for best performance, economy, and emission control.

By storing this information on one PROM, carmakers can use one basic computer for many vehicle models. To make the engine control system work for a specific model, they install the correct PROM. Some carmakers

use a single PROM chip, plugged into the computer, figure 13-37. Others (some Ford computers) employ a larger calibration module, figure 13-38. Engine computers have become economical and versatile because engineers can use a single computer hardware assembly with interchangeable PROM's to change the software. When you service engine control systems, you will learn that checking for the correct PROM installation is an important service step.

Control System Operating Modes—Open Loop and Closed Loop

You learned in chapter 5 that every control system has different operating modes. The computer does not respond to information from its sensors in exactly the same way all the time. It can ignore sensors under some conditions, or it can respond to one signal in several ways, depending on what several other sensors tell it. For example, a computer will ignore an EGO sensor if a temperature sensor says the engine is cold. It will ignore an EGO sensor if the sensor signals don't fall within the limits the computer expects for given speed, load, and temperature conditions. With the ignition on,

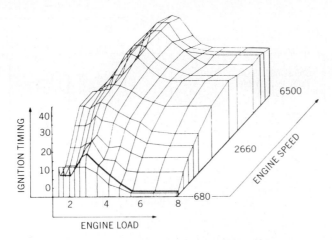

Figure 13-36. Engine mapping calculates the optimum ignition point for each combination of speed and load. (Porsche)

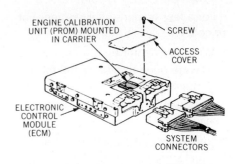

Figure 13-37. The General Motors CCC computer uses a single removable PROM. (Chevrolet)

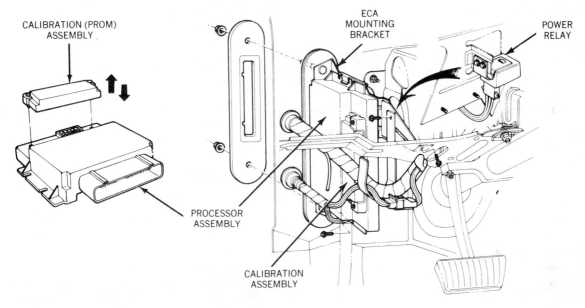

Figure 13-38. The calibration assembly (module) of this Ford EEC computer contains the system PROM. (Ford)

the computer ignores all other sensors if the rpm sensor says the engine isn't turning over.

Because of the computer's selective abilities, engineers can design a control system for two basic modes: open loop and closed loop. The most significant open-loop and closed-loop modes relate to fuel-metering feedback control. We will look at these in the following examples, but they are not the only open-loop and closed-loop functions.

Open-Loop Control. Open-loop control means that a computer—or any control device—adjusts a system

to operate in a certain way. If there is an error or a deviation in the results of the operation, a signal of the error or deviation does *not* get sent back to the computer or controller. You exercise open-loop control over your car radio when you set the volume for a certain level. The volume control switch signals the amplifier for a certain power output, and that's where it stays. If you drive through a tunnel, the volume gets weaker because the input signal gets weaker. But, the amplifier power output doesn't change until you readjust the volume control. The radio system, itself, didn't receive an error feedback signal that the volume

was too low. It relied on an outside force for adjustment.

An engine computer relies on an error feedback signal from an EGO sensor to tell it whether the air-fuel mixture passing through the engine is too rich or too lean. (You will learn how it does this later.) The computer can use the signal to readjust fuel metering, or it can ignore the signal. When it ignores the signal, the computer is operating the fuel system in open loop, figure 13-39. It signals the variable fuel-metering actuator to operate in one of several fixed modes, depending on information from other sensors. The computer operates the fuel system in open loop:

• When the engine is cold

• For a few seconds after starting, hot or cold

• With low vacuum

• At wide-open throttle or full load at any engine speed

• During idle or deceleration (some vehicles)

At other times, the computer operates the fuel system in closed loop.

Closed-Loop Control.

Closed loop means that the computer is reading and responding to an output error signal. For closed-loop fuel control, the error sensor is the EGO sensor. If the EGO sensor says the mixture is too lean, the computer adjusts the variable fuel actuator to enrich the mixture, and vice versa, figure 13-40.

Fuel metering is not the only closed-loop function performed by an engine computer. Many systems have knock sensors to detect detonation (pinging). Spark timing is a major factor that affects detonation. When the knock sensor detects detonation, it sends an input signal to the computer, which then retards timing until detonation stops. That's another kind of closed-loop control. Some systems also have electronic feedback control of turbo boost to control detonation. In fact, a simple pressure-actuated wastegate is a mechanical form of closed-loop control.

Some GM CCC systems, and others, have closed-loop idle speed control. The PROM is programmed with the desired idle speed for a particular vehicle and engine. If idle speed rises or falls from the setpoint for any reason, input from the speed sensor tells the computer to send an output signal to an idle speed control stepper motor or other actuator. In response to engine speed signals, the computer controls the stepper motor that moves the IAC valve in and out of the air passage. This changes the idle airflow and thus regulates idle speed.

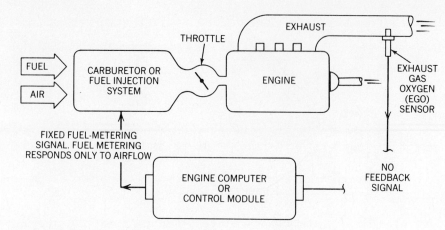

Figure 13-39. In open-loop operation, the computer does not receive, or ignores, an output error feedback signal.

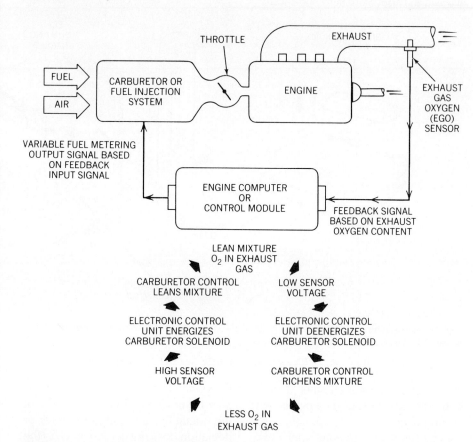

Figure 13-40. In closed-loop operation, the computer responds to the output error feedback signal and readjusts the input.

AIR-FUEL RATIO, TIMING, AND EGR EFFECTS ON OPERATION

Before we go on to look at sensors and actuators, we should review how air-fuel ratios, timing, and EGR affect overall engine operation. You have learned how they affect an engine individually. By reviewing these effects, you can see how computer control can obtain the best engine efficiency.

Air-Fuel Ratio

Figure 13-41 shows the effects of a variable air-fuel ratio with fixed timing and engine speed. With air-fuel ratios richer than 14.7:1, fuel consumption and HC and CO emissions are high, but NO$_x$ emissions are relatively low. Torque is highest at ratios of 12:1 to 16:1. Above 16:1, torque starts to drop and HC and NO$_x$ increase. HC emissions and fuel consumption increase with lean mixtures because the engine can misfire and pass fuel through the cylinders unburned. This also reduces power and torque.

The Stoichiometric Air-Fuel Ratio.

The stoichiometric air-fuel ratio of 14.7:1 provides the most complete combination of fuel and air during combustion. It also provides the best combination of performance, economy, and emission control. It is somewhat of a compromise between maximum power and maximum economy, but both of these factors are good at 14.7:1. For successful emission control, the stoichiometric ratio depends on the use of a 3-way, oxidation-reduction catalyst.

Figure 13-42 shows that a 3-way catalyst has the best combined conversion efficiency for all three pollutants at a 14.7:1 air-fuel ratio. With richer mixtures, HC and CO conversion efficiency is lower. With leaner mixtures, NO$_x$ conversion efficiency is lower. The range of conversion efficiency is quite narrow, only about ±0.05 air-fuel ratio, (that is, 14.65:1 to 14.75:1). A carburetor or injection system without feedback control cannot maintain this narrow range, but a computer-controlled system can.

Ignition Timing

Figure 13-43 shows how spark timing affects fuel consumption and HC and NO$_x$ emissions with fixed engine speed and air-fuel ratio. With timing near tdc, or slightly retarded, emissions are low, but fuel consumption is high. As timing is advanced, fuel consumption decreases, but emissions increase. During engine mapping, engineers calculate the best timing for any combination of speed and air-fuel

ratio. This is generally the point where the HC emission and fuel consumption curves cross, which also corresponds to peak torque.

Exhaust Gas Recirculation

Figure 13-44 shows that NO$_x$ emissions decrease sharply as EGR is added to the air-fuel mixture. But, as EGR increases, so do HC emissions and fuel consumption. Again, during engine mapping, engineers calculate the EGR percentage that yields the best compromise between NO$_x$ control, HC emissions, and economy. Remember that both EGR and ignition timing are important variables for detonation control on late-model engines, so engineers also consider detonation control when calculating EGR percentage.

Computer Control

Centrifugal and vacuum advance devices control spark timing in relation to engine speed and load. Airflow through a carburetor controls fuel metering similarly, and manifold vacuum can provide basic control for EGR. All of these simple controls operate more or less independently, however. A computer doesn't do anything to engine variables that mechanical controls don't do. But, a computer regulates them faster and more precisely, and can "compute" the combined effects of changing several variables simultaneously.

SYSTEM SENSORS

A sensor is an input device that converts one form of energy to another. Since a computer can only read voltage signals, an automobile sensor must convert motion, pressure, temperature, light, and other energy to voltage. Automobile sensors are switches, timers, resistors, transformers, and generators. They can send either analog or digital signals. The computer converts analog signals to digital form for processing. You also

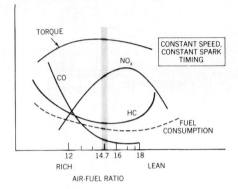

Figure 13-41. Typical fuel consumption, emission, and torque curves with changes in air-fuel ratio.

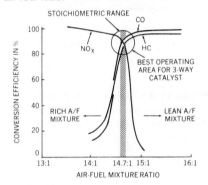

Figure 13-42. Three-way catalyst efficiency is at its best with a 14.7:1 air-fuel ratio. (GM)

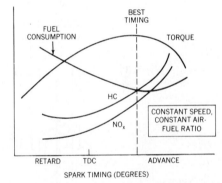

Figure 13-43. Typical fuel consumption, emission, and torque curves with changes in spark timing.

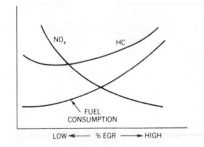

Figure 13-44. As EGR increases, NO$_x$ decreases; but HC and fuel consumption increase.

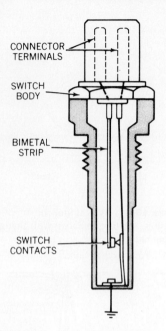

Figure 13-45. When this temperature switch closes a ground connection, signal voltage is high. When it opens the circuit, voltage is low.

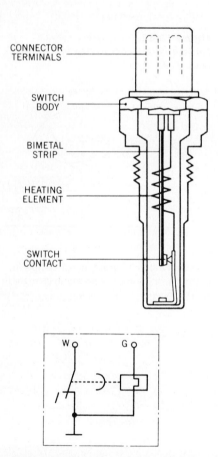

Figure 13-46. This thermo-time switch limits the operating time of the cold-start injector according to engine temperature. (Bosch)

will see some sensors referred to as **transducers**. A transducer is also a device that changes one form of energy to another and works in a system as any other sensor does.

Switches and Timers

A switch is the simplest digital sensor. A switch opens or closes a circuit and delivers a high- or a low-voltage signal, figure 13-45. One switch terminal receives input voltage from the computer. The other terminal returns a high-voltage signal when the switch closes and a low-voltage signal when it opens. The computer can respond to either a high or low signal, or both, depending on its program.

A timer, combined with a switch, can delay a signal. The timer can be electronic circuitry in the computer or it can be part of the switch. Most switch and timer combinations are thermo-time switches, as used with Bosch Jetronic and Motronic systems, figure 13-46. The switch delivers the signal that controls the cold-start injector. Closing the switch depends on temperature from the engine or from current passing through the switch. When the engine is cold, current passes through the heating winding. After a specific time, the current heats the bimetal thermostat and opens the circuit for the cold-start injector.

Resistors

Most automobile sensors are resistors. A resistor can send an analog voltage signal that is proportional to temperature, pressure, motion, or other variables. Remember, however, that a resistor can't generate a voltage. It can only modify a voltage applied to it. Therefore, automobile resistive sensors must operate with a **reference voltage** from the computer. This is a fixed voltage applied by the computer to the resistor. Most engine control systems operate with a 5-volt reference voltage (GM, Bosch, Chrysler, Ford EEC-IV, for example). Some operate with a 9-volt reference voltage (Ford EEC-I, II, and III). In any case, reference voltage must be less than minimum battery voltage to prevent inaccurate sensor signals.

The computer sends the reference voltage to the sensor. As sensor resistance changes, the return voltage changes. For example, a temperature sensor can be calibrated to send a 0-volt return signal at 0° F and a 5-volt return signal at 250° F ($-18°$ to 121° C). Every 1° F temperature change causes a 0.02-volt change in the return voltage. The computer can read these 20-millivolt increments and compute engine temperature.

A potentiometer is a variable resistor with three terminals. Reference voltage is applied to one end of the resistor, and the other end is grounded, figure 13-47. The third terminal is connected to a movable contact that slides across the resistor. Depending on whether the contact is near the supply end or the ground end of the resistor, return voltage will be

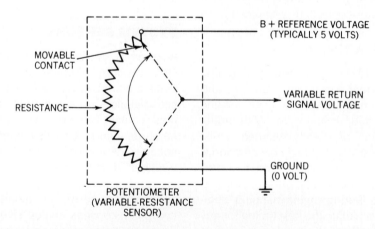

Figure 13-47. A potentiometer is a variable resistor with three terminals. Signal voltage is taken from the movable contact.

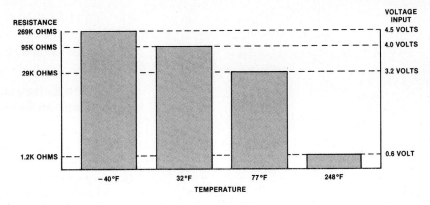

Figure 13-48. A typical thermistor resistance and temperature chart. (Ford)

high or low. Constant current through the resistor maintains constant temperature and voltage drop so that return voltage changes only in relation to sliding contact movement.

As explained in chapter 6, a thermistor is a 2-wire variable resistor whose resistance changes with temperature. Negative temperature coefficient (NTC) thermistor sensors are made of semiconductor material with high resistance at low temperature and low resistance at high temperature. Resistance does not change in proportion to temperature; that is, a given temperature change will not cause a corresponding resistance change. Figure 13-48 illustrates the relationship of resistance and temperature in a typical NTC thermistor. A passive sensor, the thermistor receives a reference voltage from the computer through one terminal and sends a return voltage to the computer through the other terminal.

A piezoresistive sensor is one whose voltage varies with pressure or force applied to it. Like a thermistor, it has two connection terminals for reference and return voltage.

Transformers

Like resistors, transformer sensors send an analog return signal to the computer in response to a reference voltage. The transformer has a movable core, and the coupling between

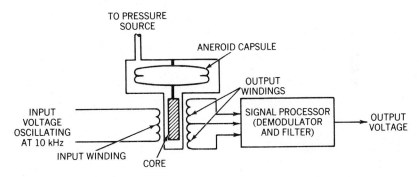

Figure 13-49. This MAP sensor is a transformer that creates a voltage differential between two output windings.

the input and output windings varies with core position. An oscillating reference voltage (usually 10 kHz) is applied to the input winding. Two output windings are balanced so that output voltage of each is the same with the core in the center position, figure 13-49. When the core moves, the output voltage of one winding is greater than the other. The two output winding voltages are processed to produce a single sensor signal voltage that is proportional to amount and direction of movement. This kind of transformer sensor is used as one type of manifold absolute pressure (MAP) sensor, as well as for other applications.

Generators

Every sensor we have seen so far sends an input signal in response to a reference voltage. A few sensors,

however, can generate a signal voltage. When you studied electronic ignitions, you learned about distributor pulse generators. These use a rotating trigger wheel to vary the reluctance around a magnetic pole piece and pickup coil, figure 13-50. Some carmakers call them **reluctance sensors**. Engine computers can use these signals as a reference for basic timing. Signal frequency also indicates engine speed.

Pulse generators also can be used to indicate crankshaft position, engine speed, and firing order. Some systems use a pulse generator or reluctance sensor in the engine block to respond to a tooth or a cutout on the harmonic balancer or the flywheel, figure 13-51. Bosch, Ford EEC-I and II, and GM MISAR systems use these sensors. Some engines have two separate sensors of this kind to indicate crankshaft speed and position. Other systems use

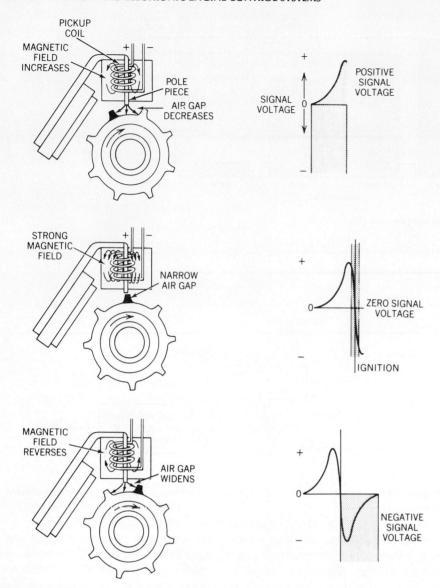

Figure 13-50. The rotating trigger wheel varies the reluctance around a pole piece and pickup coil to generate voltage.

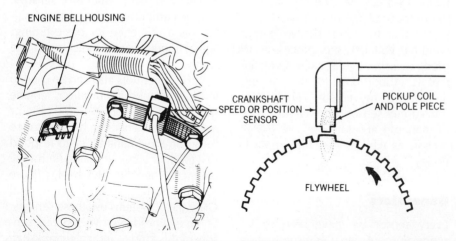

Figure 13-51. Some GM, Ford, Renault, and other Bosch systems use crankshaft position sensors in the engine block. (AMC-Renault)

a Hall-effect switch in the distributor, figure 13-52, to indicate crankshaft position and basic timing.

The Exhaust Gas Oxygen Sensor

The exhaust gas oxygen (EGO) sensor is a unique voltage generator that measures exhaust oxygen content. It generates analog signals from 0 to 1 volt by comparing the difference between oxygen in the exhaust and oxygen in the ambient air.

The EGO sensor is based on the **lambda** concept. Lambda is the Greek symbol engineers use to indicate the ratio of one number to another. For air-fuel ratio control, lambda indicates the ratio of excess air to stoichiometric air quantity. That's why

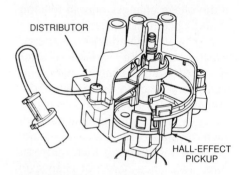

Figure 13-52. The Hall-effect switch in a Chrysler 4-cylinder distributor indicates crankshaft position and basic timing. (Chrysler)

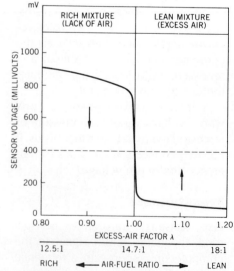

Figure 13-53. Lambda (EGO) sensor voltage at 800° C (1472° F). (Bosch)

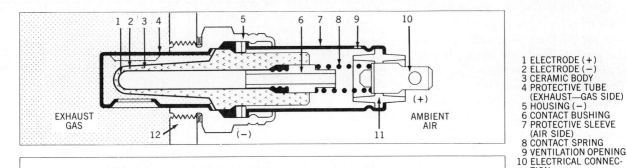

1 ELECTRODE (+)
2 ELECTRODE (−)
3 CERAMIC BODY
4 PROTECTIVE TUBE
  (EXHAUST—GAS SIDE)
5 HOUSING (−)
6 CONTACT BUSHING
7 PROTECTIVE SLEEVE
  (AIR SIDE)
8 CONTACT SPRING
9 VENTILATION OPENING
10 ELECTRICAL CONNEC-
  TION
11 INSULATING PART
12 EXHAUST PIPE WALL

Figure 13-54. The EGO sensor is installed in the exhaust manifold and exposed to ambient air, as well as to exhaust. (Bosch)

Bosch calls EGO sensors lambda sensors.

At an air-fuel ratio of 14.7:1, as much air as possible combines with fuel. There is no excess air, and there is no shortage of air. Lambda, therefore, equals 1. With a lean mixture ratio of 15, 16, or 17:1, there is excess air left after combustion. The lambda ratio of excess air to desired air is greater than 1. It may be 1.03, 1.07, 1.15, or some other number. With a rich mixture of 12, 13, or 14:1, there is a shortage of air, and the lambda ratio is less than 1. It may be 0.97, 0.93, 0.89, etc. With lambda (excess air) ratios less than 0.8 or greater than 1.20, the engine won't run. These roughly equal air-fuel ratios of 11.7:1 to 18:1.

The EGO sensor works as a **galvanic battery** to generate voltage up to about 1 volt. Its effective signal range is from about 0.1 to 0.9 volt (100 to 900 millivolts). When exhaust oxygen content is low (rich mixture), sensor voltage is high (450 to 900 millivolts). When exhaust oxygen content is high (lean mixture), sensor voltage is low (100 to 450 millivolts). Figure 13-53 shows the operating range of the sensor at a temperature of about 800° C (1472° F). Notice that sensor voltage changes fastest near a lambda ratio of 1 (air-fuel ratio of

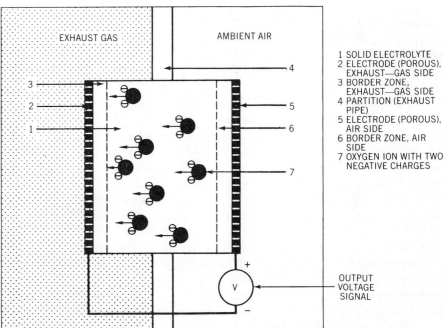

1 SOLID ELECTROLYTE
2 ELECTRODE (POROUS),
  EXHAUST—GAS SIDE
3 BORDER ZONE,
  EXHAUST—GAS SIDE
4 PARTITION (EXHAUST
  PIPE)
5 ELECTRODE (POROUS),
  AIR SIDE
6 BORDER ZONE, AIR
  SIDE
7 OXYGEN ION WITH TWO
  NEGATIVE CHARGES

OUTPUT
VOLTAGE
SIGNAL

Figure 13-55. The ZrO_2 ceramic electrolyte attracts O_2 ions to the electrodes and thus generates a voltage. (Bosch)

14.7:1), which makes it ideal for maintaining a stoichiometric ratio. The sensor must warm up to at least 300° C (572° F) before it will generate an accurate signal, and it provides the fastest switching times at about 800° C. That is the major reason for open-loop fuel control with a cold engine.

The EGO sensor is installed in the exhaust manifold, figure 13-54, and consists of two platinum electrodes separated by a zirconium dioxide (ZrO_2) ceramic electrolyte. ZrO_2 attracts free oxygen ions, which are negatively charged. One electrode is exposed to ambient (outside) air through vents in the sensor shell, figure 13-55, and collects many O_2 ions. It becomes a more negative electrode. The other electrode is exposed to exhaust gas and also collects O_2 ions. However, it collects fewer and becomes more positive. When there is a large difference between oxygen in the exhaust and oxygen in the air (rich mixture), the negative oxygen ions on the outer electrode move to the positive inner electrode. This is simple electric current (electron flow). The sensor then develops a voltage between the two electrodes. When there is more oxygen in the exhaust (lean mixture), there is less difference between O_2 ions on the electrodes and a lower voltage. Figure 13-56 summarizes the relationships of engine air-fuel mixture, exhaust oxygen content, sensor voltage, and computer response.

An important point to remember about an EGO sensor is that it *measures oxygen; it does not measure air-fuel ratio*. If the engine misfires, no oxygen is consumed in combustion. There is a large amount of oxygen in the unburned exhaust mixture, and the sensor will deliver a false "lean mixture" signal. This is one reason why computer control of ignition timing and EGR is essential for effective fuel-metering control.

All EGO sensors work on the principles explained above, but construction details differ. Some sensors have a single-wire connector for the output signal. The ground connection exists between the sensor shell and the exhaust manifold or pipe, figure 13-54. Other sensors have a 2-wire connector that provides a ground connection through the computer, figure 13-57. Single-wire and 2-wire sensors are not interchangeable. Figure 13-57 also shows a silicone boot that protects the sensor and provides a vent opening for ambient air circulation. The boot position is important for such a sensor. If it is pushed down too far on the body, it will block the air vent and create an inaccurate signal voltage.

In 1986, Chrysler introduced an EGO sensor that has no air vent. Ambient air for the inner electrode is absorbed through the insulation on the connector wiring.

Some late-model engines have heated EGO sensors. These sensors have a third wire that delivers battery current of 1 ampere or less to the sensor electrodes whenever the ignition switch is on. This current warms

Air-Fuel Mixture	Exhaust Oxygen Content	Oxygen Sensor Voltage	Computer Output Signal	Fuel Metering Change To	Idle Airflow
Rich	Low	High	Decrease Fuel Metering	Lean	Increase
Lean	High	Low	Increase Fuel Metering	Rich	Decrease

Figure 13-56. This table shows the relationships of air-fuel mixture, exhaust O_2, sensor voltage, and computer response.

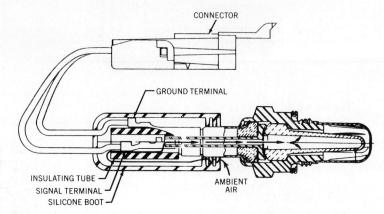

Figure 13-57. This EGO sensor has a 2-wire connector and a protective silicone boot. (AC-Delco)

the sensor faster with a cold engine and helps to maintain sensor temperature for accurate voltage signals at all times. Heated EGO sensors often are used on turbocharged engines where the sensor is installed downstream from the turbo. The turbo absorbs much of the heat energy in the exhaust, which delays sensor warmup on a cold engine and can cause the sensor to cool during long periods of idling and low-speed operation. A heated EGO sensor solves these problems.

EGO sensors are always installed in the exhaust manifolds or headpipes, but exact locations vary for different engines. Some V-type engines have separate sensors in each manifold, figure 13-58. Other V-type engines have only a single sensor. Sensors often are located low in the engine compartment, and access can be difficult. Other sensors are installed in the center of the exhaust manifold, and access is easy, figure 13-59. Engineers determine the best sensor location for accurate O_2 measurement

during laboratory testing of each engine design.

FUEL INJECTION SENSORS

In our examination of fuel injection, you haven't seen any chokes, power valves, accelerator pumps, or idle speed and mixture controls. Remember that a fuel injection system must provide enrichment and mixture control for the same engine conditions that a carburetor does. Fuel injection does it with a combination of engine sensors and auxiliary metering devices. Enrichment is provided by varying the pulse width of an electronic injector or the pressure on a mechanical injector. Cold starting is aided by coolant and air temperature sensors that tell the system to enrich the mixture. Injection pulse timing in an EFI system is governed by engine speed and crankshaft position sensors. The following sections summarize some of the common engine sensors and auxiliary metering systems.

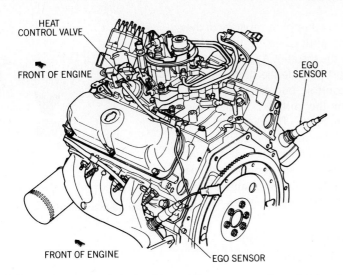

Figure 13-58. Some V-type engines have two EGO sensors, one in each exhaust manifold. (Ford)

Figure 13-59. This EGO sensor is easily accessible in the center of the manifold, at the front of the engine.

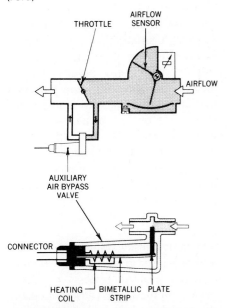

Figure 13-60. Most port injection systems have air bypass valves to aid cold starting. (Bosch)

Cold Starting

Extra air is provided by an auxiliary air bypass that works like an air bypass circuit in a carburetor. A valve opens an air passage in the intake system to allow more air into the engine, figure 13-60. The opening is controlled by a thermostatic switch or a timer, or both.

Bosch K-, D-, and L-Jetronic systems and similar port injection systems have a start valve, or cold-start injector, to add fuel to the system for starting, figure 13-61. The cold-start injector is a separate electronic injec-

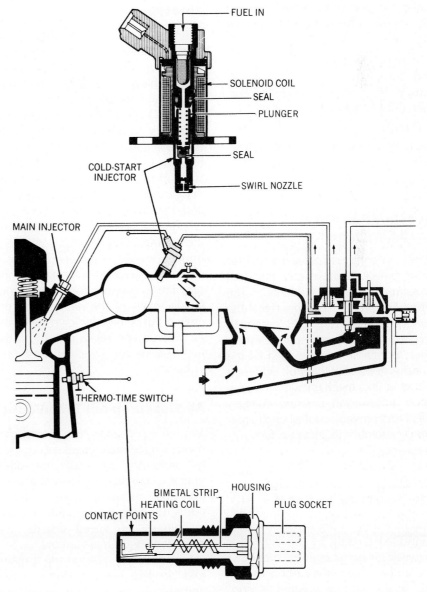

Figure 13-61. Bosch and several other port injection systems have a cold-start valve, or auxiliary injector, to deliver fuel to the manifold of a cold engine. (Volkswagen)

tor that sprays fuel into a central area of the manifold when engine temperature, speed, and airflow are low. A thermo-time switch senses coolant temperature to close the injector. Current applied to the switch heating coil opens the circuit after a prescribed amount of time.

Idle Enrichment

Idle enrichment in an electronically controlled fuel injection system results from changing the pulse width of an electronic injector or the pressure on a mechanical injector. However, the input signals from several sensors are required to allow the computer to make the proper decisions. Among the sensors involved are those that measure:

- Manifold absolute pressure (MAP) and barometric pressure. (A BMAP sensor is a dual-function sensor, measuring separate MAP and BP.)
- Throttle position
- Engine speed and crankshaft position
- Vehicle speed

Acceleration and Load Enrichment

When an engine needs extra fuel for extra power, airflow and manifold pressure change suddenly. The airflow or pressure sensors signal the control module of an EFI system to increase the injector pulse width. Thus, enrichment is provided by the same systems that control light-load metering. In a mechanical system, the same airflow and pressure changes affect fuel pressure control on the metering assembly to increase fuel volume.

AIR CONTROL SYSTEM

Fuel metering through a carburetor is controlled directly by the difference between air pressure in the fuel bowl and air pressure in the carburetor barrel. Intake air-fuel volume is con-

trolled by the pumping capacity of the engine, the airflow size of the carburetor, and the throttle. A fuel injection system must provide the same kind of mixture control, but the fuel is isolated from the airflow, behind the injection nozzles. Therefore, all systems must have a way to measure intake air volume and then meter fuel accordingly. All air control systems have a throttle to control air volume and one of the following devices to measure it:

- An airflow meter or sensor
- A manifold pressure sensor
- An air mass sensor

Throttle

The throttle in a fuel injection system works exactly like the throttle in a carburetor. Connected to the accelerator linkage, the throttle regulates the amount of air allowed into the engine. On port injection systems, the throttle is on the air inlet side of the injectors and regulates only airflow. Figures 13-17 through 13-20 show such installations. On TBI systems, the throttle is between the injectors and the manifold and controls the amount of air-fuel mixture entering the engine, figure 13-62. While the throttle regulates airflow, a sensor measures the speed of the airflow, the pressure in the manifold, or the molecular mass of the air entering the engine. All of these indicate the intake air volume and relate directly to the fuel volume the injectors must provide.

Air Measurement Techniques

You will probably read some carmaker's references to techniques used for measuring air intake and other operating conditions to regulate injection fuel metering. Two common terms to describe injection control techniques are **speed density** and **mass density**, or mass airflow.

Speed density systems use a manifold absolute pressure (MAP) sensor and engine rpm as the principal sen-

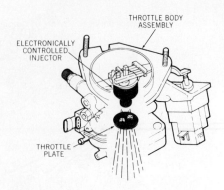

Figure 13-62. The throttle on a TBI system is between the injectors and the manifold. (Renault)

sor input signals to determine the amount of fuel to be injected. Injection is controlled by regulating injector pulse width. You learned the principle of pulse width control in chapter 6 and will review it in a later section of this chapter. Speed density systems also use input signals from temperature sensors, along with maps of engine variables such as volumetric efficiency and EGR flow. The operation of speed density systems can be sensitive variations in engine speed and EGR flow rate. Remember that the principal sensor signals in a speed density system are MAP, rpm, and temperature.

A mass density system uses a mass airflow sensor to measure the weight, or actual molecular mass, of incoming air. Air mass (mass airflow) sensors are explained in the next few pages. To start understanding them, you should know that they measure weight or mass, rather than air speed or pressure. Mass density fuel injection systems also use input signals from temperature and rpm sensors to determine injector pulse width.

Airflow Sensors

An airflow sensor is a movable plate or vane, deflected by intake airflow, figure 13-63. The Bosch K-Jetronic airflow sensor plate moves a counterweighted pair of levers that operate on the control plunger in the fuel distributor. The airflow sensor and the fuel distributor are the complete mixture control unit for the system. The sensor deflects the control plunger in proportion to airflow. The control plunger regulates fuel pump pressure to the differential pressure valve for each cylinder. Fuel control pressure on the other end of the control plunger balances airflow sensor force.

The combination of these pressures at the pressure differential valves regulates injection in relation to airflow.

The airflow sensors in Bosch L-Jetronic systems and Ford and most Japanese electronic port injection systems are a movable-vane device, attached to a potentiometer, figure 13-64. Intake airflow deflects the vane in proportion to air velocity. This moves the potentiometer to vary the return voltage of a reference voltage signal. If reference voltage applied to the sensor is 5 volts, the potentiometer will allow a 0-volt return signal at no airflow and almost a 5-volt return signal at maximum airflow. This variable voltage signal goes to the electronic module, which varies the injector pulse width in proportion to airflow.

Chrysler used a unique airflow sensor on its 1981 V-8 TBI system. Vanes at the air cleaner inlet cause the incoming air to swirl. The swirling sets up vibrating frequencies measured at a U-shaped pressure sensor farther inside the air inlet, figure 13-65. The frequencies are proportional to intake airflow and control a potentiometer signal to the electronic control module. While this airflow sensor does not look like the movable-vane or plate sensors of other systems, it delivers the same kind of information.

Manifold Pressure Sensors and Barometric Pressure Sensors

Manifold pressure sensors are used with Bendix port injection systems, Bosch D-Jetronic systems, and most TBI systems. The sensor can be a diaphragm, an aneroid bellows, or a **piezoresistive crystal**. One side of the sensor is connected to the intake

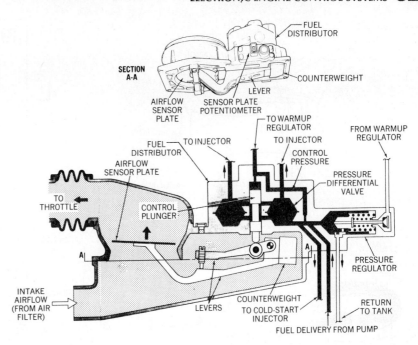

Figure 13-63. The Bosch K-Jetronic airflow sensor controls fuel pressure to the continuous injectors. (Bosch) (Audi)

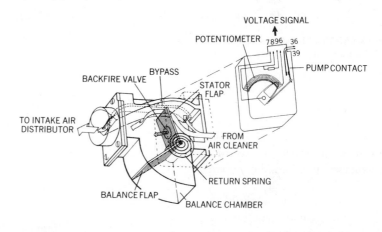

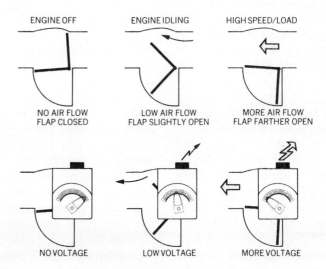

Figure 13-64. The vane airflow sensor used on Bosch, Ford, and other EFI systems sends a variable voltage signal to the electronic control module. (Volkswagen)

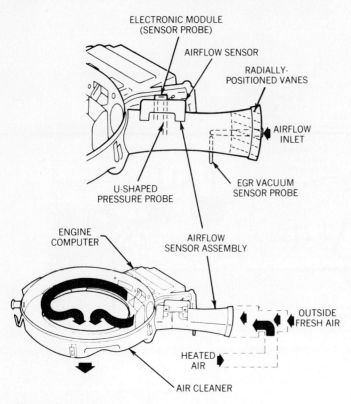

Figure 13-65. This Chrysler airflow sensor measures air volume from the frequencies generated by swirling the intake air. (Chrysler)

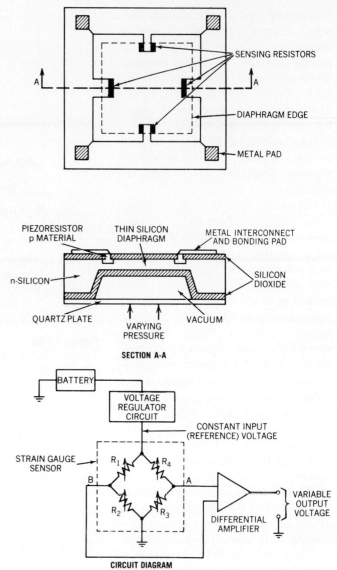

Figure 13-66. This piezoresistive MAP sensor varies signal voltage as it flexes.

manifold; the other is exposed to atmospheric pressure or sealed, figure 13-66. Pressure changes in the manifold deflect the sensor, which moves a potentiometer or otherwise varies a return voltage signal to the control module.

These sensors indicate **manifold absolute pressure**, which is another way to look at manifold vacuum. Manifold absolute pressure (MAP) is a combination of atmospheric (or boost) pressure and vacuum. Vacuum, remember, is a negative pressure. While we usually measure it in inches or millimeters of mercury, we can convert it to pounds per square inch or any other unit of pressure. *As vacuum decreases, manifold absolute pressure increases,* and vice versa. Manifold pressure also increases when a turbocharger applies boost. Manifold absolute pressure is less at high altitude, with or without boost, because atmospheric pressure is less. The combined effects of pressure and vacuum that equal manifold absolute pressure are directly proportional to intake air volume. Therefore, a sensor that converts absolute pres-

sure to a voltage signal can govern fuel injection in relation to air volume.

Figure 13-67 is a table that compares manifold pressures in absolute values and gauge values. Gauge pressure is what you see on a test gauge, whether in pounds per square inch (psi), kilopascals (kPa), or inches of mercury (in. Hg). It is pressure above or below atmospheric pressure. Absolute pressure is a measurement that includes atmospheric pressure. Thus, 0 psig equals 14.697 psia; a turbocharger boost pressure of 12 psig equals 26.70 psia (12 + 14.697).

Some sensors measure manifold

pressure and barometric pressure (atmospheric air pressure) separately. These sensors send separate signals to an electronic module or engine computer that compares them to determine the operating manifold pressure and the required amount of fuel. Most pressure sensors are mounted remotely from the engine and connected to the intake manifold by a length of tubing, figure 13-68.

Air Mass Sensor

A heated platinum wire or thin-film semiconductor sensor in the intake airflow measures the molecular mass

Pounds Per Square Inch Absolute	Pounds Per Square Inch Gauge and Inches of Mercury Gauge	Kilopascals Gauge and Centimeters of Mercury Vacuum	Kilopascals Absolute	Inches of Mercury Absolute
29.70 psia	15 psig	104.43 kPag	204.76 kPaa	60.45 in. Hg
26.70 psia	12 psig	82.74 kPag	184.07 kPaa	54.35 in. Hg
24.70 psia	10 psig	68.95 kPag	170.28 kPaa	50.28 in. Hg
21.70 psia	7 psig	48.27 kPag	149.60 kPaa	44.17 in. Hg
19.70 psia	5 psig	34.48 kPag	135.81 kPaa	40.10 in. Hg
16.70 psia	2 psig	13.79 kPag	115.12 kPaa	33.99 in. Hg
14.697 psia	0 psig/in. Hg	0.00 kPag/cm Hg	101.33 kPaa	29.92 in. Hg
13.71 psia	2 in. Hg	5.08 cm Hg	94.53 kPaa	27.92 in. Hg
12.24 psia	5 in. Hg	12.70 cm Hg	84.39 kPaa	24.92 in. Hg
11.26 psia	7 in. Hg	17.78 cm Hg	77.63 kPaa	22.92 in. Hg
9.78 psia	10 in. Hg	25.40 cm Hg	67.43 kPaa	19.92 in. Hg
8.80 psia	12 in. Hg	30.48 cm Hg	60.68 kPaa	17.92 in. Hg
7.33 psia	15 in. Hg	38.10 cm Hg	50.54 kPaa	14.92 in. Hg
5.85 psia	18 in. Hg	45.72 cm Hg	40.34 kPaa	11.92 in. Hg
4.87 psia	20 in. Hg	50.80 cm Hg	33.58 kPaa	9.92 in. Hg
3.89 psia	22 in. Hg	55.88 cm Hg	26.82 kPaa	7.92 in. Hg
2.42 psia	25 in. Hg	63.50 cm Hg	16.68 kPaa	4.92 in. Hg
0.00 psia	29.92 in. Hg	75.996 cm Hg	0.00 kPaa	0.00 in. Hg

Note: All values are taken at sea level.

Figure 13-67. Pressure relationship chart.

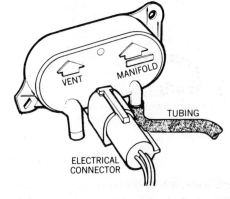

Figure 13-68. Most manifold pressure sensors are mounted away from the engine and connected to the manifold by tubing. (Ford)

of combustible air entering the engine, figure 13-69. Current from the electronic module heats the wire or film, and airflow cools it. The module tries to maintain the sensor temperature at a constant level. The extent to which the air cools the sensor varies with air velocity and temperature. These factors combine to indicate the mass volume of air entering the engine. As the sensor cools, current increases to try to maintain the desired temperature. As the sensor heats up, current decreases. The control module measures the changing current and converts it to a voltage signal to govern injector pulse width. Air mass sensors are used in Bosch LH-Jetronic systems and some similar late-model GM and Ford systems. Bosch systems use a heated wire sensor, figure 13-69. GM mass airflow (MAF) sensors are similar in design but use a heated thin-film semiconductor sensor in a hybrid electronic module.

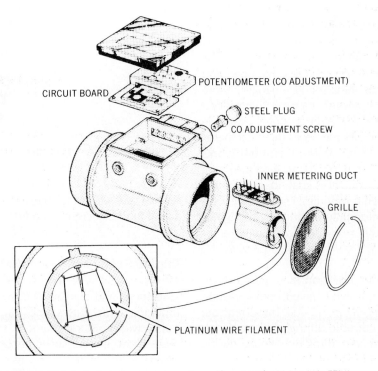

Figure 13-69. This hot-wire air mass sensor is used on Bosch LH-Jetronic EFI systems. (Volvo)

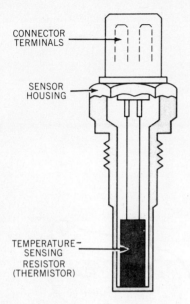

Figure 13-70. This coolant temperature sensor is a thermistor that sends a variable return voltage to the electronic control module. (Bosch)

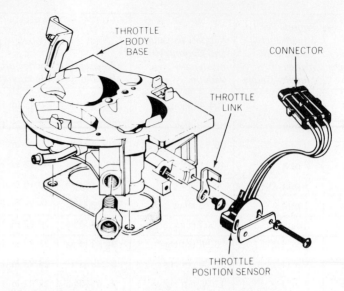

Figure 13-71. The throttle position sensor can be an on-off switch or a potentiometer. (Rochester)

Other Sensors

Here is a brief summary of other sensors used in electronic engine control systems.

Air and Coolant Temperature. All gasoline injection systems have one or more sensors to measure air and engine temperature because temperature affects intake air density and fuel requirements. These sensors can be simple on-off switches that open and close as temperature changes. More often, however, they are thermistors, figure 13-70. A thermistor is a variable resistor, whose resistance *decreases* as it is heated. The thermistor works like a potentiometer to send a varying return voltage signal to the system electronic module. The module uses this information, along with signals from other sensors, to change the injector pulse width or fuel pressure.

Throttle Position. Most gasoline injection systems have throttle position sensors, figure 13-71. These indicate closed throttle during idle and deceleration and throttle opening during acceleration and full-power operation. The throttle sensor can be a simple on-off switch or a potentiome-

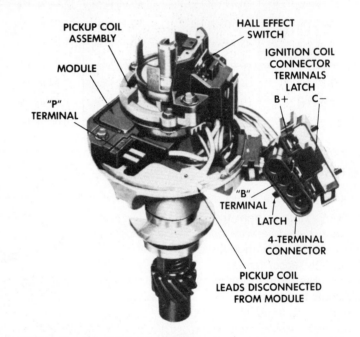

Figure 13-72. Crankshaft speed and position signals can come from switches or pulse generators in the ignition distributor. (Delco-Remy)

ter that sends a variable return voltage signal to the electronic module.

Engine Speed and Crankshaft Position. An EFI system must know engine speed and crankshaft position to time injection pulses and calculate pulse width. A mechanical system must know engine speed to operate the cold-starting and cranking-enrichment devices. Speed and position signals can come from switches or electronic pulse generators in the ignition distributor, figure 13-72, or they can come from a magnetic sensor in the engine. Most speed and position sensors mounted in the engine are located in the bell-housing. They react to changing magnetic reluctance caused by teeth or grooves on the flywheel, figure 13-73. With a breaker-point ignition, the signals are provided by a separate switching device in the distributor. With an electronic ignition; the signals can come

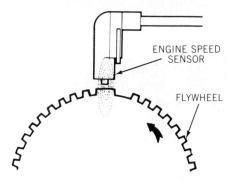

Figure 13-73. Crankshaft speed and position signals also can come from sensors mounted near the flywheel. (Renault)

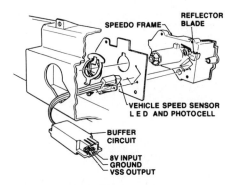

Figure 13-74. This speed sensor uses an LED and a photocell in the speedometer. (GM)

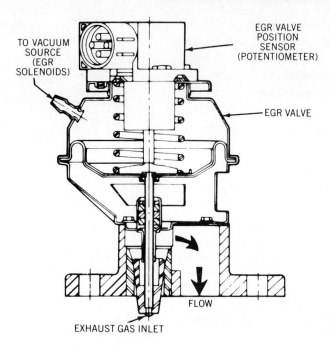

Figure 13-75. This potentiometer senses EGR valve position. (Ford)

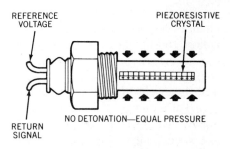

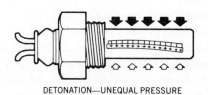

Figure 13-76. Detonation (knock) sensors have a piezoresistive crystal that flexes when detonation occurs. (Audi)

from the ignition pulse generator or Hall-effect switch, or from a separate electronic signal generator.

Vehicle Speed Sensors. Some control systems need to know vehicle speed to control torque converter lockup and transmission gear selection. Speed sensors are usually pulse generators or optical sensors in the speedometer, figure 13-74.

EGR Sensors. Knowing the EGR flow rate at any time is important for controlling timing and fuel metering, as well as EGR valve operation. Many EGR valves have a transducer that consists of a sliding-contact potentiometer on the top of the valve stem, figure 13-75. Through engine mapping, the computer knows that a certain return voltage signal equals a certain valve position, which equals a specific EGR flow rate. When combined with speed, load, and temperature signals, the computer uses this information to adjust timing, EGR, and fuel metering.

Air Conditioning Sensors. Most air conditioning sensors are switches that indicate when the compressor clutch is engaged. The A/C compressor can use 5 to 10 extra horsepower, which increases engine load. When the computer knows that the compressor is engaged, it can adjust timing, fuel flow, idle speed, and other variables to compensate for the extra load.

Detonation Sensors. You learned about detonation sensors when you studied turbochargers. Some engine control systems use detonation sensors even without turbos to retard timing and prevent pinging. Most detonation sensors contain a piezoresistive crystal, which changes resistance when pressure is applied to it. When detonation does not exist, pressure is uniform across the crystal, figure 13-76. Reference voltage is applied to the sensor, and the return signal voltage stays at its programmed value. When detonation occurs, it causes changes in the pressure applied to the sensor crystal. This changes the sen-

sor resistance and, thus, the return signal voltage.

Transmission Sensors. Late-model automatic transmissions and transaxles use electronically controlled lockup torque converters, as well as solenoids that control gear shift points. To determine when to lock and unlock the converter or shift the transmission from one gear to another, the computer looks at input from the following:

- Throttle position sensor
- Coolant temperature sensor
- Vehicle speed sensor
- Gear selector switch
- Brake switch
- Downshift pulse switch or pressure switches

Sensor input values for throttle position, coolant temperature, vehicle speed, and gear position must equal or exceed a programmed value before the computer will act. Brake and downshift input values are used to open a solenoid under specified operating conditions.

SYSTEM ACTUATORS

An actuator is an output device that changes voltage signals to mechanical action. Most engine control actuators are solenoids. Some, however, are stepper motors. As you know, a solenoid is an electromechanical dc device that is energized when voltage is applied and deenergized when it is not. A stepper motor is a dc motor that moves in incremental steps from deenergized (no voltage) to fully energized (full voltage). A typical stepper motor can have 100 to 120 steps of movement from deenergized to fully energized, depending on voltage. A solenoid is basically a digital actuator. A stepper motor can work as an analog actuator with digital signals.

Solenoid Operation

A computer controls voltage to a solenoid, but it usually does not switch the system voltage. Battery voltage is applied to one solenoid terminal, and the computer opens and closes a ground switch connected to the other terminal, figure 13-77. Thus, most actuators are grounded through the computer, and a secure computer ground connection is essential for proper system operation. The solenoid can be energized for a random

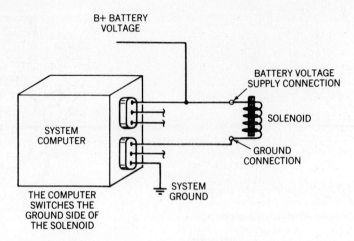

Figure 13-77. Most engine control system solenoids are grounded through the computer so the computer does not have to switch system voltage.

length of time, or it can vibrate on and off at a certain number of cycles per second.

Among the many uses that solenoids perform in fully integrated electronic engine control systems are:

- Fuel metering by modulating a fuel injector or mixture control solenoid
- Evaporative canister purging by opening and closing a solenoid in the vapor line to the manifold or carburetor
- EGR by opening and closing a solenoid-operated valve in the vacuum line to the EGR valve

Fuel-Metering Actuators

A fuel control solenoid or stepper motor normally operates so that the midpoint of its range or the 50-percent duty cycle gives a 14.7:1 ratio during closed loop. Most such actuators allow a ±2 air-fuel ratio range. That is, the system provides ratios from 12.7:1 to 16.7:1. If the system is not working correctly, however, the computer may drive the actuator to one side or the other of the midpoint to maintain a 14.7:1 closed-loop ratio. The system then may not provide the proper rich or lean mixtures for other conditions.

Stepper Motors. Stepper motor fuel control is used in some Motorcraft and Carter carburetors. The motor moves metering pins in main circuit air bleeds, figure 13-78, to control the

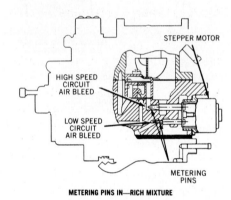

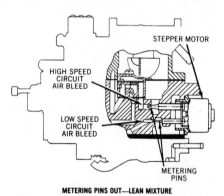

Figure 13-78. This stepper motor controls air bleeds in the high-speed and low-speed circuits to vary the air-fuel ratio. (AMC)

air-fuel ratio. Moving the pins into the bleeds enriches the mixture (less air); moving them out leans the mixture (more air). The stepper motor in a Ford 7200 VV carburetor moves a valve to control the air-fuel ratio in one of two ways:

1. In early models, the valve opens a passage to allow control vacuum to enter the fuel bowl, figure 13-79. This lowers the air pressure on the fuel and creates a leaner air-fuel ratio.

2. In later models, the valve opens air bleeds that allow additional air into the air-fuel mixture at the discharge jets.

Mixture Control Solenoids. Mixture control solenoids can control air-fuel ratios in several ways. All, however, work on the variable duty cycle principle. Some solenoids control vacuum to diaphragms in a carburetor, figure 13-80. The vacuum diaphragms move metering rods in and out of carburetor jets to regulate fuel flow, and they open and close air bleeds for idle and main-metering circuits. Some Carter carburetors have solenoids that work on a variable duty cycle to open and close air bleeds in the carburetor, figure 13-81.

Rochester carburetors used in GM C-4 and CCC systems have mixture solenoids that regulate fuel flow directly, rather than by regulating a vacuum signal. Mounted in the carburetor, the mixture solenoid controls a metering rod in the main jet, figure 13-82. It also controls a rod that opens and closes an idle air bleed, figure 13-83.

Fuel Injectors

Fuel injectors, or injection nozzles, are the principal actuators on most late-model engine control systems. Mechanical injection nozzles are not electronic devices, but they are used in electronically controlled systems. Electronic injection nozzles are specialized solenoid devices.

Mechanical Injection Nozzles. Bosch K-Jetronic is the major me-

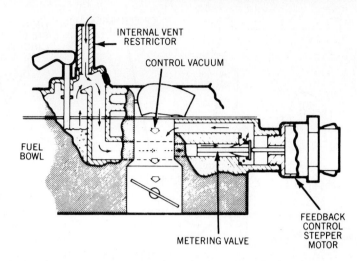

Figure 13-79. The stepper motor in Ford's early 7200 VV feedback carburetor varies air pressure on the gasoline in the fuel bowl. (Ford)

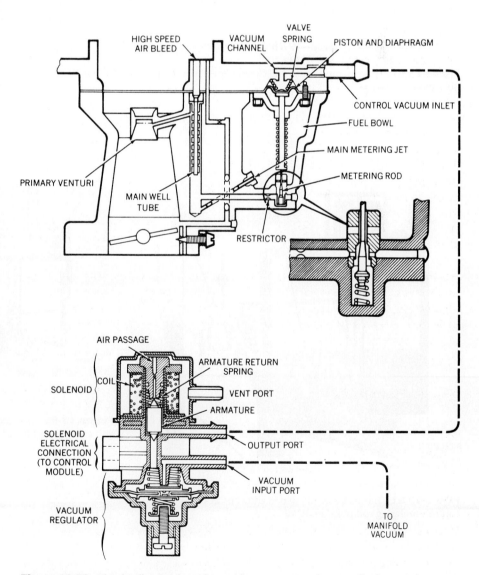

Figure 13-80. This feedback solenoid controls vacuum on carburetor diaphragms that move metering rods and open or close air bleeds. (GM)

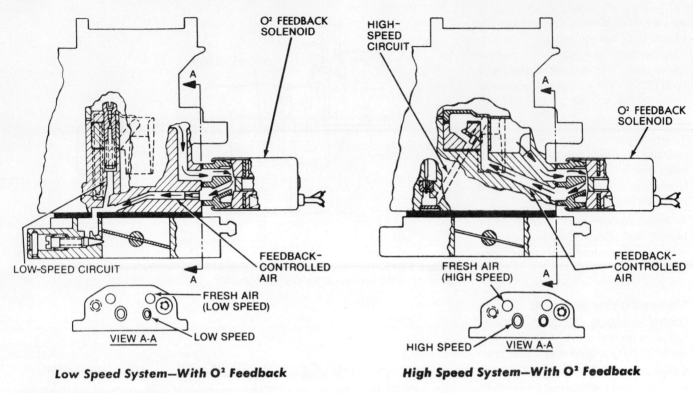

Low Speed System—With O² Feedback   *High Speed System—With O² Feedback*

Figure 13-81. This solenoid opens and closes high- and low-speed air bleeds with a variable duty cycle. (Chrysler)

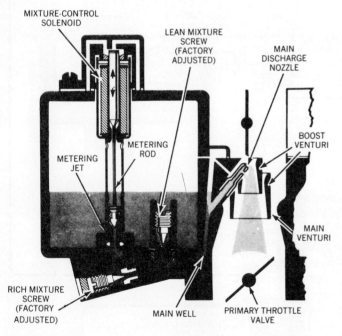

Figure 13-82. This mixture solenoid in a Rochester carburetor controls metering rod position. (GM)

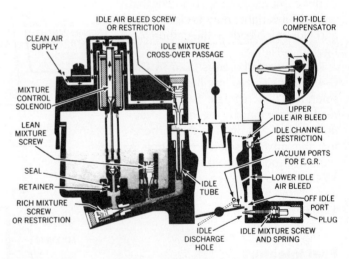

Figure 13-83. The same mixture solenoid shown in figure 13-82 also controls an idle air bleed passage. (GM)

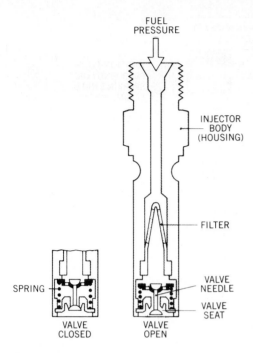

Figure 13-84. Fuel pressure and spring force work against each other to control the opening of a mechanical injection nozzle. (Bosch)

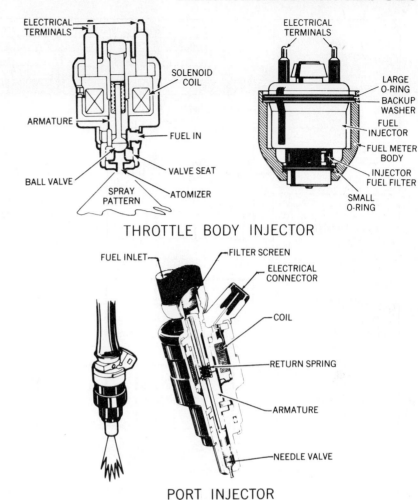

THROTTLE BODY INJECTOR

PORT INJECTOR

Figure 13-85. EFI nozzles are opened intermittently by timed solenoid action. (Rochester) (Volvo)

chanical gasoline injection system. The individual injectors, figure 13-84, have spring-loaded tips that seal the nozzles against fuel pressure. When pressure exceeds about 45 psi (310 kPa), it forces the nozzle open. Fuel pressure thus controls the amount of nozzle opening and the amount of fuel that enters the manifold. Injection pressure is controlled by the mixture control unit through a combination of pump pressure and control pressure. Under full-load operation, injection pressure may go as high as 70 psi (490 kPa). Bosch K-Jetronic nozzles inject fuel continuously while the engine is running. Fuel collects, or waits, at the intake port to mix with the air charge. Spring force and injection pressure cause the nozzle to vibrate and ensure good atomization. When the engine is off, the spring closes the nozzle to hold reserve pressure in the lines.

Electronic Injection Nozzles. A solenoid-operated electronic injector, figure 13-85, has an armature and a needle valve or ball valve assembly. A spring holds the needle or ball against the valve seat when the solenoid is deenergized. When the solenoid is

energized, it pulls the armature against spring force to unseat the valve and inject fuel. The valve moves only about 1 mm. The design of the injector tip ensures good fuel atomization and spray pattern.

The injector always opens the same distance, but the amount of fuel injected is controlled by injector pulse width. Pulse width is the amount of time that the device is energized, measured in milliseconds. The electronic module varies injector pulse width in relation to the amount of fuel a particular engine needs at any time. A short pulse width delivers little fuel; a longer pulse width delivers more fuel, figure 13-86.

Pulse width also is related to the duty cycle. The complete operating cycle of an injector or any solenoid-

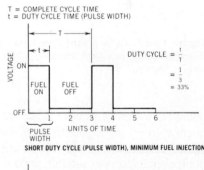

T = COMPLETE CYCLE TIME
t = DUTY CYCLE TIME (PULSE WIDTH)

$$\text{DUTY CYCLE} = \frac{t}{T}$$
$$= \frac{1}{3}$$
$$= 33\%$$

SHORT DUTY CYCLE (PULSE WIDTH), MINIMUM FUEL INJECTION

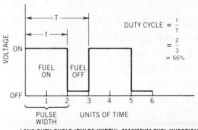

$$\text{DUTY CYCLE} = \frac{t}{T}$$
$$= \frac{2}{3}$$
$$= 66\%$$

LONG DUTY CYCLE (PULSE WIDTH), MAXIMUM FUEL INJECTION

Figure 13-86. Pulse width is the duration of injector on-time. Duty cycle is the percentage of on-time during one complete cycle.

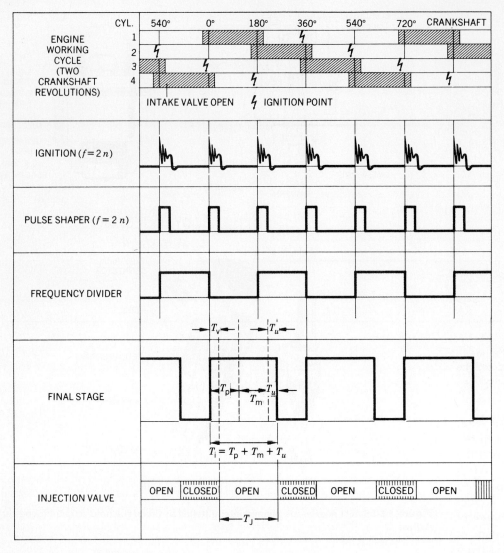

		f	IGNITION-PULSE FREQUENCY OR SPARKING RATE
		n	ENGINE SPEED
		T_p	BASIC DURATION OF INJECTION
		T_m	PULSE EXTENSION BY CORRECTIONS
		T_v	RESPONSE DELAY
		T_u	PULSE EXTENSION BY VOLTAGE COMPENSATION
		T_i	PULSE CONTROL TIME
		T_J	DURATION OF INJECTION PER CYCLE

Figure 13-87. These graphs show the relationships of engine working cycles, ignition, and injection timing for a 4-cylinder engine. All four injectors operate simultaneously in this system. (Bosch)

operated metering device is the sequence from on to off to back on again. A device can operate at any number of cycles per second, according to its design: 10, 20, 60, and so on. Each *complete* cycle always lasts the same length of time but the duty cycle is a variable percentage of total cycle time. Figure 13-86 shows two different pulse widths, or duty cycles, for the same total cycle time.

The control module calculates pulse width from information provided by sensors that measure airflow, engine speed, temperature, and throttle position. Most electronic injectors

do not inject fuel intermittently for each intake stroke. Throttle body injectors supply fuel for all cylinders from one or two nozzles, so their operating cycles and pulse widths must be matched to overall airflow and engine operation.

Electronic port injectors are usually energized in groups or all together. All injectors for 4-cylinder engines can open and close simultaneously or in groups of two. Injectors for 6- and 8-cylinder engines usually open in groups of 3 or 4 each. Injection pulses are timed so that half the fuel for each cylinder is injected each crankshaft

revolution. Figure 13-87 shows the relationships of engine operating cycles, ignition frequency, and injection timing for a 4-cylinder engine. As with a continuous injection system, the fuel waits at the intake port for the incoming air charge.

Other System Actuators

Besides controlling fuel metering and ignition timing, fully integrated electronic engine control systems regulate idle speed, EGR, evaporative canister purging, and air injection switching. Automatic transmission shifting and torque converter lockup are incorporated in some systems.

Transmission Solenoids and Switches. Since automatic transmissions were first developed, shifting and torque converter operation have depended upon hydraulic pressure within the transmission. Relying upon hydraulic pressure can lead to erratic operation for several reasons. Because both aspects of transmission operation are related to vehicle load and speed, their integration into the electronic control system assures more precise control and a quicker response to engine operating requirements.

Current systems use a series of pressure or gear switches mounted inside the transmission, figure 13-88, to provide input to the computer. Solenoids inside the transmission are used to engage and disengage the torque converter clutch, figure 13-89, and to upshift or downshift the transmission, as directed by the computer.

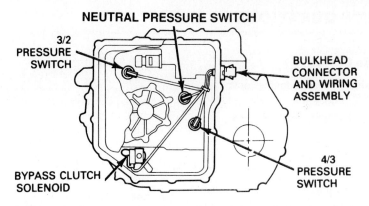

Figure 13-88. Hydraulic pressure switches and solenoids installed in the valve body of an automatic transmission or transaxle are used as sensors and actuators to control shift points and converter lockup. (Ford)

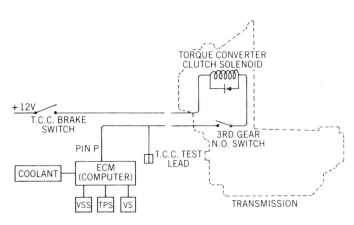

Figure 13-89. This computer-controlled solenoid opens and closes a transmission hydraulic circuit for torque converter clutch lockup. (GM)

SUMMARY

Electronic engine control systems began as single-function systems by metering fuel or controlling ignition timing. They were expanded to control a variety of engine functions, such as EGR, air injection switching, vapor canister purging, idle speed, and transmission converter and shift points. Such fully integrated control systems act as engine management systems.

Gasoline fuel injection is a proven technology that has achieved new popularity since the 1970's, due to integration into engine control systems. Gasoline injection systems use solenoid-actuated nozzles to spray fuel into the intake air charge. Gasoline injection systems meter air in relation to intake air volume, just as a carburetor does. They can be classified as port or throttle body systems, electronic or mechanical systems, and continuous or intermittent systems.

Regardless of design, all use a device to measure intake air by sensing airflow, manifold pressure, or air density. These systems do not have chokes, power valves, or accelerator pumps, but they have counterpart auxiliary devices for the same air-fuel requirements that carburetors have.

All computers perform four basic functions: input, processing, storage, and output. Early automotive computers were analog designs, but digital binary computers are more efficient and less expensive and are now used exclusively. Computers perform their function of processing sensor inputs by comparing the data to stored instructions or programs, then sending a voltage signal to the proper actuator.

The speed and precision of a computer is ideal for managing engine systems to balance fuel metering, ignition timing, and EGR operation. When this balance is obtained, the air-fuel mixture can be maintained at or close to the stoichiometric ratio of 14.7:1 for the best combination of performance, economy, and emission control.

Most sensors are switches, resistors, transformers, or generators that measure analog variables. Their analog signals are converted into digital signals by the computer's conversion circuits. Once digitized, the signals are processed by the computer according to its program, and an output voltage signal is sent to an actuator.

Actuators change the computer's output voltage signal into electromechanical motion. Actuators are generally solenoids, relays, or stepper motors.

REVIEW QUESTIONS

Multiple Choice

1. The first electronic engine control system used by a domestic carmaker was the:

  a. GM Oldsmobile MISAR system

  b. Ford EEC I system

  c. Chrysler electronic lean-burn system

  d. AMC Motronic system

2. The electronic engine control system used on most late-model GM cars is called:

  a. electronic spark and fuel control (ESFC)

  b. computer-controlled catalytic converter (C-4)

  c. computerized emission control (CEC)

  d. computer command control (CCC or C-3)

3. Mechanic A says that an engine computer receives input information, processes data, stores data, and sends output information. Mechanic B says that most late-model engine computers are based on digital microprocessors. Who is right?

  a. A only

  b. B only

  c. both A and B

  d. neither A nor B

4. Most late-model engine control systems control all of the following EXCEPT:

  a. spark timing

  b. air-fuel ratio

  c. EGR

  d. intake airflow

5. The simplest digital sensor is a:

  a. timer

  b. switch

  c. transducer

  d. solenoid

6. Most automobile engine sensors are:

  a. solenoids

  b. transformers

  c. magnetic-pulse generators

  d. resistors

7. Mechanic A says that a resistive sensor must receive a steady reference voltage. Mechanic B says that the output (return) voltage of a resistive sensor changes as resistance changes. Who is right?

  a. A only

  b. B only

  c. both A and B

  d. neither A nor B

8. Mechanic A says that an exhaust gas oxygen (EGO) sensor is a thermistor. Mechanic B says that an EGO sensor measures air-fuel ratio. Who is right?

  a. A only

  b. B only

  c. both A and B

  d. neither A nor B

9. A negative temperature coefficient (NTC) sensor is a:

  a. transducer

  b. thermistor

  c. potentiometer

  d. all of the above

10. A sensor that produces a variable output voltage in relation to force or pressure is a:

  a. potentiometer

  b. thermistor

  c. piezoresistive sensor

  d. none of the above

11. Mechanic A says that a reluctance sensor can indicate engine temperature. Mechanic B says that a reluctance sensor can indicate engine speed. Who is right?

  a. A only

  b. B only

  c. both A and B

  d. neither A nor B

12. The EGO sensor is a:

  a. thermistor

  b. potentiometer

  c. bimetal sensor

  d. galvanic battery

13. Mechanic A says that heated EGO sensors are often used on turbocharged engines. Mechanic B says that heated EGO sensors eliminate the need for air switching. Who is right?

  a. A only

  b. B only

  c. both A and B

  d. neither A nor B

14. Mechanic A says that airflow sensors are analog sensors. Mechanic B says that manifold absolute pressure (MAP) sensors are analog devices. Who is right?

  a. A only

  b. B only

  c. both A and B

  d. neither A nor B

15. Coolant and air temperature sensors do the jobs of a:

  a. carburetor choke coil

  b. carburetor power circuit

  c. vacuum advance diaphragm

  d. centrifugal advance weights

16. Mechanic A says that throttle position sensors are both load and speed sensors. Mechanic B says that a throttle position sensor can be a simple on-off switch. Who is right?

  a. A only

  b. B only

  c. both A and B

  d. neither A nor B

17. Most engine control system actuators are:

  a. transducers

  b. solenoids

  c. potentiometers

  d. thermistors

18. All of the following are kinds of gasoline fuel injection system EXCEPT:

  a. port injection

  b. precombustion chamber injection

  c. throttle body injection

  d. continuous injection

19. Mechanic A says that Bosch K-Jetronic systems are continuous injection systems. Mechanic B says that K-Jetronic systems are mechanical systems that work on differential fuel pressure. Who is right?

  a. A only

  b. B only

  c. both A and B

  d. neither A nor B

20. Bosch L-Jetronic and similar systems measure airflow with a:

  a. manifold absolute pressure sensor

  b. hot-wire air mass sensor

  c. vane-type airflow sensor

  d. barometric pressure sensor

21. Bosch LH-Jetronic and similar systems measure airflow with a:

  a. manifold absolute pressure sensor

  b. hot-wire air mass sensor

  c. vane-type airflow sensor

  d. barometric pressure sensor

22. Mechanic A says that most throttle body injection (TBI) systems measure airflow and air volume with manifold absolute pressure (MAP) or barometric pressure sensors, or both. Mechanic B says that most TBI systems also have hot-wire air mass sensors. Who is right?

a. A only
b. B only
c. both A and B
d. neither A nor B

23. Most port-type electronic fuel injection (EFI) systems are based on designs by:

a. Rochester Products Division of GM
b. Bendix Division of Allied Corporation
c. Nippondenso
d. Robert Bosch GmbH

24. The first modern port injection system on domestic cars was made by Bendix and used on:

a. 1983 and later Chevrolet Corvettes
b. 1980 and later Chrysler K-cars
c. 1973 Ford Mustang SVO models
d. 1976–79 Cadillac Sevilles

25. Mechanic A says that TBI systems are mechanical, continuous injection systems. Mechanic B says that TBI systems do not require fuel pressure regulators. Who is right?

a. A only
b. B only
c. both A and B
d. neither A nor B

26. Mechanic A says that the duty cycle of a mechanical (continuous) injection nozzle is controlled by an electronic module. Mechanic B says that the duty cycle of a solenoid-operated injector is the percentage of on-time to total cycle time. Who is right?

a. A only
b. B only
c. both A and B
d. neither A nor B

27. Electronic port injectors are usually energized:

a. continuously
b. individually in firing-order sequence
c. in groups or all together
d. at a fixed duty cycle

28. Mechanic A says that the throttle in a TBI system is between the injectors and the manifold. Mechanic B says that the throttle in an EFI system works the same as a throttle on a carbureted engine. Who is right?

a. A only
b. B only
c. both A and B
d. neither A nor B

29. All of the following are kinds of airflow sensors EXCEPT:

a. a throttle position sensor
b. a movable plate that operates a plunger in the fuel distributor
c. a platinum hot-wire sensor
d. a movable-vane potentiometer sensor

30. Manifold pressure sensors may be based on:

a. an aneroid capsule or bellows
b. a diaphragm
c. a piezoresistive crystal
d. all of the above

31. A hot-wire air mass sensor measures:

a. airflow velocity entering the engine
b. manifold absolute pressure
c. molecular mass of air entering the engine
d. all of the above

32. A cold-start injector is a:

a. mechanical, continuous injector controlled by intake airflow
b. bypass airflow injector
c. coolant-controlled detonation regulator
d. solenoid-operated auxiliary injector

33. Mechanic A says that a throttle position sensor is a variable potentiometer. Mechanic B says that some EFI systems use an on-off throttle position switch. Who is right?

a. A only
b. B only
c. both A and B
d. neither A nor B

Fill in the Blank

34. In a solenoid-operated electronic fuel injection system, the amount of fuel injected is controlled by injector _____ , or duty cycle.

35. Fuel metering through a carburetor is controlled directly by the difference between air pressure in the _____ and air pressure in the carburetor barrel.

36. The throttle in a fuel injection system regulates the amount of _____ allowed into the engine.

37. Manifold absolute pressure is a combination of atmospheric pressure and _____ .

38. An EFI system must know engine speed and _____ position to time injection pulses and calculate pulse width.

39. A thermistor is a variable resistor whose resistance _____ as it is heated.

40. A digital computer processes information in binary digits called _____ .

41. The computer's converter circuits change _____ input signals into digital information.

42. An input or output signal that is either on-off or high-low is a _____ signal.

43. The two basic operating modes for all late-model engine control systems are _____ and _____ .

44. At the stoichiometric air-fuel ratio of 14.7 : 1, HC, CO, and NO_x emissions are _____ .

45. An exhaust gas oxygen (EGO) sensor measures _____ .

46. The ratio of excess air to stoichiometric air quantity is called the _____ ratio.

47. Air and coolant temperature sensors often are a type of resistor that is called a _____ .

48. To time injection pulses and calculate injector pulse width, an EFI system must have sensors for engine _____ and crankshaft _____ .

49. In most port injection systems, idle air flow passes through an _____ passage.

50. As vacuum decreases, manifold absolute pressure _____ .

51. Bosch mechanical injection systems work on a difference between fuel pump pressure and a control pressure developed by the _____ .

PART FOUR
LIGHTING SYSTEMS, INSTRUMENTATION, AND SAFETY SYSTEMS

INTRODUCTION

Vehicle lighting, instruments, and safety systems were the next applications of electric power for automobiles after the starting, charging, and ignition systems. Electric lights replaced gas lamps on motorcars about the same time that the self-starter became commonplace. Electric instruments for fuel gauges, ammeters, and other dashboard indicators were common in the 1930's. By the 1940's and 1950's, almost all dashboard instruments used electric senders and gauges. Electric horns, windshield wipers and washers, turn signals, backup lamps, and other lighting and accessory systems are now taken for granted as important vehicle systems for safety and comfort.

Chapter 14 describes the headlamp circuits and components used on all vehicles. Many of the features of headlamp systems and other lighting systems are prescribed by law or industry standards. Basic headlamp circuits haven't changed much in 70 years, but modern lighting components and controls are a far cry from the first dim bulbs of the 1920's or the first sealed-beam headlamps of the 1940's. Late-model halogen lamps and other system features have doubled vehicle lighting safety when compared to automobiles of even a decade ago. Electronic controls for automatic lamp dimming and delayed switching are common features on many new cars. Chapter 14 concludes with a survey of electronic lighting systems on late-model vehicles.

Chapter 15 continues the survey of lighting systems by listing standard lamp bulbs and explaining basic circuit design and operation for parking and taillamps, stoplamps, turn signals, hazard flashers, backup lamps, and other safety and convenience lighting circuits.

Chapter 16 describes common electrical circuits used for instrumenta-tion, horns, windshield wipers and washers, defoggers, and engine cooling fans. Like basic lighting systems, these electrical circuits have remained quite standard for decades. You will continue to find these basic instrumentation and safety circuits on most late-model cars and trucks.

Chapter 17 introduces the modern electronic systems that have developed from the basic instruments and controls explained in chapter 16. As you compare the common electrical systems described in chapter 16 to the electronic systems in chapter 17, you will see that all of them operate to serve the same basic driver and vehicle requirements. Chapter 17 illustrates how modern electronic controls have improved the safety and convenience features on late-model cars. You also will recognize specific applications of the electronic fundamentals that you learned in Part One of this book.

14 HEADLAMP SYSTEMS AND CIRCUITS

WHAT

Automotive headlamps are an essential safety device. While they give the driver 24-hour mobility, headlamps also are important to other drivers and pedestrians. For this reason, headlamps and their circuits must be kept in good operating condition.

Although there are slight variations among carmakers, all headlamp circuits function according to a standardized design. If you understand the basic elements of a headlamp circuit and how it works, you will be able to troubleshoot virtually all such circuits.

This chapter covers headlamp types, basic circuits and control devices, and the automatic headlamp systems currently in use.

WHY

Because headlamps are so important to both driver and pedestrian safety, they have long been subject to legal requirements of state legislatures and the Federal government. Bulb-and-reflector designs were used until 1940, when sealed-beam headlamps were legally mandated for use in all states. Other than an increase of 3,000 candlepower in 1955, a changeover from two- to four-light systems in 1958, and the appearance of rectangular headlights in 1975, few changes were permitted in headlamps until 1978. That year, the National Highway Traffic and Safety Administration (NHTSA) increased the permissible light output from 75,000 to 150,000 candlepower, paving the way for the use of halogen sealed-beam headlamps, which appeared on production vehicles in 1980.

With the smaller cars of the 1980's, styling changes required the use of smaller headlamps that would provide the same or more illumination than the larger lamps they replaced. Because of styling requirements, two other changes occurred: concealed headlamps became very popular, and the composite headlamp replaced the sealed-beam lamp on many vehicles. This bulb-and-reflector design returned the headlamp to essentially where it started more than a half-century ago, although providing considerably more illumination.

The progress in the design of headlamps and their circuits in the 1980's means that service technicians must be aware of the changes and how to deal with them. Electronic control of headlamp circuits has yet to appear on production vehicles, but it cannot be far off.

Once you learn the basic operation of headlamps and circuits you will be able to service the headlamp system on any vehicle more easily.

GOALS

After completing this chapter, you should be able to:

1. Explain the differences between standard sealed-beam, halogen sealed-beam, and composite headlamps.

2. Identify the proper replacement headlamp for a given vehicle.

3. Explain how a headlamp switch controls the operating conditions of a headlamp circuit.

4. Explain the operation of a dimmer switch.

5. Identify vacuum-operated and electrically-controlled concealed headlamps and explain the difference between them.

6. Explain the operation of an automatic headlamp dimmer system.

7. Explain the operation of automatic on-off and time-delay headlamp systems.

HEADLAMP TYPES

Headlamps are categorized by design type:

- Standard sealed-beam
- Halogen sealed-beam
- Composite with replaceable halogen bulb

Sealed-beam headlamps also are categorized according to a Department of Transportation (DOT) identification or type code and trade numbers used by all manufacturers, figure 14-1. Standard sealed-beam bulbs are available in five different types for automotive use:

1. Type 1 bulbs are 5-3/4 inch (146-mm) diameter round bulbs and contain a single high-beam filament.

2. Type 1A bulbs are 4 × 6-1/2 inch (102-mm × 165-mm) rectangular bulbs and contain a single high-beam filament.

3. Type 2 bulbs are 5-3/4 inch (146-mm) or 7-inch (178-mm) diameter round bulbs and contain one high-beam and one low-beam filament.

4. Type 2A bulbs are 4 × 6-1/2 inch (102-mm × 165-mm) rectangular bulbs and contain one high-beam and one low-beam filament.

5. Type 2B bulbs are the same as Type 2, but the bulb housing is manufactured to metric dimensions of 142 × 200 mm (5.6 × 7.9 inches).

Halogen sealed-beam headlamps are offered in the same types and sizes as standard sealed-beam bulbs. In addition, they are available in a type 2E. This is a 4 × 6-1/2 inch (102-mm × 165-mm) rectangular bulb containing low- and high-beam filaments.

All sealed-beam bulbs, whether standard or halogen, have the type code molded into their lenses. Three small aiming pads also are molded into the lens at standard positions. The aiming pads are used with a mechanical aiming device, as you will learn in chapter 13 of Volume 2.

Headlamp Type & Size	Trade No.*	I.D. No.	Wattage @ 12.8 Volts High Beam	Low Beam
5-3/4 inch	4000	2C1	37.5	60
circular	4040**	2C1	37.5	60
sealed-beam	5001	1C1	50	
	H5001	1C1	37.5	
	H5006	1C1	50	
7 inch	6014	2D1	60	50
circular	6016**	2D1	60	50
sealed-beam	H6017	2D1	60	35
	H6024	2D1	60	50
4 × 6-1/2 inch	4651	1A1	50	
rectangular	H4651	1A1	50	
sealed-beam	4652	2A1	60	60
	H4656	2A1	60	60
	H4662	2A1	35	35
5-1/2 × 8 inch	6052	2B1	65	55
rectangular sealed-beam	H6054	2B1	65	35
3 × 5 inch	H4701		65	
rectangular sealed-beam	H4703		65	
aerodynamic	9004		65	45
headlamp	9005		65	
halogen bulb	9006			55

*H = Halogen
**Heavy duty

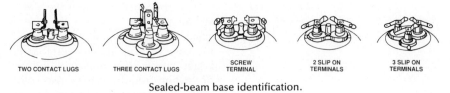

Sealed-beam base identification.

TWO CONTACT LUGS   THREE CONTACT LUGS   SCREW TERMINAL   2 SLIP ON TERMINALS   3 SLIP ON TERMINALS

Figure 14-1. Common automotive headlamp types and identification.

Standard Sealed-beam Headlamps

A standard sealed-beam headlamp consists of a filament positioned on a reflector to which a lens has been molded, figure 14-2, and all air evacuated from the unit. The headlamp must be airtight, or oxygen would cause the filament to burn up. When the light switch is turned on, battery current flows through the filament, causing it to glow white hot. The light from the filament is directed in a cylindrical beam, figure 14-3, by the polished curved surface of the reflector. Filament location in the reflector and lens design determines whether the bulb will emit a low or a high beam. The lens is a series of small prisms that changes the cylindrical beam from the reflector into an oval-shaped beam.

In a low-beam headlamp, the filament is offset in the reflector, and an **asymmetrical** lens is used to direct and spread the light beam downward and to the right. A high-beam headlamp uses a non-offset filament and a **symmetrical** lens to direct and spread the light beam upward and to the front of the vehicle. The low-beam light is used to illuminate the road directly in front of the vehicle during city driving

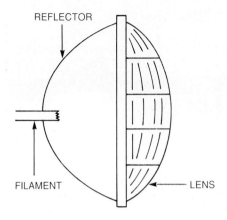

Figure 14-2. The three major components of a sealed-beam headlamp.

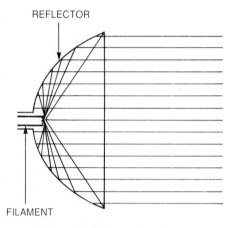

Figure 14-3. Light from the filament strikes the curved reflector surface and is reflected in a cylindrical beam to the lens.

or passing so that drivers of oncoming cars will not be blinded. The high-beam light is used in conjunction with the low-beam and illuminates the road further ahead with a reasonable degree of evenness during open-road driving.

Halogen Sealed-beam Headlamps

Halogen sealed-beam headlamps were first approved for use on 1980 domestic vehicles and initially offered as optional equipment. They provide brighter light from a power consumption approximately two-thirds of the amount required by standard sealed-beam bulbs. Halogen sealed-beams have now become standard equipment on many new cars and will gradually make the standard sealed-beam obsolete. Manufacturers recom-

mend that they be installed as replacements for older standard sealed-beam bulbs. It is not a good idea, however, to install standard sealed-beam bulbs as replacements for halogen sealed-beams because of their lower light output.

Halogen sealed-beam bulbs obtain their light by sending current through a filament enclosed in a pressure-filled capsule of a halogen gas. The bulbs are manufactured of plastic instead of glass. This reduces the weight of the bulb (an important factor with downsized vehicles) and makes it more resistant to road damage caused by flying stones and other debris.

Composite Headlamps

Composite headlamps were introduced in 1984 as a part of the aerodynamic styling trend that swept the automotive industry in the middle of the decade. This return to the bulb-and-reflector concept used before 1940 consists of a flush-mounted headlamp housing and reflector assembly with a replaceable, vacuum-sealed halogen or tungsten-halogen bulb, figure 14-4. The headlamp housings are an integral part of a vehicle's styling and thus vary widely in design.

Composite headlamps may use polycarbonate plastic or glass to form the lens part of the housing. Integral designs have the lens permanently bonded to the reflector to form a single unit, as in a sealed-beam design. Non-integral designs use a separate reflector assembly and glass lens. A tongue molded around the perimeter of the lens fits into a groove in the reflector housing. Metal clips are used to retain the lens and reflector and form a weatherproof seal. An opening in the back of the reflector of both designs accepts the replaceable halogen or tungsten-halogen bulb. The reflector design combined with the higher output bulb results in a greater amount of light output than that available from sealed-beam units. An additional advantage is that a crack or break in the lens or housing will not cause the bulb to burn out. If the lens

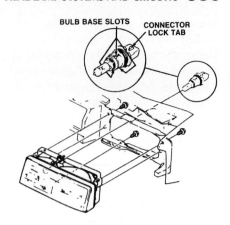

Figure 14-4. Composite headlamps are part of the vehicle's styling and use replaceable halogen or tungsten-halogen bulbs.

of an integral design is broken, however, the entire housing assembly must be replaced.

The composite headlamp housing is not sealed but is vented instead to the atmosphere. For this reason, moisture may condense on the inside of the headlamp lens during damp or inclement weather when the lamps are off. Such condensation will not affect headlamp performance, since the heat from the bulbs will dissipate the moisture quickly once they are turned on.

Bulbs used in composite headlamps, like sealed-beam headlamps, may be dual-filament designs and contain both low- and high-beam filaments, or single-filament designs for either low or or high beam. Composite headlamps with a single chamber use one bulb to provide both low and high beams. Composite headlamps with two reflector chambers require two bulbs. In this design, the outboard bulb provides the low beam and the inboard bulb delivers the high beam.

The halogen bulbs used in composite headlamps are made with quartz and are thus subject to staining from contact with normal skin oil. Manufacturers provide new bulbs in protective covers that should not be removed until installation. Bulbs that are inadvertently touched must be cleaned with a soft cloth and rubbing alcohol.

Replacing the bulb in a composite headlamp has no effect on headlamp focus or alignment. Focus is established by the position of the bulb socket; alignment is required only if the headlamp assembly is removed or replaced. However, alignment of composite headlamp assemblies requires the use of special adapters, as you will learn in chapter 13 of Volume 2.

CONCEALED HEADLAMPS

Composite headlamps are one approach to lowering the aerodynamic drag of a vehicle; concealed headlamps are another. Older designs use a movable metal or plastic door that conceals a standard headlamp, figure 14-5. The door moves up or down to expose the headlamp bulb whenever the headlamp switch is turned on. When the switch is turned off, the door moves back in place to cover the bulb. The headlamp door has a practical use in addition to styling; it protects the bulb from dirt, mud, or flying stones. Many recent designs conceal the headlamps under the body sheet metal when not in use. These "popup" designs, figure 14-6, are required by Federal law to remain off until they have completed three-quarters of their travel.

Concealed headlamps may be operated by vacuum actuators or electric motors. All, however, must have a manual actuator such as a crank or knob, figure 14-7, in case the vacuum or electric system fails. When using the manual actuator on an electric system, the battery negative cable should be disconnected. This will eliminate any possibility of the motor starting and injuring your hands.

Vacuum-Operated Concealed Headlamps

A vacuum-operated system uses a vacuum motor for each headlamp door and functions on engine vacuum stored in a reservoir, figure 14-8. Turning on the headlamp switch activates a vacuum switch or distribution valve attached to the rear of the switch, figure 14-9. The distribution valve routes vacuum to the two vac-

Figure 14-5. Headlamps may be concealed behind movable doors for styling purposes and protection from road damage.

Figure 14-6. Popup headlamps are another common concealment method used by automotive stylists.

Figure 14-7. All concealed headlamps have some form of manual control that can be activated in the engine compartment in case of system failure.

uum motors, figure 14-10, which activate the linkage to open the headlamp doors. Turning the headlamp switch off vents the distribution valve to atmospheric pressure. If the headlamp doors are spring loaded, they will close as soon as vacuum is removed from the vacuum motors. If they are not spring loaded, they will remain open unless the headlamp switch is turned off before the vacuum is removed.

Electrically Operated Concealed Headlamps

Electric systems may use one or two electric motors. Such motors are series wound with two field windings, a worm gear drive, and internal limit switches. On popup headlamp designs, the motors also contain internal ground switches to prevent the headlamps from coming on prematurely. The concealed headlamp system motor operates the headlamp assembly or door through a torsion bar or similar linkage arrangement. Electric systems generally use a relay and circuit breaker assembly to control current to each motor. Late-model systems use solid-state circuitry to control operation of the headlamp doors.

One of the systems used by Toyota on its Celica model is typical of electrically controlled concealed head-

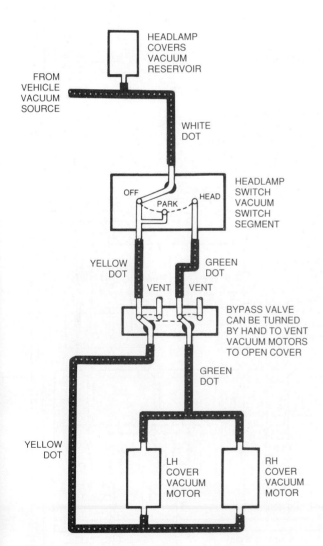

Figure 14-8. Engine vacuum stored in a reservoir is used to activate vacuum motors to open and close the headlamp doors. (Ford)

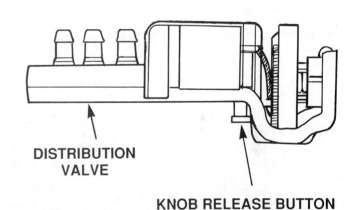

DISTRIBUTION VALVE

KNOB RELEASE BUTTON

Figure 14-9. A distribution valve on the rear of the headlamp switch activates the vacuum motor when the switch is turned on. (Ford)

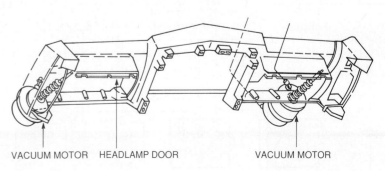

VACUUM MOTOR   HEADLAMP DOOR   VACUUM MOTOR

Figure 14-10. Vacuum-operated headlamp doors are controlled by vacuum motors and linkage. (Ford)

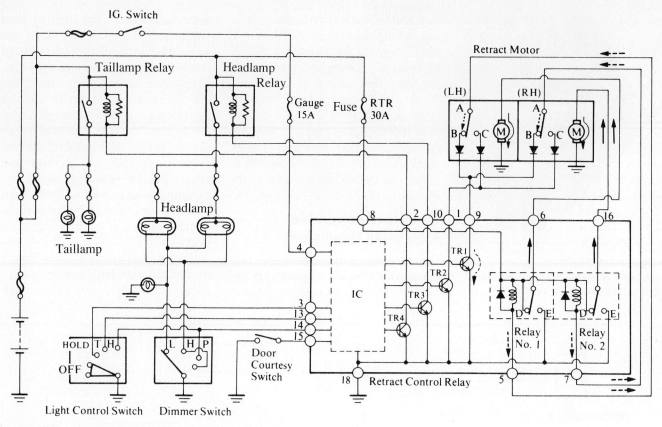

Figure 14-11. Operation of the Toyota Celica popup headlamps when the switch is turned on. (Toyota)

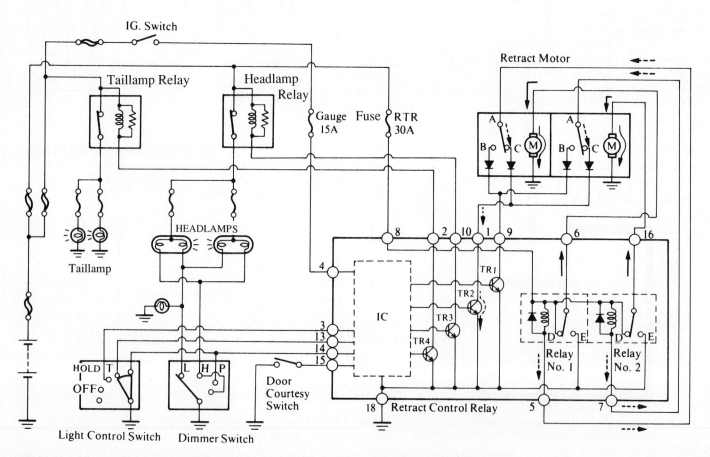

Figure 14-12. Operation of the Toyota Celica popup headlamps when the switch is turned off. (Toyota)

lamp systems in use. When the light switch is activated, figure 14-11, current flows to terminal 14 of the IC controller in the retract control relay, turning transistor TR2 on for about 10 seconds. Relay 1 and 2 turn on, and current flows to each retract motor to move the headlamps up. As soon as the headlamps are fully up, points A and C in the motor limit switch open, breaking the circuit to the number 1 and 2 relay coils. This shuts off power to the retract motors.

When the headlamp switch is turned off, figure 14-12, current to terminal 14 of the retract control relay is shut off. Transistor TR1 turns on for about 10 seconds. Relay 1 and 2 turn on and current flows to each retract motor to move the headlamps down. Once the headlamps are fully down, points A and B in the motor limit switch open, breaking the circuit to the number 1 and 2 relay coils. This shuts off power to the retract motors.

HEADLAMP CIRCUITS AND CONTROLS

We have already seen that automotive headlamps have been subject to regulation for many years by state legislatures and the Federal government. For this reason, the headlamp circuit has been virtually standardized in the automotive industry to either a single or dual headlamp circuit.

A single headlamp circuit contains a dual-filament bulb on each side of the vehicle, figure 14-13. The bulb provides both a low and a high beam. A dual headlamp circuit contains a dual-filament bulb and a single-filament bulb on each side of the vehicle, figure 14-14. One filament of the outboard bulb provides the low beam. The other outboard bulb filament and the single-filament inboard bulb provide the high beam. Bulb placement in a dual headlamp circuit is strictly controlled by state and Federal regulations. The dual-filament bulb is always mounted either outboard or above the single-filament bulb. The single- and dual-filament bulbs are manufactured so that they cannot be

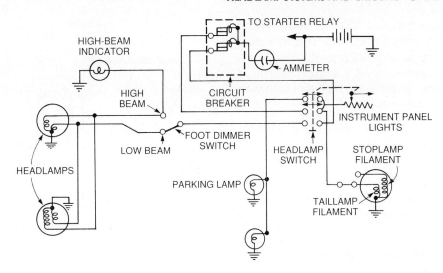

Figure 14-13. A single headlamp circuit uses a dual-filament bulb on each side of the vehicle.

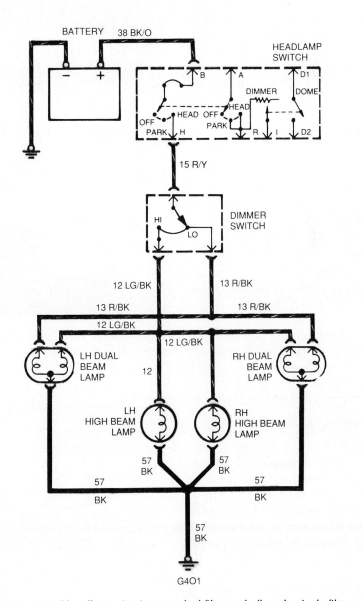

Figure 14-14. A dual headlamp circuit uses a dual filament bulb and a single filament bulb on each side of the vehicle. (Ford)

interchanged. Vehicle body styling determines whether a single or dual headlamp circuit is used.

Regardless of the type of circuit used, it must contain the following components:

- A switch to control headlamp operation
- A high-beam light
- A low-beam light
- A switch to control beam choice
- A high-beam indicator

Headlamp Switch and Circuit Breaker

The headlamp switch is the primary control component in any automotive lighting system. It is a multipurpose device that controls exterior, interior, and instrument panel lighting. Switch design may vary according to a particular vehicle's lighting system, but all perform the same function. There are three basic types of headlamp switches in general use:

1. A push-pull, knob-type switch mounted on the instrument panel, figure 14-15

2. A rocker-type switch mounted on the instrument panel, figure 14-16

3. A lever-type switch mounted on the steering column, figure 14-17

A few vehicles like the Mitsubishi Starion use a series of pushbuttons to select the switch positions, figure 14-18.

Most headlamp switches have three positions to control the following operating conditions of the headlamp circuit:

- Off
- Parking lamps
- Headlamps

Battery power is supplied directly to the headlamp switch. In some switch designs, battery power is sent only to the headlamp segment of the switch, with the remainder of the switch receiving power through a fuse in the fuse panel.

A headlamp switch is normally off (first position). When the switch is moved to its first detent (second posi-

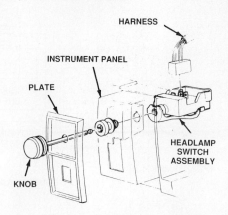
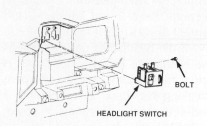

Figure 14-15. A typical push-pull headlamp switch. (Chevrolet)

Figure 14-16. A typical rocker-type headlamp switch. (Pontiac)

Figure 14-17. When the headlamp switch is mounted on the steering column, it is part of a combination or multifunction switch and is operated by a lever.

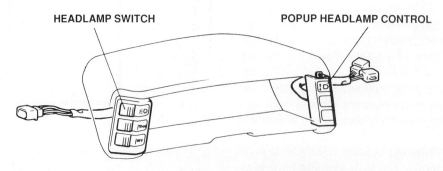

Figure 14-18. Pushbutton headlamp switches are used on some vehicles, particularly in conjunction with popup headlamps. (Mitsubishi)

tion), voltage is supplied to the instrument panel rheostat and the front and rear parking lamp and side marker circuits. Moving the switch to its second detent (third position) applies voltage to the headlamp dimmer switch. Depending upon the position of the dimmer switch, voltage is sent to either the low- or high-beam side of the circuit. Parking, side marker, and instrument panel lamps also remain on in the third position.

Many headlamp switches also contain a rheostat (variable resistor), figure 14-19. Turning the switch control knob clockwise varies instrument panel illumination from dim to bright. Rotating the knob beyond its detent turns the interior lights on. When a rocker type or stalk type headlamp switch is used, the rheostat is controlled by a separate switch.

The headlamp circuit is protected by a self-resetting, type I circuit breaker. The circuit breaker may be an internal part of the headlamp switch, figure 14-20, or it may be a separate unit installed between the switch and the battery, figure 14-13. Most headlamp circuits also contain a fusible link and a fuse to protect various parts of the system.

All headlamp circuits are required to contain an indicator lamp. The lamp is used to inform and remind the driver when the headlamps are on high-beam operation. The indicator lamp is located in a highly visible area of the instrument cluster, figure 14-21. It is wired into the circuit to provide a parallel path to ground. When the high-beam filaments are on, a small amount of high-beam current passes through the indicator lamp, turning it on.

Dimmer Switch

A 2-position dimmer switch allows the driver to switch between low- and high-beam operation. The dimmer switch is connected in series with the headlamp switch and controls the low- and high-beam current paths.

Most late model light-duty trucks and earlier passenger cars use a foot-operated, floor-mounted dimmer

Figure 14-19. Headlamp switches often contain a resistor (a rheostat) to control the illumination level of instrument panel lights.

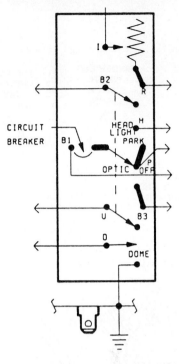

Figure 14-20. Many headlamp switches have integral circuit breakers. (Chrysler)

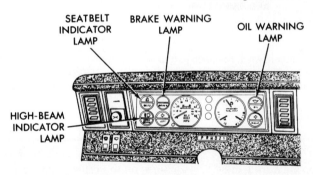

Figure 14-21. The high-beam indicator lamp is located in a prominent place in the instrument cluster. (Chrysler)

switch, figure 14-22, positioned to the left of the pedals. Many domestic cars now have the dimmer switch as part of a multifunction switch mounted on the steering column and operated by a stalk or lever, figure 14-23. This concept was introduced on imported cars in the 1970's. Other vehicles use a separate stalk- or lever-operated dimmer switch mounted in the steering column.

Dimmer switch installation in the circuit depends upon the type of circuit ground used. If the ground is provided at the headlamps, the dimmer switch will be installed in the circuit between the bulbs and the headlamp switch, figure 14-24. If the circuit uses grounded switches and

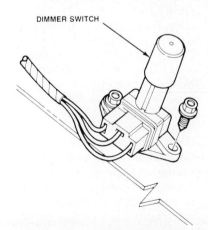

Figure 14-22. Older vehicles and most light-duty trucks use foot-operated, floor-mounted, 2-position dimmer switches to change from low to high beam and back. (Ford)

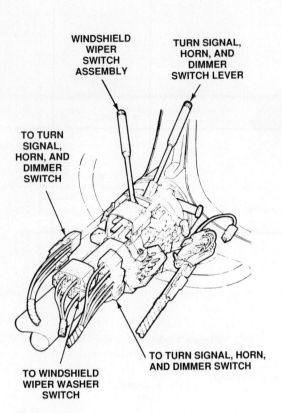

Figure 14-23. The dimmer switch has been part of the steering column multifunction switch on domestic vehicles since the late 1970's. (Ford)

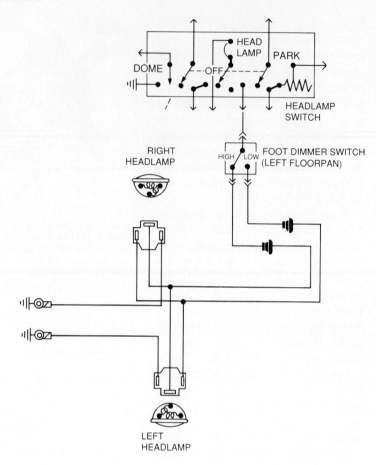

Figure 14-24. Most headlamp circuits use grounded bulbs and insulated switches. (Chrysler)

BEFORE HALOGEN, THERE WAS QUARTZ

Introduced in Europe during the mid-1960's, quartz-iodine headlamps were quick to prove their value abroad, but were never approved for use in the United States. They did find their way here, however, in the form of imported driving lamps and off-road vehicle lamps offered by Cibie and others. These were quasi-legal in many states, as long as you didn't abuse their use or irritate a traffic officer when stopped for another offense.

One of the major problems with a standard sealed-beam headlamp is its tungsten filament. The heat created by lighting the filament causes the filament to gradually self-destruct, since tiny particles of the tungsten filament vaporize. These vaporized particles are deposited, in turn, on the reflector and lens. This process gradually erodes the filament, causes the bulb to turn dark from the redeposited tungsten, and eventually results in bulb failure.

Similar in concept to the tungsten-halogen bulbs now available to American drivers, quartz-iodine bulbs solved the filament problem nicely. The tungsten filament in the bulb was enclosed in a quartz tube filled with iodine vapor. Quartz was used for the encasing tube because of the extremely high temperatures developed. The reaction of the gaseous iodine with the vaporized tungsten caused the tungsten particles to be redeposited on the filament instead of the glass parts. The end result was extended filament life and a bulb that burned brighter and longer.

The major problem with quartz-iodine bulbs was that they could not be dimmed using two filaments, as in a standard sealed-beam headlamp. The European manufacturers, however, managed to develop and incorporate an electromagnetic shutter in their quartz-iodine bulbs. This shutter was designed to drop into place electrically, masking off some of the illumination and diverting the rest downward for low-beam driving. Tungsten-halogen bulbs haven't quite caught up yet to their quartz-iodine predecessors in that respect, but there's always hope for tomorrow.

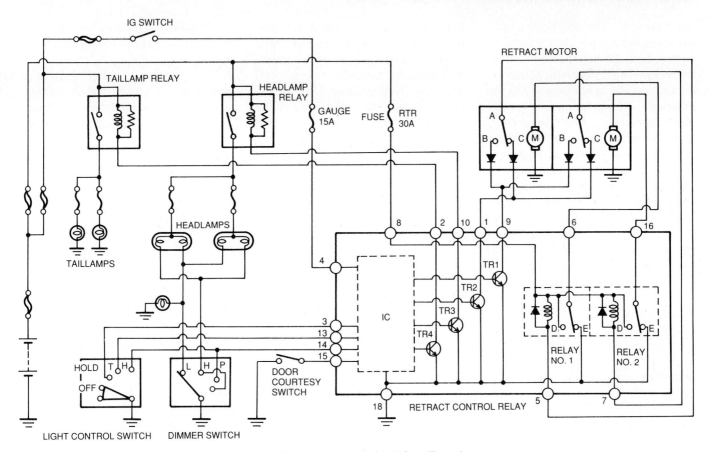

Figure 14-25. Some headlamp circuits use insulated bulbs and grounded switches. (Toyota)

insulated bulbs, the dimmer switch will be installed between the bulbs and ground, figure 14-25.

System Grounds

Two types of system grounds may be used in an automotive headlamp circuit. Most circuits are grounded directly at the headlamps, with insulated switches installed between the bulbs and the fuse panel, figure 14-24. Some circuits use a remote ground, with insulated bulbs and grounded switches, figure 14-25. Regardless of the type of ground, all headlamp filaments are wired in parallel. This prevents a burned-out filament from interrupting current flow through the other filaments.

AUTOMATIC HEADLAMP SYSTEMS

The advent of solid-state circuitry and photocells has made it possible to

control some functions of the headlamp circuit automatically. Two major systems are currently available:

- Automatic headlamp dimming or high-low beam switching
- Automatic on-off with time-delay

These systems are generally offered as options on most midpriced cars and standard equipment on luxury vehicles.

Automatic Headlamp Dimming

All domestic and some foreign carmakers have offered one or more versions of this control system. While they vary somewhat in circuit design, all work on the same principles to select the proper headlamp beam for the prevailing driving conditions.

Automatic headlamp dimmer systems generally contain the following components:

- Photocell and amplifier
- High-low beam relay

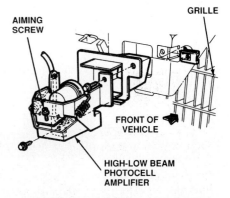

Figure 14-26. The photocell and amplifier assembly is mounted behind the grille where it can easily pick up the headlamps of oncoming vehicles. (Ford)

- Dimmer switch
- Sensitivity control device

The photocell and amplifier are positioned at the front of the vehicle, where oncoming light can be sensed, figure 14-26. When the system is operational, it holds the lights on high beam until the photocell senses that the light from the headlamps of an oncoming vehicle exceeds its sensivity threshold. The photocell amplifier energizes a relay, which switches voltage from the high-beam filaments to the low-beam filaments. Once the oncoming vehicle has passed and the photocell no longer senses the greater illumination, the amplifier deenergizes the relay, returning the voltage to the high-beam filaments. Some systems have been used that operate in just the opposite way; that is, the normal headlamp condition is low-beam. When the photocell senses the absence of light, it shifts current from the low-beam to the high-beam filament. Figure 14-27 is a block diagram of a typical automatic dimming system as used by Ford. Figure 14-28 is the electrical schematic.

The dimmer switch contains an override section that allows the driver manual control of the system. If an oncoming vehicle does not dim its lights, or if the driver wishes to overtake another vehicle in front of him, he can signal the other vehicle by applying a slight amount of pressure on the dimmer switch. This provides a ground signal through the override portion of the switch to the photocell amplifier. The amplifier turns off the voltage to the relay, which causes the high-beam filaments to light. Once the pressure is removed from the dimmer switch, it returns to normal operation.

The sensitivity control device is generally a part of the headlamp switch, figure 14-29. It uses a potentiometer to adjust the system sensitivity

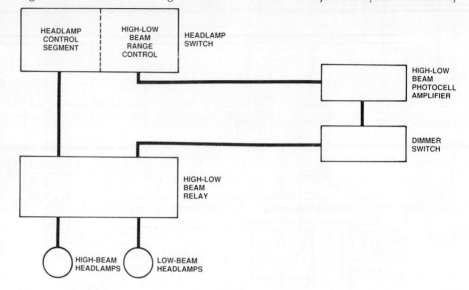

Figure 14-27. A block diagram of a typical Ford automatic headlamp dimmer system. (Ford)

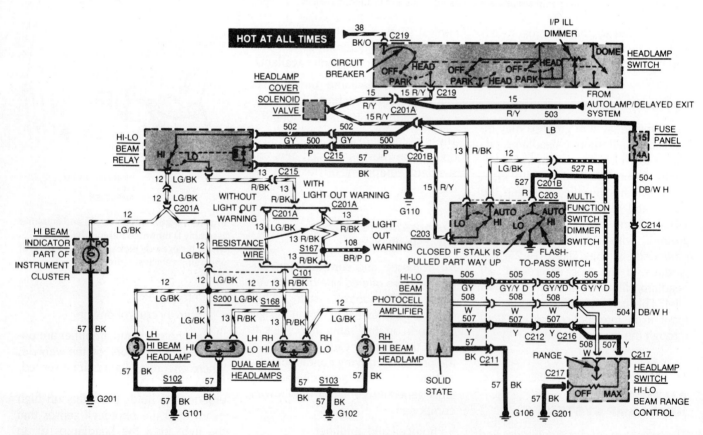

Figure 14-28. The electrical schematic of a typical Ford automatic headlamp dimmer system. (Ford)

to the surrounding ambient light. Rotating the switch knob in one direction increases the system sensitivity. This causes it to switch to low beam when oncoming vehicles are at a greater distance. Rotating the knob in the other direction decreases sensitivity. Oncoming vehicles will be closer before triggering the system. A detent position turns the system off and returns manual control over headlamp beam selection to the driver through the dimmer switch.

Automatic On-Off with Time Delay

This system electrically controls the on-off operation of the headlamps and taillamps. It also has a time-delay function that keeps the exterior lamps on for a preselected duration. The system may be called "Twilight Sentinel," "Safeguard Sentinel," or "Autolamp/Delayed Exit" according to the carmaker. Like automatic headlamp dimming circuits, they vary somewhat in circuit design, but all function according to similar principles.

Automatic on-off and time-delay systems contain the following components:

- Photocell and amplifier
- Power relay
- Time control

The photocell and amplifier unit is generally mounted under the instrument panel crash pad and upper finish panel in such a way that it receives direct outside light through the windshield. The power relay is generally installed in the engine compartment. The time control device is a potentiometer incorporated in the headlamp switch, figure 14-30, of most systems. It controls both automatic operation of the system and the length of time that the headlamps remain on after the ignition is shut off.

To follow the operation of an automatic on-off and time-delay system, we will use a typical Ford circuit, figure 14-31, as an example. When the time control is off, the off switch in the control is closed. Ground is thus applied through the control to the

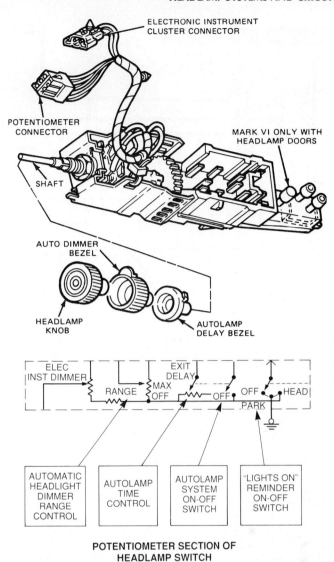

Figure 14-29. A potentiometer in the headlamp switch is used to adjust the sensitivity of an automatic headlamp dimmer system to the surrounding ambient light. (Ford)

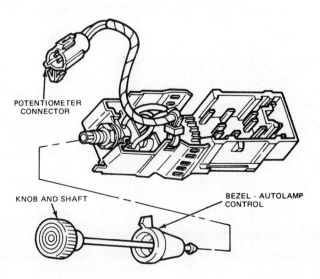

Figure 14-30. A potentiometer in the headlamp switch also provides the time-delay function in an automatic on-off headlamp system. (Ford)

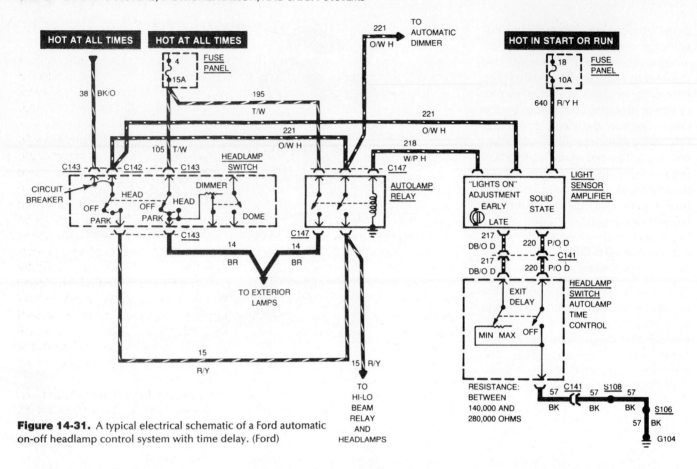

Figure 14-31. A typical electrical schematic of a Ford automatic on-off headlamp control system with time delay. (Ford)

HENRY'S UBIQUITOUS MODEL T

How much have headlamps really changed over the years? The instruction book provided with a Model T Ford dealt with the lighting system (and many other topics) in the form of questions and answers. Here are the pertinent ones dealing with the lighting system. You decide for yourself.

No. 125 How are the lights operated? The lighting system consists of two headlights and a tail light operated by a combination lighting and ignition switch located on the instrument board. The headlamp bulbs are of 6–8 volt, double filament gas filled type. The major filament is 11 candle-power, and the minor filament is 2 candle-power. The small bulb used in the tail light is of 6–8 volt, single contact, two candle-power type. All of the lamps are connected in parallel so that the burning out or removal of any one of them will not affect the other. Current for the lamps is supplied by the battery. Do not connect the

lamps to the magneto as it will result in burning out the bulbs and might discharge the magnets.

No. 126 What attention do the electric headlights require? When the car is delivered to the owner, the headlamps are properly focused and aligned, and they should require no attention other than replacement of burned-out bulbs or broken lenses, and re-focusing or re-aligning should they get out of focus or alignment. Headlights equipped with the Ford refracting lens and Ford 21 candle-power gas filled bulbs, when properly focused and aligned, pass the lighting requirements of all states, and should they get out of focus or alignment, they should immediately be re-focused and re-aligned. Headlights not equipped with the Ford refracting lens or the Ford 21 candle-power gas filled bulbs will pass the lighting requirements of all states if these lenses and bulbs are installed.

No. 127 How is the headlight lens installed? Remove the door by pressing in and turning to the left until the pins in the door rim disengage from the notches in the lamp case. You can then readily see how the lens fits into the door rim.

No. 128 What about bulb replacement? When replacing burned out bulbs, purchase genuine Ford bulbs (marked with the name FORD on the glass), as satisfactory results cannot be obtained with the many inferior bulbs now on the market. It is absolutely essential that the Ford 21 candle-power gas filled bulbs be used in the lamps equipped with the Ford Refracting Lens as the use of any other than genuine Ford bulbs may result in the lights failing to meet the lighting requirements of the various states. Care should be exercised not to touch the reflector except with a soft clean cloth.

amplifier, preventing automatic operation of the system. To activate automatic control of the system, the time control must be turned on. This provides power for the photocell amplifier through the 10-ampere fuse. The amount of light striking the photocell varies the cell's internal resistance. As the light level drops, the photocell's resistance increases. At a predetermined point, the photocell and amplifier unit turns on the power relay, which sends current to the headlamps and taillamps. When the external light level rises above the predetermined level, the photocell and amplifer unit shuts off the power relay and the exterior lamps go off.

If the exterior lamps are on when the ignition switch is turned off, voltage from the 10-ampere fuse is interrupted. This energizes a timing circuit in the amplifier, which now receives power through the headlamp switch circuit breaker to keep the relay energized. The exterior lamps remain lit for the amount of time preselected by the driver, which is determined by the resistance set on the potentiometer in the time control device. When the timer circuit shuts down, power to the relay is removed and the lights go off.

SUMMARY

Three types of headlamp bulbs are used on automobiles: standard sealed-beam, halogen sealed-beam, and composite headlamps containing a replaceable halogen or tungsten-halogen bulb. Type 1 sealed-beam headlamps contain a high-beam filament; type 2 bulbs contain both low- and high-beam filaments. Composite headlamps are a permanent part of the vehicle's styling.

Headlamps also may be concealed as a way to integrate them into body design and styling, as well as protecting them from damage. Concealed headlamps may be vacuum operated or they may use electric motors. A manual control is always provided to open and close the headlamp mechanism in case of a system failure.

All headlamp circuits must contain low- and high-beam lights, a dimmer switch, and a high-beam in icator lamp to keep the driver informed. Carmakers may use 2- or 4-lamp systems, depending upon vehicle design and styling. Most circuits use grounded lamps, but some have grounded switches and insulated lamps. Headlamp switches may be mounted on the instrument panel or incorporated as part of a combination switch on the steering column. Floor-mounted, foot-operated dimmer switches have been replaced by lever-operated switches mounted on the steering column on most late-model cars. Most headlamp circuits are protected by a fusible link, a fuse in the fuse panel, and a circuit breaker in the headlamp switch.

Headlamp beam switching and on-off operation can be controlled by photocells and solid-state modules. Such systems are found on more expensive vehicles.

REVIEW QUESTIONS

Multiple Choice

1. Student A says that some headlamp circuits have insulated bulbs and grounded switches. Student B says that some headlamp circuits have insulated switches and grounded bulbs. Who is right?

  a. A only
  b. B only
  c. both A and B
  d. neither A nor B

2. Student A says that all headlamp filaments are connected in parallel. Student B says that headlamp switches generally use a nonresetting type II circuit breaker. Who is right?

  a. A only
  b. B only
  c. both A and B
  d. neither A nor B

3. Student A says that standard sealed-beams are available only in circular headlamps. Student B says that some headlamp circuits use bulbs that have both a low- and high-beam filament. Who is right?

  a. A only
  b. B only
  c. both A and B
  d. neither A nor B

4. Student A says that a composite headlamp may use either one or two replaceable tungsten-halogen bulbs, depending upon its design. Student B says that composite headlamps are vented and may accumulate moisture inside the lens. Who is right?

  a. A only
  b. B only
  c. both A and B
  d. neither A nor B

5. Student A says that the normal skin oil found on your fingers can stain replaceable tungsten-halogen bulbs. Student B says that the multiposition dimmer switch may be mounted on the floor or on the steering column. Who is right?

  a. A only
  b. B only
  c. both A and B
  d. neither A nor B

6. Student A says that halogen sealed-beam headlamps are more damage-prone than standard sealed-beam bulbs. Student B says that halogen sealed-beam headlamps produce 30 percent less light than standard sealed-beam bulbs. Who is right?

  a. A only
  b. B only
  c. both A and B
  d. neither A nor B

7. Which of the following *is not* true of halogen sealed-beam headlamps?

  a. They may be plastic.
  b. They can be used as replacements for standard sealed-beam bulbs.
  c. They are connected in series in the headlamp circuit.
  d. They are available in circular or rectangular shapes.

8. Student A says that concealed head-lamps may be operated by a vacuum actuator or an electric motor. Student B says that all concealed headlamp systems have a manual actuator. Who is right?

a. A only

b. B only

c. both A and B

d. neither A nor B

9. Student A says that popup headlamps are required by Federal law to remain off until they have completed three-quarters of their travel. Student B says that popup headlamps are required by Federal law to be on when they start to emerge from the hood line. Who is right?

a. A only

b. B only

c. both A and B

d. neither A nor B

10. Automatic headlamp systems:

a. have a sensitivity adjustment

b. can turn the exterior lamps on and off

c. can sense oncoming cars and switch your headlamps from high beam to low beam

d. are computer-controlled on light-duty trucks under 8,500 pounds GVW

11. Student A says that turning the headlamp switch to its third detent sends power to the dimmer switch. Student B says that turning the headlamp switch to its third detent sends power directly to the headlamps. Who is right?

a. A only

b. B only

c. both A and B

d. neither A nor B

12. Student A says that all headlamp systems must have a high-beam indicator lamp. Student B says that instrument cluster illumination is controlled by a rheostat. Who is right?

a. A only

b. B only

c. both A and B

d. neither A nor B

Fill in the Blank

13. The light from a sealed-beam filament is spread symmetrically or asymmetrically by the design of the _____ .

14. The device used to adjust the sensitivity of automatic headlamp systems may be installed in the headlamp switch and is called a _____ .

15. Headlamp switches are protected either by a separate or built-in _____ .

16. If a sealed-beam headlamp is not perfectly airtight, the filament will _____ .

17. Installing standard sealed-beam bulbs as replacements for halogen sealed-beams will result in a _____ light output.

18. Installing a replaceable bulb in a composite headlamp will not affect headlamp _____ .

15 OTHER LIGHTING SYSTEMS AND CIRCUITS

WHAT

The headlamp circuit is not alone in playing an important role in driver safety. Parking lamps, side marker, clearance, and taillamps identify the front and rear of a vehicle. Stoplamps, turn signals, and backup lamps indicate a driver's intention to perform a particular maneuver. Hazard flashers signal a driver in distress.

Courtesy and convenience lighting inside the vehicle assist in entry and exit, as well as keeping the driver informed of vehicle operating conditions through the instrument panel lighting.

These other lighting circuits are equally as important as the headlamp circuit and must be kept in equally good operating condition. This chapter describes the components and explains the operation of each of these circuits.

WHY

The lighting circuits described in this chapter are important for driver safety and convenience. Like any other electrical circuit, they will require occasional service to keep them in good condition. For this reason, you must understand their operation.

These lighting circuits vary in design from carmaker to carmaker, but all follow general principles. If you know and understand these principles, you will be able to service any vehicle, regardless of manufacturer.

GOALS

After studying this chapter, you should be able to:

1. Identify a variety of common automotive bulbs according to type, base, trade number, and common use.

2. Describe the components and explain the operation of each of the following lighting circuits:

   a. parking and taillamp
   b. stoplamp and turn signal
   c. hazard warning
   d. backup lamp
   e. side courtesy and clearance lamp
   f. courtesy and convenience lamp

COMMON BULBS

Unlike headlamps, which are highly specialized types of automotive bulbs, the bulbs used in other automotive lighting circuits are smaller and more varied in design, figure 15-1. Bulbs generally can be classified by the type of base used; but since there are a number of amperage and candlepower ratings for each type of base, a particular trade number has been assigned to each bulb. These trade numbers are recognized by all bulb manufacturers.

Bulbs may contain single or dual filaments. Most bulbs are clear, allowing their use behind colored lenses when required. Manufacturers, however, provide coated amber, clear amber, and red bulbs for special applications. These are designated by adding a letter to the bulb number: A for coated amber, NA for clear amber, and R for red.

The smallest automotive bulbs have either a miniature bayonet brass base or a glass wedge base, figure 15-2. Bulbs with a brass base are used in corresponding sockets; wedge-base bulbs may use a socket or simply fit into formed metal clips that are attached to the circuit wiring.

Brass-base bulbs have two lugs on the base that retain them in their sockets. Some bulbs have an indexed base. In this design, the lugs are offset so that the bulb can be installed in the socket in only one way.

A bulb with a single contact on its base, figure 15-3, contains one filament. A bulb with a double contact, figure 15-3, contains two filaments. These are the insulated contacts for the bulb's filament. A corresponding contact inside the socket supplies the current to the bulb's filament. Dual-filament bulbs have two contacts in the socket. Ground is supplied by the base of the bulb through contact with the socket. In installations using a plastic housing, the socket is grounded by a separate ground wire.

Wedge-base bulbs generally are

Bulb Type	Base Type	Trade No.*	Candle Power	Primary Application
S8	Double-contact bayonet indexed	2057NA	24	Park
		2057A	32	Stop, signal
		1157A	32/4	Park, signal
		1157A	32/4	Park, signal
		1157	32/4	Stop, tail, signal
		1034NA	32/4	Signal
		1034A	32/4	Signal
		1034	32/4	Signal, marker
		1016	21/6	Stop, tail
		198	32/3	General
	Double-contact bayonet	1176	21/3	Stop, tail, signal
		1154	21/3	Stop, tail
		1142	21	Interior
		1076	32	Tail
		1004	15	Underhood, map
		94	15	Dome
	Single-contact bayonet	1295	50	Cornering, signal
		1156	32	Signal, backup, interior
		1141	21	Signal, interior
		1073	32	Signal, interior
		1003	15	Interior, trunk
		93	15	Dome
		89	6	Dome, courtesy, trunk
G6	Double-contact bayonet	1178	4	License
		68	3	Indicator
	Single-contact bayonet	1247	3	Indicator
		1155	3	Instrument, marker
		631	6	General
		98	6	General
		97A	4	Marker
		97	4	Marker, license
		67A	4	Indicator
		67	3	Indicator, marker, instrument
		63	3	License, parking
G4 1/2	Miniature bayonet	1898	2	Instrument
		1895	2	Instrument, marker, indicator
		257	4	Instrument
		57X	2	Interior
		57	2	Interior, marker, instrument

Bulb Type	Base Type	Trade No.*	Candle Power	Primary Application
G3 1/2	Miniature bayonet	1445	7	General
		456	2	Instrument
		53X	.75	Indicator
		53R	--	--
		53	1	Indicator
T5	Wedge	912	1	Dome, courtesy
		906	6	Dome
T3 1/4	Miniature bayonet	1893	2	Instrument
		1892	.75	Indicator
		1891	2	Indicator, marker, instrument
		1816	2	General
		1488	1.5	Indicator
		756	.31	Radio, indicator
	Wedge	558	--	Indicator, instrument
		194NA	2	Marker
		194A	2	Marker
		194	2	Marker, indicator
		193	2	Instrument
		192	3	Indicator
		168	3	Instrument
		161	1	Indicator
		158	2	Instrument
T3	Miniature end cap	212-2	12	Dome, courtesy
		212-2	6	Dome
	Flat clip	563	4	Interior
		562	6	Interior
		561	12	Interior
	Rigid loop	566	1	Interior
		564	2	Interior
T1 1/2	Miniature wedge	74	.70	Indicator
	Plastic wedge	2457NA	--	Park, stop, turn
		2457	--	Park, stop, turn
		2358NA	--	Park, stop, turn
		2358	--	Park, stop, turn

* NA = amber bulb
A = amber coated bulb
R = red bulb
X = heavy-duty bulb

Figure 15-1. Typical small bulbs for automotive use.

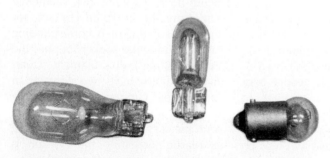

Figure 15-2. The smallest automotive bulbs may have a glass wedge base or a miniature bayonet brass base.

Figure 15-3. Bulbs with a single-contact base contain one filament; those with a double-contact base have two filaments. Note the indexing lugs on the base of the bulbs; some double-contact bulbs have offset lugs.

used for interior lights and instrument panel cluster lighting. The base and bulb are formed of glass as a single unit. The external contacts are formed by crimping the four filament wires protruding through the base around it, figure 15-4. Although the design is simple, it positions the contacts to provide direct electrical contact with the bulb's socket. The bulb is inserted by pushing it into its socket, where a molded plastic sleeve traps the filament wires against the base of the bulb. The bulb does not require indexing, since the socket has shoulders to hold it in place.

A new low-profile plastic socket design for wedge-base bulbs allows this type of bulb to replace the older brass-base design for exterior lighting on late-model vehicles. The electrical leads of the new socket enter it from the side instead of the rear, figure 15-5. This reduces the amount of space required for the socket and allows it to be used in areas where a brass-base socket would not fit. Another recent design encapsulates the wedge base and filament wires in plastic, figure 15-6. This dual-filament bulb is also used in exterior lighting applications.

PARKING AND TAILLAMPS

The parking lamps and taillamps light the vehicle for other drivers to see, allowing them to establish the length and position of the vehicle.

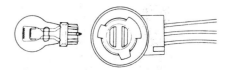

Figure 15-5. A plastic socket with leads extending from its side allows the use of wedge-base bulbs for external lighting.

Figure 15-6. Wedge-base bulbs with preformed plastic bases also are used for external lights.

Figure 15-4. Glass wedge-base bulbs are formed as a single unit with the four filament wires crimped around the base to form the external contacts.

SPECIAL BULBS FOR ACCESSORY LIGHTING

Many special bulbs are used in accessory circuits. The high-intensity bulbs once popular in driving lamps and fog lamps have been replaced by less expensive and more powerful halogen bulbs. One of the more common and useful designs was imported from Europe, where the attitude toward automotive lighting has been light-years ahead of the United States.

The peanut-size bulb carries an H-3 designation and is manufactured with a circular keyed base that will fit into the reflector socket only one way. Wire clamps are used to hold the bulb in place, and its single lead connects into the circuit with a spade terminal.

This same bulb is used on European vehicles in a supplemental high-beam headlamp. Such headlamps are used to improve the upper beam performance of 2-lamp systems. The supplemental headlamp is the same size and shape as a fog lamp, but the lens is optically designed to meet high-beam requirements instead of beam requirements instead of dropping the light in front of the vehicle, as a fog lamp does. Perhaps the supplemental high-beam concept also will be adopted in this country before too long.

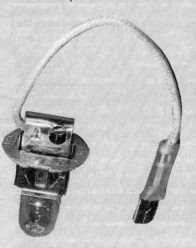

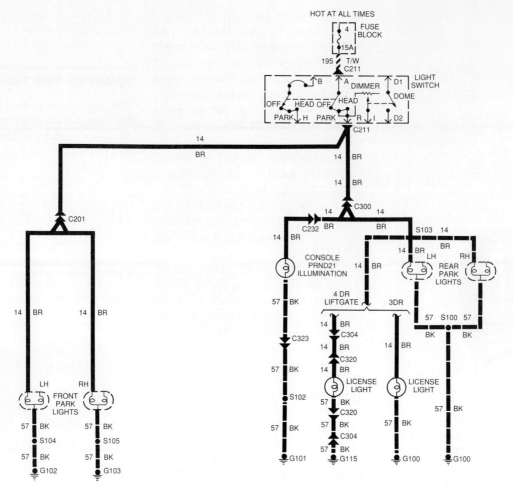

Figure 15-7. A typical parking lamp and taillamp circuit diagram. (Ford)

Circuit Diagram

A single circuit generally is used for these lamps. This allows the parking lamps and taillamps to be on at the same time. Figure 15-7 is a typical circuit diagram. The circuit is controlled by the headlamp switch. This allows the lamps to be lit independently of the ignition switch.

Switches

Parking lamps and taillamps are controlled by a set of contacts inside the headlamp switch. They can be turned on without turning the headlamps on by moving the switch to its first detent. They remain on when the switch is moved to the second detent to light the headlamps.

Power Source and Circuit Protection

Power to the circuit comes directly from the battery through the headlamp switch. The circuit is protected by a 15-ampere or 20-ampere fuse.

STOPLAMPS AND TURN SIGNALS

Stoplamps are also called brake lamps. Stoplamp lenses must always be red. A red center high-mounted stop light (CHMSL) is required by Federal law on 1986 and later passenger vehicles, figure 15-8. Turn signals are also called directional signals. Front turn signals are white or amber; rear turn signals are amber or red.

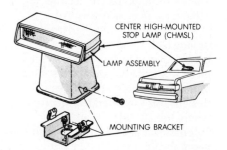

Figure 15-8. All 1986 and later passenger vehicles must have a center high-mounted stop light (CHMSL) incorporated in the stop-lamp circuit. (Chrysler)

Circuit Diagram

The stoplamps and turn signals on a vehicle may use one bulb to perform both functions or separate bulbs for each function. In circuits using a single bulb for both functions, figure 15-9, current passes through the nor-

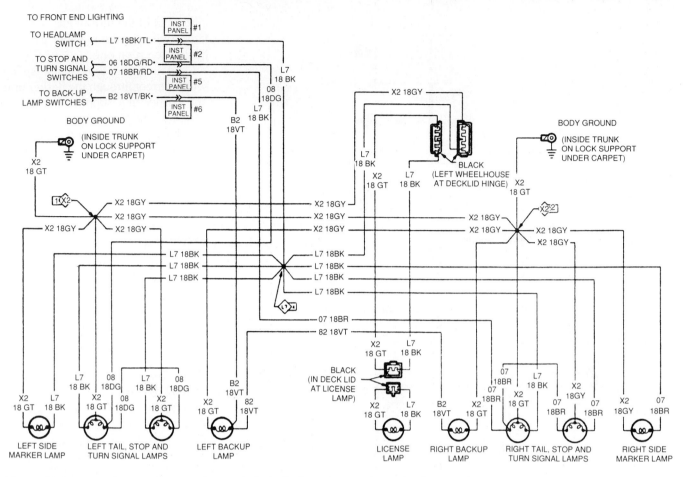

Figure 15-9. A typical circuit diagram using one bulb for both stoplamp and turn signal functions. (Chrysler)

BULB CONTACT OXIDATION

Ever replace a bulb in a parking lamp, turn signal, taillamp, or stoplamp—only to find that the new bulb doesn't work? You have tested the circuit and bulb and know that both are good, but still no light. Photographers who worked in the era of flashbulbs had the same problem with double-contact bayonet-base flashbulbs, and they came up with seat-of-the-pants solutions that have lasted to this day.

It seems that the lead contacts on the base of the bulb tend to oxidize over time, creating a thin film that acts as an insulator. This is more likely to happen with bulbs that have been in stock for long periods of time. The bright, shiny contact turns to a dull gray as its surface oxidizes. The solution, of course, is to rough up the surface of the contact before installing the bulb.

Photographers whose livelihood depended on their flashbulbs' igniting devised several different approaches to guaranteeing that a new bulb would work properly. One was to smear a dab of saliva on the contact by wiping it across the tongue before inserting it in the flashgun socket. This worked fairly well if the bulb was fired immediately, because the moisture was a good conductor. If a lengthy time passed between inserting the bulb and attempting to fire it, however, the moisture would dry and a misfire was possible.

Another trick was to pull the bulb from a pocket and wipe it rapidly across the seat of the pants on its way to the flashgun. This tended to work rather well because the materials used for clothes in those days contained coarse fibers, and well-worn trouser seats had a good polishing effect.

The best solution was a quick pass of the bulb's base across a brick or the concrete sidewalk, providing that it was done with only light pressure. Light pressure would remove the oxidation; excessive pressure would grind off too much of the lead contact and result in a gap between the bulb and socket contacts.

Photographers who had several consecutive misfires regardless of their efforts soon learned that their problem resulted from weakened springs or flattened contacts in the flashgun socket. This is the other side of "the bulb won't light" syndrome. Automotive sockets wear over time and it may sometimes be necessary to replace the socket. If this is not practical, a drop of solder on the contact points at the base of the bulb will take up slack and provide a solid connection.

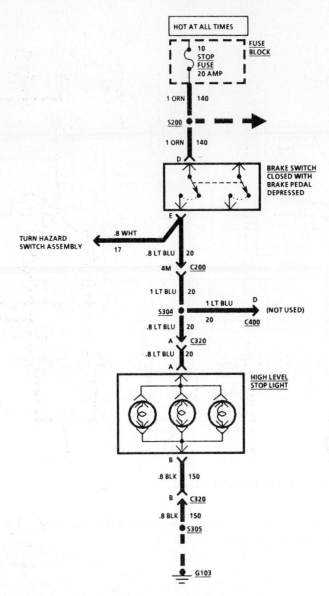

Figure 15-10. The CHMSL is connected in the circuit between the stoplamp switch and ground. (Oldsmobile)

current from the fuse block, the stoplamps will operate whether the ignition switch is on or off.

Operating the turn signal switch sends current through the flasher unit. The flasher unit supplies interrupted current to the turn signal bulbs, causing them to flash on and off rapidly. Since the turn signal switch receives current from the ignition switch, the turn signals will operate only when the ignition switch is on.

Switches

Several switches interact to transmit current to the stoplamp and turn signal circuits. The ignition switch is installed between the battery and the turn signal switch. This prevents current from flowing through the turn signal switch when the ignition switch is off. The stoplamp switch is connected directly to battery voltage through the fuse block, figure 15-11.

Cars manufactured since the mid-1960's have the stoplamp switch mounted on the brake pedal bracket, figure 15-12. Depressing the brake pedal closes the switch. The turn signal switch is operated by a lever and installed inside the steering column, figure 15-13. When the lever is moved up or down, it closes contacts inside the switch to direct current to the flasher unit and the correct turn signal lamp.

Turn signal switches are self-canceling. As the steering wheel is being returned to its straight-ahead position after completing a turn, a cam on the underside of the steering wheel contacts one of two fingers on the turn signal switch. As the cam pushes on the switch finger, it separates the switch contacts and returns the switch to its off position.

Turn Signal Flasher

A thermal flasher unit operates much like a type I self-resetting circuit breaker to provide a rapid on-off-on current for the turn signal lamps. Current passing through a bimetallic arm heats the arm enough to separate a

mally open stoplamp switch to the turn signal switch. When the turn signal switch is operated, it closes; and interrupted current is supplied to the bulb's filament through the turn signal flasher unit. This causes the bulb to flash on and off rapidly. Operating the brakes closes the normally open stoplamp switch, sending steady current through contacts in the turn signal switch to the bulb's filaments. In systems with a CHMSL, current also is sent to the single-filament bulb, figure 15-10.

When the driver signals a turn and

then brakes, brake switch current is not allowed to pass to the bulb on the signaling side. This bulb continues to receive interrupted current from the flasher unit and will flash on and off. The bulb on the other side of the vehicle receives uninterrupted current from the stoplamp switch and remains on continuously.

In circuits using separate bulbs for the stoplamps and turn signals, figure 15-11, operating the brakes closes the stoplamp switch and sends uninterrupted current to the stoplamp bulbs. Since the stoplamp switch receives

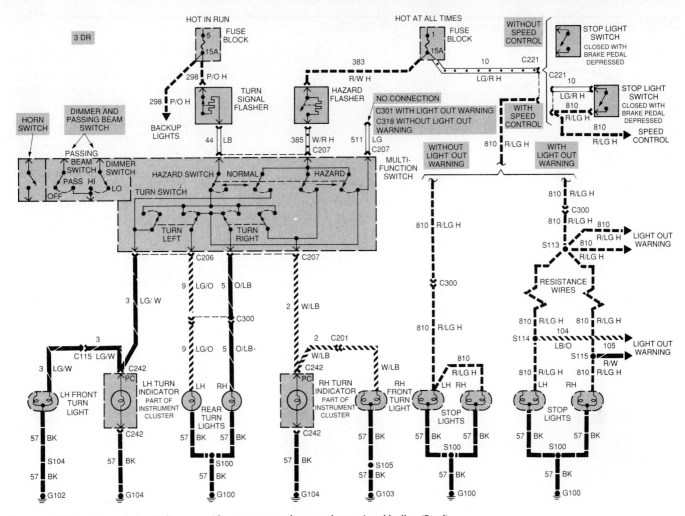

Figure 15-11. A typical circuit diagram with separate stoplamp and turn signal bulbs. (Ford)

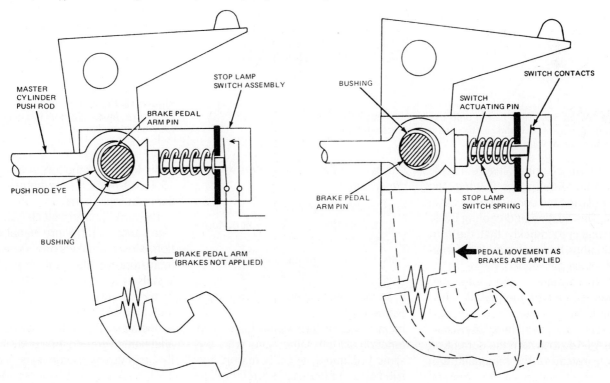

Figure 15-12. The stoplamp switch moves with the brake pedal; but since the actuating pin does not move as far as the contacts do, it closes the contacts. (Ford)

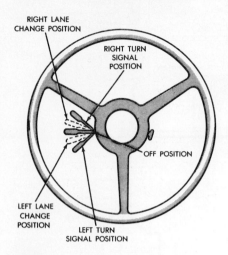

Figure 15-13. Springs and cams are incorporated in the turn signal switch to cancel the signal by separating the contacts after the turn has been completed. (Chrysler)

Figure 15-14. A thermal turn signal flasher unit contains normally closed contact points.

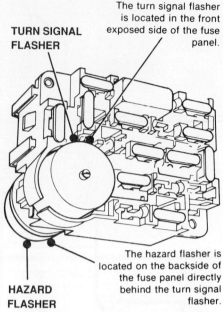

Figure 15-16. Flasher units generally are installed in the fuse block. (Chrysler)

Figure 15-15. Solid state flasher units use an integrated circuit (IC) with clock generator and can be used to control both turn signals and hazard warning lights.

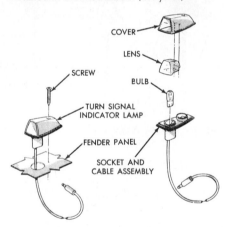

Figure 15-17. Some vehicles use a second set of turn signal indicators mounted on the front fenders. (Chrysler)

pair of contact points, figure 15-14. When the current stops flowing, the arm cools and the contact points close again. This heating and cooling cycle takes place so quickly that the turn signal lamps flash on and off approximately once per second.

Some carmakers use solid-state flashers instead of thermal flashers. A solid-state flasher uses a hybrid IC circuit and switching transistor, figure 15-15, to switch the current on and off instead of the bimetallic arm and contact points of the thermal flasher. A clock generator in the IC regulates the frequency of flashing.

This type of flasher unit offers several advantages:

• Its service life is longer.
• It is not affected by ambient temperature changes.
• Its signaling frequency is virtually independent of battery voltage.

Solid-state flashers operate independently of the current load. This means that all turn signal lamps can function at the same time with the same brightness. For this reason, the solid-state flasher can be used both to signal turns and to operate the hazard warning system. Flasher units are gen-

erally located in the fuse block, figure 15-16, or in the wiring harness under the instrument panel.

The turn signal circuit contains indicators that confirm turn signal operation. Most carmakers provide separate indicators for the right and left turn signals in the instrument cluster. One or two small bulbs light the correct indicator when the turn signal switch is operated. The bulbs provide a parallel path to ground for a portion of the flasher current. Some cars have an additional set of indicators installed on the front fenders (figure 15-17), and facing the driver.

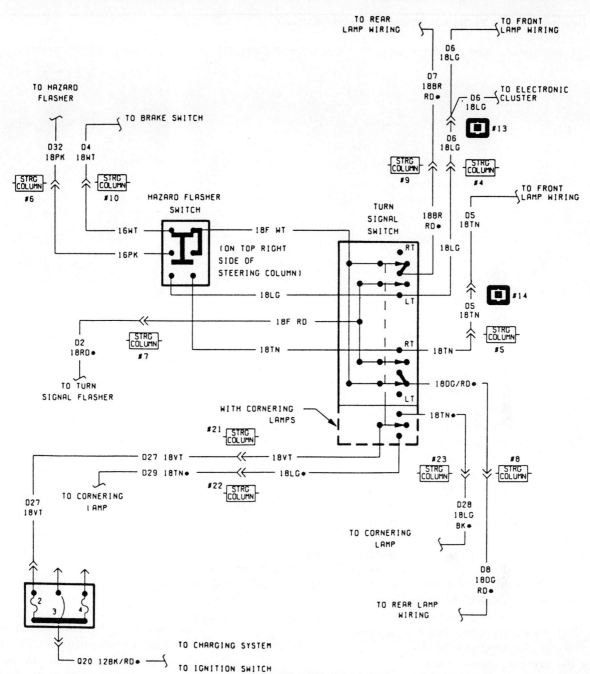

Figure 15-18. The hazard warning switch may be a separate component in the circuit. (Chrysler)

Power Source and Circuit Protection

Power is provided to the stoplamp circuit directly from the battery through a 15-ampere or 20-ampere fuse in the fuse block. The stoplamps can operate whether the ignition switch is on or off. Power for the turn signal circuit is furnished from the battery through the ignition switch when it is on. The turn signal circuit is protected by a 15-ampere or 20-ampere fuse in the fuse block.

HAZARD FLASHERS

A hazard warning lamp circuit has been included on all vehicles sold in the United States since 1967. Hazard warning lamps are used to warn other drivers of potential danger or an emergency situation.

Circuit Diagram

Sometimes called an emergency flasher system, the hazard warning lamp circuit uses the turn signal circuitry and adds its own switch and

flasher unit, figure 15-11. Battery voltage is available at one side of the hazard flasher at all times. Operating the hazard warning switch sends current to each of the turn signal bulbs at the same time.

Switches

The hazard warning lamp switch control on most vehicles is a knob located on the steering column just below the steering wheel. The system is activated by pulling the knob out on some cars, or by pushing it in on other models. The switch itself may be a separate component, figure 15-18, or a part of the turn signal switch, figure

Figure 15-19. A thermal hazard warning flasher unit contains a high-resistance coil and normally open contact points.

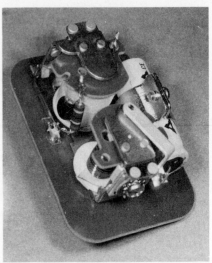

Figure 15-20. Some thermal flasher units are designed for use in either a turn signal or hazard warning circuit.

15-11. Regardless of switch design or location, its contacts send current from the fuse block through the hazard flasher to the turn signal bulbs.

Most thermal hazard flasher units are similar in appearance to thermal turn signal flashers. The hazard flasher, however, must handle a large amount of current to flash all of the turn signal bulbs at the same time. For this reason, its interior construction and operation differ from a turn signal flasher.

The thermal hazard flasher contains a movable contact mounted on a bimetallic arm, a stationary contact, and a high-resistance coil, figure 15-19. The coil is connected in parallel with the normally open contact points. Turning the hazard warning switch on sends current to the flasher unit. The high-resistance coil initially prevents the current from lighting the turn signal bulbs. But as the coil heats, it moves the bimetallic arm contact point against the stationary contact. The contact points become a parallel circuit branch and send current to the turn signal bulbs. During the period of current flow, the coil cools enough to break the circuit and shut off the bulbs. This cycle occurs approximately once every two seconds.

Some thermal flasher units are designed with dual circuitry and contact points, allowing them to be used ei-ther in the turn signal or hazard flasher circuit, figure 15-20.

If the hazard warning switch is on and the brakes are applied, the hazard warning lamps will continue to flash if the hazard switch interrupts the power from the stoplamp switch to the turn signal switch. In many circuits, this does not happen, and applying the brakes will cause the hazard warning lamps to stop flashing until the brake pedal is released.

An indicator bulb in the instrument cluster provides a parallel path to ground for part of the flasher current, notifying the driver that the circuit is working.

Power Source and Circuit Protection

Power to the circuit comes directly from the battery through the fuse block. The circuit is protected by a 15-ampere or 20-ampere fuse.

BACKUP LAMPS

Backup lamps are white and come on when the vehicle's transmission or transaxle is placed in reverse. Such lamps were used for many years before they became a mandatory safety requirement in 1971.

Circuit Diagram

Figure 15-21 shows a typical backup lamp circuit; figure 15-8 shows the backup lamps incorporated in the rear lighting circuits. Shifting the transmission or transaxle into reverse gear closes the transmission switch and sends current through the ignition switch to the backup lamps. The backup lamps will come on only when the ignition switch is on.

Switches

Most carmakers locate the backup switch on the transmission or transaxle housing, figure 15-22. On vehicles equipped with an automatic transmission or transaxle, the backup switch is generally combined with the neutral safety switch, figure 15-23. Some GM and other vehicles, however, have the combined backup lamp and neutral safety switch installed on the steering column near the gear selector lever.

Power Source and Circuit Protection

Power for the backup lamp circuit is furnished from the battery through the ignition switch when it is on. The circuit is protected by a 15-ampere or 20-ampere fuse in the fuse block.

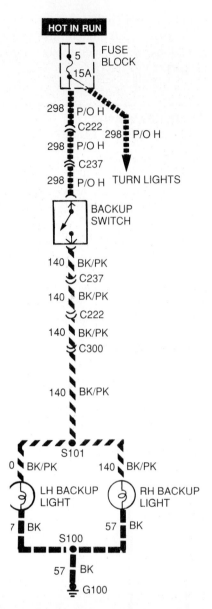

Figure 15-21. A typical backup lamp circuit. (Ford)

Figure 15-22. Backup switches are generally installed in the transmission.

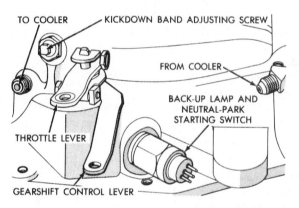

Figure 15-23. Backup switches and neutral start switches are usually combined on automatic transmissions and transaxles. (Chrysler)

SIDE MARKER AND CLEARANCE LAMPS

Side marker lamps to indicate the length of a vehicle have been a safety requirement since 1969. Carmakers meet the requirement by installing amber side marker lamps on each side of a vehicle at the front, and red side marker lamps at the rear. On vehicles using "wraparound" lamp designs, the parking lamp or taillamp bulbs provide side marker illumination.

Vehicles that exceed specified legal height and width limits are required to have clearance lamps facing to the front and rear. When used, clearance lamps are incorporated in the side marker lamp circuit and use the same color lenses as side markers.

Circuit Diagram

Side marker lamps may be independently grounded, figure 15-24, or insulated, figure 15-25. In a circuit with insulated side marker lamps, figure 15-25, the turn signal filaments provide the ground path for current. Operating the turn signal switch with the headlamp switch off sends current to both the turn signal and side marker bulbs on the signaling side of the vehicle. When the headlamp switch is on, current flow is only enough to light the side marker bulb. The turn signal bulb will not come on until the turn signal switch and flasher unit are closed. The side marker bulb cannot light, since 12 volts are applied to each end of its filament. Because there is no voltage drop, there is no current flow.

Switches

Contacts inside the headlamp switch control the side marker lamps.

Power Source and Circuit Protection

Power to the side marker lamps is provided through the headlamp

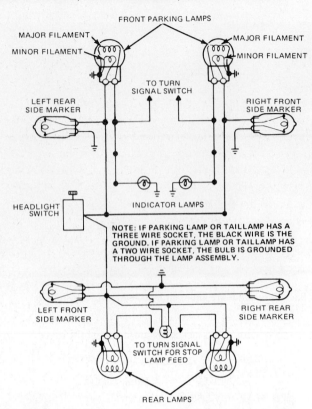

switch. The circuit is protected by a 15-ampere or 20-ampere fuse in the fuse block, which often protects other circuits.

COURTESY AND CONVENIENCE LIGHTING

Courtesy and convenience lamps include all lamps that light the interior of the vehicle. They also include instrument cluster and instrument panel lamps.

Circuit Diagram

The courtesy and convenience circuit contains door, glove box, trunk, and engine compartment lamps with their

Figure 15-24. Side marker lamps are grounded independently in this Ford circuit. (Ford)

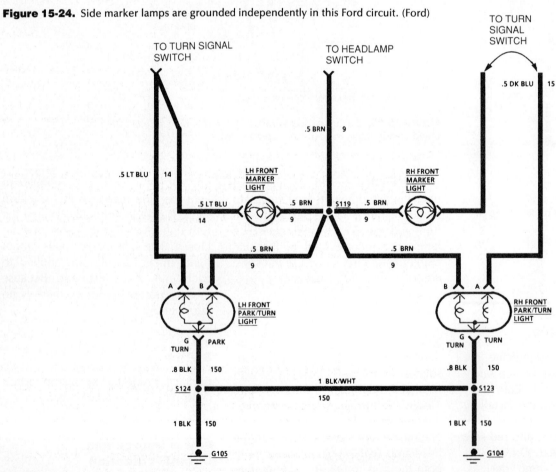

Figure 15-25. Side marker lamps are grounded through the turn signal bulb filaments in this Oldsmobile circuit. (Oldsmobile)

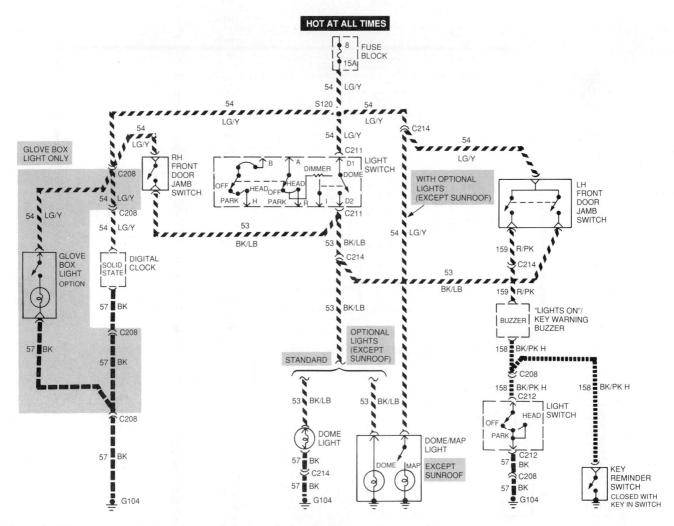

Figure 15-26. Courtesy and convenience switches may be installed between the grounded bulbs and the power source. (Ford)

own switches. Opening the door turns on the interior lamps; opening the glove box, trunk, or engine compartment turns on the respective lamp.

Some carmakers install the switches between the grounded bulb and power source, figure 15-26. Others install the bulbs between the grounded switch and power source, figure 15-27.

Switches

Courtesy and convenience lamps use a spring-loaded, push-pull switch. When a door is opened, spring tension in the switch closes its contacts. Closing the door pushes the contacts

apart, shutting off current flow. Closing any one switch completes the circuit and turns on the lamps.

Some interior lamps also have a manual switch that permits the driver or passengers to turn them on when the doors are all closed. Map lamps, reading lamps, and dome lamps are examples of lamps where a manual switch can be used to complete the circuit.

Power Source and Circuit Protection

The interior lamps in a courtesy and convenience circuit obtain power from the battery through the fuse

block. Circuit protection is usually provided by a 15-ampere fuse in the fuse block.

Solid-state Courtesy Lamps. Manufacturers offer various optional courtesy lamp systems that use a solid-state unit to light the door lock cylinder or the interior lamps at night. Figure 15-28 shows the components of a typical illuminated entry system.

The actuator contains a printed circuit board, a logic circuit, and a relay, figure 15-29. The logic circuit monitors inputs from the door handle switches and the fuse block to control relay operation.

Operating either front door handle

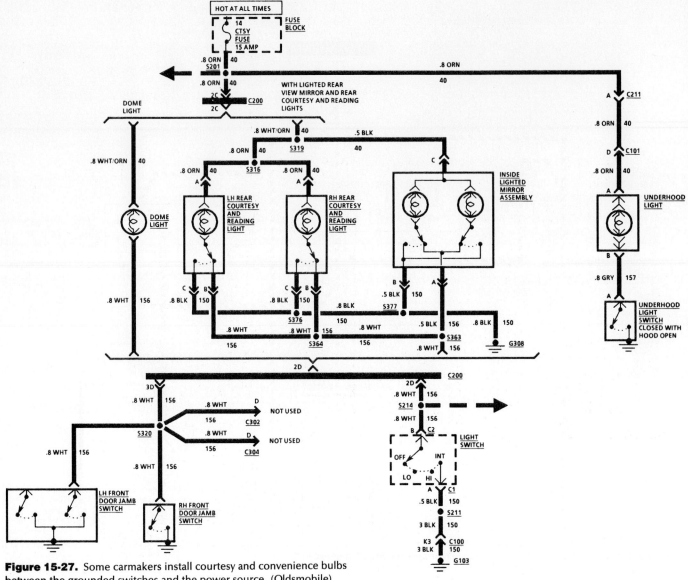

Figure 15-27. Some carmakers install courtesy and convenience bulbs between the grounded switches and the power source. (Oldsmobile)

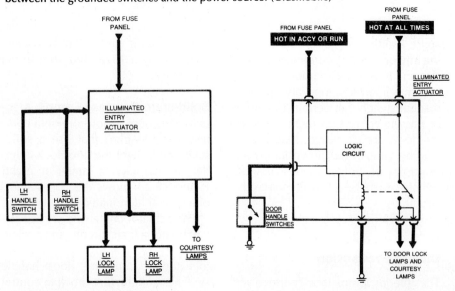

Figure 15-28. A block diagram of an illuminated entry system. (Ford)

Figure 15-29. The Ford illuminated entry actuator electrical schematic. (Ford)

closes a switch on the door latch mechanism, completing a ground path through the switch to the actuator. This turns the system on, and the actuator sends voltage to turn on the door lock lamps or interior lamps, or both. A timing circuit in the actuator logic circuit keeps the lamps lit for a specific length of time, usually 25 to 30 seconds. If the ignition switch is turned on while the timing circuit is active, it shuts off the timing sequence and the lamps turn off.

Figure 15-30 is a schematic of a typical lighted entry system used by Ford. Figure 15-31 shows the similarities in the system used by Chrysler.

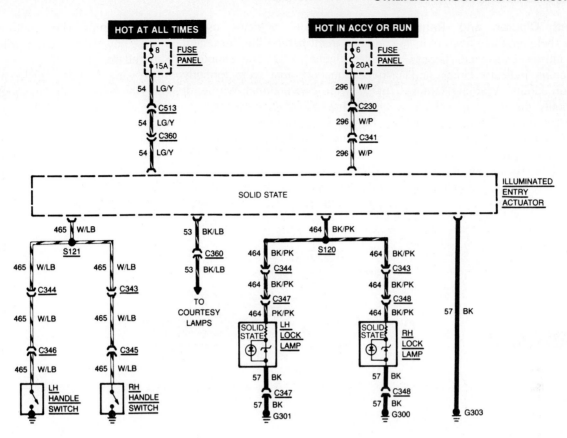

Figure 15-30. A typical illuminated entry system electrical schematic. (Ford)

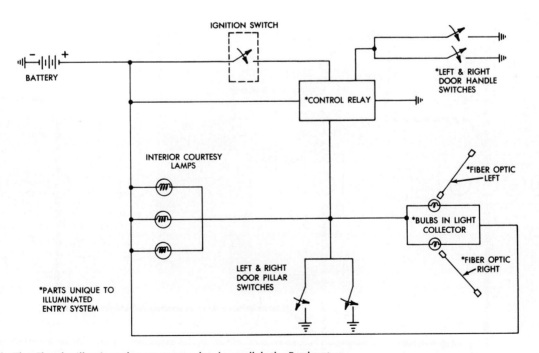

Figure 15-31. The Chrysler illuminated entry system closely parallels the Ford system. (Chrysler)

Instrument Cluster and Panel Lighting. There are three types of instrument cluster and panel lamps: warning lamps, indicator lamps, and illumination lamps. Warning lamps used to notify the driver of vehicle operating conditions are covered in chapter 16. We have already looked at indicator lamps, such as turn signal, hazard, and high-beam lamps, as we discussed these circuits. Illumination lamps are discussed below.

All late-model vehicles use a printed circuit behind the instrument cluster, figure 15-32. This simplifies the connections that were formerly made with conventional wiring. It also reduces the space necessary.

Power to the instrument cluster and panel lamps (except warning lamps) is provided through the headlamp switch. The lights receive power when the switch is moved to its first detent, turning on the parking lamps and taillamps. They continue to receive power when the headlamps are turned on.

A variable resistor called a rheostat lets the driver control the brightness of the cluster lamps. Late-model vehicles with a push-pull headlamp switch incorporate the rheostat in the switch, figure 15-33. Vehicles using a rocker-type or pushbutton headlamp switch (as well as older vehicles) have a separate rheostat for this function.

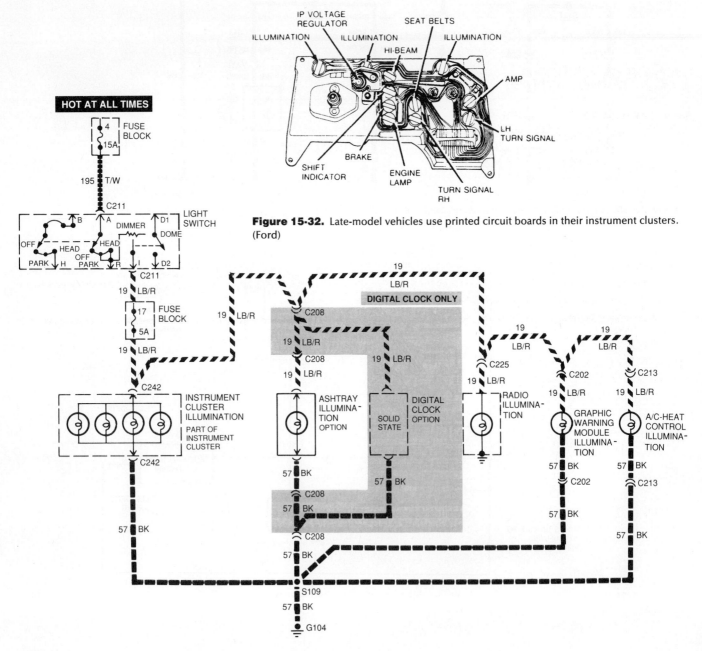

Figure 15-32. Late-model vehicles use printed circuit boards in their instrument clusters. (Ford)

Figure 15-33. The instrument panel rheostat is an integral part of push-pull headlamp switches.

SUMMARY

There are other lighting systems equal in importance to the headlamp circuit for driver safety. These are:

- Parking and taillamp circuits
- Stoplamp and turn signal circuits
- Hazard flasher circuit
- Backup lamp circuit
- Side marker and clearance lamp circuit
- Courtesy and convenience lighting circuit

These circuits must be kept in good operating condition. They use a variety of small bulbs classified by the type of base used. Bulbs may have a glass wedge or bayonet brass base. Some bulbs use indexed bases and sockets to assure correct installation. Each type of base has a number of amperage ratings, so particular trade numbers are assigned and recognized by all bulb manufacturers.

Glass wedge bulbs generally are used in interior and instrument cluster circuits. New glass wedge bulbs, however, have been designed for exterior lighting applications. Some exterior bulbs are available in red or amber colors. Single-contact bulbs have a single filament; dual-contact bulbs use a dual filament. Bulbs are grounded through their base to the socket. If a plastic housing is used, the socket is grounded by a separate ground wire.

REVIEW QUESTIONS

Multiple Choice

1. On small automobile bulbs with two contacts, the contacts are:
- **a.** grounded
- **b.** insulated
- **c.** neutral
- **d.** none of the above

2. A bayonet-base bulb designed to fit into its socket in only one way is called:
- **a.** an indexed base
- **b.** a miniature base
- **c.** a non-indexed base
- **d.** a crimped base

3. The parking lamps and taillamp circuits are usually protected by:
- **a.** a self-resetting circuit breaker
- **b.** a nonresetting circuit breaker
- **c.** twin fusible links
- **d.** a 15-ampere or 20-ampere fuse

4. Which of the following receives current through the ignition switch?
- **a.** brake switch
- **b.** hazard warning lamps
- **c.** turn signal lamps
- **d.** interior lamps

5. Flasher units transmit a rapid on-off-on current flow by acting like:
- **a.** transistors
- **b.** diodes
- **c.** capacitors
- **d.** circuit breakers

6. A thermal turn signal flasher contains:
- **a.** normally open contact points
- **b.** normally closed contact points
- **c.** a high-resistance coil
- **d.** an IC circuit

7. Which of the following *is not* contained in a solid-state flasher?
- **a.** switching transistor
- **b.** IC circuit
- **c.** clock generator
- **d.** contact points

8. Student A says that the only white lamps allowed on the rear of a vehicle are the backup lamps and license plate lamps. Student B says that turn signals must be amber or white on the front and red or amber on the rear. Who is right?
- **a.** A only
- **b.** B only
- **c.** both A and B
- **d.** neither A nor B

9. Student A says that push-pull switches are used in courtesy lamp circuits. Student B says that the switches used in courtesy lamp circuits are spring-loaded. Who is right?
- **a.** A only
- **b.** B only
- **c.** both A and B
- **d.** neither A nor B

10. Student A says that indicator lamps work by providing a parallel path to ground. Student B says that parking lamps and taillamps generally have different circuits. Who is right?
- **a.** A only
- **b.** B only
- **c.** both A and B
- **d.** neither A nor B

Fill in the Blank

11. The brightness of the instrument cluster lamps is controlled by a _____ .

12. The backup lamp switch on automatic transmission or transaxle vehicles is combined with the _____ switch.

13. Automotive bulbs are identified by their _____ .

14. Thermal flasher units contain one stationary and one movable _____ .

15. Instrument cluster connections are simplified by the use of a _____ .

16. Interior lights may have a _____ switch to complete the circuit.

17. Federal regulations require the installation of a _____ on the rear of 1986 and later vehicles.

18. If an automotive bulb number is followed by NA, it means that the bulb is _____ .

16 ELECTRICAL INSTRUMENTATION AND SAFETY SYSTEMS

WHAT

Early automobiles had few, if any, instrumentation and safety systems. Their use came about from practical necessity and from governmental regulations. The first instruments and horns were primitive in design, yet the principles behind their operation are still in use today.

Safety systems such as windshield wipers evolved over the years from hand-operated to vacuum-operated to electrically-operated devices. All do the same job, but the way in which they work has changed radically.

Electric window defoggers made their appearance more as a convenience system, but they have a definite bearing on vehicle and driver safety.

Electric cooling fans were used occasionally over the years, but became widespread with the switchover to front-wheel drive, which made it necessary to relocate the engine from a longitudinal to a transverse position in the engine compartment.

WHY

Analog instrumentation systems tell the driver important information about the operating condition of his vehicle. The speedometer tells him how fast he is driving, a fact that also makes it a safety device.

Instrument cluster gauges and warning or indicator lamps provide information about engine temperature, oil pressure, fuel level, electrical system voltage, etc. This information alerts the driver to any unusual operating conditions before they become serious.

Horns, windshield wipers and washers, and electric defoggers are important safety systems. Horns and wiper systems are mandated by law and must be kept in good operating condition.

Electric cooling fans are an engine safety system and must be kept in proper working condition to prevent the engine from overheating.

All of these systems are useful and necessary on today's automobiles, and you will have to service them from time to time. These systems vary in design from one manufacturer to another, but all follow the same principles, which you will find in this chapter. If you understand the principles, you will be able to service these systems on any vehicle.

GOALS

After studying this chapter, you should be able to:

1. Explain how the following analog instruments and devices work:
   a. speedometer
   b. bimetallic gauge
   c. electromagnetic gauge
   d. sender unit
   e. instrument voltage regulator
   f. warning and indicator lamps
   g. buzzer

2. Describe a basic horn system and explain the difference between a system that uses a relay and one that does not.

3. Explain the operation of an electric windshield wiper and washer system.

4. Describe the operation of an electric defogger system.

5. Name the components in an electric cooling fan system and describe how the system functions.

SPEEDOMETERS

The speedometers used in the early days of the automobile were driven by a shaft or cable and a set of gears connected either to the front wheel or the drive shaft. Today's analog speedometer contains an odometer and is driven by a drive gear or distance sensor in the transmission or transaxle. A flexible casing installed between the instrument and the drive gear or distance sensor contains a core, figure 16-1. The flexible casing and core assembly is called the speedometer cable and attaches to the transmission or transaxle as shown in figure 16-2. The instrument end of the cable attaches to the speedometer shaft with a threaded nut on earlier models. Late-model cables snap onto the end of the speedometer shaft in various ways, one of which is shown in figure 16-3. In some late-model

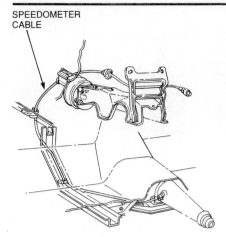

SPEEDOMETER CABLE

Figure 16-1. The analog magnetic speed-ometer is driven by a flexible cable inside a casing that connects to a driven gear in the transmission or transaxle. (Ford)

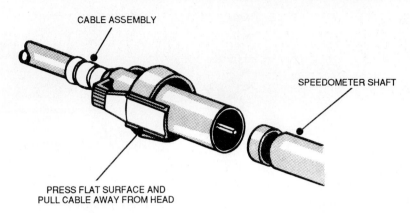

CABLE ASSEMBLY

SPEEDOMETER SHAFT

PRESS FLAT SURFACE AND PULL CABLE AWAY FROM HEAD

Figure 16-2. One end of the speedometer cable connects to a driven gear in the transmission or transaxle housing. (Ford)

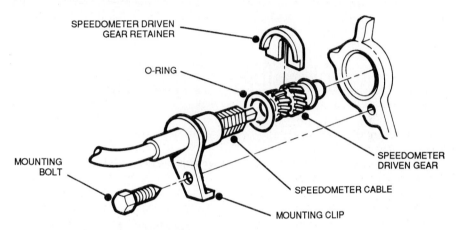

SPEEDOMETER DRIVEN GEAR RETAINER

O-RING

MOUNTING BOLT

SPEEDOMETER DRIVEN GEAR

SPEEDOMETER CABLE

MOUNTING CLIP

Figure 16-3. The other end of the speedometer cable attaches to the speedometer shaft by a snap clip or threaded nut. (Ford)

vehicles, the cable is a 2-piece unit with a threaded nut on the upper cable portion to connect to the lower cable assembly.

As the speedometer cable rotates, it turns a permanent magnet inside an iron drum in the speedometer head, figure 16-4. The drum is connected to a needle pointer. The magnetic force created by the magnet causes the iron drum to rotate against a spring retainer, which moves the pointer. The speed at which the speedometer cable and permanent magnet rotate determines how much magnetic force is applied to the drum and thus the position of the pointer.

The odometer registers the miles traveled by the vehicle and is operated by a gear on the end of the center shaft. Most odometers indicate one mile for each 1,000 revolutions of the speedometer cable. Odometer mileage is considered an indicator of vehicle condition, and state laws makes odometer "tampering" (turning the odometer back to indicate fewer miles) illegal. When a defective speedometer is replaced, the odometer on the new unit must be set to the same mileage as the one removed.

ELECTRICAL INSTRUMENTATION

Vehicle instrumentation used either analog gauges or warning and indicator lamps until the late 1970's, when

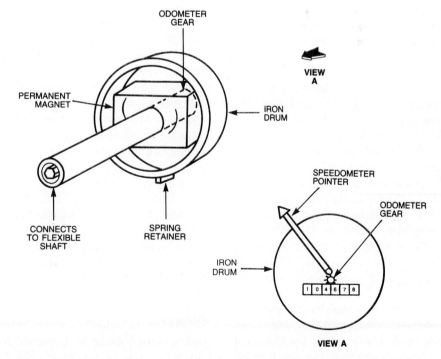

ODOMETER GEAR

VIEW A

PERMANENT MAGNET

IRON DRUM

CONNECTS TO FLEXIBLE SHAFT

SPRING RETAINER

SPEEDOMETER POINTER

ODOMETER GEAR

IRON DRUM

VIEW A

Figure 16-4. In an analog magnetic speedometer, a permanent magnet rotating inside an iron drum forces the drum to rotate against the spring retainer, moving the pointer needle. (Ford)

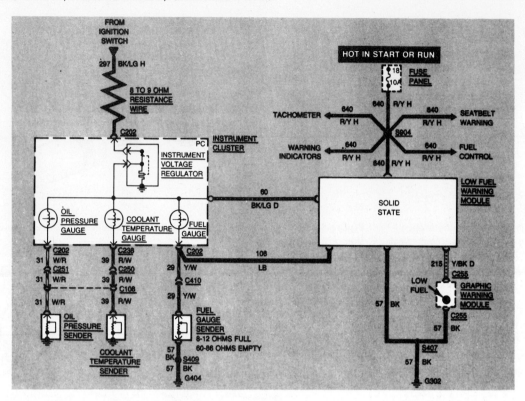

Figure 16-5. A typical fuel gauge system schematic. (Ford)

early electronic instruments first appeared. Mechanical gauges were used until World War II; postwar vehicles appeared with thermal or bimetallic electrical gauges, followed by electromagnetic gauges using either a d'Arsonval movement or a coil movement. By the mid-1980's, these were being replaced by air-core electromagnetic gauges on many vehicles. We will discuss both bimetallic and electromagnetic gauges in this section; mechanical gauges require no electrical circuit and are little more than a historical curiosity on production vehicles today. They are, however, still manufactured for use as accessory, or add-on, gauges.

The electrical instruments generally used in production automobiles are not intended to be highly accurate. Considering their simplicity and low cost, however, their indications are relatively precise. Gauges and warning or indicator lamps are electrical indicators receiving current through the ignition switch. Gauges are used to provide the driver with a scaled indication of a vehicle's operating system condition. A wide variety of gauges and warning or indicator lamps are used, ranging from engine coolant temperature indications to "fasten seatbelt" reminders.

All vehicles have a fuel gauge. They may be equipped either with temperature, oil pressure, and ammeter or voltmeter gauges, or with warning indicator lamps for these functions.

Gauges and warning or indicator lamps are operated by sender units or switches connected by wires to the gauge or lamp. Warning and indicator lamps are used instead of gauges because they are easier to understand and less expensive to manufacture. Unlike gauges, however, they are simple go/no-go devices and are unable to provide as much useful information as gauges.

Gauges

A gauge functions as an ammeter. A known voltage of approximately 5 volts is applied to each end of the gauge circuit by an instrument voltage regulator (IVR) or voltage limiter. (Coil and air-core electromagnetic gauges do not use an IVR.) The current level reading shown by the gauge changes with variations in the sender unit resistance. The higher the sender unit resistance, the lower the current level in the circuit and the smaller the indicator movement on the gauge scale. The lower the sender unit resistance, the higher the current level in the circuit and the greater the indicator movement.

We can prove this by using the typical gauge schematic shown in figure 16-5. The schematic also provides the sender unit resistance for a full and an empty tank. As you learned in chapter 1, voltage = current × resistance, or $E = IR$. If the fuel tank in the circuit shown in figure 16-5 is nearly empty, the sender unit resistance would be about 80 ohms. Since 5 volts are applied to the circuit by the IVR, the formula would read:

$$5 = I \times 80$$
$$I = 0.0625 \text{ amperes}$$

This low current would be translated on the gauge by a small pointer move-

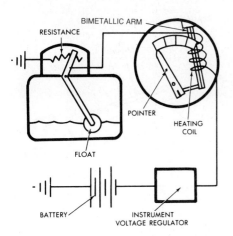

Figure 16-6. Movement of the float in the fuel tank affects a variable resistor connected to the bimetallic arm of the fuel gauge. (Ford)

Figure 16-7. The d'Arsonval movement operates on the basis of field interaction of an electromagnet and a permanent magnet.

ment, indicating a nearly empty fuel tank.

If the fuel tank in the same circuit is nearly full, the sender resistance would be about 10 ohms. Using the same formula:

$$5 = I \times 10$$
$$I = 0.05 \text{ amperes}$$

This higher current flow would be indicated on the gauge by a greater pointer movement, indicating a nearly full fuel tank.

Bimetallic Gauges. In this type of gauge, current flows through a bimetallic strip, heating one of the metals more rapidly than the other. This causes the bimetallic strip to flex in proportion to the heat it receives. The fuel level system, figure 16-6, is a typical example. It consists of a variable resistor in the fuel tank that is connected both to a float and to the instrument cluster gauge. The variable resistor is connected between ground and one end of the bimetallic arm. The other side of the bimetallic arm is connected to the voltage regulator in the cluster. The U-shaped bimetallic arm is attached to the gauge body and has a high-resistance wire wound around it. This wire acts as a heater

coil, bending the arm according to the current flowing through it.

As the fuel level in the tank drops, so does the float, increasing the resistance to electrical current flow. This causes a drop in current through the gauge coil and a decrease in the coil's temperature. The bimetallic arm straightens, pivoting the pointer attached to it toward the low end of the scale on the face of the gauge. Because the coil is on the feed leg of the U-shaped bimetallic arm, it provides built-in temperature compensation for ambient temperature changes. When temperature bends the free arm in one direction, the fixed arm is bent in the opposite direction, canceling any change caused by temperature. The bimetallic gauge always returns to a minimum reading position when the ignition is turned off.

Upon first starting the vehicle, bimetallic gauges will often climb to an abnormally high reading for a few seconds before dropping back to their correct level. This is most noticeable in cold weather, when it takes a few extra seconds for the bimetallic strips in the gauge and instrument voltage regulator to reach their cutout temperature.

Bimetallic gauges are almost indestructible because their heating ele-

ment of fine wire lasts indefinitely due to the low voltage and light current load carried. When this type of gauge malfunctions, the problem is usually caused by the instrument voltage regulator (IVR), not the gauge itself.

Electromagnetic Gauges. Magnetic field interaction is the control method used in electromagnetic gauges. Three types of movement are commonly used:

- d'Arsonval
- 3-coil or 2-coil
- Air core

The **d'Arsonval movement** consists of a permanent horseshoe magnet surrounding a movable electromagnet, figure 16-7. The two magnetic fields oppose each other, causing the electromagnet to rotate. The greater the current flow through the electromagnet's coil, the greater its field strength and the greater its rotation. A pointer attached to the electromagnet translates its movement to a scale on the face of the gauge.

A **three-coil movement** uses the field interaction of three electromagnets. The effect of the total field created by the electromagnets on a movable permanent magnet provides

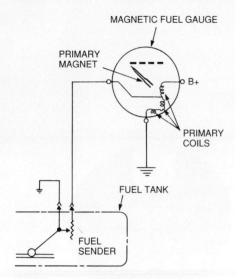

Figure 16-8. A typical late-model, 3-coil gauge design uses three primary coils and a primary magnet. (Ford)

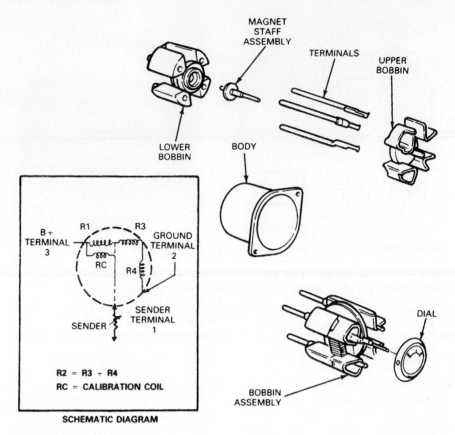

Figure 16-9. An exploded view and schematic of the 3-coil gauge design shows that some gauges use a calibration coil. (Ford)

gauge operation. In a typical late-model 3-coil gauge design, figure 16-8, one of the three primary coils is wound at 90 degrees to the other two coils. The magnetic field formed by the coils varies in direction according to the variable sender resistance connected between two of them. A permanent magnet rotates to align to the primary field.

As the permanent magnet rotates, a shaft and pointer attached to it move along the gauge scale, indicating the reading: fuel level, engine coolant temperature, or engine oil pressure, as appropriate. Figure 16-9 shows the internal components and schematic of this gauge design.

Two-coil gauge design differs according to the gauge application. When the gauge is used to indicate coolant temperature, figure 16-10, both coils receive battery voltage. One coil is grounded through the sender unit; the other is grounded directly. Sender unit resistance varies the current through one coil with changes in sender temperature, resulting in pointer movement.

A 2-coil fuel gauge operates differently. The two coils are positioned with their magnetic fields at right angles to each other. The "E" coil receives battery voltage. As the voltage reaches the end of the coil, the circuit

Figure 16-10. Inside a typical 2-coil gauge.

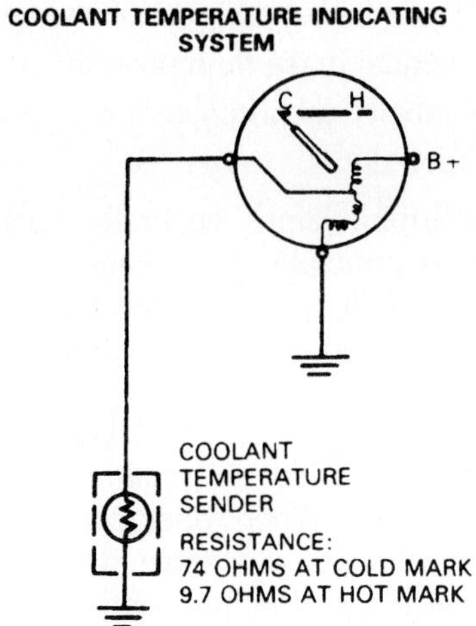

COOLANT TEMPERATURE INDICATING SYSTEM

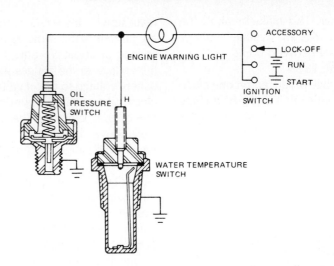

COOLANT TEMPERATURE SENDER

RESISTANCE:
74 OHMS AT COLD MARK
9.7 OHMS AT HOT MARK

Figure 16-11. A typical coolant temperature gauge system. (Ford)

Figure 16-12. The coolant temperature and oil pressure switches can share the same instrument panel warning lamp. (Ford)

divides. One path leads to ground through the "F" coil. The other path grounds through the variable resistor in the sender unit. Low sender unit resistance causes current to pass through the "E" coil and resistor, moving the pointer toward the "E" on the gauge scale. High sender unit resistance sends current flow through the "F" coil, moving the pointer toward the "F" on the gauge scale.

Gauges using the 3-coil or 2-coil design require an uninterrupted, controlled amount of voltage and rely upon system voltage of 12 volts, rather than the regulated 5 volts provided by an instrument voltage regulator (IVR) or voltage limiter. They remain at their last position when the ignition is turned off, instead of returning to a minimum reading.

An **air-core gauge** receives a varying electrical signal from its sender unit. A pivoting permanent magnet with a pointer aligns itself to a resultant field according to the resistance of the sender unit. This resistance varies the winding field strength in opposition to the reference windings. Air-core gauges are simple in design, inexpensive to manufacture, and provide greater accuracy with increased pointer travel. They offer noiseless operation that does not create radiofrequency interference (RFI), and they do not require a voltage limiter or IVR. Like 2- and 3-coil gauges, they remain

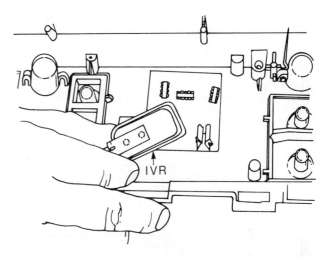

Figure 16-13. The instrument voltage regulator, or voltage limiter, is a plug-in unit that looks much like a circuit breaker. (Chrysler)

at their last reading when the ignition is turned off.

Sender Units. Sender units are variable resistors designed to be sensitive to the system they are monitoring. A coolant temperature sensor, for example, is a thermistor or bimetallic element (sensitive to temperature changes). An oil pressure sensor is a piezoresistive sensor or a pressure-operated diaphragm switch (sensitive to pressure changes). As you learned in chapter 6, a resistor sends an analog voltage signal that is proportional to the variable it is measuring. Figure 16-11 shows a typical coolant temperature gauge system; figure 16-12 shows a typical coolant temperature warning lamp system in which the oil

pressure sender unit shares the same instrument panel warning lamp.

Instrument Voltage Regulators (IVR). Instrument gauges that require a limited voltage to work properly will give inaccurate readings and may be damaged by full system voltage. Such gauges require a continuous and controlled amount of regulated voltage. This regulated voltage is supplied by an instrument voltage regulator or IVR, figure 16-13, sometimes called a voltage limiter.

The IVR supplies a reference voltage of approximately 5 volts by alternating making and breaking a circuit that is supplied with 12 volts. It works with a bimetallic strip and contact points, much like a self-resetting circuit breaker. This make-break of the circuit provides an "average" voltage by pulsating between 0 and a full 12 volts, figure 16-14.

The voltage produced on one cycle may be 4 volts; that of the next cycle may be 7 volts, etc. Since gauges react slowly, the effect of this pulsating current is the same as a constant voltage of about 5 volts. This keeps the voltage to the gauges well below battery voltage so that if voltage in the electrical system drops under the burden of other electrical loads, it is still well above the amount required to operate the gauges accurately.

The IVR contains a radio choke, figure 16-14. This coil wound with fine wire absorbs any oscillations caused by operation of the IVR contact points and prevents radio frequency interference (RFI) from affecting the radio or other electrical components.

Warning and Indicator Lamps.

Warning lamps are used to alert the driver to a potentially dangerous operating condition. Indicator lamps alert the driver to a problem. They provide information on conditions such as:

- Low oil pressure
- High engine coolant temperature
- Abnormal battery state of charge
- Unequal brake fluid pressure
- Seatbelts not fastened
- Open doors

Warning lamps generally operate on the principle of a voltage drop. A bulb will light only when there is a voltage drop across its filament. The bulb is wired into the circuit with equal voltage applied to both of its terminals under normal operating conditions. When operating conditions change, a voltage drop takes place across the filament, and the bulb will light.

Indicator lamps generally operate as a result of a switch or sender unit closing or opening. As shown in figure 16-15, closing the coolant temperature switch or the liftgate open switch completes ground to the engine indicator lamp or liftgate open indicator lamp, turning the lamp on. In this circuit, opening the oil pressure switch interrupts the circuit to the engine indicator lamp and turns it on.

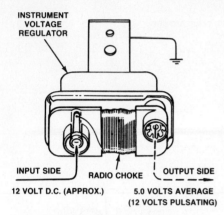

Figure 16-14. The IVR provides an "average" voltage by pulsating between 0 and a full 12 volts on the output side. An extremely fine wire coil or radio choke in the IVR absorbs oscillations created when the electrical circuit is opened and closed. (Ford)

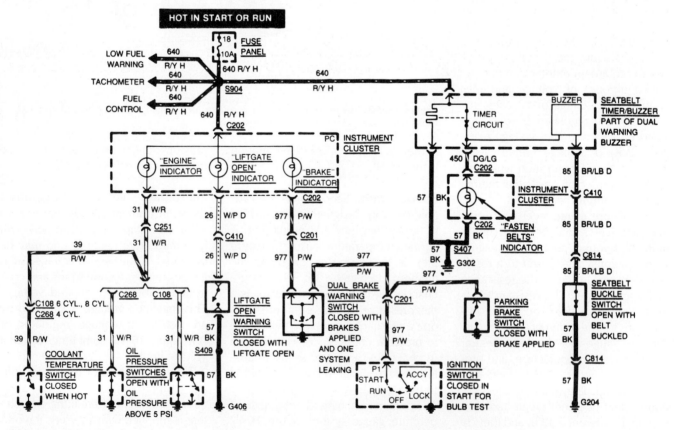

Figure 16-15. The opening or closing of a sender unit or switch operates indicator lamps. (Ford)

HOW FAST DID YOU SAY WE WERE GOING?

Sometimes we tend to take the devices we use for granted, as if everyone had always used the same ones. For example, we're all familiar with the analog magnetic speedometer, since it's been around for many years now. But Grandfather didn't have the same experience. He grew up during the years that the speedometer and other automotive instruments were evolving into the devices we take for granted today.

A variety of interesting speedometer designs preceded the analog magnetic speedometer. One early design used centrifugal control. Bell crank levers held weights on the speedometer shaft. The faster the shaft revolved, the farther the weights moved out from the shaft. Centrifugal force of the weights increased as the square of the shaft's velocity. The end of the shaft was milled and engaged a gear to which the gauge pointer was attached. This movement of the weights away from the shaft formed the basis for the gauge pointer movement.

A second early design used a calibrated current of air from an air circulator to turn a speed dial or inverted aluminum cup mounted on a pivot and set in jeweled bearings. The air circulator was a chamber containing two intermeshing aluminum gears driven by a flexible shaft connected to the front wheel or the driveshaft. Air from the chamber applied pressure against a vane connected to the inside of the speed dial. When the vehicle was not moving, the speed dial was kept at zero by a nickel-steel hairspring. As the vehicle started moving, air was applied against the speed dial vane by the air circulator and the dial moved. The amount of air applied to the vane was determined by the speed at which the air circulator was driven by the flexible shaft.

Last, but not least, was the hydraulic speedometer. This device used a centrifugal pump connected to the drive. The pump lifted a colored liquid inside a calibrated speedometer tube to show the vehicle speed.

Grandfather lived through a colorful era, but there's no doubt that he appreciated the magnetic speedometer when it appeared.

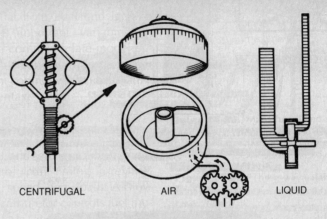

CENTRIFUGAL   AIR   LIQUID

Early speedometer designs.

Buzzers. Some warning systems include an audio signal with the visual signal. The audio signal is generally provided by a buzzer, which produces a loud warning sound under certain operating conditions, such as:

- Seatbelts not fastened
- Headlamps on with ignition key removed
- Doors open with key in ignition

Buzzers are generally constructed much like a relay but with different internal connections, figure 16-16. Closing the switch causes current to flow through the contacts and into the coil. Once the coil core is magnetized, it attracts the armature. As the armature is drawn to the coil, the contacts separate, breaking the magnetic pull from the coil. The spring-loaded arm pushes the armature up and the contacts close, making the circuit again. This cycle is repeated many times per second, generating a buzzing noise. The cycling continues until the switch is closed or until a timer shuts it off.

Figure 16-15 shows a seatbelt timer-buzzer circuit. The circuit has two separate functions. The solid-state timer circuit is powered through the fuse panel when the ignition switch is in the Start and Run positions. When the timer circuit receives voltage, the switch part of the circuit stays closed for 4 to 8 seconds. During this time, the FASTEN BELTS indicator lamp is on. The output of the timer circuit switch also is sent to the

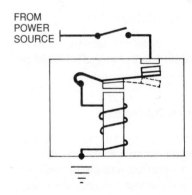

FROM POWER SOURCE

Figure 16-16. The internal construction of a buzzer.

buzzer. The seat buckle switch remains closed if the driver's seatbelt buckle is not fastened. This completes the ground path to the buzzer, which sounds until the belt is buckled or the timer circuit switch opens.

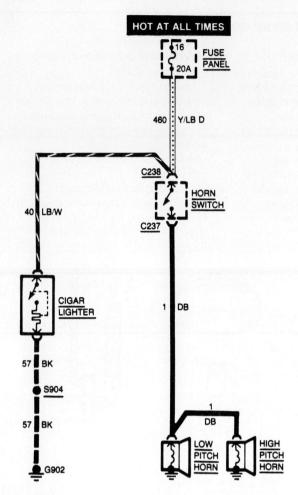

Figure 16-17. Some horn circuits operate without a relay. (Ford)

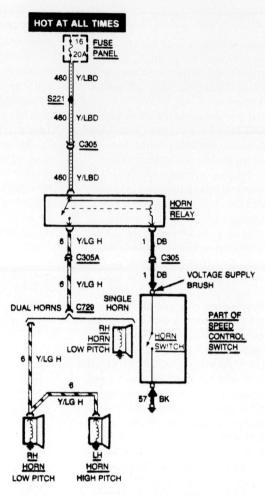

Figure 16-18. When a relay is used in the horn circuit, it is installed between the switch and horns. (Ford)

HORN CIRCUITS

The automobile horn is a safety device that allows the driver to signal pedestrians and other drivers.

Horn Operation

Horn operation is much like that of a buzzer, except that a diaphragm acts as a vibrator to create the high-pitched sound. Most electrically operated horns contain an electromagnet and diaphragm with a set of normally closed contact points wired in series with a coil. One of the points is attached to a movable armature. The horn diaphragm also is connected to the movable armature. When current is applied to the electromagnet, it attracts the diaphragm. This opens the contact points, which breaks the circuit and releases the diaphragm. Making and breaking the circuit in this way causes the diaphragm to vibrate rapidly, setting up sound waves. The pitch of the sound created by the horn is controlled by the speed of the cycling. Pitch can be adjusted by changing the spring tension on the horn armature to alter the magnetic pull on the diaphragm.

Circuit Diagram

The horn circuit is generally a simple design with a single horn wired in series with the horn switch. If two horns are installed, they are wired in parallel with each other and in series with the switch, figure 16-17. Battery current is usually sent to the horn circuit through the fuse block, although on older vehicles it may be sent from a terminal on the starter solenoid or relay. A normally open horn switch is located in the circuit between the grounded horn and the fuse block. Depressing the horn button closes the horn switch, sending current through the circuit to sound the horn.

Some circuits include a horn relay, figure 16-18. The normally open relay is located between the fuse block and the grounded horns. The horn switch is installed between the relay coil and ground. Depressing the horn switch sends a small amount of current to the relay, closing its coil and allowing a larger current to flow through the horns.

Chrysler uses an air horn system

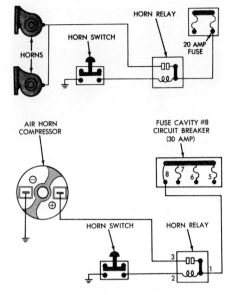

Figure 16-19. The circuit at the top is a typical Chrysler horn circuit; the one at the bottom is used with the Chrysler air horn. The circuits are identical except that the air horn circuit operates the compressor, which in turn operates the horn. (Chrysler)

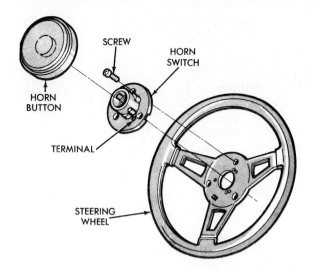

Figure 16-20. The horn switch may be located in the steering wheel under a horn button. (Chrysler)

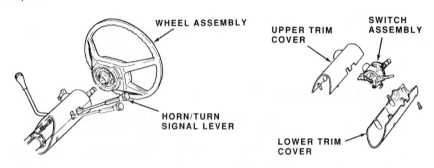

Figure 16-21. Late-model vehicles may use a multifunction horn and turn signal switch mounted on the steering column. (Ford)

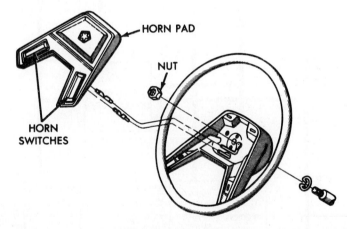

Figure 16-22. Horn switch contacts can be placed in various positions around the steering wheel. (Chrysler)

containing a compressor in its circuitry on some late-model vehicles, figure 16-19. Circuit operation is similar to the conventional horn circuit also shown in figure 16-19, but current from the relay flows to the grounded compressor, which then activates the horn.

Switches, Relays, and Circuit Protection

Horn switches are installed either in the steering wheel, figure 16-20, or as part of a lever-operated multifunction switch, figure 16-21.

When the switch is in the steering wheel, arrangement of the contact points can be varied according to steering wheel design, allowing the switch to be closed by applying pressure at one or several places on the steering wheel. Older vehicles use a separate large horn ring. Late-model vehicles may use a single button in the center of the steering wheel, figure 16-20, or multiple buttons, figure 16-22, placed at strategic points on the wheel. Horn switches that are part of a multifunction switch are gener-

ally operated by a pushbutton on the end of the operating lever. All horn systems, however, work in the same way. When pressure is applied to the switch, its contacts close and complete the circuit. Releasing the pressure allows spring tension to open the contacts and break the circuit.

Relays may be mounted on the fuse block, attached to the cowl panel, or installed near the horns in the engine compartment. Many imported cars locate the horn relay in a relay bank on the fenderwell, figure 16-23. Horn relays cannot be serviced and must be replaced if defective.

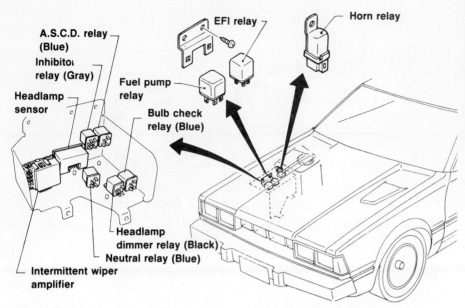

Figure 16-23. Imported cars often gang numerous relays, including the horn relay, in a relay center or box. (Nissan)

Figure 16-25. A Mercedes headlamp wiper assembly.

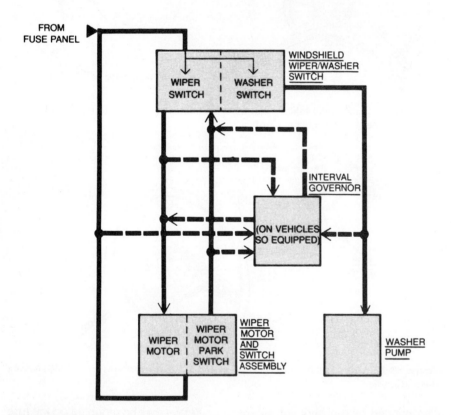

Figure 16-24. A block diagram of a typical windshield wiper and washer system. (Ford)

The horn circuit is protected by a 15-ampere or 20-ampere fuse shared with several other circuits. In some cases, the circuit also may be protected by a fusible link.

WINDSHIELD WIPERS AND WASHERS

All 1968 and later domestic and imported cars driven in the United States are required by Federal regulations to have a 2-speed windshield wiper and washer system. With the exception of American Motors, the wiper system on all domestic cars after that year is operated by an electric motor. American Motors used a wiper system operated by engine vacuum into the early 1970's before switching to an electric system. Older vehicles used either the vacuum-operated system or one operated by the power steering hydraulic system. Washer systems use an electric pump.

Two types of windshield wiper systems are used: a standard 2- or 3-speed system and a 2- or 3-speed system with an intermittent or interval feature that allows adjustment of the wiper interval period in addition to the low and high speeds. Both systems are available with either a depressed or nondepressed park. A depressed park system hides the wiper blades below the lower windshield molding; the nondepressed system parks the blades at the lower molding. Figure 16-24 is a block diagram of a typical windshield wiper and washer system.

A single-speed, rear window wiper and washer is used on many vehicles. Although completely separate from the windshield wiper and washer system, it operates in the same way. A few imported vehicles even appeared in the mid-1980's sporting headlamp wipers, figure 16-25, which proved to be a technological dead end.

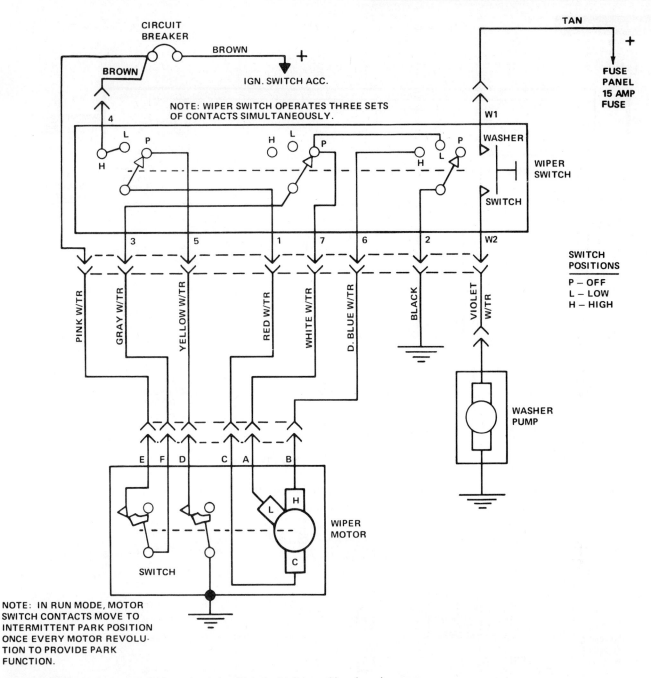

Figure 16-26. A basic 2-speed wiper circuit in which the high-speed brush and common brush oppose each other, with the low-speed brush offset to one side. (AMC)

Wiper Motors

Most 2-speed wiper motors use permanent magnetic fields, with the same bidirectional motor used for both standard and intermittent wiper systems. Wiper blade speed is determined by current flow to the appropriate brushes riding on the motor's commutator. One of the three brushes is a shared, or common, brush. It carries current whenever the motor is running. The other two brushes are placed at different positions relative to the armature to provide different speeds. Current flows to the low-speed brush for low-speed operation and to the high-speed brush for high-speed operation.

Brush placement affects motor speed and follows one of two designs:

1. The high-speed brush and common brush oppose each other, with the low-speed brush offset to one side, figure 16-26. The low-speed brush has an effect on the interaction of the magnetic fields inside the motor and causes the motor to turn slowly. The high-speed brush makes the motor turn rapidly.

2. The low-speed brush and common brush oppose each other, with the high-speed brush offset, figure 16-27, or otherwise positioned between the low-speed and common brushes, figure 16-28. Older versions of this design had the high-speed brush offset

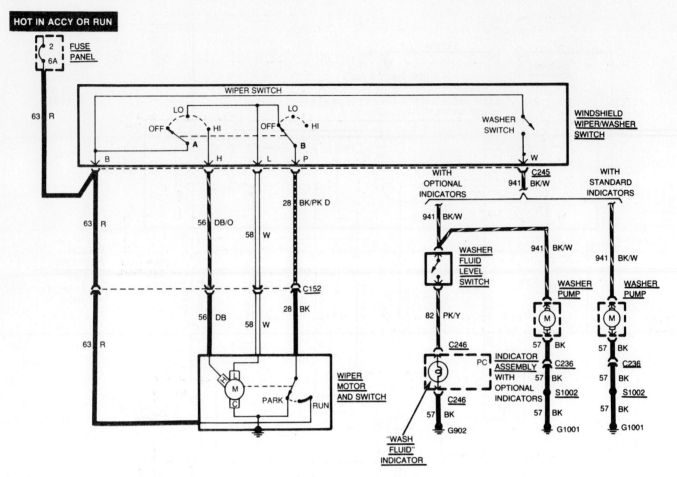

Figure 16-27. A basic 2-speed nondepressed park wiper circuit in which the low-speed brush and common brush oppose each other, with the high-speed brush offset. (Ford)

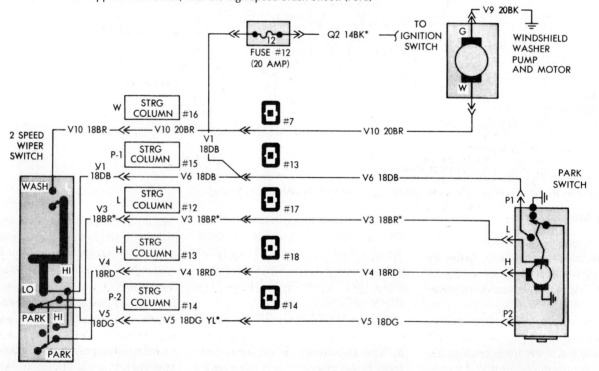

Figure 16-28. The high-speed brush is positioned between the low-speed and common brushes in this wiper circuit. (Chrysler)

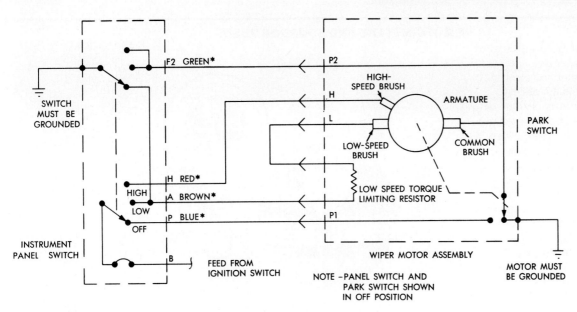

Figure 16-29. In a 3-speed wiper motor circuit, the two field coils are wound in opposite directions so that their magnetic fields oppose each other. (Chrysler)

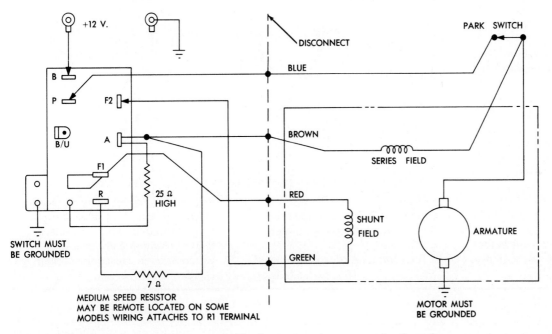

Figure 16-30. Wiper motor speed is controlled by the amount of current passing through one of the two electromagnetic fields. (Chrysler)

and used a resistor wired in series in the low-speed circuit, figure 16-29, to reduce the motor's torque at low speed.

Two electromagnetic field windings are used with some 2-speed and all 3-speed wiper motors, figure 16-30. The two field coils are wound in opposite directions; thus, their magnetic fields oppose each other. The field coil in series with a motor brush is the series field. The other field coil forms a separate circuit branch to ground and is called the shunt field.

Current through the field coils is controlled by the wiper switch. Both coils receive the same amount of current at low speed. This forms a weak total magnetic field, causing the motor to turn slowly. In a 3-speed motor at medium speed, the current flows through a resistor to one coil, weakening that coil's magnetic field but strengthening the total field in the motor. A resistor of greater value is used to obtain high speed. The greater resistance causes a further weakening of one coil's magnetic field, resulting in a much stronger total field and a higher motor speed.

OF MOTO-METERS AND BOURDON TUBES

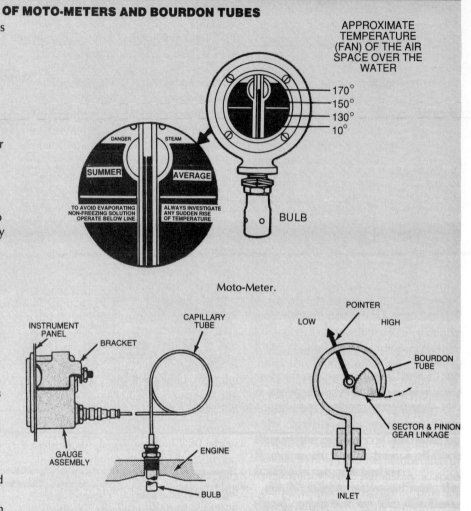

Moto-Meter.

Mechanical temperature gauge containing a bourdon tube.

In the early days of motoring, engines were cooled by water or a combination of water and alcohol, which was, incidentally, once a popular form of antifreeze. One of the first coolant temperature gauges was the Boyce Moto-Meter, which amounted to little more than a thermometer inside the radiator filler cap. The Moto-Meter contained a fluid-filled bulb under a glass tube against a graduated background that indicated operating temperature. Because the bulb did not extend into the coolant, it actually measured only the temperature of the vapor above the coolant. The Moto-Meter was used on early vehicles like Ford's Model T, where the hood did not cover the radiator. This allowed the gauge to be seen from the driver's seat. By the way, the cost of a Moto-Meter for the Model T was a prohibitive $3.50, direct from the manufacturer!

The Moto-Meter was followed by a mechanical temperature gauge containing a bourdon tube. The gauge received its signal through a capillary tube connected to a bulb mounted in the cylinder head water jacket. The gauge assembly consisted of a bourdon tube, a pointer, and a sector and pinion gear linkage. When engine temperature increased, the ether or treated alcohol in the bulb vaporized and applied pressure to the bourdon tube inlet. As the tube straightened from the pressure, the pointer rotated upscale across the dial. A decrease in coolant temperature caused the vapor to condense. This relaxed the bourdon tube, which rotated the pointer downscale.

Bourdon tube gauges were used well into the 1960's, particularly on foreign cars, before being replaced by electric gauges. They were accurate, but tended to give more problems than the Moto-Meter because vibration often caused the copper capillary tube to break.

Circuit Diagram

A typical late-model, 2-speed, non-depressed park wiper system circuit is shown in figure 16-27. Wiper motor speeds and washer operation are both controlled by one 2-segment switch. A park switch, figure 16-31, is installed in the wiper motor. Its operation is tied to motor rotation. The switch remains in the Run position for approximately 90 percent of the motor's rotation cycle. During the remaining 10 percent of each cycle (the point at which the wiper blades are at their lowest position), the switch moves to the Park position. If the wiper switch is turned off, but the wiper motor is not in the Park position, the wiper motor switch will be in the Run position. Power from the fuse block will continue to reach the low-speed brush in the motor, allowing the motor to continue to run until it reaches the Park position. At this point, the wiper motor switch will open and shut off voltage through the switch.

To drop the wiper blades below the windshield molding after parking, a depressed park wiper system uses a 2-segment motor switch, figure 16-31. When the wiper switch is turned off, but the wiper motor is not in the Park position, the Run position of the motor switch sends voltage from the fuse block back to the wiper switch, figure 16-32, which sends it to the common terminal of the motor.

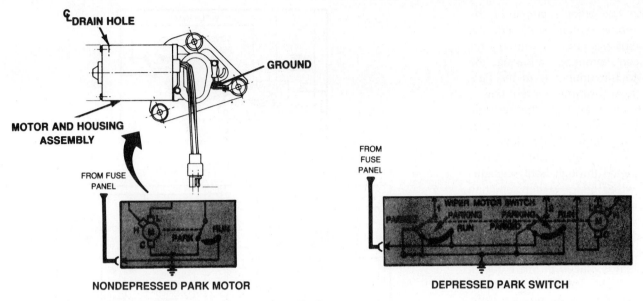

Figure 16-31. Typical park switches used in wiper motors. (Ford)

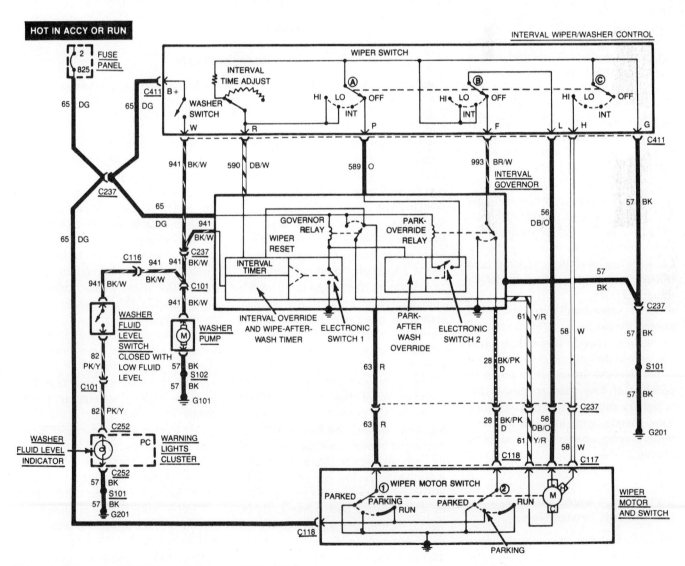

Figure 16-32. A depressed park wiper system circuit. (Ford)

Because the other segment of the wiper motor switch is closed, the wiper motor is grounded through its low-speed terminal, allowing the motor to run until it is in the Park position. At this time, current flow is momentarily reversed through the parking contacts of the wiper motor switch, moving the blades down and the switch to its Park position. Ground is completed through both segments of the wiper motor switch, shutting the motor off.

Many wiper systems offer a low-speed delay or intermittent mode that can be selected by the driver. When the system is placed in this mode, it provides an interval of 3 to 30 seconds between wiper arm sweeps across the windshield. Delay or intermittent systems send current through a solid-state module or governor, figure 16-33, which contains a potentiometer or other variable resistor and a capacitor. When the capacitor is fully charged by current sent through the potentiometer, the electronic switch or silicon-controlled rectifier (SCR) is triggered, sending current to the wiper motor. The park switch in the wiper motor shunts the SCR circuit to ground, but current continues to the motor until the wiper arms reach their Park position and open the park switch. The interval between wiper arm sweeps is determined by the capacitor's rate of charge, which is controlled through the potentiometer by the driver.

Some late-model imported cars control the delay or intermittent mode by vehicle speed. Depending upon the system design, the delay between wiper sweeps can vary from about 15 seconds at low road speeds to the wiper's normal low speed at moderate road speeds, with intervals between wiper sweeps changing as road speed changes.

Switches, Power Source, and Circuit Protection

All wiper systems use two switches: a wiper control switch in the passenger compartment and a park switch inside

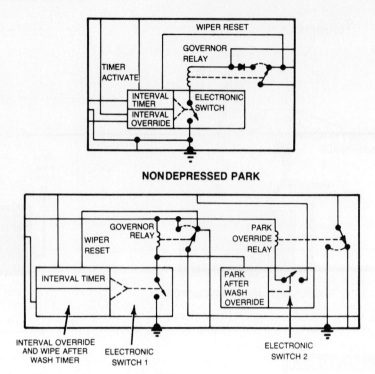

NONDEPRESSED PARK

DEPRESSED PARK

Figure 16-33. The internal construction of typical delay or intermittent solid-state modules (Ford)

the wiper motor, figure 16-24. The wiper control switch is installed between the ignition switch and the grounded wiper motor. The ignition switch must be in the Accessory or Run position before current is sent to the wiper switch. Control switches without an intermittent mode are either a 2-segment (nondepressed park) or 3-segment (depressed park) switch and generally contain the washer switch in the same housing, figure 16-34. An additional segment is added to the switch when an intermittent mode is included, figure 16-35.

With a nondepressed park system, segment A of the control switch, figure 16-34, controls power flow to the wiper motor. The Park input from the wiper motor park switch passes through segment B, figure 16-34, and is applied to the low-speed terminal of the wiper motor until the motor parks. In a depressed park system, figure 16-35, the depressed park signal from the wiper motor park switch is sent to the control switch on pin F. When the control switch is off, this signal is sent

to the wiper motor on pin L. When the control switch is set to either Low or High, the ground path to the wiper motor is completed by segment B of the switch on pin L or H. Segment C sends operating voltage to the wiper motor on pin C when the control switch is in Low or High. When the control switch is off, segment C receives the wiper motor park switch signal on pin D and sends it to the motor on pin C.

The wiper control switch may be located either on the instrument panel, or as part of a steering column multifunction switch operated by a lever or stalk. The electric washer pump is generally operated by a spring-loaded pushbutton and is controlled by contacts inside the wiper control switch. On some vehicles, the washer pump will operate as long as the switch is held in the On position.

Circuit protection is provided by a circuit breaker inside the wiper control switch and a 25-ampere or 30-ampere fuse in the fuse block. Older systems may use a separate circuit

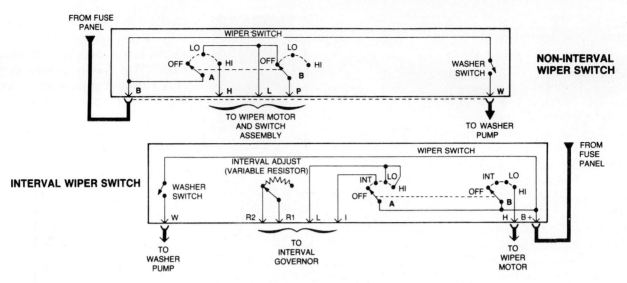

Figure 16-34. A 2-segment (nondepressed park) or 3-segment (depressed park) wiper control switch is used in systems without an intermittent mode. (Ford)

breaker instead of one integral with the switch.

Washer Pumps

Windshield cleaning fluid is drawn from the washer reservoir by the washer pump and forced through lines to nozzles, where it is applied to the windshield surface, figure 16-36. Washer pumps may be either positive-displacement or centrifugal pumps that send a steady stream of fluid, or pulse-type pumps that send intermittent streams of fluid.

Most washer pumps are mounted on the washer reservoir, figure 16-35. GM pulse-type washer pumps, however, are attached to the wiper motor, figure 16-37. Washer pumps cannot be serviced and must be replaced if defective.

Low Fluid Level Indicator

Some wiper and washer systems use a low fluid indicator lamp, figures 16-27 and 16-32. One side of an indicator lamp on the instrument panel is grounded. When the fluid level in the reservoir falls below a specified point (usually 1/4 full), the fluid level switch in the reservoir closes, sending power to the other side of the indicator lamp and turning it on.

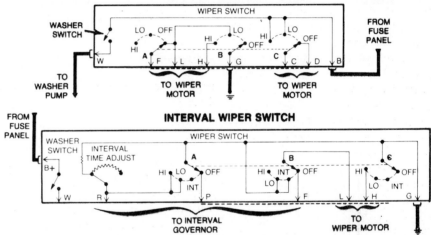

Figure 16-35. When an intermittent mode is included, the wiper control switch contains an additional segment. (Ford)

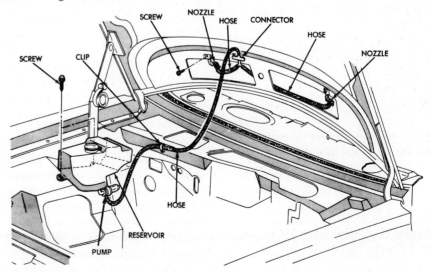

Figure 16-36. Most washer pumps are located at the bottom of the washer reservoir and send fluid to the nozzles through a system of hoses. (Chrysler)

Figure 16-37. GM pulse-type washer pumps are attached to the wiper motor.

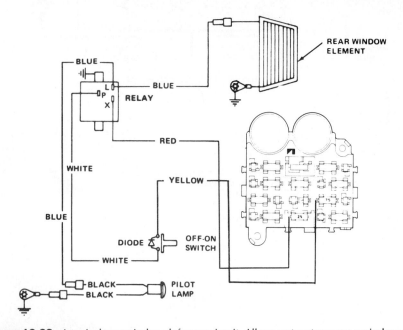

Figure 16-38. A typical rear window defogger circuit. All current systems use a window grid to heat the window surface. (AMC)

ELECTRIC DEFOGGERS

Electric defoggers heat the rear window surface to remove condensation or ice from the window. On some vehicles, the same system is used to heat the outside rearview mirror on the driver's side.

The first electric defoggers used on vehicles consisted of a motor-driven fan mounted in a box that was installed in the rear deck to blow heated air on the rear window. Controlled by a separate switch, the system operated in the same way as a heater fan. Current was passed through resistors to obtain different motor speeds. A length of resistance wire connected in parallel with the motor in the unit provided the heat when the motor was running.

The blower-type defogger was re-placed many years ago by the electrically heated window deicer or grid system that is used by all carmakers today. This system consists of two buss bars and a number of closely spaced, electrically connected grid lines applied to the inside of the window. The grid lines are made of an electrically conductive silver-ceramic material that bonds to the glass when baked on. When power is applied to the grid, it acts like a resistance wire in a toaster, heating the rear window.

Circuit Diagram

Turning on the rear window defogger switch energizes the solid-state timing circuit in the relay, figure 16-38. The timer controls the relay coil, which closes the relay contacts, allowing current to flow through the grid system for a specified length of time (usually about 10 minutes). If the vehicle is equipped with a heated rear-view mirror, current from the relay also flows through a separate fuse to the mirror heater grid. When the timer function expires, it opens the relay coil and removes power from the circuit.

The timing circuit is used because the system draws considerable power and could cause problems if accidentally left on for an extended time. Many vehicles equipped with this option use a high-output alternator. Most systems will shut down independently of the timer if the control switch or ignition switch is turned off. When this happens, the timing cycle is aborted. If the system is shut down prematurely, the control switch must be turned on a second time to reactivate the system and start a new timing cycle.

Switches, Power Source, and Circuit Protection

A single-pole, single-throw switch is used to control the electric defogger system. Some systems use a separate switch and relay; others combine the switch and relay in a single unit. System operation is indicated by an LED or lamp in the control switch knob, or

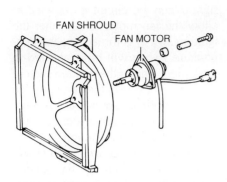

Figure 16-39. Electric cooling fans use a small motor attached to a fan shroud. (Toyota Motor Company)

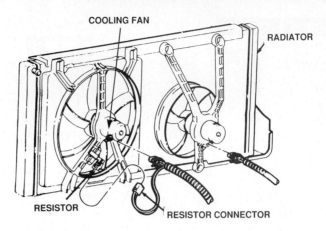

Figure 16-40. Some vehicles have separate fans to cool the radiator and air conditioning condenser. (Oldsmobile)

by a separate indicator lamp near the switch.

Power to the circuit is provided through the fuse block and the ignition switch. The circuit will operate only when the ignition switch is in the Run position. If a mirror heater is included in the circuit, it receives power through a separate fuse in the fuse block.

Protection for the heater grid circuit is provided by a fusible link located in the charging system, with the relay control system protected by a 20-ampere fuse in the fuse block.

ELECTRIC COOLING FANS

Transversely mounted engines used in front-wheel-drive (FWD) vehicles cannot cool the radiator with a crankshaft-driven fan; they require an electric cooling fan. An electric cooling fan may also be used with longitudinally mounted engines that have a crankshaft-driven fan.

The electric cooling fan system consists of a fan and electric motor attached to a fan shroud behind the radiator, figure 16-39. Some vehicles use one fan to cool the radiator and a second fan for the air conditioning condenser, figure 16-40. Dual electric fans may be used to provide extra engine cooling at idle on vehicles equipped with air conditioning or a turbocharger. Intercooled turbocharged engines often use an electric

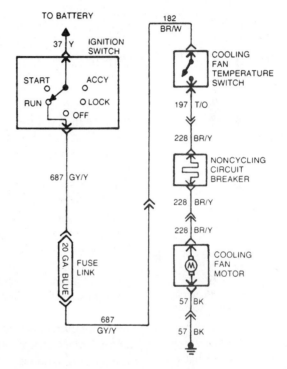

Figure 16-41. A typical cooling fan circuit controlled by a temperature switch without a relay. (Ford)

fan to cool the hot compressed intake air. This increases the density of the intake air and improves cylinder charging efficiency. Whenever more than one electric fan is used, each has its own circuit and temperature control, figure 16-40.

Circuit Diagram

Figure 16-41 shows a typical electric cooling fan circuit used on vehicles without air conditioning. Battery power is sent to the cooling fan tem-

perature switch only when the ignition switch is in the Run position. This prevents the fan from running when the ignition is off. When engine coolant exceeds the temperature setting of the switch, the switch contacts close to complete the circuit to the grounded fan motor. As coolant temperature drops, the switch contacts open and break the circuit, shutting the fan off. A nonresetting type II circuit breaker is installed in the circuit.

Electric cooling fan circuits also may use a relay, figure 16-42. The

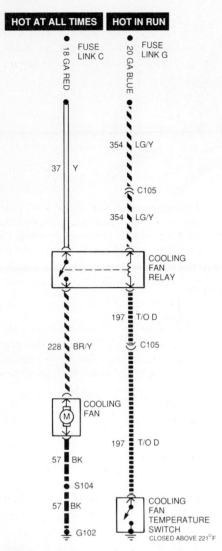

Figure 16-42. A cooling fan circuit controlled by a temperature switch and relay. (Ford)

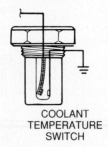

Figure 16-43. The coolant temperature switch contains a bimetallic arm and contact points. (Toyota)

relay contacts are installed between the grounded fan motor and the power source, with the temperature switch located between the relay coil and ground. When the temperature switch contacts close, a small amount of current passes through the relay coil to close the contact points, sending a larger amount of current to the fan motor.

When a relay-operated circuit is used on air conditioned vehicles, the circuit is also wired through the air conditioning relay to bypass the temperature switch and fan relay. Depending upon how the circuit is wired, the cooling fan will either run:

• Whenever the air conditioning compressor is engaged

• Whenever the air conditioning compressor head pressure is greater than a specified value

An ambient temperature sensing switch can be used to provide an "afterrun" mode, often used with turbocharged engines. If air temperature exceeds a predetermined value after the engine is shut off, the switch will allow the fan to continue running for a certain length of time. The duration of afterrun is controlled by a timer circuit in the fan relay.

A dual 3-stage fan circuit on some Toyota engines automatically switches from a series connection at low speed operation to a parallel connection during high-speed operation. Coolant temperature and air conditioning compressor operation control the back-and-forth switching between the series and parallel connections. The system is used to eliminate noise and vibration and to reduce the amount of electrical power required to maximize cooling.

Switches, Power Source, and Circuit Protection

Coolant temperature switches used with electric cooling fan circuits can be mounted in various locations. Some of the more common are the:

• Intake manifold
• Thermostat housing
• Cylinder head
• Radiator header tank

The switch operates on the principle of a bimetallic arm, figure 16-43. When engine coolant temperature reaches the calibrated value of the switch, the contact points close and complete the circuit to the relay or fan motor, depending upon circuit design. When the circuit is designed to allow the fan motor to run after the ignition switch is turned off, the temperature switch will be connected to the battery side of the ignition switch. If you are not sure of the circuit design when working around an electric cooling fan, always disconnect the motor as a safety precaution.

Power is provided to the fan circuit from the battery through the ignition switch. Circuit protection may be provided by a fusible link and circuit breaker, figure 16-41, or through one or more fusible links, figure 16-42.

SUMMARY

Electrical instrumentation provides the driver with information about the condition of the vehicle's operating systems. Speedometers operate through a flexible cable connected to a transmission or transaxle drive gear. Fuel gauges use a float and variable resistor in the fuel tank. Other gauges and lamps are operated by variable resistors or switches. Most gauges in late-model vehicles are bimetallic or electromagnetic designs. Warning or indicator lamps are less expensive and faster to read, but tell you little except that something is wrong.

The automobile horn produces a sound by using electromagnetism to vibrate a diaphragm. The horn circuit may use a relay to direct current flow to the horn, or it may be a simple series circuit without a relay. The horn switch closes the circuit in either type.

A wide variety of 2- and 3-speed windshield wiper and washer circuits are used. Rear wiper systems use a single-speed motor. Wiper motors may have permanent magnets or use electromagnetic fields. Wiper circuits may include a depressed park feature to position the blades below the windshield molding. They may have an interval wipe mode controlled by the driver or by vehicle speed. Each type of circuit is slightly different.

Electric window defoggers use a grid of conductive silver to heat the rear window for better visiblity. Some defogger systems also heat the outside mirror on the driver's side. The circuit uses a relay containing a timer circuit to prevent the heavy current drain from remaining on too long.

Electric cooling fans are used primarily on front-wheel-drive vehicles, although some rear-wheel-drive vehicles also use them. Cooling fan circuits may or may not use a relay. If the vehicle is air conditioned, the cooling fan is wired into the compressor relay to allow it to run whenever the air conditioning is on. A timer circuit in the relay can provide an afterrun feature, allowing the fan to continue running after the engine is shut off to prevent a heat soak condition.

REVIEW QUESTIONS

Multiple Choice

1. Student A says that warning lamps are used in cars because they can be arranged to display a considerable amount of information. Student B says that warning lamps are used because they are less expensive to manufacture than gauges. Who is right?

   a. A only
   b. B only
   c. both A and B
   d. neither A nor B

2. Student A says that the bimetallic strip in a gauge can be shaped to compensate for changes in ambient temperature. Student B says that internal gauge resistance compensates for temperature changes. Who is right?

   a. A only
   b. B only
   c. both A and B
   d. neither A nor B

3. Student A says that most gauges in late-model cars are an electromagnetic design. Student B says that most gauges use a d'Arsonval movement. Who is right?

   a. A only
   b. B only
   c. both A and B
   d. neither A nor B

4. Student A says that a warning lamp is activated by a voltage drop. Student B says that an indicator lamp is activated by a switch or sender unit. Who is right?

   a. A only
   b. B only
   c. both A and B
   d. neither A nor B

5. Student A says that a fuel gauge sending unit uses a variable resistor. Student B says a fixed resistor is used. Who is right?

   a. A only
   b. B only
   c. both A and B
   d. neither A nor B

6. Student A says that a buzzer uses a vibrating diaphragm. Student B says that a horn uses vibrating contact points. Who is right?

   a. A only
   b. B only
   c. both A and B
   d. neither A nor B

7. Student A says that electric cooling fans are used primarily with transverse-mounted engines. Student B says that when more than one electric cooling fan is used, each has its own circuit. Who is right?

   a. A only
   b. B only
   c. both A and B
   d. neither A nor B

8. Student A says that electromagnetic gauges use an instrument voltage regulator (IVR). Student B says that bimetallic gauges do not use an IVR. Who is right?

   a. A only
   b. B only
   c. both A and B
   d. neither A nor B

9. Student A says that a horn circuit with more than one horn must have a relay. Student B says that a horn circuit uses a relay to reduce the amount of current required to sound the horn. Who is right?

   a. A only
   b. B only
   c. both A and B
   d. neither A nor B

10. Student A says that all current windshield wiper systems use an electric motor. Student B says that some foreign cars still use a vacuum-operated wiper system. Who is right?

   a. A only
   b. B only
   c. both A and B
   d. neither A nor B

11. Student A says that all 3-speed wiper motors use permanent magnet fields. Student B says that all 2-speed wiper motors use electromagnetic fields. Who is right?

   a. A only
   b. B only
   c. both A and B
   d. neither A nor B

12. Student A says that nonintermittent wiper systems use 2-segment control switches. Student B says that intermittent wiper systems use 3-segment control switches. Who is right?

   a. A only
   b. B only
   c. both A and B
   d. neither A nor B

13. Which of the following is not used in an electric defogger system?

   a. an electric grid
   b. a relay
   c. a blower
   d. a timer circuit

14. Student A says that odometers generally indicate one mile for each 1,000 revolutions of the speedometer cable. Student B says that turning the odometer back to indicate fewer miles is illegal. Who is right?

   a. A only
   b. B only
   c. both A and B
   d. neither A nor B

15. Student A says that the park switch in a 2-speed wiper motor provides the two speeds. Student B says that speed-control brushes in the wiper motor bring the wiper arms to the windshield molding when the motor is turned off. Who is right?

   a. A only
   b. B only
   c. both A and B
   d. neither A nor B

17 ELECTRONIC INSTRUMENTATION AND SAFETY SYSTEMS

WHAT

Electronic instrumentation has made rapid strides since the introduction of the first electronic instruments in the late 1970's. This includes speedometers, odometers, tachometers, engine gauges, trip computers, menu-driven instrumentation, and electronic vehicle information centers. Various types of electronic displays are used by carmakers, as you learned in chapter 6. They also are arranged in a wide variety of ways, yet the sensors, microprocessors, and data processing are common to all systems.

Electronically heated windshields, electronically controlled cooling fans, and airbags also are becoming commonplace on today's automobiles. You will see an increasing number of such systems in the future.

WHY

Primitive electronic instruments were first used in the late 1970's. In 1980, Ford and other automakers introduced the first completely electronic instrument clusters. Drivers have accepted electronic instruments as desirable alternatives to the older analog gauges. They are more colorful, more accurate, and more useful to the driver.

Electronic instrument clusters perform the same function as the electrically controlled analog instruments they are gradually replacing: they display a variety of information required by the driver. They do this job, however, using solid-state components and circuits instead of electromechanical devices and wiring. They also can display the information in more different forms and colors than analog instruments. This chapter will introduce you to the principles of electronic instruments. As an automotive technician, you will service an increasing number of them.

This chapter will introduce you to electronic control of heated windshields, cooling fans, and airbags. Electronically heated windshields are quite similar to the electric rear window defoggers you studied in chapter 16, but the control method used is different. An increasing number of automobiles allow the onboard computer to decide whether and when the cooling fan should operate. You must be familiar with the operation of such systems because, like electronic instruments, they will eventually take the place of independently operated cooling fans.

Airbags are a mandated passive restraint system that supplement, and even may replace, the conventional seatbelt in coming years. Because of their important safety function, you should be familiar with how they work.

GOALS

After studying this chapter, you should be able to:

1. Explain the principles behind the operation of the following electronic instruments:
   a. speedometer
   b. tachometer
   c. engine gauges
   d. trip computers
   e. menu-driven instrumentation
   f. electronic information centers

2. List the components used and describe the operation of:
   a. an electronically heated windshield system
   b. an electronically controlled cooling fan

3. Describe the function, components, and operation of the following passive restraint systems:
   a. shoulder harness
   b. airbag

ELECTRONIC INSTRUMENT CLUSTERS

Analog and electronic instrument clusters work in the same way. They receive signals from different sensors and change those signals into various types of displays. An analog instrument cluster, figure 17-1, uses warning lamps and gauges with needles. These instruments inform the driver about the condition of the systems being monitored.

An electronic instrument cluster processes the sensor data through integrated circuitry in the speedometer or a microprocessor in an instrument module and then displays information using digital numbers and various types of graphs instead of gauges and needles, figure 17-2. Some electronic clusters also include incandescent warning lamps.

The needle or pointer in an analog gauge is dampened to give an "average" reading. This prevents the needle or pointer from constantly fluctuating. Electronic instruments are far more precise in their indication, since the solid-state circuitry used in them generally updates the display two to five times per second.

We will cover the principles behind electronic instrument clusters in this section.

Speedometers

Two major types of electronic speedometers are currently used. They differ primarily in the source of the speed signal. One type uses an optical speed sensor, figure 17-3. The other type uses a magnetic speed sensor, figure 17-4. The resulting display can take the form of a digital display, or what is called a quartz swing needle display, figure 17-5.

Optical Speed Sensor. The optical speed sensor used with some electronic speedometers is located in the speedometer housing behind the odometer, figure 17-3. It contains a

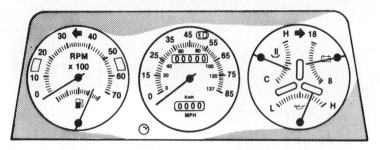

Figure 17-1. Although arrangement of the instruments may vary, analog instrument clusters use various gauges with needles and warning lamps to display information. (Chrysler)

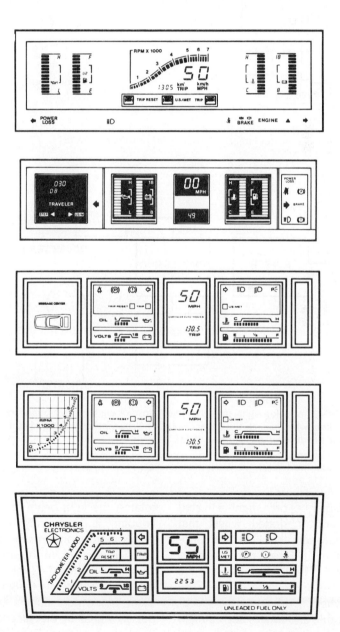

Figure 17-2. A variety of electronic instrument clusters showing the variety of displays used. (Chrysler)

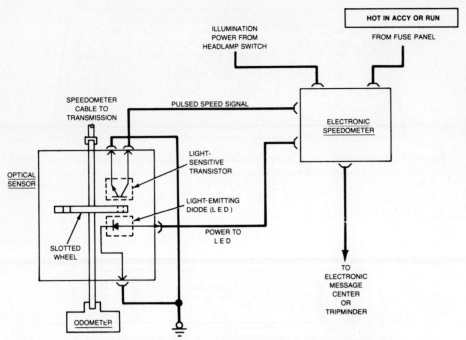

Figure 17-3. An optical sensor translates mechanical movement into an electrical signal that is sent to the speedometer integrated circuitry for processing. (Ford)

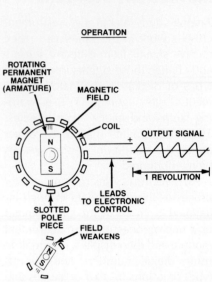

Figure 17-4. A magnetic speed sensor also translates mechanical movement into an electrical signal. (Ford)

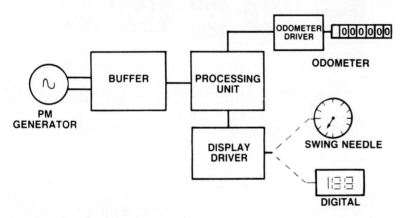

Figure 17-5. The analog signal from the speed sensor is digitized by a buffer and sent to the processing unit, which signals the driver display. The concept is the same whether the display uses a swing needle or digital readout. (GM)

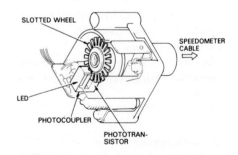

Figure 17-6. The optical sensor contains a cable-driven slotted wheel that breaks a light beam in the photocoupler to create the speed signal. (Toyota)

photocoupler, or light-activated switch, and a slotted wheel that passes between the LED and phototransistor in the photocoupler, figure 17-6. The LED emits light; the phototransistor receives light. The slotted wheel is driven by the speedometer cable and rotates according to vehicle speed. As the slotted wheel rotates, the light beam in the photocoupler is constantly interrupted. Each interruption turns the phototransistor on and off. In the speed sensor shown in figure 17-7, the phototransistor passes the on-off signal to transistor Tr_1, which sends a continuous pulsed signal to the speedometer or instrument module. To calculate vehicle speed, the IC's in the module rectify the analog input signal, count the number of pulses per second from transistor Tr_1, compare the new value with the previous one, store the new value, and display it as the present vehicle speed by sending electric current to the appropriate segments of a digital readout.

Optical speed sensors typically have 16 to 20 legs on the slotted wheel. This means that the number of positive pulses per revolution of the speedometer cable will differ according to the design of the sensor. Ford and Toyota have been major users of the optical speed sensor for speedometer operation.

Magnetic Speed Sensor. A magnetic speed sensor consists of a permanent magnet (PM) generator or magnetic reluctance pickup, figure 17-4, driven by the transmission or transaxle speedometer gear. This system does not use a speedometer cable; its output signal is sent to the speedometer or instrument module by a wire. As the PM generator or pickup rotates, changes in the electromagnetic field cause a small AC voltage to be induced in the coil. As you learned in chapter 12, this is the basis for many electronic ignitions.

Magnetic speed sensors typically generate four to eight voltage cycles or pulses per revolution of the speedometer-driven gear. The system introduced on the 1988 Chevrolet and GMC light-duty trucks, however, uses a reluctor on the transmission or transfer case output shaft and sends a constant output of 40 pulses per driveshaft revolution. Once the signal is received by the speedometer or instrument module, it receives the same processing as an optical signal and is displayed on the digital readout as present vehicle speed.

Ford, Chrysler, and General Motors have all used magnetic speed sensors for speedometer operation.

Quartz Analog Displays. The swing needle or air-core gauge used in a quartz analog display is quite similar in design to the electromagnetic gauges you studied in chapter 16. When the vehicle starts to move, the buffered signal is conditioned and sent to the microprocessor as a digitized signal. The signal is then passed through a quartz clock circuit, a gain

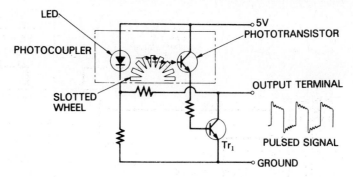

Figure 17-7. Constant interruption of the photocoupler light beam by the slotted wheel causes the phototransistor to turn on and off, turning Tr$_1$ on and off to send a pulsed signal to the speedometer or instrument module. (Toyota)

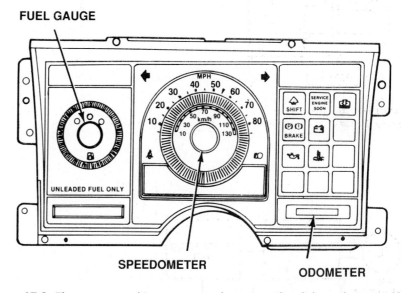

Figure 17-8. The quartz crystal instrument panel contains a disc-dial speedometer with mechanical odometer. (Chevrolet)

selector circuit, and a driver circuit. The driver circuit transmits the correct voltages to the coils in the gauge, moving the pointer and displaying the vehicle speed.

The speedometer used with 1988 and later Chevrolet and GMC light-duty trucks uses a rotating-disc dial indicator, figure 17-8, and operates in a slightly different way. The instrument cluster IC uses an integrator (a type of operational amplifier) to process the speed sensor signal into a sawtooth signal proportional to the ac input. This sawtooth signal is then sent to a Schmitt trigger, where it is converted into a dc square wave sig-

nal by a voltage divider, figure 17-9. Vehicle speed is calculated by measuring the interval between the beginning of the pulses (signal frequency). The faster the vehicle is moving, the shorter the interval between pulses. The signal is then compared to the quartz clock in the speedometer logic IC before being sent to the drive IC, where it controls two field-effect transistors (FET's), figure 17-10. The FET's function as variable resistors, controlling the current flow through the coils that rotate the indicator disc.

The speed sensor signal in this system is used by three other vehicle systems, each of which has its own

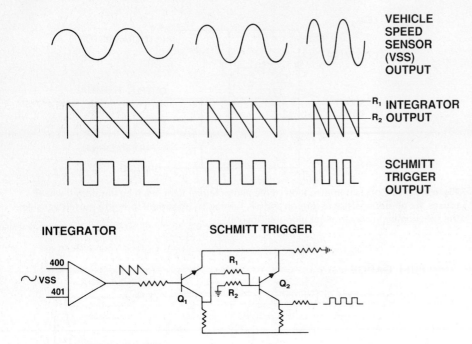

Figure 17-9. The analog speed sensor signal is digitized by passing it through an integrator and Schmitt trigger. (Chevrolet)

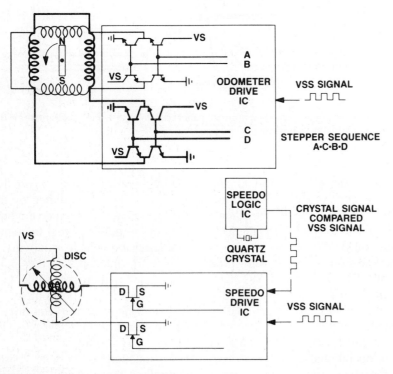

Figure 17-10. The vehicle speed sensor (VSS) signal is compared to a quartz crystal signal in the speedometer logic IC before being sent to the drive IC to operate the two field-effect transistors that rotate the indicator disc. (GM)

requirements. For this reason, the signal is conditioned in three ways:

1. An output signal of 128,000 pulses per mile is sent to the rear wheel antilock brake system.

2. A 4,000-pulse-per-mile signal is sent to the cruise control system.

3. A 2,000-pulse-per-mile signal is sent to the speedometer and odometer. The same signal is sent to the electronic control module (ECM) for transmission converter clutch control.

The rotating-disc speedometer is calibrated at the factory for individual tire sizes and axle ratios. If either is changed, the speedometer must be recalibrated accurately, or each of the systems using the speed sensor signal will be adversely affected. You will learn more about this in chapter 16 of Volume 2.

Digital Displays. The processing function used with a digital display is very similar to that described under quartz analog displays. There are, however, some small differences in operation:

• The speedometer or instrument module can display data either in English or metric. A driver-selectable switching function allows data transmission on different circuits according to the type of display desired. On vehicles destined for export, the switching function may be hard-wired as a permanent operating mode.

• An output logic circuit is used instead of a gain-selector circuit.

• The display segments and their intensity are controlled by the display driver circuit.

System configuration varies from one carmaker to another. Figure 17-11 is the schematic for the 1986 and later Oldsmobile Toronado (GM-30) instrument panel cluster (IPC). The speed sensor signal is received by the body computer module (BCM), which processes it by measuring the interval between the pulses or signal frequency to calculate the vehicle speed. The BCM transmits the calculated speed and other required information to the IPC microprocessor on

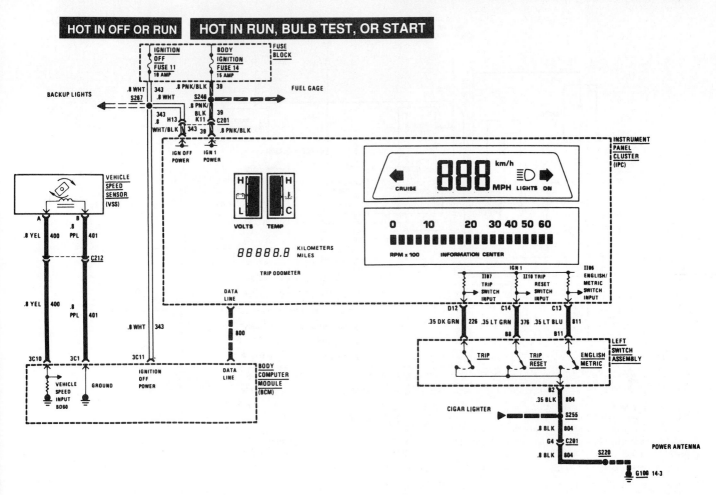

Figure 17-11. On GM vehicles with a BCM, the BCM receives the speed sensor input, calculates the vehicle speed, and sends the processed information to the IPC microprocessor, which uses it to turn on the proper display. (Oldsmobile)

the serial data link. The IPC microprocessor decodes the BCM signal and uses it to modulate the variable frequency (VF) driver circuits that turn on the required speedometer display.

Various convenience features also can be programmed into an electronic speedometer display. For example, Ford displays allow the driver to preselect a maximum road speed. This causes the word SPEED to appear in the display. If the vehicle exceeds the preselected speed by 5 mph, the display will blink the word SPEED and emit three short beeps. When vehicle speed drops back to within 5 mph of the preset speed, the word stops blinking.

A service interval reminder can be programmed into the display. When the vehicle reaches the appropriate

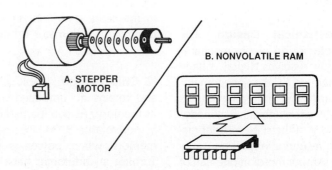

Figure 17-12. The two types of electronic odometers. (GM)

mileage, the word SERVICE will appear. The reminder is reset by depressing two buttons on the cluster at the same time. The word disappears until the next interval has been completed. Three beeps are heard to confirm the reset function.

Odometers

Two types of odometers are used with electronic speedometers. The electro-mechanical design with a stepper motor, figure 17-12A, contains a series of gear-driven number dials and

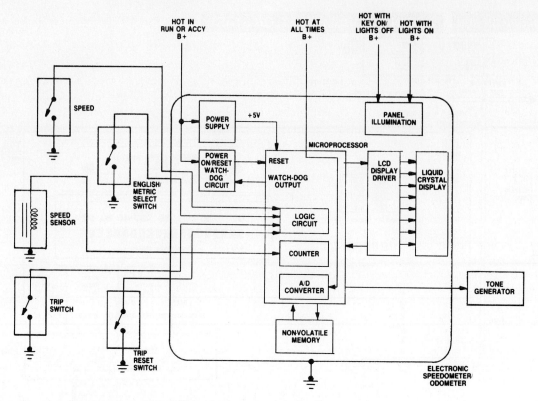

Figure 17-13. The logic circuit in this electronic odometer design is programmed to erase the trip meter display while retaining total accumulated mileage in the odometer function. This allows the trip meter to be used just as it would be in a conventional analog gauge display. (Ford)

strongly resembles the conventional odometer used with mechanical speedometers. The electronic design uses an IC chip with a nonvolatile RAM, figure 17-12B.

Electromechanical Design. The stepper motor of an electromechanical odometer receives digital voltage pulses generated by the speedometer circuit board. The incoming signals are generally passed through a divide-by-two circuit in the speedometer circuit board, resulting in their transmission to the stepper motor at one-half of the buffered speed signal entering the cluster. The result is a quite accurate compilation of accumulated mileage.

The Chevrolet and GMC quartz crystal instrument clusters described earlier use an advanced application of the stepper motor design. The stepper motor uses the converted speed sensor signal to turn the odometer drive IC on and off. An H-gate or set of

transistors drives the four stepper motor coils. The H-gate energizes the coils two at a time and constantly reverses system polarity. This causes the permanent magnet poles to rotate in the same direction, figure 17-10, turning the odometer driveshaft and related gears.

IC Chip Design. The IC chip stores and retains accumulated mileage in its memory. As you learned in chapter 5, nonvolatile RAM does not lose its memory when power is removed. Turning an odometer back to reflect fewer miles on the vehicle is one of the most common used car frauds and is strictly prohibited by law. This type of odometer cannot be turned back. In many designs, however, a faulty IC chip can be removed and a blank service replacement installed. This IC chip permanently displays an X, S, or asterisk along with the accumulated mileage to indicate that it is not the

original odometer chip. One Chrysler design uses a programmable IC chip. With this type, the mileage recorded on the faulty chip can be transferred to the new chip.

The Ford electronic speedometer and odometer system block diagram, figure 17-13, contains a dual function electronic odometer. It not only stores accumulated mileage, but also contains a trip function. When the trip reset switch is depressed, it applies a ground input to the microprocessor. The microprocessor then clears the trip odometer memory, which reverts to zero miles. The trip switch is another ground input to the microprocessor, which permits the display of total accumulated mileage (odometer function) or the miles traveled since the trip reset switch was last activated (trip odometer function).

General Motors uses a similar dual function in its GM-30 vehicles, figure 17-11. In this system, the BCM keeps track of the total accumulated mileage in its EEPROM and the trip mileage in RAM, sending the information as required to the IPC. The IPC, however, can display only one odometer function at a time. The driver must select the one he wishes to read by depressing a switch on the IPC, which then changes the display. When the driver depresses the trip reset switch, the IPC signals the BCM to reset the trip odometer mileage to zero.

Tachometers

A tachometer indicates engine rpm. While all tachometer functions must take their signal from the ignition system, there are several ways to provide a tachometer display in an electronic cluster.

Ford's electronic tachometer is one function of a multigauge, figure 17-14, and contains a built-in power supply that regulates voltage from the ignition switch to provide a 5-volt reference voltage. Three analog sensors use this reference voltage:

- Coolant temperature sender
- Fuel gauge sender
- Oil pressure sender

The module also receives inputs from the charging system voltage regulator and two ground switching sensors.

The tachometer function receives its signal from the ignition coil. Engine rpm is indicated by the number of lighted bars in a bar graph, with each bar representing 200 rpm. The bar graph will read 6,000 rpm at all engine speeds above 5,200 rpm.

Since this is a sequential multigauge, a select switch is provided in the circuitry. This switch sends a momentary ground signal to the microprocessor each time it is depressed and released. The ground signal tells the microprocessor to change the display from one gauge reading to another. The microprocessor will switch the display each time the select switch is depressed. If the driver wishes to return to a particular display, he must switch his way through the various gauge displays until it returns to the one he wants.

A power on-off watchdog circuit in the module monitors microprocessor operation and acts as an electronic circuit breaker. A pulsing output signal is sent to this circuit by the microprocessor. If the signal pulses stop while battery voltage is applied to the microprocessor, the watchdog circuit will apply a reset voltage to restart the microprocessor.

General Motors uses a slightly different approach in its GM-30 vehicles. The IPC tachometer function is combined with a PRNDL function in one gauge, figure 17-15. (The PRNDL function displays the gear range selected for vehicle operation.) The bar graph tachometer is displayed by depressing a TACH switch on the instrument panel.

The tachometer signal starts with a reference pulse from the distributorless ignition (DIS) module. Each time a spark plug fires, the DIS module sends a reference pulse to the ECM. The ECM measures the intervals between the pulses (signal frequency) and uses the data for fuel delivery and other calculations. It also transmits the rpm data to the body computer module (BCM). The IPC does not receive the rpm data directly, but acts as a bystander and listens in on the serial data link as the ECM sends the data to

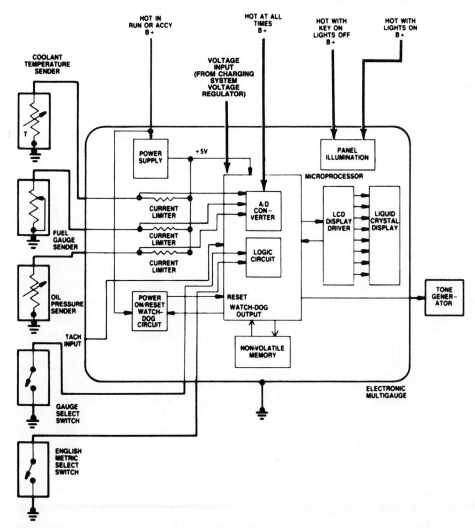

Figure 17-14. The tachometer can be a separate function, or part of a multigauge display, as shown in this rendition of the Ford electronic multigauge that provides sequential display of four gauge functions. (Ford)

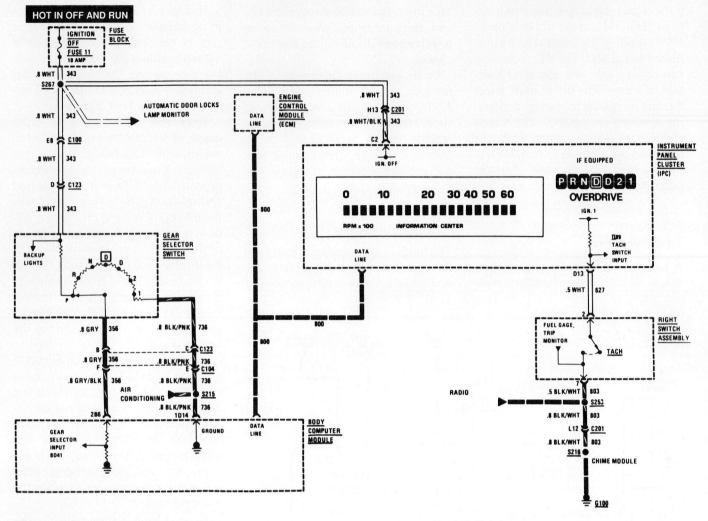

Figure 17-15. The rpm signal for this Oldsmobile tachometer is taken from the ECM as it communicates with the BCM. The ECM receives the signal from the DIS module each time a spark plug fires. (Oldsmobile)

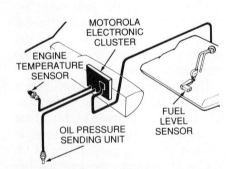

Figure 17-16. Electronic instrumentation uses the same sensors as analog mechanical instrumentation. (Chrysler)

the BCM. The IPC then processes the engine speed data to drive the tachometer display.

Engine Gauges

The gauges in an electronic cluster use the same or similar sender units as those used with conventional analog clusters, figure 17-16. The major difference between the two systems is the microprocessor installed between the sender and the gauge display. When the sender unit circuit signal changes, the microprocessor reads the change in the signal and computes a change in the display.

Fuel Gauge. The fuel gauge circuit in figure 17-17 is a good example to

show the similarity with an analog system, as well as the differences. As the fuel level changes, the sliding contact of the potentiometer sender unit moves, varying the resistance between the fuel gauge and ground. The resistance in an analog fuel gauge system is at a minimum when the tank is empty and at a maximum with the tank full. In an electronic fuel gauge system, it is just the reverse. Resistance is maximum when the tank is empty and minimum when the tank is full.

As fuel is used, the sender unit resistance decreases, increasing the sender unit voltage signal. The sender unit signal is passed through a voltage-controlled oscillator that changes it into a cycles-per-second signal to

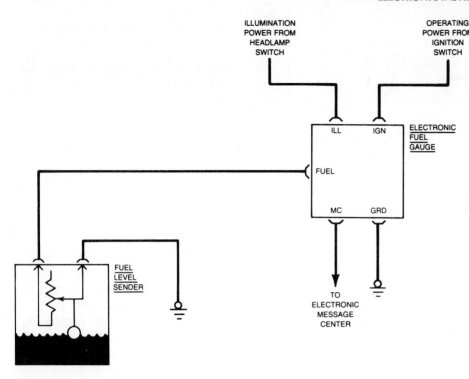

Figure 17-17. A block diagram of an electronic fuel gauge. (Ford)

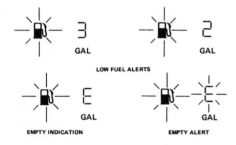

Figure 17-18. Typical low fuel level displays. (Ford)

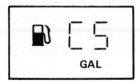

Figure 17-19. Typical fuel gauge service alerts. (Ford)

An open or a short in the circuit also can be displayed and will remain displayed until the condition has been corrected. The method of display differs according to the fuel gauge or instrument cluster design. Figure 17-19 shows one method. If the problem in the circuit is intermittent, the display will alternate between the alert and the normal display.

Temperature Gauge. The operation of an electronic temperature gauge, figure 17-20, is similar to that of the electronic fuel gauge. The temperature gauge sender unit is a thermistor. As you learned in chapter 6, a thermistor is a resistor whose resistance changes with changes in temperature. Thermistors used in temperature gauge circuits generally are negative temperature coefficient (NTC) thermistors. They have low resistance at high temperatures and high resistance at low temperatures. When a cold engine is first started, the sender unit resistance is high. This causes the sender unit to transmit a low voltage signal to the instrument module, where it is translated into a low temperature reading on the gauge display. As the engine warms up and coolant temperature increases, the sender unit resistance drops. The sender unit transmits a high voltage signal to the module, which changes the display to indicate a higher coolant temperature. If the coolant reaches a predetermined temperature, an alert function in the display flashes on and off to warn the driver of an overheating condition. This may take various forms: a flashing ISO symbol, a flashing red x, the word HOT in red, etc.

Other Gauges. Oil pressure and charging system voltage also may be displayed on electronic instrument clusters, although many systems continue to use warning lamps. When an oil pressure display is used, the instrument module receives its signal from a resistance-type sender unit installed in an oil passage near the oil filter. The circuit works the same as in an analog gauge system, with the pressure displayed in the form of a bar graph.

the microprocessor. The microprocessor counts the cycles-per-second signal from the oscillator, changing it into a signal to change the display on the instrument cluster. In some systems, the microprocessor sends an output signal to the trip minder or message center for its use.

The fuel gauge microprocessor is programmed to display various alert messages. An alert may take the form of an incandescent bulb or a symbol on the cluster. In most systems, a low-fuel alert is displayed when the sender unit indicates that there is approximately one-eighth of a tank of fuel left. The alert is generally turned on by a switch in the sender unit if a low-fuel warning lamp is used. Where the alert takes the form of a flashing fuel pump or other display symbol, it is controlled by the cluster microprocessor. The microprocessor can be programmed to flash the symbol while indicating the amount of usable fuel remaining in the tank. As the level continues to drop, the figure representing remaining fuel will change first to an E, then to a flashing E, figure 17-18.

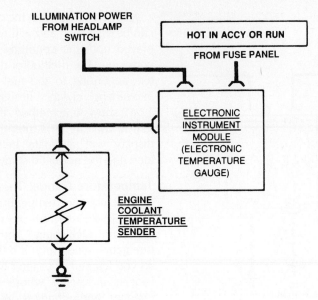

Figure 17-20. A block diagram of an electronic temperature gauge. (Ford)

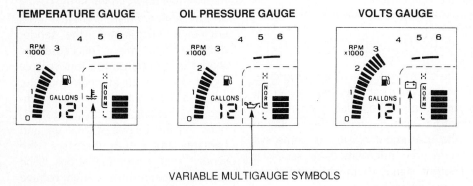

Figure 17-21. This multigauge display can be directed to show engine rpm, fuel remaining, temperature, oil pressure, and system voltage. (Ford)

Charging system voltage is calculated by comparing voltage to the instrument module against a reference voltage. The display also takes the form of a bar graph.

Some systems use a multigauge. This is generally a single display module, figure 17-21, whose function is changed by depressing a gauge select button. Because the functions are displayed sequentially, depressing the button once will change the display in figure 17-21 from temperature to oil pressure. Depressing it a second time will bring up the voltage function. To return to the temperature function, the button must be depressed three more times to run through the tachometer and fuel displays. A bar graph is used in all displays, with the function indicated by a fuel pump, a thermometer, an oil can, or a battery symbol.

Trip Computers

A trip computer is a form of calculator. All trip computers perform similar functions using speed and fuel inputs. Depending upon its design, a trip computer provides the driver with a variety of information that supple-

ments the standard vehicle instrumentation, such as:

• Average and instantaneous fuel economy
• Elapsed time and distance
• Average vehicle speed
• Distance to destination
• Estimated time of arrival
• Distance to empty with remaining fuel
• Clock functions
• Trip odometer

The more sophisticated trip computers closely parallel vehicle information or message centers, which we will look at later in this section.

The Ford Tripminder system consists of an electronic module assembly containing the circuitry, display, and keyboard. It receives a speed signal from the speed sensor (mechanical cluster) or the electronic instrument cluster microprocessor. Fuel flow data is provided by a fuel flow sensor on carbureted engines or the electronic engine control (EEC) module on fuel-injected engines. As figure 17-22 shows, the circuit is a simple one, with only two inputs to the solid-state module. The module calculates time, trip mileage and speed, fuel economy, and fuel consumption using its clock function and the two inputs. When the engine is first started and during normal driving, the Tripminder displays its clock function. The driver selects the desired display with the bottom row of buttons, figure 17-23. Each button has a dual function; depressing the button a second time brings up an alternate display. The set button changes the day, time, date, and month clock functions. The display can be changed from English to metric and back with the top center button. The reset button resets the trip function.

Chrysler has used three generations of trip computers. The Travel Computer introduced in 1983 was replaced by the Navigator in 1984. The Traveler introduced on some 1986 models replaced the Navigator in 1988.

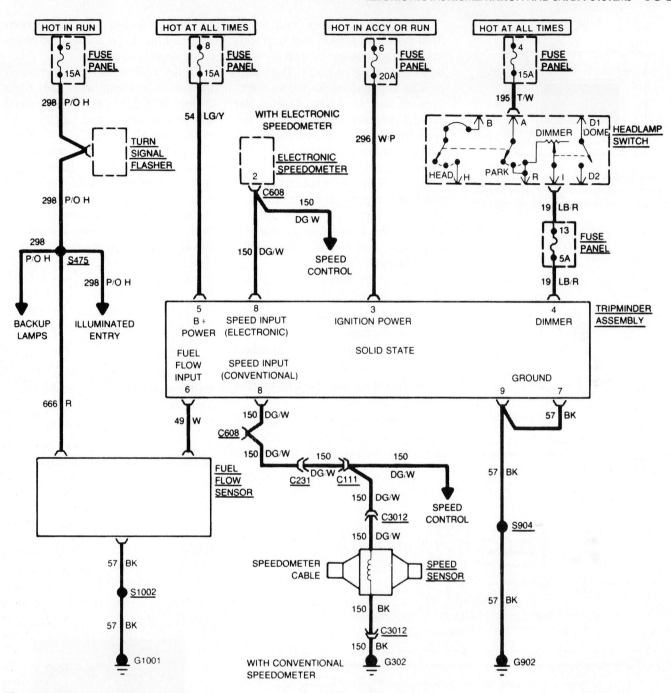

Figure 17-22. Circuit diagram of the Ford Tripminder system used with a carbureted engine. (Ford)

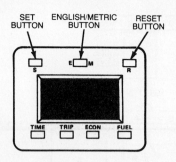

Figure 17-23. Tripminder functions are displayed on a vacuum fluorescent display and controlled by two sets of buttons. (Ford)

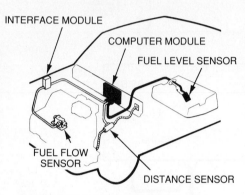

Figure 17-24. The components of Chrysler's Travel Computer system. (Chrysler)

The Travel Computer used inputs from the speed sensor, fuel tank sensor, and fuel flow sensor with an interface module, figure 17-24. The inputs provide calculations for the six functions shown in figure 17-25. The Travel Computer works much like the Ford Tripminder described earlier but has a separate switch module and display screen.

The Navigator is a second-generation trip computer that combines the separate switch module and display screen of the Travel Computer into a single unit and provides three additional outputs, figure 17-26.

The Traveler differs from the Navigator in three ways:

1. The fuel flow signal is provided by the logic module.

2. Only five functions are provided (clock functions are not included).

3. All functions are operated by two pushbuttons.

One pushbutton selects the English or metric mode. The other pushbutton lets the driver cycle through the displayed conditions. Depressing both pushbuttons at the same time resets the resettable displays.

Other carmakers' trip computers operate in a similar way. They differ mainly in the functions offered and the way in which the functions are displayed. All rely on speed sensors and fuel level sensors to provide the basic inputs used in calculating the particular displays. Late-model GM cars with a body computer module (BCM) include the trip computer functions as part of the climate control and driver information center (CCDIC), figure 17-27. The CCDIC receives its inputs from the BCM on the serial data link. The driver information center (DIC) is the lower portion of the CCDIC and has eight pushbuttons to select the desired display. Once a function has been selected, it is displayed on the liquid crystal display (LCD) panel above the pushbuttons. The DIC display panel also is used to display vehicle system diagnostics.

Menu-Driven Instrumentation

Buick uses a cathode ray tube (CRT) display on 1986 and later Riviera and other models. The CRT display combines two attributes of a personal computer: it uses touch-screen control and is menu driven. A touch-sensitive mylar switch panel on the

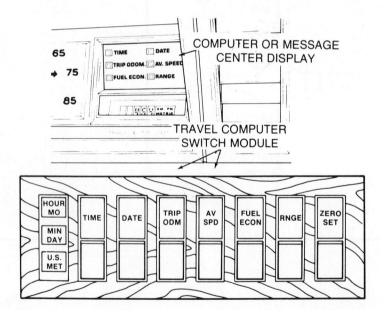

Figure 17-25. Chrysler's Travel Computer used a separate switch module located below the display window. Indicator lamps above the window light up to inform the driver which function is being displayed. (Chrysler)

Figure 17-26. Chrysler's Navigator is a second-generation trip computer offering more functions and combining the function selection and display panels in one unit. (Chrysler)

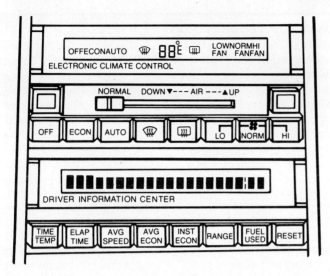

Figure 17-27. The Climate Control and Driver Information Center (CCDIC) used on many late-model GM vehicles displays driver-requested information and automatically displays driver warning messages. (Cadillac)

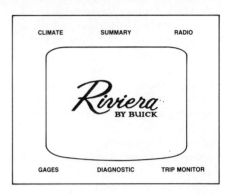

Figure 17-28. The Buick CRT displays this page when the vehicle is entered. (Buick)

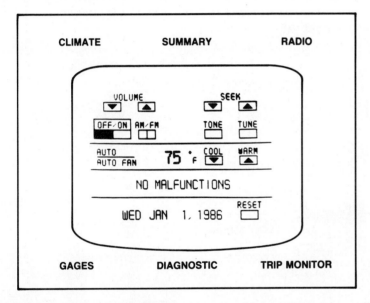

Figure 17-29. Turning on the ignition of a CRT-equipped Buick brings up the summary page. (Buick)

TRIP MONITOR PAGE

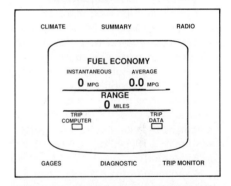

Figure 17-30. Touching the word Trip Monitor on the Buick CRT brings up this page. Further information is brought up by touching either small rectangle on the display screen. (Buick)

face of the CRT contains a series of very thin wires coded by row and column. When the CRT screen is touched in certain places, a light beam is blocked. This activates designated switches in the panel to signal the control circuitry. The requested information is then displayed on the CRT screen.

Menu-driven instrumentation uses a program that gives the driver various choices from a list or "menu" of information concerning several areas of vehicle operation. Figure 17-28 shows the first page that appears when the CRT is activated. Once the ignition is turned on, the summary page appears, figure 17-29. This gives the driver access to the functions and displays that are used most frequently.

To show how the system works, suppose that we touch the trip monitor function at the bottom right of the display. The trip monitor page will appear, with additional functions available by touching either the trip computer or trip data blocks, figure 17-30. The body computer module (BCM) performs the necessary calculations for the functions that are se-

WHAT'S NEW IN LCD TECHNOLOGY?

The twisted nematic (TN) call is used in most liquid crystal displays at the present. TN cells provide the best contrast and colors and offer the designer the most potential for graphically styled displays, as long as they remain relatively small in size. When TN cells are used for large displays, their resolution breaks down because of the pixel density and a reduction in contrast caused by using a multiplex system to light up the pixels. (Pixels are the points of color in the display image; the more pixels, the sharper and brighter the image.)

To solve the problem and permit the use of larger and more graphic LCD panels, metal-insulator-metal (MIM) technology is being applied to TN cells. In this design, every pixel has its own semiconductor switch element that supplies it with a defined voltage. This minimizes the undesirable contrast loss that occurs when pixels are driven through a multiplex arrangement.

Manufacture of TN cells with MIM technology requires that the MIM elements be applied as thin-film elements to one of the substrates in the cell. This complicates the manufacturing process because several extra steps are needed to construct the cell. Figure 1 is a cross section of a TN cell using integrated MIM elements.

A variation of the TN cell is the supertwisted (ST) nematic cell. This cell allows a higher multiplex rate to drive the pixels and gives improved electro-optic reaction. Molecules in the liquid crystal layer of a typical TN cell are twisted 90 degrees; those in the supertwisted nematic cell can be twisted up to 270 degrees. The higher multiplex rate possible with this type of cell is offset by color and temperature problems. The ST nematic cell has an inherent color that limits its uses in displays. The temperature range in which the cell will operate satisfactorily is not great enough at this time for use in automobile displays.

The greatest potential seems to rest with the ferro liquid crystal (FLC) device. An FLC has an extremely rapid switch reaction, very high multiplex rates, and a very long bistable memory. The bistable memory can retain the image even when the cell's driver is off. When the driver is turned back on, the memorized image can be written over.

The molecular order of an FLC allows two different but stable orientations without the application of voltage. The orientations result in different light transmission and opposite permanent electrical polarization. Figure 2 shows a cross section of an FLC.

The eventual goal of LCD technology is to develop cells that can create an easy-to-read display with high information density. For example, a liquid crystal shutter could be used to create a variable color display that would change speedometer readout color above a certain speed, or change the color of the fuel gauge display according to the fuel level in the tank. MIM, ST, and FLC research are all pointing in the direction of better and more useful LCD displays.

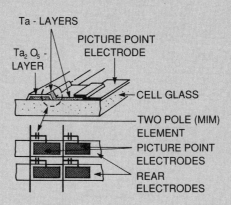

Ta - LAYERS
$Ta_2 O_5$ - LAYER
PICTURE POINT ELECTRODE
CELL GLASS
TWO POLE (MIM) ELEMENT
PICTURE POINT ELECTRODES
REAR ELECTRODES

Figure 1.

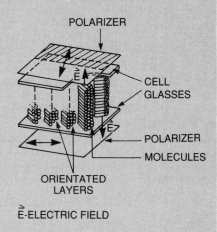

POLARIZER
CELL GLASSES
POLARIZER
MOLECULES
ORIENTATED LAYERS
E-ELECTRIC FIELD

Figure 2.

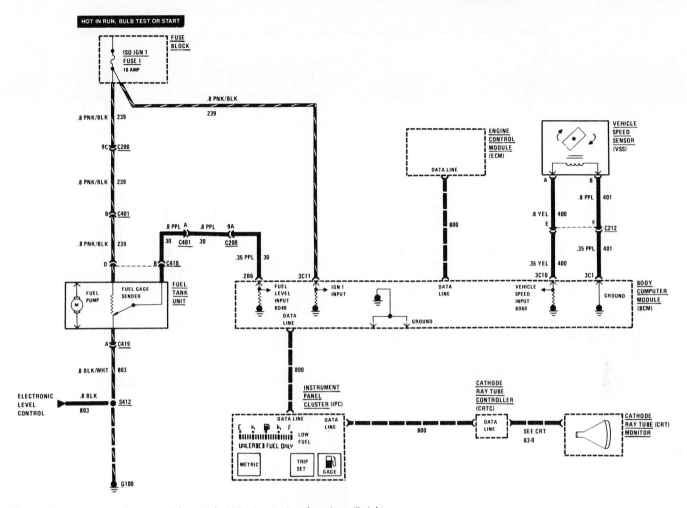

Figure 17-31. Circuit diagram of the Buick CRT trip monitor function. (Buick)

lected, transmitting the required data to the cathode ray tube controller (CRTC) for display on the CRT. Three inputs are required by the BCM to perform the trip monitor functions:

- Fuel tank level provided by the sender unit resistance
- Vehicle speed provided by the speed sensor
- Amount of fuel used provided by the ECM in the form of injector pulse width and flow rate data

Figure 17-31 is a schematic of the trip monitor function. In other modes, the CRT provides menus that let you retrieve vehicle trouble codes and check or control the gauge readings, radio, and air conditioning system.

Electronic Vehicle Information Centers (Message Centers)

The amount and type of information provided by electronic vehicle information centers, or message centers, as they are sometimes called, varies considerably among carmakers and vehicle designs. The term "message center" is loosely used to describe a display system that provides the driver with information about certain monitored systems, figure 17-32. Three major types of information are provided to the driver by most message centers:

- Trip computer function
- Operating information, such as oil pressure and coolant temperature

- Convenience information, such as burned-out bulbs and open doors

Message centers use a variety of display techniques. All message centers have a digital display for certain functions, but some of the information also may be displayed by incandescent warning lamps, a buzzer, or a chime.

The main function of a message center is to receive inputs from various sensors, process them through the control module, and display the appropriate information to the driver. If a trip computer function is included, the driver interacts with the message center as an input source. In most systems, the module input is received as a result of a switch closing to ground, a signal interpreted by the

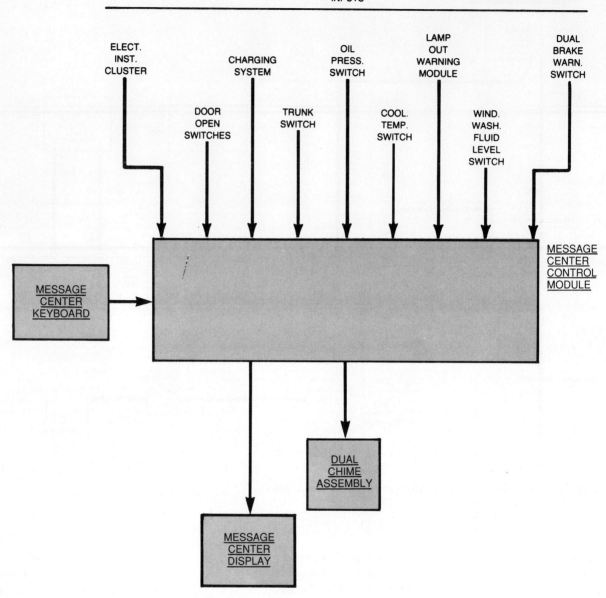

Figure 17-32. A typical message center block diagram. (Ford)

module as an abnormal condition. The module processes the input signal and sends an output signal to the display.

Figures 17-33 and 17-34 are circuit diagrams that represent the variations in message center design. The system shown in figure 17-33 provides only the trip computer and operating information functions. The system shown in figure 17-34 provides both of these functions, as well as convenience information concerning lamps, doors, and fluid level.

ELECTRONICALLY HEATED WINDSHIELDS

Windshields coated with a conductive material are used on some late-model vehicles. The conductive material can be electrically heated to melt frost and ice. This is similar to the electrically controlled rear window defogger grid system you studied in chapter 16, but is operated by a solid-state module and the onboard computer instead of a timer relay.

A standard 3-layer windshield con-

taining a plastic laminate (to provide impact protection) is coated with a mixture of silver and zinc oxide on the outside of the glass layer facing the driver. Horizontal silver bus bars are positioned at the top and bottom of the windshield. The top bus bar connects the conductive material to the ground circuits; the bottom bus bar connects to the power feed circuit. Figure 17-35 shows the system components of the system that are used on the Ford Taurus and Mercury Sable.

The engine must be running to pro-

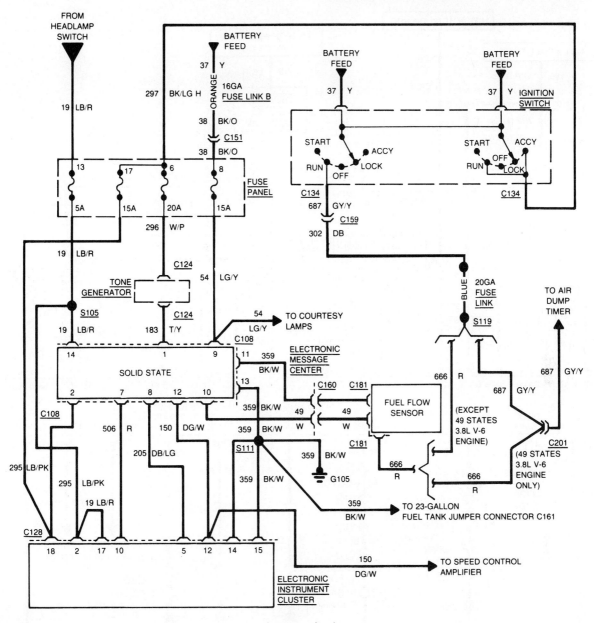

Figure 17-33. A typical two-function message center circuit schematic. (Ford)

vide alternator output and the interior of the vehicle must be below 40 degrees before the system will operate. When the system is turned on, the control module:

- Turns on an indicator lamp
- Shuts off the voltage regulator and turns on the alternator output control relay to switch alternator output from the electrical system to the windshield's power circuit
- Turns on the voltage regulator to restore alternator output

Through this process, the control module connects the windshield power circuit, figure 17-36, to the alternator output terminal through the alternator output control relay. During the 4-minute cycle that the windshield power circuit is activated, the remainder of the vehicle's electrical system depends on the battery for power.

When the battery is disconnected from the alternator, its voltage will drop to about 12 volts. This drop in

battery voltage is sensed by the voltage regulator, which responds by full-fielding the alternator. With the battery no longer in the charging circuit and the alternator providing full-field power, alternator output voltage will increase to between 30 and 70 volts, according to engine speed.

The control module monitors both the alternator and the battery. It prevents windshield overload at higher engine speeds by limiting alternator output to 70 volts. It also prevents

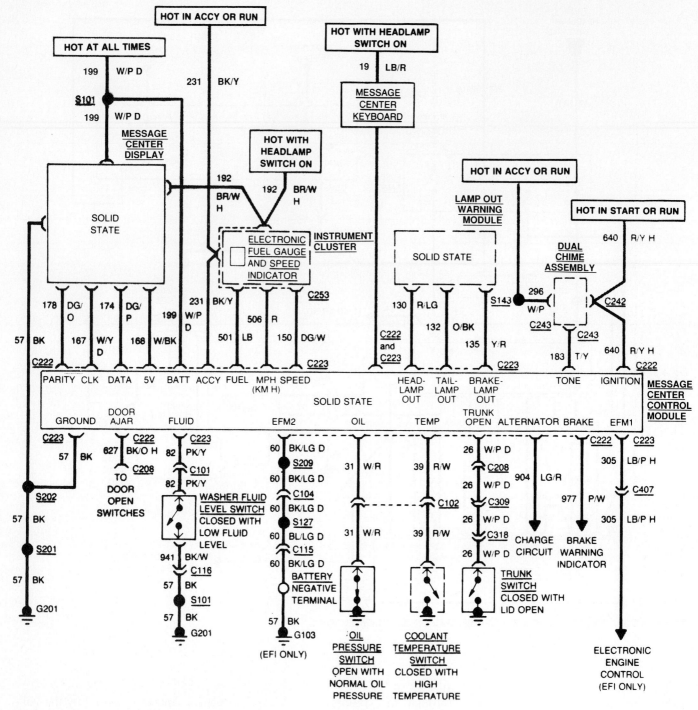

Figure 17-34. A typical 3-function message center circuit schematic. (Ford)

battery drain whenever battery voltage drops below 11 volts by cutting off power to the alternator output control relay and reconnecting the electrical system to the alternator.

The control module also is connected to the onboard computer through the same wiring used by the air conditioning compressor On signal. If the heated windshield system is turned on but the vehicle is not shifted into gear, the control module signals the onboard computer to increase engine speed to about 1,400 rpm. The higher engine speed will turn the alternator fast enough to provide the required output. When the transmission is shifted into gear, the onboard

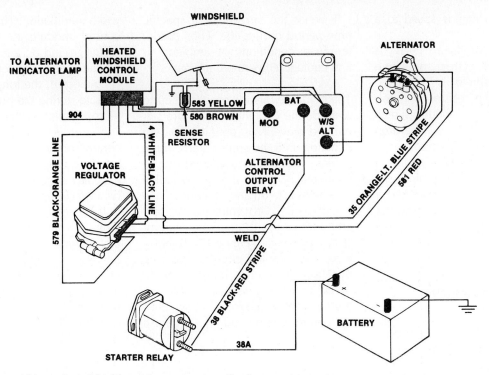

Figure 17-35. The Ford heated windshield system components. (Ford)

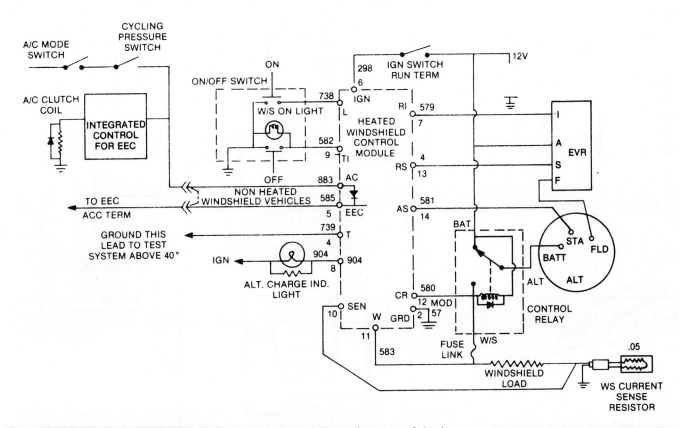

Figure 17-36. The heated windshield circuit schematic shows the low-voltage control circuit and the high-voltage power circuit. (Ford)

computer returns engine speed to a normal idle.

A sensing resistor, figure 17-37, is used to prevent system operation when the windshield is damaged. Voltage across the resistor is monitored by the control module, which turns off the system if a voltage drop (indicating a crack) is detected.

Circuit protection is provided by a 15-ampere fuse in the fuse block for the low-voltage control circuit and a fusible link at the alternator output control relay for the high-voltage power circuit.

ELECTRONIC COOLING FAN CONTROL

Although computer control of electric cooling fans is still in its early stages, it appears that there will be as many variations of the control system as there are with noncomputer-controlled cooling fans.

Fan control on late-model 4-cylinder Chrysler engines is managed by the onboard computer, which senses coolant temperature. The computer uses this input to cycle the fan on and off according to the following conditions:

• It cycles the fan on if the air conditioning clutch is engaged.
• It cycles the fan on and off at different coolant temperatures depending upon engine rpm.

• It cycles the fan on for a specific time period during idle when predetermined conditions of ambient air and coolant temperature are met.

The computer also is programmed to override the coolant temperature signal and prevent fan operation during cranking until the engine starts. If the vehicle has onboard diagnostics, a fault code 35 is set when the fan relay does not cycle on and off correctly.

Late-model GM vehicles use several approaches to computer control of the cooling fan. Figure 17-38 shows a basic fan control circuit containing dual fans. The body computer module (BCM) receives a voltage signal from the fan control module and switches the control line on and off with pulse

width modulation. This causes the fan control module to switch the fan motor ground on and off, controlling the fan speed. The longer the ground is connected, the longer the fans will operate during the pulse period. This represents the fan speed.

A current flow sensor in the fan control module tells the module when the fans are operating. A feedback generator signal to the BCM alternates between 12 volts when the fans are off to zero volts when the fans are running. This tells the BCM that the fans are operating properly. The current flow sensor also provides circuit protection. If a fan stops rotating for any reason, the sensor switches the feedback line on and off to tell the BCM that there is a problem with excessive

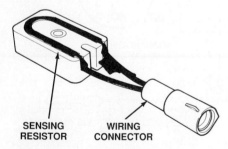

Figure 17-37. The sensing resistor is located with the alternator output control relay under the right front fender and prevents the heated windshield system from operating if the windshield is damaged. (Ford)

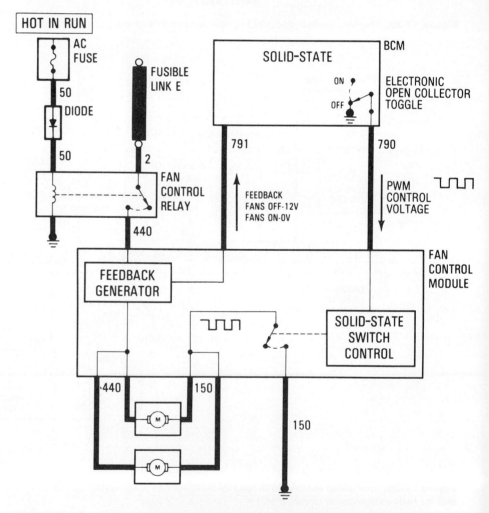

Figure 17-38. Dual cooling fans are controlled by pulse width modulation from the body computer module (BCM). A feedback generator in the fan control module tells the BCM whether or not fan operation is correct. (GM)

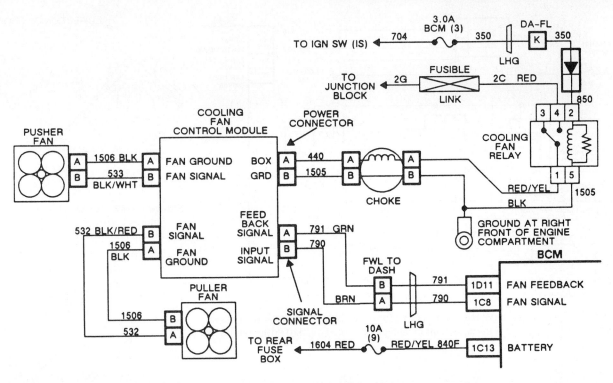

Figure 17-39. Cadillac's version of a BCM-operated cooling fan circuit uses pulse width modulation to control the fans at the higher of the two speeds calculated. (Cadillac)

current in the system. The BCM then modifies the pulse width modulation of the control line to reduce fan operation and eliminate the excessive current.

Cadillac uses a variation of this system in which the BCM controls the cooling fans based on engine coolant temperature and air conditioning system high-side temperature. This circuit is shown in figure 17-39. The BCM constantly calculates a fan speed according to coolant temperature. If the air conditioning system is on, it also calculates a second fan speed based on the compressor input, using the higher of the two fan speeds.

The BCM sends a pulse-width-modulated signal to the fan power module, which uses the signal to operate the fans. Under certain conditions, the calculated fan speed may not be used. For example, if the vehicle speed is less than 20 mph and ambient temperature exceeds 80° F, or the high-side temperature exceeds 122° F, the BCM sends the power module a 50 percent duty cycle to

prevent rapid refrigerant pressure rise at idle. When vehicle speed climbs above 25 mph, the BCM returns fan control to normal.

If the BCM signal duty cycle exceeds 90 percent, the fan power module operates the fans at 100 percent. A duty cycle of less than 10 percent results in no signal from the module and the fans remain off. Any BCM duty cycle in between 10 percent and 90 percent results in a variable output between 0 percent and 100 percent from the fan power module. If either sensor used in the system fails, the BCM provides a duty cycle signal that results in maximum fan speed. Should the BCM fail or develop an open in the signal line, the fan power module also operates the fans at maximum speed. The fan power module sends a feedback signal to the BCM. If this signal does not verify the BCM commands, the BCM will set a code B441 and display a failure message on the CCDIC.

An ECM-controlled system is used with the cooling fans on some Buick

and Oldsmobile models, figure 17-40. The standard puller-type fan runs on two speeds; the optional pusher-type fan runs at a single speed and is activated whenever the standard fan is operating at its higher speed. Fan control is not exclusive with the ECM; high speed on both fans also can be activated by the air conditioning high-pressure switch under specific conditions.

One high-speed and one low-speed relay is used with the single fan application. Systems with the optional fan have an additional high-speed relay. All relays receive power through a fusible link and are energized when the ECM or A/C pressure switch closes a ground. The low-speed relay is energized by the ECM when engine coolant temperature reaches a predetermined value, turning on the single fan. If coolant temperature climbs beyond a second predetermined value or if refrigerant pressure exceeds a specified value, the high-speed relay is energized and the fan speed increases. If the optional fan is installed,

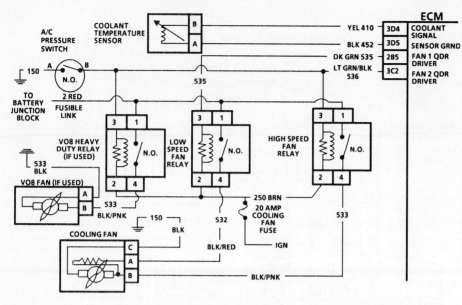

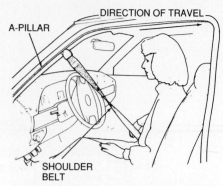

Figure 17-42. The shoulder belt or harness moves toward the A pillar when the door is opened. (Ford)

Figure 17-40. Buick and Oldsmobile use an ECM-controlled cooling fan circuit with relays energized either by the ECM or the air conditioning high-pressure switch. (Oldsmobile)

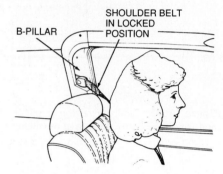

Figure 17-43. Closing the door causes the shoulder belt or harness to travel to the B pillar, where it locks in place. (Ford)

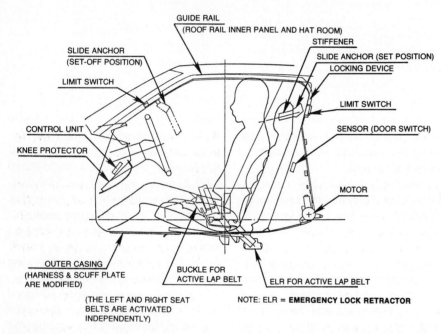

Figure 17-41. Components of a typical motorized passive restraint system. (Chrysler)

Passive Restraints

Figure 17-41 shows the components and operation of a typical motorized shoulder harness system. The system contains an inertia-lock retractor installed at the inboard side of each seat and a motor-driven track assembly located above each door opening. Some systems use a knee protector for each occupant.

When the vehicle door is opened, the outer end of the shoulder harness moves forward to a position on, or just behind, the A pillar, figure 17-42, allowing easy access for entry or exit. When the door is closed and the ignition switch turned on, the outer end of the shoulder harness moves to the rear along a track on the roof side rail to a point on the B pillar behind the occupant's shoulder, figure 17-43. This rearward movement of the shoulder harness automatically positions it on the occupant. In a 2-point system, the

it operates whenever the standard fan is running at high speed.

AUTOMATIC PASSIVE RESTRAINT AND AIRBAG SYSTEMS

Automatic passive restraints are safety systems that have been mandated by

law. Starting with the 1987 model year, a certain percentage of vehicles built by automakers contain a motorized seatbelt system that positions either the shoulder harness (2-point) or shoulder harness and lap belt (3-point) on the front seat occupants. Airbags are currently optional equipment offered by some manufacturers, but it appears likely that they eventually will be mandated by law.

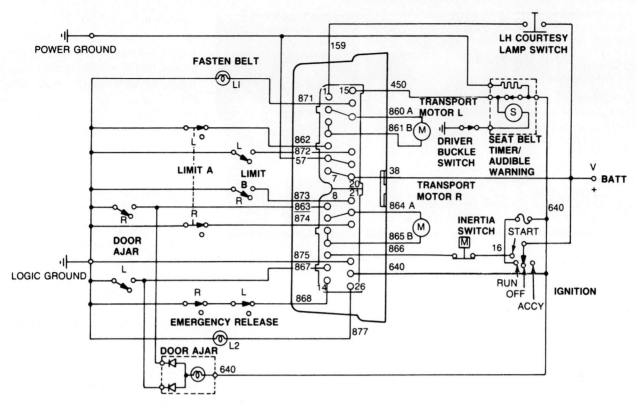

Figure 17-44. Circuit diagram of the Ford Escort passive restraint system. (Ford)

occupant must manually secure the lap belt; the 3-point system eliminates this operation. An emergency release mechanism is provided in case the system refuses to function as the result of an accident or vehicle rollover. Some systems also have a manual knob on the drive motor that can be used if the system fails with the shoulder harness in the forward position.

A passive restraint system uses an electronic control module to monitor system circuitry, figure 17-44, and control the shoulder harness movement. The module receives inputs from the following sensors:

- Door ajar switches
- Left and right limit switches
- Emergency release switch

System outputs from the module activate the drive motors to position the shoulder harness on each side and to operate the various warning indicators if the system is malfunctioning.

The door-ajar switches indicate the position of the door. The switch is open when the door is closed and

allows the harness to move to the B pillar when the ignition switch is turned on. Opening or leaving the door ajar closes the switch, and the harness remains at the A pillar regardless of ignition switch position.

The limit switches located at either end of the harness track inform the module of the harness position. When the harness moves away from the A pillar, the A switch closes. As the harness reaches the end of its travel at the B pillar, it opens the B switch and the module shuts off power to the drive motor. Opening the door causes the module to reverse the power feed to the drive motor and the harness returns to the A pillar, opening the closed A switch.

The normally closed emergency release switches open whenever one or both release levers are operated. This causes the module to turn on the instrument cluster seatbelt warning lamp, seatbelt chime, console release lever lamp, and any other indicators used in the system. It also prevents the shoulder harness retractors from locking. Returning the release levers to

their normal position closes the release switches and turns off all warning indicators.

In the Ford circuit shown in figure 17-44, the fuel pump inertia switch is wired into the system. This normally closed switch opens when the vehicle receives an impact exceeding 5 mph or rolls over during an accident and shuts off power to the fuel pump. In the passive restraint system, it prevents the shoulder harness from moving to the A pillar if a door opens during an accident. If the inertia switch is tripped, the passive restraint system will remain disabled until the switch is reset.

Airbag Systems

An airbag system is designed to supplement the driver's seatbelt system. When the airbag is activated by a head-on collision, a solid material is converted to nitrogen gas and fills an expandable bag that provides a cushion between the driver and the steering column, figure 17-45, to absorb impact energy.

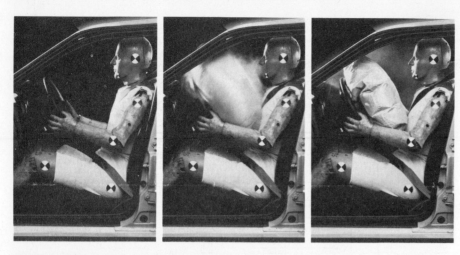

Figure 17-45. This photo sequence shows the operation of an airbag system. A sudden deceleration detected by the crash sensors causes the system to activate. The airbag is inflated to protect the driver, then almost immediately deflated. (Ford)

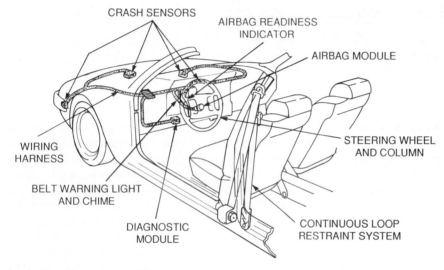

Figure 17-46. The Ford Tempo and Mercury Topaz supplemental airbag system components. (Ford)

Ford. The system used in 1986 and later Ford Tempo and Mercury Topaz models is typical and contains the following components, figure 17-46:

- Airbag module
- Crash sensors
- Diagnostic module
- Readiness indicator
- Warning lamp and chime
- Wiring harness

A similar system introduced on the 1989 Lincoln Continental provides airbags for both the driver and passenger, figure 17-47.

The airbag module contains a bag made of neoprene-coated nylon. When activated, the bag fills to a volume of 2 cubic feet in about 40 milliseconds. The bag is encased in an injection-molded plastic trim cover and liner assembly. As the bag inflates, the seams of the cover and liner assembly separate, allowing deployment of the inflating bag. A mounting plate and retainer ring are used to connect and seal the airbag

module to the inflator. A wiring shield on the mounting plate protects the wiring connection to the igniter to ensure that it will fire when triggered. Figure 17-48 shows the relationship of the airbag module components, steering column, and steering wheel.

A solid chemical gas generator inflator contains a sodium azide and copper oxide propellant, figure 17-49. When the igniter assembly is triggered, the propellant produces nitrogen gas to fill the airbag module. The nitrogen gas passes through a diffuser where it is filtered and cooled before inflating the airbag. A clock spring electrical connector, figure 17-48, in the steering wheel conducts electrical signals to the module while permitting steering wheel rotation. The igniter assembly also contains material to absorb any EMI and RFI energy that might possibly cause accidental activation of the propellant without a signal from the crash sensors.

The electrical system, figure 17-50, receives power directly from the battery and performs the following functions:

- Detects deployment level impact
- Switches electric power to the igniter
- Monitors the system to ensure readiness

The crash sensors, figure 17-51, are installed on the left and right front side members, in the upper center of the radiator support, and on the passenger compartment cowl beneath the forward part of the windshield. They function according to the direction and amount of impact. Crash sensors are normally open electrical switches designed to close when subjected to a predetermined impact. A ball inside the sensor moves through a guide tube in a direction away from the influence of a bias magnet toward a set of contact points. A dampening effect is provided by the clearance between the tube and ball. The ball must bridge the contact points to close the switch. When the switch closes, the circuit is completed and power is sent to the airbag igniter. The igniter, figure 17-52, is a combustible device that

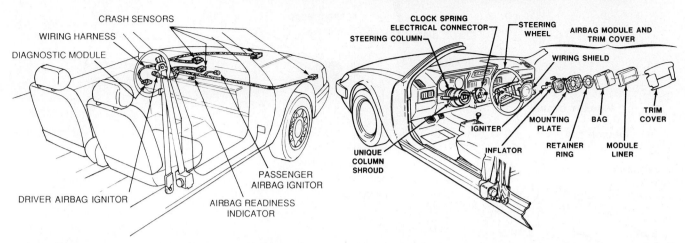

Figure 17-47. The Lincoln Continental supplemental airbag system provides airbags for both the driver and the passenger seats. (Ford)

Figure 17-48. The airbag module is contained in a module line under the steering wheel trim cover. When activated, it pops off the trim cover and expands between the steering wheel and driver. (Ford)

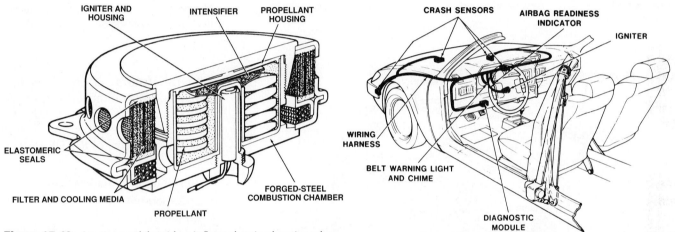

Figure 17-49. A cutaway of the airbag inflator showing location of the igniter and the solid chemical gas material. (Ford)

Figure 17-50. The airbag electrical harness. (Ford)

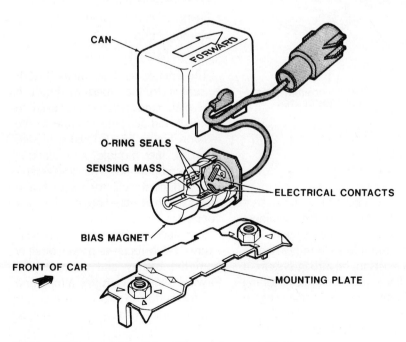

Figure 17-51. A cutaway of the airbag crash sensor. (Ford)

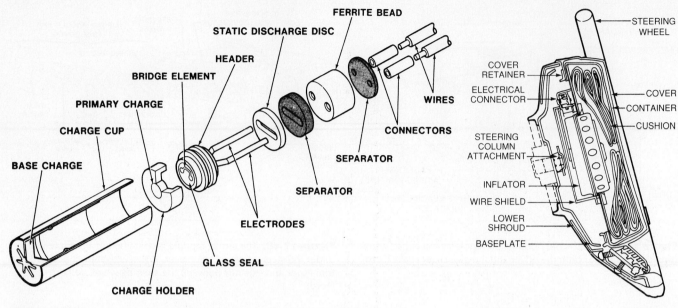

Figure 17-52. An exploded view of the airbag igniter assembly installed in the airbag inflator.

Figure 17-54. A cutaway of the SIR steering wheel module. (GM)

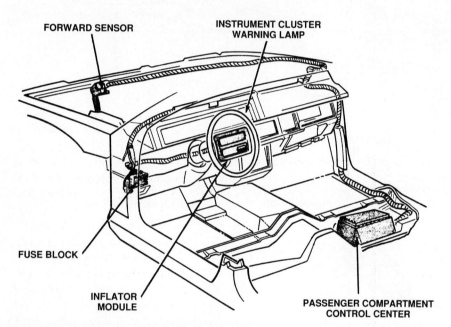

Figure 17-53. Much of the GM supplemental inflatable restraint (SIR) system is located underneath the passenger seat. (GM)

General Motors. Operation of the GM supplemental inflatable restraint (SIR) system, figure 17-53, is similar to the Ford system described above. The major components of the SIR system are:

- Inflator (airbag) module
- Crash sensors
- Arming sensor
- Control module
- Power supply (voltage converter)
- Energy reserve module
- warning lamp
- Wiring harness

The inflator module, figure 17-54, is similar to that used by Ford. A base-plate and retainer are used to connect and seal the module to the inflator. Figure 17-55 is an exploded view of the module and steering wheel components. The coil assembly conducts the electrical signals and works much like the Ford clock spring connector.

The special SIR wiring harness, figure 17-53, receives power directly from the battery and connects the forward sensor, warning lamp, and inflator module to the diagnosis center located underneath the passenger seat.

converts electric energy into thermal energy to ignite the inflator gas propellant.

The diagnostic module contains a microprocessor that runs a system self-check whenever the ignition switch is turned from Off to Run. When the self-check is completed, the module turns on the readiness indicator lamp in the instrument cluster. If the module determines that a problem exists in the airbag system, it will display a trouble code by flashing the indicator lamp and under certain conditions, may disarm the system until the problem has been corrected.

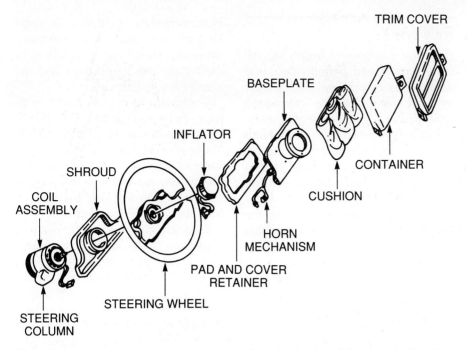

Figure 17-55. An exploded view of the SIR steering wheel and module components. (GM)

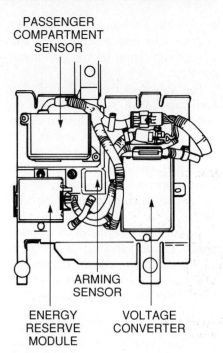

Figure 17-56. The heart of the SIR system is contained in the diagnosis center under the passenger seat. (GM)

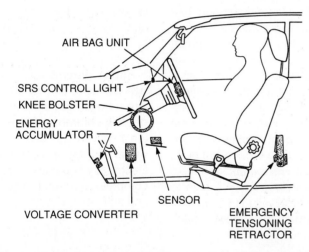

Figure 17-57. Components of the Mercedes-Benz supplemental restraint system (SRS).

The control center, figure 17-56, contains the:

• Passenger compartment crash sensor
• Control module
• Arming sensor
• Power supply (voltage converter)
• Energy reserve module

The control module microprocessor monitors the major system components and runs its self-test each time the ignition switch is turned on. If the system is performing properly, the instrument panel warning lamp will light for about 10 seconds and then go out. If the lamp does not go out after 15 seconds, does not come on, or comes on when the vehicle is running, the system requires service.

Two crash sensors, figure 17-51, are used. One is installed in front of the radiator support; the other is located in the control module assembly under the passenger seat. The crash sensors are normally open electrical switches designed to close when subjected to an impact equal to a barrier crash of about 10 mph. When the switches close, the circuit to the arming sensor in the control center is completed. The arming sensor verifies crash sensor input and signals the control module that a collision is taking place. The control module sends a deployment signal to the inflator module, and airbag deployment occurs.

The SIR system requires a minimum of 14.2 volts to operate. This required voltage is maintained by the power supply (voltage converter) unit, which boosts system voltage if battery voltage drops under 14.2 volts. The energy reserve unit is a capacitor that will provide enough voltage to deploy the system in case of a voltage drop or battery damage during impact.

Mercedes-Benz. The Mercedes-Benz supplemental restraint system (SRS) combines a 3-point seat belt with the airbag. The SRS system, figure 17-57, consists of an airbag unit in the steering column, an emergency tensioning retractor (ETR) on the passenger side, a sensor, an energy accumulator, the voltage converter, and an indicator lamp on the instrument panel.

The airbag works similarly to the Ford and GM systems described above. The ETR also contains an igniter device. During an impact with enough force, the high-pressure gas generated when the device ignites is used to operate a pulley that pulls the 3-point belt snugly against the passenger.

The SRS sensor consists of two integrated circuits and an acceleration pickup that determine the degree and direction of impact. When longitudinal deceleration of the vehicle is great enough, the sensor sends a voltage signal through a bypass filter to an amplifier, where the signal is processed to deploy the SRS system. During normal driving conditions, the sensor is disconnected from the circuit by a mercury switch.

The voltage converter provides a constant 12 volts to the sensor and energy accumulator, even if battery voltage drops as low as 4 volts. The energy accumulator works like a capacitor and acts as a backup for the battery to deliver current to the system in case of battery failure during an accident. The indicator lamp lights for approximately 10 seconds whenever the ignition is turned on to tell the driver that the system is operational.

SUMMARY

Electronic instrument clusters use the same sensors and perform the same functions as mechanical analog clusters, but can display the information faster and in a wider variety of ways. The microprocessor that controls an electronic system updates the display two to five times per second, instead of averaging the reading as an analog gauge does. The end result is more precise information provided to the driver in a more visually interesting way.

Trip computers are an onboard calculator that use a clock function and inputs from the speed and fuel sensors to calculate driver-directed information, such as average fuel consumption and estimated time of arrival. Electronic vehicle information or message centers are more sophisticated trip computers. Depending upon their design, they may provide three different functions: trip computer, operating information, and convenience information. Operating information is concerned with operating systems, such as oil pressure and coolant temperature. Convenience information informs the driver of problems such as a door left open or a burned-out bulb.

Menu-driven instrumentation uses a CRT with touch-sensitive screen to allow the driver to select the type and kind of information he needs. Such instrumentation provides the same kind of information as an electronic message center, but the method of calling up the information and the display mode differs.

Electronically heated windshields have much in common with electrically heated rear window defoggers. Those currently available use a solid-state module to disconnect the alternator from the charging system and reconnect it to the windshield circuit for a specified period of time.

Electric engine cooling fans may be controlled by the onboard computer in a variety of ways. In all designs, however, the computer relies on coolant temperature and air conditioning pressure switch signals to determine when to start and stop the fan.

Automatic passive restraints use a motorized track assembly to move the shoulder harness from one point to another. They may be 2-point or 3-point systems. Manual release switches are provided in case of a system failure or an accident.

Airbag systems use a small explosive charge to change a solid material into nitrogen gas that fills a bag in the steering column and provides a cushion between the driver and steering wheel during a head-on collision. Electrically operated crash sensors complete a circuit when impacted and activate the system.

REVIEW QUESTIONS

Multiple Choice

1. Mechanic A says that an electronic instrument cluster performs the same function as a mechanical analog cluster. Mechanic B says that an electronic instrument cluster uses the same sensors as a mechanical analog instrument cluster. Who is right?

a. A only
b. B only
c. both A and B
d. neither A nor B

2. Mechanic A says that the use of a stepper motor in an electronic speedometer prevents the odometer from being turned back. Mechanic B says that an electronic speedometer does not have to use a cable. Who is right?

a. A only
b. B only
c. both A and B
d. neither A nor B

3. Mechanic A says that the odometer in an electronic speedometer may use either a stepper motor or a nonvolatile RAM. Mechanic B says that an optical speed sensor contains a magnetic generator. Who is right?

a. A only
b. B only
c. both A and B
d. neither A nor B

4. Which of the following is not a part of an optical sensor?

a. phototransistor
b. slotted wheel
c. magnetic pickup
d. light-emitting diode (LED)

5. Which of the following is not used in a quartz analog display?

a. quartz clock circuit
b. gain selector circuit
c. driver circuit
d. output logic circuit

6. The speed sensor signal in the Chevrolet rotating-disc dial indicator system is used by four vehicle systems, each has its own requirements. How many different ways is the signal conditioned?

a. 1
b. 2

c. 3
d. 4

7. Mechanic A says that a service interval reminder can be programmed into an electronic speedometer display. Mechanic B says that some electronic clusters use incandescent warning lamps. Who is right?

a. A only
b. B only
c. both A and B
d. neither A nor B

8. Vehicle speed in GM systems is calculated by measuring the interval between the beginning of the pulses (signal frequency). Mechanic A says that the faster the vehicle is moving, the shorter the interval between pulses. Mechanic B says that the slower the vehicle is moving, the shorter the interval between pulses. Who is right?

a. A only
b. B only
c. both A and B
d. neither A nor B

9. Mechanic A says that the fuel gauge sender unit in an electronic gauge system is a thermistor. Mechanic B says that an electronic tachometer takes its signal from the ignition system. Who is right?

a. A only
b. B only
c. both A and B
d. neither A nor B

10. Mechanic A says that a trip computer is a form of calculator. Mechanic B says that all trip computers perform similar functions using speed and fuel inputs. Who is right?

a. A only
b. B only
c. both A and B
d. neither A nor B

11. Which electronic display device is used with menu-driven instrumentation?

a. LCD
b. LED
c. VFD
d. CRT

12. Which type of information is not provided the driver by most message centers?

a. trip computer information

b. operating information
c. navigational information
d. convenience information

13. Mechanic A says that the Ford electronically heated windshield receives its power from the battery. Mechanic B says that the windshield power comes from the alternator. Who is right?

a. A only
b. B only
c. both A and B
d. neither A nor B

14. The interior of a vehicle with Ford's heated windshield must be below what temperature before the system will work?

a. 40° F
b. 35° F
c. 30° F
d. 25° F

15. Which component in the Ford heated windshield system prevents the system from working if the windshield is damaged?

a. onboard computer
b. alternator output control relay
c. control module
d. sense resistor

16. Mechanic A says that some GM computer-controlled cooling fans are operated by pulse width modulation. Mechanic B says that some GM computer-controlled fan systems are operated by the BCM based on engine coolant temperature and air conditioning system high-side temperature. Who is right?

a. A only
b. B only
c. both A and B
d. neither A nor B

17. Mechanic A says that GM cooling fan systems are controlled by the BCM. Mechanic A says that GM cooling fan systems are controlled by the ECM. Who is right?

a. A only
b. B only
c. both A and B
d. neither A nor B

18. Which of the following sensors are used only in a Ford automatic passive restraint system?

a. door-ajar switches

b. limit switches

c. emergency release switch

d. inertia switch

19. Mechanic A says that opening the door of a vehicle equipped with an automatic passive restraint system will cause the belt to move toward the A pillar. Mechanic B says the belt will move toward the B pillar. Who is right?

a. A only

b. B only

c. both A and B

d. neither A nor B

20. An airbag system:

a. makes seatbelts unnecessary

b. is a passive collision protection system

c. is activated by the driver before a collision

d. all of the above

21. Mechanic A says that an airbag system will protect the driver from frontal impacts. Mechanic B says that an airbag system will protect the driver from frontal and side impacts. Who is right?

a. A only

b. B only

c. both A and B

d. neither A nor B

PART FIVE
ELECTRICAL AND ELECTRONIC ACCESSORIES

INTRODUCTION

Part Five of this book contains two chapters on automotive accessories. Chapter 18 outlines the common features of air conditioning controls and power windows, seats, and door locks that have been common options on cars and trucks for decades. The circuit installations and components of these systems are examples of carmakers' variations on the common principles that you learned in Part One of this book. There are more similarities than differences among the electrical accessories of different manufacturers.

Chapter 19 describes the electronic controls used on late-model versions of common accessory systems. Multiplex wiring systems are among the leading state-of-the-art electronic applications, and this chapter explains their installations on late-model cars.

Once again, you will see the electronic principles that you learned earlier applied to specific accessories as you compare chapter 18 to chapter 19. Electronic controls of traditional vehicle accessories will continue to multiply in the next few years. If you recognize the common features of all systems, you can keep up with the electronic revolution and remain a master automotive electronic technician.

18 ELECTRICAL ACCESSORIES

WHAT

The electrical systems that you studied in Part Four are essential to driver and vehicle safety. The electrical systems discussed in this chapter are primarily comfort and convenience features. All of these systems have been used for many years and are well defined in their design and operation.

Although there are slight variations among carmakers, most of the accessory circuits in this chapter operate according to a standard design. If you understand the basic components of an air conditioning or power window circuit and how the circuit works, you will be able to troubleshoot almost any of these circuits.

This chapter covers heating and air conditioning systems, power window, power seats, and power lock and latch systems currently in use.

WHY

Comfort and convenience systems generally are taken for granted since they are expected to work without problems and they usually do. When they do fail, however, the comfort or convenience offered by the system becomes a nuisance. Consider the power window system that fails in cold weather with a window down, or the power seat that stops working in a position that makes driving uncomfortable. When such a failure occurs, you will be expected to troubleshoot and correct the problem quickly.

This chapter explains the basic operating requirements of the more common comfort and convenience circuits. Once you understand these principles, you will be able to service such systems on any vehicle rapidly and efficiently.

GOALS

After completing this chapter, you should be able to:

1. List the components and explain the operation of:

  a. a heater system

  b. an air conditioning system

2. Explain how a power window system operates.

3. Explain the operation of:

  a. a permanent magnet motor

  b. an electromagnetic field motor

4. List the components and describe the operation of each of the following power seat systems:

  a. 2-way

  b. 4-way

  c. 6-way

5. Explain the operation of a power door lock system.

6. List the components of a power trunk release system.

ELECTRICAL HEATING AND AIR CONDITIONING CONTROLS

The heater is a basic comfort and convenience system found on almost all vehicles. It circulates hot engine coolant past a small radiator called a heater core. A motor-driven blower fan sends the hot air through ducting into the vehicle to keep the occupants warm and defrost the windshield.

Air conditioning (A/C) generally is an option but has become very popular, particularly in warm or humid areas. The air conditioning and heater systems are usually combined, using the same controls and ducting. Refrigerant from the air conditioning compressor is circulated through an evaporator. The blower fan sends the air over the cold fins of the evaporator, through the system ducting, to cool the interior of the vehicle.

Heater Systems

The electrical part of a heating system consists of a blower switch, the blower motor, and resistor block. Figure 18-1 is a circuit diagram of a simple heater system used by Ford. The circuit is wired for ground-side switching of the blower motor. In this type of circuit, the blower switch controls blower speed by sending the motor current through or around resistors on a resistor block, figure 18-2. The greater the amount of resistance, the slower the motor speed. GM and some other carmakers used a supply-side circuit during the 1970's in which the blower motor ran at low speed whenever the ignition was on. Customer complaints about blower motor noise, their inability to shut the blower motor off, and frequent resistor block replacement all were factors that led automakers to return to the ground side system shown in figure 18-1.

When the ignition switch is turned to the run position, voltage is applied to the blower motor in figure 18-1. With the blower switch off, the circuit is not grounded and the blower motor does not run. Turning the blower switch to its low speed position completes the circuit ground, sending current through the blower motor and all

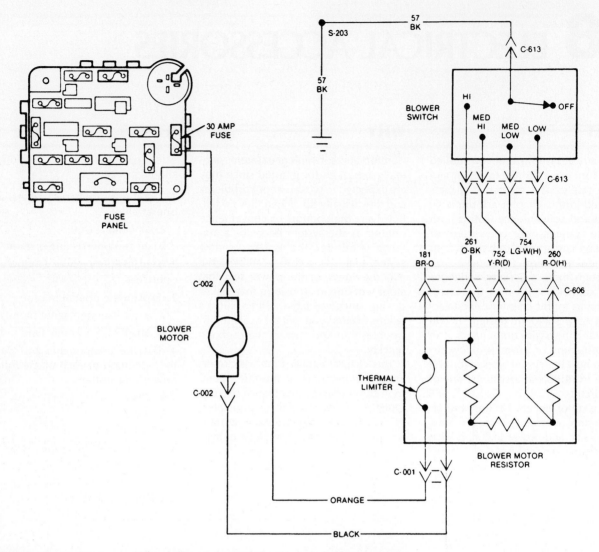

Figure 18-1. The Ford Tempo and Mercury Topaz electrical circuit is typical of heater circuits in which speed changes are made on the ground side instead of the supply side of the motor. (Ford)

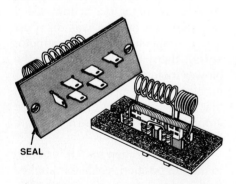

Figure 18-2. The number of resistors used on the resistor block depends upon the number of blower switch positions. (Chrysler)

three resistors. When the switch is moved to the medium-low position, current flows to the motor through two resistors; in the medium-high position, current flows through one resistor; and in the high position, current bypasses the resistor block and flows only through the blower motor.

Remember that current through the circuit always remains the same. Varying the resistance, however, changes the voltage applied to the motor. As voltage drop across the resistor block decreases from low speed to high speed, voltage across the motor increases. Higher voltage moves the same amount of current, but the motor turns faster.

Some systems (notably GM) have a relay between the blower motor and high switch position to reduce the current load carried by the blower switch. The Ford resistor block contains a thermal limiter, figure 18-3, through which current passes at all blower speeds except high speed. The thermal limiter is a protective device similar to a fuse and is installed at a specific distance from the resistors. If current passing through the thermal limiter heats it to a preset temperature (usually 212° F or 250° F) in any speed other than high blower, the wax material holding the limiter spring-loaded contacts melts. When the contacts separate, the resistor circuit opens

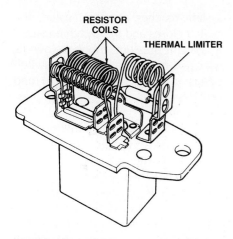

Figure 18-3. Ford resistor blocks contain a thermal limiter that acts as a circuit protection device. (Ford)

and shuts off the blower motor. Because the thermal limiter is an integral part of the resistor block and the contacts cannot be reset, the entire assembly must be replaced if the limiter opens.

Air Conditioning Systems

The electrical part of an air conditioning system uses the heater system blower switch, blower motor, and resistor block, figure 18-4. Heater circuit operation is the same as described earlier. The control assembly containing the blower switch also contains two other switches. The air conditioning on-off switch applies voltage to the electromagnetic clutch switch, turning the compressor on when the pressure switch is closed. A function clutch switch operates the compressor when the control unit function selector is in the defrost mode. On vehicles with an electric cooling fan, the fan is wired into the air conditioning circuit so that it will operate whenever the air conditioning compressor is running. A throttle kicker or idle speedup solenoid, also is wired into the air conditioning circuit. When the compressor is turned on, the solenoid increases engine idle

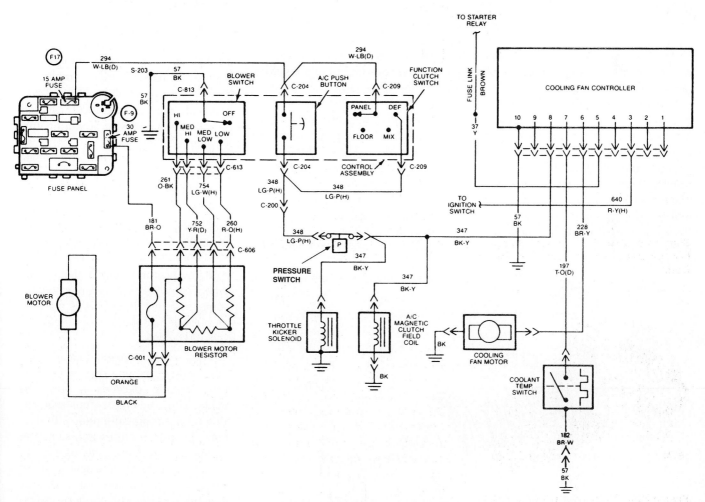

Figure 18-4. A basic manual air conditioning circuit used with Ford Tempo and Mercury Topaz models. (Ford)

speed to offset the compressor load on the engine. On many fuel-injected engines, idle speed is adjusted by an engine computer command to an idle air control (IAC) motor or an idle speed control (ISC) stepper motor.

Compressor and Clutch. The air conditioning compressor is mounted at the front of the engine and operated by a drive belt. Continuous compressor operation is a waste of energy, so most systems use an electromagnetic clutch, figure 18-5, to drive the compressor. The clutch locks and unlocks the compressor pulley to the compressor shaft. With the air conditioning off, the clutch is deenergized, and the pulley turns freely on the clutch hub or pulley bearing. When the clutch is energized, it acts like a short solenoid, magnetically drawing the drive and pulley assembly into engagement with the compressor to turn the compressor shaft.

Several late-model GM and Toyota A/C systems have variable-displacement compressors that do not require an electromagnetic clutch. System pressure and refrigerant flow are controlled by varying the compressor displacement, or output. When the system is off, the compressor is adjusted for zero displacement; it essentially freewheels with very little, if any, load on the engine.

Motors. Blower motors on older vehicles often are compound-wound or shunt-wound units. Motor speed is controlled by a rheostat that allows rpm control or by a switch providing two or more fixed speeds. Most blower motors on late-model vehicles are a permanent magnet design. Speed is controlled by introducing resistance into the motor circuit. The greater the resistance, the slower the motor speed. Figure 18-1 shows how resistor arrangement provides different speeds.

Switches and Relays. In addition to the control and magnetic clutch switches already discussed, air conditioning systems use some kind of pressure or temperature switch to control compressor operation. Such control is necessary to regulate evaporator core pressure and temperature and prevent the cooling coils from icing or getting too warm. An evaporator pressure-control valve or a suction-throttling valve installed between the evaporator and the compressor was used on many earlier air conditioning systems. Since the late-1970's, however, a clutch-cycling pressure switch or a clutch-cycling thermostatic switch has become more common.

The clutch-cycling, pressure-operated switch generally is wired in series with the clutch field coil. When pressure on the low side of the refrigerant

system reaches a certain value, the switch closes and the clutch engages. If system pressure drops below its specified minimum value, the switch opens to disengage the clutch and shut the compressor off until the pressure rises.

The clutch-cycling thermostatic switch uses a capillary sensing tube inserted in the compressor suction (inlet) line. When system temperature drops too low, it opens the compressor clutch circuit. When system temperature rises, the switch closes the circuit and the compressor clutch reengages.

Depending upon the system design, several other switches may be used in the circuit to control compressor operation. These include:

• A power steering system pressure, or cutout switch, to sense line pressure. It turns the compressor off during periods of high-power steering loads, such as parking or other sharp turns.

• A wide-open throttle (WOT) switch to shut the compressor off during full-throttle acceleration. This normally closed switch is mounted on the carburetor or accelerator pedal and wired in series with the compressor clutch circuit.

• A transmission pressure switch that overrides the WOT switch if the transmission or transaxle is in high gear.

• A low-pressure switch that opens whenever system refrigerant is low. In some systems, it also will open if ambient temperature drops below a specified value.

• A high-pressure switch that acts as a relief valve, opening only when system pressure exceeds a specified value. This shuts the compressor off. When system pressure returns to normal, the switch closes and turns the compressor back on. Systems without a high-pressure switch have a relief valve on the compressor high-side that releases system pressure. Some systems have both.

Air conditioning systems also may use various relays. These control the current to either the compressor or the

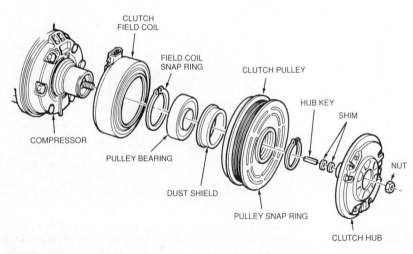

Figure 18-5. An exploded view of a typical electromagnetic clutch used with an air conditioning compressor. (Ford)

entire system, according to their function. Typical relays include:

• A time delay relay that controls current to the entire system. It is used to delay system operation briefly when the air conditioning is first turned on. In some systems, it applies current to the idle stop solenoid to increase engine idle speed. The relay also is controlled by the engine coolant temperature switch and shuts off current to the air conditioning system whenever the engine overheats.

• A compressor control or power relay that cuts off compressor operation under specific engine operating conditions, such as low engine speed, engine overheating, low ambient temperature, or full-throttle acceleration.

• A constant run relay to eliminate compressor cycling for a specified time during engine idle after the vehicle has decelerated, as when exiting a freeway and waiting at a stop light.

• An antidieseling relay to energize the compressor clutch and prevent engine dieseling when the ignition switch is turned off.

You might want to review chapter 3 if you are uncertain about switch and relay operation.

Temperature Control. Some form of control is necessary to maintain evaporator temperature at a proper level. This may be done with the clutch-cycling switch with its capillary sensing tube installed in the compressor suction line, figure 18-6, or by a thermostatic switch often called a fin thermostat, figure 18-7. This thermostatic switch is attached to the evaporator with its capillary sensing tube inserted in the evaporator fins, figure 18-8. In either system, evaporator temperature control is the same. When system temperature drops below a specified point, the switch opens the compressor clutch circuit. When system temperature rises, the switch closes the circuit, and the compressor clutch reengages.

System Control Assembly. The control assembly generally is installed in the center of the instrument panel or console. It contains driver-operated switches that control the electrical and vacuum functions, as well as mechanical levers connected to cables that operate the blend air doors and heater water valve, figure 18-9.

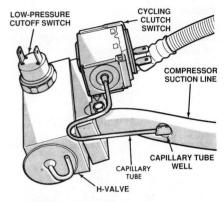

Figure 18-6. The capillary tube of a clutch-cycling switch inserted in the suction line provides evaporator temperature control. (Chrysler)

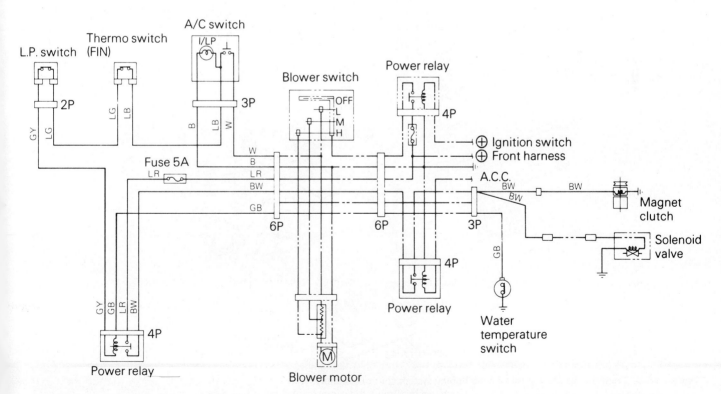

Figure 18-7. Circuit diagram of an air conditioning system that uses a thermostatic switch or fin thermostat to provide evaporator temperature control. (Mitsubishi)

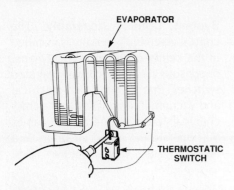

Figure 18-8. The fin thermostat is attached to the evaporator housing and gets its name from positioning of the capillary tube in the evaporator fins. (Mitsubishi)

Switch testing and replacement requires removal of the control assembly.

POWER WINDOWS

Electrically operated door windows are an optional convenience system on many automobiles. The system allows control of each window with an individual door switch. A master switch assembly allows the driver to control all windows from one position. The master switch assembly may be mounted on the driver's door or armrest, figure 18-10, or on the center console. Late-model 2-door sport coupes may not have a master switch; both individual control switches are positioned on the console, figure 18-11. Figure 18-12 shows the components of a typical power window system. Figure 18-13 is a typical circuit diagram.

A permanent magnet motor attached to the window regulator inside

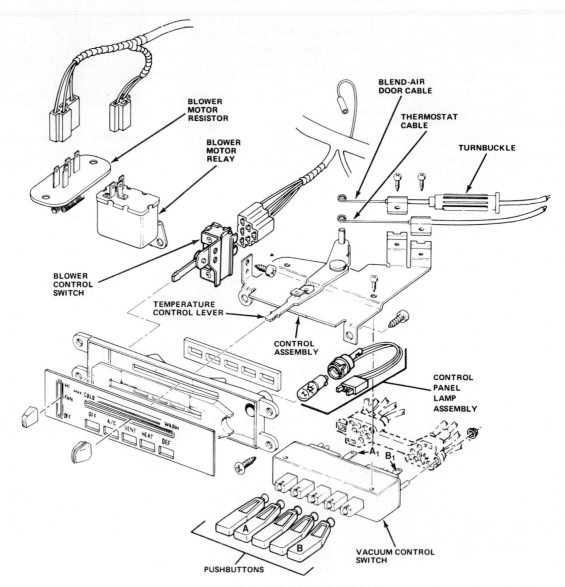

Figure 18-9. Components of a typical air conditioning system control assembly. The pushbutton marked A activates the air conditioning system by turning the compressor clutch on. Pushbutton B also turns the compressor on for the defrost mode. The electrical terminals marked A_1 and B_1 on the vacuum control assembly correspond with the pushbuttons. (Chrysler)

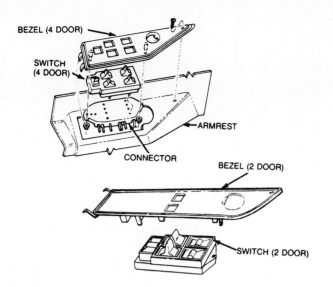

Figure 18-11. Sport coupes with console-mounted power window switches may not have a master control switch. The center switch in this arrangement is a decklid release control.

Figure 18-10. Power window master control switches may be located on the door trim panel or armrest. (Ford)

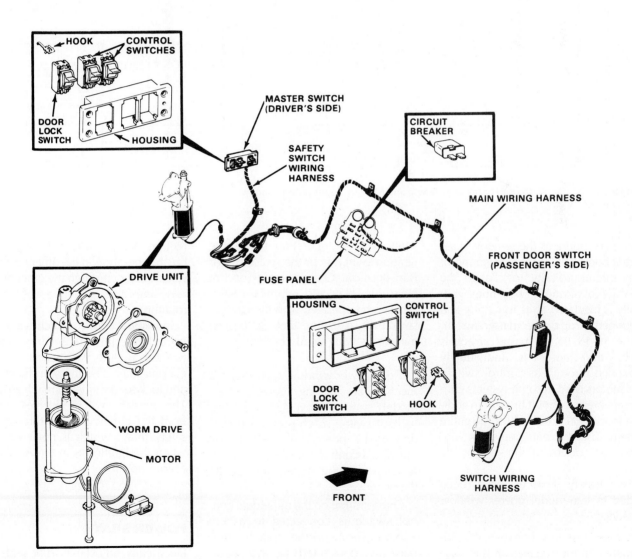

Figure 18-12. Components of a typical power window system. (Chrysler)

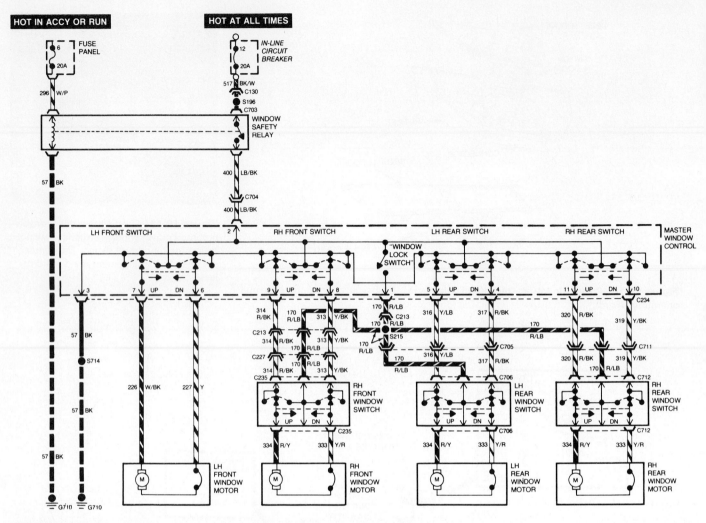

Figure 18-13. Circuit diagram of the Ford Tempo and Mercury Topaz power window system. (Ford)

each door operates the window glass in that door. The 2-wire design motor uses circuit polarity to change the direction of rotation. Each motor generally is insulated at its mounting and grounded through the master switch, figure 18-13. If no master switch is used, the motor is individually grounded through its control switch. The motors used in some systems contain an internal circuit breaker in addition to the one provided for the entire system. This prevents one stuck window from disabling the rest of the system.

Two safety features have been added to late-model power window circuits:

• A relay installed between the 30-ampere circuit breaker in the fuse block and the control switches pre-vents window operation unless the ignition switch is in the Accessory or Run position. Older vehicles do not have this relay and permit the windows to be operated with the ignition switch off, a feature that has proven dangerous with small children in the car.

• Older power window systems use a mechanical locking device; late-model systems have an electrical lockout switch. Each prevents operation of the power windows by the individual control switches. When activated, only the driver can operate the windows.

One terminal on the individual control switch is connected to battery voltage. The two other switch terminals are connected to the motor brushes. Switch operation in one di-rection sends current through one brush; operation in the other direction sends current through the other brush, reversing the direction of motor rotation.

Individual control switches are connected in series with the driver's master switch and the lockout switch. Current must pass through the master and lockout switches to reach ground. The master switch receives power from the circuit breaker through the safety relay, which is powered only when the ignition is in the Accessory or Run position.

POWER SEATS

Electrically adjustable front seats are another common optional circuit you may have to service. Three different designs have been used:

- 2-way systems
- 4-way systems
- 6-way systems

The 2-way system moves the seat forward and backward. This design was the first of the electrically adjustable seat systems but has not been used for many years. For this reason, you probably will service very few 2-way seat systems.

The GM design, figure 18-14, is typical. The series-wound motor has its two electromagnetic field windings wound in opposite directions. The forward switch position sends current through one winding. The other winding receives current from the rear switch position. Current sent through one winding turns the motor in one direction; current sent through the other winding turns the motor in the opposite direction. The seat is moved in one of two ways:

1. The motor armature shaft is connected to a transmission mounted on the seat rail. The rotary motion created by the motor is turned into linear motion to move the seat by a gear arrangement in the transmission.

2. The motor armature shaft is connected to gear drives on each seat rail by cables. The gear drives translate the rotary motion into linear motion to move the seat.

A 4-way system moves the seat forward, backward, up, and down (some designs move only the front edge of the seat up or down). The first improvement on the 2-way design, the 4-way system, was very popular at one time. It has been replaced by the 6-way design and is now found mostly on the passenger seat in some front split-seat systems.

Most 4-way power seat systems use a motor with two reversible armatures in the same housing, figure 18-15. Ford and Chrysler motors use permanent magnet fields. GM motors use series-connected electromagnetic fields, as in the 2-way motor described above. One 4-position switch, figure 18-16, operates both

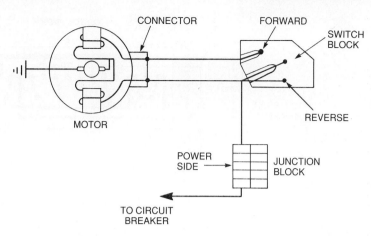

Figure 18-14. A series-wound motor with electromagnetic fields is used in GM 2- and 4-way systems.

A BLAST FROM THE PAST

Factory-installed air conditioning started to become a popular option in the late 1950's. As we know it today, automotive air conditioning is a small-size, highly efficient refrigeration system packed into the confines of an automobile. In a heat-transfer rate of Btu's per hour, an automobile A/C system ranks with the best industrial air conditioners. A/C systems are installed on about 75 percent of new cars built today.

But automobile A/C systems were introduced only 30 or 40 years ago. Did you ever wonder how drivers fought the heat as they drove across the Southwest or the Midwest plains in the 1930's and '40's? The California Car Cooler was the answer.

The car cooler was an evaporative cooler that hung from the window on the passenger's side door. You simply rolled up the window and mounted the metal case that looked like a small rocket launcher to the

window, the door frame, and the roof drip rail with adjustable clamps. Then you filled the cooler with water.

Wood fiber or cellulose material inside the cooler soaked up the water. Air entered the opening at the front of the cooler as you drove, passed through the water-soaked fiber and came out (a little bit cooler) through the opening inside the car. A/C efficiency was directly proportional to car speed. Drive fast, stay cool.

The car cooler was available for rent from one of many outlets on one side of the desert. When you reached the other side of the desert, the cooler was turned in to another outlet. They really worked, but you had to remember you had one when you pulled into a service station. If you pulled in too close to the pump with the cooler on that side, goodbye cooler and window.

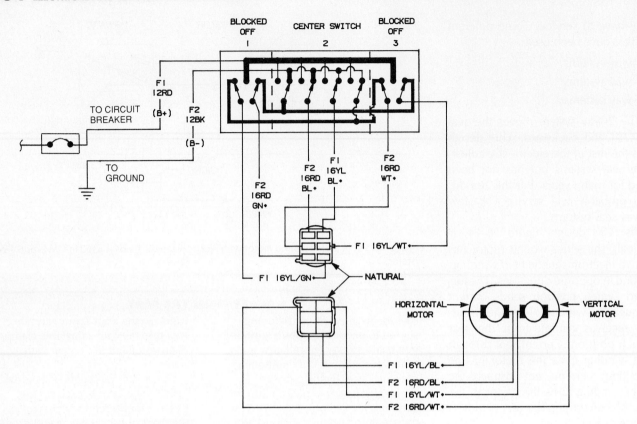

Figure 18-15. A circuit diagram of a late-model Chrysler 4-way seat system used with front split-seat designs. (Chrysler)

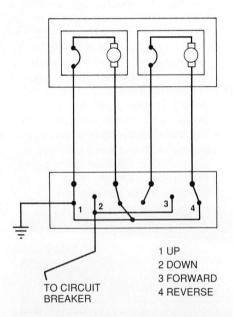

Figure 18-16. A single 4-position switch controls the two motors in a 4-way power seat system.

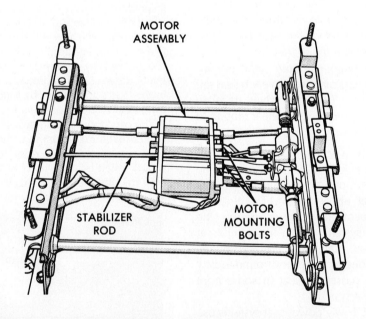

Figure 18-17. A triple-armature motor is used with all late-model 6-way seat systems. (Chrysler)

motors. The switch controls motor reversal by applying current to different motor brushes (permanent magnet) or to different field windings (electromagnetic fields). Each motor is connected to a separate transmission. One transmission moves the seat to the front or the rear. The other transmission controls up and down movement at the front of the seat.

The 6-way system adds forward and backward tilt to the forward, backward, up, and down movements of the 4-way seat. Early GM 6-way power seats use one of three solenoids to connect a single motor to one of three transmissions. Current sent through the appropriate solenoid to engage the desired transmission passes to ground through a relay. The relay contacts send current to the motor brushes in Ford and Chrysler systems. GM systems have additional switch contacts to send current to the electromagnetic motor windings.

All late-model 6-way power seat designs use a reversible, permanent magnet, 3-armature motor (often called a trimotor), figure 18-17, with flexible shafts that connect either to a rack and pinion or to a worm gear drive transmission. The control switch assembly consists of a 4-position knob that moves the seat forward, backward, up, and down, figure 18-18. Separate 2-position switches are provided for front tilt and rear tilt, figure 18-18. The control switch assembly can be installed on the side of the seat, figure 18-19, or mounted in the armrest with other system switches, figure 18-20.

The direction of current determines the direction of motor rotation. Current is applied to different motor brushes through the control switch assembly. For example, setting the 4-way switch in figure 18-21 in the Up position closes switch 3. This sends current from the circuit breaker in the fuse block through switch 3, then through switch 1 to the front height motor and through switch 7 to the rear height motor, moving the entire seat upward. Moving the 4-way switch back to the Down position opens switch 3 and closes switch 4. Current

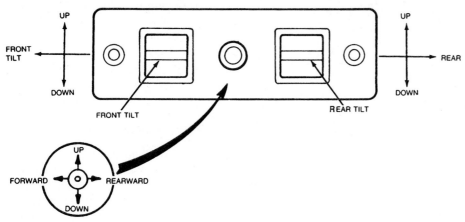

Figure 18-18. Control switch arrangement used with 6-way power seats. (Ford)

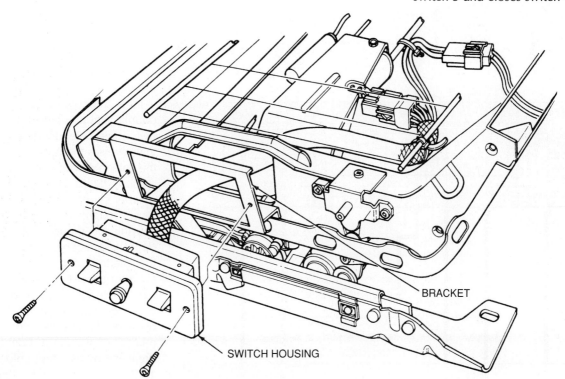

Figure 18-19. The control switch assembly may be mounted on a bracket at the side of the seat. (Ford)

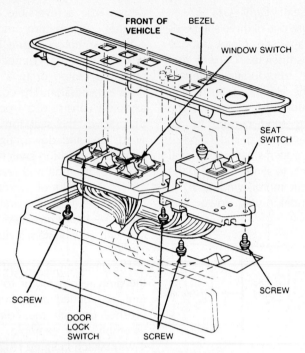

Figure 18-20. The power seat control switch often is installed in the armrest with other convenience system switches. (Ford)

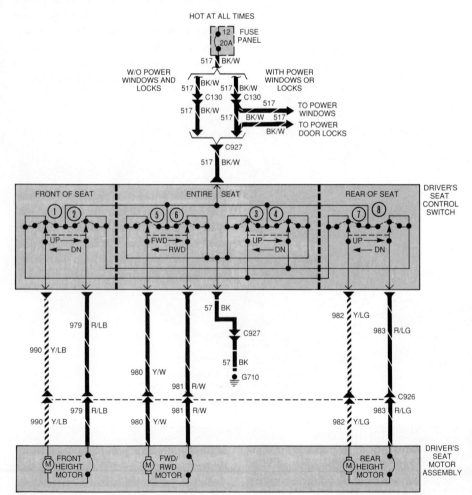

Figure 18-21. Circuit diagram of a typical 6-way power seat system. (Ford)

is sent through switch 4 to switch 2 and 8, moving the entire seat downward. Moving the front tilt switch to its Up position closes switch 1 and sends current to the front height motor to move the front of the seat upward. When the switch is placed in its Down position, switch 2 closes and reverses current to the motor, causing it to rotate in the opposite direction. The same procedure takes place when the rear tilt switch is operated.

Each armature in the motor assembly is grounded through the switch and contains its own circuit breaker as protection if power is applied during a stall condition (resulting from mechanical failure or running the motor to the limit of its travel).

POWER LOCKS AND LATCHES

Door and trunk locks and seatback latches are operated by motors and solenoids. Door and trunk locks generally are controlled by separate driver-operated switches. Seatback latch control is provided by doorjamb switches.

Door Locks

Power door lock systems generally operate either with solenoids or electric motors.

In a solenoid-operated system, a double-action solenoid is controlled by a single-pole, double-throw switch that reverses the polarity of current to the solenoid with each change of direction, figure 18-22. Reversing the polarity changes the direction of current through the solenoid windings, causing the plunger to move in the opposite direction. The movement of the solenoid plunger locks or unlocks the door according to the switch position. Some solenoid-operated systems use a relay in the circuit. The system operates as just described, but the relay controls current from the circuit breaker in the fuse block, figure 18-23. Current from the control switch flows through the relay coil and closes the relay contacts. The contacts send the current to the sole-

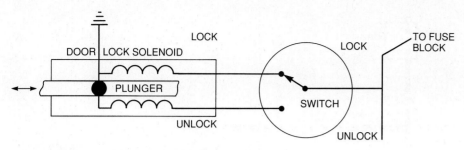

Figure 18-22. A typical solenoid-operated door lock system.

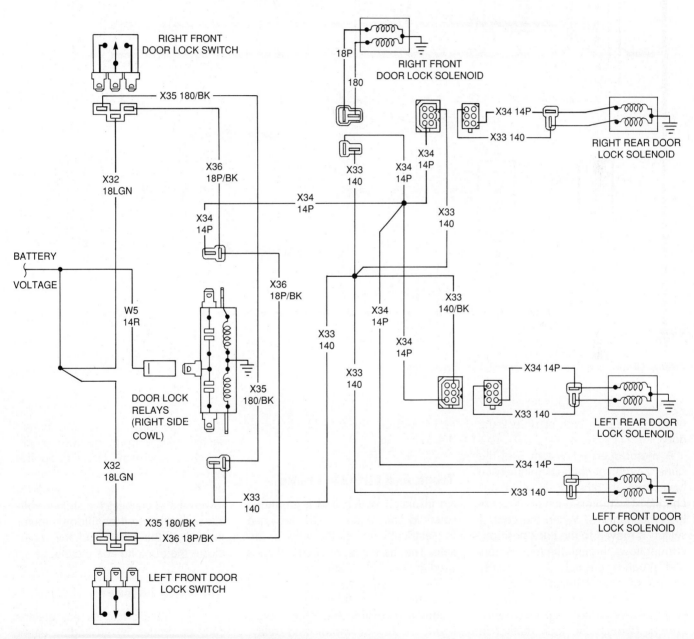

Figure 18-23. A relay-controlled, solenoid-operated door lock system. (Chrysler)

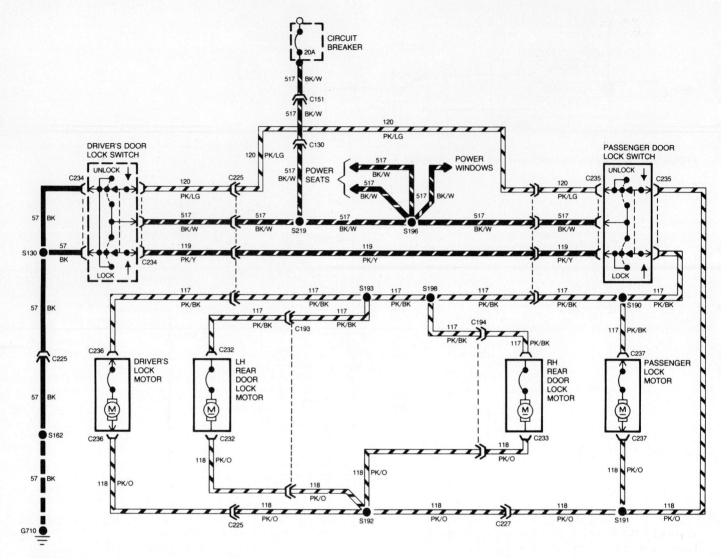

Figure 18-24. A typical motor-operated door lock system. (Ford)

noid windings to lock or unlock the door.

A motor-operated system uses the same 2-wire, permanent magnet we have seen in other systems in this chapter. The motors open or close the lock mechanisms. When the control switch is moved to the Lock position, current flows through the lock motors and grounds through the normally closed contacts of the Unlock switch, figure 18-24. Moving the control switch to the Unlock position sends current through the lock motors in the opposite direction and grounds through the normally closed contacts of the lock switch. A relay also can be used in this system to control cur-

rent flow from the fuse block circuit breaker.

Trunk And Liftgate Locks

An insulated switch and a grounded solenoid coil, figure 18-25, are used to electrically unlock the trunk or liftgate. The same type of circuit often is used to control fuel filler doors.

The more complex circuit required for a trunk lid pulldown system includes a reversible trunk lid motor, figure 18-26, or motor and relay. When a reversible motor is used, striker switches operate the system according to the position of the trunk adjust limit switch. In systems with a

relay, operating the release button sends voltage from the fuse block, energizing the relay. The relay applies power to the release solenoid, opening the trunk lid. When the trunk lid is lowered and engages the striker, voltage is applied to the pulldown motor instead of the relay, and the motor closes the trunk lid completely.

Seatback Latches

Power seatback latches are electrically controlled by grounding either doorjamb switch. When one of the front doors is opened, the doorjamb switch energizes a relay, figure 18-27. The relay sends current to the seat-

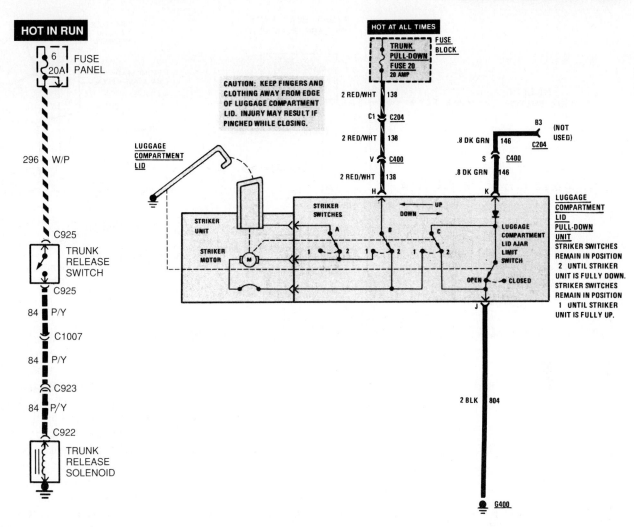

Figure 18-25. Power trunk or liftgate release systems are simple circuits with an insulated switch and grounded solenoid. (Ford)

Figure 18-26. A GM trunk pulldown circuit diagram. (Oldsmobile)

back release solenoids, which unlatch the seatbacks, figure 18-28.

SUMMARY

The systems covered in this chapter are primarily comfort and convenience systems. Heater and air conditioning systems use the same blower motor, blower control switch, resistor block, and ducting. Motor speed is controlled by sending current through the resistor block. The greater the resistance, the slower the blower motor runs.

An electromagnetic clutch is used to engage and disengage the belt-driven air conditioning compressor. The clutch is operated by a switch on the passenger compartment control assembly and locks or unlocks the drive pulley to the compressor shaft. A clutch function switch also operates the compressor when the control assembly function lever is moved to the defrost position. Various other switches and relays may be used in the air conditioning system to control the compressor under various operating conditions, such as low or high pressure, or full-throttle operation.

Late-model power window and power seat systems generally use a reversible permanent magnet motor. Older systems use a motor with elec-tromagnetic fields. With both types of motors, direction of rotation is determined by circuit polarity. When a permanent magnet motor is used, current is sent to different brushes. With an electromagnetic field motor, current is sent to different windings.

Single-pole, double-throw switches generally control these motors. A master control switch on the driver's armrest or console controls all power windows or door locks in a vehicle. Individual switches control each window or door lock and are grounded through the master switch. Current to the motor may pass through a relay in some systems.

Power seat designs offering 4-way

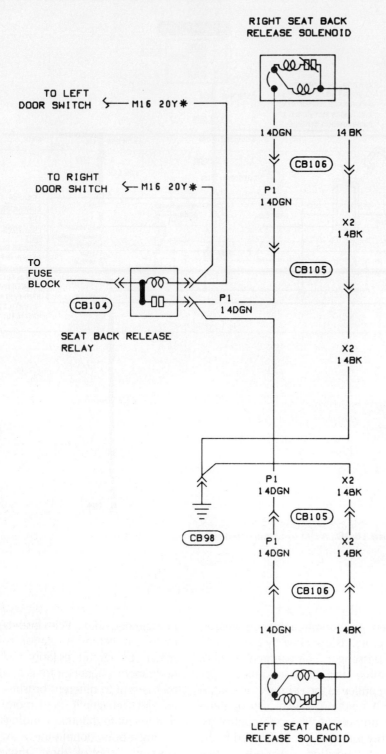

Figure 18-27. A typical power seatback latch release system. (Chrysler)

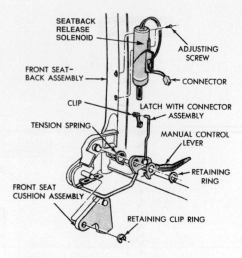

Figure 18-28. A solenoid operates the rear seatback latch. (Chrysler)

or 6-way movement use a motor assembly with 2 armatures (4-way) or 3 armatures (6-way). Rotary motion of the motor is translated into linear seat movement by rack-and-pinion or drive gear transmissions.

Power door lock, trunk lock, and seatback latch release systems use either a solenoid or a motor. Trunk release systems are simple circuits containing an insulated switch and grounded solenoid. Trunk lid pull-down circuits are more complex and include a motor and relay.

REVIEW QUESTIONS

Multiple Choice

1. Student A says that many late-model heater control circuits use ground-side switching of the blower motor. Student B says that most older circuits use supply-side switching. Who is right?

a. A only
b. B only
c. both A and B
d. neither A nor B

2. The air conditioning compressor is prevented from operating constantly by:

a. a servomagnet
b. a solenoid and relay
c. a hydromechanical clutch
d. an electromagnetic clutch

3. Student A says that high resistance in the blower motor circuit causes the fan to run fast. Student B says that high resistance causes the fan to run slower. Who is right?

a. A only
b. B only
c. both A and B
d. neither A nor B

4. Which of the following components is not shared by the air conditioning and heater systems?

a. blower switch
b. resistor block
c. control function switch
d. blower motor

5. Student A says that a relay between the circuit breaker and the control and lockout switches prevents window operation with the ignition off. Student B says that window operation with the ignition off is prevented by a mechanical lockout switch. Who is right?

a. A only
b. B only
c. both A and B
d. neither A nor B

6. Which of the following does not control the air conditioning compressor?

a. power steering cutout switch
b. transaxle pressure sensing switch
c. wide-open throttle (WOT) switch
d. SCROC thermostatic switch

7. Individual power window control switches must be connected in _____ with the master control switch.

a. shunt
b. parallel
c. series
d. compound

8. A power seat system uses:

a. stepper motors
b. omnidirectional motors
c. unidirectional motors
d. reversible motors

9. Student A says that each power window motor on most late-model cars generally is insulated at its mounting and grounded through the master switch. Student B says that it is grounded at its mounting. Who is right?

a. A only
b. B only
c. both A and B
d. neither A nor B

10. What type of protection is built into a reversible motor to prevent damage from a stall condition?

a. fusible link
b. circuit breaker
c. thermal limiter
d. overheat thermostatic switch

11. Student A says that door and trunk locks are operated by solenoids. Student B says that they are operated by motors. Who is right?

a. A only
b. B only
c. both A and B
d. neither A nor B

12. Which of the following is not found in a power door lock system?

a. solenoid
b. relay
c. electric motor
d. resistor block

13. Student A says that a reversible motor uses circuit polarity to change the direction of rotation. Student B says that current applied to different field windings in the motor changes rotational direction. Who is right?

a. A only
b. B only
c. both A and B
d. neither A nor B

14. Student A says that an air conditioning system may use an anti-dieseling relay to prevent engine dieseling when the ignition switch is turned off. Student B says that a heater system uses a throttle kicker to maintain idle speed when the blower is on. Who is right?

a. A only
b. B only
c. both A and B
d. neither A nor B

15. Student A says that late-model 6-way power seats use three solenoids and a single motor. Student B says that late-model 6-way power seats use a trimotor. Who is right?

a. A only
b. B only
c. both A and B
d. neither A nor B

16. Student A says that the low-pressure switch in an air conditioning system opens when refrigerant pressure is high. Student B says that the low-pressure switch acts as a relief valve. Who is right?

a. A only
b. B only
c. both A and B
d. neither A nor B

17. Student A says that the air conditioning compressor is cycled off during periods of high acceleration. Student B says that the compressor will not run if ambient temperature is too low. Who is right?

a. A only
b. B only
c. both A and B
d. neither A nor B

18. Student A says that most of the systems described in this chapter are protected by a circuit breaker. Student B says that the fuse block and fusible links at the starter motor are more common protective devices for these circuits. Who is right?

a. A only
b. B only
c. both A and B
d. neither A nor B

19 ELECTRONIC ACCESSORIES

WHAT

An increasing number of comfort and convenience systems are controlled either by the engine control computer, the body computer module, or a separate microprocessor module. Some of these systems have been used for many years and are well defined in their design and operation, with computer control the only new feature. Others are new developments with circuit design and operation that probably will change considerably as automotive engineers continue evolution of the systems.

Automatic temperature control systems use the same basic components found in any air conditioning system. The systems differ from the ones you studied in chapter 18 in how they are controlled. Keyless entry and factory-installed antitheft systems are becoming more common, but electronic memory seats, sunroofs, and navigation systems are just starting to appear on production cars.

WHY

The comfort and convenience systems discussed in this chapter, like those covered in chapter 18, are expected to work without problems. Generally speaking, electronic control makes them quite reliable. When they do fail, however, you will be expected to locate and correct the problem quickly.

This chapter explains the basic operating requirements of automatic temperature control systems, memory seats, electronic sunroofs, keyless entry systems, factory-installed antitheft systems, and electronic navigation. Understanding the principles behind the operation of these systems will help you to diagnose and correct a problem rapidly.

GOALS

After completing this chapter, you should be able to:

1. List the components and explain the operation of an air conditioning system controlled by:
   a. a programmer
   b. a microprocessor
   c. a body computer module (BCM)

2. Explain how a memory seat system operates.

3. Explain the operation of:
   a. an electronic sunroof system
   b. a pushbutton keyless entry system
   c. a remote keyless entry system

4. List the components and describe the operation of a typical factory-installed antitheft system.

5. Explain the principles of an electronic navigation system.

AUTOMATED TEMPERATURE CONTROL

You learned the basic components of heating and air conditioning systems and how they work in chapter 18. The same components form the basic automated temperature control system. The manual A/C system discussed in chapter 18 provides warm or cold air at a constant temperature once the driver has set the control assembly. The warm or cool air is circulated by the blower motor into the passenger compartment through ducting. Routing of the air is controlled by vacuum- or cable-operated mode door actuators and a cable-operated blend door.

An automated system can function on its own once the driver has set the control devices to tell the system what he wants it to do. There are two types of automatic air conditioning systems: semiautomatic temperature control (SATC) and electronic automatic temperature control (EATC). SATC systems are controlled by a programmer unit; EATC systems are controlled by a microprocessor or body computer module (BCM). We will look at examples of each in this section.

SEMIAUTOMATIC TEMPERATURE CONTROL (SATC) SYSTEMS

An SATC system maintains a driver-selected temperature level inside the vehicle. The system's electronic control, or programmer, senses air temperature and positions the blend-air door to maintain the passenger compartment air temperature within the preselected comfort level. The operating mode and blower speed are manually controlled by the driver.

There are many variations of SATC systems in use. The Chrysler and GM systems discussed below are typical examples.

Chrysler SATC System

Chrysler's SATC system used in 1986 and 1987 is a typical semiautomatic temperature control system and contains the following components:

• Control assembly with sliding resistor

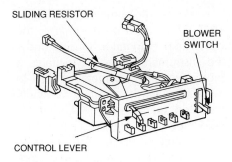

Figure 19-1. Externally, the Chrysler SATC control assembly is similar to those used with manual A/C systems. (Chrysler)

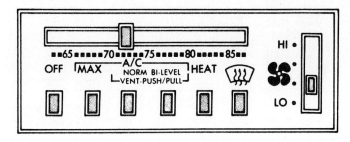

Figure 19-2. The face of the Chrysler SATC control assembly contains a temperature selector scale. Moving the lever causes a sliding resistor to send an electrical signal to the servomotor. (Chrysler)

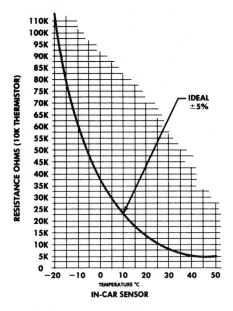

Figure 19-3. Typical resistance vs. temperature calibration curve for an in-car sensor. (Ford)

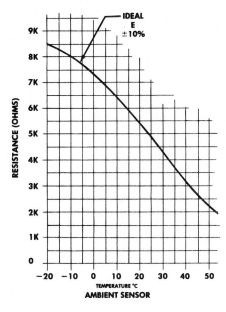

Figure 19-4. Typical resistance vs. temperature calibration curve for an ambient sensor. (Ford)

- In-car sensor
- Ambient sensor
- Servomotor (programmer)
- Aspirator system

The control assembly is similar in appearance to those used with manual A/C systems, figure 19-1, but it has a temperature range imprinted under the control lever, figure 19-2. This allows the driver to select the desired comfort level. Moving the control lever operates a sliding resistor in the control assembly, mechanically converting the lever setting into an electrical resistance value that is sent to the servomotor. Once the lever is positioned, the system can regulate the temperature of the passenger compartment in all modes except maximum A/C.

Pushbutton switches in the control assembly allow the driver to select the appropriate mode. Depending upon which pushbutton is depressed, engine vacuum is routed to vacuum actuators at the required air distribution doors (except the blend-air door, which is controlled by the servomotor).

The aspirator creates a slight vacuum that draws passenger compartment air past the in-car sensor. The in-car sensor contains a temperature-sensing thermistor that measures passenger compartment air temperature through an inverse relationship. The thermistor's electrical resistance increases as temperature decreases, and decreases as temperature increases. The ambient temperature sensor operates in the same way, but is positioned to receive outside air so that it can sense changes in the temperature outside the vehicle.

Sensor resistance value is measured by the servomotor. Figures 19-3 and 19-4 show typical calibration curves for such sensors. When resistance is high, the servomotor moves the blend-air door to allow more heat to enter. When resistance is low, the blend-air door moves in the opposite direction to reduce the amount of heat. The system operates on a variation of the feedback principle, figure 19-5, with the servomotor constantly readjusting the blend-air door position to maintain the driver-selected comfort level. Figure 19-6 is the circuit diagram.

GM C65 (Tempmatic) System

The GM Tempmatic control system maintains the vehicle's interior temperature within a range of $\pm$ 4° F. Several versions of this system are used, with each version differing according to the GM division and the car line on which the system is installed. Basic operation of the different versions is very similar to that of the Chrysler SATC system, but the control methods and programmers used are different.

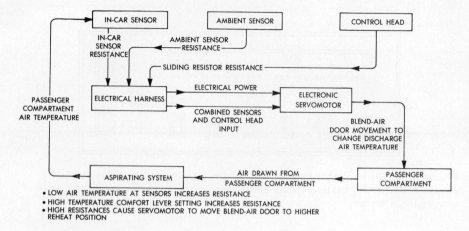

Figure 19-5. The feedback cycle used by the servomotor to maintain temperature control in the Chrysler SATC system. (Chrysler)

A typical programmer unit, figure 19-7, is mounted on the side of the heater and evaporator housing under the instrument panel. It contains a motor that is mechanically linked to the air-mix valve, and four vertically mounted vacuum solenoids that are held closed by gravity. Engine vacuum is applied to the programmer at all times. The solenoids are connected to the mode pushbuttons on the control assembly. When a pushbutton is activated, the programmer energizes the appropriate vacuum solenoid. The solenoid plunger lifts and allows vacuum to pass to the proper

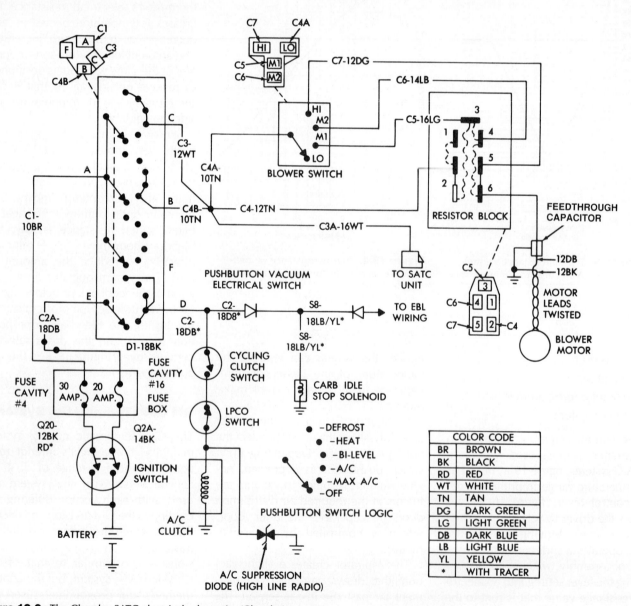

Figure 19-6. The Chrysler SATC electrical schematic. (Chrysler)

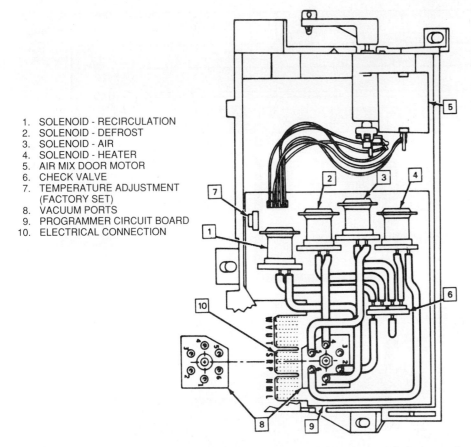

1. SOLENOID - RECIRCULATION
2. SOLENOID - DEFROST
3. SOLENOID - AIR
4. SOLENOID - HEATER
5. AIR MIX DOOR MOTOR
6. CHECK VALVE
7. TEMPERATURE ADJUSTMENT (FACTORY SET)
8. VACUUM PORTS
9. PROGRAMMER CIRCUIT BOARD
10. ELECTRICAL CONNECTION

Figure 19-7. This GM Tempmatic programmer contains four electrical solenoids that control vacuum flow to the door actuators. (Oldsmobile)

air distribution door actuator, figure 19-8.

A plastic adjustment screw is provided on the side of the programmer. The screw is connected to a potentiometer inside the programmer. If the system does not maintain the temperature within the specified 4-degree range, and all other components in the system are operating properly, this screw can be adjusted to bring the temperature within specifications.

GM C61 System

The C61 system also is produced in various versions. Disc-type thermistors are used as in-car and ambient temperature sensors and send a feedback voltage signal based on variable resistance to the programmer. A typical programmer, figure 19-9, is an integral part of the instrument panel control assembly. A rotary switch on

the base of the control assembly transmits the mode lever position into an electrical path to the compressor clutch coil. The temperature dial on the control assembly varies the resistance of a rheostat. The total resistance of the rheostat and temperature sensors is used by the programmer to determine how to control the system. The programmer also contains other major control components:

• The dc amplifier strengthens the weak signals received from the sensors before sending them to the transducer.

• The transducer changes the electrical signal received from the dc amplifier into a vacuum signal sent to the vacuum motor, which operates the rotary shaft to drive the air-mix door.

• The feedback potentiometer transmits required system corrections to the programmer circuitry.

ELECTRONIC AUTOMATIC TEMPERATURE CONTROL (EATC) SYSTEMS

As we have seen, a basic semiautomatic temperature control system is not much different from a manual one. The air distribution subsystem in both manual and SATC systems operates by means of cables and linkage. The primary difference is in the use of a programmer, electric servomotor, or control module to control the actuators.

A fine line separates the more sophisticated SATC systems from the basic EATC systems, with increasing overlap between the two, as you will see when we look at the Chevrolet and GMC light-duty truck system introduced in 1988. Some automakers apply the EATC designation to systems that closely resemble the Chrysler SATC system described earlier. Most EATC systems, however, perform the following functions (some of which also may be found in SATC systems):

• Recognize system malfunctions and display trouble codes

• Readjust interior temperature several times a second

• Provide a continuously variable blower speed signal (also may delay blower operation on cold engine starts)

• Provide the power feed to the A/C compressor clutch

The ability to run a self-diagnostic program and display trouble codes probably is the most important distinction found in a fully automatic or electronic temperature control system. We will use this as our dividing line between SATC and EATC systems. We also will divide EATC systems into two types: those controlled by an individual computer and those controlled by a multifunction body computer module (BCM).

An EATC system receives and processes inputs from:

• In-car temperature sensors
• Ambient temperature sensors
• Engine temperature sensors

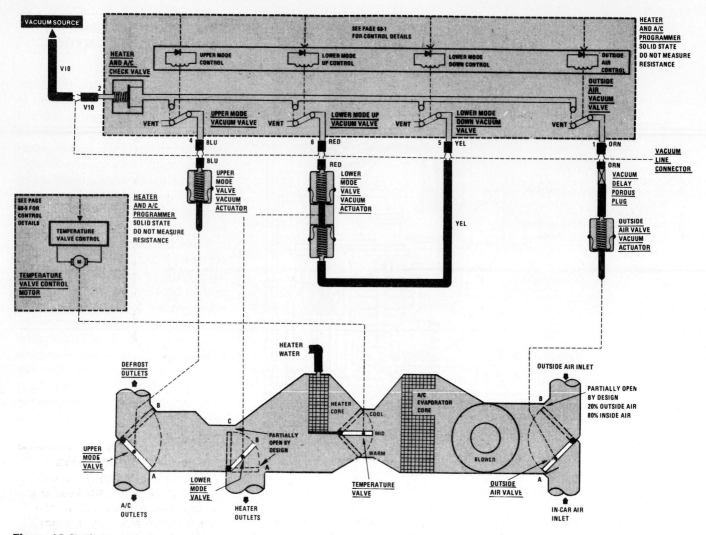

Figure 19-8. The Tempmatic printed circuit board contains the logic for solenoid and actuator operation. (Oldsmobile)

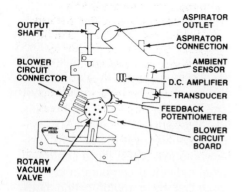

Figure 19-9. The GM C61 programmer attached to the control assembly differs considerably from that used with C65 systems. (GM)

• Temperature and function selections made by the driver

• Amount of sunlight inside the vehicle (not all systems use this input)

The inputs are processed by the system computer (electronic control assembly), figure 19-10, or BCM. The computer or BCM sends output signals to the appropriate door actuator and controls both blower motor speed and A/C clutch operation.

Sensors

Three main types of temperature sensors are used in EATC systems:

• Thermistors

• Bimetallic vacuum modulators
• Photovoltaic diodes

We already have seen how thermistors are used as in-car and ambient temperature sensors in SATC systems. EATC systems use the same sensors. They also use thermistors as A/C high- and low-side temperature sensors that allow the computer to monitor refrigerant temperature.

A second type of temperature sensor used in EATC systems is a bimetal-operated vacuum modulator. This sensor changes air temperature directly into corresponding values of modulated vacuum. The bimetal element reacts mechanically to in-car

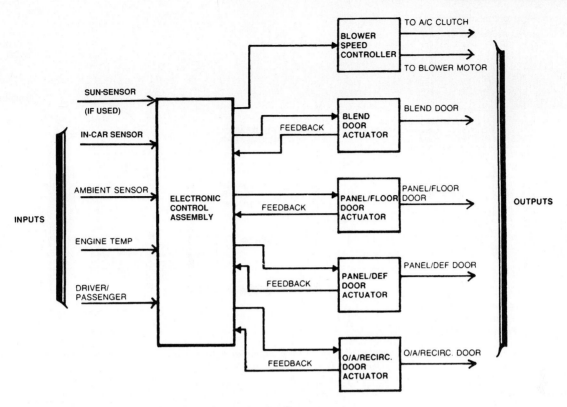

Figure 19-10. Block diagram of a typical ATC system operation. (Ford)

temperature. It controls the vacuum modulator by mechanical linkage, regulating vacuum in proportion to temperature. The entire assembly is housed inside an aspirator that draws air from the passenger compartment across the bimetal element.

Some EATC systems use a sunload sensor. This may be a photovoltaic diode used to determine the amount of sunlight present inside the vehicle, or a thermistor that senses the heat load of the sun on the vehicle. The sensor value is converted into an electrical signal sent to the computer, whose program includes a solar compensation factor for high sunload conditions.

Actuators

Many EATC systems use the same servomotors and vacuum-operated actuators found in manual and SATC systems. These are similar to the vacuum motors found in many other engine control systems.

Rotary electric motors are used as actuators in some systems to control the air distribution and blend doors. A rotary actuator contains both drive and feedback circuitry, figure 19-10. The computer uses the feedback signal from the actuator to sense the air distribution door position. If adjustment is necessary, it powers the actuator until the desired position is reached. Rotary actuators may be continuous or 2-position types.

Two types of continuous actuators are used. One type is bidirectional and can stop at any position within its 180-degree operating range. The other type rotates through 360 degrees without reversing direction. Two-position actuators operate by reversing current polarity and stop in one of two predetermined positions 180 degrees apart.

Various methods are used to produce a feedback signal. In one design, a fixed resistor is located at each actuator arm position. When the arm reaches the designated position, actuator contacts close a circuit through the resistor. The actuator will move

THE GOOD OLD DAYS

Before the introduction of sealed-beam headlamps in 1940, headlamp aiming required several additional steps. In early electric headlamps, the headlamp bulb had to be focused before the headlamp could be aimed. This was accomplished by moving the bulb and its socket back and forth in front of the reflector until the light from the bulb's filament formed a specified pattern. In addition, the reflector had to be polished and the lens cleaned to remove moisture and dirt that had entered the headlamp. The introduction of a prefocused lamp bulb greatly simplified the process by eliminating the need to reposition the bulb and socket.

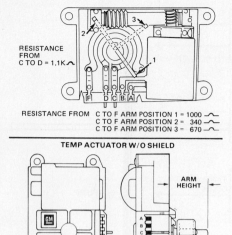

Figure 19-11. A temperature door actuator used in GM EATC systems has a hot (1) and cold (2) position. Position 3 is for system calibration. (Buick)

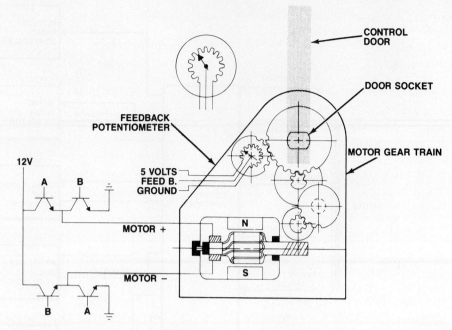

Figure 19-12. The reduction-gear control door motor is operated by an H-gate and contains a feedback potentiometer. (Chevrolet)

until the feedback circuit is closed through the appropriate resistor, shutting off the current. In another design, figure 19-11, a resistance signal from a variable resistor strip informs the computer of door position.

The computer program will change door position automatically whenever there is a change in ambient temperature or when the driver changes operating modes through the control pushbuttons. If an open develops in the feedback circuit, the actuator runs continuously until a timer circuit in the computer microprocessor shuts off current.

A permanent-magnet, reduction-gear dc motor with a gear-driven feedback potentiometer, figure 19-12, is used in the EATC system introduced on 1988 Chevrolet and GMC light-duty pickup trucks. This type of motor uses the principle of current polarity to control its direction of rotation. Current is applied, however, in a different way from the other reversible motors you have studied.

A group of four transistors called an H-gate is used to reverse current to the motor windings. When transistors A, figure 19-12, are forward biased, the motor rotates in one direction. When transistors B, figure 19-12, are for-

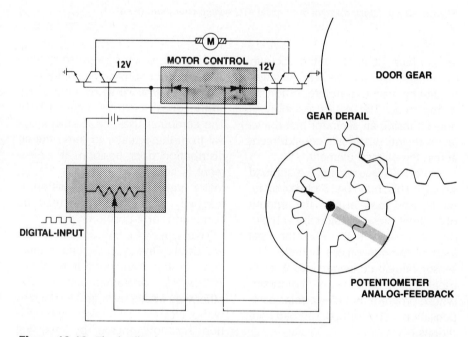

Figure 19-13. The feedback circuit in a reduction-gear control door motor uses a self-balancing bridge. (Chevrolet)

ward biased, current polarity is reversed in the motor windings, causing the motor to rotate in the opposite direction.

The final drive gear in the motor drives the feedback potentiometer, which signals door position through a 5-volt input voltage, ground, and feedback circuit, figure 19-12. The feedback circuit is a self-balancing bridge, figure 19-13. When the input and feedback voltages are balanced, no current flows in the motor control circuit. Any change in input voltage causes an imbalanced voltage condition in the motor control circuit. The appropriate pair of transistors in the H-gate are forward biased to drive the motor in the required direction. Motor operation moves the wiper in the potentiometer until the motor control circuit voltage is balanced and current flow stops in the motor control circuit.

Other Controls

EATC systems use other controls, either as separate modules and switches, or as a part of the computer program. The exact type of control and how it functions depends on the particular system, but general operation of these devices or computer programs is the same.

Blower Motor and A/C Clutch Module.
This module contains circuitry that converts low-current signals from the computer or BCM to a high-current, variable-ground feed signal to the blower motor through a relay. Blower motor speed is almost infinitely variable. In most systems, this means that up to 256 different speeds are available. A delay function in the microprocessor or BCM program allows gradual rather than abrupt changes in blower motor speed. A power transistor or solid-state relay in the module supplies voltage to operate the A/C compressor clutch.

Cold Engine Lockout Switch.
If the computer microprocessor or BCM program contains a cold engine lock-

out function, it will not operate the blower motor automatically until the air entering the passenger compartment reaches a specified temperature. With many systems, the driver can override the automatic blower feature and turn the blower on manually during this time.

The lockout function may rely on the ambient temperature sensor for its signal, or it may use a separate switch. When a separate switch is used, it generally is installed in the heater inlet or inlet hose to inform the computer or BCM of engine coolant temperature. The computer translates coolant temperature into air temperature through its program.

Power Steering Cutout Switch.
Most A/C systems use some form of switch that will shut off power to the compressor clutch coil when power steering pressure exceeds a specified value. In most EATC systems, the power steering switch also provides an input to the computer that is used for diagnostic purposes. This allows the computer to set a trouble code if the power steering switch malfunctions.

Clutch Diode.
The clutch diode protects the computer from voltage spikes that are produced by the release of the A/C compressor clutch coil.

Systems Controlled by Separate Computers

Several variations of computer-controlled EATC systems are used. The Chrysler, Ford, GM, and Chevrolet-GMC EATC systems are representative examples using different control methods. We will look at each in the following section.

Chrysler EATC System.
The Chrysler EATC system uses an individual computer with four kilobytes of memory built into the control assembly. The computer microprocessor regulates the incoming air temperature, measuring interior temperature and

adjusting the system as required every seven seconds. The control assembly microprocessor:

• Remembers the previous setting and returns to it when the vehicle is restarted
• Delays blower motor operation during cold engine starts
• Displays temperature settings in English or metric units
• Recognizes system malfunctions and sets fault codes that can be retrieved through the control assembly display
• Controls actuators by grounding their circuits

The instructions that the driver loads into the computer RAM will be lost if battery power is disconnected from the system. The system then must be reprogrammed for desired temperature settings.

The system is similar to the Chrysler SATC system discussed earlier, but uses three components not found in the SATC system:

1. Control assembly microprocessor
2. Power-vacuum module (PVM)
3. Blend-air door actuator

The PVM uses logic signals from the control assembly microprocessor to send a variable voltage signal to the blower motor, battery voltage to the A/C compressor clutch, a voltage signal to the blend-air door actuator, and vacuum to all other actuators. The blend-air door actuator is an electric servomotor that mechanically controls the blend-air door position. Figure 19-14 shows the system component relationship.

The self-diagnostic program is actuated by depressing the control assembly bilevel, floor, and defrost buttons at the same time, figure 19-15. If no faults are detected, the entire program is completed within 90 seconds. If the self-diagnostic test finds a failure, a fault code is flashed on the display panel. To resume diagnostics, press the panel button, figure 19-15. If fault code 3 is displayed, the blend-air door actuator must be serviced before

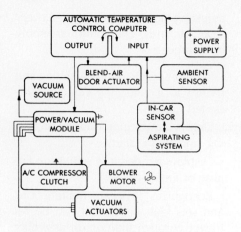

Figure 19-14. A block diagram of the Chrysler EATC system. (Chrysler)

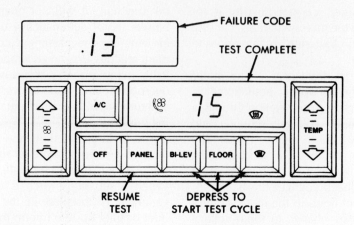

Figure 19-15. Chrysler EATC self-diagnostics flash fault codes on the control assembly display when the proper sequence of buttons is activated. (Chrysler)

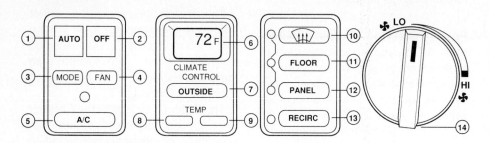

1. **AUTO—ON BUTTON**

2. **OFF—SYSTEM OFF**

3. **AUTO MODE INDICATOR**

4. **AUTO BLOWER INDICATOR**

5. **A/C COMPRESSOR OVERRIDE**

6. **DIGITAL DISPLAY WINDOW**

7. **OUTSIDE TEMPERATURE BUTTON**

8. **COOLER BUTTON**

9. **WARMER BUTTON**

10. **DEFROSTER OVERRIDE BUTTON**

11. **FLOOR OVERRIDE BUTTON**

12. **PANEL OVERRIDE BUTTON**

13. **RECIRC./OUTSIDE AIR OVERRIDE BUTTON**

14. **BLOWER SPEED OVERRIDE CONTROL**

Figure 19-16. The arrangement of control functions differs on Ford EATC control assemblies according to vehicle use. This arrangement is used with Ford Taurus and Mercury Sable models. (Ford)

the self-diagnostic test can be resumed. When the test cycle is completed, the display returns to a programmed normal defrost setting.

Ford EATC System. The microprocessor is built into the control assembly. Design and placement of the controls on the face of the assembly differ according to model year and application, figure 19-16. The control assembly microprocessor:

• Delays blower motor operation during cold engine starts

• Displays temperature settings in English or metric units

• Displays outside temperature when properly prompted

• Raises or lowers temperature in 1° F increments when properly prompted

• Recognizes system malfunctions and sets trouble codes that can be retrieved through the control assembly display

The Ford EATC system uses rotary actuators to control air distribution door positioning. Sensor inputs and actuator outputs are the same as figure 19-10 in some versions; other versions use an input from a sunload sensor and send the blower motor output signal through a high-blower relay. Figure 19-17 shows electronic control circuitry for the Ford Taurus and Mercury Sable. Circuitry differs according to model.

The self-test program is actuated by depressing two control assembly buttons at the same time, then immediately depressing another specified button, figure 19-16. The exact buttons used depend on the system application. The self-test sequence lasts for approximately 20 seconds and will flash a code on the display panel if a system failure is found. The display remains blank during the test if no problems are found. In some applications, the display reads 888 when the test is completed and the microprocessor restarts normal operation. In other applications, a final button must be depressed to signal the microprocessor to exit the self-test mode.

GM Electronic Touch Climate Control (ETCC) System. Like all other GM air conditioning systems, several versions of the ETCC system are used. The operation of all systems is similar, but they differ in the type of actuator and control device used. Air distribu-

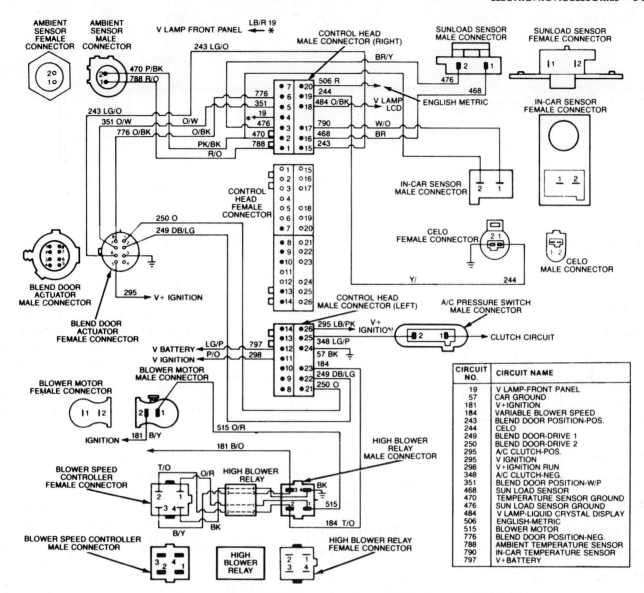

Figure 19-17. Electrical schematic of the Ford EATC control circuit used with the Ford Taurus and Mercury Sable.

CIRCUIT NO.	CIRCUIT NAME
19	V LAMP-FRONT PANEL
57	CAR GROUND
181	V+IGNITION
184	VARIABLE BLOWER SPEED
243	BLEND DOOR POSITION-POS.
244	CELO
249	BLEND DOOR-DRIVE 1
250	BLEND DOOR-DRIVE 2
295	A/C CLUTCH-POS.
295	V IGNITION
298	V+IGNITION RUN
348	A/C CLUTCH-NEG.
351	BLEND DOOR POSITION-W/P
468	SUN LOAD SENSOR
470	TEMPERATURE SENSOR GROUND
476	SUN LOAD SENSOR GROUND
484	V LAMP-LIQUID CRYSTAL DISPLAY
506	ENGLISH-METRIC
515	BLOWER MOTOR
776	BLEND DOOR POSITION-NEG.
788	AMBIENT TEMPERATURE SENSOR
790	IN-CAR TEMPERATURE SENSOR
797	V+BATTERY

tion doors are controlled by electric actuators on full-size cars. Smaller cars use vacuum-operated actuators. An electric servomotor controls the air-mix door on all models. Systems used on full-size luxury models control the blower speed through a power module, figure 19-18. These systems can store and display trouble codes if a system malfunction occurs.

All ETCC systems use a programmer unit of some type to transmit microprocessor output signals to the various actuators. Output signals to the blower motor and compressor clutch are sent through the programmer ei-

ther to a power module (luxury cars), or to a blower and A/C clutch module (others). In a system with a power module, compressor clutch ground is through the low-pressure switch. When a blower and A/C clutch module is used, power to the compressor clutch is sent through a fuse and the power steering cutout switch or a diode. The compressor ground circuit is cycled by the module.

ETCC systems with a self-diagnostic mode use feedback signals from the actuators to locate a system malfunction. If the feedback signal from an actuator is out of specifications, the

microprocessor will set a trouble code in memory. Trouble codes are retrieved and displayed on the climate control panel (CCP) by depressing the correct sequence of CCP buttons. The exact sequence and buttons used for trouble code retrieval depend upon the particular system application. You match the trouble code retrieved with the proper diagnostic chart to pinpoint the cause of the problem.

Chevrolet-GMC EATC System. This EATC system was introduced on 1988 Chevrolet and GMC light-duty pickup trucks. It is considerably different than

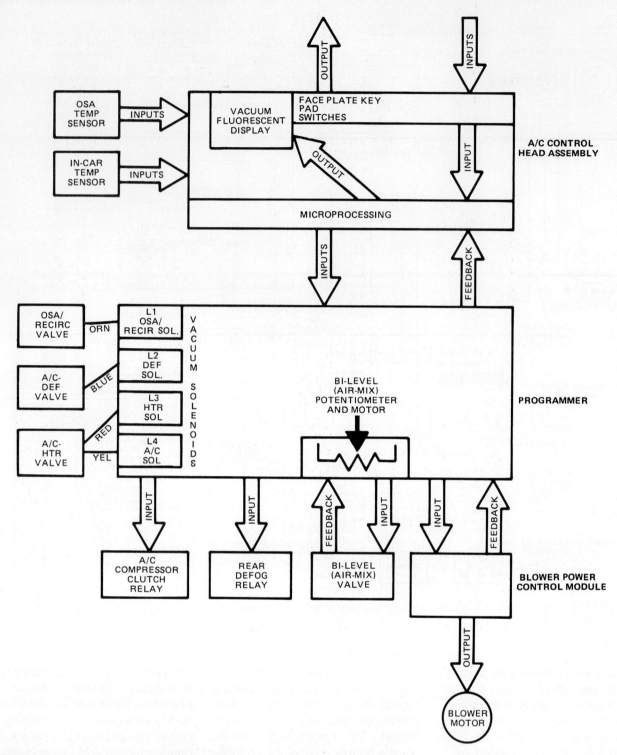

Figure 19-18. This block diagram of a typical GM ETCC system used on full-size cars shows the relationship of the control assembly, programmer, and blower module in system operation. (Buick)

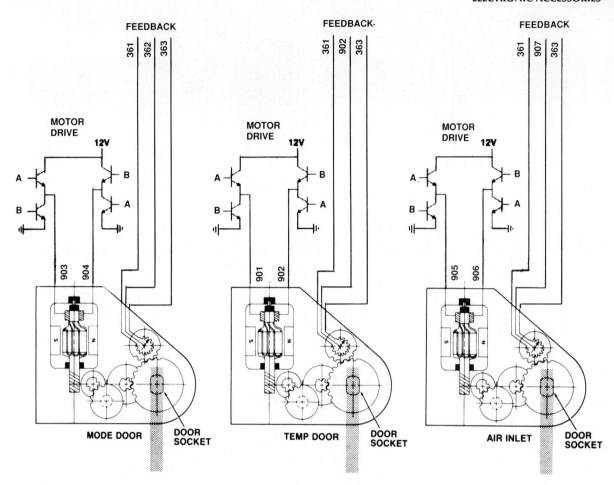

Figure 19-19. Reduction-gear actuator motors in the Chevrolet and GMC ETAS system share common input and ground circuits but have individual feedback circuits. (Chevrolet)

other GM microprocesssor-controlled EATC systems, both in the components used and how they are controlled.

The microprocessor is contained in the control assembly. It does not have a self-diagnostic function, does not have any sensors, and does not provide an infinitely variable blower speed. It is a hybrid system that fails to fit into any preconceived category.

Driver input to the control assembly tells the computer microprocessor what to do. The microprocessor operates the air distribution control doors through reduction-gear motors, figure 19-12, with a feedback potentiometer circuit, figure 19-13. The input voltage and ground are supplied to all motors through common circuits. Separate feedback circuits are wired individually to the control assembly,

figure 19-19. The microprocessor driver circuits are controlled initially by driver input. Once the system is operating, the feedback circuits provide the input used by the microprocessor to operate the driver circuits, figure 19-20.

A relay driver in the microprocessor controls two blower relays and the A/C clutch coil relay, figure 19-21. The microprocessor driver energizes the relays as required to set the blower speed or engage the compressor clutch. Power to the relay coils is transmitted on circuit 50, with the control head operating the circuit ground. Blower speed is determined by the two relays and two resistors, figure 19-22. This is similar to blower speed control in a manual A/C system, where voltage is routed through resistors on the resistor block. Energizing

both relays sends current through both resistors in series, resulting in a low blower speed. Energizing only the low relay bypasses the second resistor and gives a medium blower speed. Energizing only the high relay bypasses both resistors and sends current directly to the blower motor for a high blower speed.

BCM-Controlled Systems

Climate control is one of the primary BCM functions in GM luxury vehicles. A BCM-controlled system uses many of the same components found in other A/C systems and operates in much the same way. The primary difference between a system operated by a microprocessor in a separate control assembly and one that is controlled by

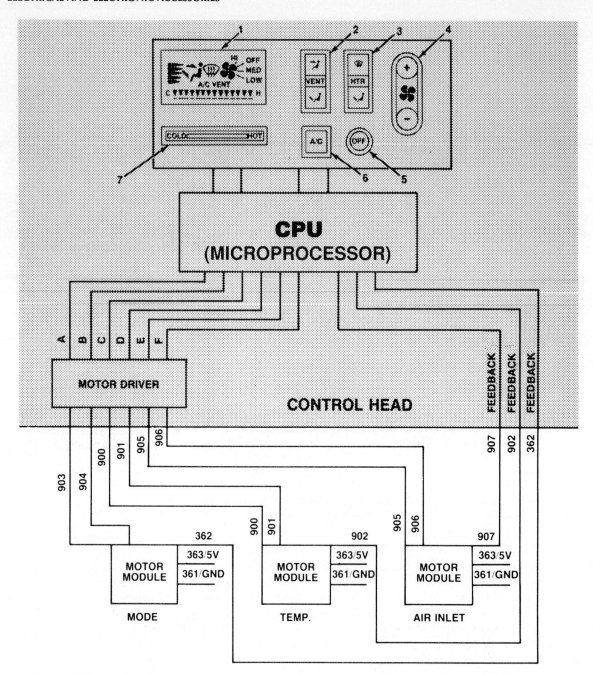

1. **Vacuum Fluorescent Display**

	Air Outlet Position Indicators
	Defrost "On" Indicator
	Fan Speed Indicator
A/C	Air Conditioning "On" Indicator
VENT	Vent "On" Indicator
C▼▼▼▼H	Temperature Position Indicator

2. Vent Function Selector Switch
3. Heater/Defrost Function Selector Switch
4. Fan Speed Selector Switch
5. System Off Button
6. Air Conditioning Function Button
7. Outlet Air Temperature Selector Bar

Figure 19-20. The microprocessor controls the motor drivers and receives feedback signals from the individual motors. (Chevrolet)

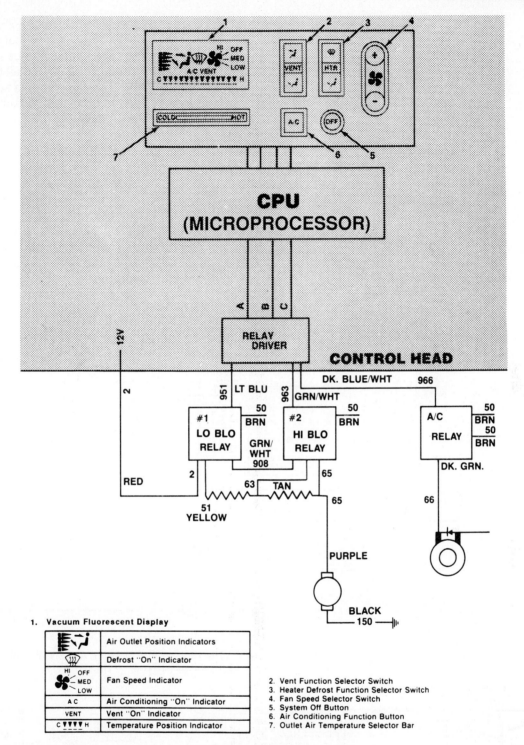

1. Vacuum Fluorescent Display

	Air Outlet Position Indicators
	Defrost "On" Indicator
	Fan Speed Indicator
A C	Air Conditioning "On" Indicator
VENT	Vent "On" Indicator
C ▼▼▼▼ H	Temperature Position Indicator

2. Vent Function Selector Switch
3. Heater Defrost Function Selector Switch
4. Fan Speed Selector Switch
5. System Off Button
6. Air Conditioning Function Button
7. Outlet Air Temperature Selector Bar

Figure 19-21. Relays and resistors control blower motor speed according to output signals from the control assembly relay driver. (Chevrolet)

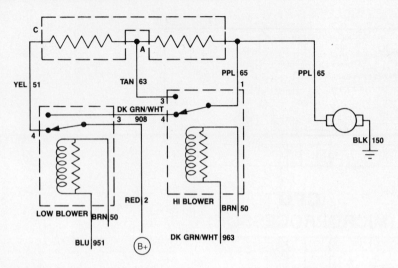

Figure 19-22. Blower speed depends upon which combination of relays and resistors are used. (Chevrolet)

the BCM, figure 19-23, is that the BCM acts as the central microprocessor and communicates with both the control assembly circuit board and the A/C programmer on a serial data link to transmit data serially (one piece after another).

Control Assemblies. The instrument panel control assembly that we have seen in all systems may be called an electronic comfort control (ECC) panel, figure 19-24, or a climate control panel (CCP), figure 19-25. The ECC or CCP contains a circuit board that translates driver requests into electrical signals that are sent to the BCM. The BCM acts as the system

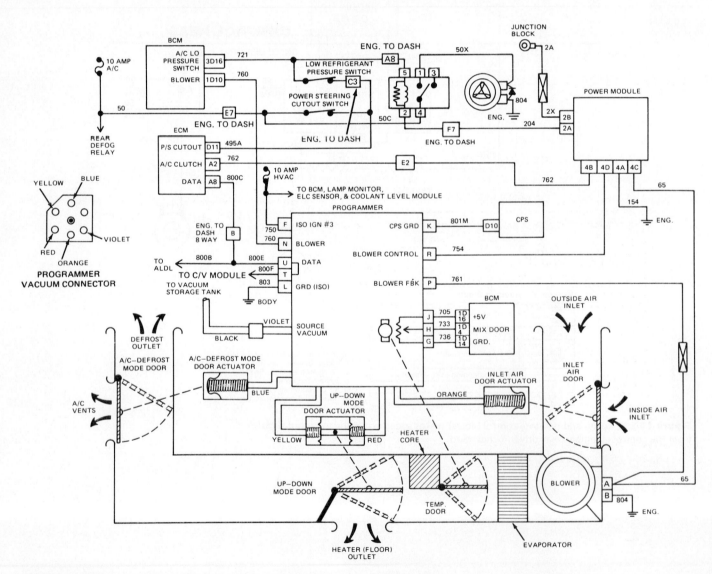

Figure 19-23. A schematic of a BCM-controlled air conditioning system. (Oldsmobile)

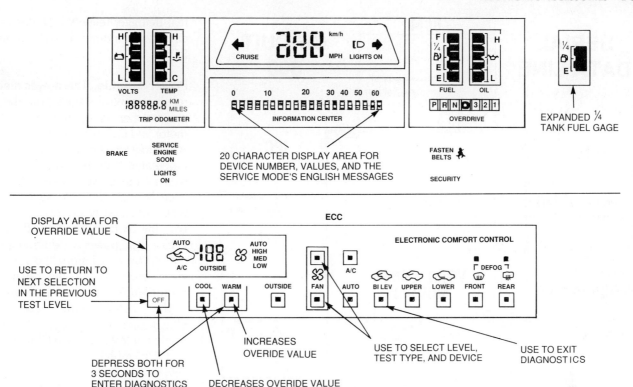

Figure 19-24. The ECC panel is part of the instrument panel control (IPC). Both are used when running the diagnostic program. (Oldsmobile)

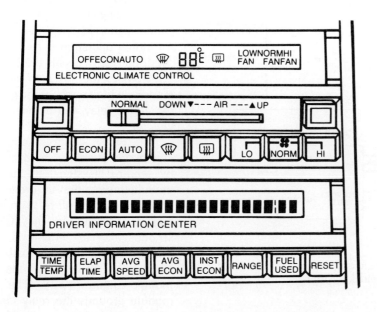

Figure 19-25. The climate control panel (CCP) is combined with the driver information system (DIS). Both are used when running the diagnostic program. (Cadillac)

microprocessor and maintains 2-way communication with the ECC or CCP panel over a serial data line or data link, figure 19-26, as you learned in chapter 5. You may want to review BCM operation as discussed in chapter 5.

A/C Programmer. The BCM also communicates on the serial data line with the A/C programmer to control air distribution and temperature. The programmer may use solenoids to direct vacuum to the air distribution mode doors and a reversible electric motor to operate the air-mix door that controls temperature, or it may use reversible electric motors to control all doors. Unlike the ECC panel, which maintains constant 2-way communication with the BCM, the A/C programmer is restricted to receiving data transmission from the BCM except for a return signal to indicate that it has received the transmission. The air-mix door motor sends a position sensor signal to the BCM that allows the BCM to monitor the door position.

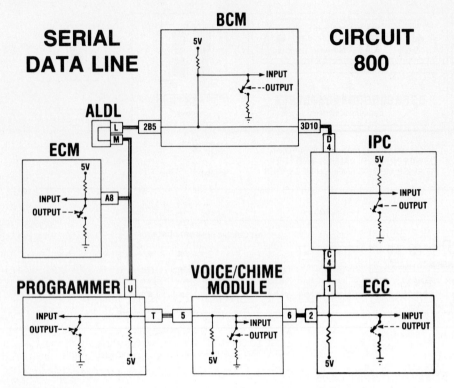

Figure 19-26. The BCM communicates with the ECC, ECM, and A/C programmer on a serial data line. (Oldsmobile)

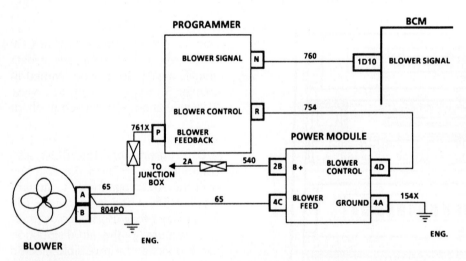

Figure 19-27. The A/C programmer monitors blower motor speed through a feedback circuit and increases or decreases blower speed as required. (Oldsmobile)

The BCM processes sensor inputs and calculates the blower speed necessary to maintain the desired passenger compartment temperature. It controls blower speed by signaling the A/C programmer on a separate circuit, figure 19-27. The A/C programmer sends a variable voltage (pulse-width-modulated) signal to the power mod-ule, which amplifies the signal and provides the high voltage required to operate the blower motor. A blower motor feedback circuit, figure 19-27, allows the A/C programmer to monitor blower motor speed, increasing or decreasing the signal voltage to maintain the desired blower speed. The A/C programmer also may control a

rear defogger relay (if included in the circuit) when directed to do so by the BCM.

Power Module. The power module receives control signals from the A/C programmer to operate the blower motor and the compressor clutch. The A/C programmer sends pulse-width-modulated (PWM) blower motor sig-nals to the power module. As you have learned, a PWM signal is one that continuously cycles on and off, with the on time varying within each cycle. The power module amplifies the PWM signal from the A/C pro-grammer to a strong output signal that is proportionate to the input signal.

The BCM controls compressor clutch operation through the elec-tronic control module (ECM) in Buick and Oldsmobile circuits. The BCM signals the ECM on the serial data line, figure 19-26, to activate the clutch. The ECM transmits this signal to the power module on a separate circuit. The power module grounds the compressor clutch relay, sending power through the relay to operate the clutch, figure 19-28. When compres-sor clutch operation is no longer de-sired, the BCM signals the ECM. The ECM passes the signal to the power module, which removes the ground to the clutch relay and deenergizes the clutch.

The BCM controls compressor clutch operation in Cadillac circuits by sending its signal to the power module through the A/C programmer. A compressor cutoff relay in the cir-cuit is energized by the ECM four seconds after the engine is started. This provides a ground path to the clutch relay coil through the power module, figure 19-29. The power module grounds the relay circuit to activate the compressor clutch. Once the compressor clutch is in operation, the ECM controls it through the cutoff relay according to vehicle operating condition.

Self-Diagnostics. The BCM-controlled A/C system is the most complex of the systems we have stud-ied. This complexity also is reflected

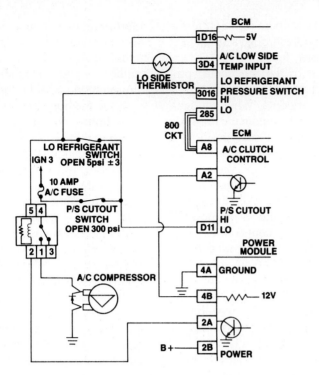

Figure 19-28. The Buick and Oldsmobile compressor clutch circuit. (Oldsmobile)

in the self-diagnostic program. If a failure occurs in any subsystem, a trouble code is set in ECM or BCM memory. The ECM and BCM both can set codes. Which one sets the code depends upon the type of failure. The codes are retrieved through the instrument panel control (IPC) display, figure 19-24, or the driver information center (DIC) display, figure 19-25, after the diagnostic mode has been entered. ECM codes are displayed first, followed by BCM codes. To diagnose possible A/C system failures, you will have to check both sets of codes, since each computer may set codes relating to A/C system operation.

MEMORY SEATS

A memory seat feature is a recent addition to power seat circuits. The

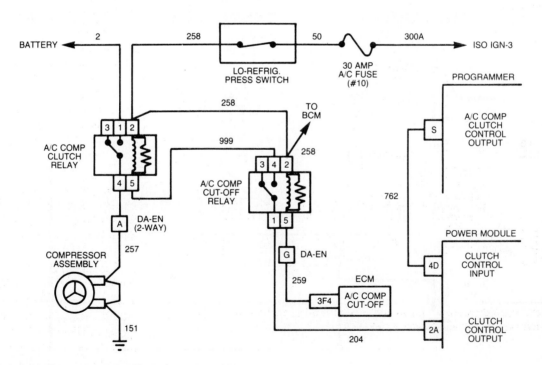

Figure 19-29. The Cadillac compressor clutch circuit. (Cadillac)

feature allows the driver to program different seat positions that can be recalled at the push of a button. Different positions can be programmed into the system memory at any time, much like a programmable radio. The systems used on the front-wheel-drive Oldsmobile 98 Regency and the 1988 Continental demonstrate the different technology in use.

Oldsmobile 98 Regency System Components and Operation

The Regency memory seat system consists of a memory module and a combined 6-way seat and memory switch assembly. The system provides automatic return of the driver's seat to one of two preset positions. Voltage is applied at all times to the seat switch

through a 15-ampere fuse and to the memory module through a 30-ampere circuit breaker, figure 19-30.

Operation of the seat motor produces electrical pulses detected by the memory module. When the ignition is on with the automatic transaxle in Park, a desired seat position is stored in memory by depressing the set memory switch and moving the memory select switch to memory position 1 or 2. Whenever the seat is moved away from the Set position, the memory module counts the motor pulses and detects the direction of movement. When the driver operates the easy exit switch to leave the vehicle, voltage is applied to both the memory 1 and 2 inputs of the module. The module responds to this signal by moving the seat to the fully down and fully back position. When the driver

returns and moves the memory select switch to the desired position, the module operates the seat to the preset position by counting motor pulses.

A memory disable function prevents the memory module from operating unless the transaxle selector lever is in Park. This prevents accidental seat operation while the vehicle is in motion. The disable function receives power through a separate 20-ampere fuse and a memory disable relay, figure 19-31. Current to the disable relay coil is sent through a 15-ampere fuse and the transaxle gear selector switch. When the selector lever is in Park, current is sent to ground through the disable relay coil. This opens the relay contact points and shuts off power to the disable input on the memory module, allowing the module to function.

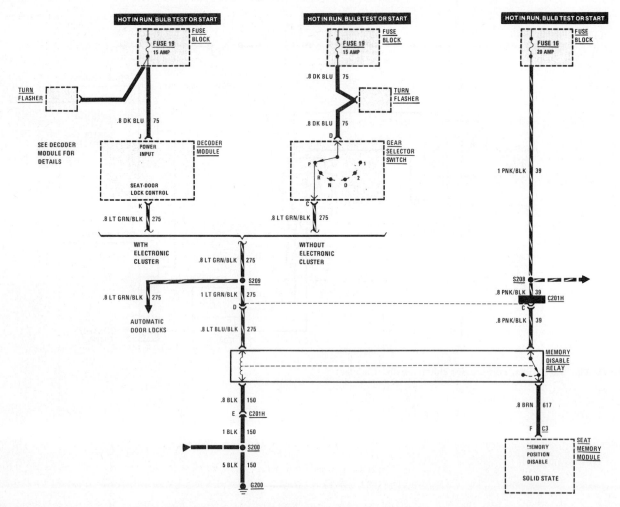

Figure 19-30. Oldsmobile 98 Regency memory seat circuit diagram. (Oldsmobile)

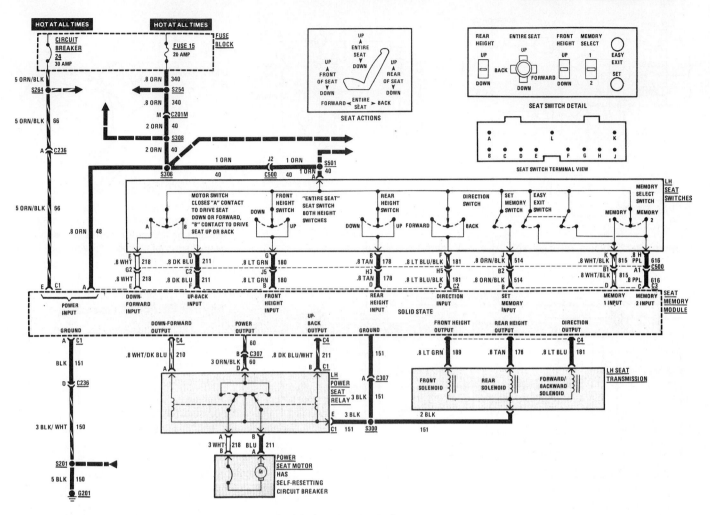

Figure 19-31. Oldsmobile 98 Regency memory seat disable function circuit diagram. (Oldsmobile)

Continental System Components and Operation

The Continental memory seat system consists of a control module with memory button control, variable resistance sensors, the doorjamb switch, and connecting wiring. The module receives battery power through the fuse block and is installed in the circuit between the 6-way control switch and the seat motor assembly. Properly programmed, the seat moves to the rear when the door is opened. After entering the vehicle, the driver depresses the appropriate seat memory button, and the seat moves to the appropriate position.

The system is programmed by moving the seat to the desired position with the 6-way seat control switch. To lock the seat position in memory, the SET button on the seat memory control

is depressed, followed by button 1. Two other positions can be programmed into the module memory in the same way. Button 2 is depressed to set the second position in memory; buttons 1 and 2 are depressed at the same time to set the third position.

Once the positions are set in the control module memory, they can be recalled by depressing the appropriate seat memory control button. Depressing button 1 recalls position 1; depressing button 2 recalls position 2. To recall position 3, buttons 1 and 2 are depressed at the same time. When a button is depressed to recall a position, the control module sends current to the appropriate seat motor to move the seat. When the seat reaches the position in memory, the module shuts off power to the seat motor.

If the battery is disconnected, the seat positions must be reprogrammed.

A loss of battery power erases the module memory. Any seat positions that were programmed are replaced by the current seat position in all three memory locations. The control module contains a self-test feature activated by a self-test button on the module. A module malfunction prevents the 6-way seat control from working.

ELECTRONIC SUNROOFS

Electronic controls have been added to electric sunroofs. The solid-state module contains two relays and a timer function that control rotation of the reversible sunroof motor according to signals from one or more sunroof limit switches. The Toyota and GM systems discussed below are typical of the electronic sunroof systems in use.

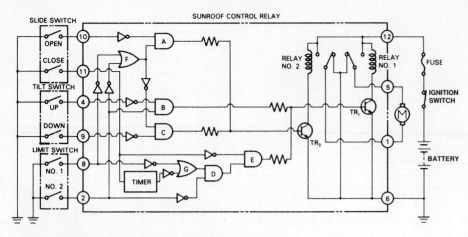

Figure 19-32. Typical Toyota electronic sunroof control circuit. (Toyota)

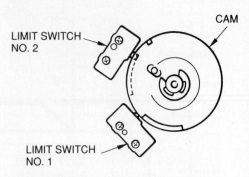

Figure 19-33. Two cam-operated limit switches on the motor inform the control relay of sunroof position. (Toyota)

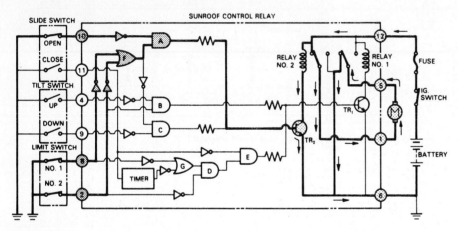

Figure 19-34. Circuit operation during sunroof opening sequence. (Toyota)

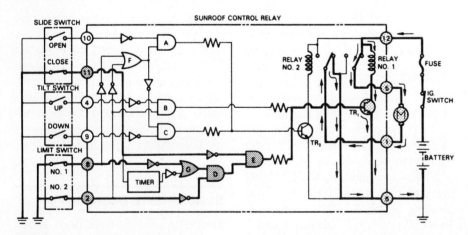

Figure 19-35. Circuit operation during sunroof closure (open more than 7-1/2 inches). (Toyota)

Toyota Sunroof Operation

Sunroof movement is controlled by the sunroof motor drive gear driven by the sunroof motor. Drive gear movement slides the sunroof forward or backward by pushing or pulling the connecting cables.

In a typical Toyota sunroof system, figure 19-32, the control relay controls sunroof motor rotation according to signals from the sunroof slide or tilt switches and the limit switches. The two limit switches attached to the sunroof motor are operated by a cam, figure 19-33, and send the position of the sunroof to the control relay.

When the slide switch is moved to the Open position, both limit switches are on. Limit switch 2 turns Tr_2 on. This energizes relay 2, and current is sent to the sunroof motor, figure 19-34, as long as the switch is held in the Open position. A clutch in the motor disengages it from the drive gear if the switch is held open longer than necessary.

Once the sunroof is open more than 7 1/2 inches and the slide switch is moved to the Close position, Tr_1 turns on, energizing relay 1. This sends current to the motor in the reverse direction, figure 19-35, and the sunroof closes as long as the switch is held in the Close position. Limit switch 2 goes off if the switch is held closed longer than necessary. This deenergizes relay 1 and shuts off the motor.

If the sunroof is open less than 7 1/2 inches, a timer function in the control module comes on, figure 19-36. When the slide switch is moved to the Close position, the timer sends a 0.5-second on signal. This turns on Tr_1, which energizes relay 1 to send current to the motor. The motor operates for 0.5 second, long enough for the rotation of the motor cam to operate limit switch 1. As soon as limit switch 1 turns on, relay 1 is energized and the motor continues to close the sunroof.

Depressing the up side of the tilt switch turns on Tr_1 and energizes relay 1, figure 19-37. Both limit switches are off, and current is sent to the motor to tilt the sunroof up as long as the switch is held in the Up position. The motor clutch disengages it from the drive gear to prevent motor damage if the tilt switch is held in the Up position longer than necessary.

When the sunroof is up and the down side of the tilt switch is depressed, Tr_2 comes on and relay 2 is energized. Both limit switches are off, and current is sent to the motor in the opposite direction, figure 19-38, to lower the sunroof as long as the switch is held in the Down position. If the switch is held closed longer than necessary, limit switch 1 turns on. When this happens, Tr_2 goes off, deenergizing relay 2. This shuts off current to the motor.

GM Sunroof Operation

Turning on the ignition switch sends power to the electronic module, rocker switch, limit switch, and motor. With the rocker switch held in the rearward position, the "open" relay is energized, figure 19-39, sending current to the reversible motor. As long as the switch is held depressed, the motor will continue to retract the sunroof until the limit switch opens. This breaks the circuit to the open relay, shutting off current to the motor.

Holding the rocker switch in the forward position energizes the "close" relay, figure 19-40, sending current to the motor in the opposite

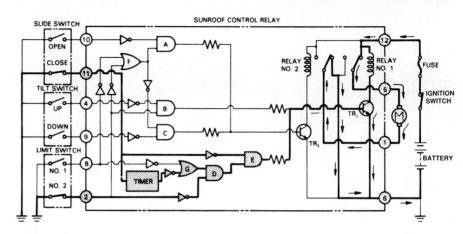

Figure 19-36. Circuit operation during sunroof closure (open less than 7-1/2 inches). (Toyota)

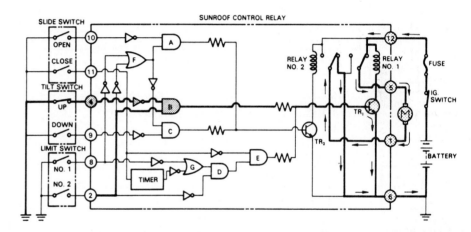

Figure 19-37. Circuit operation during sunroof tilt up. (Toyota)

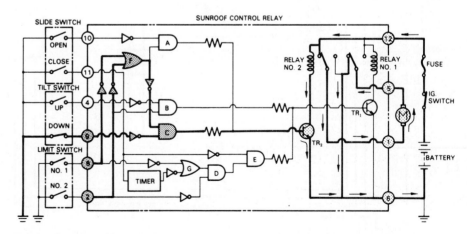

Figure 19-38. Circuit operation during sunroof tilt down. (Toyota)

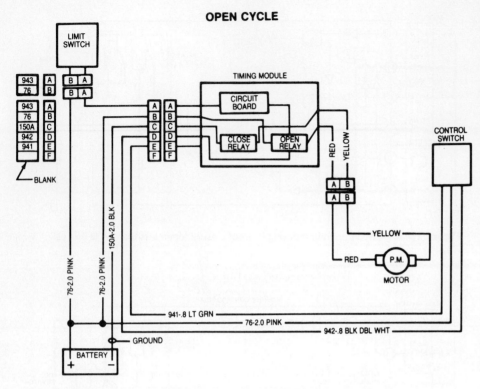

Figure 19-39. Open cycle operation of the GM electronic sunroof. (GM)

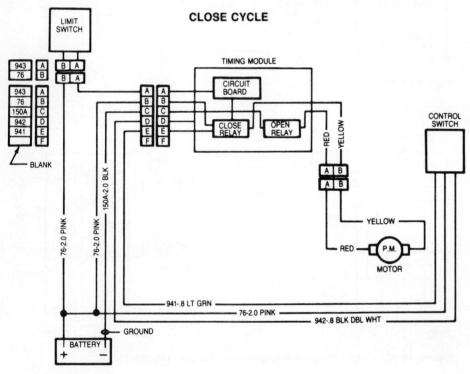

Figure 19-40. Close cycle operation of the GM electronic sunroof. (GM)

direction. The motor reverses its direction and moves the sunroof to the front. The motor will operate until the switch is released or the sunroof closes completely and the limit switch opens.

ANTITHEFT SYSTEMS

Vehicle antitheft systems have been popular aftermarket additions for many years. Some automakers have offered factory-installed antitheft options in the past, but it is just recently that such systems have been made a standard feature on the more expensive and theft-prone models.

The basic antitheft system is designed to provide a warning if a forced entry is attempted through the vehicle doors or the trunk lid. Activating the system causes the horn to sound intermittently and the exterior lights to flash for a specific period. Some models also are designed with a starter interlock feature.

The switches that operate the system are installed in the door jambs, the door lock cylinders, and the trunk lock cylinder, figure 19-41. When the antitheft system is armed, any attempt to rotate or remove the lock cylinders or to open any door or the trunk lid without a key will trip the alarm controller.

After the driver has armed the system and closed the doors, a warning lamp in the instrument cluster lights for several seconds, then goes out. Unlocking a front door from the outside with the key or turning the igni-

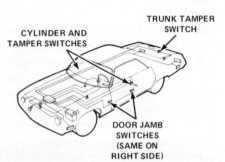

Figure 19-41. Switches in the doorjambs and lock cylinders operate a typical antitheft system. (GM)

tion switch on within a specified time disarms the system. If the alarm has been tripped, the system is disarmed by unlocking a front door with the key.

Most factory-installed antitheft systems integrate the operation of several other circuits, including the exterior lights, horn, starter, power door locks, and keyless entry, with the controller and various switches that make up the antitheft circuit. This makes an antitheft system a complex multiple circuit system that requires the automaker's circuit schematic and wiring diagram to diagnose.

Corvette Vehicle Antitheft System (VATS)

The VATS system was introduced as standard equipment on the 1986 Corvette. It acts as an ignition-disable system and can work alone or in conjunction with a version of the Delco universal theft deterrent (UTD) system, figure 19-42, called the forced entry alarm (FES) system. The VATS system does not prevent forced entry, but is specifically designed to protect the steering column lock assembly once an intruder is in the vehicle. When used on vehicles other than the Corvette, the system is called personal automotive security system (PASS).

The VATS or PASS system, figure 19-43, consists of the following components:

• Resistor ignition key
• Resistor-sensing contact
• VATS decoder module
• Starter enable relay
• Wiring harnesses

The ignition key contains a small resistor pellet. Each of the 15 different pellets used has a specific resistance value. The key is coded with a number indicating which resistor pellet it contains. Resistor pellet resistance values vary between 380 ohms and 12,300 ohms. The key must have the correct mechanical code (1 of 2,000) to operate the lock and the proper electrical code (1 of 15) to close the starter circuit.

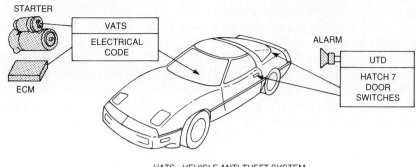

VATS - VEHICLE ANTI-THEFT SYSTEM
UTD - UNIVERSAL THEFT DETERRENT

Figure 19-42. The Delco VATS or PASS system is a resistor-key circuit that can be used alone or with a UTD system. (GM)

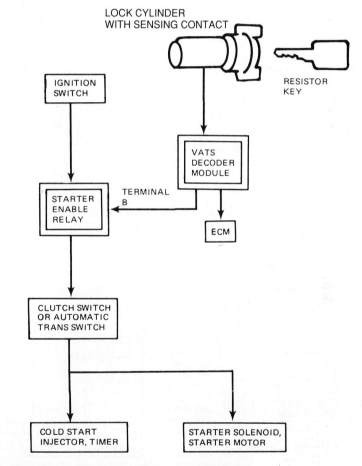

Figure 19-43. The VATS system components. (Chevrolet)

When the key is inserted in the ignition lock cylinder, the resistor pellet makes contact with the resistor-sensing contact. Rotating the lock applies battery power from the VATS fuse to the VATS decoder module. The sensing contact transmits the resistance value of the pellet to the decoder module, whose logic circuits compare the signal to a fixed resistance value in memory. If the resistor code matches the fixed value, the decoder module energizes the starter enable relay. This completes the starter circuit and signals the ECM to start fuel delivery. If the resistor code is incorrect, the decoder module circuitry shuts off for two to four minutes.

Attempting to start the engine a second time without the correct key resets the timer circuit in the decoder module. This cycle will repeat until the correct key is used. The starter-enable relay also prevents vehicle operation without the use of a key, as in cases when the lock cylinder is forcibly removed.

Delco Universal Theft Deterrent (UTD) System

The UTD system has been optional on high-line GM cars with power or automatic door locks since 1980 and is wired in various ways depending upon the vehicle and how it is equipped. You will need the exact wiring diagram to understand system operation on a particular vehicle.

The UTD system consists of the following components:

• Electronic controller
• Doorjamb switches
• Cylinder tamper switches
• Disarm switch

The electronic controller contains the circuitry, logic, and power relays that operate the system. A 2-terminal doorjamb switch is installed at each of the vehicle doors to activate the alarm whenever a door is opened with the system armed. One terminal of the switch operates the dome and courtesy lamps. The other terminal connects to the controller to activate the alarm. One terminal of the doorjamb switch used on the driver's door also operates the key warning buzzer. If the vehicle has power door locks, a diode is used to separate the circuits.

All door locks and the trunk lid lock are fitted with cylinder tamper-proof switches, figure 19-44. These switches are activated by rotation or in-and-out movement of the lock cylinders caused by an attempted forced entry. The disarm switch, figure 19-45, allows the owner to disarm the system and enter the vehicle.

Ford Antitheft Protection System

Ford's antitheft system, figure 19-46, is available on high-line models and works similarly to the Delco UTD system. When the system is armed, unauthorized entry or tampering with

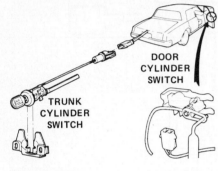

Figure 19-44. Cylinder tamper switches are activated by rotation or in-and-out movement of the lock. (GM)

Figure 19-45. The disarm switch allows the system to be deactivated without sounding the alarm. (GM)

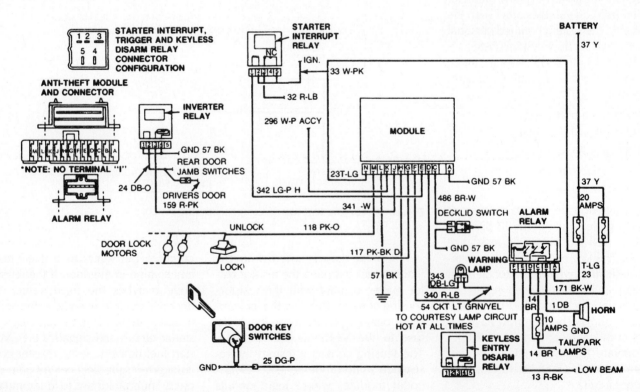

Figure 19-46. The Ford antitheft protection system circuit schematic. (Ford)

DRIVE-BY-WIRE, OR WHERE DID THE THROTTLE CABLE GO?

Throughout the decade of the 1990's, the automobile appears destined to fulfill the fantasies of the 1950's science fiction writers. Although we will not see remote control guidance of vehicles over programmed routes for some time yet, the changes in automotive technology brought about by electronics have only begun. While drive-by-wire, electronic gas pedal, and electronic accelerator are all esoteric terms, they simply describe a system in which electronics will replace the mechanical linkage between your foot and the fuel injection unit.

In principle, the system will consist of three components:

• An acceleration deflection sensor or sending unit
• An electronic control module
• A throttle actuator

The sending unit will be an integrated potentiometer, figure 1, that transmits a voltage signal to the control module proportional to the accelerator pedal movement. This signal tells the module of any changes in accelerator pedal position. Contact points in the sensor also can provide idle or kickdown signals to the module.

The module contains processing, logic, and control circuits. The digital program contains memory values and converts the analog sensor signal to a digital signal. It also receives signals from existing engine control sensors to determine engine load and speed conditions, temperature, and other related factors. After calculating the inputs, the control module sends a signal to an actuator to move the throttle plate to the correct position.

This actuator, or electronic throttle valve, can be as simple as a motor that drives the existing throttle plate, or an integrated motor with gear train, figure 2, that moves the throttle under spring load. A potentiometer at the throttle shaft can provide the control unit with a feedback signal.

Whatever form the controls take, they will eliminate mechanical wear, friction, and looseness as factors in vehicle operation, resulting in greater precision in throttle position control and more efficient use of fuel.

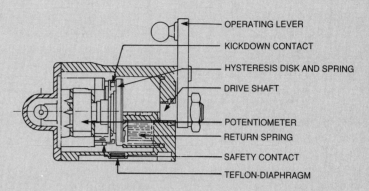

Figure 1.

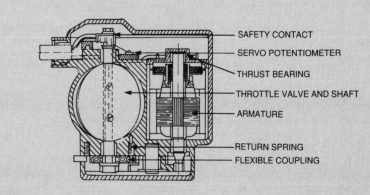

Figure 2.

lock cylinders triggers the control module. The system sounds the horn; flashes the low-beam headlamps, tail-lamps, and parking lamps on and off; and interrupts the starter circuit.

The system consists of the following components:

• Electronic control module
• Alarm relay
• Starter interrupt relay
• Indicator lamp
• Door key unlock switches
• Courtesy lamp inverter relay
• Lock cylinder tamper switch

When the ignition switch is turned off, voltage to the control module circuit 296 is removed. Opening the door applies voltage to the courtesy lamp circuit 24 through the closed courtesy lamp switch. This energizes the inverter relay, providing a ground path through the closed relay contacts and circuit 341 to the control module. The module applies a pulsating ground signal to the indicator lamp, causing it to blink. Activating the power door lock switch or pressing the last two buttons of the keyless entry keypad at the same time applies voltage to the control module on circuit 117 and to ground on circuit 118. Closing the door completes the arming sequence and replaces the pulsating ground signal to the indicator lamp with a steady signal for about 30 seconds, or until the module timer function ends.

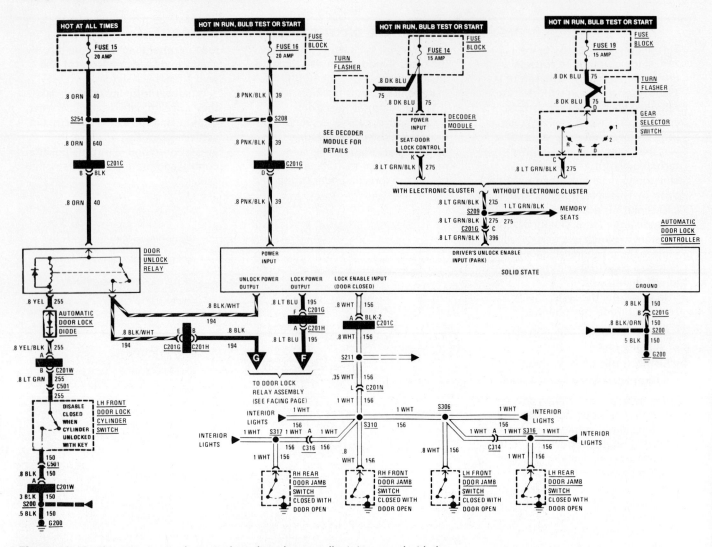

Figure 19-47. This ADL circuit schematic shows how the controller is integrated with the power door lock system in an automatic door lock system. (Oldsmobile)

If unauthorized entry or lock cylinder tampering occurs, the control module applies a pulsating ground signal to the 3-contact alarm relay on circuit 340, turning it on and off. This sends a pulsating voltage to the horn, headlamp, and taillamp circuits. The module also sends a continuous ground signal on circuit 342 to energize the starter interrupt relay. The relay contacts open and break starter circuit 32 to prevent the engine from starting.

Disarming the system with the door key provides a ground path to the control module through the door switch on circuit 25. If a keyless entry system is used, voltage is sent to the disarm relay coil on circuit 163. This energizes the coil and applies a ground through the closed relay contacts and circuit 25 to the control module.

AUTOMATIC DOOR LOCK (ADL) SYSTEM

This safety and convenience system automatically locks all vehicle doors when the transaxle gear selector is placed in Drive. Each door can be unlocked manually, or all doors can be unlocked electrically while in Drive. Moving the gear selector to park automatically unlocks all doors on some models.

System Operation

The ADL controller operates the system by monitoring the gear selector switch and the doorjamb switches. In a typical GM automatic door circuit, figure 19-47, voltage is applied through fuse 16 to the ADL controller when the ignition switch is moved to the run, bulb test, or start position. Once the doors are closed and the gear selector is placed in drive, the ADL controller sends current to ground through the lock relay coil in the lock relay assembly. Current passes through circuit breaker 24, the lock relay contacts, door lock motors, and unlock relay contacts to ground, locking the doors. The ADL controller

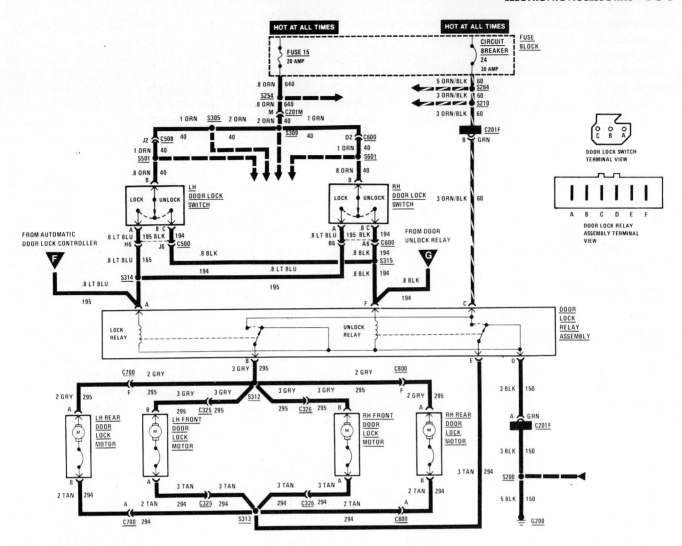

Figure 19-47. (continued)

then removes power from the relay to protect the lock motors.

When the driver stops the vehicle and places the gear selector in Park, voltage is applied to the unlock enable input of the ADL controller. Current is sent to the unlock relay coil in the lock relay assembly, unlocking the doors.

The doors are unlocked from the outside with the key. Voltage from fuse 15 is applied to the door unlock relay at all times. When the door is unlocked with the key, current from the door unlock relay goes to ground through the ADL diode and door lock cylinder switch, operating the relay. Current flows through the unlock relay contacts to the unlock relay coil

in the lock relay assembly, unlocking all doors. The ADL controller then removes power from the relay to protect the lock motors.

KEYLESS ENTRY SYSTEMS

Ford pioneered the keyless entry system on domestic vehicles. Its present keyless entry system, figure 19-48, consists of a 5-button keypad attached to the outer panel of the driver's door, a microprocessor-relay control module, and connecting wiring. Figure 19-49 shows a typical Ford keyless entry circuit diagram.

The keyless entry system performs four specific jobs and also includes

the functions of an illuminated entry system and an automatic door lock system. The system:

1. Unlocks the driver's door

2. Unlocks other doors if a specified keypad button is depressed within five seconds of unlocking the driver's door

3. Unlocks the trunk lid when a specified keypad button is depressed within five seconds of unlocking the driver's door

4. Locks all doors from outside the car when the specified keypad buttons are depressed at the same time

5. Turns on interior lamps and the illuminated keyhole in the driver's door

6. Automatically locks all doors with the driver in position, all doors closed, the ignition switch on, and the transmission or transaxle selector in reverse.

A 5-digit keypad code is printed both on the module and on a sticker attached to the inside of the trunk lid. The 5-digit code refers to the button location on the keypad, instead of the button number (the keypad buttons are numbered 1-2, 3-4, 5-6, 7-8, and 9-0 from left to right). The code used to open the vehicle is derived from the 5-digit module number. For example, if the module number is 31254, the code used to open the vehicle may be 51397, 62408, 61397, 52408, etc. Between the module number and the possible derivations from it, there are enough different number combinations from one module to prevent an unauthorized person from opening the door. When a replacement module is installed, the new module code sticker is applied over the old sticker on the trunk lid.

A calculator-type keypad installed in the driver's door is used to input the code to the module. The module is programmed to control the keyless entry, illuminated entry, and automatic door lock systems. The module connects to the keyless entry system wiring harness through two different colored 14-pin connectors. One of the 14-pin connectors also connects the module to the keypad harness.

Two different keypad harness con-

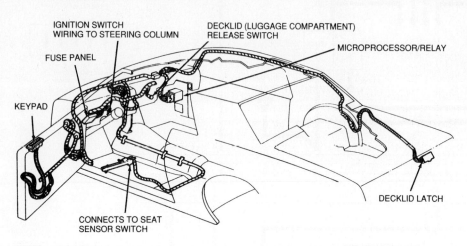

Figure 19-48. The Ford keyless entry system components and wiring harness. (Ford)

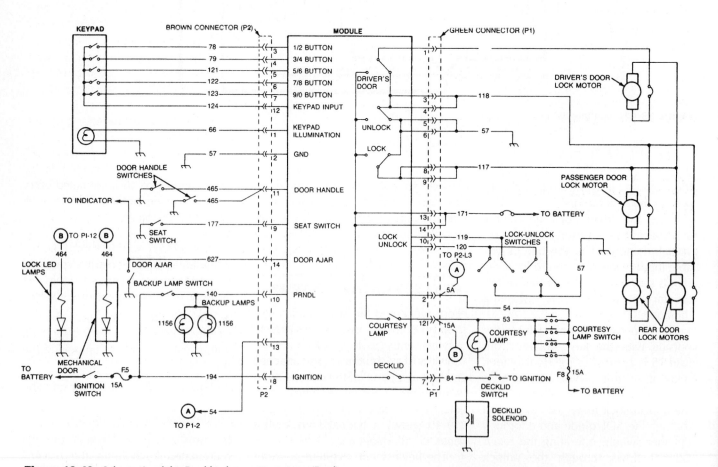

Figure 19-49. Schematic of the Ford keyless entry system. (Ford)

nector designs have been used. Early versions of the system have a curved connector; later versions use a square connector. The system works exactly the same regardless of the keypad connector used, but terminal identification of the keypad connector differs, as you will learn in chapter 18 of Volume 2.

The module uses inputs from the following components:

- Keypad buttons
- Courtesy lamp switch
- Door handles
- Driver's seat sensor
- Ignition switch
- Transmission backup lamp switch
- Power door lock and unlock switches
- Door-ajar switch

After processing the input signals, the control module sends output signals to the following actuators and lamps:

- Keypad lamps
- Door lock LED's
- Door solenoids
- Trunk release solenoid
- Courtesy lamps

The system serves as a convenient entry method when the vehicle keys are accidentally locked inside.

ELECTRONIC NAVIGATION SYSTEMS

An electronic navigation system is a position determination system. It provides the driver with necessary information about his location on a road network and gives him the ability to determine the best way of reaching his destination from wherever he is located. Any automotive navigation system must contain the following elements:

- A map database
- A display device
- A computer

There are four types of position determination or electronic navigation

systems that can provide a driver with this information:

1. Inertial navigation
2. Radio navigation
3. Signpost navigation
4. Dead reckoning

We will look briefly at each type in this chapter.

Inertial Navigation

An inertial navigation system uses three gyros, three accelerometers, control electronics, and a computer. The gyros measure the angular motion of the vehicle; the accelerometers measure vehicle acceleration. The computer controls the gyros and accelerometers, using the data they provide to calculate the position and speed of the vehicle and translate it into latitude and longitude readings. This type of system is used in commercial aviation. In their present state of development for automotive use, inertial navigation systems are extremely expensive and not really practical. They require a warmup period to become thermally stable and must be periodically realigned and calibrated to maintain their accuracy.

Radio Navigation

A radio navigation system determines position using either land- or satellite-based transmitters. Land-based systems depend upon the number and physical location of transmitting stations. Position determination requires signals from four different transmitters or satellites. It is doubtful that a land-based system will be developed to provide total area coverage of the United States or of any single state.

In theory, satellite-based systems could overcome this limitation and provide total coverage of any size area. Such a system, however, is subject to numerous technical problems, such as satellite clock errors, delays in signal transmission through the atmosphere, and satellite geometry. There also is a line-of-sight problem. The

receiver must maintain a direct line of sight with each of the four satellites it selects to obtain an accurate position signal. This is difficult in urban areas with many high-rise buildings or rural areas that are mountainous or heavily wooded.

Signpost Navigation

This system depends upon active signposts at every intersection. An active signpost is one that transmits a data code signal to the vehicle computer. There are many technical problems involved in this type of system, not the least of which is the number of signposts and data codes involved (there are at least 36,000 intersections in Los Angeles alone).

Dead Reckoning

This simple method of position determination requires only three data inputs to work: initial position, direction of travel, and distance traveled. Once the computer is provided with the initial position of the vehicle, it can calculate the current position by using distance traveled and direction of travel (which varies as a function of time).

Direction of travel can be measured by a flux-gate compass or a directional gyro. Distance traveled can be determined through the vehicle odometer, but separate sensors on the undriven wheels produce more accurate results. Even so, there are still a number of technical problems that result in a cumulative error problem, making a dead reckoning system suitable only for trips of about 2 miles.

The performance of a dead reckoning navigation system can be improved by combining it with a practical application of artificial intelligence called map matching. Map matching correlates the vehicle path with the road network to determine the vehicle's true position. It also minimizes the cumulative error problem and can bring accuracy to ±50 feet. One such system already is in use.

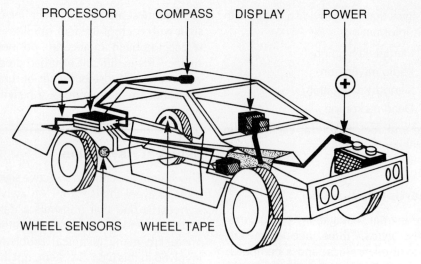

Figure 19-50. The ETAK Navigation system components. (ETAK, Inc.)

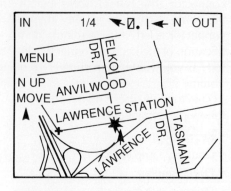

Figure 19-51. A typical ETAK map display. (ETAK, Inc.)

ETAK Navigator. The ETAK Navigator is an aftermarket installation available in San Francisco and Los Angeles. GM has equipped a fleet of vehicles with the system and is investigating it as a possible optional accessory for its high-line automobiles. The system also has potential for commercial vehicle fleet management.

The ETAK Navigator combines a flux-gate compass and two wheel sensors with a digital map base and a computer to provide an electronic map display that continuously shows the car's position on a map of the surrounding area, figure 19-50.

The driver can select a destination either by choosing two intersecting streets on the map or by entering a desired street address and the street he is presently on. The Navigator displays a map showing both the car's location and the desired destination, figure 19-51. The driver can change the scale of the map to obtain whatever detail he desires. An arrowhead symbol in the center of the display represents vehicle position. The arrowhead points toward the top of the map to indicate direction. As the vehicle is driven, the map rotates around the arrowhead. Lines that vary in brightness indicate different-sized streets, and key landmarks are labeled. Vehicle destination is indicated by a blinking star.

The digital map base is stored on a tape cassette similar to audiotape cassettes. One cassette can store the equivalent information provided on two typical paper street maps. Approximately three cassettes contain maps that cover the entire San Francisco Bay area.

The control unit contains a microprocessor with 256 kilobytes of dynamic RAM, 16 kilobytes of ROM, and 2 kilobytes of nonvolatile RAM. Directional signals from the electronic compass and distance signals from the magnetic wheel sensors are processed by the control unit, which selects the appropriate data from the tape cassette for display.

The display is a vector graphics type in which the beam draws the map and writes the identification instead of the raster scanning the entire display. The map scale on the display is variable from 1/4 mile to 10 miles. Depressing a button on the display causes it to zoom in for a closeup view of the vehicle's current location with street names included. The display also can be zoomed out to give an overview of the metropolitan area that includes vehicle location and destination. By choosing between these two extremes, a driver can tailor the map display so it only shows the information required for him to reach his destination.

SUMMARY

Automated air conditioning (A/C) systems use the same basic components found in manual A/C systems but differ in the control method. An automated system can function on its own once the control devices are set to tell the system what to do. Semiautomatic temperature control (SATC) systems use a separate programmer unit. Electronic automatic temperature control (EATC) systems may use a separate computer microprocessor or be controlled by the body computer module (BCM). Most ETAC systems have a self-diagnostic program and can set trouble codes to be used in pinpointing the location of a problem.

Thermistors, bimetal vacuum modulators, and photovoltaic diodes are used as in-car, ambient temperature, and sunlight sensors. Other inputs to the programmer, microprocessor, or BCM may include signals from a cold engine lockout or power steering cutout switch.

Actuators used to operate the air distribution doors include vacuum motors; rotary electric motors; and permanent-magnet, reduction-gear dc motors. Vacuum motors have no feedback capability. Rotary electric motors use resistors to send a feedback signal. The reduction-gear motor has a gear-driven feedback potentiometer. Blower motor speed can be controlled by a pulsed voltage signal through a separate module.

The principles used in automated temperature control are the same, but a wide variation in circuit design when the same system is applied to various car lines makes the use of the carmaker's procedures and schematics necessary to understand and diagnose a particular system.

Memory seats can be programmed like a radio. Different seat positions are recalled automatically when the door is closed, or manually by pushing a button.

Electronic sunroofs use a solid-state module containing two relays and a timer function to control rotation of a reversible motor according to signals from the system limit switches.

Antitheft systems provide a warning when a forced entry is attempted through the vehicle doors or the trunk lid. When the system is activated, it sounds the horn and blinks the exterior lights intermittently for a specific period. A starter interlock feature may be included in some systems. A supplemental system uses a lock cylinder sensor that matches the resistance in its memory with that embedded in the ignition key. If the resistances do not match, the control module disables the ignition through a starter enable relay.

An automatic door lock (ADL) system automatically locks all vehicle doors when the gear selector is placed in Drive. Moving the gear selector to Park automatically unlocks all doors.

A keyless entry system uses a numerical code and keypad to unlock the vehicle doors without a key. The system also includes illuminated entry and automatic door lock features.

Electronic navigation systems are on the horizon and will provide drivers with an electronic roadmap, allowing them to plot the best route to their destination.

REVIEW QUESTIONS

Multiple Choice

1. Student A says that an electronic automatic temperature control (EATC) system is controlled by a microprocessor. Student B says that an EATC system is BCM-controlled. Who is right?

a. A only
b. B only
c. both A and B
d. neither A nor B

2. Student A says that an in-car temperature sensor requires an aspirator system to draw passenger compartment air past the sensor. Student A says that an in-car sensor uses a pressure-sensitive piezoresistive element. Who is right?

a. A only
b. B only
c. both A and B
d. neither A nor B

3. Student A says that semiautomatic temperature control (SATC) systems use feedback circuitry. Student B says that EATC systems use feedback circuitry. Who is right?

a. A only
b. B only
c. both A and B
d. neither A nor B

4. Which of the following is not used to control an SATC system?

a. a programmer

b. electric servomotor
c. control module
d. body computer module

5. Student A says that an SATC system uses a sunlight sensor. Student B says that an EATC system uses a sunlight sensor. Who is right?

a. A only
b. B only
c. both A and B
d. neither A nor B

6. Which of the following is not used as a temperature sensor in an EATC system?

a. thermistor
b. bimetal vacuum modulator
c. potentiometer
d. photovoltaic diode

7. Which of the following is not used as an actuator in most EATC systems?

a. reduction-gear motor
b. rotary electric motor
c. vacuum motor
d. stepper motor

8. Student A says that only an SATC system can run a self-diagnostic program and display trouble codes. Student B says that only an ETCS system has this function. Who is right?

a. A only
b. B only
c. both A and B
d. neither A nor B

9. Student A says that a rotary actuator produces a feedback signal with a fixed resistor. Student B says that a variable resistor produces the feedback signal. Who is right?

a. A only
b. B only
c. both A and B
d. neither A nor B

10. Student A says that the ECM controls compressor clutch operation through the BCM. Student B says that the BCM controls compressor clutch operation through the ECM. Who is right?

a. A only
b. B only
c. both A and B
d. neither A nor B

11. Which of the following describes the diagnostics of a BCM-controlled EATC system?

a. ECM codes are displayed first.
b. BCM codes are displayed first.
c. IPC codes are displayed first.
d. DIC codes are displayed first.

12. Student A says that a memory seat system automatically returns the driver's seat to a preset position. Student B says that different positions can be programmed into the system memory at any time. Who is right?

a. A only

b. B only

c. both A and B

d. neither A nor B

13. Student A says that a memory disable function prevents a memory seat module from operating unless the transaxle selector lever is in the Park position. Student B says that the selector lever must be in the Drive position to disable the module. Who is right?

a. A only

b. B only

c. both A and B

d. neither A nor B

14. Student A says that the limit switches in an electronic sunroof system tell the module when the sunroof is open or closed. Student B says that the limit switches turn the motor off to prevent damage if the switch is held too long. Who is right?

a. A only

b. B only

c. both A and B

d. neither A nor B

15. Student A says that a resistor key antitheft system sounds the vehicle alarm if the wrong key is used. Student B says that a resistor key antitheft system disables the ignition if the wrong key is used. Who is right?

a. A only

b. B only

c. both A and B

d. neither A nor B

16. Student A says that a factory-installed antitheft system integrates the operation of several other circuits. Student B says that it is a complex multiple circuit system. Who is right?

a. A only

b. B only

c. both A and B

d. neither A nor B

17. Student A says that an automatic door lock system automatically locks all vehicle doors when the transaxle gear selector is placed in Park. Student B says that moving the gear selector to Drive automatically unlocks all doors. Who is right?

a. A only

b. B only

c. both A and B

d. neither A nor B

18. Student A says that a keyless entry system includes the functions of an illuminated entry system and an automatic door lock system. Student B says that the code stamped on the keyless entry module is the same code used to activate the system. Who is right?

a. A only

b. B only

c. both A and B

d. neither A nor B

19. The ETAK Navigator is an example of which type of vehicle position determination system?

a. inertial navigation

b. dead reckoning

c. radio navigation

d. signpost navigation

20. Student A says that the ETAK Navigator represents the vehicle on its map display as a blinking star. Student B says that a blinking arrow indicates the vehicle destination. Who is right?

a. A only

b. B only

c. both A and B

d. neither A nor B

Fill in the Blank

21. The BCM communicates with the A/C programmer on the _____ .

22. In an ETCS system with automatic blower control, the blower motor receives a _____ voltage signal.

23. The primary difference between a semiautomatic temperature control system and a manual A/C system is the method of _____ used.

24. A photovoltaic diode is used as a _____ sensor.

25. The direction of actuator rotation is based on the principle of current _____ .

26. A resistor ignition key must have the correct _____ and _____ code to operate the lock and close the starter circuit.

27. A dead reckoning navigation system can be improved by combining it with a form of artificial intelligence called _____ .

GLOSSARY

ac ripple. The small waves at the top of a rectified dc voltage oscilloscope pattern. They are the peaks of the ac voltage sine waves. Any dc voltage from a rectified ac source always has a slight ac ripple.

actuator. Any device that receives an output signal from a computer and does something in response to the signal.

adaptive learning strategy. A strategy that modifies the original program to compensate for changes in system parameters caused by various factors such as engine wear, poor fuel quality, or component malfunctioning.

after top dead center (atdc). The position of a piston after it has passed top dead center of a stroke, measured in degrees of crankshaft rotation.

air-core gauge. An electromagnetic gauge using no magnetic core. Sending unit resistance creates a field that moves a pivoting permanent magnet.

alternating current. Electric current that changes direction between negative and positive while flowing.

ambient air temperature. The air temperature surrounding the outside of the vehicle.

American Wire Gauge (AWG). One of the two standard systems for determining wire sizes based on the cross-sectional area of the conductor. The larger the wire, the lower the gauge number.

ampere. The unit used to measure the rate of electric current flow.

ampere-hour rating. The oldest battery rating method. The ampere-hour rating indicates the steady current that a battery will deliver for 20 hours at 80° F before cell voltage drops below 1.75 volts.

analog. A signal that varies proportionally with the information that it measures. In a computer, an analog signal is voltage that fluctuates over a range from high to low.

analogy. A similarity or partial resemblance in certain respects between things that are otherwise unlike.

aneroid. An evacuated metal bellows containing a vacuum that changes in length as a response to changes in atmospheric pressure.

anode. The positively charged electrode in a voltage cell.

armature. The movable part in a relay or the rotating part of a generator or motor consisting of a conductor wound around a laminated iron core.

asymmetrical. A differing pattern on each side of a centerline. The light beam of an asymmetrical low-beam headlamp is positioned farther to one side of the center than the other.

asynchronous data. Data transmission that incorporates a constant tone between sending and receiving. A start pulse precedes the transmission of new data, and a stop pulse tells the computer that the transmission has been completed.

atom. The smallest part of a chemical element that contains the characteristics of an element.

atomize. The action of breaking a liquid into a fine mist or small droplets.

available voltage. The maximum amount of secondary voltage the ignition coil can deliver.

base. The center layer of a bipolar transistor, made of doped material opposite from the collector and the emitter.

basic (initial) timing. The ignition timing setting of an engine at idle speed.

battery cells. The active units of a battery.

baud rate. Computer data transmission speed in digital bits per second.

BCI group numbers. A number used to indicate the physical features of a battery, such as size, shape, and voltage.

before top dead center (btdc). The position of a piston before it reaches top dead center of a stroke, measured in degrees of crankshaft rotation.

bias voltage. Voltage applied across a diode.

bimetal. Two strips of metal, each of which expands and contracts at a different rate when exposed to changes in temperature.

bimetal element. A strip made of different metals that expand at different rates when heated. Commonly used in circuit breakers and temperature switches to open the contacts when high current flows through the circuit.

binary system. The mathematical system that uses only the digits 0 and 1 to present information.

bipolar. The general name for NPN and PNP transistors, because current flows through semiconductor materials of both polarities. Holes and electrons are both used as current carriers.

bits. A binary digit (0 or 1). Bit combinations are used to represent letters and numbers in digital computers. Eight bits equal one byte.

bonding straps. Additional ground cables installed between the engine and chassis to provide a low-resistance ground path for various electrical circuits.

bore. The diameter of a cylinder. Also the machining process of enlarging or finishing a hole.

bottom dead center (bdc). The exact bottom of a piston stroke.

bound electrons. Five or more tightly held electrons found in an atom's valence shell.

brake horsepower (bhp). The horsepower developed at an engine's crankshaft.

brake mean effective pressure (bmep). Mean effective pressure measured as force at the engine crankshaft.

breakdown voltage. The prescribed, or designed, voltage at which a zener diode allows reverse current flow.

burn time. The time in milliseconds during which the fuel ignites and burns to develop cylinder pressure.

bus bar. A solid metal strap or bar in a fuse block that acts as a common conductor for several fuses.

475

bypass or module timing. Ignition timing provided by the module of a direct ignition system during cranking until the synchronization signal is received and ignition coil setup is achieved.

camshaft. A rotating shaft or other movable part with irregularly shaped protrusions or lobes used to produce reciprocating motion in a contacting part. In an engine valve train, camshaft motion moves a valve lifter to open a valve.

capacitance. The ability of two conducting surfaces to store voltage when separated by an insulator.

capacitive-discharge (CD) ignition. An ignition system in which primary current and voltage charge a capacitor in the ignition module until a triggering device signals a silicon-controlled rectifier (SCR) in the module to release the voltage to the coil primary winding.

case ground. A ground connector directly from the case of the device to the engine or chassis.

cathode. The negatively charged electrode in a voltage cell.

central processing unit (CPU). The calculating part of a microcomputer that makes logical decisions by comparing conditioned input with data in memory.

centrifugal (mechanical) advance. A means of advancing the ignition spark using weights in the distributor housing that react to centrifugal force.

centrifugal force. The force that tends to cause rotating bodies to move away from the center of rotation.

choke coil. A coil wound with fine wire, used to absorb oscillations in a circuit that occur when the circuit is opened or closed.

circuit. The circular, unbroken path required for electric current to flow.

claw pole. The finger, or claw, of an alternator rotor that concentrates the magnetic flux and forms the magnetic field. A claw-pole rotor has interlaced sets of claw poles to form alternating north-south poles.

clearance volume. The volume of the combustion chamber and area around the top of the piston with the piston at top dead center.

closed loop. The system operating condition when an output error signal is fed back to the system controller, which then readjusts the system to eliminate the error.

closed-loop dwell control. A feature of a

distributorless ignition in which the ignition control module adjusts dwell time to provide full coil saturation based on the previous coil buildup.

cold-cranking rotating. This battery rating indicates the amperes that a battery can supply to start an engine at low temperature. A cold-cranking rating of 500 means that a battery can provide 500 amperes for 30 seconds at 0° F before cell voltage drops below 1.2 volts.

collector. The outer layer of a semiconductor material that receives the majority current carriers in a bipolar transistor.

commutator. A segmented ring secured to one end of an armature shaft in a motor or dc generator. It acts as a rotary switch to provide a continuous current path from an external circuit through carbon brushes and the armature windings.

compound. The combination of atoms from one element with atoms of another element that share electrons to form a substance with different characteristics.

compression pressure. Pressure created by the piston as it moves from bdc to tdc on the compression stroke without having the air-fuel mixture ignited.

compression ratio. The ratio of the total volume of a cylinder and the combustion chamber to the clearance volume of the chamber alone.

computer hardware. The mechanical, magnetic, electrical, and electronic devices that make up the physical structure of a computer.

condenser. A capacitor that usually is made of two sheets of metal foil that are separated by an insulator and housed in a small metal can.

conductor. A substance that permits free electrons to move from one atom to another easily and thus allows electric current flow.

continuity. Term used to describe a continuous or unbroken electrical circuit.

conventional theory. A theory of current flow which states that electricity flows from positive to negative.

counterelectromotive force (CEMF). An induced voltage that opposes the source voltage and any increase or decrease in source current flow.

crankshaft throw. The offset portion of a crankshaft to which a connecting rod and rod bearing are attached. Each throw creates a lever with the crankshaft centerline as the pivot point (fulcrum).

cycling. The process of discharging and recharging a battery.

Darlington circuit. A current-amplifying arrangement whereby one transistor acts as a preamplifier and creates a larger base current for a second transistor.

d'Arsonval movement. A form of measuring device used in electrical gauges and test instruments. Uses a small, current-carrying coil located inside the field of a permanent horseshoe magnet. The coil rotates according to interaction of the magnetic fields.

delta stator. A 3-winding alternator stator with the ends of each winding connected to each other; there is no neutral junction. Schematically, the arrangement looks like the Greek letter delta, or a triangle. A delta stator produces high current at low speed.

demultiplexer (DEMUX). The solid-state switching device that handles the output data from the BCM to an actuator when the BCM is in the process of sequential sampling.

detented. Positions of a multiple-pole switch that allow the switch to stay in a selected position. For example, the Off, Run, Start, and Accessory positions of an ignition switch are detented.

dielectric. Insulating material used between the two conductive plates or surfaces of a capacitor.

digital. A signal that is either on or off and that is translated into the binary digits 0 and 1. In a computer, a digital signal is voltage that is either low or high, or current flow that is on or off.

diode. An electronic device made by joining P-material to N-material at a junction. It allows current flow in one direction and blocks it in the other.

direct current. Electric current that always flows in the same direction.

discrete device. An individual diode, transistor, or other electronic part that performs only one function and is connected to a circuit by wire leads.

displacement. The measurement of the volume of air moved by a piston as it travels from bottom to top of its stroke. Engine displacement is the displacement of one cylinder multiplied by the number of cylinders in the engine.

dopant. The other elements added to pure silicon and germanium in the doping process to change the electrical characteristics of the semiconductor material.

doping. The addition of a second element to a pure semiconductor. The second element has either three or five valence electrons.

double overhead cam (dohc) engine. An engine with two camshafts mounted in the cylinder head, rather than in the block. One camshaft operates the intake valves; the other operates the exhaust valves.

drain. The part of a field-effect transistor that receives the current-carrying holes or electrons. Similar to the collector in a bipolar transistor.

driver transistor. A transistor in the ignition control module that receives timing signals from the distributor signal generator and uses the signals to control the switching (power) transistors.

duplex serial data line. A data link between two computers that allows each computer to send and receive data from the other. An external clock line between the two computers controls which one sends and which one receives.

duty cycle. The percentage of time that a solenoid is energized during one complete on-off cycle during pulse width modulation.

dwell angle. The number of degrees of distributor rotation while the breaker points are closed.

dynamic range. The operating range of a sensor.

dynamometer. An instrument used to measure the torque and power output of an engine.

eddy current. Small induced current in the armature of a motor (or a dc generator) created by CEMF. Eddy currents oppose circuit current flow.

electric current. The controlled movement of electrons from one point to another.

electrical load. The working device installed in an electrical circuit. The load control current in the circuit.

electrically erasable programmable read-only memory (EEPROM). Computer memory program circuits that can be erased electrically with a voltage pulse and reprogrammed.

electrochemical. The chemical action of two dissimilar materials in a conductive chemical solution.

electrochemistry. Voltage developed by the chemical action of two dissimilar ma-terials in a conductive chemical solution.

electrode. One of two dissimilar materials placed in a conductive chemical solution to produce an electrochemical reaction.

electrolyte. The conductive and reactive substance in a voltage cell. It may be a liquid or a paste.

electromagnet. A soft iron core placed inside the coil of a current-carrying conductor.

electromagnetic. Referring to the magnetic field created by current flowing in a conductor. Also, referring to the relationship between electrical energy and magnetic energy.

electromagnetic induction. The creation of voltage and current within a conductor due to relative movement of either the magnetic field or the conductor.

electromagnetism. A form of magnetism that occurs when electric current passes through a conductor surrounding the magnet and creates a stronger magnetic field.

electromotive force. Voltage: the force that moves current through an electrical circuit.

electron. A negatively charged particle contained within an atom.

electron theory. A theory of current flow which states that electricity flows from negative to positive.

electrostatic field. The potential voltage or electrical energy between two oppositely charged points or surfaces.

element. A basic, irreducible chemical building block that makes up all types of matter.

emitter. The outer layer of semiconductor material that supplies the majority current carriers in a bipolar transistor.

engine mapping. The process of measuring the best combinations of timing, air-fuel ratio, EGR, and other controllable variables for various speeds, loads, and temperatures.

equivalent resistance. The total resistance of a parallel circuit.

erasable programmable read-only memory (EPROM). Computer memory program circuits that can be erased and reprogrammed. Erasure is done by exposing the IC chip to ultraviolet light.

excitation current. Current that magnetically excites the alternator field. During starting, it comes from the battery; when running, it comes from the alternator output.

excitation voltage. Battery or charging system voltage that delivers field current to the alternator.

farad. The unit used to measure capacitance.

feedback. The recycling of part of the system or output error signal used by a microprocessor to readjust system operation.

field-effect transistor (FET). A transistor through which current flow is controlled by voltage in a capacitive field. A unipolar transistor.

firing order. The sequence in which ignition occurs in cylinders of an engine.

firing (ionization) voltage. See *required voltage*.

fixed-dwell electronic ignition. The ignition dwell period remains relatively constant in duration and does not vary in distributor degrees as engine speed changes.

flux density. The number of flux lines per square centimeter of a particular area. It is strongest near the magnet's poles.

flux lines. Magnetic lines of force.

forward bias. Voltage applied across a diode that causes current to flow across the junction.

four-stroke cycle. The engine operating cycle in which a piston makes four full strokes (intake, compression, power, and exhaust) and 720 degrees of crankshaft revolution to develop power from the combustion process. Also called the otto cycle.

free electrons. Three or fewer loosely held electrons found in an atom's valence shell.

friction horsepower. Engine power lost to internal friction of the engine. Power consumed to overcome internal engine friction.

gain. The ratio of amplification in an electronic device.

galvanic battery. A source of dc voltage, generated by a difference in oxygen content near two electrodes.

gate. The part of a field-effect transistor that controls the capacitive field and current flow. Similar to the base in a bipolar transistor.

gross brake horsepower. Brake horsepower of an engine with only the fuel, oil, and water pumps and built-in emission controls as accessory loads.

half-wave rectification. The process of rectifying only one-half of an ac voltage (either positive or negative) and producing pulsating dc.

Hall-effect switch. A device that produces a voltage pulse dependent on the presence of a magnetic field.

heat range. A measure of the ability of a spark plug to dissipate heat from its firing end.

heat sink. Any object that absorbs and dissipates heat from another object.

hertz (Hz). A unit of frequency equal to 1 cycle per second.

hole. The place in a semiconductor valence shell from which an electron is missing. A positive charge carrier.

horsepower. Term used to describe the effort required to move 200 pounds 165 feet in one minute.

hybrid circuit. An electronic circuit built from discrete devices and IC chips.

hydrometer. A test instrument used to measure specific gravity.

ignition control module. The solid-state module through which all primary current passes in an electronic ignition.

ignition interval. The degrees of crankshaft rotation between ignition in cylinders in firing order sequence.

ignition lag. The interval between the time fuel is injected in a diesel engine until it mixes with hot compressed air and ignites; usually about 2 milliseconds.

indicated horsepower. The theoretical maximum power produced inside an engine's cylinders, calculated by measuring combustion pressure.

induced current. Current in a conductor generated by magnetic flux lines due to relative movement of either the magnetic field or the conductor.

induced voltage. Voltage in a conductor generated by magnetic flux lines due to relative movement of either the magnetic field or the conductor.

induction coil. Two conductors wound into coils, with one placed inside the other. Transformers and ignition coils are examples.

inductive-discharge ignition system. A means of igniting the air-fuel mixture in an engine cylinder based on induction of high voltage in the coil secondary winding.

inertia engagement. A general type of starter motor that uses the rotating inertia of the motor armature shaft to engage the drive pinion with the engine flywheel. A Bendix drive is the most common inertia-engagement starter drive.

insulator. A substance that prohibits free movement of the bound outer electrons from one atom to another and thus blocks electric current flow.

integrated circuit (IC). A complete electronic circuit of many transistors and other devices, all formed on a single silicon chip.

internal-combustion engine. An engine in which the air-fuel mixture is burned inside the engine power chamber.

ion. A positively or negatively charged atom that has become unbalanced by gaining or losing an electron.

keep-alive memory. Random-access memory that is retained by keeping a voltage applied to the circuits when the engine is off.

lambda. The ratio of one number to another. For exhaust gas measurement, lambda is the ratio of excess air to ideal air for complete combustion.

left-hand rule. The current flow and flux direction rule based on the electron theory of current flow. Grasping a conductor with the left-hand thumb pointing in the direction of current flow (toward +) causes the fingers to wrap around the conductor in the direction of the flux lines.

light-emitting diode (LED). A gallium-arsenide diode that releases energy as red light when holes and electrons collide.

limit-cycle control. A system that monitors its output and responds only if and when the output goes above or below predetermined limits.

linear. In a straight line.

linearity. The expression of sensor accuracy throughout its dynamic range.

linear variable differential transformer (LVDT) sensor. A sensor containing two induction coils with a movable core. As the core moves, the output voltage of one winding exceeds the other. Sensor output voltage is proportional to the amount and direction of core movement.

liquid crystal display (LCD). A display that sandwiches electrodes and polarized fluid between two pieces of glass. The application of voltage to the electrodes rearranges the light slots in the fluid and

causes light to pass through it.

logic gates. Logic circuits used by a computer to manipulate data bits. The three basic gates are the NOT, AND, and OR gates.

magnetic field. The area around a magnet in which energy is exerted because of the manner in which the atoms are aligned in the material.

magnetic flux. The lines of force that create a magnetic field.

magnetic saturation. The state that exists when the magnetic field built up around the primary and secondary coil windings by primary current reaches full magnetic strength and maximum flux density.

magnetism. A form of energy that results from the way in which atoms are aligned within certain materials, giving the materials the ability to attract other metals.

manifold absolute pressure. A combination of atmospheric pressure and vacuum.

mass density. A fuel injection control method that uses mass airflow measurement to regulate fuel metering in relation to engine air intake.

matter. Everything in the universe. Matter may exist in one of three physical forms: solid, liquid, or gas.

mean effective pressure. The average cylinder pressure developed throughout one complete 4-stroke cycle.

menu driven. Referring to a computer program that provides the user with a "menu" or list of choices. Making a choice brings up another page of the menu and requires that another choice be made. In this way, the user tells the computer what he wishes to know and the program displays the desired information.

minus rule. Minus metal on the minus (−) point means a minus-capacity condenser.

mixture. The result of mixing molecules of elements or compounds that do not share electrons.

molecule. The smallest particle of an element that can exist and retain the characteristics of the element.

momentary contact. A kind of switch that operates only when held in position. When released, it returns to its normally open or normally closed position.

MOSFET. A metal-oxide semiconductor, field-effect transistor. A type of integrated-circuit (IC) device used in a microprocessor.

multiplexer (MUX). A solid-state switching device that handles the input data from a given sensor for the BCM when it is in the process of sequential sampling.

multiplex wiring systems. An electrical circuit in which signals are transmitted by a peripheral serial bus or over optical fiber cables instead of by conventional wires. Several devices share signals on a common conductor.

mutual induction. The transfer of energy from one coil to another when both coils are placed close together.

negative-ground electrical system. An electrical system that follows the conventional current flow theory (electricity flows from positive to negative).

negative temperature coefficient (NTC) resistor. A thermistor whose resistance decreases as temperature increases—low resistance at high temperature and high resistance at low temperature.

net brake horsepower. Brake horsepower of a fully equipped engine with all accessory loads.

neutral junction. The center tap to which the common ends of Y-type stator windings are connected.

neutron. An electrically neutral particle found within most atoms.

N-material. Silicon or germanium doped with phosphorus or arsenic so that it has excess free electrons and a negative charge.

normally closed (NC) switch. A switch whose contacts are closed until an outside force opens them to complete the circuit.

normally deenergized. A condition in which voltage is not applied when the ignition is on. For example, voltage would not be applied to the windings of a solenoid until a switch closes.

normally energized. A condition in which voltage is applied when the ignition is on. For example, voltage would be applied to the windings of a solenoid.

normally open (NO) switch. A switch whose contacts are open until an outside force closes them to complete the circuit.

nucleus. The core in the center of an atom that contains the protons and neutrons.

ohm. The unit used to measure electrical resistance. If one volt moves one ampere through the circuit, the resistance is one ohm.

open-circuit (no-load) voltage. See *available voltage.*

open loop. The system operating condition when an output error signal is not fed back to the system controller.

oscillate. A rapid back-and-forth movement of voltage.

oscilloscope. A test instrument that produces a trace of electron motion on a cathode ray tube. The trace is an analog voltage representation that is proportional to amplitude and frequency.

overhead valve (ohv) engine. An engine with the intake and exhaust valves in the cylinder head above the combustion chambers.

parallel circuit. A circuit containing more than one path through which electric current can flow.

parallel data. Data transmission in which each component of the data is sent at the same time on its own line.

peripheral serial bus. A data link between two computers in which one link sends and the other link receives data transmissions.

permeability. The ease with which a material can be penetrated by magnetic flux lines. Iron is more permeable than gases such as air.

phase angle. The angular location of alternator conductors relative to the rotating field. A phase is a fraction of a complete ac cycle, usually expressed as an angle between sine waves. A 3-phase alternator has three windings 120 degrees apart and produces overlapping sine wave voltage.

photochemical reaction. The process of smog formation caused when HC and NO_x combine in the presence of sunlight and quiet air.

photoelectricity. Voltage developed by exposing a metal to light, causing electrons to flow.

piezoelectricity. Voltage developed by applying pressure to the surface of certain crystals.

piezoresistive crystal. A substance that is capable of generating a voltage when subjected to mechanical pressure.

P-material. Silicon or germanium doped with boron or gallium so that it has a shortage of free electrons and a positive charge.

PN junction. The point where two opposite kinds of semiconductor material (P and N) join together.

point gap. The maximum distance between the point contact surfaces when the

rubbing block is on the high point of the distributor cam and the points are fully open.

polarity. The possession or existence of two opposing forces or characteristics, such as the north and south poles of a magnet or the positive and negative terminals of an electrical circuit.

pole. One end of a magnet. Lines of magnetic force are concentrated around the poles.

poppet valve. A valve that opens and closes by back-and-forth linear motion.

positive engagement. A general type of starter motor that uses the positive mechanical action of a solenoid or a movable pole shoe to engage the drive pinion with the engine flywheel.

positive-ground electrical system. An electrical system that follows the electron theory of current flow (electricity flows from negative to positive).

positive temperature coefficient (PTC) resistor. A thermistor whose resistance increases as temperature increases.

potential energy. Energy that is stored or unreleased.

potentiometer. A variable resistor that acts as a voltage divider to produce a continuously variable output signal proportional to a mechanical position.

power. The measurement of the rate or speed of energy performing work.

power transistor. A transistor in the ignition control module that handles current up to 10 amperes and is used to switch primary current.

primary battery. A battery whose electrochemical reaction cannot be reversed. The battery dies when one of the electrodes is destroyed by the electrochemical action; it is not rechargeable.

primary circuit. The low-voltage circuit of an ignition system.

primary (ballast) resistor. A resistor installed in the primary circuit to stabilize ignition system voltage and current flow.

primary winding. A coil winding that uses voltage and current flow to create a magnetic field and induce a voltage in a second winding.

primary wiring. Automotive electrical system wiring that carries low voltage.

program. The job instructions for a computer.

programmable read-only memory (PROM). A computer memory IC chip that can be programmed once to store the computer program.

proportional control. A system that changes its output signal in proportion to an error signal that is determined by subtracting the feedback signal from the output signal.

proton. A positively charged particle contained within an atom.

pulse width. The amount of time that an electromechanical device, such as a solenoid, is energized. Pulse width is usually measured in milliseconds.

pulse width modulation. A continuous on-and-off cycling of a solenoid a specified number of times per second.

radiofrequency interference (RFI). Electrical impulses emitted by secondary wiring (spark plug cables) and other circuits. These impulses interfere with radio and television reception.

random-access memory (RAM). Computer read-write memory on which information can be written and from which it can be read.

read-only memory (ROM). The permanent program memory of a computer. Instructions can be read from ROM, but nothing can be written into it and it cannot be changed.

reciprocating engine. An engine in which pistons move up and down in cylinders. Combustion of an air-fuel mixture at one end of the cylinders develops power and causes a reciprocating motion. Also called a piston engine.

rectifier bridge. A single assembly that contains three or all six rectifying diodes for an alternator.

rectify. To change alternating current to direct current.

reference voltage (V_{ref}). A voltage provided by a voltage regulator in the computer to operate sensors at a constant level. The sensor modifies the signal and returns it to the computer.

relative motion. Movement of magnetic flux lines in relation to a conductor or movement of the conductor in relation to the magnetic flux lines.

relay. A device that uses a small current through an electromagnetic coil to move an armature. A relay is used to open or close a switch in a circuit carrying a larger current.

reluctance. The tendency of a material to resist the passage of magnetic flux lines.

reluctance sensor. A magnetic pulse generator that sends a voltage signal in response to varying reluctance of a magnetic field.

remote grounds. A ground connection through a wire between a device and the engine or chassis.

required voltage. The amount of secondary voltage required to jump the spark plug gap at any given time.

reserve-capacity rating. This battery rating indicates the number of minutes a fully charged battery can deliver 25 amperes before cell voltage drops below 1.75 volts.

reverse bias. Voltage applied across a diode that prevents current flow across the junction.

reverse polarity. The condition in which the ignition primary circuit has a reversed connection (usually at the coil). This causes the secondary voltage polarity at the spark plug to be reversed and force current from a positive (+) center electrode to a negative (−) ground electrode.

reversing relay. A relay that energizes a solenoid when a normally closed switch opens.

revolutions per minute (rpm). A measurement of engine rotating speed. The number of complete revolutions made by the crankshaft in one minute.

rheostat. A variable resistor used to regulate the strength of an electrical current.

right-hand rule. The current flow and flux direction rule based on conventional current-flow theory. Grasping a conductor with the right-hand thumb pointing in the direction of current flow (toward −) causes the fingers to wrap around the conductor in the direction of the flux lines.

running mates. Cylinders with crank throws in the same positions relative to firing order.

secondary battery. A battery whose electrochemical reaction can be reversed. The battery electrodes and electrolyte can be restored by reversing the current flow.

secondary circuit. The high-voltage circuit of an ignition system.

secondary winding. A coil winding that receives an induced voltage from the magnetic field created by current flow in a primary winding.

semiconductor. An element that allows electric current to flow under controlled conditions.

sensor. Any device that sends an input signal to a computer.

sequential sampling. A complex switching method involving a multiplexer and demultiplexer, which allows the BCM to deal with sensor input and actuator output in a logical manner.

serial data line. A data link between two computers that transmits the words one after another, or serially, from one computer to the other. The computers are clocked together and synchronized to the data being transmitted.

series circuit. A circuit containing a single path through which electric current can flow.

series-parallel circuit. A circuit composed of some parts in series with the voltage source and other parts in parallel with each other.

short circuit. A continuous path for current flow that changes the normal current path through the circuit. The short may be into another circuit or directly to ground.

shunt. A branch circuit or electrical connection in parallel with another branch circuit or connection through which electric current can flow.

silicon-controlled rectifier (SCR). A common type of thyristor used in automotive circuits.

sine wave voltage. The changing voltage polarity between positive and negative.

single overhead cam (sohc) engine. An engine with the camshaft mounted in the cylinder head, rather than in the block. The camshaft operates both intake and exhaust valves.

single-phase voltage. The sine wave voltage induced in one conductor during one rotor revolution.

software. The various programs in RAM and ROM that provide a microprocessor with memory and operating instructions.

solenoid. A device similar in operation to a relay, but movement of the armature or movable iron core changes electrical energy into mechanical motion.

solid-state electronics. Electronic systems based on solid semiconductor devices such as diodes and transistors.

source. The part of a field-effect transistor that supplies the current-carrying holes or electrons. Similar to the emitter in a bipolar transistor.

spark plug reach. The distance from the plug seat to the end of its threads.

spark voltage. The level to which voltage drops to sustain the spark across a plug gap once the plug fires.

specific energy. Energy that has been released to perform work and takes a different form.

specific gravity. The measurement of the density of acid as compared to water in battery electrolyte.

speed density. More correctly, speed *and* density. A fuel injection control method that uses engine speed (rpm) and air density measured by a MAP sensor to regulate fuel metering in relation to engine air intake.

starting bypass. A parallel circuit branch used to bypass the ballast resistor during engine cranking.

state of charge. The electrochemical condition of battery electrolyte and plate materials at any given time.

static electricity. Voltage that results when electrons are transferred from the surface of one material to the surface of a second material. The electrons are "at rest," or static.

stepper motor. A dc motor that moves in incremental steps between a no-voltage (deenergized) to full-voltage (energized) position.

stoichiometric ratio. An air-fuel ratio of approximately 14.7:1, which provides the most complete combustion and recombining of air and fuel.

stroke. The distance that a piston travels from bottom to top in a cylinder. Also, one complete bottom-to-top or top-to-bottom movement of a piston.

sulfur oxide. Pollution formed when the sulfur in gasoline and diesel fuel combine with oxygen.

switching transistor. See *power transistor.*

symmetrical. The same pattern on each side of a centerline. The light beam of a symmetrical high-beam headlamp is positioned the same distance on each side of the center.

synchronous data. A constant data flow with regular clock pulses that incorporates a sync pulse at the beginning of each new piece of data to tell the computer that this is a new word.

television-radio-suppression (TVRS) cables. Ignition cables containing a conductor of carbon, or of linen or fiberglass strands impregnated with graphite, designed to reduce RFI.

temperature inversion. A warm air layer in the upper atmosphere that holds smog close to the ground by preventing cooler air below it from rising.

thermistor. A variable resistor whose resistance changes when temperature changes.

thermocouple. A temperature-measuring device made of two dissimilar metals joined so that voltage is generated between two points that is directly proportional to the temperature difference between the two points.

thermoelectricity. Voltage developed by heating one metal, causing an unequal transfer of electrons to another metal.

three-coil movement. An electromagnetic gauge in which pointer movement is dependent upon field interaction of three electromagnets and the total field effect on a movable permanent magnet.

three-phase alternating current. Three overlapping, evenly spaced, single-phase ac voltage sine waves that make up the complete ac output of an alternator.

three-phase voltage. Three overlapping ac voltage sine waves generated by an alternator with a 3-winding stator. The sine waves are at equally spaced, varying phases.

threshold voltage. The minimum conduction voltage for junction diode operation.

throttling. The process of regulating the amount of air-fuel mixture entering the engine to control speed and power.

thyristor. A semiconductor switching device composed of alternating N and P layers; can also rectify alternating current to direct current.

timing (spark) advance. Ignition occurring sooner before top dead center than initial timing. Any advance in timing is measured in degrees of crankshaft rotation.

top dead center (tdc). The exact top of a piston stroke.

transducer. A device that changes one form of energy to another. For example, a transducer can change motion to voltage, or air pressure to motion. An automotive sensor, actuator, or display device is a transducer.

transistor. A 3-element semiconductor device of NPN or PNP materials that transfers electrical signals across a resistance.

turns ratio. The ratio of the number of turns in the secondary winding to the number of turns in the primary winding. The ratio is a voltage multiplier.

vacuum advance. The application of engine vacuum to advance ignition spark timing by moving the distributor breaker plate in a direction opposite to distributor rotation.

vacuum fluorescent display (VFD). A display in which anode segments coated with phosphor material are bombarded with tungsten electrons, causing the segments to glow and create the desired display.

valence shell. The outermost shell or ring of an atom.

vaporize. To change matter into a gaseous form, such as when a liquid changes into a vapor through heat or spraying.

variable-dwell electronic ignition. The ignition dwell period remains relatively constant in duration but varies in distributor degrees at different engine speeds.

volt. The unit used to measure the amount of electrical force or energy.

voltage. The electromotive force that produces current flow.

voltage cell. Two dissimilar materials suspended in a conductive and reactive substance.

voltage reserve. The difference between available voltage and required voltage.

volumetric efficiency. Expressed as a percentage, the comparison of the actual volume of air taken into an engine to the theoretical maximum amount that the engine could draw in (its displacement).

waste spark. An ignition system in which one coil fires two spark plugs at one time. The spark plug in the cylinder on compression ignites the mixture; the spark fired in the cylinder on its exhaust stroke is wasted.

watt. The unit used to measure electric power. A watt equals volts times amperes.

Wheatstone bridge. An arrangement of resistors that allows resistance to be measured by measuring current and voltage.

wiring harness. A collection of wires encased in a plastic covering or conduit and routed to specific areas of the vehicle. Most harnesses terminate in plug-in connectors.

work. The end result of released energy. It may take a variety of forms, including motion and light.

Y-type stator. A 3-winding alternator stator in which one end of each winding is connected to a neutral junction. The other end of each winding is connected between a positive and a negative diode. Schematically, the windings are arranged like a letter "Y." A Y-type stator produces high voltage at low speed.

zener diode. A diode that allows reverse current flow above a prescribed voltage without being damaged.

INDEX